Chicago

timeout.com/chicago

Time Out Guides Ltd
Universal House
251 Tottenham Court Road
London W1T 7AB
United Kingdom
Tel: +44 (0)20 7813 3000
Fax: +44 (0)20 7813 6001
Email: guides@timeout.com
www.timeout.com

Published by Time Out Guides Ltd, a wholly owned subsidiary of Time Out Group Ltd.
Time Out and the Time Out logo are trademarks of Time Out Group Ltd.

© Time Out Group Ltd 2009
Previous editions 2000, 2002, 2004, 2007.

10 9 8 7 6 5 4 3 2 1

This edition first published in Great Britain in 2009 by Ebury Publishing.
A Random House Group Company
20 Vauxhall Bridge Road, London SW1V 2SA

Random House Australia Pty Ltd 20 Alfred Street, Milsons Point, Sydney, New South Wales 2061, Australia

Random House New Zealand Ltd 18 Poland Road, Glenfield, Auckland 10, New Zealand

Random House South Africa (Pty) Ltd Isle of Houghton, Corner Boundary Road & Carse O'Gowrie, Houghton 2198, South Africa

Random House UK Limited Reg. No. 954009

For further distribution details, see www.timeout.com.

ISBN: 978-1-84670-138-2

A CIP catalogue record for this book is available from the British Library.

Printed and bound by Firmengruppe APPL, aprinta druck, Wemding, Germany.

The Random House Group Limited supports The Forest Stewardship Council (FSC), the leading international forest certification organisation. All our titles that are printed on Greenpeace approved FSC certified paper carry the FSC logo. Our paper procurement policy can be found at http://www.rbooks.co.uk/environment.

Time Out carbon-offsets its flights with Trees for Cities (www.treesforcities.org).

While every effort has been made to ensure the accuracy of the information contained within this guide, the publishers cannot accept responsibility for any errors it may contain.

Contents

Introduction

The story of Chicago is a long, convoluted and fascinating tale that raises as many questions as it answers about the city's temperament and personality. However, Chicago's character can be summarised by the myriad nicknames that have been tossed its way since 'Urbs in Horto', or 'City in a Garden', appeared as its official motto in 1837.

None of Chicago's nicknames speak as vividly of the city's persistent attempts at self-improvement as 'Paris on the Prairie'. The name arose in the wake of Daniel Burnham's Plan of Chicago, published in 1909, which set out the architect's vision for beautifying the town. A century on, the city still often announces grand schemes to prettify itself, from the successful (Millennium Park) to the contentious (the bid for the 2016 Olympics).

Similarly, no nicknames are as colourfully evocative of the town's no-nonsense work ethic as those coined in the 1916 poem 'Chicago' by Galesburg native Carl Sandburg, who tagged the town as the 'Hog Butcher for the World' and the 'City of the Big Shoulders'. The meatpacking plants at which Sandburg's poem nodded have closed, but a blue-collar toughness remains tangible outside the city's long-since-gentrified centre.

A year after Nelson Algren called Chicago a 'City on the Make' in a 1951 essay, AJ Liebling labelled Chicago the 'Second City' in the *New Yorker*, neatly summarising both Chicago's inferiority complex and New York's inbuilt arrogance (at one point, Liebling sniffs that Chicago's skyline is merely 'a theatre backdrop with a city painted on it'). In population terms, Chicago's now third behind New York and LA, but the nickname remains useful shorthand for the way it's often overshadowed by its bigger, brasher urban rivals.

However, it's one of Chicago's more infamous locals who gave the town perhaps its most appropriate nickname. Richard J Daley's 21-year reign as mayor wasn't without its controversies, but his labelling of Chicago as 'The City that Works' captures its essence: unflashy and modest, resolute and uncomplicated. Still, while Chicago might be shy about trumpeting its glory, don't mistake its self-promotional reticence for a lack of pride. From the incomparable downtown skyline to the tapestry of character-packed neighbourhoods, Chicagoans love their town, and for good reason. It works, still. *Will Fulford-Jones, Editor*

Chicago in Brief

IN CONTEXT

Opening the book, a series of features illuminates the city's past, present and future, covering everything from its origins as a trading post to the 21st-century controversies surrounding Mayor Richard M Daley. There's also an extended look at the city's incomparable architecture, still making waves more than a century after the Chicago Fire of 1871 inadvertently gave birth to the skyscraper.
▶ For more, see pp15-52.

SIGHTS

The Sights section is where you'll find coverage of all the city's major attractions: the Art Institute of Chicago and Millennium Park, Lincoln Park Zoo and the Museum of Science & Industry, and many more besides. These reviews are woven into a full guide to the city's spreadeagled array of fascinating neighbourhoods, spotlighting points of interest both mainstream and alternative.
▶ For more, see pp53-124.

CONSUME

Chicago is one of the two or three best food cities in the US, its mix of high-profile chef-led restaurants and small ethnic eateries offering almost unmatched variety. It's also a drinker's town, soaked in bars of all shapes, sizes and varieties. Shops-wise, the major stores on the fabled Magnificent Mile are the tip of a retail iceberg. Completing this section of the book is a rundown of the city's best hotels.
▶ For more, see pp125-212.

ARTS & ENTERTAINMENT

Big-name musical acts and phenomenally successful Broadway shows make their way to Chicago on a regular basis, drawing huge crowds when they arrive. But perhaps of greater interest are the strong and vital local cultural scenes, on show everywhere from storefront galleries to Symphony Center, 50-year-old comedy venues to of-the-moment nightclubs.
▶ For more, see pp213-288.

ESCAPES & EXCURSIONS

The area around Chicago isn't packed with a wealth of amazing options for those keen on escaping the buzz of the city. However, if you know where to look, it's not without its appeal: the urban delights of Milwaukee and Indianapolis, the college-town cuteness of Madison, historic Springfield, beautiful Door County and the multifarious charms of the Indiana Dunes.
▶ For more, see pp289-300.

Chicago in 48 Hours

Day 1 Downtown Delights

9AM Start by taking in one of the best views of the city: from the **Michigan Avenue Bridge** (*see p59*). If your appetite for architecture has been whetted, and if it's summer, it's a short hop to the pier from which you can catch the **Chicago Architecture Foundation**'s Architecture River Cruise (book in advance; *see p304*). Otherwise, walk south to **Millennium Park** (*see p54*), then move on to the regenerated **Art Institute of Chicago** (*see p56*).

NOON If it's Monday, Tuesday or Wednesday, there may be a free concert at the **Chicago Cultural Center** (*see p255*). If not, try Rick Bayless's **Frontera Fresco** on the top floor of Macy's (*see p147*) or, for something a bit more formal, nouveau-gastropub the **Gage** (*see p147*).

1.30PM Weather permitting, walk off your lunch by taking our tour of public art in the Loop (*see p62*). From here, stroll through Millennium Park and **Grant Park**, past the **Buckingham Fountain** (*see p56*) and on to **Museum Campus**. When you get here, take your pick from three fine attractions: the **Shedd Aquarium**, the **Field Museum** and the **Adler Planetarium** (for all, *see p68*), from which you can get tremendous views of the Loop skyline.

5.30PM No first-time visit is complete without **riding around the Loop** on one of the elevated train lines (*see p302*). Wander across from Museum Campus and pick up the Orange line at Roosevelt, taking in Chicago's business district from this most evocative of vantage points.

7PM The Loop quietens down at night, but there are plenty of dinner options west across the river in the West Loop (try **Publican** or **Blackbird**; *see pp162-164*) or south in **Chinatown** (*see pp149-151*). From here, take the train or a cab up to the 95th floor of the **John Hancock Center** (*see p79*) and a nightcap in the **Signature Lounge**. It's pretty touristy, and you'll pay heavily for your drink. However, it'll still be better value than a ride to the observation deck. And the views, especially at night, are incomparably dramatic.

NAVIGATING THE CITY

Thanks to its grid system, Chicago is easy to navigate. Ground zero is at the corner of State and Madison Streets in the Loop. Addresses on north–south roads are numbered according to how many blocks north or south of Madison they sit; the same is true of east–west thoroughfares and State Street. A street-number range of 800 corresponds to about a mile; for example, it's roughly two miles between 1 N Clark Street and 1601 N Clark Street.

The grid system also makes it easy to pinpoint the location of any address. For instance, notable main east–west streets north of Madison include Chicago Avenue. Chicago Avenue is on the axis of 800 N, which means that street addresses close to 800 N will be near the road's intersection with Chicago (for instance, Water Tower Place at 835 N Michigan Avenue is a mere block north of Michigan and Chicago). Other notable east–west streets include Division (at 1200 North),

Day 2 Exploring the City

8.30AM Start your second day in Chicago off the beaten downtown path. Start with a lush breakfast at the **Bongo Room** in Wicker Park (*see p168*), then ride the bus east along North Avenue. At the end of the line, you'll be right by the fine **Chicago History Museum** (*see p88*). But if it's a nice day, consider statue-spotting in lakeside **Lincoln Park** (*see p89*), with a detour to the **Green City Market** (*see p204*) or the **Lincoln Park Zoo** (*see p89*).

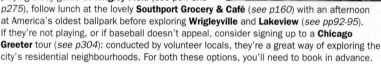

NOON If you're here when the Chicago Cubs are playing a day game at **Wrigley Field** (*see p94 and p275*), follow lunch at the lovely **Southport Grocery & Café** (*see p160*) with an afternoon at America's oldest ballpark before exploring **Wrigleyville** and **Lakeview** (*see pp92-95*). If they're not playing, or if baseball doesn't appeal, consider signing up to a **Chicago Greeter** tour (*see p304*): conducted by volunteer locals, they're a great way of exploring the city's residential neighbourhoods. For both these options, you'll need to book in advance.

5PM With any luck, there'll be time before dinner for a little shopping. If big-name brands are your thing, head to the **Magnificent Mile** to catch more or less every big name in American retail. All the major stores remain open until 7pm; many continue trading until 8pm or even 9pm. If independents are more your bag, try the cornucopia of small stores around **Wicker Park**, dealing in fashion, books, gifts and more. For more on shops, *see pp188-212*.

8PM And if you've been shopping in Wicker Park, you'll be in a pretty good place for dinner. After a cocktail at **Violet Hour** (*see p185*), take your pick from local favourites such as **Hot Chocolate**, **Bristol** and **Crust** (for all, *see pp168-169*).

10PM Still got energy? See if there are any worthwhile bands playing at the **Double Door** or the **Empty Bottle**, both within easy reach (*see p259*), or check out the DJs at **Darkroom**, **Sonotheque** or the **Debonair Social Club** (for all, *see p274*)...

North (1600 N), Armitage (2000 N), Fullerton (2400 N), Diversey (2800 N), Belmont (3200 N) and Addison (3600 N); notable north-south streets include Halsted (at 800 West), Racine (1200 W), Ashland (1600 W) and Damen (2000 W).

SEEING THE SIGHTS

Sightseeing in Chicago can be expensive. However, many of the big museums offer free admission one day a week; for a list of these free days, *see p77*.

PACKAGE DEALS

The **Chicago CityPass** (www.citypass. com) gives pre-paid, queue-jumping access to five big attractions: the trio at Museum Campus, plus the Museum of Science & Industry and a priority pass to either the John Hancock Observatory or the Willis Tower Skydeck. The pass is valid for nine days after first use and costs $69 for adults ($59 for kids). You can buy a CityPass at www.citypass.com or at any of the participating attractions.

Chicago in Profile

THE LOOP

Chicago's downtown core remains a pulsating, fascinating place, soaked in wonderful architecture but ultimately still defined by the elevated train network that rings its boundaries. Alongside its role as the financial hub of the Midwest, it's also home to one of the city's biggest attractions: **Millennium Park**.
▶ For more, see pp54-66.

THE SOUTH LOOP & CHINATOWN

The **South Loop** is an area very much in flux, its once-deserted streets now gradually filling with new apartment blocks and condo towers. To the south-east sits the trio of great museums that make up **Museum Campus**; further south sits Chicago's small, appealing and characterful **Chinatown**.
▶ For more, see pp67-73.

THE NEAR NORTH SIDE

Just north of the Chicago River lies a tourist honeypot of hotels, bars, restaurants, clubs and shops. The latter line the **Magnificent Mile**, a stretch of Michigan Avenue packed with big-name stores. To the east sits demure **Streeterville**; to the north lies the varied landscape of **River North**; and due north is the plush, moneyed **Gold Coast**.
▶ For more, see pp74-85.

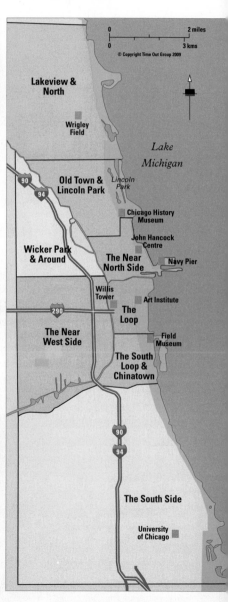

0   2 miles
0   3 kms
© Copyright Time Out Group 2009

Lakeview & North

Wrigley Field

Lake Michigan

Old Town & Lincoln Park   *Lincoln Park*

90   94

Chicago History Museum

John Hancock Centre

Wicker Park & Around

The Near North Side   **Navy Pier**

Willis Tower

290

Art Institute

The Loop

The Near West Side

Field Museum

The South Loop & Chinatown

90   94

The South Side

University of Chicago

OLD TOWN & LINCOLN PARK

One of Chicago's great glories is **Lincoln Park**, which begins at the top of the Gold Coast and stretches north for miles along the shore of Lake Michigan. You'll find everything from golf courses to beaches here, plus a zoo and innumerable statues. Several neighbourhoods run alongside the park as it progresses north; the southernmost of them are the mellow residential locales of **Old Town** and **Lincoln Park**.
▶ *For more, see pp86-91.*

LAKEVIEW & NORTH

Directly north of the Lincoln Park neighbourhood, **Lakeview** is home to the Midwest's largest gay community (in **Boystown**) and the Chicago Cubs baseball team (in **Wrigleyville**). Nearby sit quieter residential areas such as **Andersonville** and **Roscoe Village**; further north lies suburban **Evanston** and the **North Shore**.
▶ *For more, see pp92-99.*

THE NEAR WEST SIDE

Just across the river from Chicago's business district, the **West Loop** has been transformed in recent years, its warehouses and industrial buildings now joined by a slew of new clubs and restaurants and apartment complexes. Not far away sit three keystone ethnic neighbourhoods: **Greektown**, **Little Italy** and Latino-tilted **Pilsen**.
▶ *For more, see pp100-106.*

WICKER PARK & BUCKTOWN

Over the last dozen years, the twin neighbourhoods of **Wicker Park** and **Bucktown** have been gentrified beyond the point of recognition by countless bars, shops and restaurants. Change has been less dramatic to the south in **West Town** and **Ukrainian Village**, but they've risen in stature nonetheless.
▶ *For more, see pp107-112.*

OAK PARK

Roughly 20 minutes west of the Loop by train, quiet, pleasant and unabashedly suburban Oak Park has more to offer the resident than the visitor. However, it merits mention here thanks to Frank Lloyd Wright, who earned his spurs designing 25 homes in the area (including his own, now open to the public).
▶ *For more, see pp113-116.*

THE SOUTH SIDE

Chicago's sprawling South Side isn't much favoured by tourists, but there are a few pockets of interest in among its chiefly residential sprawl: in particular, the historic African American neighbourhood of **Bronzeville**, slowly on the rise, and sedate **Hyde Park**, home to the University of Chicago and the Museum of Science & Industry.
▶ *For more, see pp117-123.*

Time Out Chicago

Editorial
Editor Will Fulford-Jones
Consultant Editor Amy Carr for *Time Out Chicago*
Copy Editors Edoardo Albert, Ismay Atkins
Listings Editor Stephanie Dolan
Proofreader Mandy Martinez
Indexer Anna Norman

Managing Director Peter Fiennes
Editorial Director Ruth Jarvis
Series Editor Will Fulford-Jones
Business Manager Dan Allen
Editorial Manager Holly Pick
Assistant Management Accountant Ija Krasnikova

Design
Art Director Scott Moore
Art Editor Pinelope Kourmouzoglou
Senior Designer Henry Elphick
Graphic Designers Kei Ishimaru, Nicola Wilson
Advertising Designer Jodi Sher

Picture Desk
Picture Editor Jael Marschner
Deputy Picture Editor Lynn Chambers
Picture Researcher Gemma Walters
Picture Desk Assistant Marzena Zoladz
Picture Librarian Christina Theisen

Advertising
Commercial Director Mark Phillips
International Advertising Manager Kasimir Berger
International Sales Executive Charlie Sokol
Advertising Sales (Chicago) Vicki Pelling, Trevor
   Mikus, Mari Taisch, Erik Uppenberg, January Overton

Marketing
Marketing Manager Yvonne Poon
**Sales & Marketing Director, North America
   & Latin America** Lisa Levinson
Senior Publishing Brand Manager Luthfa Begum
Art Director Anthony Huggins

Production
Group Production Director Mark Lamond
Production Manager Brendan McKeown
Production Controller Damian Bennett
Production Coordinator Kelly Fenlon

Time Out Group
Chairman Tony Elliott
Chief Executive Officer David King
Group General Manager/Director Nichola Coulthard
Time Out Communications Ltd MD David Pepper
Time Out International Ltd MD Cathy Runciman
Time Out Magazine Ltd Publisher/MD Mark Elliott
Group IT Director Simon Chappell
Marketing & Circulation Director Catherine Demajo

Contributors
Introduction Will Fulford-Jones. **History** Victoria Cunha, Will Fulford-Jones (*Freedom Fighters* Julia Borcherts).
Chicago Today Robert K Elder. **Architecture** Madeline Nusser (*Tall Stories* Web Behrens). **The Machine** John Dugan.
On Location Will Fulford-Jones, Chris Jones. **Sights: The Loop** Lauren Weinberg (*Walk: Art in the Loop* Will Fulford-Jones; *Profile: Willis Tower* Madeline Nusser). **The South Loop & Chinatown** Will Fulford-Jones (*Profile: Field Museum* Madeline Nusser). **The Near North Side** Martina Sheehan. **Old Town & Lincoln Park** Will Fulford-Jones. **Lakeview & North** Jason A Heidemann (*Field of Dreams?* Will Fulford-Jones). **The North Shore** Will Fulford-Jones. **The Near West Side** John Dugan (*Neighbourhood Watch* Madeline Nusser). **Wicker Park & Around** John Dugan. **Oak Park** Will Fulford-Jones. **The South Side** Will Fulford-Jones (*Walk: Barack 'n' Roll* Martina Sheehan). **Hotels** Will Fulford-Jones, Jessica Herman. **Restaurants** Heather Shouse, *Time Out Chicago* staff (*In the 'Hood: Chinatown* Lisa Shames; *In the Hood: Pilsen* David Tamarkin). **Bars** Heather Shouse, *Time Out Chicago* staff (*The Brew Crew: Goose Island* Will Fulford-Jones). **Shops & Services** Kevin Aeh (*Shop Class* Lauren Weinberg; *The Vinyl Score* Brent DiCrescenzo). **Calendar** Madeline Nusser (*Profile: Neighbourhood Festivals* Judy Sutton Taylor). **Children** Judy Sutton Taylor. **Comedy** Jason A Heidemann. **Dance** Asimina Chremos. **Film** Hank Sartin. **Galleries** Lauren Weinberg. **Gay & Lesbian** Jason A Heidemann. **Music** Brent DiCrescenzo, Bryant Manning. **Nightlife** John Dugan. **Sports & Fitness** Tim McCormick. **Theatre** John Beer (*Midnight Express* Christopher Piatt, Kris Vire). **Escapes & Excursions** Ruth Welte, *Time Out Chicago* staff. **Directory** Will Fulford-Jones.

Maps john@jsgraphics.co.uk, except: page 336, used by kind permission of the Chicago Transit Authority.

Photography Martha Williams, except: pages 16, 23, 45, 49 Getty Images; page 20 ClassicStock/TopFoto; page 30 AP/Press Association Images; page 50 Kobal Collection/Warner Bros/DC Comics; page 52 Kobal Collection/Paramount; pages 165, 171 Tim Klein; page 276 David Durochik/isiphotos.com; pages 282, 284 Michael Brosilow; page 283 Anna Knott; page 286 Lara Goetsch; page 288 Margaret K Lakin. The following images were provided by the featured establishments/artists: pages 124, 225, 230, 231, 232.

The Editor would like to thank Frank Sennett, Amy Carr, Nicole Radja, Kim R Russell and the staff at *Time Out Chicago* magazine; Gregory Stepanek at the Chicago Transit Authority; and all contributors to previous editions of the *Time Out Chicago* guide, whose work forms the basis for parts of this book.

About the Guide

GETTING AROUND

The back of the book contains street maps of Chicago, as well as overview maps of the city and its surroundings. The maps start on page 321; on them are marked the locations of hotels (**❶**), restaurants (**❶**) and bars (**❶**). The majority of businesses listed in this guide are located in the areas we've mapped; the grid-square references in the listings refer to these maps.

THE ESSENTIALS

For practical information, including visas, disabled access, emergencies, lost property, useful websites and local transport, please see the Directory. It begins on page 301.

THE LISTINGS

Addresses, phone numbers, websites, transport information, hours and prices are all included in our listings, as are selected other facilities. All were checked and correct at press time. However, business owners can alter their arrangements at any time, and fluctuating economic conditions can cause prices to change rapidly.

The very best venues in the city, the must-sees and must-dos in every category, have been marked with a red star (★). In the Sights chapters, we've also marked venues that offer free admission with a FREE symbol.

PHONE NUMBERS

Chicago has a number of different area codes. The Loop and other downtown districts are covered by 312; the rest of the city is served by 773; and the suburbs surrounding the city are served by 630, 708 and 847. You don't need to use the area code if you're calling from a number with the same code. From elsewhere in the US, dial the 11-digit numbers as listed in this book.

From outside the US, dial your country's international access code (00 from the UK) or the '+' symbol (when using a mobile phone), followed by the number as listed in this guide. So, to reach the Art Institute of Chicago, dial +1-312 443 3600. For more on phones, *see p309*.

FEEDBACK

We welcome feedback on this guide, both on the venues we've included and on any other locations that you'd like to see featured in future editions. Please email us at guides@timeout.com.

Time Out Guides

Founded in 1968, Time Out has grown from humble beginnings into the leading resource for anyone wanting to know what's happening in the world's greatest cities. Alongside our influential weeklies in London, New York and Chicago, we publish more than 20 magazines in cities as varied as Beijing and Beirut; a range of travel books, with the City Guides now joined by the newer Shortlist series; and an information-packed website. The company remains proudly independent, still owned by Tony Elliott four decades after he launched *Time Out London*.

Written by local experts and illustrated with original photography, our books also retain their independence. No business has been featured because it has advertised, and all restaurants and bars are visited and reviewed anonymously.

ABOUT THE EDITOR

Will Fulford-Jones is the Series Editor of Time Out's City Guides series, and has edited more than 20 books for Time Out.

A full list of the book's contributors can be found opposite. However, we've also included details of our writers in selected chapters through the guide; the majority are regular contributors to *Time Out Chicago* magazine, published weekly and available at www.timeoutchicago.com.

If you haven't seen Blue Man Group, you haven't seen Chicago.

In Context

Chicago from the Adler Planetarium. *See pp34-44.*

History

Life by the lake.

TEXT: VICTORIA CUNHA & WILL FULFORD-JONES

The location, a boggy swampland on the edge of Lake Michigan, was far from ideal. But the efforts of those who chose to settle in what eventually became Chicago turned its geographical circumstance from a potential curse into an undoubted blessing. Ever since a Haitian traveller made his home here in the 1770s, successive residents have fought tooth and nail to turn their town into a major player. Indeed, 21st-century Chicago can only be explained by a look at the 250 years that preceded it.

EARLY SETTLERS

Missionary Father Jacques Marquette and cartographer Louis Jolliet were the first Europeans to explore the lower Lake Michigan region. In 1673, chartered and funded by the governor of New France (now Quebec), the pair attempted to follow the Mississippi and its tributaries as far as possible to the north-east. After travelling to the native village of Kaskaskia (near what is now the town of North Utica) on the Illinois River, the intrepid duo proceeded north-east on the Des Plaines River.

When they reached what the local Native Americans called 'Checagou' (believed to translate as 'wild onion', which grew in the area), Marquette and Jolliet's party floated down the Chicago River to Lake Michigan before heading north to Green Bay in autumn 1673. The trip was deemed a success, so much so that Marquette returned to the area in 1674 and spent the winter in what would later become known as Chicago before heading back to Kaskaskia in the spring. Jolliet never again visited the area.

The first permanent non-native resident of Chicago, Haitian pioneer Jean-Baptiste Point du Sable, came to the area almost exactly a century later. The son of French parents, the black Du Sable is believed to have established a fur trading post at the mouth of the Chicago River as early as 1772, marrying a Potawatomie native named Catherine around the same time. More than two decades later, Du Sable sold his property on to a fur trapper, who in turn sold it almost immediately to a trader named John Kinzie. The area's first permanent white settler, Kinzie eventually came to be known as 'the Father of Chicago'. However, it's the more unassuming Du Sable who deserves the nickname.

THEY FORT THE LAW

Fearful of further trouble after the War of Independence, the government decided a military presence was necessary, and so Fort Dearborn was built in 1803 at what is now the south end of the Michigan Avenue Bridge. Then the major western US Army garrison in the country, it occupied a strategic point near the southern end of Lake Michigan on the south side of the Chicago River, just across from the cabin built by Du Sable. Sure enough, the US was soon once more battling the British; by the summer of 1812, tensions between soldiers and natives, who were bought off by the British, were at an all-time high.

Despite efforts to appease the Potawatomie leaders, Captain Nathaniel Heald decided that safety concerns were so great, Fort Dearborn should be evacuated. Accompanied by an escort of friendly Miami natives from Indiana, the garrison began its journey along the lake, but was ambushed by natives. Heald and his wife were taken prisoner, but almost all the others who were attempting to leave the fort were executed; in all, 53 settlers and natives died. The Potawatomies returned three days later and burnt the fort.

After the war was over, trading once more began to take place in the area. Having fled during the massacre, Kinzie came back in 1816 and resumed his business activities. His descendants continued to make themselves known through their various civic and industrial ventures in the remaining years of the 19th century; his son, John H Kinzie, even stood for mayor in 1834. Today's Kinzie Street, which lies just north of the Chicago River, is testimony to his influence.

Gurdon Hubbard, another early settler, arrived from Montreal in 1818, the same year Illinois joined the union, and quickly established a fur trade route from Danville, Illinois, to Chicago. A decade later, he bought the Illinois branch of the massively profitable American Fur Company franchise; in so doing, he cemented his position on the trading ladder and set the stage for the city's future expansion. By the time Chicago was incorporated as a town in 1833, Hubbard had begun to diversify into meatpacking, shipping, insurance and real estate, while also campaigning for the construction of the Illinois–Michigan Canal. For the next three decades, his own prosperity mirrored that of his adopted home town.

IN CONTEXT

'An economic depression that swept the country in 1837, known as the Panic, threatened to put a lid on Chicago's growth.'

PIONEER CHECKPOINT

When the Erie Canal opened in 1825, it linked the Hudson River – and, thus, the East Coast – with Buffalo, New York (on Lake Erie). The canal opened up Illinois to travel and commerce, a great boon to the pioneers who were arriving from more populous areas in the east. A prime example was William Ogden, a transplanted Yankee who came west in 1835 and, two years later, became mayor of Chicago.

Meatpacking mogul Philip Armour also moved to Chicago (from Milwaukee) after the Civil War ended, and earned millions selling barrels of pork. Armour employed refrigerated train cars for shipping fresh meat, expanded the use of animal by-products, and diversified into other businesses. Meanwhile, Cyrus McCormick found Chicago to be just as hospitable to his Virginia-bred sensibilities, even borrowing money from Ogden to build the factory that would produce the mechanical reapers he had invented. During his time in Chicago, the belligerent McCormick became active in Democratic politics, and ran for Congress in 1864. Today, he's commemorated in the name of the city's convention centre.

However, few outsiders went on to have as much influence over the growth of Chicago as 'Long' John Wentworth, whose appetites for food, drink and good living matched his stature (he stood six feet six inches tall and weighed more than 300 pounds). After arriving in 1836 at the age of 21, Wentworth became the managing editor and, later, the owner-publisher of the *Chicago Democrat*, the city's first newspaper. He closed the newspaper in 1861, effectively merging it with the *Tribune* (which had been founded in 1847), but at the time, he had bigger fish to fry: having served five terms in the House of Representatives as a Democrat, Wentworth had been elected as the city's Republican mayor in 1857.

TRAINS AND BOATS AND PLAINS

An economic depression that swept the country in 1837, known as the Panic, threatened to put a lid on Chicago's growth. However, the Panic coincided with Chicago achieving city status, and things were quick to pick up after the worst had passed. In 1848, two projects were completed that between them signalled the start of Chicago's immense growth: the first telegraph line reached the city, radically improving communications, and the Illinois–Michigan Canal was finally completed almost two decades after work on it had begun, offering the city a connection to and from the Atlantic via the Great Lakes.

Because of its central location and existing trade connections, Chicago became a crucial checkpoint for railway commerce in the US. Soon, livestock, timber, grain and other goods were transported speedily through the city in previously unheard-of quantities. More and more industries established their headquarters on the south-western shores of Lake Michigan rather than at rival St Louis, roughly 300 miles away in Missouri. By 1856, Chicago had become the largest railroad centre in the country.

Chicago's steel industry was boosted by the unmatched transportation links. Situated along the banks of Lake Michigan at the mouth of the Calumet River, South Chicago became home to a number of blast furnaces. By the turn of the century, steel production in the area accounted for 50 per cent of the entire domestic output.

The employment of unskilled immigrant labour in the city's steel mills was a major factor in the growth and development of Chicago's south-east neighbourhoods. By

1870, more than half of Chicago's 300,000-strong population was foreign-born, with Germans, Irish, Bohemians and Scandinavians representing the majority of the city's new arrivals. The rapid population growth led, by necessity, to the construction of cheap, wooden buildings – at the time, timber was both cheap and easy to obtain. Fires sprang up around Chicago from time to time, but few imagined the horror that lay just around the corner.

FIRE AND RAIN

On 8 October 1871, a fire broke out adjacent to an immigrant neighbourhood that bordered the central business district. Spreading to the north-east, the blaze gained momentum, and didn't slow even upon reaching the south branch of the Chicago River. A dry summer, a concentration of wooden constructions (including roadways), and the presence of convection whirls (nicknamed 'fire devils', they enabled the blazes to leap over rivers) all stoked the inferno.

By the time it finally burned itself out in Lincoln Park, several miles north of where it had started, the blaze had carved an unprecedented trail of destruction. Over an area from Taylor Street north to Fullerton and from the river east to Lake Michigan, 17,000 buildings were destroyed, 98,000 people were left homeless and more than 300 lives were lost.

But the city's efforts to regenerate itself in the wake of the disaster were every bit as spectacular as the fire itself. Relief efforts soon gave way to rebuilding ventures; the downtown merchants wasted no time in obtaining loans and hiring crews to construct new, fireproof buildings. A mere 12 months on, 300 new structures had been erected; a few years down the line, taller, fireproof buildings stood proudly in place of the shambolic wooden structures that once made up downtown Chicago. Attracted by a blank canvas, and motivated by the enthusiasms of the city fathers, architects began to develop the extant elevator buildings into what were later termed 'skyscrapers'. The ultimate result of the fire was what remains, to this day, the finest collection of urban architecture in the US.

Another elemental problem, that of water, also needed to be addressed. Despite the seemingly unlimited supply of freshwater provided by Lake Michigan, the vast quantities of polluting matter dumped into the Chicago River were in danger of permanently befouling the city's water supplies. The eventual solution to the problem affected not only city residents but also those from downstate, since the plan involved forcing the river to run not towards but away from the lake. The sewage that had previously flowed into the clear waters of Lake Michigan would be redirected to the Mississippi by means of a channel built to extend as far as a tributary in Lockport, Illinois. This channel, later known as the Sanitary & Ship Canal, was commissioned in 1889 and opened 11 years later.

RIOT AND REFORM

But for all the successful regenerative efforts, not everything went smoothly. A nationwide railroad strike in the 1870s affected Chicago more than most, pitting out-of-work rioters against state militia units. The mayor issued warnings to those not affected by the walkout to stay at home, away from the out-of-control mobs, but not everyone heeded them. A number of protesters and civilians died in the violence.

The Haymarket Square riot of 1886 was a watershed in the struggle between self-described 'anarchist' workers and their bosses. On the night of 4 May, a public gathering to protest against the treatment of workers at Cyrus McCormick's factory turned violent when a bomb was thrown at the police. Eight officers and three protestors died in the riots, yet only eight men stood trial. Four were executed for their part in the demonstrations, but three were pardoned. The 'Haymarket martyrs', as they came to be known, inspired the socialist celebrations of ordinary workers that continue around the world each May Day.

IN CONTEXT

Throughout this period, immigrants continued to descend on Chicago, the majority from Poland, Germany, Italy and Ireland. Not all of them immediately found work, and many of those who did were forced to live in abject poverty. Jane Addams and Ellen Gates Starr decided to do something about it. The twentysomething duo, who'd met as teenagers at Rockford Female Seminary (now Rockford College), returned in 1888 from a tour of Europe inspired by what they'd seen at Toynbee Hall in London. The following year, in a mansion on Halsted Street donated by Charles Hull, they founded Hull-House to provide social services to deprived locals. One of the first such settlement houses in the US, Hull-House proved immensely influential in the late 19th- and early 20th-century push for social reform in America. In 1931, Addams' work led to her being awarded the Nobel Peace Prize.

The year after Addams and Starr opened Hull-House, the wheels were set in motion for the creation of a different but equally important Chicago institution. Founded (and, for the most part, funded) by John D Rockefeller, the University of Chicago held its first classes in 1892 on a parcel of land at 57th Street and Ellis Avenue.

Something of a progressive, university president William Rainey Harper envisioned his institution offering an equal education for both male and female students, operating a press in order to disseminate its teachings throughout the country, and using a then-novel 'quarter' system to allow for greater flexibility in the schedules of faculty and staff. However, the university is now best known for the role it played in the development of nuclear energy when, in 1942, a team led by Enrico Fermi built the first ever nuclear reactor. The event led to the Manhattan Project and the creation of the world's first atomic bomb.

FAIR'S FARE

Held just 22 years after the Chicago Fire, the World's Columbian Exposition of 1893 was a perfect opportunity for Chicago to showcase its growth. A team of planners and designers led by Daniel Burnham and Frederick Law Olmsted created a series of grand attractions in a specially created 'White City', with 46 nations providing 250,000 displays. The first ever Ferris wheel, standing 250 feet (76 metres) tall and kitted out with 36 cars, was built for the fair. However, the 'Streets in Cairo' section was the fair's most profitable attraction, due in no small part to the suggestive cavortings of an exotic dancer named Little Egypt.

IN CONTEXT

Chicago's **elevated train network**.

'For gambling and prostitution to flourish in the city, eyes had to look the other way. The politicians in charge were happy to oblige.'

More than 25 million visitors came to the city during the six months the fair was in place, putting Chicago back on the map in the eyes of outsiders who'd written it off after the fire. However, it also kicked off a more general renaissance of popular entertainment in the city that lasted long after the fair had ended. Dance halls, movie palaces, nightclubs and vaudeville shows all sprang up around the time of the event and in the years immediately after it, greatly expanding the array of cultural options available to locals.

SIN CITY

Around the time of the Columbian Exposition, the Levee district in Chicago's First Ward took corruption and decadence to levels previously unmatched in the city's already fairly rich history. Centred around State and 22nd Streets, close to modern-day Chinatown, the area was flooded with gamblers, drunks and prostitutes. The latter plied their trade in an astonishing 200 brothels, revelling in such colourful names as the Everleigh Club (run by sisters Minna and Ada), Freiberg's Dance Hall, the Library and the Opium Den.

For such activity to flourish, favours had to be granted and eyes had to look the other way. The politicos in charge of the area were only too happy to oblige. Colourfully nicknamed Chicago aldermen Michael 'Hinky Dink' Kenna and 'Bathhouse' John Coughlin got into the habit of lining their pockets with lucre from businesses grateful for their support; the duo then used some of this cash to buy votes in First Ward elections. The pair were even said to have run an unofficial office out of Freiberg's Dance Hall.

One of the beneficiaries of Kenna's and Coughlin's largesse was Charles Tyson Yerkes, who settled in Chicago in the 1880s and began to buy favours from the aldermen in a bid to gain control of the city's streetcar lines. The brash Yerkes expanded his activities into ownership of trolley cars and elevated train car lines. But eventually, the 'Traction King', as Yerkes was known, went too far when he inspired his political cohorts to introduce a bill that would extend his transit franchise for another 50 years without any compensation to the city. Although the bill was passed in 1895, it was repealed after two years of protest. Yerkes moved to New York in 1899; 48 years after his departure, the Chicago Transit Authority was created as a municipal agency to oversee the city's mass transit.

Eventually, a Vice Commission appointed by the mayor enabled enforcers to shut down brothels in the First Ward. After the Everleigh closed its doors in 1911, the rest of the Levee's bordellos, saloons and gambling houses were systematically raided until both patrons and proprietors wearied of the law's interference. A few later reopened under a cloak of darkness, but the area never again flourished.

SAM'S THE MAN

After emigrating from Britain to the US in 1881 to work as Thomas Edison's assistant, Samuel Insull proved his worth in business by increasing Edison's domestic business fourfold, before becoming president of the Chicago Edison Company in 1892. Insull was also one of the forces behind the creation of the railroad system that connects Chicago to its suburbs, now known as Metra.

However, for all his entrepreneurial spirit, the stubborn, starchy Insull's true passion was for opera. So much so, in fact, that he proposed building a new opera house for

IN CONTEXT

the town that would be financially supported by offices within its building (much like Adler and Sullivan's Auditorium Building, completed in 1889). Insull soon had the support of the major arts patrons, but insisted on looking after the entire project himself, hiring the firm of Graham, Anderson, Probst and White to design the structure.

Upon its completion, the Civic Opera House was acclaimed as a magnificent building, fêted by the city fathers who'd help fund its construction. Unfortunately, its completion came in 1929, shortly after the stock market crashed. After losing all of his companies, Insull travelled to Europe for a brief respite, before returning to the States to face court proceedings relating to fraud and embezzlement. He was acquitted, but his reputation and his finances never recovered. He died in 1938, suffering a heart attack in the Paris *métro*.

FATHER AND SON

The mayoral legacies of Carter Harrison senior and junior, which dated back to the 1870s, left large shoes to fill. The 24th mayor of Chicago (he went on to win five terms in office), the elder Harrison took charge in 1879 and presided over much of the rebuilding that followed the Chicago Fire; he later served as mayor during the World's Columbian Exposition, but was murdered in his home just three days before it ended.

The younger Harrison – elected in 1897 as the 30th mayor of Chicago, but the first born in the city – proved to be even more reform-minded than his father. Also winning five terms in office, he was known for his fair dealings with immigrant and minority groups, and was one of the driving forces behind the moral clean-up in the Levee during the early 1910s.

By 1915, Harrison Jr's star had started to wane. He was defeated in the Democratic primary by Robert Sweitzer, who in turn was roundly thrashed at the mayoral elections by William Hale Thompson. The scion of a real estate business family and a powerful friend to the likes of Al Capone, 'Big Bill' was not a clever man, but his belligerence suited the mood of the city, desperate to escape a recession.

While Thompson was an enthusiastic recipient of many minority votes, his passivity during the Chicago Race Riots that same year hurt his chances of re-election. In the summer of 1919, an isolated incident on one of Chicago's beaches set off five days of rioting between whites and blacks, leaving more than 35 people dead and hundreds more injured. Things escalated further with the death of black teenager Eugene Williams, who drowned at the segregated 29th Street beach on 27 July 1919 after a confrontation between blacks and whites reputedly prevented him from coming ashore.

Williams' death was the spark that set alight a series of violent racial battles. When word got out about it, the story soon changed: rumours spread that Williams had been stoned to death, prompting fury in the black community. After several attempts to quell the violence without force, Mayor Thompson asked the governor of Illinois for the assistance of state troops and 5,000 men were summoned to keep the peace. Coupled with his pro-German stance during World War I, the reasons for Thompson's fall from grace become obvious. He failed to win re-election in 1923.

PROHIBITION AND THE MOB

The Prohibition era in the US began when, on 16 January 1920, Congress ratified the 18th Amendment banning the manufacture and sale of alcohol. Chicago's involvement in the days prior to the amendment came chiefly through Evanston's Frances Willard, president of the Women's Christian Temperance Union for four decades.

Spurred on by the WCTU, the temperance movement gained momentum in the years after World War I: alcohol restrictions were first enacted at the community and state levels, and then across the country. However, the ideals of the 18th Amendment created hypocrisy within American society, corruption within government, and a vast increase in organised crime. Chicago was in the thick of the action.

Profile Al Capone

Chicago's mob notoriety begins with the man they called 'Scarface'.

It's the curse of Chicago's second-city status that many of its notable residents have left it for New York, travelling to find greater success in their chosen fields. Alphonse Gabriel Capone took the opposite route. Born and raised in Brooklyn during the last year of the 19th century, Capone spent his teens and early twenties bouncing around a series of ne'er-do-well New York gangs. He achieved a level of infamy, but it was only when he relocated to the Windy City that he hit the big time.

Capone's move to Chicago came at the behest of another exiled New Yorker. A former Coney Island gang leader 17 years Capone's senior, Johnny Torrio had taken a shine to the feisty young teenager back on the East Coast, and summoned the upstart to help run his bootlegging and gambling operations on Chicago's South Side. Capone soon rose through the ranks to serve as his right-hand man. And when Torrio fled to Italy in 1925, Capone picked up the reins.

Capone's takeover coincided with the return to the mayor's office, in 1927, of 'Big' Bill Thompson. Unlike the incorruptible William Dever, his predecessor, Thompson was more than happy to turn a blind eye to Capone's activities, which by then were dominated by a huge, lucrative and illegal liquor distribution network. With Prohibition in full swing, demand for alcohol was nearly unquenchable; but Capone, through a mix of business savvy and unfettered aggression, was able to meet it. When jealous North Side gangsters challenged him, he simply had them killed; most notoriously on 14 February 1929, when seven gangsters were executed in a Lincoln Park garage in what became known as the St Valentine's Day Massacre (pictured).

It took a group of outsiders to challenge Mob hegemony. US marshal Eliot Ness was charged with gathering evidence against the gangsters. Ness and his team, later nicknamed the Untouchables due to their resistance to Mob bribery, couldn't pin the St Valentine's Day Massacre on Capone. However, federal investigators did tag him with 22 charges of tax evasion.

Convicted in 1931, the same year Thompson left office, Capone ended up at Alcatraz, his empire disintegrating as he collapsed into syphilitic insanity. Following a cardiac arrest, Capone returned to Chicago in 1947 in a coffin, dead at 48 but assured of notoriety forever.

IN CONTEXT

SEE THE SIGHTS
Many Capone landmarks are gone; the garage at 2122 N Clark Street where the St Valentine's Day Massacre took place is now a garden. But a few remain on the South Side: *see p72.*

Mayor William Dever, who'd replaced Thompson in 1923, was in favour of Prohibition, and made every effort to enforce it. But then, as now, Chicago was a drinking city: Dever's attitudes were less than popular with the electorate, and opened the door to competition at the mayoral election in 1927. Opposing him was the indefatigable Thompson; raucous in his condemnation of Prohibition, he promised to reopen bars that Dever had closed.

There was more to Thompson's pro-alcohol stance than social liberalism. Under Prohibition, the Mob controlled the city's alcohol supply. During his first two terms in office, it was said that Thompson was in the pockets of the town's gangsters: first Johnny Torrio and then Al Capone. Dever was incorruptible, but Torrio and Capone were both careful to keep Thompson sweet even after he lost office in 1923. For his part, Thompson enjoyed the Mob support, not least because it helped him defeat Dever in 1927.

THE GREAT DEPRESSION

During the late 1920s and early 1930s, according to some historians, the Depression itself acted as a force for the repeal of the 18th Amendment, due to the changes it had produced within American society. In 1933, with the 21st Amendment that repealed Prohibition, it was clear that individual states would again take control of the regulation and taxation of alcohol, and that the sale of 'demon rum' would be legal once more.

During the Depression, the city's immigrant population base altered once more, a shift that was subsequently and dramatically reflected in Chicago politics. The changes began to take hold when Thompson was defeated in 1931 by Anton 'Tony' Cermak, a coal-miner's son and street vendor who had emigrated to the US from Bohemia as a child in the 1870s. It was Cermak who really set in motion the type of machine politics that typified Chicago government for much of the remainder of the 20th century (for more on this, *see pp45-48*), but he didn't get long to act out his plans. On 15 February 1933 in Miami, Cermak was struck by an assassin's bullet apparently intended for President Franklin D Roosevelt. Although he lingered for over two weeks, the wound proved fatal.

Cermak didn't live long enough to see Chicago's second World's Fair. Entitled the 'Century of Progress', it was held 40 years after the Columbian Exposition – in a neat nod to the earlier wing-ding, Daniel Burnham's two sons Hubert and Daniel were appointed to the board of trustees – and stayed open for two summers, 1933 and 1934. While not as influential as its predecessor, it proved both popular and profitable. The money raised aided the arts organisations involved in preserving the fair's exhibits, including the Museum of Science & Industry (built for the Columbian Exposition), the Adler Planetarium and the South Park Corporation (later taken over by the Chicago Park District).

After World War II, Chicago benefited from a huge boom. In 1950, its population topped 3.6 million; affluence was everywhere, as people began to move from the city to the suburbs. Five years later, the city was to reach a turning point with the election of one of the most famous American city mayors of the century.

DEUS EX MACHINE

In 1955, Richard J Daley won the first of six straight terms as mayor. Skilled in the machine politics tradition through his chairmanship of the Cook County Democratic Organization, Daley was an Irish American Democrat who gained the trust of minority and working-class voters with straight talk and a get-the-job-done attitude. But while he reigned more or less unchallenged for his first decade in office, aided in no small part by the patronage system (*see pp45-48*), his mettle was tested by spiralling crime and racial tensions, epitomised in the civil unrest triggered by the assassination of Dr Martin Luther King, Jr.

King had come to Chicago several times during the 1960s. With each visit, he flagged up more of the problems faced by minority communities: poor housing, job

discrimination, poverty, illiteracy and so on. However, he was greeted with scorn by white Chicagoans, even after several meetings with Daley in a bid to set up a Citizens Advisory Committee that could address racial tensions.

When King announced his intention to take up residence in a Lawndale slum building, the owners of the structure took him to court. Various rallies and marches led by King in white neighbourhoods led to police intervention, which in turn set the stage for the widespread burning and looting of white-owned businesses that occurred mainly in black neighbourhoods on the West Side immediately following King's death in April 1968. To stem the chaos, Daley called in the National Guard, but it was only the beginning of a turbulent year, which culminated in a national PR disaster for the mayor.

THERE'S A RIOT GOIN' ON

The Democratic National Convention of 1968 was meant to be a glorious celebration of Chicago, as the party descended on the city to choose its candidate for the upcoming presidential election. However, with both party and country split over the Vietnam War, it proved far tougher than Daley had anticipated.

When they arrived in late August, the Democrats were joined in the city by anti-war protesters. Encouraged by a group of counter-cultural mischief-makers known as the Yippies, the protestors had descended on Chicago in their hundreds to celebrate what they called the Festival of Life. Daley settled on a hard line approach to their presence, denying them permission to gather in a number of apparently sensitive locations.

Freedom Fighters

Five protesters from the '68 Democratic Convention on their legacy.

IN CONTEXT

The 1968 Democratic Convention protesters changed the way the media covered news, increased awareness of political, military and social issues and led to changes in the way primaries impact general elections. Here, five protesters (above, left to right) discuss the legacy of the events of 1968.

Michael James, then a campaigner, now owner of the Heartland Café in Rogers Park
Marilyn Katz, then head of security for the National Mobilization Committee to End the War in Vietnam [MOBE], now president of MK Communications
Nancy Kurshan, then a co-founder of the Yippies, now a retired social worker
Abe Peck, then a journalist, now professor emeritus-in-service at Northwestern University

Don Rose, then press secretary for MOBE, now a political consultant and a columnist for the *Chicago Daily Observer*

What were you hoping to accomplish?
Rose It began as an anti-Democratic Party move. The fear that we were not necessarily physically violent but destructive of what [the party was] about was quite correct. We were not demonstrators trying to say, 'Look, give us healthcare planks.' We didn't want planks; we wanted to end the war.
James I remember really wanting to have a good time... to get the kids talking about the revolution and peace, the war... smoke some dope in the park. We did have a good time until the police came

At first, the Yippies' protests passed quietly. But at the first sign of trouble, the 12,000-strong Chicago police force – supplemented, at Daley's request, by 15,000 troops from the National Guard and the US Army – waded in with nightsticks and tear gas, meeting mild dissent with fearsome violence. In the disarray, a number of journalists were gassed, beaten and arrested as they attempted to cover the melées; many disturbances were broadcast live on national TV. Daley stuck with his tougher-than-tough approach, but few Democrats stood alongside him. He, and his city, were humiliated.

The subsequent scapegoating of several protesters, in what became known as the 'Chicago Eight' trial, prolonged the embarrassment. A handful of the charges stuck at the chaotic, entertaining 100-day trial, presided over by Judge Julius Hoffman, but not for long: all the convictions were quashed on appeal in 1972. Three years later, it was established that the FBI, with the complicity of Judge Hoffman, had bugged the offices of the defendants' attorneys.

Further confrontations between police and radicals occurred in 1969 with the 'Days of Rage', during which members of the Black Panther-inspired radical group the Weathermen vandalised property and attacked police in the Loop, the Gold Coast and into Lincoln Park. That sent us into Old Town, breaking windows, hiding in gangways, police chasing us.

Peck We were a group of people trying to live our lives in a peaceful, communal way. We were trying to demonstrate… that there was a better way of living in a culture of greed.

What did you accomplish?

Katz We have a congressional delegation that was forged out of '68. It was the ending of an illusion that all of us children of the '50s grew up with: that the US was a total democracy and that our foreign policy was benign. It changed the way power was shared and policy was forged in this country.

Kurshan I think that '68… did make it more difficult for the US to militarily move wherever it wanted in the world. Our goal was really to make sure that there wouldn't be another Vietnam, and we have not succeeded in doing that, clearly. So on the one hand, I feel like we were able to put a brake on. On the other hand, we're still dealing with the same nefariousness.

What was the most memorable incident?

Rose The Tuesday night in front of the Hilton where the police lined up along the park to 'protect' the hotel from demonstrators – and the police were replaced by armed National Guardsmen who emerged from these Jeeps covered with barbed wire.

Katz The first [night] in Lincoln Park, when the phalanx of tear gas-loaded fire trucks and police came west across the park, aiming their full force at the unprepared revellers.

Knowing what you know now, what might you have done differently?

Katz Nothing!

Rose I cannot look back at '68 and say we made a tactical mistake or something I should have known to do differently. It didn't turn out exactly the way I wanted, but I can't say it was due to a mistake on our part.

Do you think people were more passionate then?

Rose If the times seemed more intense during Vietnam, I would attribute it to a more deadly war, plus the existence of the draft.

Katz I don't think the issue was passion, but a sense of possibility. We felt very empowered in the '60s, that what we did would or could make a difference. I think today there is a greater sense of desperation.

Peck Many today are passionate; we were in the crucible.

IN CONTEXT

beyond. By the time the violence had ceased, dozens of police and demonstrators had been injured. Neither side came out of it well; indeed, it was symbolic that Fred Hampton, the leader of the Chicago chapter of the Black Panthers, died in a police raid that same December. What's more, racial problems in the city continued well into the next decade, and many white residents chose to leave for the suburbs in a phenomenon termed 'white flight'.

ONWARDS AND UPWARDS

During the 1970s, the Loop was transformed into a financial centre as never before, priapic skyscrapers such as the Sears Tower springing up as testament to its economic virility. But on the whole, it was a difficult decade for Chicago, much as it was for most of the Midwest. Daley retained office, but struggled to galvanise his electorate as he had in previous decades; still in office, he died of a heart attack in 1976. In the face of economic instability, the city battled gamely on until the winter of 1978-79, when it was essentially closed by an amazing 82 inches of snow. Otherwise popular mayor Michael Bilandic was blamed by the electorate for the city's slow reaction to the blizzard, and was replaced in office the same year by Daley protégée Jane Byrne.

'Chicago's status as an industrial city may be gone, but it has regained much of the prosperity that illuminated its early years.'

As they had with Bilandic, Chicago voters quickly tired of the strident Byrne, who excelled at headline-grabbing gestures but proved less skilled at negotiating the machine politicians who still dominated the council. Chicago's first female mayor was then replaced by its first black mayor, as Harold Washington snuck through to win in a three-way heat for the Democratic nomination in 1983. But after winning office, Washington was left a lame duck when the council split into two camps: the reformers, led by Washington, and the old-school machine politicians, led by Edward Vrdolyak (*see pp47-48*).

After Washington was re-elected in 1987, things improved. The 29, as the machine politicians had become known, no longer wielded the power they once did, and Washington was able to make progress at last. After his sudden death (like Daley, he suffered a heart attack while in office), former alderman Eugene Sawyer continued with many of his reforms. But he was defeated in the 1989 mayoral primary by Richard M Daley, who has proved to be very much his father's son.

BACK TO THE FUTURE

Over the last two decades, the machine politics tradition that Byrne and Washington tried to eradicate seems to have returned in earnest. But there's little doubt that the city has improved under Daley's watch, thanks in no small part to his tireless efforts to publicise and promote it to a national and international audience.

The Loop continued to grow ever more powerful and influential during the 1990s, while the city's convention industry expanded to unprecedented levels. Daley has thrown money at city beautification schemes, in turn encouraging huge private investment in new commercial buildings and residential space. The numbers of tourists travelling to the city has also risen, attracted by Daley-sponsored measures such as the redevelopment of Navy Pier and, more recently, the late, expensive but already widely cherished Millennium Park. Chicago's status as an industrial city may be gone, but it has regained much of the prosperity that illuminated its early years.

But just as Daley inherited his father's can-do attitude towards bettering the city, so he's been dogged by controversy about alleged corruption within his administration (*see pp45-48*). For all his populism, he's often let financial muscle get in the way of sentiment: witness the demolition in 1994 of the Maxwell Street Market, breeding ground for several generations of blues musicians. The city remains one of the most racially divided in the US, a legacy of the separationist housing policies enacted by Daley Sr in the 1950s and '60s and not remedied by his successors. And then there's the curious incident of the airport in the night-time. Daley had long argued that Meigs Field airport, which occupied a prime piece of real estate just south of the Adler Planetarium, should be turned into a public park. Even so, the city was astonished when, around midnight on 30 March 2003, Daley sent bulldozers into the airfield to destroy its runways.

Yet for all the mayor's faults (perceived and otherwise), and for all the deep-cut societal problems that still exist in a city largely split along racial lines, Chicagoans in all corners of the city go about their business much as they ever have. The resilience that characterised Chicago in the days of Kinzie and Wentworth is still present today; indeed, given the difficulties the city has had to overcome (and, for that matter, has yet to address), it remains the town's dominant characteristic.

Key Events

Chicago in brief.

1673 Father Jacques Marquette and Louis Jolliet discover what later becomes Chicago.
1779 Jean Baptiste Point du Sable becomes the first permanent resident of the area.
1812 53 settlers are killed by natives in the Fort Dearborn Massacre.
1837 Chicago incorporates as a city.
1847 The Chicago River & Harbor Convention promotes commerce.
1848 The Illinois–Michigan Canal is built; the Chicago Board of Trade is established.
1871 The Chicago Fire destroys the city and claims 300 lives.
1879 The Chicago Academy of Fine Arts (later the Art Institute of Chicago) is incorporated.
1886 The Haymarket Square labour riot takes place; 11 people are killed.
1889 Jane Addams opens Hull-House; architect Frank Lloyd Wright builds his own residence in Oak Park.
1891 The Chicago Orchestra, later the Chicago Symphony Orchestra, is set up.
1892 The first elevated train service is offered to commuters.
1893 The World's Columbian Exposition opens on the South Side.
1894 Pullman train employees strike for improved working conditions.
1909 Daniel Burnham unveils his park-filled Plan of Chicago.
1915 The Eastland pleasure boat capsizes, killing 812.
1919 Race riots rage in July; 38 die.
1920 Eight Chicago White Sox players are banned from baseball after fixing the 1919 World Series.
1929 Seven bootleggers are executed in the St Valentine's Day Massacre.
1933 The Century of Progress World's Fair opens, as does the Museum of Science & Industry; Mayor Anton Cermak is killed in Miami by a gunman apparently intending to shoot President-elect Franklin D Roosevelt.

1934 John Dillinger is shot and killed at the Biograph movie theatre in Lincoln Park.
1942 Enrico Fermi conducts successful nuclear chain reaction experiments at the University of Chicago.
1953 Hugh Hefner publishes the inaugural monthly issue of *Playboy*.
1955 Richard J Daley is elected mayor; O'Hare International Airport opens.
1968 Riots take place after the murder of Martin Luther King, Jr; the Democratic National Convention is marred by violence.
1969 The Chicago Seven trial takes place; two radicals die in a Black Panther raid.
1971 The Union Stockyards close after 105 years of continuous trading.
1973 The Sears Tower opens.
1976 Mayor Richard J Daley dies while still in office.
1979 *The Blues Brothers* is filmed in the city.
1987 Mayor Harold Washington dies while still in office.
1988 Floodlights are at long last installed at Wrigley Field.
1989 Richard M Daley, son of Richard J Daley, is elected mayor of Chicago.
1992 The Chicago River floods underground tunnels, causing $1 billion of damage.
1995 Temperatures top 100 degrees for five straight days in July, killing more than 500 people.
1996 Michael Jordan and the Chicago Bulls win their sixth NBA championship.
2004 Four years late, Millennium Park opens to the public.
2005 The White Sox win the World Series for the first time since 1917.
2006 Federal investigators launch a probe into corruption at City Hall.
2008 Illinois senator Barack Obama is elected President of the US.
2009 Chicago continues to campaign for the 2016 Olympics.

IN CONTEXT

Chicago Today

Breezes blow change through the Windy City.

TEXT: ROBERT K ELDER

Loving Chicago, wrote Nelson Algren in his 1951 essay *Chicago: City on the Make*, is 'like loving a woman with a broken nose'. More than half a century after they were first published, Algren's words still ring true, but they could use a little modification. It might be more accurate to suggest that loving Chicago in the early 21st century is like loving a woman with a broken nose and plastic surgery. A great deal of plastic surgery.

Robert K Elder is a journalist, author and contributing editor at Stop Smiling *magazine. Visit www.robelder.com.*

GROWING UP

For all the apparent modernity of the city's imposing glass-and-steel skyline, much of Chicago's recent urban makeover has been a long time coming. Over the past few years, the cityscape has welcomed a number of high-profile additions: the Trump International Hotel & Tower, overlooking the Chicago River; the expansion of the Blue Cross Blue Shield Tower, close to the Aon Center; the array of Lakeshore East condo towers, in the north-east corner of the Loop.

These skyscrapers have been joined by other new landmarks, chief among them Millennium Park. With its shrapnel-like concert stage (designed by Frank Gehry), array of public art (Anish Kapoor's bean-shaped *Cloud Gate*, Jaume Plensa's *Crown Fountain*) and beautiful gardens, the park now rivals Navy Pier for visitor appeal and postcard popularity. And in the meantime, Hollywood has also rediscovered Chicago, with Christopher Nolan shooting *Batman Begins* and the lion's share of *The Dark Knight* here. So proud of this new identity is the city that it's not uncommon to hear security guards at O'Hare greet visitors by saying 'Welcome to Gotham City!'

If many of the beautifications have a hurry-up-the-neighbours-are-coming feel to them, there's a good reason: Mayor Richard M Daley's audacious bid for Chicago to host the Olympics in 2016, an attempt to bring the games to North America for the first time since the problematic Atlanta Olympics of 1996. However, even without the games, further revitalisation may be on the cards thanks to the city's $15.5-billion proposal for downtown rejuvenation that encompasses everything from a new transport hub in the West Loop and a high-speed rail link connecting the city and its two airports to further beautification of the walkways alongside the Chicago River.

Despite Chicago's city-of-tomorrow ambitions, there have been hiccups. First announced in 2005, Santiago Calatrava's Chicago Spire was designed to grow taller than the Sears Tower, renamed the Willis Tower in 2009. (So, too, was the Trump Tower, until terrorism worries led to a rethink.) But the recession has hit the developers' plans, and the Spire's future remains in doubt (*see p43*). It's far from the only building to have been held up by the stalled credit market: along the river at 111 W Wacker Drive, work on the Waterview Tower stopped in 2008 midway through construction, and completion of the long-in-development Block 37 section of the Loop has also been slow in coming. It's a city of growth, but not without growing pains.

And you can see other scars on Chicago's existing infrastructure. Take the century-old elevated train system: the city's brittle backbone, described by filmmaker Danny Boyle as 'the sexiest railway in the world'. The 'El' remains a reliable network, and retains an iconic status worldwide. But while some stations have been renovated in recent years (most notably Belmont on the Red line and some platforms on the Brown line), customers on the poorer, less visible South and West Sides have claimed that they've been passed over by the modernisation programme. And the network continues to suffer budgetary shortfalls, with unending maintenance leading to disgruntled riders.

GUN LAW

Although Chicago boasts two major-league baseball teams, a growing soccer presence and near-legendary basketball, hockey and football franchises, the city's real sport is politics. 'Chicago isn't more corrupt than any other city,' Studs Terkel once claimed. 'We're just proud of our corruption.' In Chicago, politics is entertainment, a three-ring circus kept in check by Mayor Daley (*see pp45-49*).

But for all Daley's power, he hasn't been able to stem the tide of violence, and especially gang violence, that continues to haunts the South and West Sides. The homicide rate in the city rose 15 per cent from 2007 to 2008; breathtakingly, the number of homicides in Chicago during 2008 (509) even surpassed the number of American soldiers killed in Iraq (314). The most high-profile killings came with a triple homicide involving the family of singer and Oscar-winning actress Jennifer Hudson.

IN CONTEXT

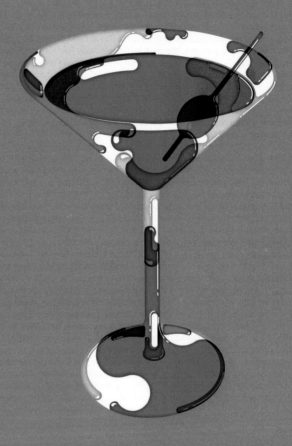

Ask New York City about New York City glamour
nycgo.com

'It's been called "America's most segregated big city", but ethnic tensions here aren't overt.'

'The real fix is going to be changing the culture, the mindset, the emotional maturity, the social fabric that a lot of these young men are operating in,' said Chicago Police Superintendent Jody Weis in a 2009 interview with *US News & World Report*. 'That fabric is torn. We've got to weave it back together and make it strong.'

While thefts and other petty crimes rise during a recession, a direct link to homicide statistics has yet to be established in Chicago. But the global economic downturn has hit Chicago in other ways. Most controversially, Mayor Daley sold off the city's parking meter infrastructure in 2008 to a private firm, which tripled parking rates in some areas, added new meters on coveted lakefront locations (many of which were frequently dysfunctional) and left locals fuming.

WINNING THE RACE
In 2000, the US Census Bureau estimated the make-up of the city's 2.8-million population as 42 per cent white and 36.8 per cent black, with a booming population of Latinos (26 per cent) and a smaller contingent of Asians (4.3 per cent); the sum total of these figures exceeds 100 per cent as some citizens identify with more than one racial group. Within these categories lies further diversity; in particular, Chicago is home to strong Polish, Asian, Puerto Rican, Mexican and Middle Eastern populations, including a thriving enclave of Assyrians (Iraqi Christians). The northern suburb of Skokie even hosted an 'Assyrian Superstar' contest via satellite television, a kind of Middle Eastern *American Idol* for Aramaic speakers.

Though Chicago has been called America's most segregated big city, ethnic tensions aren't overt. The city's African-American communities are mostly concentrated in the South and West Sides, following patterns established during the Great Migration of the early 20th century. 'There is a comfort level being among people of your own race,' one resident of historically black Bronzeville told the *Chicago Tribune* as part of a 2008 report into racial issues in the city. 'I don't think that there was any intention of segregation behind that.'

At any rate, the city's neighbourhoods are constantly in flux, and much modern segregation appears economic rather than racial. Both black Bronzeville and the largely Latino Pilsen, south-west of the Loop, have seen an influx of young hipsters seeking to establish urban arts communities in areas with cheaper rents.

THAT TODDLIN' TOWN
Most locals love their city. And 2008 offered the city a new point of pride: President Barack Obama, who seemingly escaped the grime of the city's machine politics. A self-described 'proud Chicagoan', Obama has called his adopted home town 'that most American of American cities... A city where the world's races and religions and nationalities all live and work and play and reach for the American Dream that brought them here; where our civic parades wave the colours of every culture; where our classrooms are filled with the sounds of the world's languages.'

His pride is echoed by many who've settled here. 'When I first got here, I immediately fell head over heels in love with Chicago,' local crime novelist Sean Chercover told Rick Kogan of the *Tribune* in 2008. 'The story of Chicago is the quintessential American story, complete with the inherent contradictions: the corruption and violence and racism, right alongside the optimism and opportunity and beauty.'

Which brings us back to Algren's line about Chicago's similarity to a woman with a broken nose. 'You may well find lovelier lovelies,' he added, 'but never a lovely so real.'

IN CONTEXT

Architecture

Out of disaster rose a dazzling town.

TEXT: MADELINE NUSSER

In 1871, fire wreaked havoc on Chicago, mowing it to the ground. In the months following the blaze, architects, engineers and landscapers descended on the city, then little more than a flat marsh covered in fire debris. And on this unpromising, empty landscape, a revolution fomented.

The city's flatness spurred these architects to develop both the skyscraper and the diametrically opposed Prairie School, its buildings as flat as the towers were high. Alongside these new developments, architects imported other styles, from the Paris-inspired parkways set out in Daniel Burnham's 1909 vision for the city to the excessively embellished art deco style.

In the latter half of the 20th century, the revolution slowed. Mies van der Rohe's edifices grabbed headlines, as did the famously tall likes of the Sears Tower, but the city no longer set the pace. And in the 21st century, its ambitions have all but stalled. But Chicago's skyline remains a wonder, preserved and cherished by a city that's proud of what it's given the world.

Madeline Nusser is the Around Town editor at Time Out Chicago *magazine.*

BURNING AMBITIONS

The story of Chicago's ascent from ramshackle Midwestern burg to world-class architectural showcase began in 1871, although it must have seemed like the end for those who lived in the city at the time. On the night of 8 October, a fire broke out in the barn behind the home of Patrick and Catherine O'Leary on the city's Near West Side, and raced north and east. When the blaze finally burned itself out two days later, much of the city had been reduced to smouldering ruins.

Many theories exist about the cause of the fire, from Mrs O'Leary's cow to a fiery meteorite, but most agree that poor urban planning was ultimately to blame for the way it spread. At the time, Chicago was a tinderbox: two-thirds of its 60,000 buildings were made of timber, and most of the city's 60 miles of paved streets were covered with wooden planks. In hindsight, disaster seems inevitable. But while its impact was catastrophic, the blaze inspired Chicago to rebuild as no city had done before.

THE CHICAGO SCHOOL

Refusing to be defeated by the tragedy, the city was determined to re-emerge with a daring, original vision. Once the charred buildings were cleared away, scores of architects converged on the city, drawn by the idea of working with a clean slate.

Born and educated in Boston, Louis Sullivan arrived in Chicago in 1873 and went to work for Dankmar Adler, a German émigré with a firmly established architectural practice. Despite their differences in personality, the two worked well together, Sullivan's erratic moods and artistic hauteur tempered by Adler's sober professionalism. Along with a handful of contemporaries, among them William LeBaron Jenney and Daniel Burnham, Sullivan would help define what came to be known as the Chicago School.

The Chicago School's biggest innovation was the use of an interior steel structure to distribute the weight of a building. Previously, constructing taller buildings meant thickening the load-bearing exterior masonry walls to support the weight of the upper floors. Particularly notable among such structures is Adler and Sullivan's **Auditorium Building** (50 E Congress Parkway, at S Wabash Avenue; map ❶), which combined a 4,200-seat theatre with offices and a hotel when it was completed in 1889. Owned by Roosevelt University since 1946, it remains in use as a theatre and music venue. Catch a performance by the Joffrey Ballet in order to see the spectacular interior.

The **Fine Arts Building** (410 S Michigan Avenue, at E Van Buren Street; map ❷), constructed by Solon Spencer Beman in 1885 as a showroom for Studebaker carriages, is another classic example of load-bearing masonry construction. So, too, is Burnham and John Wellborn Root's **Monadnock Building** (53 W Jackson Street, at S Dearborn Street; map ❸), completed in 1891 and the last skyscraper to be built from solid masonry construction. More than a century after its completion, it remains an impressive sight.

BUILDING UP

Most experts agree that the first official 'skyscraper' to use a steel skeletal frame was the **Home Insurance Building**, constructed in 1885 by Jenney at LaSalle and Adams Streets (and, unfortunately, demolished in 1931). Perhaps the most attractive of the steel-framed constructions still standing in the Loop is the **Marquette Building** (140 S Dearborn Street, at W Adams Street; map ❹), built by William Holabird and Martin Roche in 1895. Continuing south along Dearborn, you'll pass three other excellent examples: Burnham's 1896 **Fisher Building** (No.343; map ❺), Holabird and Roche's 1894 **Old Colony Building** (No.407; map ❻) and Jenney's 1891 **Manhattan Building** (No.431; map ❼).

Chicago School buildings are tall and rectangular with flat roofs, and often made up of three distinct elements: base, rise and capital. Their grid-like steel structure is often

IN CONTEXT

recognisable on the structure's outer surfaces. With the steel frame taking care of the heavy lifting, the exterior walls are opened up for windows and other non-load-bearing materials, most often light-coloured terracotta. The buildings generally avoid ornamentation in favour of utilitarian simplicity; it was Chicago School heavy-hitter Sullivan, after all, who declared that 'form follows function'.

The **Reliance Building**, at the south-west corner of State Street and Washington Boulevard (map ⑧), is a classic example of Chicago School innovations. Completed in 1895 by Charles Atwood and Burnham using foundations laid four years earlier by Root, the elegant Reliance makes use of a Chicago School mainstay: the oriel window, a protruding bay window that runs the length of the building and underscores its soaring verticality. With its abundance of large plate glass windows, the Reliance presaged the future of the modern-day skyscraper. It's now the **Hotel Burnham** (*see p128*).

Other Loop buildings are just as typical of the style. Take the **Santa Fe Center** (née the Railway Exchange Building; 224 S Michigan Avenue, at E Jackson Boulevard; map ⑨): when it was completed in 1904, Burnham was so proud of it that he moved his own offices there. Appropriately, it's now home to the **Chicago Architecture Foundation** (*see p304*). And don't miss Burnham and Root's majestic 1888 **Rookery** (209 S Lasalle Street, at W Adams Street; map ⑩), named for the birds that once inhabited it, or Sullivan's turn-of-the-century **Carson Pirie Scott Building** (1 S State Street, at Madison Street; map ⑪), which makes use of another common design element: the Chicago Window, a large pane of glass which is flanked by two smaller opening windows.

THE WHITE CITY

When the World's Columbian Exposition (aka the World's Fair) came to Chicago in 1893, Burnham oversaw the construction of the buildings in which the exhibits were to be housed. But the popularity of his gleaming white Beaux Arts classical constructions changed the course of architecture in the early 20th century, effectively – and ironically – outmoding the reigning Chicago School in the process.

Burnham's White City was levelled when the Columbian Exposition ended in order to make way for Meigs Field airstrip. Yet its influence remains in three classic Chicago landmarks: Shepley, Rutan and Coolidge's **Art Institute of Chicago** (111 S Michigan

Dearborn Station.

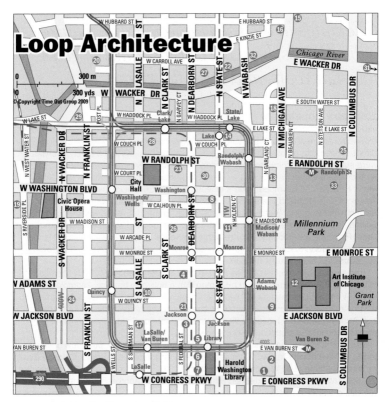

Loop Architecture

Avenue, at W Adams Street; map ⑫), completed in 1893; the ostentatious **Chicago Public Library** (78 E Washington Boulevard, at N Michigan Avenue; map ⑬), built by the same firm in 1897 and now the **Chicago Cultural Center** (*see p59*); and Rapp and Rapp's restored **Chicago Theater** (175 N State Street, at E Lake Street; map ⑭). Of a similar period, too, is Cyrus Eidlitz's beautiful Romanesque Revival **Dearborn Station** (47 W Polk Street, at Dearborn Street), completed in 1885 as one of the city's first train stations.

Burnham is now best remembered for a contribution that lasted a little longer: the 1909 Chicago Plan, which mapped out the city's development. In addition to the introduction of traffic-relieving bi-level thoroughfares around the downtown area (such as Wacker Drive), Burnham's plan minimised lakefront development, a shrewd move that resulted in the expansive lakefront parks that stretch from the South Side to the northern suburbs.

Despite Burnham's prominence and influence, some designers remained unimpressed by the Beaux Arts aesthetic, with one Wisconsin-born architect making a particular impact. Frank Lloyd Wright began his career at the office of Adler and Sullivan, but set up his own practice in Oak Park after being fired for moonlighting. It was here that he formulated what would become known as the Prairie Style of architecture; a walk around the neighbourhood, in which he built 25 homes, remains an enlightening experience. For more on Wright, *see p114* **Profile**; for his **Robie House** in Hyde Park, *see p123*.

'Buildings in the International Style feature cubic shapes, long horizontal bands of glass, low, flat roofs, and open floorplans.'

IN CONTEXT

TOWARDS MODERNISM

The Chicago School had become old hat by the 1920s, and architects began to look elsewhere for inspiration. The result was a 20-year period during which architects didn't concentrate on one style but toyed with many. Designs in a panoply of styles were submitted to a competition staged by the *Chicago Tribune* newspaper in 1922, as they searched for an architect to design their new offices. The winner was John Mead Howells and Raymond Hood's limestone-clad 456-foot (139-metre) **Tribune Tower** (435 N Michigan Avenue, at E Hubbard Street; map ⑮), a Gothic tower that arrived with flying buttresses at its ornate crown. Embedded in the walls around the building's entrance are artefacts from structures around the world, among them the Great Pyramids at Cheops and Notre-Dame Cathedral. Their presence was designed to draw attention to the paper's global reach, but they also nod towards the growing eclecticism of architectural fashion.

Just across the street is Charles Beersman's **Wrigley Building** (400 N Michigan Avenue, at E Kinzie Street; *photo p42*; map ⑯), a hulk of a building – completed in 1924 – that rises majestically over the Chicago River. The white terracotta that covers the building is cream-coloured at street level, but gets lighter towards the top. At night, when the façade is illuminated by giant floodlights, the trompe l'oeil gives the building a glorious, glowing aspect.

The American fashion for art deco never developed in Chicago, but a few buildings in the style were constructed. Chief among them is Holabird and Root's **Chicago Board of Trade Building** (141 W Jackson Boulevard, at S LaSalle Street; map ⑰), completed in 1930 (and dramatically extended a half-century later). Approach it along Lasalle for the full, dramatic effect; look up to see the crowning statue of Ceres, 45 storeys above street level. Other art deco buildings include the **Carbide & Carbon Building** (230 N Michigan Avenue, at E Lake Street; map ⑱), now the **Hard Rock Hotel** (*see p127*), and two further Holabird and Root productions: the former **Palmolive Building** (919 N Michigan Avenue, at E Walton Street), later the offices of *Playboy*; and 2 Riverside Plaza, (400 W Madison Street, at N Canal Street; map ⑲), formerly home to the *Chicago Daily News*.

And then there's the huge, art deco-styled **Merchandise Mart** (Chicago River, between N Wells & N Orleans Streets; map ⑳) the largest building in the world when it was completed in 1930. Designed by the firm of Graham, Anderson, Probst & White, the building's dramatic waterfall-style limestone façade rises 25 storeys above the river; busts of some of America's leading merchants, among them Marshall Field, A Montgomery Ward and Frank W Woolworth, line the esplanade. Commissioned by Marshall Field to house wholesale operation of his department store, it was sold to the Kennedy family in the years following the Depression. A 1991 renovation created a mall for interior design businesses on the first two floors.

GLASS AND STEEL

Despite all the local innovation, it took an outsider to kick off arguably the most striking period in Chicago's architectural history. Ludwig Mies van der Rohe arrived in the city in 1938, bringing with him the International Style. The aesthetic had its roots in the architect's native Germany but borrowed heavily from the strident simplicity of the Chicago School, ultimately carrying it to new extremes.

Tall Stories

For 150 years, Chicago has been reaching for the skies.

During its first decades, Chicago was always runner-up to Miss New York in measures of greatness. Perhaps as a result, the locals decided on an architectural strategy to prove their worth. 'Big?' went the rhetorical question. 'Bigger than yours!'

As in Europe, Chicago's earliest tall buildings were sacred sites. **Holy Name Cathedral** (733 N State Street), built in 1854, and **St Michael's Church** (1633 N Cleveland Avenue; ❶), constructed 15 years later, were two early sky-piercers, reaching 245 feet (75 metres) and 290 feet (88 metres) respectively. Reaching high towards the heavens, the spires seemed to declare a greater connection to the divine.

The next building to assume the mantle of Chicago's tallest was the first structure constructed specifically to house the **Chicago Board of Trade** (141 W Jackson Street; ❷). But when the owners removed its clock tower due to structural instability, the title passed to Burnham & Root's long-since-demolished **Masonic Temple** (at State & Randolph Streets). Its 302 feet (92 metres) made it officially the world's tallest building, but its 22 floors didn't hold the record for long: New York seized back the title in 1894 when the Manhattan Life Insurance Building was completed.

The 394-foot (120-metre) **Montgomery Ward Building** (6 N Michigan Avenue; ❸), built in 1899, was topped in 1922 by the **Wrigley Building** (400 N Michigan Avenue; ❹), which still looms 438 feet (134 metres) over the Chicago River. Two years later, it was beaten by the **Chicago Temple**

(77 W Washington Street; ❺), which in turn was defeated in 1930 by the 605-foot (184-metre) art deco monument designed to house the **Chicago Board of Trade** (141 W Jackson Street; ❻).

A futher building boom in the 1960s and '70s raised the bar once more. Built in 1965, the 648-foot (198-metre) Chicago Civic Center (now the **Daley Center**; 50 W Washington Street; ❼) was made to look feeble with the 1969 arrival of the now-iconic **John Hancock Center** (875 N Michigan Avenue; ❽), towering 1,127 feet (344 metres) over the Magnificent Mile. The Standard Oil Building (now the **Aon Center**, 200 E Randolph Street; ❾) squeaked nine feet above it in 1973. But then the very next year, Chicago reclaimed the World's Tallest title from New York thanks to the 1,451 feet (442 metres) of the Sears Tower, which was renamed in 2009 as the **Willis Tower** (233 S Wacker Drive; ❿).

The fun ended when the Council on Tall Buildings sided with some Kuala Lumpur yahoos. The Petronas Towers didn't have as many inhabitable floors as the Sears Tower; however, its spires counted while the Sears' antenna didn't. And with the apparent demise of Calatrava's plans for the Chicago Spire, the Willis Tower looks set to remain the city's king pin for a little while yet.

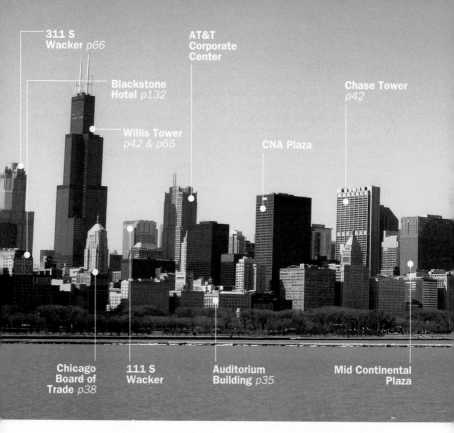

311 S Wacker *p66*

AT&T Corporate Center

Blackstone Hotel *p132*

Chase Tower *p42*

Willis Tower *p42 & p65*

CNA Plaza

Chicago Board of Trade *p38*

111 S Wacker

Auditorium Building *p35*

Mid Continental Plaza

Buildings in the International Style feature cubic shapes, long horizontal bands of glass called 'ribbon windows', low, flat roofs, and open floorplans divided by movable screen walls. Usually constructed from glass, steel and concrete, the structures are devoid of ornamentation and regional characteristics. The emphasis is on the horizontal plane, even – perhaps perversely – in skyscrapers.

After serving as director of the Bauhaus in the early 1930s, Mies came to the US in 1937 at the relatively advanced age of 51, settling first in Wyoming before, a year later, moving to Chicago in order to take up a professorship at the Armour Institute (later renamed the **Illinois Institute of Technology**). In 1939, he set about redesigning the South Side campus, creating a handful of striking buildings that demonstrated his affection for steel-framed glass and cubic abstraction. These are functional buildings, their lack of frills deliberate. 'I don't want to be interesting,' Mies once commented. 'I want to be good.'

Upon their completion in 1951, the stunning, state-of-the-art **Lake Shore Drive Apartments** (860-880 N Lake Shore Drive, at E Chestnut Street) were light years ahead of their time. An indelibly classic example of the International Style, the 26-storey twin towers were an instant commercial and critical success. A few years later, Mies turned his talents to the **Federal Center**, the unofficial name of a grouping of buildings constructed between 1959 and 1974 in the Loop (200 S Dearborn Street, at W Adams Street; map ㉑). You'll immediately recognise his signature curtain wall of glass, supported by steel black I-beams that support individual panes, emphasising the building's internal skeletal structure (and, in the process, almost turning it inside out).

Trump Tower
p44 & p135

Aon Center
p42

Heritage at
Millennium
Park

One
Prudential
Plaza

Two
Prudential
Plaza

340 on
the Park

77 W Wacker

330 N
Wabash *p41*

Legacy at
Millennium
Park

Leo Burnett
Building

Smurfit-Stone
Building

Pritzker
Pavilion
p55 & p257

Blue Cross &
Blue Shield
Tower *p31*

The grey granite that was used to pave the plaza continues uninterrupted into the lobby, creating a feeling of openness.

Mies lavished careful attention on every aspect of his creations, even going so far as to design their furniture. Take the 52-storey **330 N Wabash Building** (formerly **IBM Plaza**; 330 N Wabash Avenue, at E Wacker Drive; map ㉒), begun in 1969 and, after Mies's death the same year, completed in 1971 by one of the architect's associates. The building's voluminous glass-walled lobby, a Mies staple, is decorated with his chrome and leather Barcelona chairs, designed for an exposition in 1929.

But perhaps the most spectacular local building designed by Mies sits two hours south-west of downtown Chicago in the small town of Plano, Illinois: the **Farnsworth House** (14520 River Road, Plano, 1-866 811 4111, www.farnsworthhouse.org), completed in 1951 for Dr Edith Farnsworth (reputedly the architect's lover). This one-room, box-like house on stilts was designed by Mies to be decorated only with travertine marble floors, wooden cabinets and a rustic fireplace, and walled from the outside by mere sheets of glass. Situated on the wooded banks of the Fox River, the structure sits in striking contrast with its natural surroundings. Tours from April to November.

MOVING ON UP

Mies's influence over his contemporaries and successors is visible in a number of buildings downtown. The most notable is perhaps the **Richard J Daley Center** (55 W Randolph Street, at N Dearborn Street; map ㉓), completed as the Chicago Civic Center in 1965 to designs by Jacques Brownson of CF Murphy Associates.

Wrigley Building. *See p38.*

Designed by Bruce Graham of Skidmore, Owings & Merrill and towering 1,127 feet (344 metres) above the Magnificent Mile, the Mies-influenced **John Hancock Center** (875 N Michigan Avenue, at E Chestnut Street) became the city's tallest building when it was completed in 1969. Vaguely pyramid-shaped, the structure tapers from street level to its top floor, its visible X-shaped structural supports evenly distributing the building's weight and helping it resist the tremendous forces of wind at its higher elevations. The Hancock's lower floors are occupied by retail outlets and restaurants, with office space and apartments further up. It's topped by a bar/restaurant and an observatory (*see p79*).

Five years after the Hancock was completed, the doors opened on a second Mies-influenced, Graham-designed monster: the **Willis Tower** (originally Sears Tower; 233 S Wacker Drive, at W Adams Street; map ㉔), then became the world's tallest building (a title it relinquished two decades later). Standing a ludicrous 1,454 feet (443 metres) tall, the aluminium and amber glass tower owes a debt to the International Style with its chunky, cubist proportions. Although it's not a dynamic structure, it's easier on the eye than other cloudbusters from the same era, such as the 1,136-foot (346-metre) **Aon Center**, completed in 1973 as the Standard Oil Building (200 E Randolph Street, at N Columbus Drive; map ㉕), and the 859-foot (262-metre) **Water Tower Place** (845 N Michigan Avenue, at E Pearson Street). However, it lacks the easy elegance of the nearby **Chase Tower**, built in 1969 as the First National Bank of Chicago Building (21 N Clark Street, at W Madison Street; map ㉖).

ALTERNATIVE VIEWS

Not everyone took to Mies's aesthetic, something apparent from the two 61-storey 'corncob' towers of Bertrand Goldberg's **Marina City** apartment complex (*photo p44*; map ㉗) on the north bank of the river. Constructed of reinforced concrete, the towers were completed in 1967 and could hardly be more distinctive: the floors are cantilevered out from the main core, which houses lift shafts and rubbish chutes. A theatre built between the two towers in 1966 is now occupied by the **House of Blues** (*see p260*).

While Mies's Federal Center pushed the boundaries of what a government building should look like, Helmut Jahn's dome-shaped **James R Thompson Center** (formerly the **State of Illinois Center**; 100 W Randolph Street, at N Clark Street; map ㉘) blew away

The Best-Laid Plans...

How the city's tallest building became a giant hole in the ground.

When Santiago Calatrava's plans for a slender, twisting, 2,000-foot skyscraper on Lake Shore Drive were unveiled in 2005, everyone had a nickname for it. Some called it the Screw or the Drill-Bit; others preferred the Deformed Penis or the Birthday Candle. At any rate, the building's aggressive aesthetic inspired argument, and Calatrava's plans were pinned as the most interesting addition to Chicago's skyline in decades.

The **Chicago Spire**, as it's officially named (pictured above on an artist's mock-up), was first announced as a 115-storey hotel and condo tower, and earmarked for a site just south of Navy Pier's entrance. Debates about it raged from the get-go. Was it attractive? Who would live there? And would the skyscraper be a terrorist target? The Spire was designed as the tallest building in the country, at a time when the US still fretted over a possible repeat of 2001's terrorist attacks.

But another problem made its presence felt: money. The Fordham Corporation, the Spire's developer, was quietly unsure if it could raise enough money to get the project off the ground by the start date of mid 2007. For the project to break even, 250 condos would need to be sold in advance for $7 million each, a hefty price-tag anywhere but especially here.

By summer 2006, with Fordham unable to find the funds, Dublin-based Shelbourne Development took over. By the end of the year, they'd killed plans for a hotel and redesigned the Spire as a condo-only structure. Unit prices rose as high as $40 million, more than four times Chicago's highest condo sale. And as prices rose, the market for luxury real estate began to tank.

Although Shelbourne continued to stick to its plan to complete building by 2009, the firm ran into problems with neighbourhood residents a few weeks before construction was due to commence. Partly to appease the community, the plan grew to include a park, an exit ramp on to Lake Shore Drive, lakefront-path bridges and other big-budget additions. Ground was finally broken in late summer 2007, with Shelbourne claiming to have sold 30 percent of the Spire's 1,200 planned condos by the middle of 2008. But the credit crisis continued to deepen.

Worse was to follow when, in late 2008, Calatrava filed a lien on the property, stating that Shelbourne owed him more than $11 million. Construction stalled, leaving the project as a mere hole in the ground. As of summer 2009, no one knows when or even if work on the building will resume.

IN CONTEXT

Marina City.
See p42.

critics when it was completed in 1985. Despite its stridently modern appearance, the building pays homage to traditional government buildings, with its abstract suggestion of the classic cupola. The main attraction, though, is the 230-foot (70-metre) atrium created by the rotunda: ample lighting, exposed lift shafts and mechanics, and reflective surfaces give the space a vibrant sense of movement.

Another attention-grabbingly curvaceous modern building sits a few blocks west on the banks of the Chicago River. William E Pedersen's **333 W Wacker Drive** (map ㉙) was built between 1979 and 1983 on the bend of the river, and its curved frontage echoes the shape of the waterway in spectacular fashion. Look at it from the opposite bank or – better still – from a moving boat, from where the subtly stunning ways the light plays on the rounded frontage are best appreciated.

NEW HEIGHTS

Aside from the long-running saga surrounding **Block 37** in the Loop (map ㉚) – a long-dormant block hemmed in by State, Washington, Dearborn and Randolph Streets that's at last been developed after two decades of redundancy (*see p61*) – the most high-profile project has been the 28-acre **Lakeshore East** (map ㉛), a riverfront development on a site east of the Michigan Avenue Bridge. The first few condo towers completed as part of the development aren't memorable, but they're nonetheless notable in the way they illustrate a 21st-century Chicago trend: the way in which young professionals have returned to make their homes in the centre of the city.

Another high-profile tower has been constructed just along the river. Donald Trump's plans to build the world's tallest building fell by the wayside in the wake of 9/11. However, after a brief delay, Trump commissioned Skidmore, Owings & Merrill to construct the shorter-than-planned but nonetheless skyscraping **Trump International Hotel & Tower** (401 N Wabash Avenue, at E Kinzie Street; map ㉜; *see p135*).

For all the towering skyscrapers downtown, some impressive developments keep their extremities closer to ground level. Located east of Michigan Avenue between Randolph and Monroe Streets and unveiled in 2004, the 24-acre **Millennium Park** (*see p54*) was four years late, and, at nearly $500 million, way over budget. However, Chicagoans have taken to the completed park with great enthusiasm, and especially to Frank Gehry's **Jay Pritzker Pavilion** (map ㉝).

Millennium Park may have been late in arriving, but at least it was completed. Other projects haven't been so lucky. The slump has caused some buildings to be put on hold, the most high-profile being the Santiago Calatrava-designed **Chicago Spire** (*see p43 The Best-Laid Plans…*). And with the recession some way from receding, the question is really now about if, not when, Chicago will resume its drive upwards.

IN CONTEXT

'Mike Royko's 1971 biography of Daley portrayed the mayor as ruthless and corrupt. But by revitalising downtown, Daley prevented the kind of decline seen in other rust-belt cities.'

PROGRESS REPORTS

For all his corrupt internal practices, Daley gained a reputation for getting things done. Under his watch, construction boomed: O'Hare Airport, the Sears Tower, McCormick Place and the UIC campus were all built during his reign. But the mayor was not loved by all. Daley presided over – indeed, encouraged – a segregated city, and resisted Martin Luther King, Jr's attempts to integrate Chicago's schools. After rioting broke out in the wake of King's murder (*see pp24-25*), Daley fanned the flames of discontent when he suggested that the police reaction to the protests was too tentative.

Greater embarrassment was to follow. When US TV broadcast images of women and children being beaten and tear-gassed in the wake of anti-war demonstrations outside the Democratic Convention in August 1968, Daley was left exposed on the national stage (*see pp25-27*). The reputation of the Chicago police was permanently stained even before the Chicago Police and agents of the Cook County State's Attorney's office shot and killed Black Panther organiser Fred Hampton in 1969 under dubious circumstances.

Boss, Mike Royko's 1971 biography of Daley, portrayed the mayor as ruthless, corrupt and, on the subject of race, thoroughly unenlightened. But today, historians generally agree that by revitalising downtown and keeping some vestige of a middle class in the centre, the mayor prevented the kind of dramatic decline seen in other rust-belt cities. And though some have argued that they amount to one and the same thing, it's generally accepted that Daley tolerated corruption more than he practised it.

RAGE AGAINST THE MACHINE

In the 1970s, racial tension and the flight of the machine's ethnic base to the suburbs weakened its structure. Some of Daley's efforts in the field of public works, such as his high-rise housing projects, came to be considered failures, while his defence of residential segregation and his opposition to affirmative action in government made him increasingly unpopular with African Americans. Daley's sudden death in 1976, after 21 years in office, left a power vacuum, but his cohorts had already begun to leave the roost.

By the time Harold Washington became Chicago's first black mayor in 1983, riding in on the split loyalties of white voters and ballooning black voter registration, the machine seemed to be broken beyond repair. But Washington, himself a Democrat, was left to battle the machine when his council split along racial lines. Led by **Edward Vrdolyak**, 29 old-school white Democratic aldermen teamed up and refused to approve Washington's reform policies, but their majority wasn't sufficient to push through their own measures: they needed 30 of the council's 50 votes in order to override Washington's mayoral veto, which he was not shy about wielding. Stalemate ensued in what became known as the Council Wars.

After Washington was re-elected in 1987, the 29 dispersed, and the mayor managed to institute policies that promoted more open government and minority contracting. But Washington died in office of a heart attack that same year, and Chicagoans were soon reminded of their past with the emergence of a new yet familiar candidate for the city's top job.

IN CONTEXT

'Various scandal investigations conducted over the last few years have led closer and closer to the mayor's office.'

THE DALEY DOUBLE

Upon defeating Eugene Sawyer, Washington's replacement, in the 1989 mayoral primary, Richard J Daley's eldest son, **Richard M Daley** (pictured on page 45), won election to City Hall. His 'pin-striped machine', named for its use of lawyers and young advisors, quickly developed a powerful hold over Chicago, courting the city's most respected minority leaders and political independents with city services and contracts in order to ensure a new era of loyalty.

For many liberals, Daley represents smart, sophisticated city government, supporting gun control, gay rights and various 'green' programmes. But his programme to reform public housing, a ten-year, $5-billion plan to tear down high-rises and replace them with mixed-income row houses and condos, proved controversial.

Daley presided over an economic and cultural boom, and has been praised for revitalising the city's schools, rejuvenating downtown and restoring smaller neighbourhoods. But his rock-solid hold on the city has developed cracks. Vestiges of Chicago's patronage system have surfaced and come under attack in several major scandals. The resemblance between father and son appears to go beyond a physical likeness and a shared propensity for malapropisms.

LIKE FATHER, LIKE SON

In 2004, the *Chicago Sun-Times* broke the story of corruption in the city's Hired Truck Program, which it termed 'clout on wheels'. In a nutshell, the city was found to be hiring trucks from local firms at inflated rates, often paying them to sit idle for days or weeks at a time. The city gave around $40 million annually to these private truck companies, many based in Daley's ward; some firms were found to have kicked back donations to politicians. More than 30 people have been convicted in connection with the scheme.

Out of the scandal, another came to light. High-level Daley staffers from his secretive Intergovernmental Affairs office were found to have been practising systematic hiring, based on political connections rather than merit, for possibly thousands of City jobs. By the middle of 2006, US Attorney Patrick Fitzgerald had charged and convicted Daley's former patronage chief and three other one-time officials on charges of mail fraud.

Various scandal investigations conducted over the last few years have led closer and closer to the mayor's office. Allegations of police brutality in the city have dogged the administration for years, with a 2006 report confirming that a police torture ring acted with virtual impunity between the 1970s and the '90s. These controversies were supplemented by a series of massive cost overruns on construction projects, such as Millennium Park and the renovation of a terminal at O'Hare International Airport.

And yet despite the controversies that threatened to envelop him, Daley eased to victory in the 2007 mayoral elections more or less uncontested. Two years later, the city was enveloped in a major budget crisis, with Daley effectively privatising the city's parking meters (leasing them over 75 years to Morgan Stanley for $1.16 billion), car parks and even, in a now-failed deal, Midway Airport, all in a bid to swell the coffers. Public opinion of the mayor fell to an all-time low. But still, only a mug would bet against him winning re-election in 2011, by which time Daley will have overtaken his father and become the longest-serving mayor in the city's history. *Plus ça change.*

IN CONTEXT

Hair Today...

The rapid rise and crashing fall of Rod Blagojevich.

Born in Chicago in 1956 to a pair of Yugoslav immigrants, Rod Blagojevich rose through the ranks of the Chicago Democratic machine via connections of his alderman father-in-law. He served first under Edward Vrdolyak, leader of the 29 rebel aldermen who blocked Harold Washington's reforms (*see p47*), then as Assistant State's Attorney under Richard M Daley. In 1992, he won election to the Illinois House of Representatives. Four years later, he joined the state legislature.

In 2002, with the state's Republican party enveloped in scandal, Blagojevich became the state's first Democratic governor in a quarter-century, vowing to end what he called 'business as usual' in Springfield. Blagojevich was a confrontational absentee governor: tangling with his own party, House speaker Michael Madigan and Chicago's Mayor Daley, balancing the state's budget by sleight of hand and massive borrowing, and burnishing his own image with headline-grabbing proposals that carried little substance.

Blagojevich's administration soon fell under investigation by state and federal authorities for various influence-peddling and corrupt hiring practices. In 2006, fundraiser and advisor Tony Rezko was indicted on a variety of fraud and bribery charges (he was convicted two years later). Then, in April 2008, a *Chicago Tribune* investigation revealed that at least three of every four $25,000 donors to Blagojevich got something from the administration – jobs, contracts or favourable regulatory rulings. The machine, it seemed, was alive and well.

Eventually, Blagojevich himself became caught up in the investigation, first for allegedly shaking down a hospital for campaign funds and then for apparently intimating that the US Senate seat vacated by Barack Obama was effectively up for sale. Just as one Illinois politician was changing the course of history by winning the US Presidential election, Blagojevich and his formidable hairdo rendered the state a nationwide laughing-stock.

In early 2009, the Illinois House voted to impeach Blagojevich. But rather than accept his fate lying down, a combination of megalomania and moxie led the governor to embark on a media blitz. On the day his trial began, Blagojevich turned up in New York to plead his case on a number of US talk shows, alleging that he was the victim of a coordinated attack because of his opposition to new taxes.

It didn't help. In early 2009, the Illinois legislature removed from office its sitting governor. And in April, Blagojevich and four cohorts were indicted by a federal grand jury on a variety of corruption charges. This one looks likely to run and run...

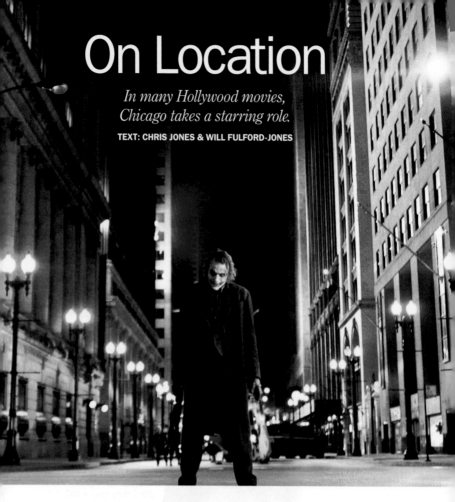

On Location

In many Hollywood movies,
Chicago takes a starring role.

TEXT: CHRIS JONES & WILL FULFORD-JONES

Chicago's role in the birth of cinema has been rather
erased by the hegemony of Hollywood, but the Windy City
was in there at the start. At the turn of the 20th century,
Chicago was home to a wide variety of production companies
and film distribution firms, with innumerable nickelodeons
standing as testament to the locals' early love of movies.

It didn't last. Legal wrangles over movie-equipment patens
and – inevitably – grumbles about the weather both helped
cause an exodus to Los Angeles, where the industry has
remained to this day. But thanks to relatively low filming
costs and a supportive city council, Chicago's versatile urban
landscape still features heavily in mainstream cinema. Here
are some of the more memorable locations that have starred
in movies down the years. Keep your eyes open, though, and
you're sure to see others on your travels around town…

STREET LIFE

LAKE SHORE DRIVE has been the site of many high-speed escapades in the movies. Tom Cruise takes to his father's Porsche and tries to elude Rebecca DeMornay's pimp while driving along here in **Risky Business**; Matthew Broderick cruises along Lake Shore in his Ferrari during **Ferris Bueller's Day Off**; and Larenz Tate and Nia Long enjoy the lakefront perspectives offered by motorbike travel during **Love Jones**. Billy Crystal and Meg Ryan drive along Lake Shore Drive in **When Harry Met Sally…**, but with a twist – they're supposed to be leaving town at the time, but the direction in which they're headed is such that they're actually heading towards it.

The polar opposite of Lake Shore Drive, **LOWER WACKER DRIVE** is a dank, sinister place, a characteristic exploited by numerous movie-makers. In John McNaughton's bleak **Henry: Portrait of a Serial Killer**, Henry and his pal Otis (Michael Rooker and Tom Townes) pretend their car has broken down on Lower Wacker before shooting the first man who stops to help them fix it. And following on from **Primal Fear** and **Thief**, the street hosts a car chase in **Batman Begins**. After taking the police on a run around the Loop (briefly getting boxed in on the top floor of the parking garage at Randolph and Lake), Christian Bale leads the cops down to Lower Wacker for a high-speed chase.

STAYING THE NIGHT

The **DRAKE HOTEL** (140 E Walton Place, Gold Coast; see p140) has long attracted a cosmopolitan crowd. Cary Grant and Eva Marie Saint grace the lobby in Hitchcock's **North by Northwest**; Julia Roberts plots against Cameron Diaz in **My Best Friend's Wedding**, with the banqueting space played by the hotel's Gold Coast Room; and Tom Cruise awaits **Risky Business** girl-for-hire Rebecca DeMornay in the Palm Court.

Despite the prominence accorded by **The Dark Knight** to both **HOTEL 71** (home to Bruce Wayne's penthouse; 71 E Wacker Drive, see p131) and the **TRUMP TOWER** (scene of the showdown between Batman and the Joker; see p135), the Drake's main hotel rival on the Chicago cinematic landscape is the **HILTON CHICAGO** (720 S Michigan Avenue, South Loop; see p132). Macauley Culkin is reunited with his family at the end of **Home Alone II: Lost in New York** in the exclusive Conrad Hilton Suite, which also features in **My Best Friend's Wedding**. Other corners of the property play the Lexington Hotel in Sam Mendes's **Road to Perdition** (the hotel's exterior is actually the **WRIGLEY BUILDING**). However, the Hilton is best known for its starring role in **The Fugitive**: its Grand Ballroom, laundry room and towering rooftop provide the backdrop for Harrison Ford's athletic escapade.

The **BLACKSTONE HOTEL** (636 S Michigan Avenue, South Loop; see p132) recently underwent a dramatic renovation. But you can see how it used to look in a couple of older Hollywood flicks. The hotel's Crystal Ballroom hosts a party in the Coen Brothers' screwball comedy **The Hudsucker Proxy**, and is also where Al Capone (played by Robert de Niro) breaks off from a eulogy to teamwork in baseball by clubbing one of his dining companions to death with a Louisville Slugger in **The Untouchables**.

RIDING THE RAILS

Nothing says Chicago quite like the clattery, rattly **EL NETWORK** (see p302); no wonder it's featured in so many Chicago-set movies. Cruise and DeMornay (them again) get intimate on board a train in **Risky Business**; Steve McQueen chases his quarry atop an El train in **The Hunter**; and in **Shall We Dance?**, Richard Gere catches sight of dance teacher Jennifer Lopez from the window of an El train during his daily commute. **The Blues Brothers** struggle to sleep with the constant rattle of trains outside their window in the now-demolished **PLYMOUTH HOTEL** (Van Buren Street, just west of State); the moviemakers paid the CTA to run extra trains to increase the effect. And no, your eyes aren't deceiving you: that is the El in **Spider-Man 2**, masquerading as New York City.

UNION STATION (210 S Canal Street, West Loop; see p302) has also played a regular role in the movies. The semi-climactic shootout between Eliot Ness (Kevin

IN CONTEXT

The Untouchables.

Costner) and Al Capone's lackeys in **The Untouchables** was shot here. The station can also be seen in **The Silver Streak**, which crashes through a model of the terminus in the 1976 movie of the same name; in **The Sting**, albeit briefly; and in 2009's **Public Enemies**, in which Johnny Depp stars as man-on-the-run John Dillinger. And Clive Owen first claps eyes on Jennifer Aniston on a commuter train bound for the station in 2005 thriller **Derailed**.

SEE YOU AT THE BAR

Hollywood has long reflected Chicago's status as a drinking town. Robert DeNiro and David Caruso prop up the bar at **CLUB LAGO** (331 W Superior Street, River North; *see p152*) in **Mad Dog and Glory**. In **About Last Night**, Rob Lowe and Demi Moore complete their sexual preliminaries at **MOTHER'S** (26 W Division Street, Gold Coast). **Prelude to a Kiss** saw Meg Ryan hook up with one of the Baldwin brothers while bartending at the **GREEN MILL** (4802 N Broadway, Uptown; *see p266*); the venerable old tavern also features in **Thief**, where it's owned by James Caan, and **High Fidelity**. And in **The Color of Money**, Paul Newman teaches Tom Cruise the tricks of the trade at various local bars and pool halls, among them the **GINGER MAN** (3740 N Clark Street, Wrigleyville) and **CHRIS'S BILLIARDS** (4637 N Milwaukee Avenue, Ravenswood; *see p280*).

THREE OTHER LANDMARKS

The urban expanse known as **DALEY PLAZA** (50 W Washington Boulevard, the Loop) has hosted befuddled Neanderthals (**The Naked Ape**), Elizabeth Shue (**Adventures in Babysitting**), and National Guardsmen, tanks and 500 extras on the lookout for Belushi and Aykroyd (**The Blues Brothers**). This latter film is also responsible for the most inventive of **WRIGLEY FIELD**'s many film appearances, when Aykroyd's driver's licence lists his home as 1060 W Addison Street – the street address of the ballpark.

The **WILLIS TOWER** (formerly Sears Tower; *see p65*) originally drew its cinematic fame from **Ferris Bueller's Day Off**, in which Matthew Broderick squeezes his face up against the glass on the Skydeck. But this shot was topped in **The Dark Knight**, during which Christian Bale stands on the building's roof looking out over the city. And yes, Bale did his own stunts. 'When you have an opportunity to stand on top of the Sears Tower wearing a Batsuit,' said Bale, 'you take it and run with it.'

Sightseeing

The Loop

Despite cash worries, Chicago's downtown continues to grow.

An unmatched architectural showcase, a high-culture hot spot and the financial heart of the Midwest, the Loop is the hub around which Chicago revolves. It's named after the route carved around it by its distinctive elevated rail tracks; you can take in the area's beguiling mix of history and modernity up close from one of these 'El' trains. But the best way to see the Loop is on foot, weaving between vertical canyons of glass and steel before adjourning to the regenerated **Millennium Park**.

The Loop's primary raison d'êtres are commercial; outside of its smattering of concert halls and theatres, it slows down after 7pm. However, of late, more locals have chosen the convenience of city living over the suburbs. Condo towers and college dorms have sprung up during the past decade, and the area's character continues to evolve.

This chapter refers to many of the Loop's architectural highlights.

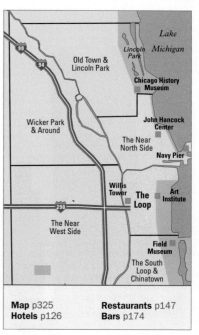

| Map p325 | Restaurants p147 |
| Hotels p126 | Bars p174 |

However, the Architecture chapter contains more detail, plus a map on which more than 30 of these buildings are marked. *See pp34-44.*

Map p325   Restaurants p147   Hotels p126   Bars p174   See pp34-44.

MILLENNIUM PARK & GRANT PARK

Millennium Park

Bordered by Randolph Street, Michigan Avenue, Monroe Street and Columbus Drive, Millennium Park was completed four years late and $300 million over budget. But as soon as the 24.5-acre project opened in 2004, on a site previously occupied by abandoned railroad tracks and parking, affection for it crushed questions about whether it violates the city's obligation to keep Grant Park 'forever open, clear and free of any buildings, or other obstruction whatever' (according to an 1836 declaration that predated the opening of the park), and whether it's big enough to contain the ego of its champion, mayor Richard M Daley. Stop by the **Welcome Center** (201 E Randolph Street, 1-312 742 1168) for maps and audio guides, or download them for free at www.millenniumpark.org.

The park's most photographed attraction is Anish Kapoor's sculpture **Cloud Gate** (aka 'the Bean'), which looms over the **McCormick Tribune Ice Rink** (*see p280*). The seams between the quarter-inch polished stainless steel plates that cover its steel support skeleton have been polished into invisibility: although it's 66 feet long and 33 feet high (20 metres by ten metres), the 110-ton structure appears to be as lightweight and fluid as the drop of mercury that supposedly inspired it. Its mirror finish reflects Michigan Avenue's historic 'streetwall', clouds, trees and your puzzled face, as you try to find yourself among the throng of tourists distorted in its trippy surfaces.

Jaume Plensa's **Crown Fountain** also improbably succeeds as both contemporary art and Chicago icon. Its two 50-foot (15-metre) towers, which contain 122,000 glass bricks, face each other across a plaza; each projects the face of one of 1,000 Chicagoans whom Plensa filmed. From time to time, the faces purse their lips and 'spit' torrents of water, to the delight of the children waiting below. The water is shut down during winter, but the striking images remain.

The *Crown Fountain* almost makes up for the hideous **Millennium Monument** at the corner of Michigan Avenue and Randolph Street, a replica of the peristyle that 'graced' the spot from 1917 to 1953. It bears a long list of 'Millennium Park founders'; basically, the rich people and corporations who provided the park's private funding. Unfortunately, you have to pass this neo-neoclassical monstrosity to reach the Welcome Center, the **Harris Theater for Music & Dance** (*see p254*) and the **McDonald's Cycle Center** (*see p279*).

Designed by Frank Gehry, the **Jay Pritzker Pavilion** (*see p257*) dominates the northern end of the park. Echoing the exploding-metal style Gehry perfected at the Guggenheim Bilbao, the outdoor concert venue's steel flourishes curl 35 to 40 feet (ten to 12 metres) into the air above the 60-foot (18-metre) bandstand. The pavilion has room for 11,000 people: 4,000 on seats near the stage, the rest on the lawn. The steel 'trellis' that shades the grass contains a state-of-the-art sound system; the chatty picnickers who attend the (mostly free) concerts don't notice.

Gehry also designed the **BP Bridge**, which snakes east from the southeastern corner of the Pritzker Pavilion's lawn to **Daley Bicentennial Plaza**, passing over Columbus Drive. Just south of it, the 2.5-acre **Lurie Garden** honours two periods of Chicago history through plants: the garden's 'dark plate' recreates the lakefront's natural prairie topography, while the orderly beds of perennial flowers that make up the 'light plate' evoke the city as it developed after the Chicago Fire.

To see the garden from above, take Renzo Piano's new 620-foot **Nichols Bridgeway** from this end of Millennium Park over Monroe Street to the third floor of the Art Institute's Modern Wing (*see p56*). Piano claims that the shape of the slender white steel and aluminium pedestrian bridge was inspired by the hull of a boat, but it's really a life raft meant to funnel scads of tourists into the museum.

Grant Park

Millennium Park has overshadowed its less flashy neighbour to the south, which was built on landfill in the 1920s and runs to Museum Campus (*see p68*). Adding insult to injury, the **Grant Park Music Festival** (*see p256*) has even decamped to the Pritzker Pavilion. Yet the 319-acre **Grant Park** retains a prominent role in the life of the city. During summer, the park hosts popular events such as the **Taste of Chicago** (*see p215*). And on the night of 4 November 2008, a quarter of a million people joined Barack Obama to celebrate his victory in the presidential election.

SIGHTS

Millennium Park.

Aside from the **Art Institute of Chicago** (*see below*), Grant Park's main point of interest is the **Buckingham Fountain**, which was donated to the city in 1927 in memory of Art Institute benefactor Clarence Buckingham. Located east of Congress Parkway, the fountain is modelled on the fountain at Versailles, but is twice the size and contains more than a million gallons of water. On summer nights, crowds gather to watch the fountain's water and light shows, during which water shoots 150 feet into the air to musical accompaniment.

For a more subtle aesthetic experience, find Richard Serra's 1988 sculpture *Reading Cones*. The width of a person is all that separates its two steel arcs, which enclose intrepid viewers in an isolating chamber. It's an unexpected oasis of solitude in Chicago's 'front yard'.

★ Art Institute of Chicago

111 S Michigan Avenue, at W Adams Street (1-312 443 3600/www.artic.edu). El: Brown, Green, Orange, Pink or Purple to Adams/ Wabash. **Open** *Sept-May* 10.30am-5pm Mon-Wed, Fri; 10.30am-8pm Thur; 10am-5pm Sat, Sun. *June-Aug* 10.30am-5pm Mon-Wed; 10.30am-9pm Thur, Fri; 10am-5pm Sat, Sun. **Admission** $18; $12 reductions; free under-12s. Free to all Feb; 5-8pm Thur; *June-Aug* 5-9pm Thur, Fri. **Credit** AmEx, Disc, MC, V. **Map** p325 J12.

The intrigue of Chicago's most noteworthy museum begins before you cross the threshold, when you meet two of the city's most beloved characters outside its Michigan Avenue entrance. Donated by Mrs Henry Field, sister-in-law to department store mogul Marshall, Edward Kemeys' two bronze lions guarded the Art Institute of Chicago since 1894. But few locals realise that the pair aren't identical twins: the south lion is said to stand in an attitude of defiance, while the north lion is reportedly 'on the prowl'.

Past these leonine doormen lies a world-class institution, one that looks the part from the moment you reach the atrium lobby. The Art Institute has the building its impressive collections deserve: built by Shepley, Rutan and Coolidge in 1892 for the World's Columbian Exposition the following year, it's as grand as it is large. The signage around the museum is good, and the free map is comprehensive enough for most visitors. However, the museum's sheer size can make it a daunting place; you may also want to invest in the excellent audio guide ($6), which provides an overview of the highlights.

Collections

In 2005, the museum started an ambitious project: a 264,000-square-foot limestone and glass building designed by Italian architect Renzo Piano. Dubbed the **Modern Wing**, Piano's building was designed to hold the Art Institute's collections of modern European painting and sculpture, contemporary art and architecture and design.

When it opened in spring 2009, the Modern Wing allowed the museum to redistributed its tightly packed collection into a more spacious and, in many ways, more logical layout. The museum's three buildings, plus the newly built Modern Wing, each feature two to three storeys of exhibition space, making it impossible to cover the country's second largest art museum in a single day. However, by prioritising the Modern Wing's modern and contemporary art, and the American 1900-1950 collection in the **Rice Building**, you'll get to see many of the Art Institute's most notable and famous works.

The Modern Wing delivers a succession of textbook classics. Numerous works by Salvador Dali (room 396) sit alongside Magritte's *Time Transfixed*, Picasso's *The Old Guitarist* (391) and countless other instantly recognisable pieces. It's also home to the **Ryan Education Center**, which has dozens of drop-in classes to keep children interested. The new wing is also accessible through Millennium Park by a quick walk over the **Nichols Bridgeway**, a pedestrian bridge that leads to **Terzo Piano**, a third-floor dining area helmed by Spiaggia chef Tony Mantuano (*see p157 and p171*). To get a seat, reservations are a must.

After this stunning beginning, move on to the **Pritzker Galleries**, where you'll find many of the Art Institute's most prized canvases. The museum has managed to accumulate amazing collections of Impressionist and post-Impressionist paintings since opening in the late 19th century, and it's here that you'll find them. Look out in particular for Caillebotte's famous *Paris Street; Rainy Day* (room 201) and Seurat's *A Sunday on La Grande Jatte – 1884* (240), at which Ferris Bueller gawped on his day off, along with other notable works such as Renoir's *Acrobats at the Cirque Fernando* and Cézanne's *The Basket of Apples*.

The American 1900-1950 Collection in the nearby Rice Building is scarcely any less impressive, containing such gems as Edward Hopper's *Nighthawks* (262), Grant Wood's *American Gothic* (263; also now immortalised in sculptural form by J Seward Johnson outside the Tribune Tower, for which *see p78*), and works by Georgia O'Keeffe (265), Winslow Homer (171) and Mary Cassatt (273).

Less celebrated but equally worthy are the new **Alsdorf Galleries of Southeast Asian Art** (140-142), also designed by Renzo Piano, and the **Medieval and Renaissance Art Collections**, all of which are of interest to more than just aficionados. And we're not done: other diversions include a paperweight collection and the **Thorne Miniature Rooms**, a collection of scale models of American, European and oriental houses spanning four centuries.

Despite the strength of its permanent collection, the Institute stages regular temporary exhibitions, some of which are more high-profile than others. Check the website and *Time Out Chicago* for details of what's on while you're in town.

Art Institute of Chicago.

The Old College Try

Two Chicago art schools show off their students to Loop enthusiasts.

The newly extended **Art Institute of Chicago** (*see p56*) wins the artistic headlines in the Loop, and with good reason. However, beyond its halls, young artists are getting useful exposure courtesy of two enterprising art colleges, who are making an appealing effort to let Loop art-lovers in on their secrets.

Chicagoans grumbled when Carson Pirie Scott closed its landmark department store in 2007 (1 S State Street, at E Madison Street). However, the Louis Sullivan-designed building, renamed the Sullivan Center in his honour, has been given fresh life by the **School of the Art Institute of Chicago** (**SAIC**), its new tenant.

Housed in the Sullivan Center, the SAIC's massive seventh-floor **Sullivan Galleries** (1-312 629 6635, www.saic.edu/exhibitions) space presents an exciting mix of work by professional artists and students. The MFA show, held every May, is a good bellwether for art's Next Big Thing. A few blocks south-east, the SAIC's **Rymer Gallery** (280 S Columbus Drive, at E Jackson Street, 1-312 629 6635, www.saic.edu/exhibitions) exhibits work by both the SAIC's high-flying faculty and international art stars. Both galleries are open to the public and admission is free.

Not to be outdone, Columbia College is keen to show off its staff and students. During the last few years, Columbia's **Leviton A+D Gallery** (619 S Wabash Avenue, at E Harrison Street, 1-312 369 8687, www.colum.edu/adgallery) and **Glass Curtain Gallery** (1104 S Wabash Avenue, at 11th Street, 1-312 369 6643, www.colum.edu/cspaces) have organised excellent shows on topics ranging from DIY culture to contemporary Palestinian art, many featuring students and faculty. And in October 2008, the school opened a shop selling fine art and other goods created by current students. For more on **ShopColumbia**, *see p207*.

MICHIGAN AVENUE

The mile-long stretch of Michigan Avenue that runs south of the river isn't Magnificent, like its counterpart to the north, but it's packed with buildings of artistic and architectural interest. What's more, the street offers glimpses of both aspects of the Loop: the hard-nosed and the tranquil. To the west stands an array of tall, imposing and often historic buildings, housing hotels, businesses and cultural institutions. And to the east are the city's parks and the lake.

Start at the **Michigan Avenue Bridge**, which affords spectacular views from its northern tip. The south-west tower houses the **McCormick Bridgehouse & Chicago River Museum** (*see p60*), which celebrates the role of the river in the city's history while also providing some fantastic views. East of the bridge, along Wacker Drive towards the lake, sit the **Lakeshore East** condo towers. The most dazzling is Jeanne Gang's **Aqua**, an 82-storey building that should be ready in 2010.

South of the bridge, you won't find much of interest until you reach the **Hard Rock Hotel** (no.230, at E South Water Street; *see p127*) – or rather, the **Carbide & Carbon Building**, the 1929 skyscraper it occupies. The building's distinctive green terracotta exterior is trimmed in gold leaf, and its awe-inspiring lobby is awash with marble and glass ornamentation.

More opulence awaits at the **Chicago Cultural Center** (78 E Washington Boulevard, at N Michigan Avenue, 1-312 744 6630, www.chicagoculturalcenter.org; *photo p60*). Built in 1897 as the city's central library, complete with two stunning Tiffany stained-glass domes and marble staircase, the centre now stages free concerts and films, superlative art shows and, on some Saturdays, civil marriage ceremonies for $10. It's also the starting point for the **Chicago Greeter** tours; *see p304*. The Randolph Street lobby contains a café with free Wi-Fi; the ground floor also houses a gift shop, the **Art*O*Mat** (a vending machine that sells works by local artists) and the **Chicago Publishers' Gallery**, a library of about 1,500 locally produced books and magazines.

Further south sits **Symphony Center** (*see p255*), home to the Chicago Symphony Orchestra. Connected by a central rotunda, its three wings encompass the 1904 Orchestra Hall, a park, a shop and an education and administration wing. Down the block is the **Santa Fe Building** (224 S Michigan Avenue, at E Jackson Boulevard), designed in 1904 by Daniel Burnham (who liked it so much that he moved his own offices here). On the ground floor is the marvellous **Chicago Architecture Foundation** (www.architecture.org; *see p304*), best known for its tours, lectures and small-scale exhibits. The gift shop is a real treat.

SIGHTS

SIGHTS

Chicago Cultural Center. *See p59.*

The **Fine Arts Building** (410 S Michigan Avenue, at E Van Buren Street) once housed the showrooms of the Studebaker Company, which in 1895 held carriages rather than cars. Soon after, it was converted into a theatre on the first floor and artists' studios above, and the words 'All Passes – Art Alone Endures' were carved inside the entrance. Frank Lloyd Wright had a studio here at one time; so did L Frank Baum, author of *The Wizard of Oz*.

When the **Auditorium Building** (S Michigan Avenue, at E Congress Parkway) was built by Adler and Sullivan, then dedicated in 1889 by President Benjamin Harrison, it was the tallest building in the world, housing a theatre (the first home of the Chicago Opera), a hotel and offices. After a spell of neglect, it was restored in the 1960s; for the programme, see www.auditoriumtheatre.org. Just south are the **Spertus Museum** (*see p61*) and the **Museum of Contemporary Photography** (*see p61*).

McCormick Bridgehouse & Chicago River Museum

Southwest tower, Michigan Avenue Bridge, at E Wacker Drive (1-312 977 0227/www.bridge housemuseum.org). El: Brown, Green, Orange, Pink or Purple to State/Lake. **Open** *May-Oct* 10am-5pm Mon,Thur-Sun. **Admission** $3; free under-5s. **Credit** AmEx, MC, V. **Map** p326 J11.

The famous 1920 Michigan Avenue Bridgehouse now serves as a museum that celebrates the river's role in building Chicago into a major metropolitan city. The five-storey space might prove difficult to traverse if you're travelling with children or grandma; however, if you make it to the top, you'll be rewarded with a unique viewpoint of the Chicago River, the bridge itself and the Trump Tower on the northern bank. The photographs, maps, newspaper

INSIDE TRACK
MONTEZ LE TRAIN

Among Chicago's multifarious nicknames was 'the Paris of the Midwest'. Even so, it's disconcerting to see one of the **Paris métro**'s famous art nouveau entrances at S Michigan Avenue and E Van Buren Street. Passers-by who spot the decorative sign, directing passengers to the Metra, may assume a pathetic attempt to bestow European elegance on the commuter railway. However, this is the real deal: Paris's RATP made the entrance's curvilinear cast-iron forms from the same moulds that Hector Guimard, their French designer, used in 1900, and donated the piece to Chicago in 2003.

articles and historical tidbits are a feast for history buffs, riverphiles or anyone with a keen interest in urban planning; the insider views of the massive gears, mechanisms and counterweights used to lift the bridge lend the place a broader appeal.

FREE Museum of Contemporary Photography

Columbia College, 600 S Michigan Avenue, at Harrison Street (1-312 663 5554/http://mocp. org). El: Green, Orange or Red to Harrison. **Open** 10am-5pm Mon-Wed, Fri, Sat; 10am-8pm Thur; noon-5pm Sun. **Admission** free. **Map** p325 J13.

Affiliated with Columbia College, the Museum of Contemporary Photography holds three floors of galleries, which encompass new work in shows and exhibitions culled from the collection of 8,500 photographs and photographic objects. Work by some of the world's best photographers and video artists is on show; the Midwest Photographers Project highlights local contemporary work.

Spertus Museum

610 S Michigan Avenue, at E Harrison Street (1-312 322 1700/www.spertus.edu). El: Green, Orange or Red to Harrison. **Open** 10am-5pm Wed, Sun; 10am-6pm Thur; 10am-5pm Sun. **Admission** $7; $5 discounts; free under-5s. Free 10am-noon Wed, 2-6pm Thur. **Credit** AmEx, Disc, MC, V. **Map** p325 J13.

Completed in late 2007 and fronted by an illuminated glass façade, the Spertus Museum's ten-storey, Kruek & Sexton-designed digs was one of the first new construction projects in decades on Michigan Avenue's 'street wall'. The building's two top floors house the museum's core-collection display and changing exhibitions in 8,000 square feet of exhibition space. The expanded displays detail the rich diversity of Jewish culture, with the 1,500 artefact-strong permanent Depot Display alongside new 19th- and 20th-century exhibits that stir the pot with often risqué contemporary artwork on Judaism. Lectures, screenings and performances also take place weekly, and often welcome drop-ins.

STATE STREET & AROUND

Macy's (no.111, at E Randolph Street; *see p188*) tops the long list of landmarks on 'That great street', the stuff of which songs are made. However, plenty of longtime locals defiantly call the block-long retail extravaganza by its original name: Marshall Field's. The store first opened on this site in 1868 (it was twice destroyed by fire, once in the Chicago Fire of 1871 and again six years later) and became the flagship shop in a pioneering nationwide chain.

When Macy's bought the store in 2005 and changed its name the following year (a century

after Field's death), Chicagoans were outraged, but not much has changed: the Tiffany mosaic dome (c1907) still stands high above one atrium, and the clock at State and Randolph, the inspiration for a Norman Rockwell painting that made the cover of the *Saturday Evening Post* in November 1945, still keeps perfect time. (The original Rockwell work hangs near the seventh-floor visitors' centre.)

The city has tried for more than two decades to turn **Block 37**, bounded by State, Washington, Randolph and Dearborn Streets (directly opposite Macy's), into a mixed-use complex. Construction work began in 2005, but the project is still far from finished: plans for a CTA 'superstation' providing a high-speed link to O'Hare stalled, and an array of proposed retail tenants have flaked out. When 22 W Washington Street, the new development's first building, opened in September 2008, it dazzled the neighbourhood with a 30-foot-wide LED screen broadcasting the television programmes of tenant CBS.

Close by sits the lovely **Chicago Theater** (175 N State Street, at W Randolph Street). You can't miss the iconic red marquee of this former movie house, which opened in 1928 and today hosts entertainers ranging from Leonard Cohen to Bob the Builder. Opposite is the **Gene Siskel Film Center** (164 N State Street, at W Randolph Street; *see p236*), one of the best arthouse cinemas in Chicago.

Facing Block 37 from the corner of State and Washington, you'll find a Chicago miracle to rival the salt stain Virgin Mary spotted in 2005 on a Kennedy Expressway underpass. (Seriously; Google it.) The **Reliance Building** (1 W Washington Street, at N State Street) was one of Chicago's most elegant early skyscrapers when it opened in 1895, but years of neglect had left it in disrepair by the time a developer

SIGHTS

Walk Art in the Loop

Spot some world-class sculptures as you scoot around downtown.

The prevalence of skyscrapers in the Loop means it's easy to walk around with your eyes to the sky. But if you snap your head back to eye level, you'll notice some striking pieces of public art. City Hall passed a groundbreaking ordinance 30 years ago, forcing those in charge of building projects to set aside a fraction of construction costs for art. Private companies followed suit, and the result has left the Loop as a sculpture garden like no other in the country.

Start at on the north-west corner of Madison and Wells.

Found under a glass-walled atrium at 200 W Madison Street (8am-7pm daily), **Louise Nevelson**'s *Dawn Shadows* (1983) is thought to have been influenced by the design of the El. Happily, Chicago's rail system is more reliable than this monstrous black form might suggest.

Go east on Madison, north at LaSalle.

The *Flight of Daedelus and Icarus*, **Roger Brown**'s vast mosaic above the entrance of 120 N LaSalle Street, tells of Icarus, who ignored his father's warnings, flew too close to the sun and then drowned after his wings melted. There may be a moral in this story for the financial industry.

Continue north.

Freeform, on the façade of the Illinois State Office Building at 160 N LaSalle Street, is one of several Loop works by local artists.

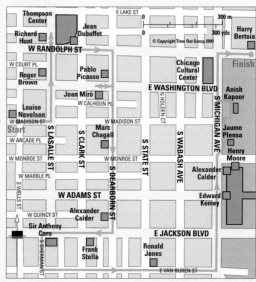

Richard Hunt has many works on display in the city, though this eye-catching abstract piece is perhaps his most prominent.

Walk back and take a left on Randolph to the Thompson Center's plaza.

Jean Dubuffet's fibreglass *Monument With Standing Beast* demands attention. Dubuffet always had affection for Chicago after a 1951 lecture he gave at the Arts Club of Chicago was rapturously received.

Move east to Dearborn and then south to Daley Plaza.

This striking piece of work is known locally only as 'the Picasso'; its creator, **Pablo Picasso**, didn't give it a title when he donated it to the city in 1967. Its lack of title helped to stoke the confusion – and, in some quarters, the contempt – that greeted its installation. It's believed to be based on the head of a woman. Or maybe a baboon.

Continue down Dearborn, then turn right into Washington.

Outside the Brunswick Building at 69 W Washington sits *Miró's Chicago*. Created by **Joan Miró** with ceramics expert Joan Artigas, it was completed in 1981.

Return to Dearborn and continue south.

He may be best known for his paintings, but Chicagoans know **Marc Chagall** more as a sculptor thanks to his vibrant, 70-foot mosaic *The Four Seasons*, now under a glass cover at Bank One Plaza.

Head south to Federal Center Plaza.
Alexander Calder was once asked why he had called his vast, hooped sculpture *Flamingo*. The questioner doubtless expected an answer swamped in allusion. Said Calder, 'It was sort of pink and has a long neck.'

Cross the road and go right on Jackson.
Between 1986 and 1997, **Frank Stella** created 266 works of art influenced by Moby-Dick. Few are more striking than *The Town-Ho's Story*, a jarring collection of mangled metal that dominates the lobby of the Ralph H Metcalfe Federal Building.

Continue east.
The shapes that make up *Chicago Fugue*, by British sculptor **Sir Anthony Caro**, allude to musical instruments. It can be seen in the lobby of 190 S LaSalle Street.

Go left on Sherman and left again on Van Buren as far as State Street.
Pritzker Park, designed by **Ronald Jones** and completed in 1991, is less sculpture and more landscape garden. However, its highlight, an interpretation of Magritte's *The Banquet*, is worthy of a detour.

Continue to Michigan, then turn left.
Edward Kemey's *Lions* have guarded the entrance of the Art Institute of Chicago for almost a century. North of the main entrance, in the Institute's McCormick Memorial Court, sit two more works by notable sculptors: *Flying Dragon*, another vast piece by **Alexander Calder**; and *Large Interior Form*, with three holes that distinguish it as a work by British sculptor **Henry Moore**.

Continue north to Millennium Park.
The two most popular pieces of public art in Chicago are two of the newest. The vast faces beamed on to **Jaume Plensa**'s *Crown Fountain (see p55)* unnerve adults but tickle kids. Everyone, though, loves **Anish Kapoor**'s *Cloud Gate (see p54)*.

Continue north and then head east on Randolph, just above the park.
Harry Bertoia's *Sounding Sculptures (pictured)* sit outside the Aon Center. Inspired by wheat swaying in the breeze on Midwest farms, the pieces are comprised of copper tubing, which make eerie music when the wind hits them.

bought it in 1996. Restoration followed, after which the building reopened as the **Hotel Burnham** *(see p128)*; it's named after Daniel Burnham, the building's architect.

South of Macy's sits Louis Sullivan's **Carson Pirie Scott** department store (1 S State Street, at E Madison Street), now home to the School of the Art Institute of Chicago; *see p59* **The Old College Try**. During renovations on the store in 2008, contractors removed a metal panel from the neighbouring building at 22 S Wabash Avenue (at E Madison Street). Behind it, to their surprise, they found ornamental work that seemed to suggest Sullivan's handiwork. Having lost several Sullivan buildings to fire of late, enthusiasts were thrilled when this 'lost' Sullivan storefront was rediscovered, especially when further research confirmed that Sullivan had indeed created the building.

Two more notable buildings sit just off State Street on Monroe. To the west is the **LaSalle Bank Theatre** (22 W Monroe Street, at S State Street), built in 1905 as the Shubert Theatre and now home to some of the biggest shows to visit Chicago. And just east of State is the **Palmer House Hilton** (17 E Monroe Street, at S State Street; *see p131*), built in 1927 by Holabird & Roche with a spectacular lobby.

A couple of blocks west, the **Marquette Building** (140 S Dearborn Street, at Marble Place) shows what Holabird & Roche could do back in 1895. The building is named after the 17th-century explorer and missionary Father Jacques Marquette, who was the first European to spend the winter in Chicago. Bas-relief panels over the main entrance, and a panoply of bronze sculptures and spectacular Tiffany glass mosaics in the two-storey lobby illustrate episodes from Marquette's journey through the Midwest – and reveal a lot about 19th-century attitudes toward Native Americans.

Due south, you'll find the world's tallest all-masonry building. When, in 1891, Daniel Burnham and partner John Root erected the 16-storey **Monadnock Building** (53 W Jackson Boulevard, at S Dearborn Street), they had to make its walls six feet thick at the base to support its weight, thinning them out as the building rose. Across the street, the **Chicago Federal Center** embodies what was cutting-edge 60 years later: the Everett McKinley Dirksen Building, the John C Kluczynski Building and the one-storey Loop Post Office were designed by Ludwig Mies van der Rohe. Mies's spare black steel and glass façades contrast with Alexander Calder's 53-foot *Flamingo*, which looks as if it could go for its own walk around the Loop at any moment.

A block south and east sits Harry Weese's **Metropolitan Correctional Center** (71 W Van Buren Street, at S Federal Street), which

SIGHTS

rises like a forbidding wedge of cheese. The top 16 floors house federal prisoners and suspects awaiting trial, which is why the windows are mere slits. Peer down on it from above, and you may see some of these inmates stretching their legs in the rooftop exercise yard; rumour has it that their wives and girlfriends sometimes entertain them by dancing on the roof of a nearby parking structure.

The **Harold Washington Library Center** (400 S State Street, at W Van Buren Street, 1-312 747 4300, www.chipublib.org), which opened in 1991, is less formally innovative but more uplifting: it's a fitting tribute to the city's first African American mayor, who appears in Jacob Lawrence's mosaic mural, *Events in the Life of Harold Washington*, which hangs in the lobby. Talks, discussions and concerts are held at the library regularly; check online for details.

RANDOLPH STREET & AROUND

Chicago government looms large on Randolph Street between LaSalle and Dearborn; never larger than at the round **James R Thompson Center** on Randolph between LaSalle and Clark (1-312 814 6684; *see also p42*), named for the former Illinois governor who commissioned it. The building was dedicated in 1985 and looks its age, due to its unfortunate salmon-and-pastel-blue colour scheme and mall-like skylit atrium. On the second floor, the **Illinois State Museum Gallery** (1-312 814 5322, www.museum.state.il.us) presents free shows that usually feature local artists.

City Hall and the adjoining **Cook County Building** sit opposite the Thompson Center, on the block bounded by Randolph, Washington, Clark and LaSalle. City council meetings are held every two weeks on City Hall's second floor; call 1-312 744 6870 if you'd like to attend.

Across the street from City Hall, located on Randolph between Clark and Dearborn, stands the **Daley Center**, named after former mayor Richard J Daley. Cook County's court system

---

INSIDE TRACK
CATCHING THE BUZZ

As part of his efforts to make Chicago greener, Mayor Daley had a green roof installed at City Hall in 2000. The space (which opens to the public during Great Chiucago Spaces & Places; *see p214*) has enabled the city to study how green roofs mitigate temperature changes. Delightfully, it's also home to approximately **200,000 bees**; their Roof Top Honey is sold at the Chicago Cultural Center (*see p59*).

---

has its headquarters in this rust-coloured high-rise, but it's best known for the untitled Picasso sculpture that dominates Daley Plaza (*see p62* **Walk**) – much to the dismay, it's said, of Daley senior, who apparently wasn't a fan of avant-garde art. A Christmas tree is put up each year in the plaza, which also plays host to the largest German holiday market outside Germany (*see p218*), a summer farmers' market (*see p204*) and the occasional political protest. The plaza's Eternal Flame Memorial, surrounded by a low metal fence, honours dead American soldiers. During the winter, the gas flame takes on an unexpected poignancy when pigeons huddle around it for warmth.

Rising 400 feet (120 metres) above ground a block south of City Hall on Washington, the **Chicago Temple** (77 W Washington Street, at N Clark Street, www.chicagotemple.org) is known as the 'Chapel in the Sky'. On an exterior first-level wall, stained-glass windows depict the history of the First United Methodist Church of Chicago. The temple's eight-storey spire is visible only from a distance.

LASALLE STREET

LaSalle Street has been the heart of the Midwest's financial industry since 1848, when a group of merchants founded the Chicago Board of Trade (CBOT) to regulate the grain futures market. In 2007, the CBOT merged with the equally storied Chicago Mercantile Exchange (CME) to form the **CME Group** (1-312 930 1000, www.cmegroup.com), the world's largest futures exchange. The group maintains lobby-level visitors' centres at 141 W Jackson Boulevard (at S LaSalle Street; 8am-4pm Mon-Fri) and 20 S Wacker Drive (at W Madison Street; 8am-4.30pm Mon-Fri), but security concerns have resulted in the closure of the trading floor to the public.

Back in the 19th century, birds nested in the run-down temporary City Hall at 209 S LaSalle Street, at W Adams Street. When Burnham and Root built a new structure there in 1888, the birds were remembered in the building's name: the **Rookery**. Two (sculpted) rooks at the LaSalle Street entrance serve as further reminders. The building's light-filled glass and marble lobby, a 1905 Frank Lloyd Wright redesign, is particularly lovely.

One Financial Place (440 S LaSalle Street, at W Congress Parkway) stands above the Eisenhower Expressway. If you're in a car, you can't miss it: traffic heading in or out of the Loop drives under the building, through arches that serve as stilts. Built in 1985 by the same architects responsible for the Sears Tower, it's home to the the Chicago Stock Exchange, the second largest in the US.

Profile Willis Tower

Now nearing 40, Chicago's most famous skyscraper gets a new name.

When it was completed in 1973, the Sears Tower received mixed reviews from critics. For years, Sears, Roebuck & Co had trouble renting out the extra space in its behemoth, eventually leaving it behind in 1992. And then, in 1998, the building lost its status as the world's tallest structure. However, despite these problems, and despite the 2009 renaming of the building in honour of a London-based insurance group, the newly rechristened **Willis Tower** (*listings p66*) has retained its status as Chicago's most iconic building.

Nine steel tubes of varying heights form the frame of the building, which is covered in black aluminium and glass. Designed by Bruce Graham from Chicago firm Skidmore, Owings & Merrill, it carries a certain grandeur, but its scale is more impressive than its appearance; the American Institute of Architects' guide to the city's buildings suggests that the tower is 'more of a structural engineering triumph than an architectural accomplishment', which seems about right.

An annual charity event offers super-fit Chicagoans the chance to climb the 2,109 steps between the ground floor and the Skydeck. In 1999, French daredevil Alain Robert went one better, climbing to the top in a little over an hour – from the outside. But those heading to the 103rd-floor Skydeck need not suffer such discomfort, thanks to the building's high-speed elevators.

After suffering through often-endless lines, visitors are faced with an overlong introductory movie and other exhibits on the building and the city. But everyone's really here for the views: on a clear day, you can see 60 miles from the Skydeck, which since 2009 has included an all-glass section that extends four feet over Wacker Drive and may leave vertigo-sufferers paralysed with fear.

In truth, the views from the John Hancock Center (*see p79*) are better, chiefly because they afford a better perspective on the Loop's skyline. The Hancock is also a more attractive building. But it's shorter. And when it comes to iconic status, at least in Chicago, size matters.

VITAL STATISTICS
Completed 3 May 1973
Storeys 108
Height 1,451 feet (442 metres)
Weight 445 million pounds (202 million kilograms)

SIGHTS

W WACKER DRIVE & THE CHICAGO RIVER

Edging up through a crowded Loop skyline that it works hard to dominate, the **Willis Tower** (formerly the **Sears Tower**; *see below*) is Chicago's most famous landmark. However, it's far from the only notable building around here. Just below it, **311 S Wacker Drive** (at W Jackson Boulevard) is the tallest reinforced concrete building in the world. Its exterior of glass and pink granite is surrounded by a neatly landscaped concourse; at night, the crown of the 65-storey structure is lit up like a Christmas tree. And to the north, Henry Cobb's curvaceous 2005 **Hyatt Center** (71 S Wacker Drive, at W Monroe Street) is one of the Loop's more feline and glamorous skyscrapers.

Home to the Lyric Opera since 1950, the 1929 **Civic Opera House** (20 N Wacker Drive, at E Madison Street; *see p253*) is centred on a lavish art deco auditorium adorned in red and orange with gold leaf accents. Its 3,500-plus capacity makes it the second-largest opera house in the country. Renovated in 1996, the building still boasts the terracotta and bronze forms of a trumpet, a lyre, and the masks of tragedy and comedy on its interior and exterior walls.

The Loop unofficially extends west over the Chicago River to encompass the **Ogilvie Transportation Center** (500 W Madison Street, at N Canal Street). Nearby **Union Station** (210 S Canal Street, at W Adams Street, 1-312 655 2385), where Amtrak stops as well as the Metra, has much more grandeur. Don't be surprised if the station, which was built in 1925 and beautifully restored in 1992, seems familiar: the famous staircase shootout at the end of *The Untouchables* was filmed there.

Heading west, you'll enter the **West Loop** and **Greektown** (*see pp100-106*). But before you get there, you'll run into Claes Oldenburg's 1977 **Batcolumn**, a 100-foot (31-metre) Cor-Ten steel baseball bat outside the **Social Security Administration Building** (600 W Madison Street, at N Jefferson Street). Critics interpret the piece as an homage to baseball, the steel industry or historical monumental columns. Still, the artist may also have been referring to the 1968 Democratic National Convention protests, where he was beaten by police.

★ Willis Tower
formerly Sears Tower
233 S Wacker Drive, at W Jackson Boulevard (1-312 875 9447/www.theskydeck.com). El: Brown, Orange, Pink or Purple to Quincy/Wells. **Open** *Apr-Sept* 10am-10pm daily. *Oct-Mar* 10am-8pm daily. **Admission** $12.95; $9.50 reductions; free under-3s. **Credit** AmEx, MC, V. **Map** p325 G12. *See p65* **Profile**.

Changing Trains

History of sorts on the El.

The **Quincy/Wells CTA station** boasts Victorian-style light fixtures, lustrous oak doors and mouldings, Corinthian pilasters and other neo-classical details on its sheet-metal walls. Yet despite appearances, none of these details are original. In the 1980s, the Illinois State Historic Preservation Office agreed to restore a Loop station to its 1897 appearance so the entire CTA system would be added to the United States' National Register of Historic Places. It chose Quincy/Wells because the station still retained some of its original features, including the fare booths.

The South Loop & Chinatown

From high society to high rises, this is a neighbourhood in flux.

While the rebirth of the West Loop has been making headlines, the **South Loop** has quietly been making a comeback of its own. As Chicagoans have moved back to the heart of the city, new apartment blocks have sprung up in the streets south of Congress Parkway, contributing to the gentrification of an area that had been neglected for years. Dozens of high-rise condo complexes have sprouted in the past few years; restaurants and supermarkets have joined them, giving the area something of a neighbourhood feel for the first time in decades.

The character of the South Loop can alter enormously within the space of a block or two. Apartment towers overlook tourist-packed **Museum Campus**; the glossy McCormick Place convention centre stands blocks from scruffy **Chinatown**, separated from it by deprived housing projects (around the intersection of Cermak Road and State Street). Change continues apace in a locale that's still to fully evolve.

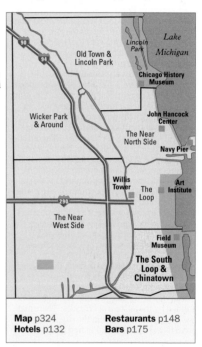

Map p324	**Restaurants** p148
Hotels p132	**Bars** p175

Map p324   **Restaurants** p148
Hotels p132   **Bars** p175

SIGHTS

PRINTER'S ROW

El: Red to Harrison.

The stretch of Dearborn Street between Congress Parkway and Polk Street is pretty quiet these days, but things were very different a century or so ago. In the late 19th century, this stretch of Dearborn became the heart of the Midwest's printing and publishing industry: Printing House Row, it was called, a nickname later shortened to **Printer's Row**. (You'd think that with all the publishers in the area, they'd have managed to put the apostrophe in the right place.) The industry has long since scattered, but many of the old buildings remain, now converted into apartments and restaurants.

At the southern end of Printer's Row, at the corner of Dearborn and Polk, stands Chicago's old railway terminus. Built in 1883, **Dearborn Station** was most famous as the starting point for trains to Los Angeles, used by those who couldn't or wouldn't travel between the two cities by car on Route 66. The last train pulled out of the station in 1971; the station is now home to shops, restaurants and other businesses that lend the locale a lift.

MUSEUM CAMPUS

El: Green, Orange or Red to Roosevelt.

Three of the country's finest museums share the grassy plot known as **Museum Campus**, jutting out into Lake Michigan at the southern edge of Grant Park (just south of Roosevelt Road). Although they've changed hugely in the intervening years, the **Shedd Aquarium**, the **Adler Planetarium** and the **Field Museum** (for all, *see below*) were erected here in time for the Century of Progress World's Fair of 1933-34; each is named after the Chicago business mogul who commissioned it. Get off the Red line at Harrison, take the sidewalk that heads east from 9th Street and Michigan Avenue, and stroll between the trio.

In 2005, **Northerly Island Park** (1400 S Lynn White Drive, 1-312 745 2910) was added to the area's recreational attractions. The island was previously occupied by Meigs Field, an airport used by the prosperous to jet in and out of downtown. On 30 March 2003, citing post-9/11 concerns over terrorism, Mayor Daley shocked the city by bulldozing the runways in the middle of the night, instantly closing the airport (and stranding a number of aircraft). These days, the redeveloped parkland offers fishing and walking opportunities, and is home to the open-air **Charter One Pavilion** (*see p257*). The island was earmarked for a central role in the city's bid for the 2016 Olympics.

A football's throw or two from here is **Soldier Field**, home to the Chicago Bears (*see p277*). Built in the early 1920s as a memorial to America's war dead, the stadium was dramatically renovated in the early 21st century, with shiny modern grandstands effectively being dropped into the framework formed by the austere old façades. There may well be uglier buildings in the city, but you'll have to work pretty hard to find them.

★ Adler Planetarium

1300 S Lake Shore Drive, at E Solidarity Drive (1-312 922 7827/www.adlerplanetarium.org). El: Green, Orange or Red to Roosevelt. **Open** *mid June-Sept* 9.30am-6pm daily. *Sept-mid June* 10am-4pm Mon-Fri (until 10pm 1st Fri of mth); 10am-4.30pm Sat, Sun. **Admission** $10; $6 discounts; free under-3. *Museum, audio tour & 1 show* $19; $15 discounts. *Unlimited shows* $25; $21 discounts. **Credit** AmEx, Disc, MC, V. **Map** p324 L14.

The name of this facility on the banks of Lake Michigan, housed in a 12-sided architectural marvel built in 1930, is only semi-appropriate: this excellent enterprise is more than just a planetarium. For a start, there are actually two planetariums here: the Definiti Space Theater, which was improved in May

2008 with the addition of a high-tech digital projector, and the Sky Theater, a more traditional experience. In addition, the Universe 3D Theater, created in January 2008, showcases similar educational space films with whiz-bang effects that only a Pink Floyd-loving stoner could fully appreciate. Between them, they offer six shows that run in rotation all day.

Most of the museum's permanent collection is accessible through a disorienting, mirrored walkway that sets the tone for what follows: it's interactive, interesting and kid-friendly but somehow never dumbed-down. The ground floor offers assorted nuggets of trivia (if the earth is a baseball, the moon is a ping-pong ball eight feet away), the 3-D Milky Way Theater and working replicas of Mars' rovers.

Shoot for the Moon features a fully-restored Gemini 12 spacecraft and more than 30 related items. Many were donated by former NASA astronaut James Lovell, who lives in the area. In part, the exhibit tells the story of Lovell's own Apollo 13 mission, the ill-fated return to earth which prompted the Tom Hanks film of the same name.

The museum also boasts the largest collection of historic, scientific instruments in the Western hemisphere. Several are located on the lower ground floor, which hosts revolving Special Topics exhibits that frame the historic astrolabes, telescopes and sundials in an informative manner. Look out for the vast Dearborn telescope, the largest in the world in its time; and Chicago's oldest planetarium, the 1913 Atwood Sphere, only 15 feet in diameter.

★ Field Museum

1400 S Lake Shore Drive, at E Roosevelt Road (1-312 922 9410/www.fieldmuseum.org). El: Green, Orange or Red to Roosevelt. **Open** 9am-5pm daily. Hours may be extended in summer. **Admission** $15; $10-$12 discounts; free under-3s. Free to all 2nd Mon of mth. **Credit** AmEx, Disc, MC, V. **Map** p324 J14.
See p70 **Profile**.

★ Shedd Aquarium

1200 S Lake Shore Drive, at E McFetridge Drive (1-312 939 2438/www.sheddaquarium. org). El: Green, Orange or Red to Roosevelt. **Open** *June-Aug* 9am-6pm daily. *Sept-May* 9am-5pm Mon-Fri; 9am-6pm Sat, Sun. **Admission**

$28.95; $21.95 reductions; free under-3s.
Credit AmEx, Disc, MC, V. **Map** p324 K14.
Housed in a beautiful, circular 1920s building on the lake, the Shedd Aquarium holds every conceivable kind of fish and water mammal. Enter through the main lobby and you'll be greeted by a large Caribbean coral reef exhibit, spectacularly plonked in the middle of a domed hall. From this central root protrude a number of branches, corridor-like exhibition spaces devoted to themes from the exotic (African tropical fish) to the everyday (invasive species found in the Great Lakes).

The displays are clearly labelled, and you can approach the exhibits in any order. Be sure to get a look at Granddad, the lungfish in the Waters of the World gallery. He was plucked from the waters of Australia in 1933 for the Century of Progress World's Fair; at an estimated age of 100 years, he's thought to be the oldest aquatic animal living in captivity anywhere in the world.

The aquarium more than doubled its visitorship in 1991 with the addition of the spectacular $45-million Oceanarium. Dominated by a vast tank, flooded with natural light and with great views of the lake, it features whales and dolphins swimming and performing shows daily. In 2008-09, it received a rehab, adding a video show and a river that runs through the faux rocks and ends in a fish-filled pool. However, although the Oceanarium's raison d'être is to recreate the conditions of the Pacific Northwest, one of its most successful exhibits was the long-running Project Seahorse, which raised awareness about the potential extinction of the species.

The other always-crowded attraction is Wild Reef. This faithful re-creation of a coral reef habitat in the Philippines contains various sections devoted to the many facets of reef life, from the creatures that inhabit the shoreline surf to those that patrol the drop-off. In one spectacular spot, shark tanks create an overhead arch, giving visitors an all-consuming diver's-eye view of the fierce predators. Amid all the fun, a few little lessons on the importance of maintaining reef habitats have also been included.

The aquarium also offers 4-D Experience movies, surprisingly fun 15-minute movies full of water squirts and air bursts, in the Phelps Auditorium. And don't miss *Man with Fish*, a painted bronze fountain (created by German artist Stephan Balkenhol) that sits just outside the aquarium. It's a humorous comment on stewardship, with an inexpressive everyman hugging a huge speckled fish.

THE PRAIRIE AVENUE HISTORIC DISTRICT

El: Red to Cermak-Chinatown.

During the late 19th century, before the city's rich and powerful moved to the North Side, the roads around 18th Street and Prairie Avenue were the grandest part of town, the centre of Chicago's high society and home to well over a hundred mansions. Only five properties from this era remain, but they provide a sense of what life must have been like among the city's privileged Victorian elite.

On the south-west corner of 18th Street and Prairie Avenue sits the **Glessner House Museum** (*see p71*), one of the key stops on a historical tour of Chicago. The property was built for John Jacob Glessner, who made his fortune in farm machinery. His neighbours

Shedd Aquarium.

SIGHTS

Profile Field Museum

A longtime local favourite continues to expand and thrive.

The **Field Museum** (*listings p68*) opened as part of the World's Columbian Exposition in 1893 as the Columbia Museum of Chicago, but was renamed after philanthropist and department store magnate Marshall Field in the early 20th century and moved to its impressive location soon after. A Chicago must-see, the museum is one of the most impressive natural science centres in the world, with a wealth of biological and anthropological exhibits alongside world-class on-site research facilities.

One big draw here is Sue, the world's largest Tyrannosaurus rex. Since she made her debut here in the late 1990s, costing the museum a cool $8.36 million at auction, Sue has become a mini-industry all by herself. Suitably awed children are normally to be found in her vicinity (near the north entrance of the museum), while parents rue the amount of Sue merchandise at the well-stocked museum shops. Despite the name, its sex is unknown: it's named after Susan Hendrickson, who unearthed the skeleton in North Dakota in 1990.

Popular though Sue is, she's by no means the whole story. The Field is too big to get around comfortably in a day, but pick up a map, plan your visit carefully, and you'll be rewarded. Among the standout exhibits are Evolving Planet, which starts with the world's oldest known single-cell organism and walks through a massive collection of dinosaur remains; Ancient Egypt, a life-sized tomb filled with real mummies and 14,000 artefacts; and the taxidermic libraries, which include the famed (and stuffed) lions of Tsavo.

Young families will find the museum a paradise for travel-weary kids. The 2007 Crown

Family PlayLab lets really young tots hold their pace with interactive displays; Underground Adventure, one of the museum's most amusing exhibits, shrinks viewers to the size of a bug in order to inspect the lives of tiny organisms. The most recent permanent additions include Ancient Americas, a staggering amount of early American artefacts displayed in an experimental politically-correct fashion, and DNA Discovery Center, a real, working biology office behind glass.

GETTING YOUR BEARINGS Time your visit to coincide with one of the free tours of the museum's highlights, held at 11am and 2pm (Mon-Fri only).

were just as wealthy: among them were the train car-designing Pullmans, whose mansion has long since vanished, and the piano-making Kimballs, whose pad at 1801 S Prairie Avenue is now home to the US Soccer Federation. To the south lived both Marshall Field, Sr and Marshall Field, Jr. However, the area's oldest house is an intruder: the **Clarke House Museum** (*see below*) originally sat on 20 acres of land at 16th Street and Michigan Avenue, and was moved to the area three decades ago.

A century after the area began to fade from prominence, it's undergoing a resurgence. Old warehouses have been converted into lofts, and new apartment complexes have sprung up from nothing. It all stands in stark contrast both to the streets that run roughly four blocks west, which are drenched in impoverished public housing, and to the hulking, ugly **McCormick Place** (E 23rd Street, at S Lake Shore Drive), which sits a few blocks south-east on the other side of Lake Shore Drive. Best accessed via the Metra service from the Randolph Street station (by Millennium Park), it's a gargantuan site, with over two million square feet of meeting space. See www.mccormickplace.com, or call 1-312 791 7000.

Clarke House Museum

1827 S Indiana Avenue, at E 18th Street (1-312 745 0040/www.glessnerhouse.org). El: Red to Cermak-Chinatown. **Open** *Tours noon, 2pm Wed-Sun.* **Admission** $10; $6-$9 discounts; free for under-5s. Free to all Wed. *Clarke & Glessner Houses* $15; $8-$12 discounts. *Prairie Avenue tour* $15. **Credit** MC, Disc,V. **Map** p324 J16.
Built in 1837 for hardware dealer Henry Clarke, this impressive property is the oldest house in Chicago. It's also the hardest place for the post office to keep track of: it's been moved twice in its long history, most recently in 1977 when the city lifted the building over a set of El tracks and on to its present (and hopefully permanent) home. Unlike the fortress-like Glessner House (*see below*), this Greek revival property was built before electricity, indoor plumbing and the Chicago Plan (*see p37*) changed the nature of architectural design in the city. Even so, the timber frame and mortise-and-tenon joints have travelled well, with ongoing restoration work enabling visitors to get a window into early upper-class life in Chicago. Tours begin at the Glessner House Museum; combined tours are available.

★ Glessner House Museum

1800 S Prairie Avenue, at E 18th Street (1-312 326 1480/www.glessnerhouse.org). El: Red to Cermak-Chinatown. **Open** *Tours 1pm, 3pm Wed-Sun.* **Admission** $10; $8-$9 discounts; free for under-5s. Free to all Wed. *Clarke & Glessner Houses* $15; $8-$12 discounts. *Prairie Avenue tour* $15. **Credit** MC, Disc, V. **Map** p324 J16.

Prairie Avenue Historic District.

A stroll through the Prairie Avenue Historic District is enjoyable in its own right, but it's incomplete without a tour of this museum. The imposing stone mansion was designed by Henry Hobson Richardson (who died in 1886, the year before it was completed). It's dark, drafty and Victorian, yet manages to maintain a certain cosiness, thanks to oak-panelled walls and gold-leaf ceilings. The house was furnished in part by local furniture maker Isaac Scott, and covered in William Morris carpets and wallpaper.

A number of Glessner's artefacts are on display in the house, among them a solid silver candlestick on the concert grand and bronze casts of Abraham Lincoln's face and hands. (The casts mysteriously disappeared in 1992, only to reappear on the doorstep a few days later after plenty of publicity.) An afternoon spent in the conservatory on the top floor, or browsing the bookshelves in the study, would make a visit here sublime. Unfortunately, you only get an hour in the house, tailed the entire time by a security guard armed with three words: 'Do not touch'. Tours begin inside the main doors on Prairie Avenue; combination tickets are available if you've also got time to see the nearby Clarke House.

National Vietnam Veterans' Art Museum

1801 S Indiana Avenue, at E 18th Street (1-312 326 0270/www.nvvam.org). El: Green, Orange or Red to Roosevelt. **Open** *11am-6pm Tue-Fri; 10am-5pm Sat.* **Admission** $10; $7 discounts. **Credit** MC, V. **Map** p324 J16.

INSIDE TRACK
THE ITALIAN CONNECTION

Before the Chinese started to arrive in what's now Chinatown a century ago, the area was home to a community of Italian Americans that included everyone from working stiffs to local mobsters: no less a figure than Al Capone was based at the **Four Deuces** (2222 S Wabash Avenue), the **Metropole Hotel** (2300 S Michigan Avenue) and the **Lexington Hotel** (2135 S Michigan Avenue), all a few blocks east of modern-day Chinatown and all now demolished. Most of the area's Italians were gone by the '60s, but a few remnants remain. **Bertucci's Corner** (300 W 24th Street, 1-312 225 2848) is a family-run restaurant that's been here since the '30s, while **St Therese Chinese Catholic Church** (218 W Alexander Street, 1-312 842 6777) contains a statue of Christ believed to have been donated by Capone's mother Therese.

The only institution in the US devoted entirely to art produced by veterans of the Vietnam conflict is a moving memorial. That said, it's a troublesome task deciding what constitutes art when the living memory is still so raw. Some pieces offer vivid representations of violence and death, with visual examples of the emotional journey many soldiers faced then and continue to face today. Still, the less literal the art, the more powerful the message. The 58,269 dog tags that hang in the foyer, gently rattling against each other, make a far more gripping expression of death than hackneyed paintings of the Grim Reaper.

Be sure to read the museum's publications: leaf through the guestbook before spending time with Mike Helbing's *Wall Drawing/Work in Progress*, a drawing created by the layered graffiti of visitors. There's meaning bound up in this museum, between a handful of mature works of art and the many very painful memories.

CHINATOWN

El: Red to Cermak-Chinatown.

A century after the Chinese first arrived, **Chinatown** remains modest. Intersected by every imaginable thoroughfare – Amtrak rail lines and the Chicago River to the west, I-55 to the south, the El network to the north and east – the district hasn't had much room to grow, which explains its oft-crowded streets. Chinese businesses dominate along Wentworth Avenue and Cermak Road: restaurants, bakeries, and small shops hawking everything from healing herbs to samurai swords. To see the area at its most vibrant, visit for the **New Year Parade** (late January or early February; *see p218*), the **Chinatown Summer Fair** (mid July) or the **Dragon Boat Races** (late July), when locals race elaborately painted wooden boats down the river to raise funds for local charities.

The Chinatown gate just west of the Cermak-Chinatown El station welcomes visitors to Wentworth Avenue, the area's main drag. On the west side of the street is the attractive **On Leong Merchants Association Building** (no.2216), also known as the Pui Tak Center. The impressively frescoed three-storey building blends styles typical of 1926, the year it was built, with traditional Chinese design elements. It never betrays the fact that it was designed by a pair of Norwegian-American architects, Christian Michaelsen and Sigurd Rognstad.

Other notable diversions in Chinatown include the **Chinese-American Museum**, which opened in 2005 (*see below*); **Chinatown Square** (2130 S Archer Avenue, 1-312 808 1745), a two-storey outdoor shopping complex erected in 1993; and **Ping Tom Memorial Park** (300 W 19th Street), a handsome and Chinese-themed riverside park tucked away behind a new housing development. However, most non-Chinese Chicagoans head here for culinary reasons: the area is packed with restaurants, including some real gems. For a few picks, *see p151*; and *see p149* **In the 'Hood** for chef Calvin Soh's tour of the area.

Chinese-American Museum of Chicago
238 W 23rd Street, at S Wentworth Avenue (1-312 949 1000/www.ccamuseum.org). El: Red to Cermak-Chinatown. **Open** 9.30am-1.30pm Fri; 10am-5pm Sat, Sun. **Admission** $2; $1 discounts. **No credit cards**.
Chinatown has more to offer than dim sum and cheap gifts, as this museum of Chinese-American history and culture proves. That said, it won't take long to get through the two floors of exhibition space. The rotating displays, some better curated than others, include travelling exhibitions from around the country, but the most fascinating shows are those culled from the personal collections of Chicago's own Chinese-American community. Past topics have included a survey of traditional Chinese furniture and clothing, an examination of Chinese Chicagoans' role in the 1893 and 1933 World's Fairs, and a look at the versatility of tofu.

Around Chinatown

Nearby, at State Street and Cermak Road, sits the **Hilliard Homes** public housing complex. Designed by Chicago's Bauhaus-trained Bertrand Goldberg in 1966 and added to the National Register of Historic Places 33 years

later, the estate comprises the most notable buildings that fall under the care of the Chicago Housing Authority. Reminiscent of Goldberg's earlier Marina City corncobs (*see p42*), the honeycomb-windowed residences were once mooted for redevelopment into luxury residences. However, they remain firmly below the poverty line, and are best admired from the safety of the El station that they overlook or from the 22 bus that runs down State Street.

There are more notable buildings nearby on Michigan Avenue (2200-2500 blocks) and parallel Indiana Avenue (2200-3500 blocks), in an area informally known as **Motor Row**. Back in the early 20th century, this was the city's main area for car sales and repair; 116 makes of automobile were sold and repaired along its streets. Many of the showrooms, some of which featured rotating display areas and elevators for the cars, occupied architecturally significant buildings; several of them have retained their terracotta façades. Originally an auto club, the third home of the *Chicago Defender* newspaper at 2400 S Michigan Avenue is a notable example of Prairie School style architecture.

Blues Heaven

2120 S Michigan Avenue, between E 21st & E 22nd Streets (1-312 808 1286/http://blues heaven.com). El: Red to Cermak-Chinatown.
Open 11am-4pm Mon-Fri; noon-2pm Sat.
Admission $10; $5 discounts. **Credit** AmEx, Disc, MC, V.
From 1957 to '67, this building was the home of the legendary Chess label and Chess/Ter-Mar studios, recording and releasing records from legendary bluesmen such as Muddy Waters, Howlin' Wolf and Buddy Guy. It's said that when the building was sold in the '70s, the new owners destroyed 250,000 records that had been abandoned here. Decades later, Willie Dixon's widow purchased the site and opened a museum and educational foundation in 1997. Today, you can tour the recording, rehearsal and office spaces, which feature guitars, memorabilia and a bit of the original soundproofing.

INSIDE TRACK TRAIN, TRAIN

Just north of Ping Tom Memorial Park (*see left*) sits a still-functioning relic of Chicago's industrial age. The imposing steel **Amtrak Bridge**, built circa 1917, is one of the few remaining vertical lift bridges of its kind. If you're lucky enough to be in the park at the right time, you'll be able to watch its massive concrete counterweights lift the suspension tracks 130 feet (40 metres) above the water as boats pass through.

Chinatown.

SIGHTS

The Near Side

Chicago's wealthy downtown is quite the tourist honeypot.

The pocket of Chicago directly north of the river and the Loop has long been a place rich in dense and fascinating contradictions. It remains so today, and is much the more interesting for its contrasts.

Once an industrial hub, **River North** has found its footing in later years as a hub for creative types, making their homes and conducting their businesses from old warehouses and factories. The serene piety of the area's **Cathedral District** is offset by the rowdy bacchanalia of many neighbouring bars and clubs. The consumerist extravagance of the **Magnificent Mile** is blocks away but worlds apart from the bleak decreptitude of the infamous Cabrini-Green estate. Nearby, in the **Gold Coast**, some of the city's oldest homes sit snuggled at the feet of soaring pioneers in Modernist design. And then there's the most wondrous contradiction: the fact that this buzzing urbanity sits within a comfortable stroll of several lovely and unexpected beaches. For millions of tourists, the experience of visiting Chicago never extends beyond the Near North Side. It's easy to see why.

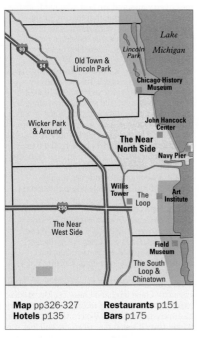

| **Map** pp326-327 | **Restaurants** p151 |
| **Hotels** p135 | **Bars** p175 |

RIVER NORTH

El: Brown or Purple to Chicago or Merchandise Mart; Red to Chicago or Grand.

These days, River North shines with more than 70 upscale art galleries, a slew of smart restaurants and some of the sleekest nightclubs in town. The presence of such businesses makes it hard to believe that, before the late 1980s, locals issued visitors with stern warnings about the rampant drug trafficking and armed robberies for which the area was known. Much of the crime spilled over from nearby Cabrini-Green, one of the nation's most notorious housing projects, which sits just north of Chicago Avenue. But these days, the elegant neighbourhoods to the east wield more influence.

The area's first boom dates back to the industrial era of the 1890s, when most of the bigger buildings were first erected. River North remained dominated by factories and warehouses until the 1970s, when, with post-industrial rust setting in, it morphed into a low-rent enclave for starving artists and other creative types. Their pioneering spirit has found a belated echo in the resurgence of the western portion of River North as a desirable business district for creative enterprises, with interior designers, dotcom start-ups, designer furniture stores and art dealers all taking leases on converted loft spaces.

The blocks bound by Chicago Avenue to the north, Wells Street to the east, Erie Street to the south and Orleans Street to the west comprise the **River North Gallery District**, home to

God Bless America. *See p78.*

large numbers of galleries and antique stores, *see p238*. In this general area, you'll also find a host of clubs, which attract both chic city dwellers and suburban weekenders; *see p267*. But despite the many hip, high-style clubs and galleries, the area is not without a few unabashed tourist traps, especially around the intersection of Clark and Ohio Streets.

Towards Michigan Avenue sit a handful of notable churches, which provide solace from the hectic streetlife and, architecturally, some relief from the vertigo-inducing skyscrapers, malls and hotels. One is the Catholic **Holy Name Cathedral** (735 N State Street, at E Chicago Avenue, 1-312 787 8040, www.holyname cathedral.org), a Victorian Gothic edifice built in 1875. A fire in February 2009 destroyed a large section of the roof, but the church remained open pending repairs. Nearby is the Episcopalian **St James Cathedral** (65 E Huron Street, at N Wabash Avenue, 1-312 787 7360, www.saintjamescathedral.org), the unusual interior walls of which are decorated with stencil patterns in more than 20 colours.

For all that, though, Chicagoans tend to associate the area with another former church, often known as 'the Castle' (632 N Dearborn Street, at W Ontario Street). Designed by Henry Ives Cobb, architect of the Fisheries Building at the 1893 World's Fair, this red granite Romanesque revival building was for years the home of the Chicago Historical Society, but now houses the **Vision/Excalibur** club (*see p269*).

Close by, the **Tree Studios** (4 E Ohio Street, at N State Street) are proof that the area's association with artists is nothing new. Built by lawyer and philanthropist Lambert Tree in 1894 and later expanded, the studios were used

by some of the city's best-known artists for decades, among them sculptor Albin Polasek, muralist John Warner Norton and painter Ruth van Sickle Ford. The complex was threatened by developers during the '90s real estate boom, but – for once – the story has a happy ending: in 2001, city fathers saved the Queen Anne and Arts and Crafts buildings from the wrecking ball, allowing artists and construction crews to re-create some of the stunning architectural details from found fragments. The ground floor now houses galleries and furniture stores, among other enterprises.

For a time, artists at Tree Studios shared their space with the **Medinah Temple Association** (600 N Wabash Avenue, at Ohio Street). Built for the national Shrine fraternal organisation in 1912, the temple was considered one of the nation's finest examples of a Middle

SIGHTS

**INSIDE TRACK
GANGLAND SECRETS**

Holy Name Cathedral (*see above*) is quietly notorious as the place where Al Capone shot gangster Dion O'Banion and, later, his successor Hymee Weiss. Until his death, O'Banion operated a flower shop across the street, providing bouquets for a number of funerals for which he was personally responsible. Sadly, visitors won't be able to find any additional gang-era history in any of the city's official whitewashed tourist literature; perhaps rampant corruption hits a little too close to home in Chicago.

Eastern-style Shrine temple. In 2003, Bloomingdale's Home & Furniture Store took over the space; the renovation that ensued preserved much of the exterior architecture and restored the interior's former glory.

Several blocks south-west of Tree Studios stands the former nemesis of Chicago's criminal contingent: **Courthouse Place** (54 W Hubbard Street, at N Dearborn Street). The former Cook County Court building was built in 1892 as the second county court facility. Over the years, it was the site of some momentous legal wrangles, including attorney Clarence Darrow's successful bid to save convicted murderers Leopold and Loeb from the death sentence in 1924. Even more chillingly, it was also once used for hangings, and is purported to be haunted. These days, it's an office building.

South of here, overlooking the river, stands Bertrand Goldberg's distinctive **Marina City** (300 N State Street). Its two iconic structures, nicknamed the Corncob Towers for obvious reasons, have made cameos in everything from Steve McQueen's final movie to a Wilco album cover. The top 40 storeys house trapezoid apartments, with the lower 20 storeys used for parking. The complex is also home to the **House of Blues** (see p260) music venue and the recently redesigned **Hotel Sax** (see p136).

East of the Corncobs along the river is The Donald's **Trump International Hotel & Tower** (see p135), completed in 2009. At one time, the 92-storey, silvery glass-curtain-wall giant was slated to become the world's tallest building, but plans were scaled back due to the sagging real estate market. Instead, upon completion, the mixed-use retail/condo/hotel became Chicago's second tallest building.

Just as Trump's new skyscraper stands as testament to a vibrant 21st-century economic optimism in Chicago, so the hulking riverfront building on its west pays tribute to earlier wealth and enthusiasm. Built in 1930 as showrooms and a wholesale office for Marshall Field's, the art-deco **Merchandise Mart** (between N Wells and N Orleans Streets, www.merchandisemart.com) is the second-largest building in the world (second only to the Pentagon), boasting an astonishing 4.2 million square feet (390,000 square metres) of floor space, as well as its own zip code. When the mart hit hard times in the 1940s, Field sold the building to Joseph P Kennedy, the father of JFK. It was the elder Kennedy who installed the outdoor Merchandise Mart Hall of Fame in 1953, honouring captains of industry with Romanesque bronze busts along the river. These days, visitors head to the Merchandise Mart for the Design Center, which boasts more than 130 showrooms of design products, and for the retail shopping area on the first two floors.

INSIDE TRACK
MUSEUM FREE DAYS

Several museums that ordinarily charge admission set aside one or more days each week where they're free to all. Timing your visit with care could save you plenty of cash. Here's when some major museums let you in for nothing...

Art Institute of Chicago p56 5-9pm Thur, Fri (hrs vary by season); throughout Feb
Chicago Children's Museum p221 5-8pm Thur; 1st Sun of mth
Chicago History Museum p88 9.30am-4.30pm Mon
Clarke House Museum & Glessner House Museum p71 tours noon-3pm Wed
DuSable Museum of African American History p121 noon-5pm Sun
Field Museum p68 9am-5pm 2nd Mon of mth, plus other one-off dates throughout the year; check website for details
Museum of Contemporary Art p81 10am-8pm Tue
Spertus Museum p61 10am-noon Tue; 2-6pm Thur

Richard H Driehaus Museum

40 E Erie Street, at N Wabash Avenue (1-312 932 8665/www.driehausmuseum.org). El: Red to Chicago. **Open** *Tours* 10am, 1pm, 3pm Tue, Wed, Sat. **Admission** $25; $12.50-$17.50 discounts. **No credit cards. Map** p326 H10.

Fund manager and philanthropist Driehaus opened this museum in 2008 to display his expansive collection of Louis Comfort Tiffany lamps and accessories, and other 19th century furnishings. Housed inside a mansion built by 19th-century liquor-magnate Samuel M Nickerson, the immaculate 'marble palace' is also a shining example of building preservation. Kids under 12 are not admitted due to the purported 'fragile nature of the historic interiors'.

THE MAGNIFICENT MILE & STREETERVILLE

El: Red to Chicago or Grand.

Michigan Avenue's Magnificent Mile is actually a Magnificent Three-Quarters-of-a-Mile, but few visitors would let that sully their impressions of the bustling commercial avenue. Every year, many of the city's 45 million visitors make it a top priority on their itineraries, spending full days collecting one rustling bag after another. While the street is a who's who of American retail, locals have complained that the stretch of 460-plus shops is in the process of losing its

SIGHTS

SIGHTS

INSIDE TRACK
AESOP'S FABLES

Tribune Tower (*see right*) is adorned with many ornate bells and whistles that often go unnoticed by harried passers-by. One notable example is the Hall of Inscriptions, as the grand entrance to the main lobby is known: intricate carvings depict symbolic imagery from Aesop's *Fables*, famous quotes heralding the ideals of a free press and some wise words from *Tribune* founder Colonel McCormick.

unique character, with independent Chicago retailers giving way to big-name chains.

In the years after World War II, developer Arthur Rubloff christened the street the Magnificent Mile as he went about renovating old buildings and erecting new ones. At the time, there wasn't anything too magnificent about it; but in due course, the road grew into its lofty sobriquet as big shops flocked. It's at its best in the run-up to Christmas, when the buildings and trees are garlanded with lights, but it's pleasant (if congested) all year round, the broad expanse of the road dotted with small flower gardens and handsome greenery.

The Magnificent Mile is best approached by walking up it from south to north, especially if you first take in the views from the southern side of the **Michigan Avenue Bridge**. After it opened in 1920, the bridge quickly became an asset to the area north of the river, making access to the Loop easier for residents and businessmen. A plaque at the south-eastern

end commemorates Fort Dearborn, the military outpost from which the city developed, and four sculptures on pylons along the bridge nod to events in the city's history: the arrival of Joliet and Marquette, trader Jean Baptiste Point du Sable's settlement, the Fort Dearborn Massacre and the rebuilding following the fire of 1871.

John Howells' and Raymond Hood's Gothic design for **Tribune Tower** (435 N Michigan Avenue), the offices of the *Chicago Tribune*, was selected in 1922 by then-publisher Colonel Robert McCormick from a field of international entries, and was completed to great acclaim three years later. The Gothic block houses the offices of the daily newspaper, the *Tribune*-owned WGN radio station (the letters stand for 'World's Greatest Newspaper') and CLTV, Chicago's 24-hour local news station. As you walk around the first level, look for the stones purportedly swiped by *Tribune* correspondents from the Alamo, the Berlin Wall, the Parthenon, and St Peter's Basilica, as well as a piece of steel from the World Trade Center and a moon rock.

Outside the Tribune Tower stands J Seward Johnson's *God Bless America*, a towering and rather eerie sculptural rendering of Grant Wood's painting *American Gothic*; *photo p75*.

Time your arrival right, and you might catch a live radio broadcast from the Tribune Tower's streetfront studio. However, mere steps away, NBC has gone one better at the **NBC 5 Streetside TV Studio** (401 N Michigan Avenue, www.nbc5.com), which stages regular live television broadcasts. The schedule usually includes a daily 5am newcast (6am on weekends), and then further news round-ups at 11am, 4.30pm and 5pm. The public is encouraged to watch from the street.

Magnificent Mile.

Across the street is the stunning **Wrigley Building** (400 N Michigan Avenue). A white terracotta-clad structure designed by Charles Beersman for Graham, Anderson, Probst & White, later responsible for Merchandise Mart, it's stood at the base of Michigan Avenue since 1924, and remains home to Wrigley. The handsome clock tower was based on the cathedral tower in the Spanish city of Seville.

Further north, Michigan Avenue has its share of breathtaking architecture, not least the formerly exclusive (and men-only) Medinah Athletic Club building that's now home to the **Hotel Intercontinental** (*see p138*). However, the main reason people flock here is for the shops. From Gap to Gucci, Apple to Armani, the Magnificent Mile is one long paean to consumerism. Some shops have their own individual premises, but many others lie within malls. For details, *see pp188-190*.

Towards the northern end of the Magnificent Mile, just across from Chicago Avenue, stand the **Water Tower** and the **Chicago Water Works** (163 E Pearson Street, at N Michigan Avenue, 1-312 744 2400), two of only a handful of structures to survive the Chicago Fire of 1871. Inside the Water Tower is the compact **City Gallery**, which favours Chicago-oriented exhibits; the Water Works across the street houses a visitors' centre, a gift shop and the **Lookingglass Theatre Company** (*see p285*). Also right here is the **Loyola University Museum of Art** (*see below*).

The Water Tower is a handsome building, but these days it's very much in the shadow of the **John Hancock Center** (*see below*) just to the north. Towering 1,107 feet (337 metres) above the Magnificent Mile and the Gold Coast, it's smaller than the Sears Tower but affords more impressive views. The criss-cross braces that form the building's outer frame were designed to keep the structure from swaying in the wind. Much of the building is residential, but the lower levels and the sunken plaza are home to shops and eateries.

Across the street from the Hancock is the impressive **Fourth Presbyterian Church** (126 E Chestnut Street, at N Michigan Avenue, 1-312 787 4570, www.fourthchurch.org), built in 1914. The interior courtyard provides a quiet contrast to the bustling din of traffic and hordes of shoppers outside. On Fridays in summer, free jazz and classical concerts take place here. A block north is the **Drake Hotel** (140 E Walton Street, at N Michigan Avenue; *see p140*), which has long been a stopover for the rich and famous. The hotel was designed to resemble a Renaissance palace: a gorgeous second-floor lobby ushers in guests, while the first floor is lined with small retail shops. This is where the **Gold Coast** (*see p82*) really begins.

★ John Hancock Center

875 N Michigan Avenue, between E Delaware Place & E Chestnut Street (1-888 875 8439/ www.hancock-observatory.com). El: Red to Chicago. **Open** 9am-11pm daily. **Admission** $15; $9-13 reductions; free under-4s. **Credit** AmEx, Disc, MC, V. **Map** p326 J9.

Though it's a few storeys shorter than the Sears Tower, Big John offers even more astonishing views. For one thing, it's far enough north to take in the Loop's skyline, and close enough to the water to allow glimpses of boats miles out on Lake Michigan. For another, the 94th-floor Hancock Observatory has an outdoor walkway: it's not for the faint of heart, but it's guaranteed to blow away the cobwebs. Buy your ticket on the ground floor and take the ear-popping, elevator ride to the observatory, where you'll soak up views from floor-to-ceiling windows. During a 2008 overhaul, the Hancock freshened up the decor and added a multimedia tour narrated by David Schwimmer, along with a nice café.

Another point in the Hancock's favour is its 96th-floor Signature Lounge. Though the restaurant below is pricey, locals like to bring out-of-town guests to the bar: even taking into account the cost, you're likely to come out ahead, as there's no admission charge and you won't have to endure the tourist kitsch of the observation deck. The secret's out, so even people arriving when the bar opens at 5pm may be met with queues for the elevator, followed by queues for a table. But if you're willing to pay more than you usually would for a drink, the views are worth the wait, particularly as the sun goes down. *Photo p80.*

Loyola University Museum of Art

820 N Michigan Avenue, at E Pearson Street (1-312 915 7805/http://www.luc.edu/luma). El: Red to Chicago. **Open** 11am-8pm Tue; 11am-6pm Wed-Sun. **Admission** $6; $5 discounts; free under-14s; free to all Tue. **Credit** AmEx, Disc, MC, V. **Map** p326 J9.

LUMA, the art gallery for local catholic college Loyola University, interprets its mission broadly: One of its efforts to 'illuminate… enduring spiritual questions' was an installation of fairy paintings. Shows are hit or miss, but some recent hits include a showing of ancient-20th century keys and locks,

SIGHTS

INSIDE TRACK CHEW ON THIS

William Wrigley, Jr founded his company as a baking powder purveyor in 1891. Packs of gum came free with each can; consumers were more interested in the candy, and Wrigley's Juicy Fruit and Spearmint were born. If you enjoy lazy weekends, thank Wrigley, Jr: he was the first US manufacturer to give employees Saturdays and Sundays off.

John Hancock Center. See p79.

and paintings from its permanent collection of medieval, Renaissance and Baroque art, including a tiny, not-to-be-missed Tintoretto.

Streeterville

As a neighbourhood founded on a garbage heap by a lunatic, it will come as no surprise to learn that Streeterville boasts one of the city's most fascinating back-stories. Loosely defined as the area south of the Hancock Center and east of Michigan Avenue, the neighbourhood takes its name from a circus-owning scoundrel who ran his steamboat aground on a sandbar near the lakeshore in 1886 and claimed the area as independent territory. Huge amounts of rubble were dumped in the lake after the Great Fire of 1871; Captain George Wellington Streeter began taking the waste (and money) from contractors and managed to expand his sandbar, which he called the 'United States District of Lake Michigan', by eight million square feet. When landfill connected the island to the shore city officials (and a wealthy industrialist) tried to stake a claim. The captain fended off the intruders with gunfire, but his mansion was finally torched by the Chicago Title & Trust Company in 1918. Two decades later, his relatives gave up the fight.

The area is these days considerably calmer than in Streeter's day, when thieves, prostitutes and marauders roamed the locale. Much of the neighbourhood is given over to expensive residential property and grand hotels, though it's also home to Northwestern University's downtown campus and, at N Columbus Drive

and W Illinois Street, **NBC Tower.** Built in 1989 but designed to blend in with the 1920s and '30s art deco skyscrapers around it, the block hosts the recordings of TV shows such as *Judge Mathis* (for tickets, call 1-866 362 8447 or see http://judgemathistv.warnerbros.com).

Located along the stretch of the river that flows into Lake Michigan, **North Pier** (435 E Illinois Street, at N Lake Shore Drive, 1-312 836 4300) doesn't compare to neighbouring **Navy Pier** (*see p81*) in terms of size and the number of attractions. But it does have peace and quiet in its favour. There are plenty of places to sit outside and watch boaters heading out to the lake. At the far eastern end, you'll find the **Centennial Fountain & Arc,** which commemorates the city's Water Reclamation District. An arc of water shoots out of the fountain and into the river – and sometimes on to passing boaters – every hour, on the hour (10am-2pm, 5pm-midnight daily, May-Sept).

This little pocket has been the site of much activity in recent years, with the establishment of new residential buildings and a handful of new shops and restaurants. E Illinois Street alone is home to **AMC River East 21** cineplex (no.322; *see p233*), the flashy **Lucky Strike Lanes** (in the same building; *see p278*) and the sprawling **Fox & Obel** food market (no.401; *see p205*). Fox & Obel is housed in the **River East Art Center** (www.rivereast artcenter.com), also home to a number of galleries. However, if it's art you're after, you're better served by the temporary shows at the low-key **Arts Club of Chicago** (201 E Ontario Street, at N St Clair Street, 1-312 787 3997) or the rather more high-profile **Museum of Contemporary Art** (*see below*).

All these buidings may yet be joined by Santiago Calatrava's **Chicago Spire** (N Lake Shore Drive, at N Water Street). However, the slump has stopped its construction. *See p43*.

FREE Arts Club of Chicago

201 E Ontario Street, at N St Clair Street (1-312 787 3997). El: Red to Chicago. **Open** 11am-6pm Mon-Fri. **Admission** free. **No credit cards**. **Map** p326 J10.

Don't let the vocal guard scare you away: this art gallery might be one of the city's snootiest members-only clubs, but its first-floor exhibitions are indeed open to the public. Established in 1916, the club was formed by wealthy art-collectors in reaction to the very traditional exhibitions then shown at the Art Institute of Chicago. The Arts Club opened to display works by avant-garde artists including a young Picasso, who'd never shown in the US, and Brancusi, whose exhibit was installed by Marcel Duchamp. Today, this mission continues. While the club no longer makes an effort to hang the utmost forward-thinking art, a solid show by a big-name contemporary artist opens every couple of months.

★ Museum of Contemporary Art

220 E Chicago Avenue, at N Mies van der Rohe Way (1-312 280 2660/www.mcachicago.org). El: Red to Chicago. **Open** 10am-8pm Tue; 10am-5pm Wed-Sun. **Admission** $12; $7 reductions; free under-12s; free to all Tue. **Credit** AmEx, Disc, MC, V. **Map** p326 J9.

While the Art Institute has a pair of lions to guard it, the MCA needs no such deterrents: the $46-million building, designed by Berlin architect Josef Paul Kleihues and opened to coincide with the MCA's 30th birthday in 1997, is imposing enough. However, while its exterior is daunting (and not universally admired), it's a different story inside: since it opened, its vast spaces have proved adaptable.

The emphasis here is on temporary shows. The MCA's scattershot approach to programming is admirable and pays plenty of dividends, both with its exhibitions and the performances that take place within its walls; there's also a sculpture garden, a Wolfgang Puck restaurant and an excellent shop hawking doo-dads from local and international designers. The 2010-11 calendar gives some idea of the variety: Italics: Italian Art Between Tradition and Revolution (Nov 2009-Feb 2010), which features Italian art from the 1960s to the present, is followed by Alexander Calder (June-Oct 2010), which explores the American master's influence on contemporary artists, which in turn will be followed by a retrospective of Chicago painter Jim Nutt (winter 2011).

FREE Pritzker Military Library

610 N Fairbanks Court, at E Ohio Street (1-312 587 0234/http://pritzkermilitarylibrary.org). El: Red to Grand. **Open** 8.30am-4.30pm Mon-Fri. **Admission** free. **Map** p326 J10.

In 2003, James N Pritzker, retired National Guard colonel and member of Chicago's affluent Pritzker family, assembled this major collection of books and materials on non-partisan military history. The result is an elegant, apolitical treasure trove of books and ephemera dating back to the Revolutionary War. An exhibition space shows off contemporary artists and the library's collection of artwork, displaying rotating exhibitions with a focus on war-related imagery several times a year. Some exhibits lack imagination yet others are quite contemplative. A wonderful lecture series flies in war experts from around the world at least once a week.

Navy Pier

Mention Navy Pier and most locals will roll their eyes or let out a groan. The attraction has a reputation as a tourist trap filled with corny theme restaurants and cheesy gift shops. For children, however, the pier is a dream come true. Little ones will be wowed by attractions such as the **Transporter FX**, a high-speed virtual reality simulator; the **IMAX Theater**, showing the latest films on enormous screens; and the whizz-bang interactive exhibits of the **Chicago Children's Museum** (*see p221*). A crazy golf course and a hand-painted musical carousel provide old-fashioned entertainment.

There's some respite for more mature audiences, too. Adults will appreciate strolling through the **Crystal Gardens** one-acre indoor palm court, taking in a play at the **Chicago Shakespeare Theater** (*see p283*) or admiring an unbeatable vista of the skyline from atop the 150-foot Ferris wheel, the pier's best attraction. The latter is made even more magical when fireworks light up the sky on Wednesday and

---

INSIDE TRACK
BOHEMIAN RHAPSODY

When the anarchists, communists, intellectuals, lunatics and general blowhards of Washington Square Park tired of delivering their soapbox tirades to the masses, they took their pontificating to the **Dill Pickle Club** across the street. Established in 1914, just south of the Newberry Library, the bar attracted a regular assortment of activists and literary figures, including Carl Sandburg, Edgar Lee Masters, Ben Hecht and others. The club's motto was, 'Step high, stoop low, leave your dignity outside'. The Newberry Library houses a collection of memorabilia from the long-gone hangout.

SIGHTS

SIGHTS

Summer Lovin' Oak Street Beach

Mingle with the city's beautiful people on the Gold Coast.

Oak Street Beach is the Riviera of Chicago's shoreline, where the city's buff and beautiful people go to sun, swim and show off. In summer, there's a flurry of activity around the volleyball nets and the lakeside paths; for a beach, the pace is relentless. Pedestrian access is via underpasses located across from the Drake Hotel.

Amenities Bathrooms, drinking fountains, a café (summer only) and volleyball posts.
Where to eat The horrendously named Oak Street Beachstro offers sustenance during summer.
Location 1000 North, Gold Coast.
More information 1-312 742 5121 or www.chicagoparkdistrict.com

Saturday evenings during summer, as well for holidays such as Independence Day.

Another top sight, one that the pier neglects to promote, is the **Smith Museum of Stained Glass Windows** (1-312 595 5024; admission free). Many of the 150-plus pieces on display were made in Chicago in the late 19th century, when the city's European immigrants made the city a hub for stained-glass artisanship.

The pier hasn't always been the glittering tourist façade it is today. It was first built as a commercial shipping pier in 1916 by Charles Frost, when it had the rather plain-sounding name of Municipal Pier No.2, as one of five quays proposed six years earlier by architect Daniel Burnham (who didn't live to see it built). The pier grew more or less deserted when most commercial ships were re-routed to a pier on the South Side; during World Wars I and II, the 50-acre site was occupied by the US Navy, before serving as the first campus for the University of Illinois at Chicago until 1965.

Following a period of dereliction, the city renovated the pier as a leisure destination in the late 1980s, a multi-million-dollar project that was completed in 1995. Boats once again leave from here, mostly of the sightseeing variety. In 2006, the Metropolitan Pier & Exposition Authority unveiled plans to overhaul the pier by adding a monorail, a rollercoaster, a floating hotel and a water park; but as a board member put it, those plans are now on 'a slow burner'.

Just outside Navy Pier to the north, off Lake Shore Drive, is **Olive Park**, a quiet green space with room for picnicking. The small **Ohio Street Beach**, just west, contains a sculpture garden honouring **Jane Addams** (*see p103*) and offers superb views of the skyline.

THE GOLD COAST

El: Red to Chicago or Clark/Division.

The Gold Coast's 24-carat moniker seems fitting when you stroll through the mansion- and luxury high rise-lined streets near the lake.

Grannies wrapped in fur coats clutch tiny yapping dogs as they dodge nannies pushing oversized strollers down the pristine sidewalks; well-dressed ladies-who-lunch window-shop in expensive and exclusive boutiques.

But the farther you travel from the lake, the less luxurious the scene becomes; especially the area surrounding the intersection of Division and Rush Streets, home to more restaurants and bars per square foot than any other corner of Chicago since the 1920s. On weekends, the bars on Division Street are a rowdy, booze-soaked whirlpool in which tourists, conventioneers, suburbanites and college freshmen happily drown their dignity. The 1986 film *About Last Night* was set here. Meanwhile, Rush Street is now dubbed the 'Viagra Triangle' on account of its popularity with greying men on the prowl for younger women.

The neighbourhood's upmarket reputation was established by entrepreneur Potter Palmer, founder of the grand **Palmer House Hotel** (*see p131*), when he built a $250,000 'mansion to end all mansions' in 1882 on what now equates to 1350 N Lake Shore Drive. The area had been marshland up until the hotelier's arrival, but when a string of rich and influential Chicagoans followed in his wake, the locale soon came to replace **Prairie Avenue** (*see p69*) as the preferred address of Chicago's elite.

As the Gold Coast's cachet grew, it became a destination to which many Chicagoans aspired. The area attracted the Roman Catholic Church; the city archbishop resides at an expansive red-brick building on State Street (*see p85*). Just blocks away, Hugh Hefner chose the building at 1340 N State Street for his **Playboy Mansion**, though he eventually moved his headquarters and his bunnies to California. Palmer's mansion was torn down in 1950 to make room for one of the area's multiple high-rises, some of which are of architectural merit. However, many of the Gold Coast's early stately homes have been left standing, in styles from Tudor to art deco.

Technically, the Gold Coast is bounded by Chicago and North Avenues, Clark Street and

Lake Michigan. While the northern half of this area is chiefly residential, the southern block is mostly commercial.

Oak Street & around

Away from the **Oak Street Beach** (*see p82* **On the Beach**), the Gold Coast's other attractions are less frenetic. Oak Street itself is the city's high-end fashion strip (*see p194*); walking west along it will lead you to within a stone's throw of **Washington Square**, a green space bound by Delaware, Walton, Dearborn and Clark streets. Throughout its history, the square saw spirited demonstrations from all kinds of lively orators and protestors, until Mayor Richard J Daley cracked down on it in the 1960s. These days, it's a calm place for 364 days a year. The exception is the last Sunday of July, when the square hosts the lively, politicised Bughouse Debates in tribute to the park's past life. The debates are organised by the **Newberry Library** (*see below*), Chicago's research library for the humanities.

FREE **Newberry Library**
60 W Walton Street, between N Dearborn & N Clark Streets (1-312 943 9090/www.newberry. org). El: Red to Chicago. **Open** 8.15am-5pm Mon, Fri, Sat; 8.15am-7.30pm Tue-Thur. **Admission** free. **No credit cards**. **Map** p326 H9.
Neither the patrician setting nor the classic architecture of the Newberry Library, designed by Henry Ives Cobb and completed in 1893, betray its mission to bring highbrow culture to the plebs. Founded in 1887 by banker Walter L Newberry, it's not a lending library but a research centre that contains a vast variety of texts covering local history, literature, genealogy and cartography texts, along with a collection of Jefferson's letters. It's open to anyone; all you need is a reading card, which will require a photo ID, proof of address and a reason for wanting to search a specific collection. The small but exceptional exhibitions generally revolve around historical or literary themes, and are always free.

Astor Street

The grandeur of leaded-glass bay windows, elaborately carved frescoes, soaring turrets and meticulously manicured streetfront gardens make it seem as if time forgot about Astor Street. In truth, it was a 1975 Chicago Landmark designation that fought off time, engaging the street in a brutal battle between old and new.

Architecturally, Astor Street is an old-fashioned anomaly nestled among a forest of modern high rises, many of which have not aged well. Running north from Division Street, close by the colourful and exuberant **Lake Shore Drive Synagogue** (70 E Elm Street, 1-312 337 6811, tours by request), the handsome street makes for an enjoyable and quiet stroll past magnificent mansions that, for the most part, are immaculately preserved by their current residents.

Astor Street offers a glimpse into an era when Chicago's wealthiest citizens jostled for

Astor Street.

SIGHTS

Summer Lovin' North Avenue Beach

Mingle with the city's beautiful people on the Gold Coast.

Seething during the summer months with sexy singles playing beach sports and muscle-bound men on bikes, North Avenue Beach basically equates to the West Coast minus the surf. If you're not into scoping and getting scoped, you might find this strip of sand a bit run-down. Still, it's worth it for the beautiful skyline views of the city. And even if you don't play volleyball, it's worth checking out the action, which can get both very skilled and highly competitive.

Amenities The big boat-shaped building houses bathrooms, showers and a host of services (beach towel and bike rental, for instance). You'll also find a newspaper stand, a café and other temporary fixtures.
Where to eat Open in summer, Castaways Bar & Grill serves until 11pm. All the cafés and hot-dog stands close at 5pm.
Location 1600 North, Gold Coast.
More information 1-312 742 5121 or www.chicagoparkdistrict.com

bragging rights by engaging in a contest to build more luxurious mansions than their neighbours. It went up in the world after the Great Chicago Fire of 1871, when the city was forced to rebuild. However, the quarter-mile stretch of road didn't come into its own until the turn of the 20th century. Unlike the barn-like palaces that languished on Prairie Avenue, the mansions built on Astor Street by the likes of Cyrus McCormick and the Goodmans were more akin to overgrown townhouses. Most of the properties were built in the Queen Anne, Romanesque or Georgian Revival architectural styles, though their gaudy coats of arms, turrets and balconies were later dubbed 'Stockyard Renaissance' by one wag.

From the late 19th century until World War II, the street was home to many of the richest men and women in the city. But after the war,

the lure of the North Shore put the area on the skids: many of the buildings were knocked down in the 1960s to make room for the faceless high-rise condo buildings that stud the Gold Coast. However, community protest prevailed and Landmark District status was secured in 1975, the first such area in Chicago; the homes are now largely in excellent shape.

Even the apartment towers along Astor Street carry with them a little class. Take the pair at **no.1260** and **no.1301**, for example: built in the early 1930s by Philip B Maher, they're almost identical examples of art deco luxury, the artful minimalism of their design providing a bridge between the new and old Gold Coasts. And at the same intersection (with Goethe Street) stands **Astor Tower**, no.1300, the most eye-catchingly modern building on the road. Built in 1963 by one-time Astor Street resident Bertrand Goldberg (who also built Marina City; *see p77*), the 28-storey tower sits perched on a small glass box and some precariously slender columns. Even amid the real estate market's plunging prices, some units still fetch well over $1 million.

Before continuing up Astor Street, it's worthwhile taking a stroll east to the former home of the **Three Arts Club** (1300 N Dearborn Street), built by Holabird & Root in 1914 to resemble a Tuscan villa. Before it closed in 2007, the enterprise harkened back to an era when society women felt the need to protect young ladies from the 'wicked city' by giving them a refuge in which to study music, art or drama. The club sold the building several years ago, with a heavy heart, after anticipated public funding for renovation did not materialise, but continues its mission of supporting artists via awards and fellowships.

From there, head back to Astor Street and continue north to no.1355, which is also known as **Astor Court**. This Georgian mansion was designed by Howard Van Doren Shaw in 1914 for William O Goodman, who funded the construction of the Goodman Theatre in the Loop (*see p284*) in tribute to their late playwright son. The marble archway and spiked fence give it a hint of Versailles, as does the tantalising glimpse through a gate of a lost-in-time courtyard.

Next door is one of the real landmarks on the street, the **Charnley-Persky House** (no.1365). A simple but compact building, it was built in 1892 and designed by the great Frank Lloyd Wright while he was still working under the auspices of Louis Sullivan's firm (he was later fired for moonlighting on his own projects). A mix of the duo's styles, combining Wright's sweeping horizontal lines and Sullivan's ornamentation, it's now the headquarters of the Society of Architectural Historians, which conducts tours of the house every Wednesday at noon and every Saturday at 10am (and also at 1pm from April to November). Wednesday tours are free; Saturday tours cost $8-$15 and also include the exterior and interior of nearby **Madlener House**, and an exterior walking tour of the 1400 block of North Astor Street. Call 1-312 915 0105 or see www.charnleyhouse.org.

Across the junction with Schiller Street sits the **Ryerson House** (no.1406), which was designed by David Adler in 1922 for steel magnate Joseph T Ryerson. Its look was patterned, mostly successfully, after Paris hotels. Just beyond it stands a tall, skinny slice of art deco simplicity: completed in 1929 by the firm of Holabird & Root, the **Russell House** (no.1444) faces the world with a sleek stone façade imported from France and carved

decorative panels. Opposite, the **Fortune House** (no.1451) was built in the Jacobethan style in 1910 by Howard Van Doren Shaw.

At the junction with Burton Place stands the imposing edifice of the palazzo that former mayor Joseph Medill built for his daughter, Mrs Robert Patterson, in 1893. The orange brick walls, terracotta trim and inviting courtyard of no.1500 have all aged well, though the property has now been divided into frighteningly exclusive condominiums. Just west off Astor Street, the thick, immovable **Madlener House** (4 W Burton Place) was built in 1902 by Richard Schmidt. Its interior can be seen as part of the Saturday tours of Charnley House (*see above*).

Its postal address is 1555 N State Parkway, but the **Archbishop's Residence** stretches an entire block along Astor Street. This 1885 Queen Anne mansion is built of red brick with sandstone trim and has 19 chimneys poking up to the sky. At the top of Astor Street, either turn right in the direction of the **International Museum of Surgical Science** (*see below*), or wander left along W North Avenue. At no.59 is one of the city's oldest and most expensive private schools, the **Latin School of Chicago**. Founded in 1888, it counts guitarist Roger McGuinn and sculptor Claes Oldenburg among its alumni. Just across the road is the **Chicago History Museum** (*see p88*) and the **Old Town** neighbourhood (*see p86*).

International Museum of Surgical Science

1524 N Lake Shore Drive, between E North Boulevard & E Burton Place (1-312 642 6502/www.imss.org). El: Red to Clark/ Division. **Open** *May-Sept* 10am-4pm Tue-Sun; *Oct-Apr* 10am-4pm Tue-Sat. **Admission** $10; $6 reductions; free to all Tue. **Credit** AmEx, MC, V. **Map** p327 H7.

Not everyone will appreciate the assortment of surgery-related artefacts at this unusual museum. Indeed, many will probably shudder at the sight of a 3,000-year-old Peruvian skull drill or the Civil War-era amputation kit. Still, as with a gruesome car accident, it's difficult not to at least peek, even if only through your fingers. Operated by the neighbouring International College of Surgeons since 1954, the rather creepy International Museum of Surgical Science also houses a rare (working) iron lung; a re-created X-ray lab that includes Emil Grubbe's turn-of-the-century equipment; oddly captivating surgery-related murals by Gregorio Calvi di Bergolo; and, for the kids, a walk-in re-creation of a 19th-century apothecary. A small gallery features revolving anatomy- and surgery-related contemporary art exhibitions. If your stomach starts to turn, make a dash for outside: the façade of the lakefront mansion, which was designed by renowned architect Howard Van Doren in 1917, is also worth a look.

SIGHTS

Old Town & Lincoln Park

Once bohemian, now sedate: two of Chicago's more demure locales.

Similar in spirit yet nonetheless quite distinct, the adjoining residential neighbourhoods of **Old Town** and **Lincoln Park** carry broad appeal for a certain type of Chicagoan who finds River North too brash but Wicker Park too edgy. Both neighbourhoods grew increasingly affluent in the 1980s and early '90s, since when they've settled into comfortable middle age.

Old Town and Lincoln Park are dominated by handsome residential housing, with a handful of commercial drags – North Avenue and Wells Street in Old Town, Lincoln Avenue and Clark Street in Lincoln Park – giving focus to the communities. However, for visitors, the main appeal lies alongside the lake in the shape of Lincoln Park itself, which begins at North Avenue and runs five miles north along the waterfront. It's easy to lose a summer's afternoon just wandering around its vast, appealing pastures; many locals often do.

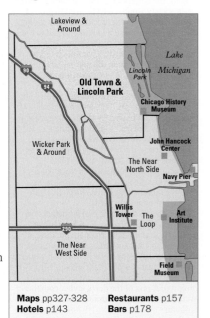

| **Maps** pp327-328 | **Restaurants** p157 |
| **Hotels** p143 | **Bars** p178 |

OLD TOWN

El: Brown or Purple to Sedgwick; Red to North/Clybourn.

Once a trading spot for Indian tribes, the neighbourhood now known as Old Town was properly settled by German immigrants, who were pushed north following the Chicago Fire of 1871. At the time, the stretch of land between North Avenue, Clark Street, Armitage Avenue and Larrabee Street was little more than a patchwork of gardens and cow pastures, but it was redeveloped after the blaze; the influx of German shops and restaurants along North Avenue earned it the moniker 'German Broadway'. After World War II, the

neighbourhood was finally considered venerable enough to assume its current name.

The development of the Cabrini-Green public housing project along Division Street and the collapse of industry in the area in the 1950s changed the face of Old Town's south-west corner. Home to 20,000 people, the project became a symbol of the city's neglect of its urban poor, the extremes of gang violence and the local drug trade. Ever-conscious of its public image (and ever aware of the escalating price of real estate), the city has begun to tear down the development's main towers and relocate its residents, a programme of enforced gentrification that's not been without its critics. Nearby, upmarket apartment blocks, grocery stores and coffee shops have sprouted.

Crilly Court.

Nonetheless, approximately 4,700 people remain in the complex, many of them enduring long waiting lists for hard-to-come-by government housing elsewhere.

The downturn of Old Town made it financially viable territory for movers and shakers in the 1950s counterculture, who began to lend the neighbourhood a new character. During the following decade, the area became a kind of Midwestern equivalent to New York's Greenwich Village and San Francisco's Haight. The likes of Miles Davis and John Coltrane played (and recorded) at the Plugged Nickel (1321 N Wells Street); just down the road sat Mother Blues (No.1305), a no less important music venue at the time. Folk singers also descended on the district, to the **Old Town School of Folk Music** on Armitage Avenue (*see p261*) and the Earl of Old Town pub at 1615 N Wells Street. Just opposite the latter, Mike Nichols' and Elaine May's **Second City** crew (*see p228*) went about defining modern sketch comedy after emerging from the ashes of the Compass Players troupe.

It couldn't last, and didn't. As has been the case with many such fashionable and forward-thinking neighbourhoods across the world, Old Town proved too attractive for its own good. As its reputation rose, so did the rents, and the hippies, beatniks and folkies were gradually forced to look elsewhere. The cutting edge is conspicuous by its absence in what is now a relatively affluent and cultured part of town. Along Wells Street and Armitage Avenue sits a slew of smart restaurants and one of the city's longest string of boutiques. Still, some of the old

raffishness remains in the **Old Town Ale House** (*see p179*), a glorious imbiberie that continues to draw a democratic mix of working stiffs, theatrical luvvies, rabblerousing twentysomethings and hopeless old soaks.

Bona fide sights and attractions are largely absent from Old Town, but a wander around its confines is nonetheless an agreeable way to lose track of an afternoon. It remains a handsome place, nowhere more so than in the historic **Old Town Triangle**. Hemmed in by Wells Street to the east, North Avenue to the south and a vaguely diagonal line connecting the Lincoln Avenue/Wisconsin Street junction with the corner of North and Larrabee, this cosy district has retained many of its 19th-century cottages, built in the three decades after the Chicago Fire. It's easy to see why the locals are so proud of their neighbourhood.

One such street is **Crilly Court**, constructed by developer Daniel F Crilly in the middle of an entire block he purchased in the early 1880s. Between 1885 and 1893, Crilly built row houses on the west side of the block and four-storey apartment buildings on the east, carving the names of his four children above the doors. Some five decades later, son Edgar renovated the buildings, closing off the alleys to form a series of courtyards. The renovation was one of the first in the Old Town Triangle, and the younger Crilly is credited with leading the way in the historical preservation of the locale.

Several homes near Crilly Court have their own historic significance. The residence at **216 W Menomonee Street** is believed to have been a 'fire relief cottage', built by the city following the Chicago Fire (at a cost of $75) to provide shelter for homeless residents. Just north are two other frame houses built in the 1870s for the Swiss-born Wacker brewing family. Frederick's son Charles, then a member of Chicago's planning commission and the man after whom Wacker Drive is named, lived in the carriage house at **1836 N Lincoln Park West**, while his father resided in the Swiss chalet-style residence at 1838. Down the street, the row houses at **1828-1834 N Lincoln Park West** were designed by Dankmar Adler and Louis Sullivan in 1884 and 1885. Displaying Sullivan's love of geometric ornamentation, they're rare examples of his early residential work.

One of the oldest buildings in Old Town is also one of its tallest. Built in 1869 on land donated by beer baron Michael Diversey, the Romanesque **St Michael's Church** (1633 N Cleveland Avenue, at W North Avenue, 1-312 642 2498, www.st-mikes.org) was partially gutted by the Chicago Fire, but rebuilt in next to no time by the Germans who worshipped in it. Local tradition dictates that if you can hear the ringing of the bells (the largest of which weighs an amazing 6,000 pounds or 2,800 kilos), you're in Old Town. The interior, open to the public, contains a carved wooden altar and stained-glass windows; outside are stone columns and several roofs with intricate brickwork.

A few streets away sits the **Midwest Buddhist Temple** (435 W Menomonee Street, at N Hudson Avenue, 1-312 943 7801, www.midwestbuddhisttemple.org), a modernist structure built in the early 1970s by Japanese immigrants who began to settle in the area. The one-storey concrete base is topped by a pagoda-like roof; inside sits a sizeable gold Buddha. The congregation, still about 80 per cent Japanese, hosts an annual Ginza Holiday in the middle of August, celebrating Japanese culture, dance, music and food.

Heading east, it's hard to miss the enormous **Moody Church** (1609 N LaSalle Street, 1-312 943 0466, www.moodychurch.org), named after the 19th-century evangelist Dwight L Moody and completed in 1925. Directly beyond it is the south-western corner of **Lincoln Park** (*see p89*), and the excellent **Chicago History Museum** (*see below*).

★ Chicago History Museum

1601 N Clark Street, at W North Avenue (1-312 642 4600/www.chicagohistory.org). El: Brown, Purple to Sedgwick. **Open** 9.30am-4.30pm Mon-Wed, Fri, Sat; 9.30am-4.30pm Thur; noon-5pm Sun. **Admission** $14; $12 discounts; free under-13s. Free to all Mon. **Credit** AmEx, DC, Disc, MC, V. **Map** p327 H7.

Founded in 1852, the Chicago Historical Society is the city's oldest cultural institution. After a massive refurbishment, it returned in 2006 with a younger, more populist identity. Permanent exhibitions, which are now presented thematically rather than chronologically, include old favourites such as Chicago's first locomotive, the table upon which Lincoln signed the Emancipation Proclamation, and George Washington's inaugural suit. Of the new displays, City in Crisis remembers some of the city's disasters, such as the Chicago Fire of 1871, the Eastland boat disaster and the race riots of 1919. Conversely, City on the Make and My Kind of Town recall some of the city's more positive moments,

Lincoln Park.

such as its rapid growth and early industry, as well
as great moments in sports and recreation.

The temporary exhibitions are just as interesting
and varied, taking in everything from Chicago
sports memorabilia to local photography. The
spruced-up building still houses a tastefully stocked
gift shop; the selection of books, in particular, is
impeccable. A programme of lectures, discussions
and tours rounds things out nicely.

LINCOLN PARK

*El: Brown or Purple to Armitage, Diversey or
Fullerton; Red to Fullerton.*

In the middle of the 19th century, the area
around **Lincoln Park** contained little more
than a smallpox hospital and a conveniently
located cemetery. Today, it's one of Chicago's
most desirable neighbourhoods, its popularity
due in no small part to the picturesque, 1,200-
acre lakefront space from which it takes its
name. The park runs along Lake Michigan
from North Avenue (1600 N) up to Hollywood
Avenue (5700 N) on the edge of Andersonville.
The neighbourhood, however, extends only as
far as Diversey Avenue (2800 N), running
westwards all the way to the Chicago River.

The park

The same urban utopian spirit that inspired
the design for New York's Central Park made
Lincoln Park a reality. Named after Abraham
Lincoln in the wake of his 1865 assassination,
the park was created on drained swampland
(and the city's cemetery) over several decades.
Not even the Chicago Fire put a stop to its
construction, which continued into the 20th
century with the addition of several of its most
beloved institutions and the extension of the
park far into northern Chicago. It's grown into
one of the city's most cherished sites.

Lincoln Park is laced with paths that invite
aimless strolling or unimpeded cycling (*see
p304*), but also has facilities for other activities.
There are playing fields and golf courses, tennis
courts and chess tables; you can even rent a
paddleboat on the South Pond, from a kiosk
right by the historic **Café Brauer** (2021 N
Stockton Drive, 1-312 742 2400). The park is

undoubtedly at its best on weekdays during
summer, when it's a relatively peaceful place.
Even at weekends, though, it's not too hectic:
its immense size and reach mean the crowds
tend to spread out along its length.

When the city began work on the park in the
1860s, it decided to move all the bodies from the
cemetery to other locations in the north of the
city. Most went quietly, as one might expect
dead people to go. However, the family of
hotelier Ira Crouch went to court to prevent the
city from shifting their beloved's corpse. Much
to their surprise, and to the city's irritation,
they won; as a result, the **Couch Mausoleum**
stands near the junction of LaSalle and Clark
Streets, not far from the world's oldest statue of
the president who lends his name to the park.

The park's main attraction, and the one area
that can get a little too busy in summer, is the
Lincoln Park Zoo (*see below*), a small and
much beloved operation located at around 2200
N (near Webster Avenue). Just north of the
elephant house sits the **Alfred Caldwell Lily
Pool**, built in 1889 and redesigned four decades
later by the Prairie School architect whose name
it bears. Restored in 2005, it's now a National
Historic Landmark, and well worth a look.

Just north of the zoo's main entrance is the
Shakespeare Garden, which contains a
variety of flowers and plants mentioned in the
Bard's plays. The garden also contains the
Bates Fountain, a popular cooling destination
in summer, and a bronze bust of the playwright
that dates back to 1894; it's one of more than 20
sculptural monuments dating from the late 19th
century, maintained with funds raised by an
advocacy group (*see p90* **The Bronze Age**).

The broad lawn leads to the **Lincoln Park
Conservatory** (1-312 742 7736), a Victorian
greenhouse erected in 1892. The four halls of
the conservatory retain a variety of climates
and allow plants from all over the world to
flourish. The conservatory is open 9am-5pm
daily, and admission is free. Just across from it
is the **Notebaert Nature Museum** (*see p91*).

Lincoln Park Zoo

*2200 N Cannon Drive, at W Webster Avenue (1-
312 742 2000/www.lpzoo.org). El: Brown, Purple
or Red to Fullerton.* **Open** *Zoo buildings: Apr,
May, Sept, Oct 10am-5pm daily. June-Aug 10am-
6.30pm daily. Nov-Mar 10am-4.30pm daily. Zoo
grounds: Apr, May, Sept, Oct 10am-5pm daily.
June-Aug 10am-6pm Mon-Fri; 9am-7pm Sat, Sun.
Nov-Mar 10am-4.30pm daily.* **Admission** free.
No credit cards. Map p328 H5.

Compared to its competitors, it's small. That said,
there are few Chicagoan activities more enjoyable
than strolling through Lincoln Park Zoo on a sunny
weekday afternoon. It opened in 1868 after the park
was presented with two swans by New York's Central

SIGHTS

The Bronze Age

Lincoln Park is awash in statues. Here are five of its more interesting memorials.

ABRAHAM LINCOLN

The man after whom Lincoln Park is named is memorialised in it by *Standing Lincoln*, the work of Irish-American sculptor **Augustus Saint-Gaudens**. The figure, set on a plinth designed by Stanford White, was unveiled in 1885, two decades after Lincoln's death. Based in Vermont at the time, Saint-Gaudens used a local farmer named Langdon Morse as his model. Brits who think the statue looks familiar aren't dreaming – there's a replica in London's Parliament Square.
Location At the south end of the park, close to the Chicago History Museum.

JOHANN WOLFGANG VON GOETHE

The great German writer never visited Chicago before his death in 1832 at the ripe old age of 82. No matter. At the dawn of the 20th century, Chicago's community of German immigrants decided he deserved a tribute anyway. The competition to design the statue was won, appropriately, by a German: **Herman Hahn**, who cast Goethe in the form of a Greek god with an eagle on his knee above a plaque memorialising him as 'The mastermind of the German people'. Hahn presumably intended the figure to look heroic; through 21st-century eyes, though, he looks rather camp.
Location Near the intersection of Diversey Parkway and Stockton Drive.

ULYSSES S GRANT

Native of Galena, Illinois, Civil War hero and the 18th US president, Grant gets his tribute in the form of a suitably grand statue by Italian-American sculptor **Louis Rebisso**. Grant sits astride a horse, looking out across the park like he owns the place. In truth, he has a greater claim to Grant Park in the Loop, named after him and home to another dominating statue of this most dominating of men.
Location Cannon Drive, near the southern entrance to the park.

HANS CHRISTIAN ANDERSEN

Chicago's Swedish community has long been fairly prominent in the city, especially in Andersonville. Their Danish neighbours, though, are really only celebrated in the statue of their most famous storyteller. The seated bronze figure of Hans Christian Andersen in the park was created by **John**

Ulysses S Grant.

Gelert, an obscure sculptor better known for his monument to the police killed during the Haymarket Riots; it stands outside the Chicago Police Department headquarters at 3510 S Michigan Avenue on the South Side.
Location Close to Café Brauer, around the 2000 block of N Cannon Drive.

GREENE VARDIMAN BLACK

As the inventor of a foot-powered dental drill and the first man to use nitrous oxide as a dental anaesthetic, Winchester, Illinois native Greene Vardiman Black (1836-1915) is widely regarded as the founding father of modern dentistry. **Frederick C Hibbard**'s statue portrays him as a fairly severe-looking figure, but wisely omits any depictions of his presumably agonised patients.
Location The intersection of North Avenue and Astor Street.

Park; 141 years later, it's one of the oldest zoos in the country, its 35-acre site home to a thousand species.

The Kovler Lion House remains popular; so, too, does the Regenstein African Journey, which re-creates an African landscape and houses a variety of species native to the continent. Another top draw is the Regenstein Center for African Apes. The zoo is a world leader in gorilla breeding, with around 50 born here since 1970. Added in 2005, the Pritzker Family Children's Zoo features a re-created wooded environment complete with beavers, wolves and bears. All told, it's an attractive place, and it's a wonder it's still free: since 1995, it's been run not by the city but by the Lincoln Park Zoological Society, with two-thirds of its income coming from private sources.

Notebaert Nature Museum

2430 N Cannon Drive, at W Fullerton Avenue (1-773 755 5100/www.naturemuseum.org). El: Brown, Purple or Red to Fullerton. **Open** 9am-4.30pm Mon-Fri; 10am-5pm Sat, Sun. **Admission** $9; $6-$7 discounts; free under-3s. Free to all Thur. **Credit** AmEx, Disc, MC, V. **Map** p328 H5.
Its location, along Lincoln Park's North Pond, is ideal. Its $31-million, 73,000sq ft (6,600sq m) building is grand. And the fanfare that greeted its opening in 1999 was enormous. Still, the Notebaert Nature Museum is a bit of a disappointment, due chiefly to the fact that few of its exhibits are as exciting as they should be. Highlights include the Hands-On Habitat, which aims to teach kids about how animals live, and Birds of Chicago, a show of 100 Illinois bird specimens, some dating back to the 1900s. The temporary exhibitions also occasionally hit the mark. But the museum's main selling point is the Judy Istock Butterfly Haven, a glass-topped space populated by more than 75 species of butterfly. The most attractive parts of the museum are the outdoor pond and walkway through the artfully restored native prairie; these can be enjoyed for free, leaving the admission fee to be invested in a good lunch at North Pond (*see p158*), one of Chicago's premier eateries.

The neighbourhood

Lincoln Park began to take off as a residential neighbourhood in the late 1970s, after the Puerto Rican Young Lords turf gang that once rumbled around its streets began to disperse. These days, it's a sought-after address among the North Side's burgeoning population of youngish urban professionals and career-focused post-collegiates with money to burn. (This image of Lincoln Park locals has become something of a cliché, but is still grounded in truth.) As with Old Town, its neighbour to the south, Lincoln Park doesn't contain many sights per se, but it's no less appealing for all that. Wide, tree-lined streets lead – if you're lucky – to attractive corner bars and appealing shops, frequented by a mostly laid-back bunch.

The neighbourhood is anchored by **DePaul University**, the campus of which ebbs quietly out from around the intersection of Fullerton and Sheffield Avenues. The college connection is most obvious along the nearby stretches of Lincoln Avenue and Clark Street, dotted with sports bars and low-key party palaces that get flooded with people, and alcohol, on weekends. Armitage Avenue and Halsted Street are more easygoing alternatives.

Although Lincoln Park is more famous, fans of Chicago resident L Frank Baum will want to visit nearby **Oz Park** (*see p222*).

Over half of the buildings in Lincoln Park were built between 1880 and 1904. These days, there's a battle raging between preservationists, who want to hang on to the area's heritage, and developers, who'd prefer to tear parts of it down and start again. Quaint Victorian houses are increasingly having to fight for attention with giant new mansions, but they're winning the battle. One of the highlights is the **Francis J Dewes Mansion** (www.dewesmansion.com), built at 503 W Wrightwood Avenue (at N Hampden Court) for a local beer baron in 1896.

Just west of the zoo (*see p89*) is the site of the infamous **St Valentine's Day Massacre**, where, on 14 February 1929, seven members of Bugs Moran's gang were executed against a garage wall by Al Capone's henchmen. Though Moran escaped (he'd overslept), the killings broke his resistance and cemented Capone's position at the forefront of Chicago's lucrative organised crime world. Film fans will have seen a fictional and comical version of the massacre at the beginning of *Some Like it Hot*. The garage, at 2122 N Clark Street, has since been replaced by a lawn. But the incident still resonates: the nearby **Chicago Pizza & Oven Grinder Company** (2121 N Clark Street, at W Dickens Avenue, 1-773 248 2570) tells the tale on its menus.

Several blocks north-west is the site of yet another fabled gangland killing: that of John Dillinger, a professional criminal who had escaped from police custody in Crown Point, Indiana, where he was awaiting trial for the murder of a cop. He'd been pinned as Public Enemy Number One by the FBI, who tracked him down to the **Biograph Theatre** (2433 N Lincoln Avenue, at W Fullerton Avenue) on 22 July 1934. As he left a screening of *Manhattan Melodrama*, police shot him dead; bystanders dipped their skirts and handkerchiefs in his blood as souvenirs. The Biograph closed as a cinema several years ago, but was recently taken over by the **Victory Gardens Theater** (*see p286*). Dillinger, meanwhile, is remembered on the anniversary of his death each year with a parade from the **Red Lion Pub** (2446 N Lincoln Avenue, at W Montana Street, 1-773 348 2695) to the site of his grisly demise.

SIGHTS

Lakeview & North

A jumble of communities compete for attention on Chicago's North Side.

The sight of 40,000 baseball fans cheering in unison, the sound of a drag queen's stiletto heels hitting the pavement, the smell of Italian, Swedish, Asian and Indian food wafting through the air, the touch of warm sand in your toes on a perfect beach day… Welcome to **Lakeview**, the undisputed hub of Chicago's North Side and a mecca for yuppies and guppies, swingers and singles, movers and shakers and so much more. If Lincoln Park presented a perfect snapshot of city life in the '80s, Lakeview happily eclipsed it during the Clinton era.

But urban bliss ain't cheap. Many Lakeview denizens flew the coop starting in the early 2000s when they realized that lakefront living could be enjoyed at a significantly lower price by moving north, and the area now lacks a little of the edge it once retained. Further north and west, **Uptown**, **Edgewater**, **Andersonville** and **Ravenswood/Lincoln Square** all merit attention if time allows.

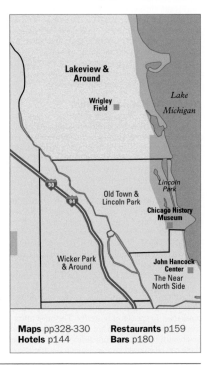

Lakeview & Around

Wrigley Field

Lake Michigan

Old Town & Lincoln Park

Lincoln Park

Chicago History Museum

Wicker Park & Around

John Hancock Center

The Near North Side

Maps pp328-330   **Restaurants** p159
Hotels p144   **Bars** p180

LAKEVIEW

El: Brown to Belmont, Southport or Wellington; Purple to Belmont or Wellington; Red to Addison or Belmont.

Lakeview is said to have taken its name from a hotel built in 1853 by James Rees and EE Hundley. Having completed the construction, the pair struggled to decide on a name until their friend Walter Newberry turned up to see the place. Impressed by the waterside vistas, Newberry suggested that they call it the Hotel Lake View. The name eventually carried over to the neighbourhood itself.

At the time Rees and Hundley were building, the area was countryside, farmed by European immigrants. Things changed in 1854, when cholera swept Chicago and many locals fled

north to escape it. As there were no roads to the area from Chicago, Rees and Hundley laid down a plank thoroughfare. Lake View Plank Road, as it was plainly christened (it's since morphed into modern-day Broadway), spurred on immediate and dramatic expansion of the area.

During the following three decades, the now-incorporated Lakeview Township stretched as far north as Devon Avenue and all the way to Western Avenue in the west. In 1887, it lost its independence and was annexed by the city. The event led to the area shrinking, with its northern reaches having been absorbed into Andersonville, Edgewater, Buena Park, North Center, St Ben's, Lincoln Square and Uptown. Today, Lakeview is officially bordered by Diversey Parkway to the south, Irving Park Road to the north and Ashland Avenue to the west, with the lake as the eastern boundary.

In truth, Lakeview is a jumble of micro-neighbourhoods crammed into one. **Boystown** (*see p243*), the epicentre of gay life in Chicago, hugs the lakefront and stretches west to Clark Street where it turns into **Wrigleyville**, home of the Chicago Cubs and a seemingly infinite number of sports bars. Further west lies the charming **Southport Corridor**, a yuppified stretch of chic clothing shops and restaurants anchored by the historic Music Box Theater. Beyond it, **Roscoe Village** revels in self-satisfaction with its cosy Main Street feel.

For a time, Lakeview had a hip cachet; the punky shops around Belmont and Clark, such as the **Alley** (3228 N Clark Street, at W Belmont Avenue, 1-773 883 1800, www.thealley.com), are testament to an edgier past, as was the presence at 3448 N Greenview Avenue of Smashing Pumpkins singer Billy Corgan (he sold up and moved out years ago). However, the district has since grown more affluent and less cutting-edge, and is nowadays visited mainly for its reliable restaurants, its baseball team and its lakefront. In summer, the park offers a multitude of activities (jogging, tennis) and inactivities (snoozing on the grass).

The hubs of Lakeview's culture, nightlife and commerce are the stretches of Clark, Halsted and Broadway Streets to the north and south of Belmont Avenue, home to an array of clothing stores, kitschy shops, gay and straight bars and restaurants. Among the best are the **Unabridged Bookstore** (*see p192*) and **Uncle Fun** (*see p194*), which offers a selection of bizarre knick-knacks, kitsch and gag gifts.

Close at hand are two very different cinemas. The 1912 **Vic Theatre** is a former vaudeville house that stages touring rock acts alongside the rowdy Brew & View movie nights (*see*

Dinkel's. *See p95*.

p234). Meanwhile, the more demure **Music Box** (*see p236*) is an over-the-top, Italian Renaissance-inspired spot. The main theatre, seating 750, uses trompe l'oeil paintings of garden walls to create the illusion of sitting in an outdoor courtyard, with a ceiling covered with stars and moving cloud formations.

Wrigleyville

Central Lakeview was changed forever in 1914 with the construction of **Wrigley Field** (*see p94*). On game days (the Cubs play here 81 times a year; more if they reach the play-offs), Lakeview morphs from a sedate, cultured enclave to a wild, beer-soaked bacchanal. Cubs culture rules near the junction of Clark and Addison: sports bars dominate the area. Even Boystown gets in on the act: the **North End** (3733 N Halsted Street, at W Bradley Place, 1-773 477 7999) is a gay sports bar.

However, not every hangout around here focuses on baseball. Chief among the avoiders is the **Metro** (*see p261*), originally a Swedish community centre but now one of the country's favourite indie-music venues. The adjoining **Smart Bar** (*see p272*) was a key centre in the emergence of both the industrial and house scenes. A few doors down sits the **Gingerman** (3740 N Clark Street, between W Waveland Avenue & W Grace Street, 1-773 549 2050), where the ambience is rather gentler than at

Field of Dreams?

Could the Cubs consider leaving their longtime home?

Located at the corner of Clark and Addison Streets, Weeghman Park was built in 1914 for the Chicago Whales baseball team of the Federal League. When both league and team folded two seasons later, owner Charles Weeghman bought the Chicago Cubs team of the thriving National League and moved them across town; then, in 1920, he sold the team and the ballpark to Philip Wrigley. Six years later, the name of the stadium was changed to Wrigley Field, a name it retains today.

As baseball has reinvented itself of late, many of the sport's famous old ballparks have been torn down. Aside from the Cubs, just five of the 29 major league teams play in facilities built before 1987, and only one of these ballparks – Fenway Park in Boston, which also dates to 1914 – is more than 50 years old. But Wrigley Field is different. From the ivy on the outfield walls (planted in 1937 by maverick executive Bill Veeck) to the in-game doodlings of organist Gary Pressy, the Cubs glory in the park's old-fashioned traditions. The stadium dominates its surroundings to the point that even the neighbourhood itself now takes its name: thanks in no small part to real estate agents who were quick to spot the park's appeal to homebuyers, the streets around the park are now universally known as Wrigleyville.

On the face of it, the Cubs leaving Wrigley is unthinkable. The ballpark is perhaps the team's greatest asset, able to draw crowds paying high ticket prices even when, as has often been the case in franchise history, the team flat-out stinks.

But in recent years, Wrigley's future has looked less assured. Apparently keener on comfortable modernity than comforting tradition, some fans have begun to wonder whether the Cubs shouldn't up sticks to a shiny new facility in the suburbs. And so have some of the players. 'You come into a ballpark like [new Yankee Stadium] and you see great things,' grumbled pitcher Carlos Zambrano in 2009. 'You wish that Chicago would build a new stadium for the Cubs.'

Just as pertinent for the ballpark's future is the team's ownership. After a protracted sale process, longtime owners the Tribune Company at last looked set to divest themselves of the Cubs and Wrigley Field in 2009, but with few guarantees as to the future of either the team or its ballpark. As the park approaches its centenary, Wrigley Field's future has never seemed shakier.

► *For more on the Chicago Cubs and Wrigley Field, see p275.*

months, the century-old **Ravinia Festival** in Highland Park (*see p256*) provides an outdoor home for the Chicago Symphony Orchestra and the Hubbard Street Dance Company, but also mixes in a variety of pop acts. Unlike at many music festivals, the cheap seats are a big draw here, offering concertgoers a chance to spread out and picnic on the lawn (concertgoers are encouraged to bring their own food and drink). But if you want to see the musicians while you hear them, you'll need to pony up for the pavilion seats.

Further north sits **Six Flags Great America & Hurricane Harbor** (I-94/I-294 from Chicago, exit at Route 132, 1-847 249 4636, www.sixflags.com), a vast, loud and exhausting amusement park in the suburb of **Gurnee**. After a day at this thrillfest, most parents (and a fair few kids) come away sunburned, footweary and broke.

And then further north, not too far from the Wisconsin border at the town of **Zion**, sits **Illinois Beach State Park** (1-847 662 4811, www.dnr.state.il.us). Whether you choose overnight accommodation at a fully equipped inn, beachside camping or just a day trip, it's not hard to take it easy at this clean and uncomplicated lakeside beach park that stretches six miles and covers 4,000 acres. Nearby **Tempel Farms** (17000 Wadsworth Road, Wadsworth, 1-847 623 7272, www.tempel farms.com) breeds Lipizzan horses, which give full dressage performances in July and August.

★ FREE Bahá'í Temple House of Worship

100 Linden Avenue, Wilmette (1-847 853 2300/ ww.bahai.us). El: Red, then Purple to Linden. **Open** *Auditorium* 6am-10pm daily. *Visitors' centre* May-Oct 10am-10pm daily. Nov-Apr 10am-5pm daily. **Admission** free. **No credit cards.** No visit to the North Shore is complete without taking in this enormous, whitewashed temple, which resembles nothing so much as the world's largest lemon squeezer. Inspiring prayer, devotion and countless photo ops – and visible for miles – this 164ft (50m) spiritual dome is magnificent when illuminated at night; its surrounding manicured garden adds to its beauty by day. It was completed in 1953 as a place of prayer and meditation for the Bahá'í faith, which advocates the 'oneness of God, the oneness of mankind and the oneness of religion'.

FREE Chicago Botanic Garden

1000 Lake Cook Road, Glencoe (1-847 835 5440/www.chicagobotanic.org). Metra: Glencoe. **Open** *June-Aug* 7am-9pm daily. *Sept-May* 8am-sunset daily. **Admission** free. **No credit cards.** A variety of planting styles has delighted visitors to the Botanic Garden since 1972. The sprawling yet calm oasis is beautifully maintained, with trails that encourage walkers and cyclists to linger. Highlights include a walled English garden; the series of islands that make up the Japanese gardens; a 15-acre prairie; summertime carillon concerts; and the Lenhardt Library, which houses around 28,000 horticulture titles, many extremely rare. There's also a pleasant restaurant, plus galleries that host rotating exhibitions of botanic-themed art. Note that although admission is free, parking costs $15 (reduced to $7 for seniors on Tuesdays); take the Metra to avoid the charges.

▶ *There's more of this sort of thing at the Garfield Park Conservatory; see p106.*

Illinois Holocaust Museum & Education Center

9603 Woods Drive, at Old Orchard Road, Skokie (1-847 677 4640/www.ilholocaustmuseum.org). El: Yellow to Skokie. **Open** 10am-5pm Tue, Wed, Fri; 10am-8pm Thur; 11am-4pm Sat, Sun. **Admission** $8; $5-$6 discounts; free under-5s. **Credit** AmEx, MC, V.
When a group of neo-Nazis planned to march in heavily Jewish Skokie in the 1970s, local Holocaust survivors banded together to create an educational group, the Holocaust Memorial Foundation of Illinois. After ten years of planning, the foundation opened a Stanley Tigerman-designed museum in April 2009. It houses more than 11,000 artefacts, several of which are on display in a 10,000-square-foot main exhibit on the Holocaust and genocide. The museum may open on Mondays in the future.

Baha'i Temple House of Worship.

The Near West Side

Art meets commerce in this round-the-world stew of cultures.

The contrast between the rough and the new makes the Near West Side – loosely speaking, the streets due west of the Loop and due south of Ukrainian Village/West Town – one of the most dynamic areas of the city.

The area facing the greatest flux at present is the **West Loop**. The streets rattle with tough urban authenticity, courtesy of freeways carving their way above ground level and the rumble emanating from the Lake Street El tracks, but they're also increasingly upscale, thanks to the arrival of new bars and restaurants in the locale.

In an arc below the West Loop stand three neighbourhoods originally settled by immigrants: **Greektown**, **Little Italy** and **Pilsen**. Many of the original settlers have long since moved to the suburbs, but their replacements – some Latino, some upwardly mobile anglo – have given the area a dynamic new feel.

It's easy to explore the West Loop, Greektown, Little Italy and Pilsen by foot along their main streets. The commercial areas of each neighbourhood are increasingly busy with activity, but it's wise to keep your wits about you when venturing into the long stretches of no man's land that separate them.

Map p330   Bars p181
Restaurants p162

THE WEST LOOP

El: Green or Pink to Ashland or Clinton.

The Loop's western boundary is officially marked by the Chicago River. Unofficially, though, the area has come to extend several blocks further, as far as the twin transport hubs of **Ogilvie Transportation Centre** and **Union Station**. Trains serving both stations funnel commuters to and from the city each day; Union Station, a Beaux Arts-style building designed by Daniel Burnham, is by far the more handsome of the two.

The West Loop really begins beyond these two transport hubs, west of the Kennedy Expressway. For years, these streets were an uninviting maze of warehouses and garment factories, but the last ten years have seen them transformed into some of the hottest real estate in this post-industrial town, a development craze that encompasses both residential conversions and new businesses.

Along **Randolph Street** between Halsted and Racine Streets, a string of highly regarded restaurants compete for attention with bars, clubs and lounges. As they do so, old-line wholesalers such as the **Puckered Pickle Company** look on with bemusement and occasional irritation. Randolph also hosts a monthly antique market between May and October and a street festival with music and food in summer, further attempts to drag the neighbourhood away from its roots.

SIGHTS

Oprah's **Harpo Studios.**

The **Fulton Market** area is also in flux, to say the least. During the day, the streets are full of trucks and men in white jackets working in the meatpacking industry and lunching at greasy diners. Come sundown, though, it's a nightlife hot spot with several clubs and some of the city's most talked-about fine dining establishments, such as **Publican** (*see p164*).

It's a similar story along **Lake Street** between Halsted and Morgan Streets, where meat and veg cash-and-carry outposts share the street with nightclubs and the seemingly obligatory loft apartments. But, from the looks of it, the meat business is still in good shape. For a vision of the area's bone-hacking present, check out the **Peoria Packing Butcher Shop** (1300 W Lake Street, at N Elizabeth Street, 1-312 738 1800), where piles of raw meat and pigs' feet are heaped in refrigerated rooms for the benefit of eager bargain hunters.

Before real estate prices spiralled, a colony of artists had discovered the West Loop; indeed, the current boom was partly brought about by their arrival and the kudos that came attached to it. A number of galleries remain in the district, clustered at Peoria and Washington and in the Fulton Market area between Peoria and Racine (*see pp241-242*). They have an impact on local culture, but it's dwarfed by that of **Harpo Studios** (1058 W Washington Boulevard, 1-312 591 9222, www.oprah.com), from where the most powerful woman in American media shoots her shows and oversees her empire. In theory, visitors can book free tickets to recordings of *The Oprah Winfrey Show* by phone, but it's notoriously difficult.

About a mile west on Madison Street is the massive **United Center** (*see p277*). The home to the famed Chicago Bulls basketball team and the Chicago Blackhawks hockey team, it also welcomes big-time music acts and circuses (which sometimes amount to the same thing). The once-bleak blocks around the arena are sprouting with new development, but it's still not currently an area in which to linger.

GREEKTOWN

El: Blue to UIC-Halsted.

In the late 1970s, there were more than 125,000 Greeks in Chicago. It's a different story today, though you might not know it from a walk along Halsted Street from Monroe Street south to Van Buren Street – this stretch remains the Midwest's biggest Hellenic commercial area. Scattered between welcoming Greek restaurants is an eclectic array of shops selling everything from baklava and Greek pop music to candles and evil eye stones (at the fabulously odd **Athenian Candle Company** (300 S Halsted Street, at W Jackson Street, 1-312 332 6988). The **Hellenic Museum & Cultural Center** (*see p102*) provides what remains of the community with an anchor.

On Adams Street, one block east of Halsted and across the freeway, sits the decidedly un-Greek **Old St Patrick's Church** (700 W Adams Street, at S Desplaines Street, 1-312 648 1021, www.oldpats.org; *photos p102*). Dating to 1856, it was one of the first churches in America built to serve Irish immigrants; having survived the Chicago Fire in 1871, it's also the oldest church building in the city. The interior is decorated with muted stained-glass windows and a mix of pagan and Christian symbols. Each July, the church hosts the **World's Largest Block Party** (*see p216*).

SIGHTS

Old St Patrick's Church. *See p101.*

SIGHTS

Hellenic Museum & Cultural Center

801 W Adams Street, at S Halsted Street (1-312 655 1234/www.hellenicmuseum.org). El: Blue to UIC-Halsted. **Open** 10am-4pm Tue-Fri; 11am-4pm Sat. **Admission** $5; free under-12s. **Credit** AmEx, MC, V. **Map** p330 F12.

While work has stalled on the Hellenic Museum & Cultural Center's intended new home, on the site of the former N Turek & Sons hardware store at 333 S Halsted Street, operations have moved to this temporary space. This shrine to immigrant Greek culture derives many of its pieces from the collections of local Greek families, but it's not only of interest to those with Greek ancestry. The 2008 Cyprus Revealed display, which featured ancient, hand-painted ceramics and rare medieval maps from the old country, is one example of the kind of noteworthy temporary exhibitions favoured here. The art on show, on the other hand, isn't quite as dazzling.

UIC & AROUND

El: Blue to UIC-Halsted.

Stroll down Halsted south from Greektown and you'll soon find yourself surrounded by the brutalist architecture of the **University of Illinois at Chicago (UIC)** campus, built in the 1960s and an ever-expanding interruption to the historic neighbourhoods that surround it. The campus has been a controversial fixture

since it was developed, and the passing years haven't calmed the ire of those who've long opposed it. The most contentious development in recent years has been the University Village project of residential and retail development, in part because it's sparked further changes in the nearby Pilsen neighbourhood. Tucked away from all the fresh concrete is the **Jane Addams Hull-House Museum** *(see right)*.

A couple of blocks south of Hull-House lies the former site of **Maxwell Street Market**, where European settlers joined Jewish merchants and traders in setting up shop at the turn of the 20th century. During the Great Migration, southern blacks settled there and gave birth to the Chicago blues *(see p103* **Electric Feel**.

In the early 1990s, UIC got permission from Mayor Daley to raze the entire site, demolishing landmarks such as Nate's Deli (where Aretha Franklin bursts into song in *The Blues Brothers*) as the campus expanded. Bloodied but unbowed, the multi-ethnic market has since been forced to move twice; it's now on the stretch of Desplaines Street between Roosevelt and Harrison – just north, incidentally, of where Ms O'Leary's cow is reputed to have started the Great Chicago Fire. On Sundays from 7am to 3pm, you can find stalls selling everything from power tools to bootleg DVDs, plus a parade of Mexican food stands.

FREE Jane Addams Hull-House Museum
800 S Halsted Street, at W Polk Street (1-312 413 5353/www.uic.edu/jaddams/hull). El: Blue to UIC-Halsted. **Open** 10am-4pm Tue-Fri; noon-4pm Sun. **Admission** free. **No credit cards.** **Map** p330 F14.

After an 1888 visit to London's Toynbee Hall, a pioneering settlement house that provided social services for a working-class neighbourhood, a pair of young women named Jane Addams and Ellen Gates Starr returned to Chicago vowing to start something similar. A year later, Hull-House opened its doors. It began as a relatively small operation, but eventually expanded to include educational facilities, social assistance offices, and the city's first swimming pool, public kitchen and gymnasium. One beneficiary of the music programme was a young Benny Goodman, who learned to play clarinet there.

The fame of Hull-House grew, inspiring other socially conscious people in the US just as Addams herself had been inspired by Toynbee Hall. She died in 1935, aged 74, but her work is commemorated in the two structures that remain of her 13-building complex. In the original 1856 mansion (donated to Addams by Charles Hull, hence the name) sit displays of paintings that once hung at the settlement, pottery and tableware created at Addams' community art programme, and her desk. In 2007, the museum added History on Call, voice narratives on the house's holdings accessible by dialling a number from your cellphone. Next door is the dining hall, which now holds photographs, exhibits and a slide-show introduction to the American labour movement and the social problems faced by the West Side's immigrants. Enlightening and inspiring.

LITTLE ITALY

El: Blue to Polk or Racine; Pink to Polk.

Sauntering west from Halsted on Taylor Street will lead you into Little Italy. It's said that pizza first made its way from Naples to the US in this once-thriving district. However, like Greektown, it's a shadow of its formerly charismatic self, with the Italians who once lived here forced out by the construction of the Eisenhower Expressway or driven away by the creation of the UIC's Circle Campus. What remains is a nostalgia trip, but it's not an unenjoyable one.

Aside from the **National Italian American Sports Hall of Fame** (*see p104*), the main attractions are culinary, with most of the action along Taylor Street between S Morgan Street and S Ashland Avenue. There are prime people-watching opportunities at

---

Electric Feel

How Maxwell Street Market helped revolutionise the blues.

The Great Migration brought thousands of southern blacks to Chicago in the early 20th century. But this great movement of people would also lead to a musical revolution, as these Mississippi Delta migrants brought with them the blues.

The blues of the South was acoustic and country-style, but it found a large audience among the city's steel mills and meatpacking factories in the 1920s. Opportunities for the hustling musician were incredible, but other migrants struggled. As a result, the songs were often laments of the hard times endured by new arrivals in Chicago.

Blues music found a home in the city's 'black belt' of Bronzeville, but also in the immigrant-dominated Near West Side, and specifically on Maxwell Street's Sunday market day. Calling the area 'Jew Town', as it was dominated by stores owned by Jews arrived from Europe, blues musicians found that they could play to large audiences at the market and make some decent money while they worked their way up to playing at the established clubs. After World War II, there were even fly-by-night record labels in Chicago that signed acts directly off Maxwell Street.

But the market also demanded something extra: volume. To be heard in the busy, bustling street, blues players realised they needed electric instruments, like the electric guitars made by Silvertone, and amplifiers. This new mode of performance required an alliance with the Jewish shopkeepers, who traded musicians electricity for promoting their wares on the sidewalk.

In the 1940s, the louder guitar-and-amp set-ups came into vogue on Maxwell Street, in clubs and, eventually, recordings. By the '50s, Chicago's urban electrified take on the blues was in full bloom, with Muddy Waters, Little Walter, Bo Diddley and Howlin' Wolf all in their prime. It's doubtful it would have sounded quite the same without the influence of market forces.

SIGHTS

INSIDE TRACK HOME AT LAST

The three-storey brick building at 1322-1324 W Taylor Street opened in 1938 as the **Jane Addams Homes**, the first federal government housing project in Chicago. The site has been chosen as the location for the National Public Housing Museum, due to open in 2012; see www.publichousingmuseum.org for updates on the museum's progress.

the **Rosebud Café** (no.1500, 1-312 942 1117, www.rosebudrestaurants.com). Sandwiches and gourmet goods can be procured at the perennial **Conte di Savoia** deli (no.1438, 1-312 666 3471, www.contedisavoia.com). In summer, folk queue for flavoured ices at **Mario's Italian Lemonade** (1068 W Taylor Street, at S Carpenter Street, no phone, closed Oct-Apr).

To the west, Little Italy has a maze of fascinating residential sidestreets that reward exploration. From Taylor, head north on Loomis to view the classic Chicago three-flats and stoops that line the street, then turn east on Lexington to enjoy the beautiful old homes that overlook **Arrigo Park**, a peaceful green that stands out amid the brick, stone and stucco.

South of Little Italy, one modern structure stands out amid a stretch of empty lots. The former **Illinois Regional Library for the Blind & Physically Handicapped** (1055 W Roosevelt Road) has been converted into a bank, but retains its 165-foot (50-metre) window and unique curving shape.

FREE **National Italian American Sports Hall of Fame**

1431 W Taylor Street, at S Bishop Street (1-312 226 5566/www.niashf.org). El: Blue to Racine. **Open** 9am-5pm Mon-Fri; 11am-4pm Sat, Sun. **Admission** free. **No credit cards. Map** p330 D14.

This Little Italy museum honours more than 200 sports heroes with a collection that includes Mario Andretti's racing car and Rocky Marciano's championship belt. Piazza DiMaggio, a small plaza dedicated to every Italian American's favourite son, lies directly across the street and makes a convenient picnic spot for an espresso from Conte di Savoia.

PILSEN

El: Blue or Pink to 18th.

Pilsen was originally settled in the 1800s by German, Czech, Polish and Yugoslavian immigrants drawn to work on the railroads. In 1857, under orders from Mayor Wentworth,

police forced Bohemians out of the Near North Side to join them. (The neighbourhood's name is an echo of the Czech city of Plzen.) By the late 19th century, industrialisation and its concomitant social pressures had transformed the locale into a hub of labour activism. But as immigrant quotas began to restrict the influx of Southern and Eastern Europeans in the 1920s, Pilsen's Mexican heritage took root.

Isolated to a degree by the Chicago River and railroad tracks, Pilsen is coming out of its shell. For decades, it's been a vibrant Latino cultural centre, home to the largest Mexican and Mexican American community in the Midwest. But an influx in recent years of artists and students has brought change, and change has in turn brought strife. The conflict is not a simple matter of ethnicity; Muppies (Mexican yuppies) are among the gentrifiers. But the character of the area is shifting, and fast.

Pilsen's main commercial activity takes place on **W 18th Street** between S Racine Avenue and S Paulina Street, where street vendors abound and salsa music pours out of passing vehicles. Bilingual visitors can pick up Neruda in the original Spanish at **Libreria Girón** (2141 W 21st Street, at S Leavitt Street, 1-773 847 3000, www.gironbooks.com); hipsters will want to peruse the periodicals at **Golden Age** (1744 W 18th Street, at S Wood Street, 1-312 850 2574, www.shopgoldenage.com); and there's also a designer T-shirt joint, **OMD** (1419 W 18th Street, at S Blue Island Avenue, 1-312 563 9663, www.omdchicago.com), that's high on Latino attitude. There's also plenty of great food around here, too; for chef Rick Bayless's picks in the area, *see p165* **In the 'Hood**.

A sizeable artistic community inhabits the blocks around the intersection of 18th and Halsted Streets; many artists rent from the Podmajersky family, which has supported creative entrepreneurs and historic preservation in the community for generations. Scenesters tend to congregate at the **Skylark** (2149 S Halsted Street, at W 21st Street, 1-312 948 5275), a boho bar with a fine beer selection, or blend in with the clubby and largely recycled decor at **Simone's** (960 W 18th Street, at Morgan Street; *see p182*).

Other notable buildings include the old **Schoenhofen Brewery** (W 18th Street & S Canalport Avenue), built in 1902 and a well preserved example of American architecture's movement away from revivalist styles. Designed by Richard E Schmidt and Hugh Garden, disciples of Frank Lloyd Wright, it sits on an artesian spring-fed well that's some 1,600 feet (500 metres) deep, and could conceivably brew again in the future. A few blocks away, the **National Museum of Mexican Art** (*see below*) provides Pilsen with a cultural focus.

Neighbourhood Watch

Pilsen's many murals unite the community.

When Mexicans and Mexican Americans settled in the Pilsen neighbourhood in the 1960s, wall murals emerged as a powerful form of community expression. Influenced by the Mexican muralists of the 1910 Revolution, among them Diego Rivera and Jose Orozco, Pilsen's street painters advocated civil rights and praised the virtues of a united neighbourhood.

The landscape has altered dramatically since the 1960s. Most of the murals from the '60s and '70s have vanished, including many of the more politically charged works that bemoaned the Vietnam War and Latino struggles. Fortunately, though, several artists from that generation are alive and well and still making murals, alongside a younger generation who've picked up the torch.

In 1994, a group headed by longtime muralist **Hector Duarte** painted a small mural entitled *Alto al desplazamiento* at 18th and Bishop Streets. In it, a claw reaches out from behind two Latino workers. The name of the mural loosely translates as 'Stop the gentrification', a sentiment still widely voiced today.

To the north of Damen station, **Juan Chavez**'s glass mosaic collage *Vida Simple* (Damen Avenue & Cullerton Street) depicts Pilsen residents atop a collage of

buildings, plants and gesturing hands. Co-commissioned by the CTA and the city's Public Art Program, it's one of two mosaics that Chavez has made for the Chicago transport system.

Finally, **Francisco Mendoza**'s Orozco Community Academy mosaics (1645 W 18th Place, at S Paulina Street) include portraits of Mexican and Chicano people made from coloured bits of tile. Among them are Frida Kahlo stoically posing, and neighbourhood folk hitting the books at the library.

These are just three examples, but the neighbourhood is full of them. Keep your eyes open as you wander through the area, and you may even see a muralist at work.

SIGHTS

Czech it Out

Pilsen's Bohemian past proves hard to shift.

It's easy to forget that Pilsen was founded by the Irish and Germans and then settled by Bohemian and Czech immigrants. After all, their descendants moved on a long time ago. But on 20 April 1857, migration *to* Pilsen was encouraged – with a billy club – when Chicago Mayor Wentworth led the 'Battle of the Sands', sending police in to the Near North Side to boot poor Bohemian families out. The Bohemians duly left, but thrived in their new home. By 1910, Pilsen had become the largest Bohemian community in the US, but it also eventually welcomed almost 30 European ethnic groups.

The neighbourhood is now dominated by Mexican Americans and other Latino immigrants, but a few buildings remain that illuminate the Pilsen of the past. The handsome and historic **APO Building** (1438 W 18th Street, at S Laflin Street) was a community centre for the Czech population. Today, in a sign of the changing make-up of the district, it houses the art gallery and printmaking workshop **La Casa de la Cultura Carlos Cortez** and hosts an unsuitably lively Día de los Muertos event around Halloween.

Nearby, the fascinating **Plzensky Sokol** (1812 S Ashland Street, at W 18th Street), was once a school and athletic club for Czech and Polish immigrants before it became a dancehall. It's now an outlet for Mexican crafts called Rancho Viejo, but the former stage, balcony and dancefloor are still visible.

It's an easy walk from the north to Pilsen, albeit a slightly grim one, but the locale's southern edge is blocked off by the Chicago River and an array of shipping, storage and trucking facilities. The area is served by the El but it's notoriously hard to hail a cab out of Pilsen at night, so be sure to bring a taxi company number with you.

★ FREE National Museum of Mexican Art
1852 W 19th Street, at S Damen Avenue (1-312 738 1503/www.nationalmuseumof mexicanart.org). El: Blue or Pink to 18th Street. **Open** 10am-5pm Tue-Sun. **Admission** free. **No credit cards**.

This Pilsen staple changed its name from the Mexican Fine Arts Center Museum in 2006, but remains one of Chicago's most enjoyable community museums. The permanent displays are intriguing; in particular, Mexicanidad: Our Past is Present, which offers a whistle-stop tour of Mexican arts and culture with the aid of music, art, religious artefacts and other ephemera. Several of the galleries are given over to temporary exhibits, such as a recent display from the Bank of America Collection featuring Mexican artists such as Diego Rivera and Gabriel Orozco as well as Americans who worked south of the border, including Paul Strand and Harry Callahan. All the exhibits come with informative and engaging captions in English and Spanish.

Call ahead for details of music, dance and other performances, especially if you're here during the annual Day of the Dead festival (*see p217*). Open all year, the crafts-packed Tienda Tzintzuntzan gift shop is one of the best museum stores in town.

EAST GARFIELD PARK
El: Green to Conservatory–Central Park Drive.

Precious little of note surrounds the district of East Garfield Park, isolated between the rapidly smartening West Loop and handsome Oak Park. For visitors, it merits inclusion here for the wonderful **Garfield Park Conservatory** (*see below*), easily and safely accessible from its own El station. But otherwise, the area is best avoided: it's sketchy in places and downright unsafe in others.

★ FREE Garfield Park Conservatory
300 N Central Park Avenue at Fulton Boulevard (1-312 746 5100/www.garfieldconservatory.org). El: Green to Conservatory/Central Park. **Open** 9am-5pm Mon, Tue, Thur-Sun; 9am-8pm Wed. **Admission** free. **No credit cards**.

The Garfield Park Conservatory was described as 'landscape art under glass' when it opened in 1908. Its contents are certainly impressive, but the architecture itself is notable. Between the building's haystack shape and walls of stratified stonework, landscape architect Jens Jensen considered the Fern Room in particular, with its 'prairie waterfall' (a stone and water element within a glass structure) to be one of his greatest achievements.

Inside, roughly 120,000 plants representing some 600 species occupy the conservatory's 1.6 acres; four times a year, flower shows herald the change in seasons. In 2008, the conservatory opened Sugar from the Sun, an exhibit on photosynthesis, which is explored in living displays (which is to say plenty of plants but a scant few text panels).

Wicker Park & Around

It's still Chicago's neighbourhood du jour, but things continue to evolve.

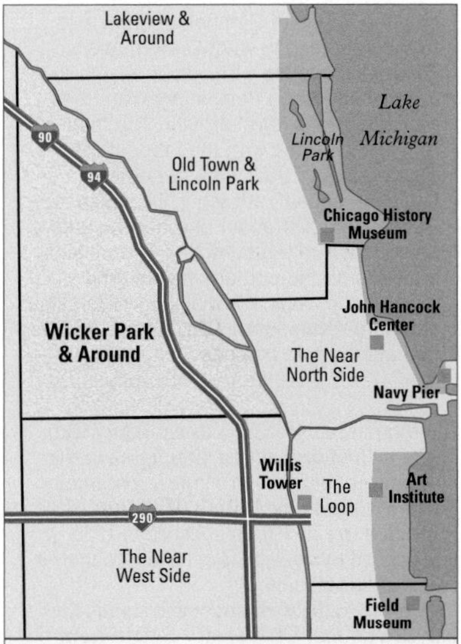

There's a downside to being cool: everyone wants a piece of you. In the 1960s, **Wicker Park** was one of Chicago's most notoriously unapproachable neighbourhoods. A few decades later, it's an extremely fashionable address for those wanting a faintly edgy backdrop to their property investments. Settled mainly by waves of Eastern European immigrants, **Bucktown** and **Ukrainian Village** continue to lend the area a distinctly Slavic feel. But they, too, are both riding the road towards gentrification.

The borders of the neighbourhoods are far from rigid. Beginning where Milwaukee Avenue meets the Kennedy Expressway, the Milwaukee Avenue corridor trails Chicago Avenue west to Western Avenue, and then follows Milwaukee north until around Armitage. The portion south of Division Street is known as West Town, and contained within the area is Ukrainian Village. Above it, bordered roughly by Division Street and Western, Ashland and Bloomingdale Avenues, is Wicker Park. And north of Wicker Park and up to Fullerton Avenue is Bucktown.

Map p331	**Restaurants** p166
Hotels p144	**Bars** p182

Map labels: Lakeview & Around · Lake Michigan · Lincoln Park · Old Town & Lincoln Park · Chicago History Museum · John Hancock Center · Wicker Park & Around · The Near North Side · Navy Pier · Willis Tower · The Loop · Art Institute · The Near West Side · Field Museum

UKRAINIAN VILLAGE & WEST TOWN

El: Blue to Chicago or Division.

Eastern European immigrants first moved to the area now known as **Ukrainian Village** in the years after the Chicago Fire of 1871, with Ukrainians and Russians in particular developing healthy communities in the neighbourhood. Many of the area's Eastern Europeans began to resettle in the suburbs during the rapid urban expansion of the 1950s and '60s. However, a noteworthy population continues to make its homes in the area, which remains one of the city's largest east Slavic population bubbles.

The Ukrainians have since been joined by Puerto Ricans and Mexicans, who first came to the streets between here and Wicker Park seeking solid blue-collar work in the then-thriving apparel industry. Many arrived too late: the jobs had begun to move overseas, and the area became something of a vacuum. But the Spanish-language billboards that dot the streets speak of a Puerto Rican and Mexican influence that still holds steady in this part of town.

Any tour of the area should begin at the south-west corner of Milwaukee Avenue and Augusta Boulevard, where you'll find the **Polish Roman Catholic Union of America**. The building is the home of the oldest Polish fraternal organisation in the

SIGHTS

INSIDE TRACK
PUERTO RICAN CHICAGO

The spiritual centre of **Puerto Rican Chicago** is not hard to find: just look for the steel Puerto Rican flag that hangs over Division Street as it heads into the neighbourhood of Humboldt Park (close to the intersection with Western Avenue). The park explodes with colourful activity in June when Puerto Ricans celebrate their heritage for six days straight. The festival roughly coincides with the feast of the patron saint of San Juan, but it has a pan-Latin appeal, attracting Dominicans, Cubans and just about anyone who enjoys salsa music in the outdoors. The musical offerings on the outdoor stages tend towards the tropical but also include salsa crooners, Latin house DJs, reggaeton acts and plenty more besides.

US, established in 1873; Vincent Barzynski, one of its founders, was a vital figure in the development of Chicago's Polish community. It's now home to the **Polish Museum of America** (*see p110*); established in 1935 and opened two years later, it's the country's oldest ethnic museum.

A block to the west and north stands the **Northwestern University Settlement House** (1400 W Augusta Boulevard, at N Noble Street), home base of the organisation founded by sociologist Charles Zeublin. A lesser-known cousin of **Hull-House** (*see p103*), it played a major role in the development of American social services. The building was designed by architect Irving K Pond, who earned a name as a developer of settlement houses; it still houses several social service organisations.

To the north-west, the three-way intersection of Milwaukee, Division and Ashland marks the **Polonia Triangle**, known throughout the city's history as Polish Downtown and the one-time heart of Polish Chicago. On the west side of the corner sits a fountain dedicated to writer Nelson Algren, who lived in the area. The large white terracotta building, now a bank and clothing store, was once the home of *Dziennik Zwiazkowy*, Chicago's largest Polish-language daily newspaper, as well as the Jan Smulski Bank Polski. Just to the east, at **1520 W Division Street**, is a large grey building that once housed the Polish National Alliance, the largest fraternal Polish organisation in the country. Further west is the handsome **Division Street Russian & Turkish Baths** (1914 Division Street, at N Winchester Avenue, 1-773 384 9671,

www.chicagorussiansauna.com), which opened in 1906 and remains one of the country's few traditional bathhouses still in operation.

On the corner of Evergreen and Noble stands the gigantic **St Stanislaus Kostka** (1351 W Evergreen Avenue, at N Noble Street, 1-773 278 2470, www.ststansk.com), completed in 1881 and home to Chicago's first Polish-Catholic congregation. Modelled after a church in Krakow, St Stanislaus boasted one of the largest congregations in the US – close to 5,000 families – at the turn of the 19th century. The church was dedicated and served by Barzynski until his death in 1899. Outside service hours, it's open only by appointment.

One block north of the church runs **Blackhawk Street**, which will take you back to Ashland. Though redevelopment has reared its ugly head, a few pre-20th century homes remain, built at the height of the area's economic prosperity. The oldest homes are easily distinguished by the fact that they were constructed below sidewalk level, an oddity resulting from an 1850 decision by the city to raise sidewalks to facilitate better drainage.

The heart of Ukrainian Village, though, is further west. At the south-west corner of Haddon and Leavitt stands the **Holy Trinity Orthodox Cathedral** (1121 N Leavitt Street, at W Haddon Street, 1-773 486 6064), the first Orthodox/Greek Rite church to drop anchor in the community. Founded in 1892 by Carpatho-Ukrainian immigrants as St Vladimir's Russian Orthodox Church, it was redesigned by Louis Sullivan to resemble a Slavic church, with Tsar Nicholas II donating $4,000 towards the construction. The new church was consecrated in 1903 and was designated a cathedral by the Russian Orthodox Church two decades later. Added to the National Register of Historic Places over 30 years ago, it's open to visitors by appointment.

A couple of blocks away, on the north-eastern corner of Oakley and Cortez, is **St Volodymyr Ukrainian Orthodox Cathedral** (2238 W Cortez Street, at N Oakley Avenue, 1-773 278 2827). Built in 1911, it marks the proper entrance to Ukrainian Village, and was the first religious institution formed by local Ukrainians in the area. Call ahead if you want to look around.

From here, head south on Oakley until you come to Rice Street. You can't miss the huge, Byzantine-styled **St Nicholas Ukrainian Catholic Cathedral** (2238 W Rice Street, at N Oakley Avenue, 1-773 276 4537, www.stnicholascathedralukrcath.org), modelled after the Basilica of St Sophia in Kiev, Ukraine. Completed in 1915, it was founded by Uniate Catholics, who hailed from Galicia and Carpatho-Ukraine. The interior is among

Division Street Russian & Turkish Baths.

773.394.0500

European SPA & Turkish Bath

Chicago's most elaborate, with ornate paintings, an enormous Greek chandelier and carpentry dominating the interior cupolas and imparting a distinctive Byzantine flavour. Call ahead to look around, or show up for a service.

St Nicholas was the community centre for Ukrainians until 1968, when a split in the parish over the use of the Gregorian and Julian calendars divided the congregation and sent many to the **Sts Volodymyr & Olha Church** (2245 W Superior Street, at N Oakley Avenue, 1-312 829 5209, www.stsvo.org). The church is a modern Byzantine edifice with golden cupolas and a gigantic mosaic depicting the conversion of the Ukraine to Christianity in AD 988 by St Volodymyr. It's also a piece of living history: the Eastern Rites are still conducted here in Ukrainian. Pop your head in between 9am and 4pm on weekdays. The **Ukrainian Institute of Modern Art** (*see p110*) is a block north.

From here, wander east along Chicago Avenue, past an array of authentic Ukrainian and Russian businesses, towards the south-east corner of the neighbourhood. At Chicago and Ashland stands the **Goldblatt Bros** building (1609 W Chicago Avenue, at N Ashland Avenue), established as a discount department store in 1914 by two sons of Polish immigrants. From this store, Maurice and Nathan built an impressive empire that stretched to more than 40 locations by the '70s. After years of neglect and requests from locals to spare it from demolition, the restored building now houses city workers and occasional art exhibits; some locals also cast ballots here at the 2008 elections.

**INSIDE TRACK
RENEGADE CRAFT FAIR**

The **Renegade Craft Fair** (www.renegade craft.com), a gathering of 300 craftsmen and artists from around North America, takes place each September along Division Street. It's an incredible place if you're in the market for handmade courier bags, silkscreen art, stuffed toys, stationery and knitted versions of just about anything. It's a weekend of low-key, feel good commerce, but Renegade also retain a year-round presence at its shop (1924 W Division Street, at N Damen Avenue, www.renegadehandmade.com).

Polish Museum of America

984 N Milwaukee Avenue, at W Augusta Boulevard (1-773 384 3352/www.polishmuseum ofamerica.org). El: Blue to Chicago. **Open** 11am-4pm Mon-Wed, Fri-Sun. **Admission** $5; $3-$4 reductions. **No credit cards. Map** p331 D9.

While it does a fine job of explaining the history of the city's Polish settlers, the Polish Museum of America has a colourful history in its own right. The museum opened in 1937, but its collection expanded dramatically when exhibits sent by the Polish government to New York for the 1939 World's Fair became stuck in the US after Poland was invaded. The museum purchased many of the artefacts for its archives, which grew more when Ignacy Paderewski, noted Polish pianist and the first prime minister of a free Poland, left many personal effects to the museum in 1941. Paderewski was exiled to the US when war broke out; a plaque recognising his contribution to the city stands at the entrance of Wicker Park.

These days, the dark, dusty museum complements its permanent collection with temporary shows, most of which feature odds and ends from Chicago's Polish community. Staff are only too happy to explain the history of Chicago's Polish community, or to recommend one of the many Polish restaurants in Little Warsaw, further up Milwaukee Avenue.

FREE Ukrainian Institute of Modern Art

2320 W Chicago Avenue, at N Oakley Avenue (1-773 227 5522/www.uima-art.org). Bus: 66. **Open** noon-4pm Wed, Thur, Sat, Sun. **Admission** free. **No credit cards. Map** p331 A9.

As its name suggests, this operation is devoted to modern and contemporary art by Ukrainian artists. One of the city's better-kept secrets, the not-for-profit organisation has a small permanent collection, which usually takes second billing to notable temporary shows on topics such as graphics and war art. One recent exhibition was devoted to Russian cubist sculptor Alexander Archipenko.

Ukrainian National Museum

2249 W Superior Street, at N Oakley Avenue (1-312 421 8020/www.ukrainiannationalmuseum. org). Bus: 49, X49, 66. **Open** 11am-4pm Thur-Sun. **Admission** *Suggested donation* $5. **No credit cards.**

Located in the heart of Ukrainian Village, this sweet little museum houses traditional clothing, musical instruments, agricultural tools and folk art from the Eastern European nation. A library houses some 16,000 books and periodicals, and cultural archives.

WICKER PARK & BUCKTOWN

El: Blue to Damen, Division or Western.

In centuries gone by, the main artery of Wicker Park was the road which is now known as **Milwaukee Avenue**. The route was first worn into a pathway by several tribes of Native Americans, who used it to gain access to the game-rich outer prairies. In the mid-19th century, the neighbourhood became a home to industry of various stripes: first a major steelworks near Ashland and Armitage, and later an array of clothing, furniture, musical instrument and cigar manufacturers and a fair few breweries.

At roughly the same time that Ukrainians and Russians were moving into West Town and what became known as Ukrainian Village, the neighbourhoods to the north were also settled by immigrant communities. Unwelcome residents in Anglo lakeside Chicago, German immigrants built stately houses in the area around the plot of recreational land which was called **Wicker Park**; directly north of there, the Poles moved into **Bucktown**. Paved after the Chicago Fire, Milwaukee Avenue (and, later, the Metropolitan West Side Elevated Railroad) connected these new European settlements with downtown.

Artists and musicians began to move to the area during the 1980s, often displacing residents even poorer than themselves. The seeds they planted for a Greenwich Village-style bohemian enclave blossomed into a vibrant music and arts scene in the '90s. But, as is usually the case with such ground-up cultural regeneration, the 'hood has since gone dramatically upscale, making it even more of a destination than ever.

Wicker Park and Bucktown are still hip, but they're also increasingly affluent and commercial. Luxury condos house young professionals, and a high density of strollers, joggers and dog-walkers lend the district a gentrified feel. Damen, Division and Milwaukee

---

INSIDE TRACK BEER BARONS

German beer barons built ostentatious mansions in Wicker Park in the 1860s on what was then known as Ewing Place; some survive today along Hoyne and Pierce Avenues, an area known as **Beer Baron Row**. But the existence of the mansions begs the question: what happened to Chicago brewing? In short, the Chicago Fire. After the Chicago Brewery burned to the ground in 1871, Milwaukee's already robust brewing industry suddenly had a monopoly, and Wisconsin-based brewers such as Schlitz immediately increased their market shares in the city. However, the city does once again boast a handful of breweries: *see p178, p183* and *p184* **The Brew Crew**.

SIGHTS

Beer Baron Row. See p112.

Avenues are lined with high-end boutiques, dining destinations and concept bars scattered among the established outposts of bohemia – record shops, cafés and vintage stores. The creative classes still live here, and come here to play here too, but there's a sense that the funky frontier lies elsewhere: in Pilsen, perhaps, or Logan Square.

Wicker Park

From the Goldblatt Bros building (*see p109*), wander north up Ashland and then north-west up Milwaukee towards the bewildering '**Six Corners**' intersection of Milwaukee, North and Damen. This is the beating heart of the Wicker Park neighbourhood, but also the junction at which the local gentrification is at its most pronounced. A liver-boggling number of nightclubs, bars and restaurants sit within a stone's throw of here.

And yet for all the moneyed development that's swept the area in the last half-decade or so, many iconic old buildings still remain – relics from previous periods of prosperity but also, at the same time, veterans of intermittent depressions and recessions. Perhaps chief among these landmarks is the **Northwest Tower** (1600 N Milwaukee Avenue, at W North Avenue), a triangular, 12-storey art deco building that was completed just before the Depression in 1929 by the architectural firm Holabird & Root. The one-time centre of Wicker Park's business activity, it was lying virtually empty by 1970, but a restoration plan in 1984 again filled the building with offices and

businesses. A developer now hopes to turn it into a 90-room boutique hotel, though straitened economic circumstances may result in a delay to his plans.

Across the street from the Northwest Tower stands the two-block-long, three-storey **Flat Iron Building** (1579 Milwaukee Avenue, at W North Avenue), a less venerable structure than its neighbour but one that has also found a new lease of life in recent years as Wicker Park has gradually evolved. Much of the building is occupied by young artists, but its arty coffee shop has been replaced in recent years by a new Bank of America; useful shorthand, perhaps, for the changes in the neighbourhood as a whole. A large proportion of the neighbourhood's galleries sit within a stone's throw or two from here; for details, *see p242*.

South of the Milwaukee–Damen–North intersection, things get a little quieter. For a glimpse into Wicker Park's history, wander along **W Pierce Avenue**, lined with large homes built by earlier German and Polish residents. The **Gingerbread House** (no.2137) was constructed in 1888 by Herman Weinhardt; across the street stands the **Paderewski House** (no.2138), built two years earlier and since renamed after the Polish pianist who once entertained a crowd from the verandah of the property. And at **no.2141** stands a house adorned with an Orthodox cross on top. Built in the late 19th century, it was once the home of the archbishop of the Russian Orthodox Holy Virgin Protection Church. There are more handsome old mansions on

SIGHTS

nearby Hoyne Avenue between Pierce and Schiller: known as **Beer Baron Row** (*photo p111*), it was once a retreat for Chicago's prosperous brewers.

Further south along Damen Avenue, you'll find the plot of land that gives the area its name. Although it's named after German Protestants Charles and Joel Wicker, **Wicker Park** was actually donated by Mary L Stewart in 1870, but Charles Wicker is nevertheless commemorated by a life-size bronze statue. The figure was dedicated in 2006 and depicts the businessman, politician, and developer wielding a broom, which evidently was his habit. Community activists have noticed that the statue's placement coincided with the emergence of a more sanitised neighbourhood, but few bemoan the loss of the crack dealers

that once made this a dangerous corner of the city. Today, you're more likely to encounter farmers' markets and designer Doug Wood's tasteful gardens.

The literary-minded should walk one block south of the park to **Evergreen Avenue**, aka Nelson Algren Honorary Boulevard. Algren, author of *The Man with the Golden Arm* and one of Chicago's most accomplished writers, lived at no.1958 from 1959 to 1975. The city erected a Historical Wicker Park monument to help the curious locate the house; a plaque commemorates his residency. Further south on Damen (at Division Street) is the **Rainbo Club** (*see p183*), formerly favoured by Algren but now a popular haunt for local hipsters, artists and musicians. For more Wicker Park literary history, *see below*.

Read All About It

Wicker Park's literary lions live on in bookstores at home and abroad.

Perhaps because of the neighbourhood's historic role as a refuge for new arrivals, the working man and the otherwise down-and-out, many of Chicago's literary giants have held an affinity for the area around Wicker Park. The literary legacy here is such that one can easily get a flavour of the neighbourhood as it existed during the 20th century from some of the best novels of the era, not to mention some powerful pieces of literary documentary. The irony, of course, is that recent gentrification means struggling writers can no longer afford to live here.

Take Nobel Prize-winner **Saul Bellow**, for example, who moved with his family from Quebec to Humboldt Park when Solomon Bello (as he was born) was aged nine. For a time, the Bellows lived on Cortez Street in Ukrainian Village; Bellow attended high school in Humboldt Park. He later wrote *The Adventures of Augie March*, much of which is set in Chicago, and went on to reminisce about his upbringing in days when the unmistakable scent of the stockyards drifted north.

Studs Terkel regularly turned his attention to the Windy City, venturing west to research his social and oral histories of Chicago. His book *Division Street* captured what he called 'a cross-section of urban

thought' in its interviews with the aspirational migrants, the upwardly mobile and the just-plain-regular folks that all help make Chicago what it is.

But there's no writer more closely associated with Wicker Park than **Nelson Algren** who lived, worked and drank in the neighbourhood. In part, his books *The Man with the Golden Arm* and *Chicago: City on the Make* were set here. Goldblatt Bros (*see p109*), St Stanislaus Kostka (*see p108*) and the now-defunct department store Wieboldt's all make appearances in Algren's novels under fictional names; other churches and parks are referred to by their real names. The writer may also have taken his lover, Simone de Beauvoir, to **Phyllis' Musical Inn** (*see p185*) or the **Rainbo** (*see p183*), two of his favourite watering holes. For a map of these and other Algren sights, visit www.nelsonalgren.org.

The Nelson Algren Committee was formed in the late 1980s to recognise the author who took up the cause of Chicago's outsiders. At the time of its founding, Algren's novels were all out of print; they're now all available once more. In 2009, the organisation celebrated an Algren centennial, secure in the knowledge that it had helped Algren regain his place in the literary pantheon.

SIGHTS

Oak Park

Head out west for Hemingway and Wright, the stars of the suburbs.

Heading west on the Green line, you'll pass some of the city's most deprived areas once you've crossed the Chicago River. From the window of the El train, you'll see abandoned public housing, empty warehouses, boarded-up storefronts and trash-littered vacant lots. But towards the end of the line, it's another story.

The first town over the city limits as you head west from downtown, **Oak Park** is one of Chicago's oldest suburbs, and one of its most handsome. The village grew up in the years following the Great Fire of Chicago, and still feels slightly old-fashioned. Yet it's more than just a cute suburb. Oak Park doesn't work hard to please visitors, but it's worthy of diversion all the same.

AROUND OAK PARK

El: Green to Harlem, Oak Park or Ridgeland.

Three Green line El stops serve the suburb of Oak Park, with the line itself following the east–west route of Lake Street: Ridgeland station lies at its eastern extremity, while Harlem/Lake station in downtown Oak Park is at the end of the line. Aside from the kid-oriented **Wonder Works** (*see p222*), and a smattering of shops along Harrison Street close to the junction of Ridgeland Avenue (very close to the Austin stop on the Blue line, but also an easy walk from the Ridgeland Green line station), there's not much east of Oak Park Avenue; so to cover the most interesting parts of the town, get off at the Oak Park station and carve an anti-clockwise loop, heading north, west and south.

Emerge from the train at Oak Park station and you'll be within a stone's throw of the intersection of Oak Park Avenue and Lake Street, the heart of the area's commercial activity. There are a few shops south of here on Oak Park Avenue; **Oak Park Records** (179 S Oak Park Avenue), for instance, one of a dying breed of neighbourhood record stores. But most of the action is a touch further north; among the bijou stores are expensive female fashion boutique **Ananas** (109 N Oak Park Avenue, 1-708 524 8585), olive-oil specialist **Olive & Well** (1-708 848 4230, www.oliveandwell.com) and the family-friendly **Magic Tree**

Bookstore (141 N Oak Park Avenue, 1-708 848 0770, http://magictreebooks.com).

Further north along Oak Park Avenue are the **Ernest Hemingway Birthplace & Museum** (*see p116*), a pair of buildings dedicated to one of the two famous residents to whom Oak Park owes much of its tourist appeal. Just opposite, at 211 N Oak Avenue, is a bistro apparently named after the author, but bizarrely spelled with two 'M's.

If you head north from here, then west on Chicago Avenue, you'll find evidence of the area's other most famous son: Frank Lloyd Wright, who got his start in Oak Park and built 25 homes around the junction of Chicago and Forest Avenues. For more on Wright, *see p114* **Profile**. After you've explored the Wright stuff, reward yourself with a sundae at the historic **Petersen's Ice Cream Parlor** (1100 Chicago Avenue, 1-708 386 6131, www.petersenicecream.com).

Turning left from Chicago on to Harlem Avenue will lead you towards further evidence of Oak Park's independent mindset, with a number of small local shops thriving despite the presence nearby of chains. **Barbara's Bookstore** (1100 Lake Street; *see p191*), for instance, which retains a loyal customer base and the family-owned **Lake Theatre** (1022 Lake Street, 1-708 848 9088, www.classic cinemas.com), which books art films as well as Hollywood blockbusters. From here, at the intersection of Harlem and Lake, you can catch the Green line train back to Chicago.

Profile Frank Lloyd Wright

America's most famous architect got his start in Chicagoland.

The majority of eye-catching and headline-grabbing buildings in Chicago are priapic, sky-piercing affairs. Spend a mere five minutes walking around the Loop and it'll become apparent why the city is known as the home of the skyscraper. It's perhaps ironic, then, that Chicagoland's most celebrated architect made his name not by designing grandiose public buildings or flashy towers, but by constructing isolated residences for rich suburbanites, shuttered from the prying eyes of the common man. Nowadays, **Frank Lloyd Wright**'s style is taken for granted. A century ago, it was virtually revolutionary.

Raised in Wisconsin, Wright arrived in Chicago in the years following the Great Fire and went to work in the offices of Adler and Sullivan, where he was assigned to the firm's residential design department. Eschewing the Beaux Arts style so popular at the time, Wright's residential designs reflected both his own interest in other architectural cultures and the influence of his bosses, both forward-thinking architects in their own right.

In 1893, though, Wright was fired from Adler and Sullivan for moonlighting and set up his own practice at his home in suburban Oak Park, which he shared with his wife Catherine Tobin and their six children.

At his home studio, Wright spent the next decade defining what would come to be known as the Prairie Style, building more than 20 homes for his Oak Park neighbours. Miraculously, all of them survive today.

Mostly constructed of light-coloured brick and stucco, Wright's early Prairie Style homes are low, ground-hugging, rectangular structures featuring broad gabled roofs, sweeping horizontal lines and open, flowing floor plans. Wright was careful that they should blend in with their surroundings, imitating the wide open and flat topography of the Midwest plains. Common features include enclosed porches, stout chimneys and overhanging eaves.

Among the more notable Wright-designed properties in Oak Park are, chronologically, the relatively early **Parker** and **Gale Houses** (1019 and 1027 W Chicago Avenue); the **Thomas**

House (210 N Forest Avenue), considered Wright's first true Prairie Style home; the **Moore House** (333 N Forest Avenue), which Wright himself reworked almost three decades after its 1895 completion; the **Hills House** (313 Forest Avenue), reconstructed after a fire in 1977; and the **Gale House** (6 Elizabeth Court), one of the last homes he built in the area. None of them is open to the public (they're all occupied), but you can see the exteriors simply by strolling around the neighbourhood. For more insight, get an audio tour from the **Frank Lloyd Wright Home & Studio** (*see p116*), or join one of the weekend guided tours (booking may be required).

Wright also designed Oak Park's **Unity Temple** (*see p116*), a liberal Protestant church that recently celebrated its centenary (and is currently raising funds for a much-needed restoration). Both of Wright's parents belonged to the Unitarian Church, which encourages followers to approach religion through nature, science and art in the belief that such disciplines reveal the underlying principles of God's universe. Indeed, Wright's respect for natural elements and precise geometry is apparent in the designs of his homes and the temple.

Wright left his home studio in 1909 and sold the property in 1925. Five decades later, the building had been so abused and altered by subsequent owners that it barely resembled the architect's original design. In 1974, the Frank Lloyd Wright Home & Studio Foundation was formed to acquire the property, oversee a $3-million restoration that returned the property to its 1909 appearance, and eventually open it to the public as a museum and education centre dedicated to the architect's work. Tours of the Frank Lloyd Wright Home & Studio offer fascinating insights into Wright's early life and creative influences. If you're lucky, you'll get one of the more entertaining tour guides, who won't gloss over the soapy details of Wright's philandering ways. Joint tickets are available with the aforementioned guided tours of Oak Park; see www.wrightplus.org for full details of the many tours available.

One of the last designs to come out of Wright's Oak Park studio was the **Robie House** (*see p123*), which is located near the University of Chicago on the city's South Side. Wright began work on the home of Chicago industrialist Frederick C Robie in 1909, a project the architect would later proclaim 'the cornerstone of modern architecture'.

When asked what his best building was, the self-aggrandising Wright always answered, 'My next one'. He may have had a point: New York City's Guggenheim Museum was the last structure he designed before his death in 1959. Although Wright went on to design notable buildings all over the country, the small town where he got his start remains a fascinating place to see him in action.

SIGHTS

SIGHTS

Ernest Hemingway Birthplace & Museum

Birthplace *339 N Oak Park Avenue, between Erie Street & Superior Street.* **Museum** *200 N Oak Park Avenue, between Ontario Street & Erie Street (1-708 848 2222/www.ehfop.org). El: Green to Oak Park.* **Open** 1-5pm Tue-Sun; 10am-5pm Sat. **Admission** $8; $6 discounts; free under-5s. **No credit cards.**

Looked after by the Hemingway Foundation, the Oak Park house where Ernie emerged has been open to the public for years. The displays include photographs, furnishings, memorabilia and the like, with all the items connected to Hemingway's childhood years in some way. A museum two blocks away continues the theme with videos, books, posters and other Ernestabilia. All very well and good, of course, but the fact that Hemingway himself despised Oak Park, leaving as soon as he could (aged 18, for Kansas City, Missouri, and a job on a newspaper) and memorably referring to it as a place of 'wide lawns and narrow minds', is skimmed over. Hemingway may have been in Oak Park, but Oak Park certainly wasn't in Hemingway.

Frank Lloyd Wright Home & Studio

951 Chicago Avenue, between N Forest Avenue & Woodbine Avenue, Oak Park (1-708 848 1976/www.wrightplus.org). El: Green to Oak Park. **Open** *Tours* (45mins) 11am, 1pm & 3pm Mon-Fri; every 20mins, 11am-3.30pm Sat, Sun. **Admission** $15; $5-$12 discounts; free under-4s. **No credit cards.**
See p114 **Profile.**

Oak Park Conservatory

615 Garfield Street, between S Clarence & S East Avenues (1-708 386 4700/www.oprf.com/ conservatory). El: Green to Oak Park. **Open** 2-4pm Mon; 10am-4pm Tue-Sun. **Admission** *Suggested donation* $2. **No credit cards.**

Much more than just a greenhouse, this 73-year-old glass structure contains three large themed rooms (highlighting tropical, fern and desert plants). A 5,000sq ft (450sq m) building, which opened in 2000, provides space for social and educational events. Next door, Rehm Park has a play area for children, tennis courts and a pool.

Pleasant Home/Historical Society of Oak Park & River Forest

217 S Home Avenue, at Pleasant Street (1-708 383 2654/www.oprf.com/phf). El: Green to Oak Park. **Tours** *Mar-Nov* 12.30pm, 1.30pm & 2.30pm Thur-Sun. *Dec-Feb* 12.30pm & 1.30pm Thur-Sun. **Admission** $5; $3 discounts; free under-5s. **No credit cards.**

Designed in 1897 by Prairie School architect George W Maher, Pleasant Home is used primarily for meetings and wedding receptions. However, there's also a photograph and document archive here, plus a charming little local museum with exhibits relating to long-time local resident Edgar Rice Burroughs and the ubiquitous Mr Hemingway. You can only visit the museum and home as part of a tour.

Unity Temple

875 Lake Street, at N Kenilworth Avenue (1-708 383 8873/www.unitytemple-utrf.org). El: Green to Oak Park. **Open** 10.30am-4.30pm Mon-Fri; 1-4pm Sat, Sun. *Tours* 1pm, 2pm & 3pm Sat, Sun. **Admission** $8; $6 discounts; free under-5s. **Credit** AmEx, MC, V.

This Unitarian Universalist church, which was designed by Lloyd Wright in 1905 and eventually completed in 1908, is notable for its striking first-floor sanctuary and community room. Also of interest are the physical expressions of Wright's notions of divinity and sacred space found throughout (such as light fixtures, leaded glass windows and furniture); his love of music is reflected in the regular concerts that are held here. During the week, you can take a self-guided tour; at weekends, it's guided tours only. An interesting lecture-series on the temple's creator and his influence is held between February and October.

Also in the area

Brookfield Zoo

3300 Golf Road, at 31st Street & 1st Avenue, Brookfield (1-708 485 0263/www. brookfieldzoo.org). Metra: Hollywood (Zoo Stop). **Open** *May-early Sept* 9.30am-6pm daily. *Early Sept-May* 10am-5pm daily. **Admission** $12; $8 discounts; free under-2s. Free to all Tue-Thur, Sat, Sun Oct-Feb & Tue-Thur Mar-Sept. **Credit** AmEx, Disc, MC, V.

Brookfield Zoo, about five miles from Oak Park, is worlds apart from its compatriot in Lincoln Park (*see p89*) in terms of geography, tone and size. Over 200 acres of land are dedicated to keeping more than 400 species of wildlife. Cages are largely eschewed in favour of letting the animals roam free, to the delight of the kid-heavy crowds. The dolphin shows in the Seven Seas Panorama are predictably popular. And, of course, everyone loves the inquisitive meerkats. Parents should come prepared for an expensive time in the well-stocked gift shop afterwards. Parking costs an additional $8.

The South Side

From economic deprivation to academic excellence, all human life is here.

Cherry-pick moments from its history, and the South Side may seem like the most important region of Chicago. Huge academic progress has been made over decades at the University of Chicago; the country's cultural history was rewritten with the emergence of the electric blues; and, in the shape of Barack Obama, Chicago's South Side delivered to the country its first African-American president.

However, such landmark moments don't tell the whole story. Pockets of affluence and influence dot the South Side, most notably in collegiate **Hyde Park**, where the Museum of Science and Industry is one of Chicago's top attractions. But huge swathes of the South Side still suffer from economic decay and high crime rates, partly as a result of public-housing policies enforced by the city council that were historically segregationist. There's plenty to see here, but also a number of stretches that are best avoided.

Map p332   **Bars** p187
Restaurants p173

THE NEAR SOUTH SIDE

El: Red to Cermak-Chinatown.

The streets immediately beyond the **South Loop** and **Chinatown** (*see p67*), which end around I-55, are either uninspiring or downright shady. However, there are a few notable landmarks here, chief among them the **Wood-Maxey-Boyd House** at 2801 S Prairie Avenue (near E 28th Street). This Queen Anne-style building was saved from demolition during the 1950s and again in 2003, when owner Alva Maxey-Boyd faced down the city and won. Her neighbours weren't as tough or as lucky: after a programme of systematic demolition, this is the only house on the block.

Given the vast amounts of ink and paper that have been expended on describing the Ludwig Mies van der Rohe buildings in the Loop and on

the Near North Side, it's somewhat surprising that his designs for the main campus of the **Illinois Institute of Technology** (IIT) are generally overlooked – this is, after all, one of the more important modernist sites in the country. Guided tours of the site ($5) are run at 10am and 1pm every day except Sunday, with self-guided audio tours ($5) also available (10am-3pm Mon-Sat). All tours depart from the ultra-postmodern **McCormick Tribune Campus Center** (3201 S State Street, at S 32nd Street), itself designed by noted Dutch architect Rem Koolhaas. The giant graphic of a head pays tribute to Mies with a wink and a nudge; the stainless steel tube around the El trains helps to reduce the noise emanating from them. For more, call 1-312 567 5025 or see http://www.iit.edu/giving/mies. The site is easily accessible by catching the 29 bus that runs down State Street.

INSIDE TRACK
SALUTE TO THE PIONEERS

Chicago's black population swelled
substantially during the Great Migration,
the name given to the relocation of
countless thousands of African Americans
from the South to northern cities during
the 1920s and '20s. Their pioneering
spirit is honoured with a **15-foot bronze
statue** at King Drive and 26th Place. The
work of LA artist Alison Saar, it denotes
a man carrying a suitcase and waving
goodbye; he's wearing a suit made from
shoe-soles, representing the hard journey
endured by many who made the trek.

BRONZEVILLE

El: Green to 35th-Bronzeville-IIT.

Taking as its approximate borders Wentworth
and Cottage Grove Avenues, and 26th and 51st
Streets, Bronzeville emerged as a product of
racial segregation and de facto residential
restrictions. The neighbourhood came to be
symbolic of the Chicago Renaissance, a period
of African-American cultural flowering in
the city, before fading under the weight of
underinvestment and neglect. In recent years,
it's begun to make a comeback, but this long-
beleaguered district still has a little way to go.

African Americans began to settle in the
area in the late 19th century, joining the Irish
Americans who already called it home. By the
1920s, the area had become a 'Black Metropolis':
two major waves of migration brought some
200,000 southerners to the South Side, and the
area prospered. Around this time, the area was
christened Bronzeville by the *Chicago Bee*, an
African American newspaper that elected a
'mayor' for the district every year.

It didn't last. The Depression and ongoing,
city-approved segregation contributed to a
downturn in the area's fortunes (as chronicled
by local resident Richard Wright in his 1940
novel *Native Son*). The city's response was to
drop more than 30 blocks of public housing on
the neighbourhood and starve it of investment
and attention, two acts that essentially rubber-
stamped its earlier segregationist policies
and invited economic decline. The district
degenerated throughout the 1970s and '80s.

Bronzeville still hasn't recovered from all
these years of neglect and blight. Parts of the
area remain decidedly sketchy, especially
at night. However, an array of new local
businesses are trying to turn the area around.
At E 47th Street and S King Drive, a complex

houses contemporary American eaterie **Blu
47** (1-773 536 6000) and the **Spoken Word
Café** (1-773 373 2233). Nearby, at the corner of
47th Street and King Drive, the old Regal
Theater has been converted into the **Harold
Washington Cultural Center** (4701 S
King Drive, at E 47th Street, 1-773 373 1900,
www.haroldwashingtonculturalcenter.com),
a controversy-blighted arts enterprise.

Some relics from Bronzeville's glory
days have survived into the 21st century.
The **Chicago Defender Building** (3435 S
Indiana Avenue, at E 35th Street) was built as a
synagogue, but went on to house the newspaper
that agitated for civil rights and encouraged the
Great Migration. Not far away sit the elaborate
offices of its competitor, the *Chicago Bee* (3647-
3655 S State Street, at E 36th Street). Opposite
each other at the corner of 35th Street and King
Drive are the old **Supreme Life Offices**,
once the home of the country's first African
American insurance agency, and the **Victory
Monument**, erected in 1926 to honour black
soldiers who fought in World War I.

BRIDGEPORT

El: Orange to Halsted; Red to Sox-35th.

Originally and fatefully dubbed Hardscrabble,
Bridgeport (south from 26th Street to Pershing
Road, between Wentworth and Ashland

**Victory
Monument.**

Walk Barack 'n' Roll

Get to know Obama's Chicago by following in his footsteps – literally.

even gave it a nod – albeit under the alias Smitty's – in *Dreams from My Father.*
Continue south on Blackstone to 53rd Street and turn left.
Peer through the window of **Valois** (1518 E 53rd Street, 1-773 667 0647), a cafeteria-style restaurant that attracts everyone from working Joes and ageing African Americans to University of Chicago profs and students, as chronicled in Mitchell Duneier's book *Slim's Table.* Obama was once a regular.
Go right on Lake Park, right on 54th Street and left on Harper.
The first apartment Obama rented as a young community organiser in the late '80s stands at **5429 S Harper Avenue.** The building's a little tattered but full of charm.
At 54th Place, turn right, then head south on Dorchester Avenue and west on 57th Street.
Another former Obama hangout, the **Medici on 57th** (1327 E 57th Street, 1-773 667 7394, www.medici57.com) has grasped on to its patron's coattails. A glass case on one wall enshrines a selection of OBAMA EATS HERE T-shirts; each table has an OBAMA 2008-engraved wood cutting board. If you ask what his favourite dishes are, your scarcely seen server might walk away mumbling something about the Secret Service making it hard for the president to drop in.
Continue west on 57th, then go south on Woodlawn Avenue and walk through the Midway Plaisance.
Obama taught at the **University of Chicago Law School** (1111 E 60th Street) for more than a decade, beginning in 1992. The building doesn't bear any trace of his presence, but a plaque seems inevitable.

SIGHTS

Start at 5046 S Greenwood Avenue.
The Obamas are currently making their home on Pennsylvania Avenue in DC. But in Chicago, the family calls this two-storey, red-brick mansion home. If you gawk through the evergreens too long or snap pictures from too close an angle, expect to hear the security staff guide you away with a well-rehearsed, 'Please take your pictures from the other side of the street.'
Head down Hyde Park Boulevard and turn south on Blackstone Avenue.
For the past 20 years, Obama has engaged the services of the **Hyde Park Hair Salon & Barber Shop** (5234 S Blackstone Avenue, 1-773 493 6028, www.hydeparkhairsalon. net) to keep his perfectly trimmed, close-cropped 'do looking politician-perfect. The shop has seen a spike in business since the rock star-like rise of Obama, who

Obama's first apartment.

INSIDE TRACK
AN UNLIKELY MEMORIAL

Given his racist tendencies, it's ironic that 19th-century politician **Stephen A Douglas** once owned the land now occupied by Bronzeville. Douglas died in 1861, the year after he was defeated by Abraham Lincoln in the presidential elections; two decades later, he was commemorated at 35th Street and Cottage Grove Avenues with an ostentatious tomb, a 46-foot (14-metre) column topped by a statue of the man himself.

Avenues) grew up around the Illinois–Michigan Canal as a settlement of Irish Americans willing to work for land. During the early and mid-20th century, it was known for its hostility to outsiders and for the gangs that enforced its boundaries. However, such behaviour didn't prevent it from exerting a huge influence over the development of the city; indeed, it might even have helped. For it was from here that the fabled Democratic political machine cranked into action. For more on this era, *see p45*.

Centred around Halsted Street, Bridgeport has maintained a working-class Irish character, but is now home to communities of Mexican Americans and Lithuanian Americans. And while Bridgeport remains tight-knit, an influx of condo conversions and an assortment of 'space available' signs on nearby warehouses tell their own story. The **Polo Café** (3322 S

Morgan Street, at W 33rd Place, 1-773 927 7656, www.polocafe.com), a former candy shop, has become a focal point for the new district.

However, most Chicagoans visit Bridgeport to take in a Chicago White Sox baseball game at **US Cellular Field** (S Wentworth Avenue & E 35th Street; *see p276*), a hulking concrete bowl built in the early 1990s. Aesthetically, it's not a patch on Wrigley Field, but the fans don't mind. After all, since it opened, the Cubs haven't been a patch on the White Sox, who won the World Series in 2005.

HYDE PARK

Metra: 55th-56th-57th Street.

With the University of Chicago as its anchor, Hyde Park enjoys a reputation as an oasis of intellectualism and community activism. The neighbourhood is much more low-key than the equivalent, college-dominated districts on the North Side counterparts; largely geared towards the middle-class families that have settled here, it has far fewer bars, restaurants and nightclubs than, for example, DePaul-dominated Lincoln Park. But its true campus culture and geographic isolation – it's ringed by rather more deprived areas – also makes it feel much more self-enclosed.

The campus of the **University of Chicago** is at the heart of Hyde Park, both figuratively and literally. Many of the buildings are neo-Gothic, but several newer structures are worthy of attention. Chief among them is Cesar Pelli's flowing and airy **Gerald Ratner Athletic**

DuSable Museum of African American History.

Gerard N. Lew

Dr. Margaret T.G. Burroughs

Center, which houses a pool visible from the sidewalk between 55th and 56th Streets on Ellis Avenue. In addition to the **Oriental Institute** (*see p123*), the campus is home to a pair of galleries. The **Renaissance Society** (5811 S Ellis Avenue, at E 58th Street, 1-773 702 8670, www.renaissancesociety.org) offers modern-art shows, while the **Smart Museum of Art** (*see p124*) boasts an enviable permanent collection. For a tour of the campus, *see p122* **Walk**.

As you might expect, the leafy streets around the college are dotted with bookstores (*see p190*). Close by sits **Robie House** (*see p123*), a Frank Lloyd Wright masterpiece. Other attractions sit further away. To the east, in lakefront Jackson Park, sits the **Museum of Science and Industry** (*see below*), one of the city's premier family-friendly museums. And to the west, in Washington Park, is the **DuSable Museum of African American History** (*see below*). Both parks are ideal for finding pensive pauses unavailable in other parts of the city, rather like the district as a whole.

DuSable Museum of African American History

740 E 56th Place, at E 57th Street (1-773 947 0600/ www.dusablemuseum.org). Metra: 55th-56th-57th Street. **Open** *Jan-May* 10am-5pm Mon-Sat; noon-5pm Sun. *June-Dec* 10am-5pm Tue-Sat; noon-5pm Sun. **Admission** $3; $1-$2 discounts; free under-6s; free to all Sun. Credit AmEx, MC, V. **Map** p332 X17.

When the DuSable Museum opened in the early '60s, African-American history was suffering serious neglect at the hands of the nation's cultural institutions. The seeds of change were planted when, in 1961, printmaker and schoolteacher Margaret Burroughs cleared the furniture out of her South Side home's living room, replaced it with an enviable collection of African-American art and artefacts, and hung a shingle outside reading 'African American Museum'. And so the DuSable was born.

One of the country's first museums dedicated to black history, the DuSable is now housed in a stately former Park District building in Washington Park. Revolving exhibitions spotlight everything from African-American entrepreneurship and the civil rights movement to traditional quilt-making techniques. The museum also focuses on Chicago's own African-American community, with an ongoing exhibit on the life of Bronzeville beauty product pioneer Annie Malone, the first African-American millionaire. Organisation and interpretive materials don't seem to be of utmost importance, but the helpful staff compensate.

★ Museum of Science & Industry

5700 S Lake Shore Drive, at 57th Street (1-773 684 1414/www.msichicago.org). Metra: 55th-56th-57th Street. **Open** 9.30am-4pm Mon-Sat;

11am-4pm Sun. **Admission** $13; $9-$12 discounts; free under-2s. **Credit** AmEx, Disc, MC, V. **Map** p332 Z17.

If you're into exhibits loaded with interactive features, this expansive Hyde Park operation should be just the ticket. Built in 1893 as the Palace of Fine Arts for the World's Columbian Exposition, the building was converted to its present incarnation in the 1920s. Although it's a fair way from downtown, the Museum of Science & Industry is deservedly one of the city's top attractions.

The challenge for every science museum is not only to track the history of technological progress, but also to keep pace with it. While some of the whiz-bang exhibits are good – notably the new **Fast Forward** display, which features cuisine made by ink-jet printers and instant-messaged hugs – there are some real clunkers here, too. The 30 computers and 25 projectors in **Networld** are so underwhelming that the exhibit's archaic facts about the internet seem particularly noteworthy.

Overall, the museum's focus is broad, as witnessed by low-tech displays such as **Colleen Moore's Fairy Castle** (ground floor, by the yellow stairs), a gaudy but fabulous multi-room miniature that's just a bit too big to be called a doll's house. Nearby, the huge John Deere combine harvester and the cow poop display in the recently rehabbed **Farm Tech** (ground floor, by the red stairs) are equally amazing. The long queues that form outside the **Coal Mine** (main floor, by the rotunda) hide an exhibit that kids enjoy immensely, at least if they don't go mad during the boring wait on the staircase. Go during the earlier portion of your visit, as seats on 'Old Ben #17' often fill to capacity and the exhibit closes earlier than the rest of the museum.

Of all the vehicles in the museum, the **1934 Pioneer Zephyr** train (Great Hall) is one of the highlights, as is the not-to-be-missed **U-505 German** submarine (ground floor). One of only five

---

INSIDE TRACK
UNION STOCK YARDS

For years, Bridgeport's economy was driven by meat. Opened in 1865, the **Union Stock Yards** was the centre of the country's meatpacking industry, and eventually grew to cover an area constrained by Pershing Road, Halsted Street, 47th Street and Ashland Avenue. Upton Sinclair's 1906 book *The Jungle* passed damning judgment on the slaughterhouse conditions, but the yards continued to thrive. It closed in 1971, but its presence is commemorated by the Stockyards Gate over Exchange Avenue (at Peoria Street), next to a memorial to firefighters who died in a fire here in 1910.

surviving World War II subs in the world, it recently underwent a $35-million overhaul that afforded it its very own vast underground chamber. It's now surrounded by lots of interpretive materials, short films and various artefacts that were found on board when, in June of 1944, it was captured by American seamen off the coast of West Africa. The vast exhibition is included with admission but the on-board tour requires additional tickets ($5).

Elsewhere in the museum, young visitors especially will wander around, wide eyed with wonder, at the interactive science displays, whether whispering to a friend across the hall at the **Whispering Gallery** (main floor), watching **Earth Revealed**'s NASA real-time footage of the planet from afar (main floor), or seeing a chick hatch before their eyes in the hatchery (main floor). It's easy to get disoriented, and it'll take at least a day to see anything close to all that the museum has to offer, even without temporary pop-culture inspired blockbusters such as the popular 2009 show *Harry Potter: The Exhibit*. Still, it's well worth your time. *Photo p124.*

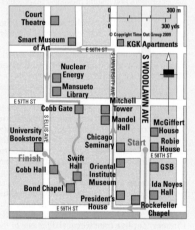

Walk Back to School

Explore the collegiate territory of Hyde Park.

Begin at the corner of 58th Street and Woodlawn Avenue.

Just south of Frank Lloyd Wright's **Robie House** (*see p123*) sits the relatively new **Charles M Harper Center** (1101 E 58th Street). Designed by Rafael Vinoly, it's in part a modern reinterpretation of its Wright-designed neighbour. Approach the Harper Center from the south to see how the two buildings interact. It's just a pity that from this angle, Robie House is overshadowed – literally – by the altogether less distinguished **McGiffert House** (5751 S Woodlawn Avenue).

Head south down Woodlawn Avenue until you get to the junction of Woodlawn and 59th Street.

It looks pretty big out front, but the churchy **Ida Noyes Hall** (1212 E 59th Street) is even bigger once inside. It was built in 1916 as a women's hall of residence; these days, it holds a cinema and a pool.

Across the way you'll find the **Rockefeller Memorial Chapel** (5850 S Woodlawn Avenue, http://rockefeller.uchicago.edu), which is named after the man whose cash funded the building of the university. Built to the Gothic designs of Bertram Goodhue in 1928, the chapel is notable for its stained glass, a surfeit of exterior statues and its clanging carillon.

Walk a block west down Woodlawn, then take the next right up University.

Past the **President's House** (5855 S University Avenue) and the **Oriental Institute Museum** (*see p123*) sits the **Chicago Theological Seminary** (1164 E 58th Street, www.ctschicago.edu). Visit the quietly lovely **Thorndike Hilton Memorial Chapel** and the **Seminary Co-operative Bookstore** (5757 S University Avenue; *see p192*) downstairs.

Continue north up University Avenue to the south-west corner with E 57th Street.

If you're lucky, your visit to Hyde Park will coincide with a concert at **Mandel Hall** (*see p255*). Some top-notch classical ensembles perform in its beautiful auditorium.

Walk north up University Avenue for a block.

George and William Keck designed the three-flat, International-style **Keck-Gottschalk-Keck Apartments** (5551 S University Avenue) for themselves and Professor Louis Gottschalk in 1937. It's now a designated Chicago landmark known for the external blinds attached to its street-facing windows.

Turn left on to E 56th Street.

The **Smart Museum of Art** (*see p124*) is the second university museum that you'll find en route. On the left sits an unappealing block of residences, but at the intersection with Ellis Avenue, your gaze may well be drawn to the modern,

SIGHTS

★ Oriental Institute Museum

*University of Chicago, 1155 E 58th Street, at
S University Avenue (1-773 702 9520/http://
oi.uchicago.edu). Metra: 55th-56th-57th Street.*
Open 10am-6pm Tue, Thur-Sat; 10am-8.30pm
Wed; noon-6pm Sun. **Admission** *Suggested
donation* $5; $2 under-12s. **No credit cards**.
Map p332 X17.
This University of Chicago-run archaeological treasure trove thankfully forgoes the current museum
trend of providing hokey interactive displays that
pander to the PlayStation generation's short attention spans. Instead, it allows some stunning architectural finds to speak for themselves in
old-fashioned glass display cases. Years ago, John
D Rockefeller bankrolled the institute so archaeolo-
gist and Egyptologist James Breasted and his col-
leagues could lead expeditions to excavate lost
civilisations. The vast collection that resulted, which
includes cuneiform tablets, mummies and larger-
than-life stone statues from Egypt and the Near
East, evokes all the mystery and intrigue any whip-
cracking, fedora-wearing action hero could handle.

The space is divided into galleries themed around
the great civilisations of Mesopotamia, Egypt and
Persia, along with newer galleries that take in the
Palestine and Nubia collections. Among the highlights are the hard-to-miss, 16-foot, solid-stone,
human-headed winged bull that guarded King
Sargon II's palace court more than 2,700 years ago,
and the equally imposing 3,000-year-old King Tut
statue that was uncovered in Thebes.

FREE Renaissance Society

*5811 S Ellis Avenue, between E 58th & 59th
Streets (1-773 702 8670/www.renaissance
society.org). Metra: 55th-56th-57th Street.*
Tours 10am-5pm Tue-Fri; noon-5pm Sat,
Sun. **Admission** free. **No credit cards**.
Map p332 X17.
Despite the name, you won't find any Michelangelos
here: this gallery, which is unaffiliated with the
University of Chicago but inhabits a space inside its
Cobb Hall, has specialised in new and cutting-edge
art since it opened in 1915. The 'Ren' introduced
Alexander Calder and Fernand Léger to the US and
still stages some of the most daring, conceptual-
heavy shows in Chicago. The gallery also sells
affordable, unique editions and artists' books.

★ Robie House

*5757 S Woodlawn Avenue, at E 58th Street
(1-708 848 1976/www.wrightplus.org). Metra
55th-56th-57th Street.* **Tours** 11am-3pm Sat,
but closed Oct 2009-May 2010. **Admission**
$12; $10 discounts. **Credit** AmEx, Disc, MC, V.
Map p332 Y17.
If you have even a basic knowledge of the history of
architecture, you'll know who's behind this place.
Commissioned by Chicago industrialist Frederick C
Robie and completed in 1910, this is Frank Lloyd
Wright at his finest. A masterpiece of the Prairie
Style, the house features dramatic horizontal lines,
cantilevered roofs, expansive stretches of glass and
Wright's signature open floorplan. Tickets for some
tours are available in advance; otherwise, it's first
come, first served.

For the 100th anniversary, the house is receiving
a much-needed facelift. Tours look likely to be suspended from October 2009 until around May 2010;
check the website for further updates.
▶ *For Wright's work in Oak Park, see p131.*

---

eye-catching curves of the **Gerald
Ratner Athletics Center**.
Turn left down Ellis Avenue.
A Henry Moore sculpture, **Nuclear
Energy**, stands on the site of Stagg Field,
the former football field. It was here, on
2 December 1942, that Enrico Fermi
conducted the first successful nuclear
experiment. Moore's statue was unveiled
exactly 25 years later. The **Joe & Rika
Mansueto Library**, designed by Helmut
Jahn, will open here in 2010.
Turn left into E 57th Street.
The Gothic **Cobb Gate** makes for a
grand entrance to the college, and made
for an equally grand exit for Billy Crystal
and Meg Ryan when they set off for New
York City from here in *When Harry Met
Sally*. Ask a savvy student to explain the
collegiate myth that has grown up around
the figures on the gate.
Continue south to the roundabout.
The portentous **Swift Hall** is home to
the university's Divinity School. It figures,
then, that right next to it should be the
Bond Chapel, all dark woods and studied
calm. Close by, **Cobb Hall** is the oldest
building on campus, dating back to
1892. It takes its name from Henry Ives
Cobb, the architect who designed 18
of the college buildings. Inside, the
university mounts exhibitions of
unapologetically modern art in the
Renaissance Society (*see right*).
*Cut through the passageway between
Cobb Hall and the Administration
building and then head north up
Ellis Avenue.*
The Barnes & Noble-run **University
of Chicago Bookstore** (970 E 58th
Street, 1-773 702 8729) draws a mix
of students needing textbooks and
tourists needing souvenirs.

SIGHTS

Museum of Science & Industry. *See p121.*

FREE Smart Museum of Art
University of Chicago, 5550 S Greenwood Avenue, at E 55th Street (1-773 702 0200/http://smartmuseum.uchicago.edu). Metra: 55th-56th-57th Street. **Open** 10am-4pm Tue, Wed, Fri; 10am-8pm Thur; 11am-5pm Sat, Sun. **Admission** free. **Map** p332 X17.
The Smart Museum of Art houses a dizzying collection of more than 10,000 objects, spanning 5,000 years from ancient Shang Dynasty bronzes to modern works of art. The mind reels, stepping from Shinto prints in one room to Anselm Kiefer in the next.

THE PULLMAN DISTRICT

Metra: 111th Street.

The Pullman District (roughly bounded by 104th, 115th, Cottage Grove and Langley Streets) is the preserved remains of the first model planned industrial community in the US. Tycoon George Pullman conceived a workers' utopia to be built alongside his new railcar factory, and set about creating it on a 3,000-acre site. Erected from 1880, the 1,300 structures included houses, shops, churches, parks and a library for his employees. Sadly, Pullman's dream turned into a nightmare when workers' dissatisfaction resulted in a destructive strike. As a result, the town was annexed by Chicago in 1898, though Pullman wasn't around to see it happen; he'd died a year earlier.

Much of the original town is gone, destroyed by overzealous construction workers and, in the case of the old clock tower, arsonists (it burned down in 1998). Still, the buildings that remain give a decent impression of what this community was like. The Hotel Florence, the Greenstone Church and some rowhouse-lined sidestreets are all either intact or have been restored in what is now a National Landmark District. Start your visit at the **Historic Pullman Foundation Visitor Center**.

INSIDE TRACK
SOUTH SIDE LUXURY

Looming over the northern edge of Hyde Park, the **Powhatan Apartments** building (E 50th Street & S Chicago Beach Drive) is a world apart from the undistinguished and poverty-soaked high-rises that dot the South Side. It was built in the 1920s, just before the Great Depression put a lid on developers' hopes to reinvent the area. The art deco detailing is by Charles L Morgan, a graphic artist and friend of Frank Lloyd Wright.

Historic Pullman Foundation Visitors Center

11141 S Cottage Grove Avenue, at S 112th Street (1-773 785 8901/www.pullmanil.org). Metra: 111th Street. **Open** 11am-3pm Tue-Sun. **Tours** *May-Oct* 1.30pm 1st Sun of mth. **Admission** *Suggested donation* $5; $3-$4 discounts; free under-6s. **Credit** AmEx, MC, V.
The Pullman City visitors' centre houses historic photos and Pullman-related items, such as a buffet table from the Pullman mansion, ornamental decor from the old Hotel Florence and the 'Perfect Town' award given to Pullman.

Consume

Threadless. *See p199.*

Hotels

Historic luxury or 21st-century chic? Your call…

For more than a century, a handful of grand
old hotels such as the Drake gave Chicago's
well-heeled visitors somewhere suitably smart
to drop their bags. Over the last decade, though,
the hotel sector has played catch-up with the
old-timers, adding new style to a once-tired scene.
Familiar names and longtime favourites, such
as the **W**, the **Hard Rock** and the three popular
Kimpton Group hotels, have been joined in
the city by bright new operations, such as the
Affinia and the **Dana**. And happily some of
the veterans have even been revived: witness
the 2008 reopening of the landmark **Blackstone**, and the recent sprucing-up
of the **Palmer House Hilton**.

CONSUME

INFORMATION & PRICES

The prices given in this chapter refer to the
rack rates for standard double rooms. These
rates should at least offer an idea about what
you can expect to pay at a given hotel, but do
note that rates can vary wildly within the city
and even within a single property. At peak
season and during major conventions, bargains
may be hard to find. Conversely, though, great
deals are often available at quieter times. Note
that all prices given in this chapter, and given
by hotels on their own websites, will exclude
the city's crippling hotel tax of 15.4 per cent.

Before booking, always check the hotels'
own websites, where many of the best deals are
exclusively available. It may be worth building
a little flexibility into your schedule: by arriving
a day later, for instance, you could save money
on the same room at the same hotel. It's also
worth checking online systems such as **www.
hotels.com, www.priceline.com, www.
lastminute.com, www.expedia.com** and
Chicago-based **Hot Rooms** (1-773 468 7666,
www.hotrooms.com), all of which offer regular
deals. However you book, always ask about
cancellation policies when booking.

We've listed a selection of services for each
hotel at the bottom of each review, detailing
everything from in-room entertainment options
to the cost of parking. Prices for internet access
and parking are for any given 24-hour period
unless stated.

We've listed only those hotels within a
reasonable distance of downtown. Other chain
hotels can be found further out, especially
around O'Hare. For a list of main hotel
chains, *see right* **The Chain Gang**.

The Loop
Deluxe

Fairmont Chicago
*200 N Columbus Drive, at E Lake Street, IL
60601 (1-866 540 4409/1-312 565 8000/
www.fairmont.com). El: Brown, Green, Orange,
Pink or Purple to State/Lake; Red to Lake.* **Rates**
$159-$489 double. **Rooms** 687. **Credit** AmEx,
Disc, MC, V. **Map** p325 J11 ❶
A feeling of refined romance pervades in these cushy
digs: oversized bathrooms, separate dressing rooms,
fluffy robes and in-room spa services complete with
champagne and chocolate-covered strawberries.
From standards to suites, all 687 rooms offer ample
space and an organic, modern feel, but if you sign
up for the Gold floor, you'll also gain access to a

> ❶ Red numbers given in this chapter
> correspond to the location of each hotel
> on the street maps. *See pp324-332.*

About the author
Jessica Herman writes for The Get section in
Time Out Chicago *magazine.*

private lobby. At the end of the evening, settle down in the lobby's wine, chocolate and cheese lounge, the Eno Wine Room, for a nightcap. Extra cash allows for a hot stone massage in the spa.
Bar. Business centre. Concierge. Disabled-adapted rooms. Gym. Internet (wireless & cable, $14.95/day). Parking ($49/day). Restaurant. Room service. Spa. TV (pay movies).

Renaissance Chicago Hotel
1 W Wacker Drive, at N State Street, IL 60601 (1-800 468 3571/1-312 372 7200/www. renaissancehotel.com). El: Brown, Green, Orange, Pink or Purple to State/Lake; Red to Lake. **Rates** $289-$369 double. **Rooms** 543. **Credit** AmEx, Disc, MC, V. **Map** p326 H11 ❷
This 27-storey hotel has 543 rooms, including 40 sprawling suites that are bigger than many condos. Neutral colours and standard furnishings give guestrooms a tasteful yet generic feel; the bay windows provide impressive views of the skyline, river and Lake Michigan. A funky fountain and a textured wall hanging add some interest (albeit a somewhat dated aesthetic) to the public areas. The location is perfect for the restaurants of River North, but those who prefer to eat in are well served by the contemporary American fare in Great Street.
Bar. Business centre. Concierge. Disabled-adapted rooms. Gym. Internet (free wireless in public spaces; $9.95/day via cable in rooms). Parking ($45/day). Pool. Restaurants (2). Room service. Spa. TV (pay movies).

Swissôtel
323 E Wacker Drive, at N Columbus Drive, IL 60601 (1-800 654 7263/1-312 565 0565/ www.chicago.swissotel.com). El: Brown, Green, Orange, Pink or Purple to State/Lake; Red to Lake. **Rates** $189-$389 double. **Rooms** 632. **Credit** AmEx, Disc, MC, V. **Map** p326 J11 ❸
Though not as Swiss as it once was (it's now owned by the Raffles group of Singapore), this outpost of the global chain still offers up European-style

breakfasts in Geneva, its breakfast-only eaterie, as well as cheese and chocolate fondue in the lobby. Otherwise, the hotel is a high-tech operation, from the ergonomically designed furniture to the 42nd-floor fitness spa offering jaw-dropping lake views. Even the building is modern: the hotel occupies a triangular glass high-rise. If you're planning to host a gathering with 2,000 of your closest friends, check out the hotel's most recent addition: a 30,000sq ft events centre.
Bar. Business centre. Concierge. Disabled-adapted rooms. Gym ($15/day). Internet (wireless and cable, $9.95/day). Parking ($49/day). Pool (indoor). Restaurants (2). Room service. TV (pay movies).

Expensive

Hard Rock Hotel
230 N Michigan Avenue, at E South Water Street, Chicago, IL 60601 (1-866 966 5166/1-312 345 1000/www.hardrock.com). El: Brown, Green, Orange, Pink or Purple to State/Lake; Red to Lake. **Rates** $149-$409 double. **Rooms** 379. **Credit** AmEx, Disc, MC, V. **Map** p325 J11 ❹
The Hard Rock delivers the company's expected blend of upscale hotel chic and baby boomer-friendly rock 'n' roll graverobbing, with an unexpected side order of hipster-pleasing trendiness in the Base Bar. The rooms are slick and appealing, if expensive; customers are a democratic mix of business travellers and weekending style mavens. Despite the modernity, the hotel does have strong ties to the city's past: it's housed within the Carbon & Carbide Building, an art deco landmark built in 1929 by the sons of Daniel Burnham. The building's exterior colours, so the story goes, are designed to mimic a dark green champagne bottle with gold foil.
Bar. Business centre. Concierge. Disabled-adapted rooms. Gym. Internet (wireless, free). Parking ($46/day). Restaurants (2). Room service. TV (DVD, pay movies).

CONSUME

The Chain Gang

Hotel chains with additional branches around Chicagoland.

EXPENSIVE & MODERATE
Hilton 1-800 445 8667/www.hilton.com.
Hyatt 1-888 591 1234/www.hyatt.com.
Marriott 1-888 236 2427/ www.marriott.com.
Radisson 1-888 201 1718/ www.radisson.com.
Ramada 1-800 272 6232/ www.ramada.com.
Sheraton 1-800 325 3535/ www.starwoodhotels.com.

BUDGET
Best Western 1-800 780 7234/ www.bestwestern.com.
Comfort Inn 1-877 424 6423/ www.comfortinn.com.
Holiday Inn 1-800 465 4329/ www.holidayinn.com.
Motel 6 1-800 466 8356/ www.motel6.com.
Travelodge 1-800 578 7878/ www.travelodge.com.

Hotel Allegro.

Hotel Allegro

171 W Randolph Street, at N LaSalle Street, IL 60601 (1-800 643 1500/1-312 236 0123/ www.allegrochicago.com). El: Blue, Brown, Green, Orange, Pink or Purple to Clark; Red to Lake. **Rates** $179-$299 double. **Rooms** 483. **Credit** AmEx, Disc, MC, V. **Map** p325 H12 ❺

One of three Kimpton hotels in the Loop (the others are the Monaco and the Burnham; *see below*), the Allegro benefited from a renovation in 2008-09, adding a handsome new sign and sprucing up the rooms with the firm's trademark blend of modernity and faintly retro chic. As at the other hotels in the chain, guests enjoy a daily wine hour in the lobby (5-6pm) and an in-room yoga channel; staff are both charming and well-drilled. 312 Chicago offers Italian-American specialities, with Encore Lunch Club & Liquid Lounge dealing in food and cocktails.
Bar. Business centre. Concierge. Disabled-adapted rooms. Gym. Internet (wireless, free). Parking ($45 self, $49 valet/day). Restaurant (2). Room service. TV (DVD, pay movies).

★ Hotel Blake

500 S Dearborn Street, at E Congress Parkway, IL 60605 (1-312 986 1234/www.hotelblake.com). El: Blue or Red to Jackson; Brown, Green, Orange, Pink or Purple to Library. **Rates** $169-$449 double, $650-$1,200 suite . **Rooms** 162. **Credit** AmEx, Disc, MC, V. **Map** p325 H13 ❻

Housed in the recently renovated former 19th-century headquarters of the Morton Salt Company in the heart of Printers Row, the Blake has a historic exterior that belies the chic, contemporary digs that lie within its walls. The 162 spacious rooms have retained their crown moulding but have otherwise been brought gently up to date with casually handsome furnishings and hi-tech fittings. A 24-hour complimentary business centre and fitness room are other attractions; the upmarket, carnivore-focused Custom House (*see p146*) provides sustenance.
Bar. Business centre. Concierge. Disabled-adapted rooms. Gym. Internet (wireless, free). Parking ($39/day). Restaurant. Room service. TV (pay movies).

★ Hotel Burnham

1 W Washington Street, at N State Street, IL 60602 (1-877 294 9712/1-312 782 1111/ www.burnhamhotel.com). El: Blue to Washington; Brown, Green, Orange, Pink or Purple to Randolph/Wabash; Red to Lake. **Rates** $199-$299 double. **Rooms** 122. **Credit** AmEx, Disc, MC, V. **Map** p325 H12 ❼

This architectural treasure morphed several years ago from the Reliance Building into the Hotel Burnham, named in honour of the architect whose firm created it. The restoration job was beautiful (this is a National Historic Landmark, after all), but it didn't leave the building stuck in the 19th century: the Kimpton Group has brought its usual exuberance to the design of the guestrooms and suites, doing them out with rich indigo blue and gold fabrics mixed with mischievous cherubs and musical figures. Grab a sidewalk table for some tasty fare at Café Atwood, above-par as these things go.
Bar. Business centre. Concierge. Disabled-adapted rooms. Gym. Internet (wireless, free). Parking ($42/day). Restaurant. Room service. TV (pay movies).

Hotel Monaco

225 N Wabash Avenue, at E Wacker Drive, IL 60601 (1-866 610 0081/1-312 960 8500/ www.monaco-chicago.com). El: Brown, Green, Orange, Pink or Purple to State/Lake; Red to Lake. **Rates** $199-$299 double. **Rooms** 192. **Credit** AmEx, Disc, MC, V. **Map** p325 H11 ❽

Its facilities and location have made it popular with business travellers, but this funky Kimpton hotel rewards those who are just here to relax. Guests let go of their stress with the help of free chair massages and wine, served nightly around a limestone fireplace in the lobby. Serenity also beckons in the 192 stylishly decorated rooms, where windowsills filled with plush pillows are referred to as 'meditation stations'. Another nice gimmick: guests are offered a 'pet' goldfish for the duration of their stay. The South Water Kitchen dishes up comfort food.
Bar. Business centre. Concierge. Disabled-adapted rooms. Gym. Internet (wireless, free). Parking ($40/day). Restaurant. Room service. TV (pay movies).

…And, Relax

Hotel spas offer plenty of ways to forget your cares and worries… at a price.

There's luxury. And then there's the sort of sybaritic unlocking of your body's stress centres that you'll enjoy at Chicago's best spas, many of which are inside hotels…

It's no surprise that the sprawling **Spa at Trump Chicago** (*see p135*) has raised the bar for pampering in Chicago. High-rollers will want to book a 90-minute Gem Stone service, during which you'll be massaged with a sapphire-, ruby- or diamond-infused organic oil. Signature-service guests are greeted by a personal concierge who oversees every moment of their visit. Book a 60-minute service and you'll get free access to the Trump's gym, which offers amazing views over the city.

The Trump isn't the only place charging a pretty penny: facials and massages at the **Palmer House Hilton**'s **Spa Chakra** (*see p131*) start at $210. However, the steep prices include the cost of a 15-minute footbath, built-in gratuities and a make-up refresher in the salon. The spa specialises in massages that pair essential oils with massage techniques; for instance, the Indian version incorporates a blend of spices, cedar oil and elemi aromatic extract with ayurvedic body-treatment techniques.

The **James**'s **Spa by Asha** (pictured; *see p138*) encourage guests to come early so they can enjoy an aromatherapy foot bath in the dimly lit lounge. While you soak your peds, a therapist will wrap a heated pillow around your neck and massage your feet and calves. The pretreatment ritual is so relaxing, it's almost a buzz-kill to have to get up for your scheduled service. Almost.

The **Fairmont Chicago**'s **mySpa** (*see p126*) also has a taste for aromatherapy. The chi-chi AromaHarmony massage uses seven scented oils to balance your chakras and energise your body. When you're done being rubbed and oiled, you can count on walking out looking as good as you feel; employees in the dressing room offer quick, complimentary make-up touch-ups.

Bliss at the **W Chicago City Center** (*see p131*) is a spa in the sky with 16 treatment rooms, four movie-while-you-manicure stations with DVD players and a full slate of massage, nail and body treatments. Try the signature triple layer oxygen facial, said to clean, calm, hydrate and illuminate. Sure, prices are as lofty as the lake views, but how often can you say you had your feet filed with a diamond dust-covered paddle?

CONSUME

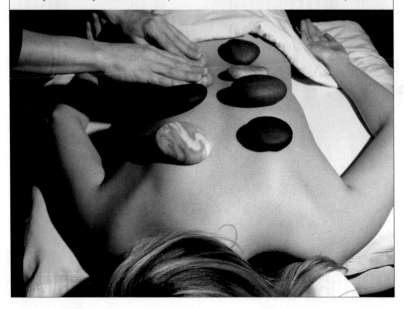

Discover the city from your back pocket

Essential for your weekend break, 25 top cities available.

POCKET SIZED *from* £6.99 / $11.95

Palmer House Hilton.

CONSUME

Hotel 71

71 E Wacker Drive, between N Wabash & N Michigan Avenues, IL 60601 (1-312 346 7100/ www.hotel71.com). El: Brown, Green, Orange, Pink or Purple to State/Lake; Red to Lake. **Rates** $159-$279 double. **Rooms** 307. **Credit** AmEx, Disc, MC, V. **Map** p325 J11 ❾

With more than 300 rooms, this isn't quite the 'boutique hotel' advertised on the website, but it's still a handsome place. Hotel 71 is housed in a newish skyscraper, and it shows: the rooms are a very generous size, and modern amenities abound. The decor is also modern, but not belligerently so: the colours are muted and the furniture is comfortable. The hotel overlooks the river; views from some of the rooms offer low-key panoramas of the city. There's no restaurant or bar, but there are options nearby. *Business centre. Concierge. Disabled-adapted rooms. Gym. Internet (wireless, free). Parking ($43/day). Room service. TV (pay movies).*

Palmer House Hilton

17 E Monroe Street, at S State Street, IL 60603 (1-800 445 8667/1-312 726 7500/www.hilton. com). El: Blue or Red to Monroe; Brown, Green, Orange, Pink or Purple to Madison/Wabash. **Rates** $159-$279 double. **Rooms** 1,639. **Credit** AmEx, Disc, MC, V. **Map** p325 J12 ❿

The Palmer House burned to the ground in the fire of 1871 just two weeks after opening. Undaunted, Potter Palmer rebuilt the place; it was back in business by 1873, and is now the longest continuously operating hotel in America. After a regeneration, the opulent Beaux Arts lobby remains a showpiece, with frescoes worthy of a museum, a ceiling by 19th-century muralist Louis Pierre Rigal and some

tremendous people-watching. The smallish standard rooms can't compete but they're in good shape. *Bar. Business centre. Concierge. Disabled-adapted rooms. Gym. Internet (wireless, $14.99/day). Parking ($35 self, $51 valet/day). Pool (indoor). Restaurant. Room service. Spa. TV (pay movies).*

★ TheWit

201 N State Street, at E Lake Street, IL 60601 (1-312 467 0200/www.thewithotel.com). El: Brown, Green, Orange, Pink or Purple to State/Lake; Red to Lake. **Rates** $199-$349 double. **Rooms** 298. **Credit** AmEx, Disc, MC, V. **Map** p325 H12 ⓫

TheWit falls under the Doubletree umbrella, but don't be fooled by its corporate identity: this is one of the city's most dynamic new hotels. The drama starts in the airy open-plan lobby; from the covetable tables directly above the front desk, you can peek at the trains running around the Loop. The rooms are attractive and modern, decorated with playful touches and high-tech amenities (HDTVs, all-modcon internet connectivity, touch-screen phones). Best of all are the views from the vast glass windows in all rooms – from some corner suites and the spectacular 27th-floor Roof lounge, you can see both the lake and the river. Recommended. *Bars (2). Business centre. Concierge. Disabled-adapted rooms. Gym. Internet (wireless & cable, $9.95-$18.95/day). Parking ($45). Restaurants (2). Room service. Spa. TV (pay movies).*

W Chicago City Center

172 W Adams Street, between S LaSalle & S Wells Streets, IL 60603 (1-877 946 8357/1-312 332 1200/www.starwoodhotels.com). El: Brown, Orange, Pink or Purple to Quincy/Wells. **Rates**

$239-$629 double. **Rooms** 369. **Credit** AmEx, Disc, MC, V. **Map** p325 H12 ⑫

One glance at the glam, two-storey lobby inside this Beaux Arts building, and it's obvious that this is a see-and-be-seen kind of setting. Cocktail waitresses in short black skirts serve seasonal drinks to guests lounging at white leather banquettes beneath spinning disco balls, while a DJ provides an upbeat loungey soundtrack. Renovations have left the hotel with a new lighter look – floating beds draped with faux fur throws, crisp white linens and tasteful pops of colour. Although this W lacks the heavenly day spa Bliss, guests still get a taste of spa-like pampering thanks to Bliss products in the bathroom.

Bar. Business centre. Concierge. Disabled-adapted rooms. Gym. Internet (wireless, $14.95/day). Parking ($51/day). Restaurant. Room service. TV (DVD, pay movies).

Moderate

Central Loop Hotel

111 W Adams Street, at S Clark Street, IL 60603 (1-866 744 2333/1-312 601 3525/ www.centralloophotel.com). El: Blue to Monroe. **Rates** $89-$259 double. **Rooms** 108. **Credit** AmEx, Disc, MC, V. **Map** p325 H12 ⑬

Tucked away above the Elephant & Castle pub-restaurant, this slightly unusual operation lacks the high-concept design-school charisma that defines many of its nearby competitors. However, it's a tidy little spot, and the price is most definitely right. It's basically a business hotel: frills are at a premium (the rooms are smallish, for instance, as are the TVs and the bathrooms), but everything is kept in perfect condition, all the rooms have desks, wireless is free (as is laundry) and the rates are very much on the low side for the locale. Worth considering.

Bar. Business centre. Concierge. Disabled-adapted rooms. Gym. Internet (wireless and cable, free). Parking ($20 self, $30 valet/day). Restaurant. Room service. TV (pay movies).

Silversmith

10 S Wabash Drive, at E Madison Street, IL 60603 (1-877 227 6963/1-312 372 7696/ www.silversmithchicagohotel.com). El: Blue or Red to Monroe; Brown, Green, Orange, Pink or Purple to Madison/Wabash. **Rates** $169-$309 double. **Rooms** 143. **Credit** AmEx, Disc, MC, V. **Map** p305 H12 ⑭

This 143-room hotel on Jewelers Row was operated by the Crowne Plaza group until relatively recently, and its rather weary design aesthetic is still very much in evidence through the property. The building's exterior is handsomely clad in dark green, highly glazed terracotta, and was built to house silversmiths (hence the name) and jewellers. Inside, though, it's all a bit grey, the olives and browns in the decor not enhanced by the lack of natural light in many of the rooms.

Bar. Business centre. Concierge. Disabled-adapted rooms. Gym. Internet (cable, free). Parking ($42/day). Restaurant. Room service. TV (pay movies).

The South Loop & Chinatown

THE SOUTH LOOP

Expensive

★ Blackstone

636 S Michigan Avenue, at E Balbo Avenue, IL 60605 (1-800 468 3571/1-312 447 0955/ www.blackstonerenaissance.com). El: Red to Harrison. **Rates** $199-$449 double; $1,500-$3,500 suite. **Rooms**: 332. **Credit** AmEx, Disc, MC, V. **Map** p325 J13 ⑮

Built a century ago, this hotel was one of the grandest in Chicago for years. By the late 1990s, it had collapsed into decrepitude, but the Marriott group embarked on a comprehensive and ultimately very successful programme of renovations that reimagined the hotel's former glory for a 21st-century audience. The rooms are capacious and modern, but not inappropriately so, and the luxury is tastefully done throughout. The beautiful, antique-packed suite 915 is a little different from the others: this is the 'smoke-filled room' of US political legend, where a group of senators met in secret to settle on the nomination of Warren Harding as president. There are plenty of nods to history elsewhere in the building (check out the artworks on the wall), but the Mercat de la Planxa restaurant is resolutely modern.

Bar. Business centre. Concierge. Disabled-adapted rooms. Internet (wireless, $13/day). Parking ($47/day). Restaurant. Room service. TV (pay movies).

Hilton Chicago

720 S Michigan Avenue, at E Balbo Drive, IL 60605 (1-800 445 8667/1-312 922 4400/ www.chicagohilton.com). El: Red to Harrison. **Rates** $179-$429 double. **Rooms** 1,544. **Credit** AmEx, Disc, MC, V. **Map** p325 J13 ⑯

Back in 1927, the Stevens was the largest hotel in the world. Although it's gone through countless changes since then, not least in its name, it remains something of a beast. The vast public spaces are decorated with fine art, flowers and plush carpets; an 'executive' level in the tower has its own check-in and levels of pampering consistent with the prices. Thanks to a staff exchange programme with Ireland, its pub, Kitty O'Shea's, has at least a hint of authenticity. A free shuttle runs to the Magnificent Mile.

Bars (2). Business centre. Concierge. Disabled-adapted rooms. Gym ($18/day). Internet (wireless,

CONSUME

Blackstone.

$19.99/day; $7.50/hour). Parking ($43 self, $50 valet/day). Pool (indoor). Restaurants (2). Room service. Spa. TV (pay movies).

Budget

Essex Inn
800 S Michigan Avenue, at E 8th Street, IL 60605 (1-800 621 6909/1-312 939 2800/ www.essexinn.com). El: Red to Harrison. **Rates** $99-$279 double. **Rooms** 254. **Credit** AmEx, Disc, MC, V. **Map** p324 J14 ⑰
The 1999 makeover of this '70s-style hotel, located in the shadow of the hulking Hilton, has placed it squarely in the 'best buy' category, although neither the bland interior nor the unbecoming frontage are likely to win any design awards. The Savoy Bar & Grill offers a full menu, and the hotel shuttles guests free of charge to the Magnificent Mile. But the key attraction here is the wonderful indoor pool with a retractable glass roof, offering million-dollar views of Lake Michigan, Museum Campus and Soldier Field.
Bar. Business centre. Concierge. Disabled-adapted rooms. Gym. Internet (wireless, $5.95/day). Parking ($37 valet/day). Pool (indoor). Restaurant. Room service. TV.

CHINATOWN & AROUND

Expensive

Wheeler Mansion
2020 S Calumet Avenue, at E Cullerton Street, IL 60616 (1-312 945 2020/www.wheeler mansion.com). El: Red to Cermak-Chinatown. **Rates** $235-$265 double. **Credit** AmEx, Disc, MC, V. **Map** p324 J16 ⑱

One of the few mansions to survive the Chicago Fire, the Wheeler is typical of the elegant domiciles that once housed the city's elite. Built in 1870 for Calvin T Wheeler, the president of the Chicago Board of Trade, this opulent mansion had fallen on hard times and was slated to become a parking lot until preservationists snapped it up in 1999 and turned it into a classy B&B. A five-minute walk from McCormick Place, the 11-room inn is an intimate alternative to convention-centre lodging. Daily gourmet breakfasts and turn-down service are included, along with Egyptian cotton linens and robes.
Concierge. Internet (cable, $14.99/day). Parking (free). TV.

Moderate

Hyatt Regency McCormick Place
2233 S Martin Luther King Drive, at E Cermak Road, IL 60616 (1-800 633 7313/1-312 567 1234/http://mccormickplace.hyatt.com). El: Red to Cermak-Chinatown. **Rates** $150-$400 double. **Rooms** 800. **Credit** AmEx, Disc, MC, V.
The only hotel adjoining McCormick Place, this Hyatt offers 800 rooms to convention-going patrons. The convenience to conventioneers is obvious; while the hotel is a bit removed from the city, prices are fair. Chinatown is a short taxi ride away, and an hourly shuttle is available for downtown access. Although the Cermak-Chinatown El train stop looks close, it's not an enjoyable walk, especially at night.
There's a more central Hyatt Regency in the Loop, with a massive 2,019 rooms (151 E Wacker Drive, at N Michigan Avenue, 1-800 233 1234, 1-312 565 1234).
Bar. Business centre. Concierge. Disabled-adapted rooms. Gym. Internet (cable, $9.95/day). Parking ($27 self, $38 valet/day). Pool (indoor). Restaurant. Room service. TV (pay movies).

CONSUME

Airline flights are one of the biggest producers of the global warming gas CO_2. But with **The CarbonNeutral Company** you can make your travel a little greener.

Go to **www.carbonneutral.com** to calculate your flight emissions then 'neutralise' them through international projects which save exactly the same amount of carbon dioxide.

Contact us at **shop@carbonneutral.com** or call into the office on **0870 199 99 88** for more details.

CarbonNeutral®flights

The Near North Side

RIVER NORTH

Deluxe

★ Trump Chicago

401 N Wabash Avenue, between Kinzie & Hubbard Streets, IL 60611 (1-877 458 7867/ 1-312 588 8000/www.trumpchicagohotel.com). El: Red to Grand. **Rates** *from $310 double; from $675 suite.* **Rooms** 339. **Credit** AmEx, Disc, MC, V. **Map** p326 H11 ⑲

The Donald originally hoped that his first Chicago skyscraper would be the world's tallest building. A post-9/11 change of plan has capped the design at a more manageable height, but it's still a dominant sight along the Chicago River. The hotel is every bit as luxurious as you'd expect from a Trump property, with all mod cons present and correct in the rooms, but it's perhaps a little more understated. The rooms, the bar and the 16th-floor restaurant (*see p155*) are all fairly sober. Still, given the often-amazing views, they don't need to be showy. The gym has panoramic views over the city; there's also a lovely spa.

Bar (2). Concierge. Disabled-adapted rooms. Gym. Internet (wireless, free). Parking ($42/day). Pool (indoor). Restaurant. Room service. Spa. TV (DVD, pay movies).

Expensive

Amalfi Hotel

20 W Kinzie Street, at N State Street, IL 60610 (1-877 262 5341/1-312 395 9000/www. amalfihotelchicago.com). El: Red to Grand. **Rates** $209-$409 double. **Rooms** 215. **Credit** AmEx, Disc, MC, V. **Map** p325 H11 ⑳

The 215-room Amalfi Hotel welcomes guests by sitting them down at an individual check-in desk with what it grandly calls an 'experience designer', who might suggest a complimentary Amalfitini cocktail in the Ravello lounge. Pretensions aside, staff do load your visit with plenty of value-added amenities, such as free high-speed internet access, no annoying extras for local calls, and a nightly reception with complimentary drinks. The Amalfi also delivers on comfort, with fine Egyptian cotton sheets, pillow-top mattresses, plush terry robes and even slippers.

Business centre. Concierge. Disabled-adapted rooms. Gym. Internet (wireless, free). Parking ($43/day). Room service. TV (DVD).

Dana

660 N State Street, at W Erie Street, IL 60654 (1-888 301 3262/1-312 202 6000/www. danahotelandspa.com). El: Red to Chicago. **Rates** $245-$495 double. **Rooms** 216. **Credit** AmEx, Disc, MC, V. **Map** p326 H10 ㉑

This new-build hotel opened in 2008, offering res-olutely up-to-the-minute facilities leavened with a little quasi-spiritual attitude (the hotel literature suggests that its name translates from Sanskrit as 'the pleasure of giving'). The rooms aren't huge but they are appealing, crisp modern decor set off by enor-mous TVs, glass-walled bathrooms (with fantasti-cally powerful showers) and, higher up, great views. The hotel is topped by the Vertigo lounge, which occasionally hosts DJs; the restaurant downstairs is an unlikely mix of steakhouse and sushi bar. Further appeal is provided at a handsome spa. *Photo p136.*

CONSUME

Trump Chicago.

Dana. *See p135.*

Bars (2). Gym. Internet (wireless and cable, free). Parking ($38/day). Restaurant. Spa. TV (pay movies).

★ Hotel Felix
111 W Huron Street, at N Clark Street, IL 60654 (1-877 848 4040/1-312 447 3440/ www.hotelfelixchicago.com). El: Red to Chicago. **Rates** $169-$229 double. **Rooms** 225. **Credit** AmEx, Disc, MC, V. **Map** p326 H11 ㉒

The Felix opened in 2009, bringing a green sensibility to a building that opened in 1926 but had fallen on hard times. The structure's exterior remains from the old school; inside, though, it's all change, from the low-key lobby (highlighted by a handsome water feature and a fireplace) to the hotel's own spa and the crisp and appealing guestrooms. Environmental friendliness covers the water-saving showers, but doesn't preclude against modern convenience: there's free wireless everywhere.

Bar Business centre. Concierge. Disabled-adapted rooms. Gym. Internet (wireless and cable, free). Parking ($32-$42/day). Restaurant. Room service. Spa. TV (pay movies).

Hotel Sax
333 N Dearborn Street, at W Carroll Avenue, IL 60610 (1-877-569-3742/1-312 245 0333/ www.hotelsaxchicago.com). El: Red to Grand. **Rates** $200-$350 double. **Rooms** 353. **Credit** AmEx, Disc, MC, V. **Map** p326 H11 ㉓

Familiar to previous visitors as the House of Blues, this hotel, in the shadow of the Marina City towers, has been reinvented with a new but still faintly musical name. (The House of Blues music venue, incidentally, remains open; *see p260*.) The

renovation has toned down some of the HoB's garish colour schemes, especially in the rooms, which are an appealing mix of light and dark shades supplemented by the obligatory flatscreen TVs and other high-tech modern amenities. Set back from the rather awkward lobby is the Crimson Lounge, a multi-purpose bar-restaurant-club; more unusual is the Studio, a Microsoft-branded electronic games room.

Bar. Business centre. Concierge. Disabled-adapted rooms. Gym. Internet (wireless, free). Parking ($42/day). Restaurant. Room service. TV (pay movies).

Moderate

Comfort Inn & Suites Downtown
15 E Ohio Street, between N State & N Wabash Streets, IL 60611 (1-888 775 9223/1-312 894 0900/www.chicagocomfortinn.com). El: Red to Grand. **Rates** $179-$249 double. **Rooms** 130. **Credit** AmEx, Disc, MC, V. **Map** p326 H10 ㉔

Fashioned from a gutted transients' hotel, this branch of the Comfort Inn chain retains many original 1920s art deco elements. A shabby-chic lobby features a cheerful gas fireplace and a mahogany Tudor-style beamed ceiling, with hot orange accents to brighten up the woodwork. The rooms aren't as interesting but they're in decent shape.

Concierge. Disabled-adapted rooms. Gym. Internet (cable, free). Parking ($25/day). TV (pay movies).

Hampton Inn & Suites
33 W Illinois Street, at N Dearborn Street, IL 60610 (1-800 426 7866/1-312 832 0330/

*www.hamptoninnchicago.com). El: Red
to Grand.* **Rates** $169-$350 double.
Rooms 232. **Credit** AmEx, Disc, MC, V.
Map p326 H11 ㉕

Yet another chain-affiliated hotel striving for individuality. Built in 1998, this 230-room property is
mindful of Chicago's architectural heritage; the
Prairie-style touches are deliberately reminiscent
of Frank Lloyd Wright. Guests are treated to
displays of artefacts from historic buildings, such
as a stair stringer from Adler and Sullivan's
Chicago Stock Exchange building. The guestrooms
look exactly the same as those in pretty much any
other Hampton Inn.
*Business centre. Concierge. Disabled-adapted
rooms. Gym. Internet (wireless, free). Parking
($42/day). Pool (indoor). Room service.
Restaurants (2). TV (pay movies).*

Hilton Garden Inn

*10 E Grand Avenue, at N State Street, IL
60611 (1-800 445 8667/1-312 595 0000/
www.chicagodowntownnorth.gardeninn.com).
El: Red to Grand.* **Rates** $109-$379 double.
Rooms 357. **Credit** AmEx, Disc, MC, V.
Map p326 H10 ㉖

North America's largest Hilton Garden Inn offers
spacious if colourless guestrooms at prices that are
pretty low for the area. All the rooms have refriger-
ators and microwaves, and a 24-hour pantry in the
lobby stocks microwaveable cuisine if you can't be
bothered to leave the building. The hotel offers
complimentary access to the nearby Crunch Fitness
club. In a word? Reliable.

There's also a Hilton Suites in the shadow of the
John Hancock Center on the Gold Coast (198 E
Delaware Place, at N Mies van der Rohe Way, 1-800
445 8667, 1-312 664 1100).
*Bar. Business centre. Disabled-adapted rooms.
Gym. Internet (cable, free). Parking ($29 self,
$44 valet/day). Pool (indoor). Restaurant.
Room service.*

Budget

Ohio House

*600 N LaSalle Street, at W Ontario Street,
IL 60610 (1-866 601 6446/1-312 943 6000/
www.ohiohousemotel.com). El: Red to Grand.*
Rates $109-$129 double. **Rooms** 50. **Credit**
AmEx, Disc, MC, V. **Map** p326 H10 ㉗

This timeworn motel seems straight from a 1960s
movie set, offering no-frills rooms at budget rates in
a desirable location. Penny pinchers will appreciate
the coffee shop, which offers mammoth breakfasts
(two each of eggs, pancakes, bacon and sausages)
for a few bucks. A large room above the office – the
management calls it a 'suite' – includes a refrigera-
tor, microwave and sleeper sofa, and could conceivably hold a family of five or six.
Internet (wireless, $9.99/day). Parking (free).

THE MAGNIFICENT MILE & STREETERVILLE

Deluxe

Omni Chicago

*676 N Michigan Avenue, at E Huron Street, IL
60611 (1-800 843 6664/1-312 944 6664/www.
omnihotels.com). El: Red to Chicago.* **Rates** $229-
$899 suite. **Rooms** 347. **Credit** AmEx, Disc, MC,
V. **Map** p326 J10 ㉘

This 347-suite property is apparently favoured by
Oprah when she needs somewhere to house her talk-
show guests. Guests can choose from a variety of
spacious suites, some of which come with stow-
away treadmills, a 'get fit kit' and a refreshment centre stocked with healthy snacks; all come with plush
robes, plasma TVs, wet bars and, a true rarity, windows that open. Sun worshippers can take advantage of two fifth-floor sundecks. The 676 restaurant
and bar serves Northern Italian and American food.
*Bar. Business centre. Concierge. Disabled-adapted
rooms. Gym. Internet (wireless, free). Parking
($48/day). Pool (indoor). Restaurant. Room
service. Spa. TV (DVD, pay movies).*

Park Hyatt Chicago

*800 N Michigan Avenue, at W Chicago Avenue,
IL 60611 (1-800 778 7477/1-312 335 1234/
www.parkchicago.hyatt.com). El: Red to Chicago.*
Rates $345-$545 double. **Rooms** 198. **Credit**
AmEx, Disc, MC, V. **Map** p326 J10 ㉙

Little expense has been spared at this 198-room
Magnificent Mile property, housed in the lower third
of a slender, 67-storey residential tower. High-tech
to the core, guestrooms have DVD players, flat-
screen LCD televisions and iPod connectivity, along
with black leather Eames chairs and 300-thread-
count linens. NoMI's garden terrace is a happening
place on summer nights; at other times, the lounge
is an ideal spot to rub Rolexes with the out-crowd.
*Bar. Business centre. Concierge. Disabled-adapted
rooms. Gym. Internet (wireless, free). Parking
($45/day). Pool (indoor). Restaurant. Room
service. Spa. TV (DVD, pay movies).*

★ Peninsula Chicago

*108 E Superior Street, at N Michigan Avenue, IL
60611 (1-866 288 8889/1-312 337 2888/www.
chicago.peninsula.com). El: Red to Chicago.*
Rates $475-$650 double. **Rooms** 339. **Credit**
AmEx, Disc, MC, V. **Map** p326 J10 ㉚

This swanky icon is less about gaudy frills than
extreme comfort. As you soak in a marble tub, you
may feel equally sybaritic. High-tech bedside control
panels mean guests don't need to get up to draw the
curtains or adjust the temperature. Afternoon tea in
the sun-drenched lobby is a refined treat; the G&T
brigade gathers nightly around the fireplaces in the
bar. Grab dim sum at Shanghai Terrace (*see p156*),
a modern version of a 1930s Shanghai supper club.

CONSUME

Bar. Business centre. Concierge. Disabled-adapted rooms. Gym. Internet (wireless, free). Parking ($49/day). Pool (indoor). Restaurants (4). Room service. Spa. TV (DVD, pay movies).

Expensive

★ Allerton
701 N Michigan Avenue, at E Huron Street, IL 60611 (1-877 701 8111/1-312 440 1500/www.theallertonhotel.com). El: Red to Chicago. **Rates** $105-$499 double. **Rooms** 443. **Credit** AmEx, Disc, MC, V. **Map** p326 J10 ③①
Travellers visiting Chicago after a long absence may be in for a serious bout of déjà vu upon catching sight of this historic 443-room hotel. Built in 1924 as Michigan Avenue's first high-rise, the hotel had its brickwork restored as part of a major refurbishment. The interior was also overhauled in 2008, lending a handsome new look to decor that had grown tired down the years. The hotel's famous 'Tip Tap Tap' sign still glows from its roof; it's a slight shame that neither the restaurant nor the lounge provide diversions, though neither take its name.
Bar. Business centre. Concierge. Disabled-adapted rooms. Gym. Internet (wireless, $9.95/day). Parking ($51/day). Restaurant. Room service. TV (DVD, pay movies).

Conrad Chicago
521 N Rush Street, at E Ohio Street, IL 60611 (1-800 266 7237/1-312 645 1500/ www.conradchicago.com). El: Red to Grand. **Rates** $255-$455 double. **Rooms** 411. **Credit** AmEx, Disc, MC, V. **Map** p326 J10 ③②
Shopaholics will appreciate the location of this 311-room, Hilton-operated player, perched above the Shops at North Bridge mall. Each guestroom is decked out with a 42-inch flat-screen TV, a state-of-the-art sound system and 500-thread-count Pratesi linens; guests get to choose their pillows from an extensive menu. In warm weather, kick back on the smart outdoor couches on the hotel's terrace, while sipping a cocktail or tucking into some tapas. Movies play in the background on Sunday nights.
Bars (2). Business centre. Concierge. Disabled-adapted rooms. Gym. Internet (wireless and cable, free). Parking ($32 self, $51 valet/day). Restaurants (3). Room service. TV (DVD, pay movies).

InterContinental Chicago
505 N Michigan Avenue, at E Grand Avenue, IL 60611 (1-800 972 2492/1-312 944 4100/ www.chicago.intercontinental.com). El: Red to Grand. **Rates** $189-$449 double. **Rooms** 792. **Credit** AmEx, Disc, MC, V. **Map** p326 J10 ③③
A dramatic four-storey rotunda greets guests entering this architectural showpiece, which started out in 1929 as the Medinah Athletic Club. The stock market crash put an end to its first incarnation (the

opulent pool, where Johnny Weissmuller trained, has survived), before the property reopened in 1944 as a hotel. But although it hangs on to its history, the hotel is constantly upgrading itself: witness the emergence of Eno, where patrons can indulge in flights of wine, cheese and chocolate. The 792 guestrooms are suitably luxurious.
Bars (2). Business centre. Concierge. Disabled-adapted rooms. Gym. Internet (wireless, $12.95/day). Parking ($53/day). Pool (indoor). Restaurant. Room service. TV (pay movies).

★ James Chicago
55 E Ontario Street, at N Rush Street, IL 60611 (1-877 526 3755/1-312 337 1000/ www.jameshotels.com). El: Red to Grand. **Rates** $239-$599 double. **Rooms** 297. **Credit** AmEx, Disc, MC, V. **Map** p326 H10 ③④
One of the most fashionable hotels in the city continues to draw the crowds several years after its opening: to Primehouse David Burke, its all-conquering steakhouse, and to the oft-buzzing J Bar, but also to the surprisingly capacious hotel side of the operation. The 297 sleek, fashionable rooms all come with large-screen TVs, stereo systems and good-sized bathrooms; the roll call of amenities is led by an impressive gym and spa. And all this just a block from Michigan Avenue.
Bars (2). Business centre. Concierge. Disabled-adapted rooms. Gym. Internet (wireless, free). Parking ($37 self, $50 valet/day). Restaurant. Room service. Spa. TV (DVD, pay movies).

Sheraton Chicago Hotel & Towers
301 E North Water Street, at N Columbus Drive, IL 60611 (1-877 242 2558/1-312 464 1000/www.sheratonchicago.com). El: Red to Grand. **Rates** $159-$379 double. **Rooms** 1,209. **Credit** AmEx, Disc, MC, V. **Map** p326 J11 ③⑤
This darling of the convention circuit is a behemoth, boasting 1,209 rooms and the largest hotel ballroom in the Midwest. An equally spacious lobby with imported marble and rich wood accents has huge picture windows overlooking the river, making it a sedate spot in which to sip a cup of coffee from the Java Bar. For something stronger, head to stylish Chibar, which has views of the Centennial Fountain that throws arcs of water across the river in summer. The aquatic theme continues with the lobby's quiet, perpetual waterfalls in black granite.
Bar. Business centre. Concierge. Disabled-adapted rooms. Gym. Internet (wireless, $12.95/day). Parking ($34 self, $48 valet/day). Pool (indoor). Restaurants (3). Room service. TV (pay movies).

W Chicago Lakeshore
644 N Lake Shore Drive, at E Ohio Street, IL 60611 (1-877 946 8357/1-312 943 9200/ www.starwoodhotels.com). El: Red to Grand. **Rates** $199-$499 double. **Rooms** 520. **Credit** AmEx, Disc, MC, V. **Map** p326 K10 ③⑥

The city's second W hotel has come a long way from its previous incarnation as a Days Inn. At these prices, so it should have. If you've stayed at a W before, the cool vibe and the sleek, casually expensive decor will be familiar. An indoor pool adjoins the outdoor sundeck, and the Bliss Spa provides pampering from head to toe. The Asian-influenced look has the young urban professional crowd swarming to both its lobby bar and lofty lounge. *Bars (2). Business centre. Concierge. Disabled-adapted rooms. Gym. Internet (wireless, $14.95/day). Parking ($48/day). Pool (indoor). Restaurant. Room service. Spa. TV (DVD, pay movies).*

Moderate

Courtyard by Marriott
165 E Ontario Street, at N St Clair Street, IL 60611 (1-800 321-2211/1-312 573 0800/ www.marriott.com). El: Red to Grand. **Rates** $199-$309 double. **Credit** AmEx, DC, Disc, MC, V. **Map** p326 J10 ③⑦

While other Streeterville hotels have been painstakingly renovated of late, this surprisingly sleek 24-storey property was recently built from scratch to recall the art deco style of 1930s Michigan Avenue. The lobby features warm crimsons and cherry wood accented with granite and brushed chrome, as well as a chandelier of fluted blown-glass tubes. Just off the lobby, Viand is a contemporary American brasserie with a friendly bar. *Bar. Business centre. Concierge. Disabled-adapted rooms. Gym. Internet (free via cable in rooms). Parking ($26 self, $36 valet/day). Pool. Restaurant. Room service.*

Doubletree
300 E Ohio Street, at N Fairbanks Court, IL 60611 (1-866 778 8536/1-312 787 6100/ www.doubletreemagmile.com). El: Red to Grand. **Rates** $159-$229 double. **Rooms** 500. **Credit** AmEx, Disc, MC, V. **Map** p326 J10 ③⑧

Guests who stayed in this hotel a few years ago when it was a Holiday Inn won't recognise the place since its makeover. Sure, the lobby still feels a tad dated, but noteworthy details – signature cookies on arrival, Neutrogena bath products, the Markethouse restaurant – compensate for the lack of style. Guests have access to the adjoining Lakeshore Athletic Club (for a fee), tennis courts and second-floor spa. During the warmer months, take the children out at night for an outdoor movie screening by the pool. *Bar. Business centre. Disabled-adapted rooms. Gym. Internet (cable, $9.95/day). Parking ($41/day). Pool. Restaurant. Room service. TV (pay movies).*

Embassy Suites Chicago Downtown Lakefront
511 N Columbus Drive, at E Ohio Street, IL 60611 (1-888 903 8884/1-312 836 5900/ www.chicagoembassy.com). El: Red to Grand. **Rates** $149-$429 suite. **Rooms** 455. **Credit** AmEx, Disc, MC, V. **Map** p326 J10 ③⑨

A signature atrium soaring 17 storeys high, lends a wide-open feel to this all-suites hotel. Room rates include cooked-to-order breakfasts and complimentary early-evening cocktails. You can stretch your budget further by taking advantage of the suite's tiny 'kitchen' (a mini-fridge and a microwave). During the week, the hotel is particularly popular with business travellers and those who oversee their expense accounts; on weekends, economy-minded families take over. There's a sister operation on State Street (no.600, at E Ohio Street, 1-800 362 1779, 1-312 943 3800). *Bar. Business centre. Concierge. Disabled-adapted rooms. Gym. Internet (wireless and cable, $14.95/day). Parking ($41 self, $49 valet/day). Pool (indoor). Restaurant. Room service. TV (pay movies).*

★ Inn of Chicago
162 E Ohio Street, at N St Clair Street, IL 60611 (1-800 557 2378/1-312 787 3100/ www.innofchicago.com). El: Red to Grand. **Rates** $179-$229 double. **Rooms** 360. **Credit** AmEx, Disc, MC, V. **Map** p326 J10 ④⓪

The dreary name belies a surprisingly handsome hotel – especially in the hip and loungey lobby, replete with chocolate brown and zebra print seating, gold forest-theme wallpaper and glass bead window embellishments. The 360 rooms don't offer many frills, but they do feel fresh and clean and feature a soothing, blue, green and brown colour scheme. Guests can work out for free in the small, stuffy fitness room; and handily there's free Wi-Fi in the lobby. *Bar. Business centre. Concierge. Disabled-adapted rooms. Gym. Internet (wireless, $9.95/day). Parking ($36 self, $41 valet/day). TV (pay movies).*

Red Roof Inn
162 E Ontario Street, at N St Clair Street, IL 60611 (1-800 733 7663/1-312 787 3580/ www.redroof-chicago-downtown.com). El: Red to Grand. **Rates** $79-$189 double. **Rooms** 195. **Credit** AmEx, Disc, MC, V. **Map** p326 J10 ④①

You'll usually find this economy lodging chain along the nation's highways or in the far-flung suburbs. But here's one in the heart of the city: just a block east of fashionable Boul Mich, and perhaps the only Red Roof Inn with chandeliers in the lobby. Renovated in 2001, the rooms are clean, comfortable, cheap and devoid of any individuality. Adjoining the hotel is the Coco Pazzo Café, a branch of the fine Coco Pazzo mini-chain. *Bar. Disabled-adapted rooms. Internet (wireless, $5.99/day). Parking ($36/day). Restaurant. TV (pay movies).*

CONSUME

THE GOLD COAST

Deluxe

Drake

*140 E Walton Place, at N Michigan Avenue,
IL 60611 (1-800 553 7253/1-312 787 2200/
www.thedrakehotel.com). El: Red to Chicago.*
Rates $209-$389 double. **Rooms** 532. **Credit**
AmEx, Disc, MC, V. **Map** *p326 J9* ⓐ

A traditional old-money stomping ground favoured
by Chicago socialites, this stately icon exudes old-
school style, with velvet seats in elevators, enormous
chandeliers and a spectacular flower arrangement in
the picturesque lobby. A stay in one of the guestrooms, which have been accommodating celebrities
and heads of state since 1920, feels a bit like crashing a rich aunt's downtown condo. Make a point of
meeting your ladies for high tea at the classic Palm
Court or take a worthy date for a martini at the Coq
d'Or downstairs; if you're lucky, you'll catch the slick
lounge singer exercising his vocal cords.

*Bars (4). Business centre. Concierge. Disabled-
adapted rooms. Gym. Internet (cable, $10/day).
Parking ($49 valet). Restaurants (4). Room
service. TV (pay movies).*

Four Seasons

*120 E Delaware Place, at N Michigan Avenue,
IL 60611 (1-800 332 3442/1-312 280 8800/
www.fourseasons.com). El: Red to Chicago.*
Rates $475-$675 double. **Rooms** 343. **Credit**
AmEx, Disc, MC, V. **Map** *p326 J9* ⓐ

You can practically smell the money at this opulent
hotel. The public spaces are decked out with Italian
marble, glittering crystal and exquisite woodwork;
rooms and suites come with classy furnishings,
high-end toiletries and twice-daily maid service.
Those in search of edibles and potables will find
ample refreshment at Seasons, a clubby cigar bar
and lounge with a companionable fireplace, a waterfall and views of the Magnificent Mile. The swimming pool is covered by a skylight and surrounded
by Romanesque columns.

*Bar. Business centre. Concierge. Disabled-
adapted rooms. Gym. Internet (wireless, free).
Parking ($33 self, $46 valet/day). Pool (indoor).
Restaurants (3). Room service. Spa. TV (DVD,
pay movies).*

Ritz-Carlton Chicago

*160 E Pearson Street, at N Michigan Avenue,
IL 60611 (1-800 621 6906/1-312 266 1000/
www.fourseasons.com/chicagorc). El: Red to
Chicago.* **Rates** $425-$625 double. **Rooms** 435.
Credit *AmEx, Disc, MC, V.* **Map** *p326* ⓐ

While the lavish lobby, with its gushing fountain
and massive skylight, takes on an ethereal quality,
granny-ish upholstered sofas and chairs lend a
slightly stuffy vibe (a facelift is on the way). Happily,
the 435 richly appointed rooms, which take up the

top 15 floors of Water Tower Place, look brand-
spanking-new after a recent renovation: leather-
lined cabinetry, modern graphic wallpaper, silk
chaise longues and more. Leave room in your toi-
letry case to snag some extra bottles of the
L'Occitane shower products. The Spa at the Carlton
Club offers more than 25 treatments.

*Bar. Business centre. Concierge. Disabled-
adapted rooms. Gym. Internet (wireless, free).
Parking ($35 self, $45 valet/day). Pool (indoor).
Restaurants (2). Room service. Spa. TV (DVD,
pay movies).*

Sofitel Chicago Water Tower

*20 E Chestnut Street, at N Wabash Avenue,
IL 60611 (1-877 813 7700/1-312 324 4000/
www.sofitel.com). El: Red to Chicago.* **Rates**
$195-$395 double. **Rooms** 415. **Credit** *AmEx,
Disc, MC, V.* **Map** *p326 H9* ⓐ

The radical prism-shaped design of this 32-storey
building by French architect Jean-Paul Viguier is a
striking addition to the Chicago skyline. The hotel
opened in a plum Gold Coast location in 2002, with
415 sleekly designed rooms featuring spacious marble bathrooms. As French as the croissants baked
daily on the premises, the Sofitel offers haute cuisine
in a cool, modern setting at the Café des Architectes.

*Bars (2). Business centre (2). Concierge. Disabled-
adapted rooms. Gym. Internet (wireless and cable,
$9.99/day). Parking ($47/day). Restaurant. Room
service. TV (pay movies).*

Expensive

★ Affinia

*166 E Superior Street, at N Michigan Avenue,
IL 60611 (1-866 233 4642/1-312 787 6000/
www.affinia.com). El: Red to Chicago.* **Rates**
$179-$359 double. **Rooms** 215. **Credit** *AmEx,
Disc, MC, V.* **Map** *p326 J10* ⓐ

The first Chicago hotel from the New York-based
Affinia chain is a neat and tidy reinvention of a formerly tired Streeterville operation named the
Fitzgerald. The generous-sized rooms and suites
come with a cultured look, dark carpets set off by
pleasing accessories and, in the bathroom, love-it-
or-hate-it shiny red wallpaper. At the top of the hotel
is C-View, a nice bar with an appealing open-air

INSIDE TRACK B&B BREAKS

Bed and breakfast is an increasingly
popular option in Chicago, especially
among travellers keen to avoid the big
downtown properties and their big
downtown prices. The **Chicago Bed &
Breakfast Association** (www.chicago-bed-
breakfast.com) has an online calendar of
availability at several B&Bs in the city.

Affinia.

deck; there's a restaurant just off the lobby. One other nice touch: in advance of their stay, guests can log on to myaffinia.com and make special room requests, covering everything from hypoallergenic pillows to fitness equipment.
Bars (2). Concierge. Disabled-adapted rooms. Gym. Internet (wireless, $9.95/day). Parking ($48/day). Restaurant. Room service. TV (DVD, pay movies).

Hotel Indigo
1244 N Dearborn Parkway, at W Goethe Street, IL 60610 (1-800 972 2494/1-312 787 4980/ www.ichotelsgroup.com). El: Red to Clark/ Division. **Rates** $159-$379 double. **Rooms** 165. **Credit** AmEx, Disc, MC, V. **Map** p327 H8 ❹
Original artwork from Chicago neo-Impressionist Bill Olendorf is the only remnant held over from the renovation of this 1929 hotel, formerly the Claridge. Whimsical wall murals, hardwood floors and a bold colour palette make for a refreshing change from standard hotel decor. The colourful, cheery tone is set by the inviting lobby, filled with well-stuffed chairs. The well-equipped fitness centre and window-front bar are further bonuses.
Bar. Business centre. Concierge. Disabled-adapted rooms. Gym. Internet (wireless, free). Parking ($37/day). Restaurant. Room service. Spa. TV (DVD, pay movies).

Millennium Knickerbocker
163 E Walton Place, at N Michigan Avenue, IL 60611 (1-866 866 8086/1-312 751 8100/

www.knickerbockerhotel.com). El: Red to Chicago.* **Rates** $209-$309 double. **Rooms** 306. **Credit** AmEx, Disc, MC, V. **Map** p326 J9 ❹
Formerly Hugh Hefner's Playboy Towers, this regal property now caters to a more refined crowd. Guests and locals fill the ruby-coloured velvet bar stools in the two-storey lobby bar, which features a pianist five nights a week. Even if you're not invited to the party, pop into the lobby-level ballroom to check out the lit-up dance floor beneath the dripping chandelier and gilded ceiling. Thanks to a recent refit, all the guestrooms come with a contemporary look in a warm, neutral palette with pops of pink, modern amenities and rainshower heads in the bathroom.
Bar. Business centre. Concierge. Disabled-adapted rooms. Gym. Internet (free wireless in public spaces; $9.95/day wireless in rooms). Parking ($49/day). Restaurant. Room service. TV (pay movies).

Raffaello
201 E Delaware Place, at N Seneca Street, IL 60611 (1-800 983 7870/1-312 943 5000/www.chicagoraffaello.com). El: Red to Chicago. **Rates** $229-$399 double. **Rooms** 175. **Credit** AmEx, Disc, MC, V. **Map** p326 J9 ❹
A $20-million renovation of this landmark building in Streeterville has improved things enormously. The old hotel was looking a bit tired by the time it closed in 2005; its replacement is rather more eye-catching. The opulent lobby has Mediterranean touches, and there's a hydroponic garden on the green roof. The spacious guestrooms come with 500-thread-count bedding.
Business centre. Disabled-adapted rooms. Gym. Internet (cable and wireless, $9.95/day). Parking ($23 self, $47 valet/day). Restaurant. Room service. Spa. TV (DVD).

Sutton Place
21 E Bellevue Place, at N Rush Street, IL 60611 (1-866 378 8866/1-312 266 2100/ www.suttonplace.com). El: Red to Clark/Division. **Rates** $179-$499 double. **Rooms** 246. **Credit** AmEx, MC, V. **Map** p326 H9 ❺
The classy detailing in this hotel, here since 1988 but still looking pretty sharp for its age, extends to each of the 246 guestrooms, appointed with DVD players, flat screen TVs, CD collections, deep-soaking tubs and fluffy robes. Six penthouse suites have floor-to-ceiling windows and their own private balconies, offering a great vantage point from which to spy on Gold Coasters as they shop away the day and party hard by night. Guests won't need to go far to party themselves: downstairs sits the Whiskey Bar & Grill.
Bars (2). Business centre. Concierge. Disabled-adapted rooms. Gym. Internet (wireless, $9.95/day). Parking ($45/day). Restaurant. Room service. TV (DVD, pay movies).

CONSUME

Talbott Hotel

20 E Delaware Place, at N Rush Street,
IL 60611 (1-800 825 2688/1-312 944 4970/
www.talbotthotel.com). El: Red to Chicago. **Rates**
$169-$499 double. **Credit** AmEx,
Disc, MC, V. **Map** p326 J9 ⑤

Quite possibly the only hotel in the world with a life-sized cow mounted on its frontage (a remnant of the city's bovine-themed public art display a few years back), this boutique hotel is reminiscent of a small, upmarket European inn. The classically furnished guestrooms (with canopied beds) and the granite and marble lobby were treated to a massive renovation in 2006. Guests get complimentary passes to a nearby health club.
Bar. Business centre. Concierge. Disabled-adapted rooms. Internet (wireless, free). Parking ($31 self, $48 valet/day). Restaurant. Room service. TV (DVD).

Westin

909 N Michigan Avenue, at E Delaware Place,
IL 60611 (1-800 228 3000/1-312 943 7200/
www.westin.com). El: Red to Chicago. **Rates**
$199-$439 double. **Rooms** 752. **Credit** AmEx,
Disc, MC, V. **Map** p326 J9 ⑤

Hotels are basically in the business of selling sleep. Acknowledging this, the nationwide Westin group equips its hotel rooms with what it calls the Heavenly Bed, designed to encourage zzzzs. By and large, it lives up to its name. The 752 guestrooms include 23 suites. Steaks and seafood are served up in the 300-seat Grill on the Alley. The other Westin in Chicago, the **Westin River North** (320 N Dearborn Street, 1-800 937 8461, 1-312 744 1900), offers more of the same.
Bar. Business centre. Concierge. Disabled-adapted rooms. Gym. Internet (free wireless in public spaces; $12.95 wireless and via cable in rooms). Parking ($49/day). Room service. TV.

Moderate

Gold Coast Guest House

113 W Elm Street, at N Clark Street, IL 60610
(1-312 337 0361/www.bbchicago.com). El: Red to
Clark/Division. **Rates** $119-$219 double. **Rooms**
4. **Credit** AmEx, Disc, MC, V. **Map** p326 H9 ⑤

Housed in a 19th-century Victorian townhouse (built just after the Great Fire had ravaged the town), this B&B is a welcome oasis of good-value accommodation in a swanky neighbourhood. Sally, the friendly owner, is happy to chat with guests over a glass of wine in the lush garden. Be sure to book ahead, as there are only four guestrooms. Guests looking for more privacy and longer stays should ask about Sally's nearby studios and one-bedroom apartments.
Business centre. Internet (wireless, free). Parking ($25/day). TV (DVD).

Seneca

200 E Chestnut Street, at N Mies van der Rohe
Way, IL 60611 (1-800 800 6261/1-312 787
8900/www.senecahotel.com). El: Red to Chicago.

CONSUME

Make Yourself At Home

Leave the hotel life behind with an apartment stay in the city.

If money's tight on your trip to town, or the thought of eating out for every meal sounds more like a penance than a pleasure, then renting an apartment might be your saving grace. But finance and food aren't the only reasons to consider staying in an apartment instead of a hotel. Renting a place in a new city, even if only for a long weekend, can bring you a little closer to the experience of actually living there.

Vacation Rentals by Owner (www.vrbo.com) and the sublet section of **Craigslist** (http://chicago.craigslist.org) are both good places to start your search. But if you'd like your hotel pre-vetted, two Chicago-based companies offer an ample supply of properties all over town. Both companies provide plenty of pictures online for every property, so you should have a fairly good idea of where you'll be staying before you book.

At Home Inn Chicago (www.athomeinn chicago.com) rents about 125 privately-owned apartments; most are between the Loop and the Gold Coast, but some are as far north as Rogers Park. Rates for a studio start at $99 per night, rising to $135 during peak season (15 March-15 December), and go all the way up to $700 a night for a three-bedroom duplex. The minimum stay is usually two nights, though busy weekends may require a three-night commitment. Send a grocery list and the company will stock the fridge with your favourite basics for an additional $20.

Elite Chicago Rentals (www.elitechicago rentals.com) is a newcomer by comparison, but already rents out over 100 properties; the Gold Coast and Streeterville areas are particularly well covered. Prices are a little higher than At Home Inn Chicago, though; and unless you're staying Monday through Wednesday, Elite requires a three-night stay.

Windy City Urban Inn. *See p144.*

Rates $165-$295 double. **Rooms** 190. **Credit** AmEx, Disc, MC, V. **Map** p326 J9 ⑤④
Don't let the doorman and classical music in the tastefully elegant lobby fool you: the Seneca's prices are refreshingly low for this part of town. The hotel's deluxe one-bedroom suites arguably represent the best value in this 1924 building.
Bars (2). Disabled-adapted rooms. Gym. Internet (wireless, free). Parking ($48/day). Restaurants (3). TV.

Whitehall Hotel
105 E Delaware Place, at N Michigan Avenue, IL 60611 (1-800 948 4255/1-312 944 6300/www.thewhitehallhotel.com). El: Red to Chicago. **Rates** $149-$299 double. **Rooms** 222. **Credit** AmEx, Disc, MC, V. **Map** p326 J9 ⑤⑤
The 222-room Whitehall occupies a landmark building, developed in 1928 to house luxury apartments. The panelled lobby retains its clubby English look, while a stylish Italian eaterie, Fornetto Mei, has supplanted the private dining club that used to be here. Its sidewalk atrium is a great place for people-watching in this moneyed neighbourhood. The rooms feature mahogany furniture and Chippendale desks.
Bar. Business centre. Concierge. Disabled-adapted rooms. Gym. Internet (wireless and cable, $9.95/day). Parking ($45/day). Restaurant. Room service. TV (pay movies).

Old Town & Lincoln Park
LINCOLN PARK
Budget

Days Inn Chicago
644 W Diversey Parkway, at N Clark Street, IL 60614 (1-888 576 3297/1-773 525 7010/www.daysinnchicago.net). El: Brown or Purple to Diversey. **Rates** $110-$156 double. **Rooms** 133. **Credit** AmEx, Disc, MC, V. **Map** p328 F4 ⑤⑥
Belying its parent company's longstanding reputation for midmarket blandness, the main Days Inn location in Chicago is a handsome place, kept in fine fettle after a renovation several years ago. The lobby offers guests a bright entrance; the comparatively good-looking rooms are nicely kept and relatively spacious. Best of all: the plum location, at the busy intersection of Broadway, Clark and Diversey on the cusp of Lincoln Park and Lakeview. Continental breakfast is served in a comfortable sitting area; the hotel also offers complimentary admission to Bally's health club next door.
Disabled-adapted rooms. Internet (wireless, free). Parking ($22/day). TV (pay movies).

★ Windy City Urban Inn

607 W Deming Place, at N Clark Street,
IL 60614 (1-877 897 7091/1-773 248 7091/
www.windycityinn.com). Bus 22, 36. **Rates**
$125-$255 double. **Rooms** 9. **Credit** AmEx,
Disc, MC, V. **Map** p328 F4 ⑤⑦

Visitors will find a home away from home at this
Victorian mansion owned by local TV newsman
Andy Shaw and his wife Mary. Tucked away on a
quiet, leafy street in Lincoln Park, the six cosy
guestrooms and three apartments (in the neighbouring coach house; there may be a minimum-stay
requirement at busy times) are themed on and
named after local writers, from the tough-talking
Nelson Algren to the more demure Gwendolyn
Brooks. Guests are invited to grab a book and a
glass of sherry and lounge in the ivy-covered garden or snuggle up by the fireplace. *Photo p143.*
Concierge. Internet (wireless, free). Parking
($12/day). TV (DVD).

Lakeview & Around

LAKEVIEW

Budget

City Suites

933 W Belmont Avenue, at N Sheffield Avenue,
IL 60657 (1-800 248 9108/1-773 404 3400/
www.cityinns.com). El: Brown, Purple or Red to
Belmont. **Rates** $129-$289 suite. **Rooms** 45.
Credit AmEx, Disc, MC, V. **Map** p329 E3 ⑤⑧

This 45-room boutique hotel in a part-gentrified,
part-bohemian neighbourhood is right next to the
Belmont El station, from where it's a 15-minute train
ride to downtown. Walk four blocks north, meanwhile, and you'll be at Wrigley Field. The hotel itself
has an appealing art deco feel; its suites include
sleeper sofas, armchairs and spacious workstations
with Wi-Fi. A continental breakfast is included, but
Ann Sather and its peerless Swedish pancakes and
cinnamon rolls are temptingly close to the hotel.
Concierge. Internet (wireless, free). Parking
($22/day). TV.

Majestic

528 W Brompton Avenue, at N Lake Shore
Drive, IL 60657 (1-800 727 5108/1-773 404
3499/www.cityinns.com). Bus 145, 146, 151.
Rates $109-$329 suite. **Rooms** 53. **Credit**
AmEx, Disc, MC, V. **Map** p329 G1 ⑤⑨

Set on a quiet, tree-lined residential street within
walking distance of the delightful Lincoln Park Zoo,
the Majestic is housed in a building dating from the
1920s, and offers 29 rooms and 24 suites fitted out
with microwaves and wet bars. It's not especially
handy for the El, but buses along nearby Lake Shore
Drive get you to the Magnificent Mile in about 15
minutes. As with its sister properties City Suites

and the Willows, guests are greeted each morning
with a complimentary breakfast.
Concierge. Internet (wireless, free). Parking
($22/day). TV.

Willows

555 W Surf Street, at N Broadway, IL 60657
(1-800 787 3108/1-773 528 8400/www.
cityinns.com). El: Brown or Purple to Diversey.
Rates $109-$279 double. **Rooms** 54. **Credit**
AmEx, Disc, MC, V. **Map** p329 G3 ⑥⓪

This quaint, 54-room hotel near the busy intersection of Clark and Diversey has an old-fashioned
French country feel. Fans of minor hotel curiosities
(and, for that matter, of vintage private-eye movies)
will enjoy riding in the original 1920s Otis elevator,
creaks and all. Room rates include a continental
breakfast and complimentary cookies every afternoon at 4pm. Good value.
Concierge. Internet (wireless, free). Parking
($22/day). TV.

FURTHER NORTH

Budget

House 5863

5863 N Glenwood Avenue, at W Ardmore
Avenue, Uptown, IL 60660 (1-773 944 5555/
www.house5863.com). El: Red to Thorndale.
Rates $99-$179 double. **Rooms** 5. **Credit**
AmEx, Dics, MC, V.

This relatively new B&B fits right in with its surrounding hip yet down-to-earth North Side neighbourhood. From the dark red brick exterior, the
plasma-screen TV in the lobby and the modern
design of the guestrooms – outfitted in a primarily
black-and-white palette with low-to-the-ground furnishings – the place eschews that stale vibe some
older B&Bs exude. Relax in the outdoor garden,
which can be reserved and catered for any event, or
take a walk to the nearby lakefront.
Business centre. Internet (wireless, free). Parking
($20/day).

Wicker Park & Around

WICKER PARK & BUCKTOWN

Budget

House of Two Urns B&B

1239 N Greenview Avenue, at W Division Street,
IL 60622 (1-877 896 8767/1-773 235 1408/
www.twourns.com). El: Blue to Division. **Rates**
$109-$189 double. **Rooms** 6. **Credit** Disc, MC, V.
Map p331 D8 ⑥①

Wicker Park's reputation as an artistic enclave
fits perfectly with this friendly, off-beat B&B.
Named after the urn motif found in the stained-glass

CONSUME

Ray's Bucktown B&B.

window and façade, this 1912 brownstone has four rooms with eccentric themes such as European antique plates or the tale of the princess and the pea. Some rooms have shared baths. Sweet smells still fill this former Polish bakery in the morning, when the owner whips up a full breakfast for guests. Those looking for more privacy can book one of three apartments across the street.
Business centre. Concierge. Internet (wireless, free). Parking (free). TV (DVD).

★ Ray's Bucktown B&B

2144 N Leavitt Street, at W Webster Avenue, IL 60622 (1-800 355 2324/1-773 384 3245/ www.raysbucktownbandb.com). El: Blue to Western. **Rates** $119-$199 double. **Rooms** 10. **Credit** AmEx, Disc, MC, V. **Map** p331 B5 ⑥
Sitting several worlds away from B&B's traditionally chintzy image, Ray Reiss's Bucktown operation is a B&B for the 21st century. The rooms are crisp, fresh and modern, and the facilities are awesome: aside from Wi-Fi throughout the building, rooms have TiVo-equipped televisions, and there's even a photographic studio available to rent. A two-night minimum is usually in effect, though one-night stays can sometimes be accommodated.
Internet (wireless, free). Parking (free). TV (DVD).

★ Ruby Room

1743-1745 W Division Street, at N Wood Street, IL 60622; (1-773 235 2323/www. rubyroom.com). El: Blue to Division. **Rates** $135-$225 double. **Rooms** 8. **Credit** AmEx, MC, V. **Map** p331 C8 ⑥
The steam shower alone warrants a splurge on one of the Ruby Deluxe suites at this spa's neighbouring B&B, but the king-size beds, topped with pillow mattresses and feather beds, and minimalist yet inviting aesthetic lend a sense of luxury to each of the eight rooms. You won't find a phone or TV in this joint; a stack of books (think: a primer on healing crystals), a CD player and Wi-Fi access provide the only in-room entertainment. It's bring your own everything as far as food goes, but don't worry: the area is full of restaurants, cafés and bars, and staff can provide plenty of recommendations. Stop next door at the spa for a haircut, crystal energy healing treatment or massage.
Internet (wireless, free). Spa.

Wicker Park Inn

1329 N Wicker Park Avenue, at W Wolcott Avenue, IL 60622 (1-773 486 2743/ www.wickerparkinn.com). El: Blue to Damen. **Rates** $139-$199 double. **Rooms** 6. **Credit** AmEx, MC, V. **Map** p331 C8 ⑥
You won't find the usual frilly curtains and old-fashioned furniture at this modern B&B, located on a tree-lined street of turn-of-the-century row houses in the city's hippest 'hood. The six guestrooms each have private bath, television and free wireless internet access. Wake up to a shot of espresso and a continental breakfast buffet brought in fresh from a nearby bakery.
Internet (wireless, free). Parking (free). TV.

Restaurants

From celeb chefs to corner cafés and most places in between.

For decades, residents of the City of Big Shoulders have had famously healthy appetites. But in the last couple of decades, the city's dining scene has come into its own. The cosy local restaurants, ethnic eateries and comfort-cooking operations for which the city has long been renowned have been joined by an array of high-end eateries; alongside them sit a terrific variety of mid-range spots, many offering creative and seasonally slanted reinventions of dishes from both home and abroad. With San Francisco and New York, Chicago now counts as one of the best cities for dining in the US; whatever your taste and budget, you won't go hungry.

THE LOCAL SCENE

Stephanie Izard earned Chicago some chef cred by taking home the prize on Bravo's Emmy-winning show *Top Chef* in 2008. But even before her success, chef-driven dining was big news in the city. Highlights include the off-the-wall DIY no-server system at Michael Carlson's tiny **Schwa** (*see p170*); the playful American cooking of Graham Elliot Bowles at his near-eponymous River North restaurant (*see p154*); the contemporary Latin and Med creations of Randy Zweiban at **Province** (*see p164*); Ryan Poli's accessible, seasonal fare at **Perennial** (*see p157*); and the groundbreaking molecular gastronomy of Grant Achatz at **Alinea** (*see p157*), Chicago's answer to El Bulli.

Elsewhere, midscale-casual restaurants such as the **Bristol** (*see p168*), **Mado** (*see p169*), **Avec** (*see p162*), **HotChocolate** (*see p169*) and **Lula Café** (*see p172*) have been bringing seasonal flavours to the fore in impressive fashion. They're all democratic places, tax brackets mingling comfortably in the often-full rooms. But if you're looking to rub elbows with a few locals, the influx of eateries offering communal dining make a great icebreaker. Whether over steaming bowls of noodles at **Urban Belly** (*see p172*), bodacious burgers at **Duchamp** (*see p168*) or Belgian

beers at **Publican** (*see p164*), there's no better community organiser than great food.

Elsewhere, homesickness cures are offered in innumerable ethnic enclaves: **Chinatown** for Chinese food and **Pilsen** for Mexican eats; **Greektown** and **Little Italy** for Greek and Italian; **Andersonville** for Swedish fare and **Lincoln Square** for German cooking; and, further out, Indian cooking on **Devon Avenue** on the far north side and more Italian treats along Harlem Avenue in **Elmwood Park**. And that's without tackling Chicago's deep-dish pizzas and hot dogs (*see p153* **A Dog's Life**)…

Essential information

Competition for tables at some smart and/or hip restaurants can be fierce. If in doubt, call ahead and book, especially at weekends. Few restaurants operate a dress code, but men may be asked to don a jacket and tie in some posh spots downtown; call to check if you're in doubt.

Prices given throughout the chapter are for an average main course. We've used the $ symbol to denote operations offering particularly good value: restaurants with main courses for around $10 or less, plus cafés, diners and other similarly cheap operations.

> ❶ Blue numbers given in this chapter correspond to the location of each restaurant on the street maps.
> *See pp324-332.*

About the author
Heather Shouse *is the Eat & Drink editor of* Time Out Chicago *magazine, and the Chicago reporter for* Food & Wine *magazine.*

CONSUME

New restaurants open all the time in Chicago. For the latest news and reviews, see the weekly *Time Out Chicago* magazine.

Restaurants

THE LOOP

$ Cafecito
26 E Congress Parkway, between S State Street & S Wabash Avenue (1-312 922 2233/http://cafe citochicago.com). El: Brown, Orange, Pink or Purple to Library; Blue or Red to Jackson. **Open** 7am-9pm Mon-Fri; 10am-6pm Sat, Sun. **Sandwich** $5. **Credit** MC, V. **Map** p325 H13 ❶ Cuban
You don't have to claim a bunk at the adjacent youth hostel to get your hands on one of this café's terrific Cuban sandwiches. There's no confusion over the star of the show: the Cubano's crusty bread is toasted just right, its roast pork juicy, its pickles thick, and its mustard and gooey cheese plentiful. And once it's devoured, only a potent *cortadito* will keep you from slumping on the café's comfy couch.

★ Custom House
500 S Dearborn Street, at W Congress Parkway (1-312 523 0200/www.customhouse.cc). El: Brown, Orange, Pink or Purple to Library; Red to Harrison. **Open** 11.30am-2pm Mon-Fri; 5-10pm Mon-Sat; 5-9pm Sun. **Main courses** $29. **Credit** AmEx, Disc, MC, V. **Map** p325 H13 ❷ Contemporary American
There's much disagreement over which meal this restaurant does best – great breakfast buffets, wonderful lunches, splurgeworthy dinners – and the ever-changing seasonal menus make the decision even tougher. Chef Shawn McClain is no slouch with high-quality steaks and chops, but the specials really are special: Ahi tuna drizzled with caper-raisin vinaigrette; or Hawaiian marlin with littleneck clams, housemade bacon and sweet corn chowder.
▶ *For the Hotel Blake, in which it sits, see p128.*

★ $ Frontera Fresco
Macy's 111 N State Street, 7th Floor, at E Washington Street (1-312 781 2955/www. fronterafresco.com). El: Blue to Washington; Brown, Green, Orange, Pink or Purple to Randolph/Wabash. **Open** 11am-5pm Mon-Sat. **Main courses** $7. **Credit** AmEx, Disc, MC, V. **Map** p325 H12 ❸ Mexican
Macy's brought Rick Bayless into the fold with the addition of this carry-out counter offering tortas, quesadillas, tamales, salads and soups, but with fillings that counter most fast-food notions. Smoked pork loin and applewood bacon top the torta Cubana, Amy's All-Natural Chicken Chorizo shows up in a quesadilla, and steak joins garlicky mushrooms and chipotle sauce for an earthy huarache.
▶ *For Bayless's Frontera Grill, see p154.*

★ Gage
24 S Michigan Avenue, at E Madison Street (1-312 372 4243/www.thegagechicago.com). El: Brown, Green, Orange, Pink or Purple to Madison/ Wabash. **Open** 11am-2pm Mon-Fri; 10am-3pm Sat; 10am-noon Sun. **Main courses** $30. **Credit** AmEx, Disc, MC, V. **Map** p325 J12 ❹ Gastropub
Owner Billy Lawless and chef Dirk Flanigan have a hit on their hands with this Loop take on a British gastropub. Flanigan's food is rich and aggressively flavourful, from the perfect-for-snacking Scotch egg to the Gage burger, served a juicy medium-rare and dripping with melted onion marmalade and gobs of stinky Midwestern camembert. The whiskey list is lengthy, beer options reach beyond the basics and wines are accompanied by clever descriptions.

$ Hannah's Bretzel
180 W Washington Street, at N Wells Street (1-312 621 1111/www.hannahsbretzel.com). El: Blue, Brown, Orange, Pink or Purple to Washington. **Open** 7am-5pm Mon-Fri. **Main courses** $9. **Credit** AmEx, MC, V. **Map** p325 H12 ❺ Café
This tiny Euro-chic café bills itself as an organic carry-out restaurant, but note that the word healthy is nowhere to be found. Warm, whole-grain pretzels – baked throughout the day on the premises – may indeed be good for you; no doubt the organic salads are, too. Sandwiches, such as the Black Forest ham and gruyère on soft 'bretzel' bread, aren't unhealthy, either. But doctors probably wouldn't condone the wall dedicated to chocolate, on which you'll find more than 175 different bars.

Park Grill
11 N Michigan Avenue, at E Madison Street (1-312 521 7275/www.parkgrillchicago.com). El: Blue or Red to Monroe; Brown, Green, Orange, Pink, Purple to Madison/Wabash. **Open** 11am-9.30pm daily. **Main courses** $19. **Credit** AmEx, Disc, MC, V. **Map** p325 J12 ❻ Contemporary American

---

**INSIDE TRACK
SNACK ATTACKS**

Running out of steam somewhere between Neiman Marcus and Filene's Basement? You need a sugar hit. State Street bargain-hunters should duck into Macy's for the royaltines at **Sarah's Pastries & Candies** (*see p188*), while Magnificent Mile shoppers ought to make a beeline for the gelato and *cannoli* at Italian deli **L'Appetito** (*see p206*) or the unusual, although always delicious, chocolates sold at **Vosges Haut-Chocolat** (*see p206*). Fight off the munchies in the Loop with a visit to **Garrett Popcorn Shop** (*see p206*).

Park Grill's location overlooking the Millennium Park Ice Rink has its pros and cons: watching flailing skaters is transfixing, but with food this good, you might want to focus on your meal. Seasonal offerings may include whisper-thin beef carpaccio sprinkled with Parmesan and juicy capers or jumbo lump crab cake with yellow-curry sauce. The Kobe burger is also a treat, melted gorgonzola topping thick-as-your-fist beef between buttery brioche. Strap on skates to get your heart pumping again.
▶ *For the ice rink itself, see p280.*

Russian Tea Time
77 E Adams Street, between S Michigan & S Wabash Avenues (1-312 360 0000/www.russian teatime.com). El: Blue or Red to Jackson; Brown, Green, Orange, Pink or Purple to Adams/ Wabash. **Open** 11am-9pm Mon-Thur, Sun; 11am-midnight Fri, Sat. **Main courses** $24. **Credit** AmEx, Disc, MC, V. **Map** p325 J12 **❼ Russian**
A classy choice for the symphony set and couples looking to indulge themselves, this institution proves that excess is best. Slide into a cosy booth and start the assault with borscht, sour cream-slathered dumplings and caviar blini, followed by creamy beef stroganoff or oniony, nutmeg-laced, ground beef-stuffed cabbage rolls. Be sure to order a flight of house-infused vodkas (pepper, pineapple, ginger, coriander and more).

Vivere
71 W Monroe Street, between S Clark & S Dearborn Streets (1-312 332 7005/www.vivere chicago.com). El: Blue or Red to Monroe; Brown, Green, Orange, Pink or Purple to Adams/ Wabash. **Open** 11.30am-2.30pm Mon-Fri; 5-10pm Mon-Thur; 5-11pm Fri, Sat. **Main courses** $20. **Credit** AmEx, Disc, MC, V. **Map** p325 H12 **❽ Italian**
The best of the three restaurants that make up the multi-level Italian Village, Vivere boasts a menu as contemporary as its decor. That's quite a feat, given that the room looks like an Italian Baroque version of Alice's Wonderland. The menu is a balance of classics and interesting twists applied to housemade pastas, seafood stews and grilled game. The best part about the kitchen offering half-orders of pasta is that you can get two: try the sage-scented, pheasant-filled agnolottini and the rigatoni alla bolognese.

$ Wow Bao
175 W Jackson Street, at S Wells Street (1-312 334 6395/www.wowbao.com). El: Blue or Red to Jackson; Brown, Orange, Pink or Purple to Quincy/Wells. **Open** 6.30am-5.30pm Mon-Fri. **Main courses** $6. **Credit** AmEx, Disc, MC, V. **Map** p325 H13 **❾ Asian**
Are breakfast *bao*, stuffed with egg, bacon and cheese (or, more successfully, egg with a peppery crumbled sausage), the new Wheaties? Probably not. Still, there's plenty to enjoy here. Potstickers are fine;

better to go with the Thai curry-chicken rice bowl with its mild, yet aromatic and complex, yellow curry. Or just stick with the *bao*, steamed buns stuffed with fillings such as slightly spicy kung pao chicken or the sweet and rich barbecue pork.

THE SOUTH LOOP & CHINATOWN
The South Loop

$ Canady le Chocolatier
824 S Wabash Avenue, between E 8th & E 9th Streets (1-312 212 1270/www.canadyle chocolatierchicago.com). El: Red to Harrison. **Open** noon-9pm Mon-Sat; noon-6pm Sun. **Ice-cream** $2.50. **Credit** MC, V. **Map** p324 H14 **❿ Ice-cream**
It's always encouraging to find little ice-cream shops that make their own products, and this gelato gem also makes dozens of varieties of filled chocolates and truffles. Go for broke and get a cup of gelato for now (the pistachio and the tiramisu are our favourites) and a custom-selected box of sweets for later (try the ginger truffle and the *dulce de leche* chocolate). The shop also does custom gelato cakes that will reduce the folks at Baskin-Robbins to tears.

$ Double Li
228 W Cermak Road, between S Wentworth & S Archer Avenues (1-312 842 7818). El: Red to Cermak-Chinatown. **Open** 10.30am-10.30pm daily. **Main courses** $9. **Credit** AmEx, Disc, MC, V. **Map** p324 H16 **⓫ Chinese**
Mr Li, the amiable owner, used to guide diners through specials written on the wall in Chinese only. However, they've now made it onto the English-language menu, adding to the many fantastic Szechuan options available for those looking to get out of a fried-rice rut. Both the fish with cabbage in chilli oil and the mapo tofu pack plenty of earthy spice via a fistful of Szechuan peppercorns. And if softshell or blue crabs are on offer, get them.

$ Epic Burger
517 S State Street, between E Congress Parkway & E Harrison Street (1-312 913 1373/www.epic burger.com). El: Red to Harrison. **Open** 11am-10pm Mon-Thur; 11am-mid Fri, Sat; 11am-9pm Sun. **Main courses** $6. **Credit** AmEx, Disc, MC, V. **Map** p325 H13 **⓬ American**
This burger joint makes much of its Slow Food principles (beef and chicken are all-natural, hand-cut fries are cooked in trans fat-free vegetable oil)... but is the food up to much? It's pretty good. Burgers are hand-formed to almost an inch thick and cooked to a nice pinky medium. Opt for aged cheddar, bacon and egg toppings, and be sure to add on to your order the earthy, skin-on fries.
▶ *A fine burger alternative is offered at Custom House; see p147.*

$ Manny's Coffee Shop & Deli

*1141 S Jefferson Street, at S Grenshaw Street
(1-312 939 2855/www.mannysdeli.com). El:
Blue to Clinton.* **Open** 5am-8pm Mon-Sat.
Main courses $10. **Credit** AmEx, Disc, MC, V.
Map p324 G14 ⓮ **American/cafeteria**

The city's most quintessential restaurant is not a
steakhouse or a lab-like kitchen putting out cutting-
edge cuisine. It's a cafeteria. Decide what you want
before you get in line at this 66-year-old institution.
You'll pass plates of Jell-O and chicken salad, but the
line moves quickly. Our advice? Grab one of the oversized corned beef or pastrami sandwiches, a potato
pancake on the side and a packet of Tums for dessert.

Mercat a la Planxa

*638 S Michigan Avenue, between E Harrison
Street & E Balbo Drive (1-312 765 0524/www.
mercatchicago.com). El: Green, Orange or Red
to Roosevelt.* **Open** 6.30am-11pm Mon-Thur;
6.30am-midnight Fri, Sat; 6.30am-10pm Sun.
Tapa $10. **Credit** AmEx, Disc, MC, V. **Map**
p325 J13 ⓮ **Catalan**

The *croquetas* are crispy, the filet mignon has a
great salty crust and the *sous vide* pork belly melts
in the mouth like ice-cream. And yet there's still
something missing; often the service, which can be
rather on the aloof side. The best time to visit is
when chef de cuisine Michael Fiorello unleashes the

In the 'Hood Chinatown

Calvin Soh on how to eat in the Asian haven without getting your duck cooked.

No matter how low the buying power of the
US dollar goes, it's still a heck of a lot
cheaper to buy exotic Asian ingredients in
Chicago than in Singapore. At least that's
how Calvin Soh sees it. He should know: as
chef de cuisine at Shanghai Terrace, the
Singapore native is no stranger to birds'
nests, wild ginseng and dried abalone. To
find these and more familiar Asian items,
Soh heads to Chinatown.

Soh is such a regular at the **Ten Ren Tea
& Ginseng Co** (2247 S Wentworth Avenue,
1-312 842 1171) that he often hangs out
there on his day off, chatting with the
owner-manager (Mr Fine to you). Among
the large, copper-coloured canisters, Soh
points to Osmanthus Oolong tea as one
of his favourites. The $139-per-pound price
might induce sticker shock, but a pound of
tea brews 200 cups. 'When I'm stressed
out in the restaurant, I make a pot of this
to help me relax.'

For the best Peking duck in the city,
Soh heads toward the end of the block to
Tao Ho Yee Food Co (2422 S Wentworth
Avenue, 1-312 225 9828). What the
miniscule takeout shop lacks in decor, it
more than makes up for with the quality
of its duck, which is served at the Ritz-
Carlton and Four Seasons. Arrive early in
the morning (8am) or at noon – the shop
cooks its ducks in two daily shifts. Better
yet, call a day ahead and reserve one.

Sometimes even Peking duck isn't
enough to cure Soh's homesickness,
so when the pangs hit hard, he heads to
Penang (2201 S Wentworth Avenue, 1-312
326 6888). 'This is where I can find food
that's most similar to what I could eat
back home,' he says. Here among the tiki

lounge decor, he always orders *roti canai*,
an Indian-style pancake he often ate for
breakfast growing up ('It's crispy and really
nice with curry sauce').

Like many of Chicago's foodies, when
Soh craves Chinese food he heads to Tony
Hu's restaurants, including **Lao Shanghai**
(2163 S China Place, 1-312 808 0830) –
Soh's a big fan of its *xiao long bao* or 'juicy
buns' – and **Lao Beijing** (2138 S Archer
Avenue, 1-312 881 0168). 'For Chinese
food in Chinatown, chef Tony is the best,'
he beams.

Just like any great dinner, a Chinatown
tour should end with something sweet.
Soh goes to **Captain Café & Bakery**
(2161 S China Place, 1-312 791 0888),
where he wolfs down mini mooncakes and
the flaky, sweet-and-savoury egg cakes with
a pickled duck egg hidden inside. But Soh
doesn't go too far overboard on the sugar.
'An important part of food is to create a
comfortable feeling after the meal is
eaten,' he points out.

▶ For Soh's **Shanghai Terrace**, *see p156.*

CONSUME

Experience Nick's Fishmarket

A Chicago area culinary landmark, Nick's Fishmarket is famous for serving the freshest seafood, premium dry-aged steaks and award-winning wines for over 30 years.

In our main dining room, servers donned in tuxedos are experts at providing the highest level of service to the most discerning diners and help to set the tone for an elegant night on the town.

Our location in the heart of the Theatre District makes Nick's Fishmarket and Grill the ideal destination for your pre- or post-theatre plans.

Nick's Fishmarket Grill offers a more casual, yet chic, dining option. Stop in for a quick lunch while sightseeing or celebrate with a drink at our bar after a long day of shopping. Try our Signature Cocktails and special Bar Bites menu.

51 South Clark
Chicago, IL
312.564.5555
reallynice.com/**nicks**

Private Dining Rooms are also available for both business meetings and social gatherings. We have room sizes to fit your needs.

more adventurous seasonal sidewalk-café menu, which specialises in *bocadillos* (like duck ham with blue cheese) and charcuterie.
▶ *The restaurant is in the Blackstone Hotel, for which see p132.*

$ Yolk
1120 S Michigan Avenue, between S 11th Street & S Roosevelt Road (1-312 789 9655/www.yolk-online.com). El: Green, Orange, Red to Roosevelt. **Open** 6am-3pm Mon-Fri; 7am-3pm Sat, Sun. **Main courses** $9. **Credit** AmEx, Disc, MC, V. **Map** p324 J14 ⓯ **Diner**
No matter the schizophrenic nature of Chicago's ever-fluctuating weather, things will always remain bright and sunny in this blue-and-yellow, breakfast-and-lunch-only spot. Enormous omelettes are good standbys, but don't discount the quirkier fare: 'bacon waffles' add bits of bacon to waffle batter for tasty results. For lunch, the patty melt is a greasy, cheesy, delicious mess, exactly as it should be. Avoid the lacklustre housemade pecan and cinnamon rolls.

Chinatown

★ $ Lao Sze Chuan
2172 S Archer Avenue, between W Wentworth & W Princeton Avenues (1-312 326 5040/www.lao szechuan.com). El: Red to Cermak-Chinatown. **Open** 11.30am-midnight daily. **Main courses** $10. **Credit** AmEx, Disc, MC, V. **Map** p324 H16 ⓰ **Chinese/Szechuan**
This place is the best spot for Szechuan cuisine in town, evident from the nightly queues of heat-seekers. The kitchen uses plenty of Szechuan pepper, dried chillis, garlic and ginger to create addictive flavours; favourites include Chengdu dumplings, crispy Chinese eggplant with ground pork, twice-cooked pork, *ma po* tofu, Szechuan prawns and 'chef's special' dry chilli chicken.

$ Shui Wah
2162 S Archer Avenue, between W Wentworth & W Princeton Avenues (1-312 225 8811). El: Red to Cermak-Chinatown. **Open** 8am-midnight daily. **Main courses** $10. **Credit** AmEx, Disc, MC, V. **Map** p324 H16 ⓱ **Chinese**
Check off your dim sum order on the provided paper and you'll soon be stuffed with all the classics, from Chiu Chow-style (meaning, hailing from Hong Kong and its surrounding region) dumplings to memorable salt-and-pepper squid. Come 3pm, the dim-sum menu is replaced by dinner offerings; best bets include clams in slightly spicy black-bean sauce, salty egg tofu with four types of mushrooms and Japanese-ish eggplant with beef.

$ Spring World
2109-A S China Place, at S Wells Street, Chinatown Square (1-312 326 9966). El: Red to Cermak-Chinatown. Bus: 18, 21, 62. **Open**

INSIDE TRACK
DIM SUM AND THEN SOME

Let's say your night out involves a bit of food and drink, and let's say that maybe you had a bit too much of said drink. It's the morning after, and you need dim sum, the Chinese hangover cure of choice. In Chinatown, the best spots for the stuff include **Shui Wah** (*see below*), **Happy Chef** (2164 S Archer Avenue, 1-312 808 3689) and **Phoenix** (2131 S Archer Avenue, 1-312 328 0848).

10.30am-10pm daily. **Main courses** $10. **Credit** Disc, MC, V. **Map** p324 G16 ⓲ **Chinese/Cantonese**
If the gloopy, corn-starch-heavy dishes of traditional Cantonese restaurants aren't doing it for you, head to Spring World. Try the hand-shredded chicken with spicy sesame vinaigrette dotted with peanuts, garlic, sesame seeds and spring onion slivers, or the crispy whole tilapia topped with tangy garlic-ginger-chilli paste. Other favourites include crispy scallion cake, perfect for dipping in chilli sesame oil.

$ Three Happiness Restaurant
209 W Cermak Road, between S Wentworth & S Archer Avenues (1-312 842 1964). El: Red to Cermak-Chinatown. Bus: 18, 21, 62. **Open** 24 hrs daily. **Main courses** $8. **Credit** AmEx, Disc, MC, V. **Chinese**
This isn't the giant Three Happiness on the corner of Wentworth Avenue; it's worth stressing this because the difference is monumental. Ignore the far-from-spotless decor (or lack thereof) and skip the so-so appetisers in favour of black pepper beef with rice noodles (ordered 'crispy'), stir-fried Dungeness crab in chilli-seafood XO sauce, crispy salt-and-pepper shrimp and Cantonese-style crispy-skin chicken.

THE NEAR NORTH SIDE
River North

Aigre Doux
230 W Kinzie Street, between N Wells & N Franklin Streets (1-312 329 9400/www.aigre douxchicago.com). El: Brown or Purple to Merchandise Mart. **Open** 5-10pm Mon-Thur; 5-11pm Fri, Sat. **Main courses** $30. **Credit** AmEx, Disc, MC, V. **Map** p326 G11 ⓳ **Contemporary American**
Husband-and-wife team Mohammad Islam and Malika Ameen have entrenched themselves in River North, giving Merchandise Mart folks an after-work haunt (a bar-bites menu tops out at $10) while also maintaining dining-destination status. Dishes might include oxtail ravioli exploding with juicy meat.

Bin 36

*339 N Dearborn Street, at W Kinzie Street
(1-312 755 9463/http://bin36.com).* **El:** *Red to
Grand.* **Open** 6.30am-10pm Mon-Wed; 6.30am-
midnight Thur; 6.30am-1am Fri; 7am-1am Sat;
7am-10pm Sun. **Main courses** $22. **Credit**
AmEx, Disc, MC, V. **Map** p326 H11 ⑳
American/wine bar

This swanky institution gives wine top billing.
Choose from 50 wines by the glass to pair with a
menu of rich American bistro-style dishes. Though
the seasonal menu changes often, you can expect
dishes such as an earthy, creamy truffled cheese fondue; a meaty mushroom timbale livened up with
pesto oil; fluffy hand-made gnocchi; and skate wing
as crisp and golden as an autumn apple.

▶ *The same folks run the Bin Wine Café in
Wicker Park; see p168.*

Brasserie Jo

*59 W Hubbard Street, between N Dearborn &
N Clark Streets (1-312 595 0800/www.brasserie
jo.com).* **El:** *Red to Grand.* **Open** 5-10pm Mon-
Thur; 5-11pm Fri, Sat; 4-9pm Sun. **Main
courses** $22. **Credit** AmEx, Disc, MC, V.
Map p326 H11 ㉑ **French**

Chef Jean Joho's brasserie is casual in both design
and spirit. The menu of simple Alsatian food
matches: the classic salad lyonnaise, rife with chewy
lardons, is a solid starter, but it can't compete with
the crispy, onion-filled tarte flambé (free from the
bar on Tuesdays). The chicken in the creamy riesling coq au vin arrives with a delectable pile of
doughy, salty *kneffla*.

▶ *For more fine French food, try Café des
Architectes; see p156.*

Café Iberico

*739 N LaSalle Street, between W Superior Street
& W Chicago Avenue (1-312 573 1510).* **El:**
Brown, Purple or Red to Chicago. **Open** 11am-
11.30pm Mon-Thur; 11am-1.30am Fri, Sat; 11am-
11pm Sun. **Tapa** $7. **Credit** AmEx, Disc, MC, V.
Map p326 H10 ㉒ **Tapas**

The wait at this always-packed tapas joint can be
long and annoying, but once you get inside, things
go pretty quickly. Cheap plates of *patatas bravas*
and *croquetas de pollo* (creamy chicken and ham frit-
ters) arrive at the table almost immediately, dropped
like afterthoughts by overworked servers. But with
a plate of manchego and a pitcher of sangria to tide
you over, you won't even notice the wait.

★ Chicago Chop House

*60 W Ontario Street, between N Dearborn & N
Clark Streets (1-312 787 7100/www.chicagochop
house.com).* **El:** *Red to Grand.* **Open** 5-11pm
Mon-Thur; 5-11.30pm Fri; 4-11.30pm Sat; 4-11pm
Sun. **Main courses** $30. **Credit** AmEx, Disc,
MC, V. **Map** p326 H10 ㉓ **American**

This century-old brownstone is a quintessential
Chicago steakhouse. Conventioneers and local businessmen with fat expense wallets head upstairs for
white-tablecloth service, pricey wines and 48- or 64-
ounce porterhouses fit for a king. Alternatively, head
to the subterranean piano bar, where every inch of
wall is covered with vintage photos of Capone and
crew, and the high wooden tables are packed with
loud storytellers and uncompromising carnivores.

Club Lago

*331 W Superior Street, at N Orleans Street (1-
312 951 2849/www.clublago.com).* **El:** *Brown or*

Frontera Grill. *See p154.*

A Dog's Life

The classic Chicago hot dog brooks no arguments.

Order a hot dog in Chicago, and you'll need to accede to time-honoured tradition. Hold the ketchup and forget the pork: you'll get an all beef dog (steamed or boiled) on a poppy-seed bun, topped with mustard, relish, chopped onions, tomato wedges, a pickle spear, sport peppers and celery salt. But how these particulars came to form the classic Chicago dog is part speculation, part marketing schtick and part gossipy hearsay. And the guy who's heard most of these stories is Bruce Kraig, president of the Culinary Historians of Chicago and author of *The Hot Dog* (Reaktion Press).

'The best I got from various interviews from old-timers,' says Kraig, 'was that the Chicago dog as we know it was invented in the 1910s, and the toppings came from competition among Greek and Italian vendors, who needed to add value to their product during the Depression.' But before that, the hot dog – *sans* seven toppings – made its Chicago debut at the 1893 World's Columbian Exposition, trotted out under the Vienna name by a couple of Austrian immigrants looking to cash in on the Eastern European frankfurter.

More than a century later, the Vienna company is still the main game in town, supplying franks to 85 per cent of Chicago's hot-dog stands. But what of those seven toppings? As Kraig explains, it's all down to Chicago's immigration stew.

'Sausage is German in origin and so is mustard, but buns are American; Germans would eat it with bread, but not a bun. Sport peppers are basically *giardiniera*, as is relish, which is Italian. Dill pickles are German. Tomatoes and onions are Mediterranean, so that's Greek and Italian; these came from guys that turned their produce carts into hot-dog carts on Maxwell Street. Chicago was once a major producer of celery; celery salt became a substitute. The poppy-seed bun, which is Jewish and was introduced locally by Rosen's bakery, didn't appear until after World War II.'

Makes sense, but why have locals rejected ketchup? The solid red line Chicagoans have drawn between themselves and those who 'ruin' a dog with ketchup is so notorious that it's infiltrated the National Hot Dog & Sausage Council, whose Hot Dog Etiquette guide includes the rule, 'Don't use ketchup on your hot dog after the age of 18.'

Bob Schwartz, a senior vice-president at Vienna, is such a disciple of the rule he's written a book called *Never Put Ketchup on a Hot Dog*. 'The real reason not to use it is because the sweetness and acidity doesn't blend well with the other toppings,' he says. 'Sure, there are several stories, but very simply, it's just legend. And when the legend becomes stronger than the fact, you print the legend.'

▶ If you only eat one hot dog while you're here, get it from **Hot Doug's** (3324 N California Avenue, at W Roscoe Street, 1-773 279 9550, www.hotdougs.com).

CONSUME

Purple to Chicago. **Open** 11am-10pm Mon-Thur; 11am-11pm Fri, Sat. **Main courses** $15. **Credit** AmEx, Disc, MC, V. **Map** p326 G10 ❷ **Italian**
Yuppies may come and go from this ever-changing neighbourhood, but Club Lago always remains the same. Now in the hands of Guido and Giancarlo Nardini, grandsons of the original owner, the restaurant offers food that's as basic and hearty as it was in 1952. A boiler in the adjacent building exploded in 2009, leaving a substantial hole in the restaurant and causing it to close. However, the brothers are determined to rebuild. History rarely tastes so good.
▶ *There's more old-school Italian cooking at nearby Gene & Georgetti; see p154.*

Crofton on Wells

535 N Wells Street, at W Ohio Street (1-312 755 1790/www.croftononwells.com). El: Red to Grand. **Open** 5-10pm Mon-Sat. **Main courses** $34. **Credit** AmEx, Disc, MC, V. **Map** p326 G10 ❷
Contemporary American
Suzy Crofton, the owner, manager, sommelier and chef of this contemporary-looking restaurant, spends as much time here as her many job titles suggest. Her seasonal American cooking has inspired a couple of dishes that regulars won't let her take off the menu (usually heavy on seasonal offerings), such as the jumbo lump crabmeat crab cake. The service is among the most attentive in the city.

★ Frontera Grill

445 N Clark Street, between W Hubbard & W Illinois Streets (1-312 661 1434). El: Brown or Purple to Merchandise Mart; Red to Grand. **Open** 11.30am-2.30pm Tue-Fri; 5.20-10pm Tue; 5-10pm Wed, Thur; 5-11pm Fri, Sat; 10.30am-2.30pm Sat. **Main courses** $25. **Credit** AmEx, Disc, MC, V. **Map** p326 H11 ㉖ **Mexican**

Most celeb chefs branch out to other cities, leaving the original restaurant at home to suffer. Rick Bayless kept close to the kitchen and chose to expand in other ways (books, TV shows). Lucky Chicago. Frontera offers a vibrant slice of Mexico City, a place to chow down on *ceviches*, earthy *mole*, wood-grilled steak tucked into housemade tortillas and, of course, insanely good margaritas. *Photo p152.*

▶ *For more on Bayless, see p165* **In the 'Hood**.

Fulton's on the River

315 N LaSalle Street, at the Chicago River (1-312 822 0100/www.levyrestaurants.com). El: Brown or Purple to Merchandise Mart. **Open** 11am-9pm Mon-Thur; 11am-10pm Fri; 5-10pm Sat. **Main courses** $40. **Credit** AmEx, Disc, MC, V. **Map** p326 H11 ㉗ **American**

Fulton's is as much about the view as it is about the food. Fortunately, both are worth a visit. The menu – equal parts seafood and steakhouse – is nothing out of the ordinary, but everything is of exquisite quality. King crab legs from the extensive raw bar are fresh and sweet, filet mignon is tender, and a side dish of roasted butternut squash with pumpkin butter and goat's cheese is so decadent you can skip dessert. Make your trip worth the price and ask for a window seat.

Gene & Georgetti

500 N Franklin Street, at W Illinois Street (1-312 527 3718/www.geneandgeorgetti.com). El: Red to Grand. **Open** 11am-11pm Mon-Thur; 11am-midnight Fri, Sat. **Main courses** $35. **Credit** AmEx MC, V. **Map** p326 G10 ㉘ **Steakhouse**

Since 1941, this old-school River North steakhouse has been serving diners steaks and Italian classics in a dimly lit, cosy restaurant. The murals on the walls are as appealing as the menu and impeccable service. Of course, a hearty, juicy steak is the main

draw: go for the filet mignon or loin. Tasty non-steak options include calf's livers, veal vesuvio and an eggplant parmigiana (for vegetarians).

★ Graham Elliot

217 W Huron Street, at N Wells Street (1-312 624 9975/www.grahamelliot.com). El: Brown or Purple to Chicago. **Open** 5-10.30pm Mon-Sat. **Main courses** $32. **Credit** AmEx, Disc, MC, V. **Map** p326 G10 ㉙ **Contemporary American**

Quite how much you'll love Graham Elliot Bowles's dressed-down solo project depends on your tolerance for quirky. Want whoppers with your peanut butter brownie and Nilla wafers on peach cobbler? You'll be happy. Still, even doubters should be silenced when it really works, as with the massive pork prime rib with watermelon, grits, greens, a root-beer-based barbecue sauce and corn nuts for crunch.

Hub 51

51 W Hubbard Street, at N Dearborn Street (1-312 828 0051/www.hub51chicago.com). El: Red to Grand. **Open** 11.30am-midnight Mon-Wed; 11.30am-2am Thur, Fri; 11.30am-3am Sat; 5pm-midnight Sun. **Main courses** $20. **Credit** AmEx, Disc, MC, V. **Map** p326 H11 ㉚ **Contemporary American**

This mid-scale River North catch-all offers a menu ranging from open-faced BLTs to halibut tacos. The crowd is as varied as the eats – tourists, ladies who lunch and local working stiffs rub elbows – and everyone seems content with the large portions and boisterous scene. Braised pork tacos with housemade tortillas are a surprise hit, and plump *maki* do the trick if sushi cravings hit.

Japonais

600 W Chicago Avenue, at N Larrabee Street (1-312 822 9600/www.japonaischicago.com). El: Brown or Purple to Chicago. **Open** 11.30am-2.30pm Mon-Fri; 5-11pm Mon-Thur; 5-11.30pm Fri, Sat; 5-10pm Sun. **Main courses** $25. **Credit** AmEx, Disc, MC, V. **Map** p326 F9 ㉛ **Japanese**

Spend more than a million bucks building a restaurant in an undeveloped stretch of town, and you too can have a spot capable of transporting Chicagoans to a distant land. The Ian Schrager-esque space is swank, sexy and vibrant, and the food is also worthwhile. The modern Japanese cuisine centres around superb-quality raw fish, presented simply as sashimi or whacked out into tasty rolls. Don't leave without having the Kobe carpaccio.

Joe's Seafood, Prime Steaks & Stone Crab

60 E Grand Avenue, at N Wabash Avenue (1-312 379 5637/www.joes.net/chicago). El: Red to Grand. **Open** 11.30am-9.30pm Mon-Thur; 11.30am-10.30pm Fri; 11am-10.30pm Sat; 11am-9.30pm Sun. **Main courses** $40. **Credit** AmEx, Disc, MC, V. **Map** p326 H10 ㉜ **American**

INSIDE TRACK BAR NONE

Dining alone can be one of the best, most relaxing ways to unwind from the day, provided you aren't surrounded by canoodling couples. One neat trick: eat at the bar. At places such as **Naha** (*see p155*), **Le Bouchon** (*see p168*), **Avec** (*see p162*) and **Bin Wine Café** (*see p168*), you'll get the same menu as the rest of the room, but privacy to enjoy it in peace.

Graham Elliot.

When you're paying through the nose for a steakhouse experience, you should feel like a king. The service should be top-notch, the atmosphere should be classy and the food should be stellar. Joe's hits each mark. Start with one of the signature stone crabs, the sugar prawns and a delicious chopped salad that could feed two. Go straight to the bone-in New York strip, perfect when charred medium-rare. Blackened mahi mahi is juicy and just spicy enough.

Lux Bar

18 E Bellevue Place, at N Rush Street (1-312 642 3400/www.luxbar.com). El: Red to Clark/Division. **Open** 11am-midnight Mon-Fri; 8am-midnight Sat, Sun. **Main courses** $15. **Credit** AmEx, Disc, MC, V. **Map** p326 H9 ❸ **American**
Both the food and space at Lux seem to be imported from a simpler era, with dishes such as luscious filet mignon 'sliders' and impossibly crispy, impeccably juicy fried chicken presented without fanfare. The straightforward approach can sometimes backfire, such as with the bland turkey burger; but for the most part, this spot's a gem, especially for those who appreciate well-made cocktails and solid food.

★ Naha

500 N Clark Street, at W Illinois Street (1-312 321-6242/www.naha-chicago.com). El: Red to Grand. **Open** 11.30am-2pm Mon-Fri; 5.30-9.30pm Mon-Thur; 5.30-10.30pm Fri, Sat. **Main courses** $35. **Credit** AmEx, Disc, MC, V. **Map** p326 H10 ❹ **Contemporary American**
Chef Carrie Nahabedian delivers an upscale experience minus the pomp, courtesy of a snazzy room, great service and a seasonal menu that reads like a who's who in regional, sustainable foods. The menu

changes daily: expect anything from seasonal veggies accompanying a wild Copper River Alaskan salmon to slow-roasted salmon with morels, sugar snap peas and cipollini onions.

Quartino

626 N State Street, at W Ontario Street (1-312 698 5000/www.quartinochicago.com). El: Red to Grand. **Open** 11.30am-1am Mon-Sat; 11.30am-midnight Sun. **Small plate** $9. **Credit** AmEx, Disc, MC, V. **Map** p326 H10 ❸ **Italian**
This cavernous, rustic Italian dining room is decked out with reclaimed wood and subway tiles, vintage mirrors and mismatched chairs. To ensure authenticity on the plate, chef John Coletta produces housemade *salumi* such as beef bresaola, spicy *soppressata* and duck prosciutto served with housemade *giardiniera* and *mostarda*. The pizza is among the better thin-crust versions in town. Living up to the name, the affordable, half-Italian, half-global wine list is offered in quarter, half and full litres.

Sixteen

401 N Wabash Avenue, at E Kinzie Street (1-312 588 8030/www.trumpchicagohotel.com). El: Red to Grand. **Open** 6.30am-2pm Mon-Sat; 5.30-9.30pm Mon-Thur, Sun; 5.30-10pm Fri, Sat; 11am-3pm Sun. **Main courses** $35. **Credit** AmEx, Disc, MC, V. **Map** p326 H11 ❸ **Contemporary American**
The stately dining room on the 16th floor of the Trump Tower is impressive, but the close-up view of architectural gems like the Wrigley Building and Tribune Tower, and the supremely polished, doting staff, both come at a price. Frank Brunacci's artistically presented food includes dishes such as fresh

pasta and escargots in cream sauce with truffles and lamb loin cooked *sous vide* and plated with trumpet mushrooms, salsify and harissa.

▶ *For the hotel in Trump Tower, see p135.*

The Magnificent Mile & Streeterville

$ Eppy's Deli
224 E Ontario Street, between N St Clair Street & N Fairbanks Court (1-312 943 7797). El: Red to Grand. **Open** 9am-7pm Mon-Fri; 9am-6pm Sat, Sun. **Sandwich** $7. **Credit** AmEx, MC, V. **Map** p326 J10 ③ **American**
'Larry the Jew' is at the helm of this slick garden-level operation, which has all the chutzpah of a New York Jewish deli but none of the grit. Ordering your sandwich on the marbled rye is the best bet; whether you choose the thinly sliced turkey or celery-flecked tuna salad, the goods are piled on thick and high.

$ King Café
900 N Michigan Avenue, between E Walton Street & E Delaware Place (1-312 280 6122/www.kingcafechicago.com). El: Red to Chicago. **Open** 7.30am-8pm Mon-Fri; 8am-8pm Sat; 8am-6pm Sun. **Sandwich** $7. **Credit** AmEx, Disc, MC, V. **Map** p326 J9 ③ **Café**
If you're going to eat in a mall, it might as well be the 900 Shops. Restaurateur Joe King serves contemporary café food: butternut squash soup redolent of baking spices; a meaty lobster roll on a tasty grilled roll; and hearty, chewy oatmeal-raisin cookies. The food is a step above what you'd find in other malls, and so are the prices. In other words, just like the shops themselves.

▶ *For the mall, see p190.*

Markethouse
611 N Fairbanks Court, at E Ohio Street (1-312 224 2200/www.markethousechicago.com). El: Red to Grand. **Open** 6am-2pm, 5-10pm daily. **Main courses** $26. **Credit** AmEx, Disc, MC, V. **Map** p326 J10 ③ **Contemporary American**
At Markethouse, executive chef Scott Walton and chef de cuisine Thomas Rice produce flavourful, smart and well-executed comfort classics, updated with seasonal flair. Tender Berkshire pork chop over German-style red cabbage topped with sweet-and-sour quince is a standout, while pastrami cured salmon and a salad of apples, beets, rocket and blue cheese are fantastic starters.

★ NoMI
800 N Michigan Avenue, between W Chicago Avenue & W Pearson Street (1-312 239 4030/www.nomirestaurant.com). El: Red to Chicago. **Open** 6.30am-10.30am Mon-Fri; 11.30am-1.30pm daily; 6-9pm Mon-Thur, Sat, Sun; 6-9.30pm Fri. **Main courses** $36. **Credit** AmEx, Disc, MC, V. **Map** p326 J9 ④ **French/Asian**

The view of Michigan Avenue from the seventh floor of the Park Hyatt is great, but what's going on inside this French-Asian restaurant impresses even more. Christophe David's menu changes each season, but there are always creative options: morels served with Virginia ham from Washington State, say. End your meal with something from the restaurant's vintage tea list.

▶ *For the hotel, see p137.*

Pizzeria Due
619 N Wabash Avenue, between E Ohio & E Ontario Streets (1-312 943 2400). El: Red to Grand. **Open** 11am-1.30am Mon-Thur, Sun; 11am-2.30am Fri, Sat. **Main courses** $15. **Credit** AmEx, Disc, MC, V. **Map** p326 H10 ④ **Pizza**
This crowd-pleasing sister to the original Uno features a cosy dining room/bar that reeks of that 'old Chicago' feel, complete with the black-and-white tiled floor and historical photos lining the walls. Knife-and-fork, deep-dish pizza is its sole raison d'être, with a rich crust that gets crisp from its time in a traditional black-iron pan. Tourists love it; but, secretly, so do jaded locals.

▶ *The original, Pizzeria Uno, is at 29 E Ohio Street (1-312 321 1000).*

Shanghai Terrace
Peninsula Chicago, 108 E Superior Street, between N Michigan Avenue & N Rush Street (1-312 573 6744/www.peninsula.com). El: Red to Chicago. **Open** 5-11pm Mon-Sat. **Main courses** $20. **Credit** AmEx, Disc, MC, V. **Map** p326 J10 ④ **Chinese**
It's not usually worth paying through the nose for Chinese food in Chinatown, particularly when good Chinatown options abound. However, this gorgeous fourth-floor terrace, brimming with fresh flowers and offering a view of the historic Water Tower, is hard to beat, and the elevated takes on five-spiced duck, drunken baby chicken and wok-baked lobster mostly surpass expectations.

▶ *For more on chef Calvin Soh, see p149* **In the 'Hood.**

The Gold Coast

★ Café des Architectes
Sofitel, 20 E Chestnut Street, at N Wabash Avenue (1-312 324 4000/www.cafedesarchitectes.com). El: Red to Chicago. **Open** 6am-11pm daily. **Main courses** $30. **Credit** AmEx, Disc, MC, V. **Map** p326 H9 ④ **French**
Martial Noguier's dishes – delicate *hamachi* carpaccio, sumptuous short ribs, peppery tenderloin au poivre – brim with intricate flavours and textural details, all wrapped up in an exciting, singular package. Desserts from pastry chef Suzanne Imaz, who worked with Noguier at one sixtyblue, follow suit. Very impressive, all told.

CONSUME

★ Spiaggia

980 N Michigan Avenue, between E Oak Street & E Walton Place (1-312 280 2750/www. spiaggiarestaurant.com). El: Red to Clark/ Division. **Open** 6-9pm Mon-Thur, Sun; 5.30-10.30pm Fri, Sat. **Main courses** $42. **Credit** AmEx, Disc, MC, V. **Map** p326 J9 **❹** **Italian**
Want to have the best Italian fine-dining experience in town? Splurge here, a favourite of Barack and Michelle Obama. Tony Mantuano marries imported Italian foodstuffs with top-notch American ingredients and a deep understanding of cuisine from north Italy. Wood-roasted filet mignon with marrow and herb crust is served with hen of the woods mushrooms and roasted red pearl onions.
▶ *For more on Tony Mantuano, see p171*
In the 'Hood.

OLD TOWN & LINCOLN PARK

Old Town

★ Alinea

1723 N Halsted Street, between W North Avenue & W Willow Street (1-312 867 0110/www.alinea-restaurant.com). El: Red to North/Clybourn. **Open** 5.30-9.30pm Wed-Fri; 5-9.30pm Sat, Sun. **Degustation** $145. **Credit** AmEx, Disc, MC, V. **Map** p327 F7 **❹** **Contemporary American**
Gourmet anointed Alinea the no.1 restaurant in the country. So what's all the fuss? Grant Achatz's food, a well-orchestrated ride that plays with textures, temperatures and notions of 'normal' cuisine while somehow remaining grounded in season, flavour

and flawless execution. Past dishes have included squab with peppercorn custard. But you never know what'll steal the show when you're in the audience.

Black Duck

1800 N Halsted Street, at W Willow Street (1-312 664 1801/www.blackducktavern.com). El: Red to North/Clybourn. **Open** 5pm-2am Mon-Fri, Sun; 5pm-3am Sat. **Main courses** $25. **Credit** AmEx, Disc, MC, V. **Map** p327 F7 **❹** **Gastropub**
The stretch of Halsted Street that lays claim to this classy tavern is packed with upscale eateries. More gastropub than sports bar, Black Duck keeps the scene grounded. Grab one of the tables that surround the beautiful, dark-wood bar and start with a Black Duck martini and plate of scallops wrapped in salty bacon. Move on to the New York strip seasoned simply with salt, pepper and rosemary.

★ Perennial

1800 N Lincoln Avenue, at N Clark Street (1-312 981 7070/www.perennialchicago.com). El: Brown or Purple to Sedgwick. **Open** 5-9pm Mon-Thur, Sun; 5pm-2am Fri, Sat; 10am-2pm Sat, Sun. **Main courses** $23. **Credit** AmEx, Disc, MC, V. **Map** p327 H7 **❹** **Contemporary American**
Chefs Giuseppe Tentori and Ryan Poli have a wizardly knack for injecting the essence of summer into the dishes at Perennial: gazpacho brims with the fresh flavours of red pepper; grilled lamb chops have the charred taste of a backyard grill. The menu has just as many hits as misses (go for the chicken wings, but leave the seasonal tart). Still, in a room this cheerful, it's hard to feel anything but content.

CONSUME

Café des Architectes.

Lincoln Park

★ Charlie Trotter's

816 W Armitage Avenue, between N Halsted and N Dayton Streets (1-773 248 6228/www. charlietrotters.com). El: Brown or Purple to Armitage. **Open** 6-9pm Tue-Thur; 5.30-9pm Fri, Sat. **Degustation** $125. **Credit** AmEx, Disc, MC, V. **Map** p328 F6 **43 Contemporary American**

Trotter remains one of the best chefs in the country, proving nightly that not only did he train the younger talent in town, but he can still school them. À la carte doesn't exist here, so go full throttle with the impeccable, contemporary eight-course tasting menu and tack on wine pairings; the team hits them out of the park. Trotter changes the menu every other week or so.

Fattoush

2652 N Halsted Street, between W Wrightwood & W Schubert Avenues (1-773 327 2652/www. fattoushrestaurant.com). El: Brown or Purple to Diversey. **Open** noon-9pm Mon, Wed, Thur; noon-10pm Fri, Sat; noon-8pm Sun. **Main courses** $17. **Credit** AmEx, Disc, MC, V. **Map** p328 F4 **49 Middle Eastern**

The dining room is full of tables dressed with blinding white linens that are, most of the time, empty. But don't let that give you pause. The meze – creamy houmous, steaming spinach pies, crunchy salads – are all potent with sharp, tangy lemon juice, while the aromatic *kibbeh* are packed with cinnamon. The kebabs are more like thin steaks than cubes, but juicy nonetheless. Save room for the four kinds of sticky, flaky baklava.

Half Shell

676 W Diversey Parkway, between N Orchard & N Clark Streets (1-773 549 1773/www.halfshell chicago.com). El: Brown or Purple to Diversey. **Open** 11.30am-11pm daily. **Main courses** $16. **No credit cards. Map** p328 F4 **50 Seafood**

'We close when we feel like closin'' and 'Nothin' but cash, no exceptions' are among the oh-so-perfect-for-the-setting sayings heard in just one night at this 40-year-old, subterranean restaurant. Grab a table in the tiny Christmas light-strewn room, and start out with the Mulligan stew and an order of crispy calamares. If you're looking to crack some crab, splurge on the massive, meaty king legs.

★ L20

2300 N Lincoln Park West, at W Belden Avenue (1-773 868 0002/www.l2orestaurant.com). El: Brown, Purple or Red to Fullerton. **Open** 6-10pm Mon, Wed, Thur; 5-11pm Fri, Sat; 5-9pm Sun. **Degustation** $135. **Credit** AmEx, Disc, MC, V. **Map** p328 G5 **51 Seafood**

Laurent Gras doesn't overlook a single detail at this homage to all things oceanic – from the first feel of the velvety menu to that last bite of macaroon, the chef is in control. À la carte exists only in the lounge; the restaurant offers four- and 12-course menus of inspired options such as salted cod purée with ribbons of smoked gelatin and sliced geoduck with a touch of fresh wasabi. Don't fill up on fish: you'll want to eat as much anchovy-stuffed brioche as you can.

North Pond

2610 N Cannon Drive, between W Fullerton Parkway & N Lake Shore Drive (1-773 477 5845/www.northpondrestaurant.com). Bus:

L20.

76, 151, 156. **Open** *Oct-May* 5.30-9.30pm
Wed-Sun; 10.30am-1pm Sun. *June-Sept* 11.30am-
1.30pm Tue-Fri; 10.30am-1pm Sun; 5.30-9.30pm
Tue-Sun. **Main courses** $40. **Credit** AmEx,
Disc, MC, V. **Map** p328 G4  **Contemporary
American**
Okay, so technically you're not eating outside. But
when you're only a few feet from a pond in the middle of Lincoln Park, you're as close to nature as it
gets in the city. Even more so when you sample chef
Bruce Sherman's elevated contemporary menu, con-
cocted with as much locally grown organic food as
he can find. Dishes might include English peas with
minted goat's cheese gnocchi.

★ Riccardo Trattoria
*2119 N Clark Street, between W Dickens &
W Webster Avenues (1-773 549 0038/www.
riccardotrattoria.com). El: Brown, Purple or Red
to Fullerton.* **Open** 5-10pm Mon-Thur; 5-11pm
Fri, Sat; 5-9pm Sun. **Main courses** $20. **Credit**
AmEx, Disc, MC, V. **Map** p328 G6 ❻ **Italian**
Chef Riccardo Michi's family founded the Bice
restaurant empire in Milan, so he knows a thing or
two about regional Italian food. Don't miss the *orec-
chiette* with wild-boar sausage, garlicky *rapini* and
pecorino cheese, or the rack of lamb. If you're fortu-
nate, the Italian waiters might cap off your meal
with a slice of ricotta cheesecake.

LAKEVIEW & NORTH
Lakeview & Wrigleyville

$ Chicago Diner
*3411 N Halsted Street, between W Roscoe Street
& W Newport Avenue (1-773 935 6696/www.
veggiediner.com/wp). El: Brown, Purple or Red to
Belmont.* **Open** 11am-10pm Mon-Thur; 11am-
10.30pm Fri; 10am-10.30pm Sat; 10am-10pm Sun.
Main courses $11. **Credit** AmEx, Disc, MC, V.
Map p329 F2 ❺ **Vegetarian**
Even non-vegetarians know the Chicago Diner. The
vibe is normal, everyday, albeit with soy milk, tofu
and tempeh on the giant menu. Waits for weekend
brunch can get painful, but patient non-meat-eaters
are rewarded with dense and fairly flaky soy mar-
garine biscuits and sweet blueberry-lemon muffins
made with vegan egg substitute. The back patio is
an outdoor oasis.

$ Crisp
*2940 N Broadway, between W Oakdale & W
Wellington Avenues (1-877 693 8653/www.crisp
online.com). El: Brown or Purple to Diversey.*
Open 11.30am-9pm Tue-Thur, Sun; 11.30am-
10.30pm Fri, Sat. **Main courses** $8. **Credit**
AmEx, MC, V. **Map** p329 F3 ❺ **Korean**
The chicken at Crisp is fresh, of good quality and
comes slathered in three different sauces: a sticky
barbecue, a hot sauce-laced Buffalo and a sesame

Mixteco Grill.
See p160.

soy glaze dubbed 'Seoul Sassy'. The latter is a winner; but even unadorned, the chicken stands out for
its juicy meat and crunchy black pepper-dotted
crust. There's also a decent *bibimbap* and Korean-
style burritos. But really, the chicken is the thing.

HB Home Bistro
*3404 N Halsted Street, between W Roscoe Street
& W Newport Avenue (1-773 661 0299/www.
homebistrochicago.com). El: Brown, Purple or
Red to Belmont.* **Open** 5-10pm Tue-Thur;
5-10.30pm Fri, Sat; 5-9pm Sun. **Main courses**
$19. **Credit** AmEx, Disc, MC, V. **Map** p329 F2 ❺
Contemporary American
The Food Network hype surrounding the Hearty
Boys has died down a little, so you'll probably be
able to grab a table in this funky-cosy Boystown
BYOB. Ever-changing seasonal dishes from chef
Joncarl Lachman might include a creamy mushroom
soup with lavender and thyme; and Kefta-spiced
lamb pie alongside almond-garlic mashed potatoes.
HB's signature cupcake flight, however, happily
remains unchanged.

Mia Francesca
*3311 N Clark Street, between W Aldine Avenue
& W Buckingham Place (1-773 281 3310/www.
miafrancesca.com). El: Brown, Purple or Red to
Belmont.* **Open** 5-10pm Mon-Thur, Sun; 5-11pm
Fri, Sat; 11.30am-2.30pm Sat, Sun. **Main
courses** $15. **Credit** AmEx, Disc, MC, V.
Map p329 F2 ❺ **Italian**

CONSUME

Loyalists from the neighbourhood dig in to huge oval platters of cool, caper-studded carpaccio; pastas tossed with lemony cream and asparagus; and the best garlic spinach in town. Couples and families happily wait at the bar, somehow oblivious to the chaos of the always-packed room and the obligatory wait even for those with a reservation. A very amiable Italian spot.

★ Mixteco Grill

1601 W Montrose Avenue, at N Ashland Avenue (1-773 868 1601). El: Brown to Montrose. **Open** 5-10pm Tue-Thur; 5-11pm Fri, Sat; 5-9pm Sun; 10am-2.30pm Sat, Sun. **Main courses** $17. **Credit** AmEx, Disc, MC, V. Mexican
The *moles* here steal the show. *Sopes* get a dose of the brooding, smoky *mole rojo*, and white fish gets treated with a lighter, sprightly *mole verde*. And while its not a *mole*, the smooth *poblano* sauce pooled around perfectly grilled shrimp is so marine, there's almost no need the seafood. In fact, protein is all but superfluous when you have a bowl of *mole* and some handmade tortillas. *Photo p159.*

$ Southport Grocery & Café

3552 N Southport Avenue, between W Eddy & W Addison Streets (1-773 665 0100/www.southport grocery.com). El: Brown to Southport. **Open** 8am-4pm Mon-Fri, Sun; 8am-5pm Sat. **Main courses** $9. **Credit** AmEx, Disc, MC, V. **Map** p329 D1 ⑤⑧ Café
Go ahead and believe the hype about the cupcake: it's moist, it's substantial but it's not heavy, and the thick, sugary icing hides deep flavours of chocolate and vanilla. For brunch, try sweet and savoury French toast with rosemary-roasted ham. Later, try the fillet of cod, fried up crispy and golden and plated on *challah* with creamy citrus-caper mayo. Eat up, but save room for one of those cupcakes.

$ TAC Quick Thai

3930 N Sheridan Road, between W Dakin Street & W Irving Park Road (1-773 327 5253). El: Red to Sheridan. **Open** 11am-10pm Mon, Wed-Sat; 11am-9.30pm Sun. **Main courses** $8. **Credit** AmEx, MC, V. Thai
The once-tiny Thai joint has more than doubled in size. Luckily, the kitchen isn't having any trouble keeping up with the crowds that flood the simple room. Sure-fire flavour explosions include tart and smoky pork-and-rice sausage; ground chicken with crispy basil and preserved eggs; wrap-ready pork meatballs served with rice papers, fierce chillis, garlic cloves, fresh basil and mint, diced banana and apple; and the best beef noodle dish in town, the brisket-packed 'boat noodles'.

Terragusto on Addison

1851 W Addison Street, between N Lincoln & N Wolcott Avenues (1-773 248 2777/www.terra gustocafe.com). El: Brown to Addison. **Open**
6-10pm Wed-Fri; 5-10pm Sat; 5-8.30pm Sun. **Main courses** $17. **Credit** AmEx, Disc, MC, V. **Map** p330 C1 ⑤⑨ Italian
Theo Gilbert has a master plan for his customers: They're going to sit down and eat a four-course Italian meal made with local, organic, sustainable ingredients. And they're going to like it. *Ripiene* (filled pasta) are delicate and delectable; pan-fried polenta is a luscious base for bitter *rapini* and sweet onions. But do you really need four courses? No. Save yourself the stomach-ache – and the cash – and settle for three.

★ Wakamono

3317 N Broadway, between W Aldine Avenue & W Buckingham Place (1-773 296 6800/www. wakamonosushi.com). El: Brown, Purple or Red to Belmont. **Open** 4-11pm daily. **Small plates** $7. **Credit** AmEx, MC, V. **Map** p329 F2 ⑥⓪ Japanese
This cool-conscious place focuses on small plates of dishes, such as fresh tofu sprinkled with chilli oil and peanuts. Prosciutto topped with *ponzu* sauce, or crunchy toasted shallots and charred asparagus are brilliant, if unexpected, combinations of flavours. And the always-fresh sushi is simply impeccable. Yet the biggest surprise is the service: unlike across the street at sister restaurant Ping Pong, the servers here actually smile.

Roscoe Village

Volo

2008 W Roscoe Street, between N Damen & N Seeley Avenues (1-773 348 4600/www.volo restaurant.com). Bus: 50, 77, 152. **Open** 6-10pm Mon-Thur; 6pm-midnight Fri, Sat. **Small plates** $10. **Credit** AmEx, MC, V. **Map** p330 B2 ⑥① Contemporary American
Stephen Dunne's best dishes at this small-plates wine bar are the rich ones – intense duck confit with haricots vert and lentils, seared diver scallops topped with caviar and crispy leeks – but seasonal specials such as peekytoe-crab salad with preserved lemon and avocado suit just fine, too. The varied wine list is well thought out, with plenty of food-friendly flights available.

Andersonville, Edgewater & Uptown

★ Anteprima

5316 N Clark Street, between W Berwyn & W Summerdale Avenues (1-773 506 9990/http:// anteprimachicago.net). Bus: 22, 92. **Open** 5.30-10pm Mon-Thur; 5.30-11pm Fri, Sat; 5-9.30pm Sun. **Main courses** $20. **Credit** AmEx, Disc, MC, V. Italian
What's not to like about this cute Andersonville bistro? Well, the veal meatballs aren't too hot; but other than that, very little. Don't miss the balsamic

Anteprima.

and honey-laced quail, perfectly roasted so that the crispy skin gives way to juicy, well-seasoned meat; the tender, lemon-kissed, grilled octopus; or the *salumi* plate. Save room for the perfect endings of vanilla bean-speckled lemon *panna cotta* and chocolate tart lined with a buttery hazelnut crust.

$ Coffee Studio
5628 N Clark Street, at W Olive Avenue (1-773 271 7881/www.thecoffeestudio.com). El: Red to Bryn Mawr. **Open** 6.30am-9pm daily. **Coffee** $3. **Credit** AmEx, MC, V. **Café**
Andersonville is nuts about this coffee shop, which offers a colourful variety of organic, sustainable menu items. The quiche selection, featuring hearty wild mushroom pies, is definitely a draw, as are the handful of can't-believe-it's-vegan desserts. The smooth, expertly pulled shots of espresso and smart, mid-century modern design make this the sexiest coffee shop on the block.

Great Lake
1477 W Balmoral Avenue, between N Clark Street & N Glenwood Avenue (1-773 334 9270). El: Red to Berwyn. **Open** 5-9pm Tue-Sat. Main courses $18. **Credit** MC, V. **Pizza**
Warning: everything at this high-design pizzeria is tiny. The space fits one communal table and a shelf of carefully selected sundries, while the menu consists of only four pizzas (and, a create-your-own option isn't one of them). Perhaps most importantly, the pizza oven is also small, allowing for only one pizza to be cooked at a time. Could it be worth the wait? Thanks to the puffy, chewy crust; the house-pulled mozzarella; layers of fresh, earthy mushrooms; and an eye for detail, the answer is yes.

★ Hopleaf
5148 N Clark Street, between W Winona Street & W Foster Avenue (1-773 334 9851/www. hopleaf.com). El: Red to Berwyn. **Open** 5-11pm Mon-Thur, Sun; 5pm-midnight Fri, Sat. **Main courses** $18. **Credit** AmEx, Disc, MC, V. **Gastropub**
Carnivores can exercise their organic options with the likes of smoky brisket sandwich or grilled Dakota beef flank steak at this bar-restaurant (speciality: Belgian beers). Other highlights, if in season, might include roasted spring chicken with oven-roasted artichokes; and CB&J, a grilled sandwich of housemade cashew butter, fig jam and morbier cheese on sourdough bread.

★ $ Pasticceria Natalina
5406 N Clark Street, between W Balmoral & W Catalpa Avenues (1-773 989 0662/www.p-natalina.com). Bus: 22, 92. **Open** noon-9pm Wed-Fri; 9am-7pm Sat; 11am-7pm Sun. **Pastries** $3.50. **Credit** MC, V. **Café**
On weekends, start with the savoury items – you won't regret digging into the fiercely herbal mint-and-pea *fazzoletti*. But the focus of this Sicilian bakeshop is on desserts such as the *sfogliatelle* cookie (delicate layers of pastry encase orange-kissed ricotta) and the *barca di crema*, a square of puff pastry filled with cream and topped with amarena cherries that's intoxicatingly delicious.

$ Svea
5236 N Clark Street, at W Farragut Avenue (1-773 275 7738). El: Red to Berwyn. Open 7am-2.30pm Mon-Fri; 7am-3.30pm Sat, Sun. **Main courses** $7. **No credit cards**. **Swedish**

Sweet Things

Hard as it may be, sometimes you simply have to make room for dessert…

Sometimes you've stuffed yourself so silly at dinner you need a nice stroll before you can even think about looking at a dessert menu. If that's the case, make your sweet stop count with some picks for the city's crème de la crème de la crème.

Natalie Zarzour is a stickler for the details. The baker-owner of Sicilian-leaning sweet shop **Pasticceria Natalina** (*see p161*) knows just what it takes to make the perfect **cannoli**: a delicate shell, a filling of whipped sheep's milk ricotta, candied citrus folded into the filling, tiny chips of dark chocolate, unsalted pistachios and, last but not least, Zarzour says 'they gotta be filled to order.'

Even if you're not dripping money like most of the well-heeled regulars at **Spiaggia** (*see p157*; Obama's among them), you owe it to yourself to stop in for some coffee and **gelato** at the bar. The staff spends more than three hours each morning spinning 25 flavours of gelati and sorbetti, painstakingly cleaning the machine between each batch to avoid flavour overlap. Chocolate, vanilla, pistachio, espresso are the constants.

But the change of seasons brings maple-candied-walnut and pumpkin in fall, blood orange and quince in winter, and blueberry and cherry in summer.

Savvy Division Street shoppers already know that the best bargain along the strip isn't found on a dress rack: it's behind the gleaming cases of **chocolate** emporium **Coco Rouge** (*see p168*), which rotates concoctions so creative Willy Wonka would be impressed. In cold weather, the thick-as-pudding hot chocolate is unbeatable; year-round, try chocolates and truffles spiked with smoky scotch, fiery red chillies or fragrant saffron.

The name of Mindy Segal, the pastry chef at **HotChocolate** (*see p169*), has become synonymous with sweets in this town, and her style is based more on the weather than her own whim. Among her **seasonal desserts**, winter sees citrus turned into multiple forms, summer brings out berry-based plates, and spring is time for strawberry-rhubarb and Meyer lemon. Purists are in luck: Segal's stellar brioche doughnuts with hot fudge are available all year-round.

Fancy-shmancy breakfast food, the kind with goat's cheese in the omelettes and too much fruit in the pancake batter, is a bit much on mornings after the night before. On those days, head to this Andersonville diner for hearty, no-nonsense food. The Viking Breakfast – two eggs, three Swedish pancakes with lingonberry compote, *falukorv* sausage and toast – is an excellent hangover cure; later in the day, try the Swedish meatballs.

THE NEAR WEST SIDE
The West Loop & Greektown

★ Avec
615 W Randolph Street, between N Jefferson & N Desplaines Streets (1-312 377 2002/www.avec restaurant.com). El: Green or Pink to Clinton. **Open** 3.30pm-midnight Mon-Thur; 3.30pm-1am Fri, Sat; 3.30-11pm Sun. **Small plates** $10. **Credit** AmEx, Disc, MC, V. **Map** p330 F12 ❷ **Mediterranean**
Owner Donnie Madia and chef Paul Kahan's tiny space looks like a sauna, has communal seating, doesn't take reservations and is as loud as hell. But it's a must-eat spot for in-the-know foodies. Small mainstays such as chorizo-stuffed dates and salty

brandade are unbeatable; wood oven-roasted curried pork shoulder with dried apricots, prunes, slab bacon and apricot mustard is another favourite.

★ Blackbird
619 W Randolph Street, between N Jefferson & N Desplaines Streets (1-312 715 0708). El: Green or Pink to Clinton. **Open** 11.30am-2pm Mon-Fri; 5.30-10.30pm Mon-Thur; 5.30-11.30pm Fri, Sat. **Main courses** $33. **Credit** AmEx, Disc, MC, V. **Map** p330 F12 ❸ **Contemporary American**
Paul Kahan's minimalist chic restaurant is as popular as ever, with chef Mike Sheerin feeding the way-too-cool-for-school crowd and pastry chef Tim Dahl indulging their sweet teeth. You'll find evidence of the duo's handiwork at this creative eaterie in dishes such as crispy veal sweetbreads and cool Meyer-lemon mousse flanked by nibs of dehydrated olive, fennel and grapefruit pieces.

De Cero
814 W Randolph Street, at N Green Street (1-312 455 8114/www.decerotaqueria.com). El: Green or Pink to Clinton. **Open** 11.30am-2pm Mon-Fri; 5-10pm Mon-Thur; 5-11pm Fri, Sat; 5-9pm Sun. **Main courses** $16. **Credit** AmEx, Disc, MC, V. **Map** p330 F11 ❹ **Mexican**

This *taquería* fancies itself as edgy and upscale. Battered fish tacos don't quite fit the bill, but they make for a delicious guilty pleasure. More refined tacos include the ahi tuna, coupled with a mango salsa and bursting with bright, fresh flavours, and the chorizo, with a kick tempered by cool crema. Fresh corn tamales shine with straight-off-the-cob flavour that goes perfectly with one of the tart hibiscus margaritas.

$ Ina's
1235 W Randolph Street, between N Racine Avenue & N Elizabeth Street (1-312 226 8227/ www.breakfastqueen.com). Bus: 20. **Open** 7am-3pm Mon; 7am-3pm, 5-9pm Tue-Fri; 8am-3pm, 5-9pm Sat; 8am-2pm Sun. **Main courses** $9. **Credit** AmEx, Disc, MC, V. **Map** p330 E12 **65** **American**
Judging from the queues at the weekends, people seem willing to wait forever for scrapple (a crispy, slightly spicy polenta-like dish flanked by eggs and chorizo) and Heavenly Hots (sour cream pancakes with fruit compote). But that same comfort-food theme can also be found at dinner, when Ina cooks her famous fried chicken and, on weekends, a 'Friday night in Brooklyn' special of matzo-ball soup and brisket.

Meiji
623 W Randolph Street, between N Jefferson & N Desplaines Streets (1-312 887 9999/http:// meijirestaurant.com). El: Green or Pink to Clinton. **Open** 11.30am-2.30pm Mon-Fri; 5-10.30pm Mon-Wed; 5-11.30pm Thur-Sat. **Nigiri** $6. **Credit** AmEx, Disc, MC, V. **Map** p330 F12 **66** **Japanese**

This sophisticated sushi spot also dabbles in traditional Japanese dishes such as egg-custard soup. On the sushi side, both novices and traditionalists will be happy: over-the-top rolls bursting with cream cheese and tempura crunch are balanced by incredibly fresh, razor-thin sashimi cuts of fatty tuna and fluke, as well as harder-to-come-by seasonal cuts such as *shirauo*, slick slivers of white fish – commonly called ice fish – served in a cucumber cup.

$ 9 Muses
315 S Halsted Street, between W Jackson Boulevard & W Van Buren Street (1-312 902 9922). El: Blue to UIC-Halsted. **Open** 11am-2am Mon-Fri; 11am-3am Sat. **Main courses** $7. **Credit** AmEx, Disc, MC, V. **Map** p330 F12 **67** **Greek**
It's a good sign that this trendy, clubby sort of restaurant is packed with young Greeks: their presence suggests that the Hellenic munchies, like the Florina peppers (two roasted red peppers stuffed with creamy feta), *loukanika* (a pork-lamb sausage) and huge gyro platters, are on the mark. If you can stop yourself from talking by shovelling in the food, nobody will know you don't belong.

One Sixtyblue
1400 W Randolph Street, between N Ada Street & N Ogden Avenue (1-312 850 0303/www.one sixtyblue.com). El: Green or Pink to Ashland. **Open** 5.30-9.30pm Mon-Thur; 5.30-10.30pm Fri, Sat. **Main courses** $25. **Credit** AmEx, MC, V. **Map** p330 D11 **68** **French**
The kitchen at One Sixtyblue has won a deserved reputation for its contemporary French fare grounded by seasonal American products. Dishes

Publican. *See p164.*

might include chilled ahi tuna tartare with mango or wild striped bass with manila clams, baby purple artichokes and crispy bacon. Sweets such as house-made truffles and a white chocolate-coconut mousse with lime foam are tasty endings; alternatively, relax in the lofty dining room with a port and a cheese plate starring America's finest.

Province

161 N Jefferson Street, between W Randolph & W Lake Street (1-312 669 9900/http:// provincerestaurant.com). El: Green or Pink to Clinton. **Open** 11.30am-10.30pm Mon-Thur; 11.30am-11.30pm Fri; 5-11.30pm Sat. **Main courses** $17. **Credit** AmEx, Disc, MC, V. **Map** p326 F11 **American/Latin American**
Big is the key word at Randy Zweiban's Province, an American restaurant with Latin touches. House-smoked *sable ceviche* has a powerful smoky brini-ness, a taco filled with rich, oily tuna and fiery serrano-chile salsa and rabbit confit gets paired with a thick marcona-almond emulsion. When a dish dis-appoints, it's not because it's bad, but rather because it simply cannot compete with the more aggressive food on the table.

★ Publican

837 W Fulton Market, between N Green Street & N Peoria Street (1-312 733 9555/http://the publicanrestaurant.com). El: Green or Pink to Clinton. **Open** 3.30-10.30pm Mon-Thur; 3.30-11.30pm Fri, Sat; 10am-2pm, 5-10pm Sun. **Share plate** $19. **Credit** AmEx, Disc, MC, V. **Map** p330 F11 **Gastropub**
The third project from the team behind Blackbird (*see p162*) is a minimalist, golden-hued, beer hall-like space. Pork is king of chef Brian Huston's menu; to come here and not order the impeccable charcu-terie is to miss the point. But non-swine entrées come off just as well, whether in shareable plates of lightly charred half-chicken paired with thick rounds of summer sausage or pan-seared whole loup-de-mer stuffed with bitter greens. The Belgian-heavy beer list is worth some exploring. *Photo p163.*

Santorini

800 W Adams Street, at S Halsted Street (1-312 829 8820/www.santorinichicago.com). El: Blue to UIC-Halsted. **Open** 11am-10pm Mon-Thur, Sun; 11am-midnight Fri, Sat. **Main courses** $17. **Credit** AmEx, Disc, MC, V. **Map** p330 F12 **Greek**
The Kantos family serves food that's impeccably fresh, importing organic olive oil and oregano from the family farm in Sparta. Like most of the seafood, the whole, grilled red snapper needs nothing more than a squeeze of lemon to show off its delicate flesh and subtle flavour. You may jump every time some-body screams 'Opa!' and a ball of flaming *saganaki* cheese erupts at nearby tables, but if your nerves can handle it, your taste buds will thank you.

Veerasway

844 W Randolph Street, between N Green & N Peoria Streets (1-312 491 0844/www. veerasway.com). El: Green or Pink to Clinton. **Open** 5-9pm Mon-Wed, Sun; 5-10pm Thur; 11.30am-2pm, 5-10pm Fri; 5-10pm Sat. **Main courses** $16. **Credit** AmEx, Disc, MC, V. **Map** p330 F11 **Indian**
This modern Indian spot does a nice job updating the fiery cuisine with snazzy street snacks (try the fried banana peppers stuffed with lentils and paneer) and cocktails (the cardamom-packed Bengali Tiger is delicious). Heat-seekers should request extra fire with classics such as lamb rogan josh, while those looking for something new will find it with the juicy tamarind-date glazed chicken.

Little Italy & Heart of Chicago

$ Al's #1 Italian Beef

1079 W Taylor Street, between S Carpenter & S Aberdeen Streets (1-312 226 4017/www.als beef.com). El: Blue to Racine. **Open** 9am-11pm Mon-Thur; 9am-midnight Fri; 10am-midnight Sat; 10am-11pm Sun. **Main courses** $4. **No credit cards. Map** p330 E14 **American**
Having opened in 1938, this Al's is the oldest, and the only direct descendent of the original (a wooden stand at Laflin and Harrison). These days, you'll find Italian beefs all over town, but there's something special about eating one at this surviving piece of Little Italy. A six-inch bun piled with tender, thinly sliced beef is only better as a 'combo' (topped with chargrilled sausage), 'dipped' in beef jus and fin-ished with hot giardiniera.

Francesca's on Taylor

1400 W Taylor Street, at S Loomis Street (1-312 829 2828/www.miafrancesca.com). El: Blue to Racine. **Open** 11.30am-2.30pm Mon-Fri; 5-9pm Mon; 5-10pm Tue-Thur; 5-11pm Fri, Sat; 4-9pm Sun. **Main courses** $15. **Credit** AmEx, Disc, MC, V. **Map** p330 D14 **Italian**
The portions are generous, the room is comfortable and the food is reliable. This, plus the place's ability to glide from family-friendly pasta joint to romantic trattoria as the night progresses, is what packs 'em in every night. Good bets include crispy calamares, *quattro stagioni* pizza and rosemary-laced roasted chicken. The food isn't going to conjure any memo-ries of travels to Italy, but it's a safe bet in Little Italy's increasingly less-Italian landscape.

RoSal's

1154 W Taylor Street, between S May Street & S Racine Avenue (1-312 243 2357/www.rosals. com). El: Blue to Racine. **Open** 4-9pm Mon-Thur; 4-11pm Fri, Sat. **Main courses** $18. **Credit** AmEx, Disc, MC, V. **Map** p330 E14 **Italian**
Typically, we'd tell the server to save the speech, but here, it's somehow still charming when the bubbly

In the 'Hood Pilsen

Frontera Grill's Rick Bayless tours his favourite Mexican spots.

'There are two flavour profiles in Mexican food,' says Rick Bayless between bites of a taco at Pilsen's **Don Pedro Carnitas** (1113 W 18th Street, 1-312 829 4757): home food and street food. 'Street food almost always has this super well-cooked fatty element in it that is completely balanced by straight, bright acid. The street-food balance in Mexico is about the fatty [being] as strong as the acid. And that's why all the salsas in Mexico are not based on tomatoes – they're based on tomatillos. Because they're hugely more acidic.'

Bayless's passion for Mexican food first came to public attention in the late '70s, when he appeared in a PBS series about the cuisine. He opened Frontera Grill in the mid '80s, since when his empire has spread to include fine-dining restaurants and snack counters, cookbooks and supermarket sauces. But through it all, he's remained faithful to Chicago, and is still a regular visitor to the Mexican enclave of Pilsen.

On the way to **Restaurant La Casa Del Pueblo** (1834 S Blue Island Avenue, 1-312 421 4664), Bayless puts in a good word for that Mexican institution, the grocery-store eaterie. 'If you have a Mexican grocery near you, the taquería inside is really a good bet, typically.' La Casa is next door to its grocery-store counterpart, and is not so much a taquería as it is a *fonda* – a Mexican diner. All kinds of home-style Mexican dishes are displayed cafeteria-style, including *chicharrónes en salsa verde* (pork rinds soaked in a green-chilli sauce; 'an acquired taste,' admits Bayless).

From here, it's only a short stroll to **Taquería Cardona's** (1451 W 18th Street, 1-312 492 8059) for a *huarache*, a flat oval of *masa* (tortilla dough) topped with *cecina*. It's covered in iceberg lettuce – probably an American addition, Bayless says – but that does little to interfere with the intricate beefy and briny flavour of the chopped *cecina*.

And finally, it's off to **Kristoffer's Cafe** (1733 S Halsted Street, 1-312 829 4150), a coffee shop/bakery to which Bayless has been tipped off by a friend. The *tres leches* cake is rumoured to be great, but Bayless looks little dubious. There are all kinds of three-milks (condensed, evaporated and regular) cake, some in sacrilegious

CONSUME

variations (eggnog, caramel, piña colada). 'Here in the United States,' he mutters, 'we tend to want 31 flavours of everything.'

It turns out that the tres leches isn't good. It's *more* than good: sumptuous without being soggy, satisfying without being overly sweet. Bayless sits at the table and falls into deep thought, forking cake into his mouth in silence. Finally, he walks up to the counter and asks to speak to the couple who own the place. He doesn't have to introduce himself; they've been excited since he walked in. Now, as he gets ready to address them, they hold on to each other in nervous anticipation.

'I've eaten a lot of tres leches in Mexico,' he tells them. 'And this – this is the best one I've ever had.'

▶ For Bayless's **Frontera Grill**, see p154.

girl 'from da neighborhood' explains how namesake owners Roseanne and Salvatore came to open their Little Italy spot. Cuteness aside, the food's among the best to be found on the Taylor Street strip. Start with the lightly charred but tender grilled calamari; and go for the veal *saltimbocca* with a side of spinach for the main event.

Pilsen

$ El Milagro
1927 S Blue Island Avenue, between W 19th & W Cullerton Streets (1-312 421 7443/www. el-milagro.com). El: Pink to 18th. **Open** 7am-6.30pm Mon-Sat; 7am-5pm Sun. **Main courses** $4. **Credit** AmEx, Disc, MC, V. **Mexican**
This Pilsen café is covered in bright purple, yellow and orange paint inside and out. What does it have to be so cheery about? Mainly, it's one of the city's most successful purveyors of corn and flour tortillas. And employees know how to put those tortillas to good use: piling them with tender chicken legs submerged in *mole rojo*, or sumptuous, slow-cooked beef in a rich tomato sauce. Satisfying tamales are available for a more portable meal.

$ Nuevo León
1515 W 18th Street, between S Laflin Street & S Ashland Avenue (1-312 421 1517/www.nuevo leonrestaurant.com). El: Pink to 18th. **Open** 7am-midnight Sat, Sun. **Main courses** $10. **No credit cards.** **Mexican**
Since 1962, the Gutierrez family has been running this mecca of Mexican food, starting every dinner with an unexpected amuse-bouche. Don't fill up: there's a lot more where that came from, such as roasted chicken pieces covered in a thick, dark, intense *mole*, and *tacos de chorizo*. The waitresses hustling back and forth between two rooms are cheerfully brisk but will bring anything you ask except alcohol – you've got to bring the mescal yourself.

WICKER PARK & AROUND
Ukrainian Village & West Town

Flo
1434 W Chicago Avenue, between N Greenview Avenue & N Bishop Street (1-312 243 0477/ www.eatatflo.com). **Open** 8.30am-10pm Tue-Thur; 8.30am-11pm Fri; 9am-11pm Sat; 9am-2.30pm Sun. **Main courses** $11. **Credit** AmEx, Disc, MC, V. **Map** p331 D9 **Café**
Folk-art collectors Renée and Rodney Carswell's funky, casual dining room is an all-day draw for those after an interesting meal at a reasonable price. Brunch and breakfast standouts include New Mexico-influenced tongue-scorchers such as green-chilli enchiladas and *huevos rancheros*, perfect when balanced with fresh-fruit smoothies and strong cof-

fee. At dinner, local and often organic produce appear as salads and sides for comforting classics such as fish tacos and roasted chicken *mole*.

★ Green Zebra
1460 W Chicago Avenue, at N Greenview Avenue (1-312 243 7100/www.greenzebrachicago.com). El: Blue to Chicago. **Open** 5.30-10pm Mon-Thur; 5-11pm Fri, Sat; 10.30am-2pm, 5-9pm Sun. **Main courses** $12. **Credit** AmEx, MC, V. **Map** p331 D9 **⑦ Vegetarian**
Shawn McClain's moss-coloured, minimalist house of Zen is the only upscale dining experience that local vegetarians can truly call their own. Scrubbed-up brunch classics at Green Zebra include German-style pancakes with Granny Smiths and caramelised-banana crêpes with ricotta and Wisconsin honey. Chef de cuisine Molly Kipp's superseasonal dinner menu is always updated: you may find agnolotti with stinging nettles, or roasted halibut with fingerlings, fennel and asparagus.

★ $ Lovely: A Bake Shop
1130 N Milwaukee Avenue, between W Thomas Street & W Haddon Avenue (1-773 572 4766/ www.lovelybakeshop.com). El: Blue to Division. **Open** 7am-7pm Mon-Fri; 9am-6pm Sat; 9am-4pm Sun. **Pastries** $3. **Credit** MC, V. **Map** p331 D9 **⑬ Café**
Brooke Dailey and Gina Howie, two friends who met at the French Pastry School, are behind this comfortable bakery filled with vintage tables and knick-knacks. The treats are more than a match for the decor: from cakey, star-shaped muffins to flaky pain au chocolat, the pastries are just as sweet and delicious as they should be. And their brownies? Tinged with crème fraiche and dark chocolate, they're some of the most decadent in town.

May Street Market
1132 W Grand Avenue, at N May Street (1-312 421-5547). El: Blue to Grand. **Open** 5-10pm Mon-Sat. **Main courses** $21. **Credit** AmEx, Disc, MC, V. **Contemporary American**

> ### INSIDE TRACK
> ### THE BRUNCH BUNCH
>
> Few American cities dive into weekend brunch with as much enthusiasm as Chicago. Among the best brunches in the city are those served at **Perennial** (*see p157*) in Old Town; the **Southport Grocery & Café** (*see p160*) in Lakeview; **Ina's** (*see p163*) and the **Bristol** (*see p168*) in the West Loop; **Flo** (*see left*) and **Green Zebra** (*see above*) in Ukrainian Village; and **HotChocolate** (*see p169*) and the **Bongo Room** (*see p168*) in Wicker Park.

CONSUME

Bristol. *See p168.*

Alex Cheswick's Grand Avenue restaurant is a destination for lovers of contemporary food. Regulars tend to fall back on signature favourites such as the Maytag blue cheese-cake appetiser, but don't ignore the bar menu, which showcases Cheswick's talent with burgers (good luck deciding between the turkey and beef versions). Also available at the bar: a shareable Spanish and American cheese plate that makes the wait for a table more tolerable.

Paramount Room

415 N Milwaukee Avenue, between W Kinzie & W Hubbard Streets (1-312 829 6300). El: Blue to Grand. **Open** *3pm-midnight Mon-Wed; 11.30am-2am Thur, Fri; 11am-2am Sat; 11am-10pm Sun.* **Main courses** $15. **Credit** AmEx, MC, V. **Map** p330 F11 ⑳ **Gastropub**
Chef Stephen Dunne focuses on elevated bar food at this West Town spot. Some of his food (fried pickle spears, a Wagyu burger) acts merely as a sponge for the impressive beer list. But the duck confit is sublime, the fish-and-chips are crisp and flavourful, and the crab salad is light and inspired. The ultimate beer and food pairing comes at dessert with the Black & Tan Float, a root-beer float made with Guinness ice-cream.

$ Shokolad

2524 W Chicago Avenue, at N Maplewood Avenue (1-773 276 6402). Bus: 49, X49, 66. **Open** *8am-7pm Tue-Fri; 9am-7pm Sat; 10am-7pm Sun.* **Main courses** $7. **Credit** AmEx, Disc, MC, V. **Café**
Well-heeled women chat over coffee and cake, a handful of sugar-rushing kids scrape the bottom of their fruit parfaits, and neighbourhood elders, including men of the cloth, tuck into good bowls of borscht, all to the tune of Ukrainian chatter. The younger of the mother-daughter team behind the casual spot is right to recommend her mom's baked goods, but the savoury crêpes, buttery panini and delicious soups are all worth a visit.

$ Twisted Spoke

501 N Ogden Avenue, at W Grand Avenue (1-312 666 1500/www.twistedspoke.com). El: Blue to Grand. **Open** *11am-2am Mon-Fri; 9am-3am Sat; 9am-2am Sun.* **Main courses** $9. **Credit** AmEx, MC, V. **American**
When you begin brunch by showing your ID at the door, you know you're in the right place for a bloody Mary. Spicy and sweet, garnished with salami and completed with a beer back, it's practically a meal in itself. But don't let it distract you from the food. Breakfast tacos are a good way to spice up your egg intake, and the Spoke's signature 'Fatboy' burgers are thick, juicy and perfectly tender.

West Town Tavern

1329 W Chicago Avenue, at N Throop Street (1-312 666 6175/www.westtowntavern.com). El: Blue to Chicago. **Open** *5-10pm Mon-Sat.* **Main courses** $22. **Credit** AmEx, MC, V. **Gastropub**
Would that every neighbourhood had a cosy spot like this: unfussy food, fun wines, and jeans and suits mingling *sans* attitude. Chef-owner Susan Goss and husband Drew keep customers coming back weekly for nightly specials, such as the killer buttermilk biscuit-and-fried chicken platter made with Goss's great-grandma's recipe. On other nights, the staple menu – antipasto plates, skillet-roasted mussels – is supplemented by seasonal specials.

Wicker Park & Bucktown

Bin Wine Café

1559 N Milwaukee Avenue, between W Honore Street & W North Avenue (1-773 486 2233/ http://binwinecafe.com). El: Blue to Damen. **Open** 5-10pm Mon-Thur; 5-11.30pm Fri; 10am-11.30pm Sat; 10am-10pm Sun. **Small plates** $13. **Credit** AmEx, Disc, MC, V. **Map** p331 C7 ⓰ **Wine bar**
The focus at this cosy storefront by the folks behind Bin 36 is wine and John Caputo's global cuisine. The dinner menu is full of delicious seasonal plates, such as winter's slow-roasted pork ribs with blood-orange barbecue sauce and summer's seared Montana ruby red trout with sweet corn salsa. But it's the brunch that's really filling. With must-trys such as chocolate-chip pancakes and blue crab-and-spinach quiche, you'll probably be too full for dinner.

$ Bongo Room

1470 N Milwaukee Avenue, at W Evergreen Avenue (1-773 489 0690). El: Blue to Damen. **Open** 7.30am-2pm Mon-Fri; 9am-2pm Sat, Sun. **Main courses** $10. **Credit** AmEx, Disc, MC, V. **Map** p331 C8 ⓱ **Café**
Hungover musicians, early-rising soccer moms and everybody in between flocks to this bright, cheery spot for fancy morning cocktails and the outrageous sweet brunch specials: chocolate tower French toast, for instance, a creamy, luxurious pile of chocolate bread smothered in what's essentially melted banana crème brûlée. Prepare to wait in line.

Le Bouchon

1958 N Damen Avenue, between W Homer Street & W Armitage Avenue (1-773 862 6600/www.lebouchonofchicago.com). El: Blue to Damen. **Open** 5.30-11pm Mon-Thur; 5pm-midnight Fri, Sat. **Main courses** $20. **Credit** AmEx, Disc, MC, V. **Map** p331 B6 ⓲ **French**
It's small and crowded, and you'll have to wait at the bar even with a reservation. But Le Bouchon is the closest thing Chicago has to that adorable little bistro in Paris. Regulars have their never-fail favourites: the flaky, caramelly onion tart; the robust onion soup with a gluttonous amount of gruyère; the butter-topped steak flanked by perfectly crisp frites; the simple profiteroles. Only ruder waiters could make for a more French experience.

★ Bristol

2152 N Damen Avenue, between W Shakespeare and W Webster Avenues (1-773 862 5555/ www.thebristolchicago.com). El: Blue to Western. **Open** 5.30-10pm Mon-Thur; 5.30pm-midnight Fri; 10am-2pm, 5.30pm-midnight Sat; 10am-2pm, 5-10pm Sun. **Main courses** $16. **Credit** AmEx, MC, V. **Map** p331 B5 ⓳
Contemporary American
There's a benefit to eating at the communal tables of this charming, simple restaurant: it's easy to scope

out chef Chris Pandel's dishes before committing to ordering. So if you see somebody swooning over the combination of crisp, acidic fruit and creamy Manchego in the heirloom apple salad, the fried sardines with pickled tomatoes or the devastatingly delicious egg-and-ricotta-filled raviolo, order it. But for help on the stellar beer list, put yourself in the hands of the capable servers. *Photo p167.*

Club Lucky

1824 W Wabansia Avenue, at N Honore Street (1-773 227 2300/http://clubluckychicago.com). El: Blue to Damen. **Open** 11.30am-10pm Mon, Tue; 11.30am-11pm Wed, Thur; 11.30am-midnight Fri; 5pm-midnight Sat; 4-10pm Sun. *May-Sept* also 11.30am-5pm Sat, 10am-2.30pm Sun. **Main courses** $18. **Credit** AmEx, Disc, MC, V. **Map** p331 C7 ⓴ **Italian**
The nearby condo dwellers with children in tow may be a different crowd than the Polish regulars who once frequented this joint post-Prohibition, but the owners have gone out of their way to restore the original cocktail-culture look of the '50s. The place is always packed, thanks to a dependable, old-school, family-style Italian menu with standouts such as grilled calamares and chicken vesuvio. If you're kidphobic, go late for the lounge vibe of Sinatra standards and signature martinis.

$ Coco Rouge

1940 W Division Street, at N Winchester Avenue (1-773 772 2626). El: Blue to Division. **Open** noon-10pm Tue-Sat; noon-8pm Sun. **Desserts** $6. **Credit** AmEx, MC, V. **Map** p331 B8 ⓵ **Desserts**
See p162 **Sweet Things.**

Crust

2056 W Division Street, at N Hoyne Avenue (1-773 235 5511/www.crustorganic.com). El: Blue to Division. **Open** 5-10pm Mon-Thur; 11.30am-midnight Fri-Sun. **Main courses** $12. **Credit** AmEx, Disc, MC, V. **Map** p331 B8 ⓶ **Café**
The motto of Crust is 'Eat Real'. 'Eat simple and good' is more like it: that's the general take on salads composed of impeccably fresh vegetables; tender pulled pork topped with crunchy slaw on soft housemade brioche; and pizzas (appearing on the menu as 'flatbreads'), which have a bubbly, half-inch-thick crust that's slightly, pleasantly chewy. When it's topped with béchamel, caramelised onion, bacon and caraway seeds, like the 'Flammkuchen', it can be very good indeed.

Duchamp

2118 N Damen Avenue, at W Charleston Street (1-773 235 6434/www.duchamp-chicago.com). El: Blue to Western. **Open** 5-10pm Mon-Thur, Sun; 5-11pm Fri, Sat. **Main courses** $17. **Credit** AmEx, Disc, MC, V. **Map** p331 B6 ⓷ **French/American**

Mado.

Duchamp has all the elements of a great restaurant: a modern but cosy room, an incomparable patio, and an established chef putting out French and American classics. The problem is that the food only lives up to its potential half of the time. For every great dish (tender braised pork shoulder; sweet, spicy and crispy chicken wings), there's a lacklustre one (pasty gnocchi; under-seasoned fish and chips). Thankfully, the rest of the experience outweighs even the most disappointing bites.

Enoteca Roma

2146 W Division Street, between N Hoyne Avenue & N Leavitt Street (1-773 342 1011/ www.enotecaroma.com). **Open** 5pm-midnight Mon-Fri; 10am-3pm, 5pm-midnight Sat, Sun. **Main courses** $16. **Credit** AmEx, Disc, MC, V. **Map** p331 B8 **88** Italian

Cop a seat among the greenery and dive into the wine list; it's playful, varied (not limited to Italian bottles) and built for food. Topped with toothsome ingredients such as brie and honey, cannellini beans and black olive purée, the bruschetta varieties are the favourite sons of the extensive menu, but don't overlook the Roman-style pizzas and Letizia's soft, salty focaccia with spicy mustard.

★ HotChocolate

1747 N Damen Avenue, at W Willow Street (1-773 489 1747/www.hotchocolatechicago.com). El: Blue to Damen. **Open** 11.30am-2pm Wed-Fri; 5.30-10pm Tue, Wed; 5.30-11pm Thur; 5.30pm-midnight Fri; 10am-2pm, 5.30pm-midnight Sat; 10am-2pm, 5.30-10pm Sun. **Main courses** $14. **Credit** AmEx, Disc, MC, V. **Map** p331 B7 **89** Contemporary American

Don't let the name fool you – it's not just desserts here. Chef de cuisine Mark Steuer and pastry chef Mindy Segal are both sticklers for season, so expect an everchanging assortment of dishes from cold-weather classics such as brined, bone-in pork chop with sautéed spaetzle to springy pan-seared trout with citrus, radishes and fennel. Segal shines with finales such as Thoughts on Cherries, a tasting plate of the fruit done four ways, and at brunch.

★ Mado

1647 N Milwaukee Avenue, at W Caton Street (1-773 342 2340/www.madorestaurant chicago.com). El: Blue to Damen. **Open** 5-10pm Tue-Thur; 5-11pm Fri, Sat; 10am-2.30pm, 5-9pm Sun. **Main courses** $19. **Credit** AmEx, Disc, MC, V. **Map** p331 B7 **90** Mediterranean

The combination of exemplary ingredients and minimalist preparation is at the heart of every dish at this simple BYOB spot; it turns out to be an excellent way to cook. The kitchen allows Jerusalem artichokes, dressed with lemon and parsley, to show off their crunchy earthiness, scallops (prepared *crudo*-style with grapefruit) to boast their clean, natural sweetness, and housemade beef-shank terrine to exhibit its lingering richness.

Mana Food Bar

1742 W Division Street, between N Paulina & N Wood Streets (1-773 342 1742/www.manafood bar.com). El: Blue to Division. **Open** 4-10pm Mon-Thur; noon-11pm Fri, Sat; noon-9pm Sun. **Small plates** $6. **Credit** AmEx, Disc, MC, V. **Map** p331 C8 91 **Vegetarian**

Susan Thompson and Jill Barron of De Cero have teamed up again at this spot, where global vegetarian fare is gobbled up by diners lounging on chunky wood stools and dark booths. It's not cheap – two people will spend around $50 to leave full – so to leave both replete and happy, choose wisely. Try the small portions of simple yellow squash 'pasta', asparagus ravioli in spicy tomato sauce and the brown rice-mushroom sliders.

★ Mirai Sushi

2020 W Division Street, between N Damen & N Hoyne Avenues (1-773 862 8500/www.mirai sushi.com). El: Blue to Division. **Open** 5-10pm Mon-Thur; 5-11pm Fri, Sat. **Nigiri** $4. **Credit** AmEx, Disc, MC, V. **Map** p331 B8 92 **Sushi**

Signatures such as *yukke toro* (fatty tuna tartare with quail egg and housemade soy sauce) and *kani nigiri* (seaweed filled with baked spicy crab) aren't exclusive to Mirai Sushi, but the funky neighbourhood and surrounding post-dinner bar choices are. The prices are $2-$5 less than at Japonais, with which Mirai shares a head chef, so use the extra dough to attack the specials sheet, which often offers supremely fresh flights of tuna and whitefish of varying fattiness.

Piece

1927 W North Avenue, between N Wolcott & N Winchester Avenues (1-773 772 4422/www.piece chicago.com). El: Blue to Damen. **Open** 11am-10.30pm Mon-Wed; 11am-11pm Thur; 11am-12.30am Fri, Sat; 11am-10pm Sun. **Main courses** $14. **Credit** AmEx, Disc, MC, V. **Map** p331 C7 93 **Pizza**

Two things keep Piece from going the route of sports-bar-beer-bong culture: it serves excellent house brews and makes expertly executed pizzas. The crispy pies hold a lot of weight, so after you choose your pizza style – red, white or New Haven-style 'plain' (red sauce, no mozzarella) – start piling on the toppings. Wash it down with a pitcher of the crisp Golden Arm, and you'll never disparagingly say 'pizza and beer joint' again.

Restaurant Takashi

1952 N Damen Avenue, between W Homer Street & W Armitage Avenue (1-773 772 6170/ www.takashichicago.com). El: Blue to Western. **Open** 5.30-10pm Tue-Thur; 5.30-10.30pm Fri; 5-10.30pm Sat; 5-9.30pm Sun. **Main courses** $22. **Credit** AmEx, Disc, MC, V. **Map** p331 B6 94 **Japanese**

Takashi Yagihashi has transformed the former Scylla space into a Zen den showcasing food that deftly combines his Japanese heritage with French training and American ingredients. Flavours are subtle and balanced; presentation is delicate and often beautiful. Yagihashi's frequent use of local seasonal produce means that sunny days may bring a summer roll with shrimp, smoked salmon, caviar and a caper-golden raisin dressing, while winter ushers in a shrimp roll or pork belly with steamed bun.

Rodan

1530 N Milwaukee Avenue, between N Damen Avenue & N Honore Street (1-773 276 7036/ www.rodan.ws). El: Blue to Damen. **Open** 6-11pm daily. **Main courses** $13. **Credit** AmEx, Disc, MC, V. **Map** p331 B7 95 **Asian/Latin American**

It's easy to dismiss Rodan as a scenester sipping spot, but the South American/Southeast Asian menu from co-owner Maripa Abella is worth a visit even if slick digs aren't your bag. Grab a window seat and start brunch with the Vietnamese coffee with powdered sugar-topped, beignet-like doughnuts. Pan-Latin classics such as black bean *arepas* and *huevos rancheros* are delicious, too, but for real savouriness, come at night when dinner specials (steaming bowls of Asian noodle soup, say) are under five bucks.

★ Schwa

1466 N Ashland Avenue, at W Le Moyne Street (1-773 252-1466/http://schwarestaurant.com). El: Blue to Division. **Open** 5.30-10.30pm Tue-Sat. **Degustation** $55 or $110. **Credit** AmEx, Disc, MC, V. **Map** p331 C7 96 **Contemporary American**

Fewer than 30 diners can fit in this tiny restaurant at one time, and all of them must have had reservations weeks in advance. The menu is more of a suggestion: Schwa serves what it wants and doesn't get into too many descriptions of what those dishes are. You'll be treated to the likes of its take on *pad thai*, with marinated slivers of jellyfish standing in for noodles; rich beer-cheese soup; and sumptuous venison paired with a white chocolate foam.

Smoke Daddy

1804 W Division Street, between N Wood & N Honore Streets (1-773 772 6656/www.thesmoke daddy.com). El: Blue to Division. **Open** 11.30am-11pm Mon-Wed, Sun; 11.30am-1.30am Thur-Sat. **Main courses** $15. **Credit** AmEx, Disc, MC, V. **Map** p331 C8 97 **American**

CONSUME

In the 'Hood Harlem Avenue

Spiaggia's Tony Mantuano steps out of his glass castle and on to Harlem Avenue.

The main drag of Harlem Avenue, in the far-west neighbourhood of Elmwood Park, was once thick with Italian immigrants. Most of them have long since scattered far and wide, but a handful of Italian-run speciality shops and cafés remain in the area. The neighbourhood remains a favourite hangout of Tony Mantuano, chef-partner of Magnificent Mile gem Spiaggia.

We start at **Caputo's Grocery** (2560 N Harlem Avenue, 1-708 453 0155), a quick stop for cheap Italian produce. Mantuano points out good deals on Andy Boy Farm's rapini, cubanelle frying peppers and fresh fava beans, as well as pork belly for $2.69 a pound ('Apparently, no one told them it was in vogue'). After ogling the fish and bantering with owners Dominick Conenna and Vince DeVito at nearby **Mercato del Pesce** (2623 N Harlem Avenue, 1-773 889 7909), Mantuano's ready for lunch.

'If I'm with the family, I'll go to **Caponie's** (3350 N Harlem Avenue, 1-773 804 9024) for a pretty good Italian-American pizza cooked in a wood-burning oven,' Mantuano confides. But today, there's a Diavolo sandwich at **Riviera Italian Foods** (3220 N Harlem Avenue, 1-773 637 4252) with his name on it. Behind the counter, owner Carmelo Pugliese builds it with nothing but foods he makes himself, stacking spicy soppressata, coppa, mozzarella and

giardiniera on to a torpedo roll while the chef scans the aisles for Giuseppe Cocco noodles, his preferred brand of dry pasta.

Just as Mantuano's finishing off the sandwich at a sidewalk table, a silver-haired guy wearing a T-shirt with a map of Italy pops his head out of next door's **Societa San Pietro & Paolo** (3222 N Harlem Avenue, no phone) and insists Mantuano come in for an espresso. The guy introduces himself as 'Nicky' and motions to the man behind the bar. 'Hey, Rocky, pull a couple!' In minutes, tiny cups of espresso appear. Impressed by the brew, Mantuano learns the beans come from nearby **Caffe Italia** (2625 N Harlem Avenue, 1-773 889 0455). 'This would be perfect with those sesame-seed cookies across the street,' Mantuano says, motioning to **Palermo Bakery** (3317 N Harlem Avenue, 1-773 777 5957). 'They make them the best, browned and crisp.'

'The best,' Nicky says, 'is this soppressata from Carmelo next door.' He gestures to the sliced-into sausage lying on butcher paper on the bar. As if on cue, Carmelo appears, still in his apron, and looks sheepish as the men in the bar brag about him. Nicky turns to Mantuano. 'You're a chef so you know your stuff. So tell him – isn't this stuff the best?'

▶ For Mantuano's **Spiaggia**, see p157.

CONSUME

Gluttony grabs hold in this kitschy kitchen, and it doesn't let go until the band plays its last bluesy rockabilly note. So skip the brisket, ignore the chicken, and resist filling up on the sweet-potato fries: instead, reserve your hunger for the Rib Sampler, a huge plate of baby back ribs, spare ribs and rib tips that's so big it might intimidate.

Humboldt Park & Logan Square

$ Feed

2803 W Chicago Avenue, at N California Avenue (1-773 489 4600/http://feedrestaurantchicago. com). Bus: 66. **Open** 8am-10pm Mon-Fri; 9am-10pm Sat; 9am-9pm Sun. **Main courses** $7. **No credit cards. American**

There's a fine line dividing kitsch from authenticity, and this homely chicken shack sits right in the middle. Despite the crowds of gay Moby-lookalikes, Starter-jacket-clad teenagers and yuppie moms, Feed still looks and feels the way you'd imagine a rural Kentucky chicken shack does.

$ Kuma's Corner

2900 W Belmont Avenue, at N Francisco Avenue (1-773 604 8769/www.kumas-corner.com). El: Blue to Belmont. **Open** 11.30am-2am Mon-Fri; 11.30am-3am Sat; noon-midnight Sun. **Main courses** $10. **Credit** AmEx, Disc, MC, V. **American**

The servers here sport more ink than a Bic factory, and the metal is cranked up so loud you can't hear yourself talking, but therein lies Kuma's Corner's charm. Squeeze through the ass-to-elbows crowds and up to the long bar, where you might be in for a lengthy wait. What's the draw? The Slayer burger,

for one – a pile of fries topped with a half-pound burger, chilli, cherry peppers, Andouille, onions and Jack cheese, on a pretzel bun. That, and the menu of highbrow brews.

★ Lula Café

2537 N Kedzie Boulevard, between W Linden Place & W Albany Avenue (1-773 489 9554/ www.lulacafe.com). El: Blue to Logan Square. **Open** 9am-10pm Mon, Wed, Thur, Sun; 9am-11pm Fri, Sat. **Main courses** $20. **Credit** AmEx, MC, V. **Café**

For a sunny brunch or breakfast at this neighbourhood favourite, vie for a seat at a small table indoors or on the sidewalk café, where planters spill over with the same herbs you'll find in your eggs Florentine or red-pepper strata. At night, try specials that range from artichoke-and-Meyer-lemon soup with a dollop of caviar and bits of roasted squab breast to striped marlin with pickled ramps.

★ Urban Belly

3053 N California Avenue, at W Barry Avenue (1-773 583 0500/www.urbanbellychicago.com). El: Blue to Belmont. **Open** 11am-9pm Tue-Sun. **Main courses** $12. **Credit** AmEx, Disc, MC, V. **Asian**

You'd think a dish called the Urbanbelly Ramen would be this noodle bar's signature. No, the best dish is the rice-cake noodles: chewy, mini-Frisbee-shaped noodles topped with a juicy, perfectly fried chicken breast and bits of mango, which help cool the fiery, chilli-spiked broth. Like the rich lamb-and-brandy dumplings, it's the kind of dish with which you'll want to take your time. But the crowds wanting your seat dictate that you should eat fast and go.

CONSUME

Café 103.

INSIDE TRACK NICE BUNS

When a burger craving hits, accept no substitute. Finding the best in town depends on your type of vibe, so know that burgers at **Kuma's Corner** (*see p172*) come with a side of metal (the head-banging, tattooed kind, not steel); **HotChocolate** (*see p169*) offers a neighbourhood feel with their egg-topped patty; **Twisted Spoke**'s two-handed gut-buster (*see p167*) is served up in biker-chic digs; and **Moody's** (*see p181*) can either be a beer garden party in summer or a recluse's fireside friend in winter.

THE SOUTH SIDE

Blu 47
4655 S King Drive, at E 47th Street (1-773 536 6000). El: Green, Red to 47th. **Open** 5-10.30pm Tue-Sun; 10am-2.30pm Sun. **Main courses** $18. **Credit** AmEx, Disc, MC, V. **American**
Don't look for any signs marking this Bronzeville lounge and restaurant. Just follow the train of cars in line for valet. This upscale eaterie is hidden on the second floor of a nondescript commercial complex, but the varied menu and vibe make it a spot worth seeking out. You'd be hard-pressed to find anything elsewhere like chef David Blackmon's bayou catfish.

★ Café 103
1909 W 103rd Street, at S Longwood Drive (1-773 238 5115/www.cafe103.com). Metra: 103rd Street. **Open** 11am-3pm, 5-10pm Tue-Sat. **Main courses** $24. **Credit** AmEx, Disc, MC, V. **American**
This small, simple and slightly upscale BYOB proves that creative and contemporary food isn't confined to the North Side. The menu is kept to about a dozen items to focus on freshness and seasonality. In summer, heirloom tomatoes are paired with crispy walleye and English peas, in a mixed green salad with goat's cheese, black grapes and walnuts.

$ Chant
1509 E 53rd Street, at S Harper Avenue (1-773 324 1999/www.chantchicago.com). Metra: 55th-56th-57th Street. **Open** noon-10pm Mon; 11.30am-midnight Tue-Thur; 11.30am-1am Fri, Sat; 11am-10pm Sun. **Credit** AmEx, Disc, MC, V. **Map** p332 Y16 **98** **Asian**
After years of operating as Noodles Etc, this South Side spot relaunched in 2007 in a new space with a bigger menu and a full-service bar. Popular dishes from the old menu are still available. But some creative newer options are winners, among them the beef Massaman curry, a tender steak fillet topped with a creamy, peanut curry sauce and potatoes.

La Petite Folie
Hyde Park Shopping Center, 1504 E 55th Street, at E 55th Place (1-773 493 1394/http://lapetite folie.com). Metra: 55th-56th-57th Street. **Open** 11.30am-2pm Tue-Fri; 5-9pm Tue-Sun. **Main courses** $23. **Credit** AmEx, Disc, MC, V. **Map** p332 Y17 **99** **French**
A mid-life career change prompted chef Mary Mastricola to open this almost-hidden, slightly upscale restaurant eight years ago. The French wine list provides affordable choices, and the trusty menu gets updated with seasonal additions every month or so. Early autumn eats include boneless rabbit filled with truffled hazelnut mousse, monkfish paella with jumbo shrimp and trout Grenobloise.

$ Medici
1327 E 57th Street, at S Kimbark Avenues (1-773 667 7394/www.medici57.com). El: Red to 55th. **Open** 11am-11pm Mon-Thur; 11am-midnight Fri; 9am-midnight Sat; 9am-11pm Sun. **Main courses** $9. **Credit** MC, V. **Map** p332 Y17 **100** **American**
Bring a Sharpie and an appetite for burgers when you hit this University of Chicago hangout. Among the surprisingly good takes on typical student fare are speciality burgers and shakes, as well as great late-night salads. Go for the simple but classic Ensalada Kimba – blue cheese, apples and pecans over crisp romaine. The restaurant also serves freshly baked pastries from its sister bakery next door.

Park 52
5201 S Harper Avenue, at E 52nd Street (1-773 241 5200/www.park52chicago.com). Bus: 6, 15, 28, 55. Metra: 51st-53rd Street. **Open** 5-10pm Mon-Wed; 5pm-midnight Thur-Sat; 11am-9pm Sun. **Main courses** $21. **Credit** AmEx, Disc, MC, V. **Map** p332 Y16 **101** **American**
Jerry Kleiner has brought mid-scale swank and classic American eats to Hyde Park's Harper Court, making for a nice night out for locals who desperately need more options. If grilled steak, roast chicken, iceberg wedge salad and the like don't excite, stick to chef Chris Barron's specials menu, which includes seasonal flavours which are bought from local farmers' markets.

★ $ Zaleski & Horvath Market Café
1126 E 47th Street, between S Woodlawn & S Greenwood Avenues (1-773 538 7372/www.zh marketcafe.com). Bus: 2, 15, 47. **Open** 7am-7pm Mon-Fri; 8am-6pm Sat, Sun. **Main courses** $8. **Credit** AmEx, MC, V. **Map** p332 X15 **102** **Café**
A couple of Hyde Park veterans and a sandwich maker from the suburbs joined forces to open this casual but high-quality grocery store and sandwich shop. The shelves are stocked with gourmet groceries, but the crowds tend to gather at the deli counter for the quince paste and Spanish jamón sandwiches or the panini.

CONSUME

Bars

Fancy a drink? You're in good company.

America's favourite pastime – no, not baseball but drinking – remains a draw for Chicagoans, who take pride in the city's vast variety of watering holes. Hardcore boozehounds relish the dive bars and local taverns; connoisseurs, meanwhile, are well served both by an array of beer-specialist bars and the increasing number of sleeker hangouts at which bartenders have been replaced by self-described 'mixologists'.

Bars and clubs in Chicago have either a 2am or 4am licence. In general, the city is cracking down on 4am licences, which are generally limited to dance clubs and bars that have been around forever. However, all bars get an hour's extension on Saturday, which means the 2am bars close at 3am, and the 4am joints stay open until 5am. Although if you're still drinking at that time, chances are you don't know or care what the time is anyway...

CONSUME

THE LOOP

Base Bar

Hard Rock Hotel, 230 N Michigan Avenue, at E Lake Street (1-312 345 1000). El: Brown, Green, Orange, Pink or Purple to State/Lake; Red to Lake. **Open** 3pm-2am Mon-Thur, Sun; 11am-2.30am Fri; noon-midnight Sat. **Credit** AmEx, Disc, MC, V. **Map** p325 J11 ❶

This is the Hard Rock, so expect to lounge on low-slung leather chairs and couches among a young after-work crowd, sipping a Bellini to the tunes of the Killers and such. But since it's the Hard Rock, you can also expect to see a tourist mom in a hot pink T-shirt pushing a ginormous stroller. As the night wears on, the crowds get hipper, the beats get louder and the tourists get some sleep.

▶ *For the hotel, see p127.*

★ Cal's Liquors

400 S Wells Street, at W Van Buren Street (1-312 922 6392/www.drinkatcalsbar.com). El: Brown, Orange, Pink or Purple to LaSalle/Van Buren. **Open** 11am-7pm Mon-Thur; 11am-2am Fri; 8pm-3am Sat. **No credit cards. Map** p325 G13 ❷

Cal himself slings insults and Old Style beer at this Loop dive (under the El), where a handful of stools are warmed by bike messengers, construction workers and the occasional gritty punk coming to check out bands with names like Urinal Mints and Rabid Rabbit that bang out music from a tiny corner.

Kasey's Tavern

701 S Dearborn Avenue, between W Harrison & W Polk Streets (1-312 427 7992/www. kaseystavern.net). El: Red to Harrison. **Open** 11am-2am Mon-Fri; 11am-3am Sat; noon-2am Sun. **Credit** AmEx, Disc, MC, V. **Map** p325 H13 ❸

The people-watching at Kasey's is almost as good as it is from the benches around the Printer's Row fountain, but this popular watering hole's got beer. And pizza. You'll recognise the same Irish-English-pub vibe from up north, and you may spy a frat rat. But generally, the crowd, like the bookish, lofty-artsy neighbourhood, is definitely mixed, especially when it comes to baseball loyalties.

Living Room

W Chicago City Center, 172 W Adams Street, between S LaSalle & S Wells Streets (1-312 332 1200). El: Brown, Orange, Pink or Purple to Quincy/Wells. **Open** 11am-midnight daily. **Credit** AmEx, Disc, MC, V. **Map** p325 H12 ❹

The bar at the Loop's W Hotel attracts both local and visiting scenesters. Expect lounge-worthy leather chairs, models moonlighting as waitresses

> ❶ Green numbers given in this chapter correspond to the location of each bar on the street maps. *See pp324-332.*

and sexed-up singles looking to clink cosmos. And while the well-stocked bar lives up to its name with dozens of whiskeys, bartenders also make mean martinis and Manhattans for the nostalgic set.
► *For the hotel, see p131.*

17 West

17 W Adams Street, between S State & S Dearborn Streets (1-312 427 3170/www.berghoff. com). El: Blue or Red to Monroe. **Open** 11am-9pm Mon-Thur; 11am-10pm Fri, Sat. **Credit** AmEx, MC, V. **Map** p325 H12 ⑤
What used to be the Berghoff is now essentially a cleaner version of its former self, and with a frilly martini list to boot. The room is a little airier since the dividing wall was taken down, but the century-old German pub was always about that gorgeous, room-length bar. And the mix of tourists, after-work suits and afternoon men won't notice the renovations when they're bellying up to it.

Wine Bar at the Walnut Room

Macy's, 111 N State Street, 7th Floor, at E Washington Street (1-312 781 3125). El: Blue to Washington; Brown, Green, Orange, Pink or Purple to Randolph/Wabash. **Open** 10am-9pm Mon-Sat; 10am-8pm Sun. **Credit** AmEx, Disc, MC, V. **Map** p325 H12 ⑥
The newest attraction at the decades-old Walnut Room is really just a corner of the dining area. But it's a nice corner, full of the restaurant's characteristic dark wood and formal-yet-friendly service. Nicer still is the wine list, which touts the bar's pricing policy: the bottles are priced for retail, not restaurant service. Good value, needless to say.
► *For Macy's itself, see p188.*

THE SOUTH LOOP & CHINATOWN

Reggie's Music Joint

2105 S State Street, at E 21st Street (1-312 949 0120/www.reggieslive.com). El: Red to Cermak-Chinatown. **Open** 11am-2am Mon-Fri, Sun; 11am-3am Sat. **Credit** MC, V. **Map** p324 H16 ⑦
In case you missed all the concert posters, the flat screens showing performance footage or the corner stage (which, more often than not, has a band on it), music is the theme of this South Side pub. But with such a good beer selection and a friendly staff, you don't need to be into the tunes to enjoy the night.

THE NEAR NORTH SIDE

River North

Angels & Kings

710 N Clark Street, between W Huron & W Superior Streets (1-312 482 8600/www.angels andkings.com). El: Red to Chicago. **Open** 9pm-2am Mon, Wed-Fri; 8pm-3am Sat. **Credit** AmEx, Disc, MC, V. **Map** p326 H10 ⑧

Angels & Kings.

Bull & Bear.

Local lad Pete Wentz of Fall Out Boy owns this long, narrow bar, so what do you think it'll be like? Full of people dressed like truckers and drinking PBR? With a stage decked out with two leather chairs and a gothic, almost-naked-save-for-the-thick-eyeliner go-go dancer writhing on it? Could be.

Bull & Bear

431 N Wells Street, between W Illinois & W Hubbard Streets (1-312 527 5973/www.bullbear bar.com). El: Brown or Purple to Merchandise Mart. **Open** 11am-2am Mon-Fri; noon-3am Sat; noon-2am Sun. **Credit** AmEx, Disc, MC, V. **Map** p326 H11 ❾

There's something ironic about a stock market-themed bar opening in the middle of an economic crisis, complete with bottles of Dom and Cristal listed under 'Liquid Assets'. The cocktails and upscale bar food – truffle fries with lemon aioli, for instance – are well executed if you have cash to burn, but you'll need to plunk down real dough for one of the talked-about booths with table-side beer taps.

Clark Street Ale House

742 N Clark Street, between W Superior & W Chicago Streets (1-312 642 9253). El: Red to Chicago. **Open** 4pm-4am Mon-Fri, Sun; 4pm-5am Sat. **Credit** AmEx, Disc, MC, V. **Map** p326 H10 ❿

There are people who hang out at this dim Near North pub without ever ordering a drink, but it seems a shame to miss out on the two dozen beers on tap – mostly domestic gems, such as Great Lakes Brewing Company's Elliot Ness. So order a beer and settle down next to the friendly locals who drop on to wooden stools just to chat with the bartender.

Fado

100 W Grand Avenue, between N Clark Street & N LaSalle Drive (1-312 836 0066/www.fado irishpub.com). El: Red to Grand. **Open** 11.30am-1.30am Mon-Thur; 11.30am-2.30am Fri; 10am-3am Sat; 10am-1.30am Sun. **Credit** AmEx, Disc, MC, V. **Map** p326 H10 ⓫

It's true, Fado is part of a chain, but, if you can, don't hold that against it. All three floors of this dark, wood-filled and slightly over-stylised Irish pub are packed with young professionals busily getting sloshed and loosening their ties and their tongues. After trying the Black Velveteen, a smooth and sweet blend of Guinness and cider, you might even want to join them.

★ Green Door Tavern

678 N Orleans Street, between W Erie & W Huron Streets (1-312 664 5496/http:// greendoorchicago.com). El: Brown or Purple to Chicago. **Open** 11.30am-2am Mon-Fri; 11.30am-3am Sat; noon-8pm Sun. **Credit** AmEx, Disc, MC, V. **Map** p326 G12 ⓬

If you're into slick, minimalist lounges or enormous, bass-heavy clubs, you may find it hard to believe that this River North stalwart has anything to offer. But poke around and you'll find a nice dining room to the side, a pool room in the back and a jukebox that caters to most tastes.

Motel Bar

600 W Chicago Avenue, at N Larrabee Street (1-312 822 2900/www.themotelbar.com). Bus: 66. **Open** 3.30pm-2am Mon-Fri, Sun; 3.30pm-3am Sat. **Credit** AmEx, MC, V. **Map** p326 F9 ⓭

This low-lit lounge is nothing like any motel you're likely to find by the highwayside, but the throwback classic cocktails, the 'room service' comfort food menu, the unpretentious staff and the varied jukebox (in lieu of a DJ turning it into a club) all work nicely. The massive outdoor patio is simple and sparse, with a few candles for light.

★ Pops for Champagne

601 N State Street, at E Ohio Street (1-312 266 7677/www.popsforchampagne.com). El: Red to Grand. **Open** *3pm-2am Mon-Fri, Sun; 1pm-2am Sat.* **Credit** *AmEx, Disc, MC, V.* **Map** *p326 H10* ⓮

Pops is sleeker, shinier and more grown-up than its old Lincoln Park location, and that's a good thing for its older, jazz-loving crowd. The young Lincoln Parkers who used to stop by for a glass of wine may be out of luck: not only is this not their crowd anymore, it's also out of their price range.

▶ *There's a jazz club in the basement; see p266.*

Redhead Piano Bar

16 W Ontario Street, between N State & N Dearborn Streets (1-312 640 1000/www.redhead pianobar.com). El: Red to Grand. **Open** *7pm-4am Mon-Fri, Sun; 7pm-5am Sat.* **Credit** *AmEx, Disc, MC, V.* **Map** *p326 H10* ⓯

For the piano-bar fiend who likes his joints a little more Grace than Will, this underground spot should hit all the right notes. But although the guys here aren't gay, they're at least dressed well: bouncers inspect outfits as well as ID, and flip-flops and T-shirts don't get in.

▶ *For more singalongs, head to the Zebra Lounge; see p178.*

Rockit Bar & Grill

22 W Hubbard Street, between N State & N Dearborn Streets (1-312 645 6000/www.rockit barandgrill.com). El: Red to Grand. **Open** *11.30am-1.30am Mon-Fri; 10.30am-2.30am Sat; 10.30am-1.30am Sun.* **Credit** *AmEx, Disc, MC, V.* **Map** *p326 H11* ⓰

INSIDE TRACK GETTING HIGH

There are few better ways to escape the city streets than to elevate yourself – literally. Head to a rooftop patio for a view with your brew; most are partially enclosed for year-round use, so you can leave the parkas in the hotel. **C-View** (*see p178*), **Whiskey Sky** (at the W Lakeshore; *see p138*) and **Vertigo** (*see p177*) are best for see-and-be-seen swankness, while the wooden deck at the **Bottom Lounge** (*see p258*) offers an escape in case the band downstairs isn't destined for greatness.

Most of the guys who go to this sporty, sceney homage to stainless steel don't seem to care what the food tastes like – it's more of a tits-and-beer thing. But if they'd pay attention, they'd find that the antibar food offers gems, such as mildly spicy braised lamb lettuce wraps and perfectly golden roasted chicken. The bar ain't too shabby, either, with nearly 30 types of beer either on tap or in bottles.

SushiSamba Rio

504 N Wells Street, at W Illinois Street (1-312 595 2300/www.sushisamba.com). El: Brown or Purple to Merchandise Mart. **Open** *11.30am-11pm Mon, Tue, Sun; 11.30am-1am Wed; 11.30am-2am Thur, Fri; 11.30am-3.30am Sat.* **Credit** *AmEx, Disc, MC, V.* **Map** *p326 H10* ⓱

Not only is the plush rooftop patio with a 40-foot bar, sharp sound system, sofas and stools perfect for a nightcap (or night-starter), it's great for sashimi as well. On Wednesdays after 10pm, this slick spot turns bootyrific for Favela Nights, a weekly party driven by Rio rhythms and a rotating cast of performance artists.

Swirl Wine Bar

111 W Hubbard Street, between N Clark & N LaSalle Streets (1-312 828 9000/www.swirlwine barchicago.com). El: Brown or Purple to Merchandise Mart; Red to Grand. **Open** *5pm-2am Tue-Thur; 5pm-4am Fri; 7pm-5am Sat.* **Credit** *AmEx, MC, V.* **Map** *p326 H11* ⓲

Since drinking on an empty stomach is a one-way ticket to drunk-dialling your ex, it's a relief to learn that this wine bar, which carries 25 wines by the glass, puts just as much focus on the food. The housemade *empanada* hides mushrooms inside its flaky crust; pizza topped with caramelised onions and pears goes perfectly with an off-dry riesling.

▶ *Other worthwhile wine bars include Bin 36 (see p152), Juicy Wine Co (see p182) and the Tasting Room (see p181).*

Vertigo

Dana Hotel & Spa, 2 W Erie Street, at N State Street (1-312 202 6060/www.danahotelandspa. com). El: Red to Grand. **Open** *5pm-2am Wed-Sat.* **Credit** *AmEx, Disc, MC, V.* **Map** *p326 H10* ⓳

You'd think the focus of this bar, which sits on the 26th floor of the Dana Hotel, would be the view. But there's a lot more to distract drinkers – the roaring fire pit, the classic cocktails (curiously served in plastic glasses) and the incredibly short shorts on the servers. DJs play from time to time.

The Magnificent Mile & Streeterville

★ Bar at Peninsula Hotel

108 E Superior Street, 5th Floor, between N Michigan Avenue & N Rush Street (1-312 573 6766/www.peninsula.com). El: Red to

The Brew Crew Goose Island

Chicago's biggest brewery continues to grow.

In 1986, fortysomething company man John Hall was waiting for a delayed plane when he stumbled on an article about microbrewed beer. Call it inspiration or call it a mid-life crisis, but Hall decided there and then that Chicago needed such a brewery and that he was just the man to start it, despite the fact that he had precisely no experience in the industry.

Fast-forward two decades, and Goose Island has grown from an on-a-whim start-up to one of the 30 largest breweries in the country. Hall's original bar (*see p178*) has grown into a buzzing gastropub, and now boasts a Wrigleyville sibling. The business is now so big that most of the beer is now brewed out of a newish

plant in West Town under the supervision of Greg Hall (John's son).

Honker's Ale remains the best-seller, a deeply moreish and surprisingly creamy-tasting pale ale. Other perennials include a pungent **IPA** and the richly flavoured **Nut Brown Ale**. Some beers are seasonal: **Christmas Ale**, for instance, and the less charismatic summery wheat beer **312**. Others are brewed in what amount to limited editions, such as the glorious **Pere Jacques**. Many Chicago bars stock Honker's and IPA, but you may need to head to the brewpub for the rare stuff.

▶ *For more on Goose Island, including information on stockists and tours, see www.gooseisland.com.*

Chicago. **Open** 5pm-1am Mon-Thur, Sun; 3pm-1am Fri, Sat. **Credit** AmEx, Disc, MC, V. **Map** p326 J10 ⑳

Escort a date to the Peninsula's dark, clubby cocktail bar and you probably won't go home alone. All the manly bases have been covered – a glowing fireplace, a stogie-stocked humidor, high-backed bar stools and cosy couched conversation nooks. Sip well-crafted cocktails, bubbly by the glass or whiskeys from obscure distillers.
▶ *For the hotel, see p137.*

Billy Goat Tavern

430 N Lower Michigan Avenue, at E Kinzie Street (1-312 222 1525/www.billygoattavern.com). El: Red to Grand. **Open** 6am-2am Mon-Fri; 10am-2am Sat, Sun. **No credit cards. Map** p326 J11 ㉑

This subterranean tavern – there are other locations, but this is the only one worth a visit – was the inspiration for John Belushi's Olympia Café skits on *Saturday Night Live* in the '70s, and drinkers can still get a 'cheezborger' with a side of schtick. Sam Sianis, nephew of the Greek immigrant who founded the haunt in 1934, still hollers out orders from behind the U-shaped counter. Weekends are a tourist crush, but weekday lunch still offers glimpses of hungry reporters, cops and other downtown characters. Just remember: no fries, *cheeps*; no Pepsi, Coke.

C-View

Affinia Hotel, 166 E Superior Street, between N St Clair Street & N Michigan Avenue (1-312 523 0923/www.c-houserestaurant.com). El: Red to Chicago. **Open** 5-11pm Mon-Wed, Sun 5pm-midnight Thur-Sat. **Credit** AmEx, Disc, MC, V. **Map** p326 J10 ㉒

The namesake 29th-floor view is the thing at this tiny rooftop bar – at least, that's what everybody says. But though the patio section is nice, the view of the skyline isn't beautiful enough to fight for a seat there. Especially when you can sit at the stylish indoor bar and get just as much beauty out of the delicious lavender-lemon-tequila cocktail.

The Gold Coast

★ Zebra Lounge

1220 N State Street, at W Division Street (1-312 642 5140). El: Red to Clark/Division. **Open** 6pm-2am Mon, Sun; 5pm-2am Tue-Fri; 6pm-3am Sat. **Credit** AmEx, Disc, MC, V. **Map** p327 H8 ㉓

Around the corner from Division Street's jackass bar scene sits this cosy one-room saloon, tucked inside the Canterbury Court apartments. Singles, socialites and even sexagenarians pack themselves in at busy weekends. The zebra theme is a bit reckless but distinctive. The ultrared lighting, on the other hand, makes you wonder if students from the Art Institute are going to emerge from behind the bar with developed film. A nightly piano player keeps the Zebra refreshingly unhip with old-school favourites.

OLD TOWN & LINCOLN PARK

Old Town

Goose Island Brew Pub

1800 N Clybourn Avenue, at W Willow Street (1-312 915 0071/www.gooseisland.com). El: Brown or Purple to Armitage; Red to North/ Clybourn. **Open** 11am-1am Mon-Thur, Sun; 11am-2am Fri, Sat. **Credit** AmEx, Disc, MC, V.

The beer selection alone is enough of a draw to this amiable brewpub, where you could happily spend an afternoon nursing a malty Smoked Porter. But pair your drink of choice with a Paulina Market sausage sampler of locally made links, and things look even better. There's another in Wrigleyville (3535 N Clark Street, at N Addison Street, 1-773 832 9040)

▶ *For more on the beers, see left.*

★ Old Town Ale House

219 W North Avenue, at N Wieland Street (1-312 944 7020/www.oldtownalehouse.net). El: Brown or Purple to Sedgwick. **Open** 8am-4am Mon-Fri; 8am-5am Sat; noon-4am Sun. **No credit cards. Map** p327 G7 ❷

Among the framed drawings of regulars cluttering the wooden walls of this saloon-style staple are posters boasting that you're in '*le premiere* dive bar' of Chicago. It's hard to tell where this place gets off speaking French, but it's been around since 1958, so it's earned bragging rights. The clientele are a democratic mix of buttoned-down yuppies and old soaks.

Lincoln Park

★ Delilah's

2771 N Lincoln Avenue, between W Schubert Avenue & W Diversey Parkway (1-773 472 2771/ www.delilahschicago.com). El: Brown or Purple to Diversey. **Open** 4pm-2am Mon-Fri, Sun; 4pm-3am Sat. **Credit** AmEx, Disc, MC, V. **Map** p328 E4 ❷

One of the city's best spots for rock 'n' roll doesn't have a stage. Instead, this Lincoln Park favourite has one of the best jukeboxes in town and brings in

DJs on some nights who know their Buzzcocks from their Bauhaus. Add an insane whiskey selection, more than 200 beers (Belgians, microbrews, seasonals), and you have a bar to call home.

▶ *There are also film screenings here; see p236.*

Grand Central

950 W Wrightwood Avenue, between N Wilton & N Sheffield Avenues (1-773 832 4000). El: Brown, Purple or Red to Fullerton. **Open** 4.30pm-2am Mon-Fri; 10am-3am Sat, 10.30am-3pm Sun. **Credit** AmEx, Disc, MC, V. **Map** p328 E4 ❷

As its name implies, and as its location next to the El tracks underscores, the feel here is that of a bar inside a Depression-era train station. Stained-glass ceiling lights emit an amber glow; small black-and-white ceramic tiles line the floor. But the centrepiece – despite the prevalence of flat-screen TVs and crazy-drunk locals on weekends – is the piano that sits on a circular stage behind the long front bar.

Maeve

1325 W Wrightwood Avenue, at N Wayne Avenue (1-773 388 3333/www.maevechicago.com). El: Brown, Purple or Red to Fullerton. **Open** 4pm-2am Mon-Fri; noon-3am Sat; noon-2am Sun. **Credit** AmEx, Disc, MC, V. **Map** p328 D4 ❷

This smallish, sports memorabilia-free spot boasts more class than most Lincoln Park watering holes: dark woods, dim lighting and candle-topped tables. So go ahead, quietly sip a glass of pinot while you wait for a table at adjacent Rose Angelis. But skip the after-dinner martini: by that time, the place will be packed with loud, horny thirtysomethings.

CONSUME

Old Town Ale House.

Sedgwick's Bar & Grill

1935 N Sedgwick Street, between W Armitage Avenue & W Wisconsin Street (1-312 337 7900/ www.sedgwickschicago.com). El: Brown or Purple to Sedgwick. **Open** 11.30am-2am Mon-Fri; 10am-3am Sat; 10am-2am Sun. **Credit** AmEx, Disc, MC, V. **Map** p328 G6 ㉘

On most nights, this cosy space is an after-work stopover for biz-caz yuppies escaping their Old Town high-rises. Brews, yummy comfort food and muted big-screen sports highlights abound. All those things happen on Tuesdays, too, with a little euchre thrown into the fold. League play occupies most of the pool tables, but you'll always have a seat.

★ Webster's Wine Bar

1480 W Webster Avenue, between N Clybourn Avenue & N Dominick Street (1-773 868 0608/ www.websterwinebar.com). Bus: 9, 74. **Open** 5pm-2am Mon-Fri; 4pm-3am Sat; 4pm-2am Sun. **Credit** AmEx, Disc, MC, V. **Map** p328 D5 ㉙

Many moviegoers, on their way to the Webster Place theatre, have stopped in here for a pre-show cocktail and never made it to the film. After all, when tasting pours are this affordable (and interesting), it's easy to pretend it's for educational purposes and stay all night, soaking up the dark, cultured vibe and munching on tasty cheese platters.

LAKEVIEW & NORTH

Lakeview & Wrigleyville

For gay bars in Boystown, *see pp247-248.*

Ginger's Ale House

3801 N Ashland Avenue, at W Grace Street (1-773 348 2767/www.gingersalehouse.com). El: Brown to Addison. **Open** 11am-2am Mon-Fri, Sun; 11am-3am Sat. **Credit** AmEx, MC, V.

A Irish-ish pub that's one of the best spots in town to watch televised soccer. *See p185* **Inside Track**.

▶ *If it's too busy, try the nearby, sports-friendly Globe (1934 W Irving Park Road, at N Wolcott Avenue, 1-773 871 3757, www.theglobepub.com).*

Harry Caray's Tavern

3551 N Sheffield Avenue, between W Cornelia Avenue & W Addison Street (1-773 327 7800/ www.harrycaraystavern.com). El: Red to Addison. **Open** 11am-2am Mon-Fri; 10am-3am Sat; 10am-2am Sun. **Credit** AmEx, MC, V. **Map** p329 E1 ㉚

The bro-tastic meat market that was Hi-Tops is gone, and in its place is this classy Cubs pub that should have sports fans with taste renewing their faith in the Wrigleyville scene. Countless flatscreen televisions and a bust of the bar's bespectacled namesake share the woody space with unexpectedly-hip-for-a-sports-bar touches such as a co-ed sink area and a create-your-own burger menu.

Hungry Brain

2319 W Belmont Avenue, between N Oakley & N Western Avenues (1-773 935 2118). El: Brown to Paulina. **Open** 8pm-2am Tue-Sun. **No credit cards.**

This converted theatre keeps its artsy charm with thrift-store finds galore. An old piano, couches and a coffee table sit on the small stage (which gets occasional use for one-night shows). Art-school dropouts flank the Ms Pac-Man game and great jukebox, and friendly bartenders serve cheap beers with a smile.

Murphy's Bleachers

3655 N Sheffield Street, at W Waveland Avenue (1-773 281 5356/www.murphysbleachers.com). El: Red to Addison. **Open** 11am-2am daily. **Credit** AmEx, Disc, MC, V. **Map** p329 E1 ㉛

Function trumps form and comfort at this woody, cavernous Cub corral and outdoor stable, er, patio behind Wrigley Field. For the Cubs' 81 home games a year, it's packed to the gills, but Wrigleyville's frat-shack contingent keep it humming even in winter.

Vines on Clark

3554 N Clark Street, at N Eddy Street (1-773 327 8572). El: Red to Addison. **Open** 11am-2am Mon-Fri; 11am-3am Sat; 11am-10pm Sun. **Credit** AmEx, Disc, MC, V. **Map** p329 E1 ㉜

When does the combination of metal patio furniture, brick flooring and industrial-sized trash cans qualify as a popular beer garden? When your beer garden and rooftop patio are a fly ball from Wrigley Field. Beer goggles don't only make people more attractive.

Roscoe Village

Village Tap

2055 W Roscoe Street, at N Hoyne Avenue (1-773 883 0817). Bus: 50, 77, 152. **Open** 5pm-2am Mon-Thur; 3pm-2am Fri; noon-3am Sat; noon-2am Sun. **Credit** AmEx, Disc, MC, V. **Map** p330 B2 ㉝

Roscoe Village has gentrified over the last few years, and the same goes for its watering holes. Still, it's one of the best places in town to grab a beer, chat with the friendly bartenders and test your alcohol-addled vocabulary with a game of Scrabble.

Andersonville, Edgewater & Uptown

For gay bars in Andersonville, *see pp246-247.*

★ Carol's Pub

4659 N Clark Street, between W Wilson & W Leland Avenues (1-773 334 2402/www.carols-pub.com). El: Red to Wilson. **Open** noon-4am Mon; 9am-2am Tue; 11am-4pm Wed-Fri; 11am-5am Sat; 11am-midnight Sun. **No credit cards.**

This honky-tonk offers $1.50 domestics on Mondays, country karaoke on Thursdays and house band Diamondback on weekends. There's a pool

Tiny Lounge

table in the back, a greasy grill turning out a stream of late-night burgers and a Hank Williams-filled jukebox to round out the grit fest.

Moody's Pub
5910 N Broadway, between W Rosedale & W Thorndale Avenues (1-773 275 2696). El: Red to Thorndale. **Open** 11.30am-1am Mon-Fri; 11.30am-2am Sat; noon-1am Sun. **No credit cards**.
This beer garden is one of the best in Chicago, but only if you can deal with ass-to-elbow crowds. Try this beer-and-burger haven in winter, but remember to bring a flashlight to read the menu: the place is dark enough that you could carry on an affair while your spouse is sitting across the room.

Lincoln Square & Ravenswood

Glunz Bavarian Haus
4128 N Lincoln Avenue, at W Warner Avenue (1-773 472 4287/www.glunzbavarianhaus.com). El: Brown to Irving Park. **Credit** MC, V.
Deutschland takes a lot of pride in its beer. So before you get schnitzel-faced at this friendly German restaurant, sample the brews. Consult the German-American family at the next table on the topic, and you'll be singing 'Deutschland über Alles' in no time.

Ten Cat Tavern
3931 N Ashland Avenue, at W Byron Street (1-773 935 5377). El: Brown to Irving Park. **Open** 3pm-2am Mon-Fri, Sun; 3pm-3am Sat. **No credit cards**. **Map** p330 D0 ㉞

Drinking at the Ten Cat is a little like getting into the DeLorean and travelling back to 1955. Eclectic, mismatched furniture and a blues-heavy jukebox set the mood for kicking back or rackin' 'em up at the two vintage tables. Just be careful, McFly: the bartenders won't hesitate to embarrass you on the felt.

Tiny Lounge
4352 N Leavitt Street, at W Montrose Avenue (1-773 463 0396). El: Brown to Montrose. **Open** 7pm-2am Mon-Fri, Sun; 7pm-3am Sat. **Credit** AmEx, MC, V.
The original Tiny Lounge closed in 2005 to make way for a new train station. Version 2.0, though, is slicker but still pretty appealing, thanks to cushy, circular booths, an extensive martini list and the conspicuous lack of a TV. A good neighbourhood option.

THE NEAR WEST SIDE
The West Loop & Greektown

Dugan's Pub
128 S Halsted Street, between W Washington Boulevard & W Randolph Street (1-312 421 7191/http://dugansonhalsted.com). El: Green to Clinton. **Open** 2pm-4am Mon-Sat; noon-4am Sun. **Credit** AmEx, Disc, MC, V. **Map** p330 F12 ㉟
Who knew the Irish and the Greeks got along so well? Early in the evening, this friendly watering hole seems to be filled with people waiting for a table at Greek Islands. Later, off-duty cops start filing in; not so much to keep the peace, but simply to grab a beer and a handful of free popcorn.

★ Fulton Lounge

955 W Fulton Street, at S Morgan Street (1-312 942 9500/www.fultonlounge.com). Bus: 8, 65. **Open** 5pm-2am Tue-Fri; 5pm-3am Sat. **Credit** AmEx, Disc, MC, V. **Map** p330 E11 ③

Saturday nights at this Fulton warehouse district hot spot are packed, so expect to wait to get in and again at the bar. Opt for a weekday when there's space to take in the charming bookshelves, exposed brick walls and diverse crowd. Only then can you see what all the fuss is about.

Tasting Room

1415 W Randolph Street, at N Ogden Avenue (1-312 942 1313/www.thetastingroomchicago.com). El: Green or Pink to Ashland. **Open** 4pm-1am Mon-Fri; 4pm-2am Sat. **Credit** AmEx, Disc, MC, V. **Map** p330 D12 ③

Out of the way? Yeah. A tad snobby? Sometimes. Still a great wine bar? For sure. You'd be hard pressed to find another wine bar in Chicago with a better list. And even harder pressed to find one with as good a view of the skyline.

Little Italy & Pilsen

Drum & Monkey

1435 W Taylor Street, at S Bishop Street (1-312 563 1874/http://thedrumandmonkeychicago.com). El: Pink to Polk. **Open** 11am-2am Mon-Fri, Sun; 11am-3am Sat. **Credit** AmEx, Disc, MC, V. **Map** p330 D14 ③

This immaculately detailed Irish pub, formerly the Four Corners, might be the last thing you'd expect on the spaghetti strip of Taylor Street, but soon it'll be top of your 'places to swig pints and shovel eats' list. Just ask any of the UIC doctors who are regulars.

★ Simone's

960 W 18th Street, at S Morgan Street (1-312 666 8601/www.simonesbar.com). El: Pink to 18th. **Open** 11.30am-2am daily. **Credit** AmEx, Disc, MC, V.

This Pilsen hangout looks nothing like your typical Bucktown bar. Instead, the hyper-recycled materials used to outfit the establishment make it feel like the inside of a pinball machine. And it's this innovative design – coupled with the better-than-average cocktails – that ensure you won't get bored.

WICKER PARK & AROUND
Ukrainian Village & West Town

Club Foot

1824 W Augusta Street, between N Wood & N Honore Streets (1-773 489 0379). El: Blue to Division. **Open** 8pm-2am Mon-Fri, Sun; 8pm-3am Sat. **No credit cards. Map** p331 C9 ③

Fans of *I Love the '80s* will be in heaven here, surrounded by walls plastered with vintage concert T-shirts and glass cases jam-packed with collectible toys. During the week, there's room to take it all in, but weekends get crammed with locals playing pool to a DJ's mix of punk, indie rock and occasional polka. Yes, polka. After all, this is Ukrainian Village.

Empty Bottle

1035 N Western Avenue, at W Cortez Street (1-773 276 3600/www.emptybottle.com). Bus: 49, 66, 70. **Open** 5pm-2am Mon-Wed; 3pm-2am Thur, Fri; noon-3am Sat; noon-2am Sun. **No credit cards. Map** p331 A9 ④

This music venue and bar has increasingly turned to booking adventurous electronic, indie hip-hop and experimental-music acts. Just remember that it's more about the head-bobbing of hipsters than serious dancefloor action, so boogie at your own risk.
▶ *For the music side of the operation, see p259.*

Exit

1315 W North Avenue, at N Ada Street (1-773 395 2700/www.exitchicago.com). El: Red to North/Clybourn. **Open** 9pm-4am Mon-Fri, Sun; 9pm-5am Sat. **Credit** AmEx, MC, V.

Thursday is fetish night and Monday it's punk rock, but pretty much any evening you stumble on this haunt for the black-clad you'll see that the freaks indeed do come out after dark. Like any clique, it tends to have an insider feel, but brave souls looking for their Ministry and PBR fix have to start somewhere. Beware: there's a $5 cover on weekends.

Gold Star Bar

1755 W Division Street, between N Wood Street & N Hermitage Avenue (1-773 227 8700). El: Blue to Division. **Open** 4pm-2am Mon-Fri, Sun; 3pm-3am Sat. **No credit cards. Map** p331 C8 ④

Truly a neighbourhood hangout, this tried-and-true East Village bar is frequented by those who appreciate Claudio the tamale guy, a jukebox that stocks both white-hot jazz and doom metal, a cheap pool table, equally cheap drinks and a crowd who really couldn't care less if you show up in sweats.

★ Happy Village

1059 N Wolcott Avenue, at W Thomas Street (1-773 486 1512). El: Blue to Division. **Open** 4pm-2am Mon-Fri; noon-2am Sat, noon-11pm Sun. **No credit cards. Map** p331 C9 ④

A gurgling goldfish pond, picnic tables and a lush lawn all around is the scene at this West Town dive. But when it rains (or at 11pm, when the garden closes), pack up the ciggies and head inside, where the smell of whiskey and cheap beer hangs in the air, and the jukebox coughs out the Cars and Madonna.

Inner Town Pub

1935 W Thomas Street, at N Winchester Avenue (1-773 465 5568/www.innertownpub.com). El: Blue to Division. **Open** 3pm-2am Mon-Fri, Sun; 3pm-3am Sat. **No credit cards. Map** p331 B9 ④

The Brew Crew Two Brothers

A pair of Chicago siblings get their kicks tinkering with artisan beers.

Like most artists, Jason and Jim Ebel of the Two Brothers Brewery finance their passion with reliable money-makers. From their brewery in the western Chicago suburb of Warrenville, the Ebels kick out five solid beers year round. Sold in most liquor stores and better bars in Chicago, **Domaine DuPage** is the duo's biggest seller, and its success has enabled the brothers to play around with interesting artisan beers that only get a limited run in local bars and liquor stores. But you'll need to be quick. When the 3,000 bottles of special releases such as **Philosopher's Stone**, a tart black

saison, and **10**, a Belgian-style *kriek lambic*, are gone, they're gone for good.

In addition to experimenting with special projects, the Ebels also brew beers that are released at each change of season. **Northwind Imperial Stout** is a hearty winter warmer, **Dog Days** is a golden lager that ushers in summer, and the fresh-hopped **Heavy Handed IPA** is built for autumn. You can try some of their brews at the brewery's Tap House, or as part of a free Saturday tour.

▶ *For more on Two Brothers, including information on stockists, tours and the Tap House, see www.twobrosbrew.com.*

With more clutter than your eccentric aunt's house, this former speakeasy serves cheap booze and warm salted nuts in true dive fashion. Indie-rockers on their way to Empty Bottle shows take advantage of free pool, while a smattering of toothless old-timers keep it gritty with war stories and phlegmy coughs.

★ Juicy Wine Co
694 N Milwaukee Avenue, at W Huron Street (1-312 492 6620/http://juicywine.com). El: Blue to Chicago. **Open** 4pm-1am Mon-Thur; 4pm-2am Fri, Sat; 11am-midnight Sun. **Credit** AmEx, MC, V.
Walking into Rodney Alex's wine bar – with its wall of well-chosen, well-priced bottles and warm yet impeccably contemporary wood tones – is like walking into the coolest wine bar in London, or the coolest wine bar in New York… only guess what? It just happens to be the coolest wine bar in Chicago. The food's pretty good, too.

★ Matchbox
770 N Milwaukee Avenue, between N Carpenter Street & N Ogden Avenue (1-312 666 9292). El: Blue to Chicago. **Open** 4pm-2am Mon-Fri, Sun; 4pm-3am Sat. **Credit** AmEx, MC, V.
If the thought of being crammed in this tiny boxcar of a bar makes you nervous, relax. The patio practically doubles capacity, and is the perfect spot in which to throw back one of its margaritas, made with fresh lemon and lime juice, top-shelf liquors and powdered sugar, and poured with a heavy hand.

Rainbo Club
1150 N Damen Avenue, between W Haddon Avenue & W Division Street (1-773 489 5999). El: Blue to Division. **Open** 4pm-2am Mon-Fri, Sun; 4pm-3am Sat. **No credit cards.**
Map p331 B8 ④

The bittersweet reality of many great little dives is that they lose charm when overrun by masses of clingers-on. Somehow, this Ukrainian Village spot has managed to remain an underground favourite. The local artists and musicians who frequent it hold on to terra firma with cheap drink in hand, awaiting a turn in the photo booth while nodding to everything from Aesop Rock to Black Sabbath.

Wicker Park & Bucktown

Beachwood Inn
1415 N Wood Street, between W Beach Avenue & W Julian Street (1-773 486 9806). El: Blue to Division. **Open** 4pm-2am Mon-Fri; 3pm-3am Sat; 3pm-2am Sun. **No credit cards.**
Map p331 C8 ④
No hipsters, no yuppies, no class-drawing lines – just regular neighbourhood folks in this one-room watering hole, taking turns on the pool table or playing Scrabble and Connect Four. The scatterbrained decor (old snow sports, sports crap, beer memorabilia) is as random as the jukebox, which offers pre-'90s tunes from the Pretenders to Michael Jackson.

Chaise Lounge
1840 W North Avenue, between N Honore Street & N Wolcott Avenue (1-773 342 1840/http://chaiseloungechicago.com). El: Blue to Damen. **Open** 4pm-2am Mon-Fri; 2pm-3am Sat; 2pm-midnight Sun. **Credit** AmEx, Disc, MC, V. **Map** p331 C7 ④
This is both a bar and a restaurant, featuring dishes such as Tuscan bean salad with fried pancetta, and beet-and-goat's-cheese napoleon. But it's the rooftop deck (covered in chillier months) and alfresco patio that steal the show, at least for those looking to rub elbows with Miami Beach dweller-wannabes.

CONSUME

The Brew Crew Half Acre

From Milwaukee to Lincoln Avenue, meet Chicago's newest brewery.

Gabriel Magliaro and his pals had a vision: bringing great beer to the masses. They also had a problem: no money. Their clever solution was to form a brewing company, Half Acre, but tap Wisconsin's Sand Creek Brewery (in Black River Falls) to contract-brew their dream beer rather than set up their own operation from scratch.

The term contract brewing may sound foreign, but it's not totally uncommon. Magliaro likes to point out that it's how Samuel Adams got its start, but he quickly follows up that he and his partners are in no way hoping to become 'big-time beer'.

Nonetheless, Half Acre is growing. Having launched in 2007 with the full-bodied **Half Acre Lager**, the brewery branched out in 2008 with the richer, darker **Over Ale**; both are available in selected Chicago bars. And then, in 2009, it opened its very own Chicago brewery up on Lincoln Avenue, complete with tasting room and retail space. The range of beers looks set to expand along with the business; look out for seasonal brews and special editions during your stay.

▶ *For more on Half Acre, including information on stockists, see www.halfacrebeer.com.*

★ Charleston

2076 N Hoyne Avenue, between W Charleston Street & W Dickens Avenue (1-773 489 4757/ www.charlestonchicago.com). El: Blue to Western. **Open** 3pm-2am Mon-Fri; 2pm-2am Sat, Sun. **No credit cards. Map** p331 B6
Hipsters, yuppies, freaks, dirty old men and bluegrass bands pack this tchotchke-ridden corner tap, which is easily one of Bucktown's favourites. None of the above descriptions fit your personality? No worries. Between the piano, Wi-Fi access and live music, you'll find something that suits.

★ Danny's Tavern

1951 W Dickens Avenue, between N Damen & N Winchester Avenues (1-773 489 6457). El: Blue to Damen. **Open** 7pm-2am Mon-Fri, Sun; 7pm-3am Sat. **No credit cards. Map** p331 C6
The floors of this converted Bucktown house shake so much from the weight of hot-footed trendsetters that you'd think the place is seconds from caving in. Most of the dancing is set to a mix of hip hop, electro and rock on the weekends (and the insanely popular first-Wednesday-of-the-month funk party called Sheer Magic), but there are plenty of nooks and crannies to sit back, relax and people-watch.

Debonair Social Club

1575 N Milwaukee Avenue, between W Honore Street & W North Avenue (1-773 227 7990/ www.debonairsocialclub.com). El: Blue to Damen. **Open** 9pm-2am Tue-Fri, Sun; 9pm-3am Sat. **Credit** AmEx, MC, V. **Map** p331 C7
Early in the evening at this bi-level hangout, a bit like a starter club for Wicker Park's post-collegiate bar hoppers, the video art on the wall is the room's main source of light, giving off a cool, sultry cocktail-lounge vibe. But it's the calm before the storm:

when celebrity DJs stop by, the place gets packed with clubby scenesters and frantic bass lines. So if you're here for the quiet, enjoy it while you can.

Empire Liquors

1566 N Milwaukee Avenue, between W Honore Street & W North Avenue (1-773 278 1600/ www.empireliquors.com). El: Blue to Damen. **Open** 9pm-2am Wed, Thur; 8pm-2am Fri; Sat 8pm-3am. **Credit** AmEx, Disc, MC, V. **Map** p331 B7
Black walls, wiry chandeliers and more guyliner than a My Chemical Romance concert make this an angsty addition to the hood. The scene can get a little overwhelming in front, but if you snag a seat in the private(ish) room in back you'll be golden – or at least as golden as a goth kid can get.

Estelle's

2013 W North Avenue, at N Milwaukee Avenue (1-773 782 0450/www.estelleschicago.com). El: Blue to Damen. **Open** 7pm-4am Mon-Fri, Sun; 7pm-5am Sat. **Credit** AmEx, MC, V. **Map** p331 B7
There are some evenings when you just don't want to have to take the trouble of making sure you're cooling with the cool cats. Well, then head to this low-key sanctuary. No one's trying to out-cool anyone here (though late at night, they're definitely trying to pick each other up), so feel free to strike up a conversation with a stranger over some tasty late-night bar eats, served until 4am.

Flat Iron

1565 N Milwaukee Avenue, at N Damen Avenue (1-773 365 9000/http://theflatironchicago.com). El: Blue to Damen. **Open** 4pm-4am daily. **Credit** AmEx, MC, V. **Map** p331 B7

When this place was the Note, the focus was on the bands on stage. Now, those bands are gone, and the focus is on… nothing. The dark bar, now decorated with street-art murals, is roomy and a little divey, and it's as low-key and basic as a bar can get. And that's exactly what the neighbourhood needs.

Handlebar Bar & Grill

2311 W North Avenue, between N Oakley & N Claremont Avenues (1-773 384 9546/http:// handlebarchicago.com). El: Blue to Damen. **Open** 10am-midnight Mon-Thur; 10am-2am Fri, Sat; 10am-11pm Sun. **Credit** MC, V. **Map** p331 A7 ⑤

The multiple bike racks at the back are packed with every kind of two-wheeler imaginable no matter the time of year at this biker bar (and by 'biker', we mean those who self-power their locomotion, rather than relying on the internal comustion engine). Eco-minded folks chat over tasty vegan fare, check out each other's rides and sample the diverse draft beers.

Lemmings

1850 N Damen Avenue, between W Moffat & W Cortland Streets (1-773 862 1688). El: Blue to Damen. **Open** 4pm-2am Mon-Fri; noon-3am Sat; noon-2am Sun. **Credit** AmEx, Disc, MC, V. **Map** p331 B6 ⑥

Don't take the name too literally: there's a nice crowd here, but the joint isn't actually packed tight with followers, so you can usually find a seat from which to soak up the comforting vibe. It's still low-key, but you'll usually find someone willing to take you on at pool or Ms Pac-Man.

★ Map Room

1949 N Hoyne Avenue, between W Homer Street & W Armitage Avenue (1-773 252 7636/www. maproom.com). El: Blue to Western. **Open** 6.30am-2am Mon-Fri; 7.30am-3am Sat; 11am-2am Sun. **Credit** MC, V. **Map** p331 B6 ⑤

You couldn't fit another beer on the killer list or another Bucktown local around the pool table here, especially on Tuesdays, aka 'International Night'. This weekly party brings in food from a different ethnic spot around town – plates are free with an order of two drinks. In the morning, the place functions as a coffee house.

INSIDE TRACK GOAL!

Whether they call it football, soccer, *futbol* or some other variant, fans from abroad need a place to cheer on their team. Happily, the city is full of expats who wouldn't dream of missing a game. European diehards find fellow supporters at **Ginger's Ale House** (*see p180*), **Fado** (*see p176*) and **Small Bar** (*see p185*), all of which screen big matches live.

Moonshine

1824 W Division Street, between N Honore Street & N Marion Court (1-773 862 8686/ www.moonshinechicago.com). El: Blue to Division. **Open** 11am-2am Mon-Fri; 10am-3am Sat; 10am-2am Sun. **Credit** AmEx, Disc, MC, V. **Map** p331 C8 ⑤⑥

True to its Prohibition-era theme, this bar serves its beer in mason jars. But there's nothing redneck about the seven booths outfitted with individual plasma-screen TVs. Those are likely to get more use during quieter weeknights when couples and small groups stop in for beers, burgers and televised games. Weekends can be a madhouse, with blaring DJ-driven music and scoping singles taking over.

Phyllis' Musical Inn

1800 W Division Street, at N Wood Street (1-773 486 9862). El: Blue to Division. **Open** 4pm-2am Mon-Fri; 4pm-3am Sat. **No credit cards.** **Map** p331 C8 ⑥⑦

One of Wicker Park's first spots for live music refuses to go the way of cover bands, instead booking local acts that play original rock. They're not always great, but the garden patio is. A scrappy mix of chairs and tables, a basketball hoop and groups of friends shooting the breeze over cheap drinks makes for a classic summer night.

Quencher's Saloon

2401 N Western Avenue, at W Fullerton Avenue (1-773 276 9730/www.quenchers.com). El: Blue to California. **Open** 11am-2am Mon-Fri, Sun; 11am-3am Sat. **No credit cards.** **Map** p331 A5 ⑤⑧

This 25-year-old beer bar has one of the most diverse crowds in town. The well-heeled eye each other on weekends, local beer nerds meet to taste the 200 choices on weeknights and drunk punks wander in whenever. Luckily, they peacefully co-exist in two spacious rooms, all in the name of beer. Daytime crowds enjoy the laid-back vibe, thanks to free popcorn and comfortable couches.

Small Bar

2049 W Division Street, between N Damen & N Hoyne Avenues (1-773 772 2727/www.thesmall bar.com). El: Blue to Division. **Open** 11am-2am Mon-Fri, Sun; 11am-3am Sat. **Credit** AmEx, Disc, MC, V. **Map** p331 B8 ⑤⑨

This welcoming neighbourhood joint is far from small – it's a decent-sized, airy space that opens up on to a sidewalk patio. If they wanted a more literal and descriptive name, maybe Beer Bar (named for the 90-beer-strong list), Scenester Bar (it's not Rainbo, but close) or Cash Bar (obscure beer ain't cheap, kids) would have been more accurate.

★ Violet Hour

1520 N Damen Avenue, between W Le Moyne Street & N Wicker Park Avenue (1-773 252 1500/www.theviolethour.com).

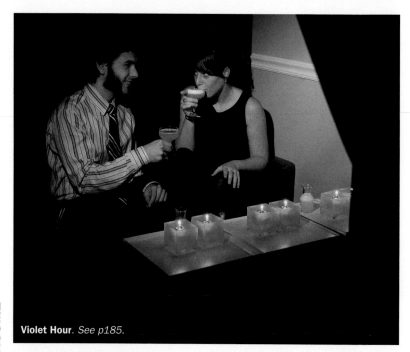

Violet Hour. *See p185.*

El: Blue to Damen. **Open** 6pm-2am Mon-Fri,
Sun; 6pm-3am Sat. **Credit** AmEx, MC, V.
Map p331 B7 ⑥
This cocktail lounge is exactly what you'd expect
from a bar that takes its name from *The Waste
Land*: pristine (the carefully constructed cocktails
are excellent), pretentious (you won't find a sign on
the door – just look for the long queues) and, ultimately, completely and unarguably gorgeous.

Zakopane
*1734 W Division Street, between N Hermitage
Avenue & N Wood Street (1-773 486 1559). El:
Blue to Division.* **Open** 7am-2am Mon-Sat; 11am-
2am Sun. **No credit cards.** **Map** p331 C8 ⑥
If you're lucky, you'll stumble in on a night when
the Anna Kournikova lookalike bartender is working, pouring vodka drinks with a heavy hand. But
any night will do at this wood-panelled, Polish-
owned watering hole. The old drunks are quick to
challenge you at pool, and the young Poles are
obsessed with the jukebox that spits out Polish versions of early-'90s American chart toppers.

Humboldt Park & Logan Square

Burlington
*3425 W Fullerton Avenue, between N Bernard
Street & N St Louis Avenue (1-773 384 3243).*

El: Blue to Logan Square. **Open** 7pm-2am Mon-
Fri; 7pm-3am Sat; noon-2am Sun. **Credit** AmEx,
Disc, MC, V.
This Logan Square bar has everything you could
ask for – that is, as long as you don't ask for too
much. The spare, dim room has plenty of hipster
atmosphere (but no hipster snobbery), ample seating at a wood-panelled bar and a delicious beer on
tap that you can't get anywhere else – just point to
the unmarked draft handle adorned with antlers.

★ Green Eye Lounge
*2403 W Homer Street, at N Western Avenue (1-
773 227 8851/www.greeneyelounge.com). El:
Blue to Western.* **Open** 3pm-2am Mon-Fri; noon-
3am Sat; noon-2am Sun. **Credit** AmEx, Disc, MC,
V. **Map** p331 A6 ⑥
There's no pretence here – in fact, the Green Eye's
self-proclaimed addition to the 'hood is 'cheap drinks
for reasonable people'. Locals head here for Goose
Island drafts, a small outdoor patio (in the summer)
and its prime spot right next to the Blue line.

Whirlaway Lounge
*3224 W Fullerton Avenue, between N Kedzie
Boulevard & N Sawyer Avenue (1-773 276
6809/www.whirlaway.net). El: Blue to Logan
Square.* **Open** 4pm-2am Mon-Fri, Sun; 4pm-
3am Sat. **No credit cards.**

This Logan Square watering hole glows with charm – or is it the string of Christmas lights behind the bar? Either way, retired rock stars put away beers next to their disciples under the soft lights, snapshots of regulars and the warm smile of the maternal owner-bartender, Maria.

★ **Whistler**
2421 N Milwaukee Avenue, between W Fullerton Avenue & W Richmond Street (1-773 227 3530/ www.whistlerchicago.com). El: Blue to California. **Open** 6pm-2am Mon-Thur; 5pm-2am Fri; 5pm-3am Sat; 5pm-2am Sun. **Credit** AmEx, MC, V.
From the outside, this place looks like a gallery (which, technically, it partially is). On the inside, it's open and loftlike, with a permanent stage for live music. But behind the bar, a bartender is skillfully making cocktails like a rosemary collins. One sip and there's no doubt that despite everything else going on, the cocktails are the reason to stick around.

THE SOUTH SIDE

Cove Lounge
1750 E 55th Street, between S Hyde Park Boulevard & S Everett Avenue (1-773 684 1013). Bus: 6, 55, X55. **Open** 10am-2am Mon-Fri; 11am-2am Sat; 11am-midnight Sun. **No credit cards. Map** p332 Z17 ⑥③
The payoff from the nautical theme hinted at by this blue-collar hangout's name is decidedly small. Aside

from a light fixture made from a ship's wheel and anchor-shaped coat hooks, this is your standard shot-and-a-beer dive. The crowd is composed primarily of 'townies', with a bit of overflow from the student-heavy crowd at nearby Jimmy's (*see below*).

Schaller's Pump
3714 S Halsted Street, at W 37th Street (1-773 376 6332). El: Red to Sox-35th. **Open** 11am-2am Mon-Fri; 4pm-3am Sat; 4-9pm Sun. **No credit cards.**
There's no better place to cheer on your team than this down-home, blue-collar institution near US Cellular Field. Arrive at least a half-hour before game time if you're planning on eating the just-like-Mom-made classics. Add doting servers, cheap beer and a living room-like atmosphere, and you've got the best sports experience short of front-row tickets.

Woodlawn Tap
1172 E 55th Street, between S University & S Woodlawn Avenues (1-773 643 5516). Bus: 28, 55. **Open** 10.30am-2am Mon-Fri; 11am-3am Sat; 11am-2am Sun. **No credit cards. Map** p332 X17 ⑥④
Just off the University of Chicago campus, Jimmy's (as it's affectionately called by those in the know, after dearly departed original owner Jimmy Wilson) is the favoured spot for the scholars to rub elbows with undergrads and working-class regulars. Cheap burgers are washed down with even cheaper beer.

Think Local, Drink Global

Leave Chicago without leaving Chicago at a neighbourhood bar with a difference.

Forget love or music: whether you're sipping *soju* in a sleek Korean lounge or downing Tecates in a boisterous Little Village *vaquero* bar, drinking is the international language. Bars are different all over the world, but Chicago's famous melting-pot make-up allows for plenty of globetrotting opportunities without leaving the city limits.

Polish party spot the **Martini Club** (4933 N Milwaukee Avenue, 1-773 202 9444) nestles in the blue-collar 'hood of Jefferson Park, but it tries to draw an upscale, clubby crowd with gilded mirrors, a translucent bar with red under-lighting, leather booths and exposed brick. In a city that abounds with Polish shot-and-beer joints, the bar reaches out to those whose names may not end in -ski while still retaining its Polish roots.

Italian joints in Chicago are as prevalent as potholes, and they're just as hit-or-miss. Head north-west, though, and you'll find

plenty of character at **Café Cappuccino** (3719 N Harlem Avenue, 1-773 725 9553), an unassuming bar and restaurant in a strip mall. Older guys yell Italian invectives into their cellphones while groups of young men apprise both the women who walk past and the soccer game on TV, as Euro-disco versions of '80s classics blare at nightclub decibels.

Push on the door between popular eateries Blackbird and Meiji (*see pp162-163*), head up the stairs and soon you'll hear the faint sounds of exotic pop music, laughter and maybe even a few toasts of '*gumbae*'. Congratulations: you've found the Korean **Nara Lounge** (623 W Randolph Street, West Loop, 1-312 887 9999). In this low-lit, cosy space, Korean expats show up around midnight, refill *soju* glasses often and counter the buzz with a never-ending stream of *anju*, share-sized plates heaping with crimson sauces and spicy-sweet snacks.

CONSUME

Shops & Services

A Magnificent city for shopping

Throughout its proudly blue-collar history, Chicago has occasionally lacked a little high style. But, reflecting the changes in the city itself, Chicago is now something of a fashion hub. Recent openings from the likes of **Marc Jacobs**, **Michael Kors** and **Joe's Jeans** have lured fashionistas into major shopping districts (*see p189* **Where to Shop**), while a bevy of local boutiques continues to show off the local retail talent. And there's plenty to appeal to non-fashionistas, from great vintage record shops to upscale spas. Indeed, the only downer comes courtesy of the sales tax: at 10.25 per cent, it's the highest of any big city in the US.

CONSUME

General

DEPARTMENT STORES

★ Barneys New York
15 E Oak Street, Gold Coast (1-312 587 1700/www.barneys.com). El: Red to Clark/Division. **Open** 10am-7pm Mon-Sat; noon-6pm Sun. **Credit** AmEx, MC, V. **Map** p326 H9.
Barneys has been offering Chicago shoppers its New York City sophistication for years, and in the spring of 2009 it offered even more by moving across the street from its old location and doubling in size. Professionals and socialites with deep pockets head here for top designer and private-label apparel: clothing, jewellery, bags, shoes and accessories, spread over 90,000sq ft of sleek retail space.
► *Up in Lincoln Park, the two-storey Barneys New York Co-Op (2209-2211 N Halsted Street, at W Webster Avenue, 1-773 248 0426) is a hipper, more youthful and slightly cheaper version.*

Bloomingdale's
900 N Michigan Shops, 900 N Michigan Avenue, at E Walton Street, Magnificent Mile (1-312 440 4460/www.bloomingdales.com). El: Red to Chicago. **Open** 10am-8pm Mon-Sat; 11am-7pm Sun. **Credit** AmEx, MC, V. **Map** p329 J9.
On a Magnificent Mile awash with tradition, Bloomies is all about having fun. A must for the

younger shopper, its six levels are packed with fashions for the free-spirited; in particular, don't miss the often surprisingly well-stocked clearance racks.
► *There's a Bloomingdale's Home & Furniture Store in River North (600 N Wabash Avenue, between W Ontario & W Ohio Streets, 1-312 324 7500).*

Macy's
111 N State Street, at E Randolph Street, the Loop (1-312 781 1000/www.macys.com). El: Blue to Washington; Brown, Green, Orange, Pink or Purple to Randolph/Wabash; Red to Lake. **Open** 10am-8pm Mon-Sat; 11am-6pm Sun. **Credit** AmEx, Disc, MC, V. **Map** p325 H12.
It's been a few years since this chain took over the beloved Marshall Field's name, and Chicagoans finally seem at peace with the change. After all, they can still enjoy the nine levels of this landmark

---

INSIDE TRACK
MACY'S MAKE-UP

Visit the Fresh counter at **Macy's** (*see above*) on State Street for a gratis facial every Wednesday and Thursday. The aesthetician whisks you away into a candle-lit back room for 45 minutes, treating your skin to a bevy of Fresh products. And it's all no strings attached: you don't have to pay a penny for a product (unless you want to). Aim to book a week in advance.

About the author
Kevin Aeh edits The Get for Time Out Chicago magazine.

Where to Shop

Chicago's best shopping neighbourhoods in brief.

THE LOOP
There's not much notable retail activity in the Loop, but bargain-hunters should hightail it to **State Street**, where a number of department stores and clothing shops offer steals.

OLD TOWN & LINCOLN PARK
In the village-like streets of these two smartening neighbourhoods, independent clothing boutiques happily coexist next to outposts of national niche brands. Fertile shopping drags include **Clark Street**.

THE NEAR NORTH SIDE
Between the Chicago River and Water Tower Place, **Michigan Avenue** – aka the Magnificent Mile – is a consumerist paradise, packed with enormous department stores and multi-level flagships for countless big-ticket brands. As you might expect, it's packed on weekends.

The nearby **Gold Coast** isn't named for the colour of shoppers' credit cards but it might as well be. The boutiques on **Oak Street** sell the poshest clothes that (someone else's) money can buy.

LAKEVIEW & AROUND
The chains that have encroached upon Lincoln Park haven't all made it up to Lakeview, which is still dominated by interesting independent stores. **Clark Street** contains its fair share of stores, especially north of Belmont.

WICKER PARK & AROUND
This part of town is awash with arty stores selling cool clothing, high-design home decor and funky accessories, plus a handful of great bookstores and music shops. Much of the action is around the three-way junction of **Damen, North and Milwaukee Avenues**.

department store, impressively stocked with clothes, furniture, iPods (sold from vending machines) and everything in between. Sample the Frango mints, gaze at the Tiffany-domed atrium and check the various stores-within-a-store, including shirtmaker Thomas Pink and bath-and-body import Lush.
▶ *The seventh floor holds several worthwhile eating options; see p147 and p175.*

Neiman Marcus
737 N Michigan Avenue, at E Chicago Avenue, Magnificent Mile (1-312 642 5900/www.neiman marcus.com). El: Red to Chicago. **Open** 10am-7pm Mon-Sat; noon-6pm Sun. **Credit** AmEx, Disc, MC, V. **Map** p326 J10.
Neiman Marcus woos shoppers with a refreshingly airy interior, *haute* fashions from classic establish-ment names such as Chanel to up-and-comers, lux-urious accessories and tempting baked goods. Money is generally no object for the wealthy folks who shop here, resulting in a pricing structure that's led wags to nickname it 'Needless Markup'.

Nordstrom
55 E Grand Avenue, at N Michigan Avenue, Magnificent Mile (1-312 464 1515/www. nordstrom.com). El: Red to Grand. **Open** 10am-8pm Mon-Sat; 11am-6pm Sun. **Credit** AmEx, Disc, MC, V. **Map** p326 J10.
Nordstrom is known for its wide range of fashions, particularly in footwear, and its attentive customer service. If you happen to be in town during one of

its famous half-yearly sales, be prepared to spend at least a full afternoon here – check in your bags with the store concierge and get power-shopping. The in-store café is perfect for a lunchtime wind-down.
▶ *Prices are lower at Nordstrom Rack, the store's discount offshoot (24 N State Street, at W Madison Street, the Loop, 1-312 377 5500).*

Saks Fifth Avenue
Chicago Place, 700 N Michigan Avenue, at E Superior Street, Magnificent Mile (1-312 944 6500/www.saksfifthavenue.com). El: Red to Chicago. **Open** 10am-7pm Mon-Sat; noon-6pm Sun. **Credit** AmEx, Disc, MC, V. **Map** p326 J10.
Favoured by Chicago's upper crust since 1929, five years after it first opened in New York City, Saks Fifth Avenue favours traditional fashions over the wilder trends. Expect to find a wide range of high-quality apparel for women and children, supple-mented with stylish accessories.
▶ *Just across the street sits Saks' equally classy menswear store (no.717).*

Sears
2 N State Street, at W Washington Street, the Loop (1-312 373 6000/www.sears.com). El: Blue to Washington; Brown, Green, Orange, Pink or Purple to Randolph/Wabash; Red to Lake. **Open** 9am-8pm Mon-Sat; 11am-6pm Sun. **Credit** AmEx, Disc, MC, V. **Map** p325 H12.
Although it's hardly a style destination, Sears offers affordable fashions for men, women and children,

CONSUME

with regular bargains on wardrobe staples such as Levi's 501s. What it lacks in exciting clothes, the department store makes up for with its wide selection of products including washing machines and kitchen curtains.
Other locations throughout the city.

MALLS

Century Shopping Center
2828 N Clark Street, between W Diversey Parkway & W Surf Street, Lakeview (1-773 929 8100). El: Brown or Purple to Diversey. **Open** 10am-9pm Mon-Fri; 10am-6pm Sat; noon-6pm Sun. **Map** p328 F4.
A small neighbourhood mall highlighted by an indie cinema and a Bally's Total Fitness (1-773 929 6900, www.ballys.com), plus Aveda (1-773 883 1560, www.aveda.com), Express for Men (1-773 665 2192, www.expressfashion.com) and Victoria's Secret (1-773 549 7405, www.victoriassecret.com).

Chicago Place
700 N Michigan Avenue, at E Superior Street, Magnificent Mile (1-312 266 7710/www.chicagoplace.com). El: Red to Chicago. **Open** 10am-7pm Mon-Fri; 10am-6pm Sat; noon-5pm Sun. **Map** p326 J10.
Saks Fifth Avenue (*see p189*) is the main attraction at this mall, which is undergoing something of a makeover. New tenants, Zara among them, made their Michigan Avenue debut in 2009; check the website for the full line-up of stores.

900 Shops
900 N Michigan Avenue, at E Walton Street, Magnificent Mile (1-312 915 3916/www.shop 900.com). El: Red to Chicago. **Open** 10am-7pm Mon-Sat; noon-6pm Sun. **Map** p326 J9.
The six-floor 900 N Michigan mall is a relatively upscale operation, which offers the city's only full-scale Bloomingdale's (*see p188*) alongside branches of Gucci (1-312 664 5504, www.gucci.com), J.Crew (1-312 751 2739, www.jcrew.com), Club Monaco (1-312 787 8757, www.clubmonaco.com) and a handsome Michael Kors boutique (1-312 640 1122, www.michaelkors.com).

Shops at North Bridge
520 N Michigan Avenue, at E Grand Avenue, Magnificent Mile (1-312 327 2300/www.theshops atnorthbridge.com). El: Red to Grand. **Open** Jan-mid Apr 10am-7pm Mon-Sat; 11am-6pm Sun. Mid Apr-Dec 10am-8pm Mon-Sat; 11am-6pm Sun. **Map** p326 J10.
Nordstrom (*see p189*) is the flagship at this 100-store development on the Magnificent Mile, but midmarket to upscale stores such as Hugo Boss (1-312 660 0056, www.hugoboss.com), Oilily (1-312 822 9616, www.oilily-world.com), jeweller Erwin Pearl (1-312 321 1445, www.erwinpearl.com), Lucky Brand Jeans

(1-312 464 0829, www.luckybrand.com), Sephora (1-312 494 9598, www.sephora.com) and a vast Lego Store (1-312 494 0760, http://shop.lego.com) also appeal to the largely non-native shoppers.

Water Tower Place
835 N Michigan Avenue, at E Chestnut Street, Magnificent Mile (1-312 440 3166/www.shop watertower.com). El: Red to Chicago.
Open 10am-9pm Mon- Sat; 11am-6pm Sun. **Map** p326 J9.
American Girl Place (1-877-247-5223, www.americangirl.com) moved into this shopping centre in autumn 2008, but the mall isn't just full of little girls clutching dolls. It's also a destination for fashionistas, who frequent Betsey Johnson (1-312 280 6964) and Canadian retailer Aritzia (1-312 867 9230, www.aritzia.ca), as well as staples Banana Republic (1-312 642 7667, www.bananarepublic.com), French Connection (1-312 932 9460, www.frenchconnection. com) and Abercrombie & Fitch (1-312 787 8825, www.abercrombie.com).

Westfield Old Orchard
4999 Old Orchard Center, off Route 41 (via I-94), Skokie (1-847 674 7070/www.westfield. com/oldorchard). **Open** 10.30am-8.30pm Mon-Fri; 10am-9pm Sat; 11am-6pm Sun.
As suburban malls go, this one's more pleasing than most, with branches of the Apple Store (1-847 679 1801, www.apple.com), Aveda (1-847 679 1863, www.aveda.com), Lucky Brand Jeans (1-847 674

(1-630 820 7085) via big chains including Gap (1-630 499 5068, www.gap.com) and Banana Republic (1-630 851 5135, www.bananarepublic.com).

Gurnee Mills
6170 W Grand Avenue, off I-94/I-294 (exit at Route 132, W Grand Avenue), Gurnee (1-847 263 7500/www.gurneemillsmall.com). **Open** 10am-9pm Mon-Fri; 10am-9.30pm Sat; 11am-7pm Sun.

JC Penney (1-847 855 0470, www.jcpenney.com), Nike Factory Store (1-847 855 0857, www.nike.com) and TJ Maxx (1-847 855 0146, www.tjmaxx.com) draw bargain hunters; an Abercrombie & Fitch Outlet (1-847 855 2819, www.abercrombie. com) and a Disney Outlet (1-847 856 8239, www.disney.com) are among the 100-plus stores that keep them coming to this not terribly pleasant mall.

Specialist
BOOKS & MAGAZINES
General

Water Tower Place.

See also p193 **After-Words New & Used Books**.

★ Barbara's Bookstore
1218 S Halsted Street, between W Roosevelt Road & James M Rochford Street, Gold Coast (1-312 413 2665/www.barbarasbookstore.com). El: Blue to UIC-Halsted. **Open** 9am-10pm Mon-Fri; 10am-10pm Sat; 10am-8pm Sun. **Credit** AmEx, Disc, MC, V. **Map** p326 H9.

This small chain opened its flagship store over by UIC in 2003, since when it's drawn a local clientele both from on the campus and beyond it. The solid stock is complemented by a calendar of author readings, a children's story hour at 11am on Saturday mornings and other special events.

Other locations Macy's (*see p188*); 1100 Lake Street, Oak Park (1-708 848 9140).

3103, www.luckybrand.com), Sephora (1-847 329 1494, www.sephora.com) and Abercrombie & Fitch (1-847 679 6372, www.abercrombie.com).

Woodfield Shopping Center
5 Woodfield Mall, off Route 53 S (Woodfield Road exit), via I-90, Schaumburg (1-847 330 1537/www.shopwoodfield.com). **Open** 10am-9pm Mon-Sat; 11am-9pm Sun.

Five department stores, including a Sears (1-847 330 2356, www.sears.com) and a Nordstrom (1-847 605 2121, www.nordstrom.com), are joined by Crate & Barrel (1-847 619 4200, www.crateandbarrel.com), inspiring apothecary CO Bigelow (1-847 517 7167, www.bigelowchemist.com) and a Mac-packed Apple Store (1-847 240 6280, www.apple.com). This was once the largest mall in the country.

Outlet malls

Chicago Premium Outlets
1650 Premium Outlets Boulevard, off I-88 (exit at Aurora, Farnsworth Avenue North), Aurora (1-630 585 2200/www.premiumoutlets. com/chicago). **Open** 10am-9pm Mon-Sat; 10am-6pm Sun.

Drive about an hour outside the city limits to shop at 100-odd outlet stores, from posh brands such as Salvatore Ferragamo (1-630 236 9720, www. ferragamo.com) and DKNY (1-630 236 8900, www.dkny.com) to hipster favourites such as Diesel (1-630 236 5514, www.diesel.com) and Converse

CONSUME

CONSUME

Barnes & Noble
1130 N State Street, at W Cedar Street, Gold Coast (1-312 280 8155/www.barnesandnoble. com). El: Red to Clark/Division. **Open** 9am-8pm Mon-Sat; 10am-7pm Sun. **Credit** AmEx, Disc, MC, V. **Map** p326 H9.
In a gratifying break from the norm, the on-the-ball staffers at this wood-panelled store often make a genuine effort to find the book you're looking for. The magazine section is large and varied.
Other locations 1 E Jackson Boulevard at S State Street, the Loop (1-312 362 8792); 1441 W Webster Avenue, at N Clybourn Avenue, Lincoln Park (1-773 871 3610).

Borders Books & Music
150 N State Street, at Randolph Street, the Loop (1-312 606 0750/www.borders.com). El: Brown, Green, Orange, Pink or Purple to State/Lake; Red to Lake. **Open** 8am-9pm Mon-Fri; 9am-9pm Sat; 10am-8pm Sun. **Credit** AmEx, Disc, MC, V. **Map** p326 J9.
When Borders closes its Magnificent Mile branch in 2010, this State Street operation will be the chain's most central Chicago store. The firm's usual broad selection of stock is available here, including a good local-interest collection and a solid range of magazines from home and abroad.
Other locations 2817 N Clark Street, at W Diversey Parkway, Lakeview (1-773 935 3909); and throughout the city.

★ Powell's
1501 E 57th Street, between S Harper Avenue & S Lake Park Avenue, Hyde Park (1-773 955 7780/www.powellschicago.com). Metra: 55th-56th-57th Street. **Open** 9am-11pm daily. **Credit** MC, V. **Map** p332 Y17.
The three branches of this chain between them offer an agreeably browsable selection of remaindered books and second-hand stock. The Hyde Park and South Loop locations, both about as big as each other, have strong academic collections, while the Lakeview operation has a large art and photography selection.
Other locations 828 S Wabash Avenue, at W 8th Street, South Loop (1-312 341 0748); 2850 N Lincoln Avenue, at W Wolfram Street, Lakeview (1-773 248 1444).

Seminary Cooperative Bookstore
5757 S University Avenue, between E 57th Street & E 58th Street, Hyde Park (1-773 752 4381/www.semcoop.com). Metra: 59th Street. **Open** 8.30am-9pm Mon-Fri; 10am-6pm Sat; noon-6pm Sun. **Credit** AmEx, Disc, MC, V. **Map** p332 X12.
The Seminary Coop is revered by local academics, but general readers are sure to find something unusual and inspiring to read within its impeccably stocked shelves. There are obscure texts galore,

Quimby's Bookstore.

leaving even the most intrepid bookworm happy. The 57th Street location offers a slightly smaller selection in a slightly airier location.
Other locations Newberry Library Bookstore, 60 W Walton Street, at N Dearborn Street, Gold Coast (1-312 255 3520); 57th Street Books, 1301 E 57th Street, at S Kimball Avenue, Hyde Park (1-773 684 1300).

Unabridged Bookstore
3251 N Broadway Street, between W Melrose Street & W Aldine Avenue, Lakeview (1-773 883 9119/www.unabridgedbookstore.com). El: Brown, Purple or Red to Belmont. **Open** 10am-9pm Mon-Fri; 10am-7pm Sat, Sun. **Credit** AmEx, Disc, MC, V. **Map** p329 F2.
This indie bookstore largely reflects the make-up of the neighbourhood in which it sits: it's particularly strong on gay and lesbian literature. You'll find a large selection of hard-to-find LBGT magazines as well as autographed copies of books by writers such as David Sedaris and Augusten Burroughs.

Specialist

Prairie Avenue Bookshop
418 S Wabash Avenue, between E Van Buren Street & E Congress Parkway, the Loop (1-312 922 8311/www.pabook.com). El: Blue or Red to Jackson; Brown, Orange, Pink or Purple to Library. **Open** 10am-6pm Mon-Fri; 10am-4pm Sat. **Credit** AmEx, Disc, MC, V. **Map** p325 H13.

One of the Midwest's most impressive architectural bookstores stocks 15,000 titles on architecture, interiors, city planning and graphic design. Get cosy in the sit-around furniture by Frank Lloyd Wright, Mies van der Rohe and Le Corbusier.

▶ For more on the city's architecture, see p34.

Quimby's Bookstore
1854 W North Avenue, at N Wolcott Avenue, Wicker Park (1-773 342 0910/www.quimbys. com). El: Blue to Damen. **Open** noon-9pm Mon-Thur; noon-10pm Fri; 11am-10pm Sat; noon-6pm Sun. **Credit** AmEx, Disc, MC, V. **Map** p331 B7.
Find the newest in small press, underground and self-published magazines at this Wicker Park staple, or check out the decent comic and book selections.

★ Women & Children First
5233 N Clark Street, at W Foster Avenue, Andersonville (1-773 769 9299/www.womenand childrenfirst.com). El: Red to Berwyn. **Open** 11am-7pm Mon, Tue; 11am-9pm Wed-Fri; 10am-7pm Sat; 11am-6pm Sun. **Credit** AmEx, Disc, MC, V.
This welcoming, queer-friendly spot is as much a community meeting place as it is a bookstore. Readings, for women and children alike, draw established authors and up-and-coming activists.

Used & antiquarian

After-Words New & Used Books
23 E Illinois Street, between N State Street & N Wabash Avenue, River North (1-312 464 1110). El: Red to Grand. **Open** 10.30am-10pm Mon-Thur; 10.30am-11pm Fri; 10am-11pm Sat; noon-7pm Sun. **Credit** AmEx, MC, V. **Map** p326 H11.
This two-storey shop offers new, used and out-of-print volumes. Customers can access the internet by the hour using store computers, and are even able to order customised stationery.

★ Myopic Books
1564 N Milwaukee Avenue, at N Damen Avenue, Wicker Park (1-773 862 4882/www.myopic bookstore.com). El: Blue to Damen. **Open** 11am-1am Mon-Sat; 11am-10pm Sun. **Credit** MC, V. **Map** p331 C7.
Staff at this three-storey shop are serious about the no-cellphones policy, which makes for a quiet environment. Everything from foreign fiction to cookbooks is represented. Prices are fair, staff tremendous, and the shop is open until 1am most nights.

CHILDREN
Fashion

Gap Kids can be found within the four-storey Gap flagship store on Michigan Avenue (555 N Michigan Ave, 1-312 494 8580, www.gap.com),

while cheery Dutch import **Oilily** has a shop in the Shops at North Bridge (*see p190*; 1-312 527 5747, www.oililyusa.com).

★ Grow
1943 W Division Street, at N Damen Avenue, Wicker Park (1-773 489 0009/www.grow-kids.com). El: Blue to Damen. **Open** 10am-6pm Tue, Wed, Fri, Sat; 10am-8pm Thur; noon-5pm Sun. **Credit** AmEx, Disc, MC, V. **Map** p331 B8.
This hip, modern Wicker Park store sells nursery furniture and organic children's attire. The goods all come with sleek and sometimes retro aesthetics.

Psychobaby
1630 N Damen Avenue, at W North Avenue, Wicker Park (1-773 772 2815/www.psychobaby online.com). El: Blue to Damen. **Open** 10am-6pm Mon-Wed, Fri, Sat; 10am-8pm Thur; 11am-5pm Sun. **Credit** AmEx, Disc, MC, V. **Map** p331 B7.
Tots and toddlers get outfitted in funky fashions at this Wicker Park operation, where the clothes are a real antidote to traditional frilly togs. Educational toys, shoes and books round out the selection.

Threadless Kids
1905 W Division Street, at N Wolcott Avenue, Wicker Park (1-773 698 7042/www.threadless kids.com). El: Blue to Damen. **Open** 10am-7pm Mon-Sat; noon-5pm Sun. **Credit** AmEx, Disc, MC, V. **Map** p331 C8.
Little ones can get into the graphic T-shirt craze thanks to racks of mini versions of this popular company's screen-printed merchandise, which is designed and then voted for online by the public.

Toys & games

For the **Lego Store**, *see p190* Shops at North Bridge. There's also an **FAO Schwarz** inside the Macy's on State Street; *see p188*.

Quake
4628 N Lincoln Avenue, at W Eastwood Avenue, Uptown (1-773 878 4288). El: Red to Lawrence. **Open** 1-6pm Mon, Wed-Fri; noon-6pm Sat; noon-5pm Sun. **Credit** MC, V.
The place to find that elusive Mystery Date game or that *Nightmare Before Christmas* figurine, along with retro lunchboxes, *Star Wars* swag and board games from the 1960s and '70s.

★ Rotofugi
1953 W Chicago Avenue, at N Damen Avenue, West Town (1-312 491 9501/www.rotofugi.com). Bus 50, 66. **Open** noon-8pm Mon-Sat; noon-5pm Sun. **Credit** AmEx, Disc, MC, V. **Map** p331 B10.
Grown-up kids rush to this Japanese-inspired toy shop to pick up limited-edition vinyl dolls, plush toys and poseable figures. There's almost always a cool art exhibition on show.

CONSUME

Timeless Toys

4749 N Lincoln Avenue, at W Lawrence Avenue, Lincoln Square (1-773 334 4445/www.timeless toyschicago.com). El: Brown to Western. **Open** 10am-6pm Mon-Wed, Sat; 10am-7pm Thur, Fri; 11am-5pm Sun. **Credit** AmEx, Disc, MC, V.

Angelina Jolie helped put this years-old toyshop in the pages of national gossip mags when the paparazzi photographed her shopping here while in town shooting a movie. Its inventory is comprised of classic (wooden trains, puzzles), educational (science kits) and imaginative toys (costumes, puppets).

★ Uncle Fun

1338 W Belmont Avenue, at N Southport Avenue, Lakeview (1-773 477 8223/www.unclefunchicago. com). El: Brown, Purple or Red to Belmont. **Open** noon-7pm Mon-Fri; 11am-7pm Sat; 11am-5pm Sun. **Credit** AmEx, MC, V. **Map** p329 D2.

Children young and old will love digging through drawers jammed full of plastic squirt cameras, fake puke and other novelty toys from the 1970s and '80s, all at fairly reasonable prices.

ELECTRONICS & PHOTOGRAPHY

The Magnificent Mile is home to the **Apple Store** (no.679, at E Erie Street, 1-312 981 4104, www.apple.com) and a major **Nokia** store (no.543, at E Grand Avenue, 1-312 670 2607, www.nokiausa.com). Nearby, there's also a branch of **Bang & Olufsen** (609 N State Street, 1-312 787 6006, www.bang-olufsen.com).

Central Camera

230 S Wabash Avenue, at E Jackson Boulevard, the Loop (1-312 427 5580/www.centralcamera. com). El: Blue or Red to Jackson; Brown, Green, Orange, Pink or Purple to Adams/Wabash. **Open** 8.30am-5.30pm Mon-Fri; 8.30am-5pm Sat. **Credit** AmEx, Disc, MC, V. **Map** p325 H12.

The knowledgeable service and lack of appealing decor here haven't changed much during Central Camera's century in business, but the stock certainly has: these days, it's packed with digital imaging equipment, as well as more old-fashioned gear. The repair service is a valued extra.

Saturday Audio Exchange

1021 W Belmont Avenue, at W Kenmore Avenue, Lakeview (1-773 935 4434/www. saturdayaudio.com). El: Brown, Purple or Red to Belmont. **Open** 5.30-9pm Thur; 10.30am-5.30pm Sat; noon-4pm Sun. **Credit** AmEx, Disc, MC, V. **Map** p329 E2.

Thanks to great prices and smart, unpushy staff, this local fave thrives despite the fact that it's only open three days a week. Brands include Denon, Musical Fidelity and Blu-ray; stock is a mix of new and used equipment.

FASHION

Designer

A stroll down the fashionable sidewalk of E Oak Street between State Street and Michigan Avenue turns up the big design names, among them the likes of **Hermès** (no.110, 1-312 787 8175, www.hermes.com), **Jil Sander** (no.48, 1-312 335 0006, www.jilsander.com), **Kate Spade** (no.56, 1-312 654 8853, www.kate spade.com), **Prada** (no.30, 1-312 951 1113, www.prada.com), **Ultimo** (no.116, 1-312 787 1171, www.ultimo.com) and **Yves Saint Laurent** (no.51, 1-312 751 8995, www.ysl.com).

The north end of N Michigan Avenue, between Superior and Oak Streets, is another important fashionista destination, not least as it is home to the world's largest **Ralph Lauren** (no.750, 1-312 280 1655, www.polo.com), plus **Giorgio Armani** (no.800, 1-312 751 2244, www.armani.com), **Gucci** (in the 900 N Michigan Shops, 1-312 664 5504, www.gucci. com), **J Mendel** (no.919, 1-312 981 1725, www.jmendel.com) and **Chanel** (no.935, 1-312 787 5500, www.chanel.com).

Head to the now gentrified Wicker Park/ Bucktown area for the city's latest designer invasion, thanks to the Chicago debut of a **Marc by Marc Jacobs** boutique (1714 N Damen Avenue, 1-773 276 2998, www.marc jacobs.com). Other big name designers who've opened up shop in the neighbourhood include **Nanette Lepore** (1623 N Damen Ave, 1-773 489 4500, www.nanettelepore.com) and Chicago native **Cynthia Rowley** (1653 N Damen Avenue, 1-773 276 9209, www.cynthiarowley.com).

Blake

212 W Chicago Avenue, between N Wells Street & N Franklin Street, River North (1-312 202 0047). El: Brown or Purple to Chicago. **Open** 10.30am-7pm Mon-Fri; 10.30am-6.30pm Sat. **Credit** AmEx, Disc, MC, V. **Map** p326 G10.

You'll need to be buzzed in to browse the pricey frocks from Dries Van Noten, Marni and others, but the selection is worth the initial awkwardness. That said, the easily intimidated should head elsewhere, as the staff's attitude can be just as chilly as the shop's stark interior.

INSIDE TRACK
IKRAM & OBAMA

Like Michelle Obama's style? Compliment Ikram Goldman, the owner of **Ikram** (*see p195*): she helped Mrs Obama choose her Inauguration dresses.

CONSUME

Cynthia Rowley.

Connect

1330 N Milwaukee Avenue, at N Paulina Street, Wicker Park (1-312 890 3684 /www.connect-chicago.com). El: Blue to Division. **Open** 11am-7pm Mon-Sat; noon-5pm Sun. **Credit** AmEx, Disc, MC, V. **Map** p331 C8.

There are two ways to get the goods at this eco-friendly retailer: shop at the store and walk out the door with your purchases, or order through Connect's in-house interactive showroom, where you'll get a ten per cent discount, and then have the clothes delivered via bike couriers the same week. *Photo p197.*

Eskell

1509 N Milwaukee Avenue, at N Honore Street, Wicker Park (1-773 486 0830/www.eskell.com). El: Blue to Damen. **Open** 11am-7pm Tue-Sat; 11am-5pm Sun. **Credit** AmEx, Disc, MC, V. **Map** p328 E5.

Young arty types depend on Eskell to find tiny designer labels, many from New York's hippest enclaves. The house line displays beautiful use of pattern and texture in its rock-'n'-roll-meets-hippie dresses and separates.

Guise Chic

2128 N Halsted Street, between Dickens & Webster Avenues, Lincoln Park (1-773 929 6130/www.guisechic.com). El: Brown or Purple to Armitage. **Open** 9.30am-8.30pm Mon-Fri; 9.30am-7pm Sat; 10am-6.30pm Sun. **Credit** AmEx, Disc, MC, V. **Map** p328 F6.

In addition to carrying designers duds including items by J-Brand, Aka and Delman for women, and Tom Ford and Helmut Lang items for men, this space also offers salon services in the back of the boutique.

Hejfina

1529 N Milwaukee Avenue, at W North Avenue, Wicker Park (1-773 772 0002/www.hejfina.com). El: Blue to Damen. **Open** 11am-7pm Tue-Sat; noon-6pm Sun. **Credit** AmEx, Disc, MC, V. **Map** p331 C7.

Cool and sleek, this lifestyle boutique provides fashions for men and women; many are from international designers and most are exclusive to the store.

Helen Yi

1645 N Damen Avenue, at W North Avenue, Bucktown (1-773 252 3838/www.helenyi.com). El: Blue to Damen. **Open** 11am-7pm Mon-Sat; noon-5pm Sun. **Credit** AmEx, MC, V. **Map** p331 B7.

Make sure your credit card balance is in good shape when you visit this spacious women's boutique. After you've seen the lovely clothes from Chloé and other top designers, you'll struggle not to splurge.

Ikram

873 N Rush Street, at E Chicago Avenue, Gold Coast (1-312 587 1000/www.ikram.com). El: Red to Chicago. **Open** 10am-6pm Mon-Sat. **Credit** AmEx, Disc, MC, V. **Map** p326 J10.

Ikram Goldman learned the rag trade at Ultimo before opening her boutique. The global scope of the high-end fashions, flirty footwear and unique jewellery found in this shop are fresh off the pages of *Vogue.*

Jake

939 N Rush Street, at W Oak Street, Gold Coast (1-312 664 5553/www.shopjake.com). El: Red to Chicago. **Open** 10am-7pm Mon-Fri; 10am-6pm Sat; noon-6pm Sun. **Credit** AmEx, MC, V. **Map** p326 H9.

CONSUME

The best-dressed men and women in Chicago have Jake at the top of their must-shop list. The owners attend fashion shows in Paris and New York to find graceful, modern lines from the likes of 3.1 Phillip Lim, Band of Outsiders and Opening Ceremony.

★ Joe's Jeans
1715 N Damen Avenue, at W St Paul Avenue, Bucktown (1-773 252 1715/www.joesjeans.com). El: Blue to Damen. Bus: 50, 56, 72. **Open** 11am-6pm Mon, Tue; noon-5pm Wed, Thur; 11am-7pm Fri, Sat; noon-6pm Sun. **Credit** AmEx, Disc, MC, V. **Map** p331 B7.
This hip denim label chose Chicago as the location for its first retail shop. In addition to the afore mentioned jeans, you'll find vintage coffee table books, jewellery and apothecary goods scattered throughout the sleek interior.

Maria Pinto
133 N Jefferson Street, at W Randolph Street, West Loop (1-312 648 1350/www.mariapinto. com). El: Green to Clinton. **Open** 10am-6pm Tue, Wed, Fri; 10am-7pm Thur; 10am-5pm Sat. **Credit** MC, V. **Map** p325 F12.
With rich bamboo flooring, light fixtures from Italy and a hand-painted mural inspired by one of Maria Pinto's subtle lace patterns, the Chicago-based designer's store creates the perfect home for the elegant evening dresses Michelle Obama – a longtime Pinto fan – has been photographed wearing.

Michelle Tan
1872 N Damen Avenue, at W Cortland Street, Bucktown (1-773 252 1888/www.michelletan. com). El: Blue to Damen. **Open** 11am-7pm Tue-Sat; noon-5pm Sun. **Credit** MC, V. **Map** p331 B6.
Local womenswear designer Tan specialises in unconventional cuts, unfinished hems and minimalist colours. She also sells complementary pieces by other rising local and international designers.

P.45
1643 N Damen Avenue, at W North Avenue, Wicker Park (1-773 862 4523/www.p45.com). El: Blue to Damen. **Open** 11am-7pm Mon-Sat; noon-5pm Sun. **Credit** AmEx, Disc, MC, V. **Map** p331 B7.
This super-hip shop, which features a wonderful sweeping interior created by famous local designer Suhail, is a piece of SoHo in Chicago. The young proprietresses of the industrial-chic space buy exclusive designs from local and New York up-and-comers, which they sell at hefty prices.

★ Robin Richman
2108 N Damen Avenue, at W Webster Avenue, Bucktown (1-773 278 6150/www.robinrichman. com). El: Blue (O'Hare branch) to Western. **Open** 11am-6pm Tue-Sat; noon-5pm Sun. **Credit** AmEx, Disc, MC, V. **Map** p331 B5.

A shopping pioneer in Bucktown for hip women's clothing. Antique-looking items (handsome bags, semi-precious jewellery and the like) make the atmosphere both rustic and ravishing.

Roslyn
2035 N Damen Avenue, between W McLean & W Dickens Avenues, Bucktown (1-773 489 1311/www.roslynboutique.com). El: Blue to Damen. **Open** 11am-7pm Tue-Sat; noon-5pm Sun. **Credit** AmEx, Disc, MC, V. **Map** p331 B6.
At Roslyn, the racks of women's clothes are organised by label, each accompanied by a biography. You'll appreciate the nuance: most of the pricey pieces are by rising (read: just-out-of-school) designers.

Scoop
1702 N Milwaukee Avenue, at W Wabansia Avenue, Wicker Park (1-773 227 9930/www. scoopnyc.com). El: Blue to Damen. **Open** 11am-7pm Mon-Sat; noon-6pm Sun. **Credit** AmEx, Disc, MC, V. **Map** p331 B7.
There's something for the whole fashionable family here, including Jimmy Choo slingbacks, Earnest Sewn denim for kids and John Varvatos sweaters for men. Prices aren't cheap, but there's often a good selection of items on sale.

Discount

See also p191 **Outlet malls**.

Beta Boutique
2016 W Concord Place, between N Damen & N Milwaukee Avenues, Bucktown (1-773 276 0905/ www.betaboutique.com). El: Blue to Damen. **Open** 11am-7pm Thur, Fri; 11am-6pm Sat; noon-5pm Sun. **Credit** AmEx, Disc, MC, V. **Map** p331 B7.
Frugal fans of fashion will find plenty to love in this shop. Prices on hundreds of contemporary designer pieces (mostly women's, but some items for men are available) are whittled down by 40-90%. The shop's occasional sales offer even greater deals.

General

Many of the country's familiar chains are down on Michigan Avenue, among them cheap-chic staple **H&M** (no.840, at E Chicago Avenue, 1-312 640 0060, www.hm.com), posh and preppy **Banana Republic** (no.744, at E Chicago Avenue, 1-312 642 0020, www.banana republic.com) and **Gap** (no.555, at W Grand Avenue, 1-312 494 8580, www.gap.com). Cheap and cheery **Old Navy** has a store in the Loop (35 N State Street, at W Washington Street, 1-312 551 0522, www.oldnavy.com).

The Gold Coast is home to high-concept, high-priced chains **Anthropologie** (1120 N State Street, at E Cedar Street, 1-312 255 1848, www.anthropologie.com), **Ugg** (909 N Rush

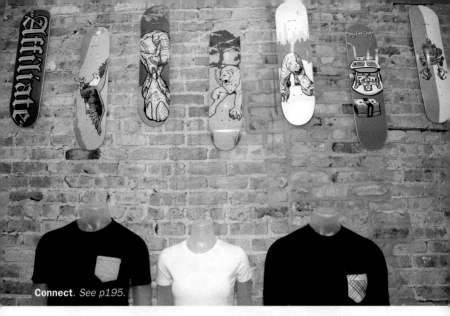

Connect. *See p195.*

Street, 1-312 255 1280, www.uggaustralia.com), the **Original Penguin** (901 N Rush Street, at E Delaware Place, 1-312 475 0792, www.original penguin.com) and **Diesel** (923 N Rush Street, at E Walton Street, 1-312 255 0157, www. diesel.com). Wicker Park, meanwhile, contains branches of **Urban Outfitters** (1521 N Milwaukee Avenue, at N Damen Avenue, 1-773 772 8550, www.urbanoutfitters.com), the **Levi's Store** (1552 N Milwaukee Avenue, at W North Avenue, 1-773 486 3900, www.levi.com) and the increasingly ubiquitous **American Apparel** (1563 N Milwaukee Avenue, at N Damen Avenue, 1-773 235 6778, www.americanapparel.net).

Akira
1837 W North Avenue, at N Honore Street, Wicker Park (1-773 489 0818/www.akirachicago. com). El: Blue to Damen. **Open** noon-9pm Mon-Fri; 11am-9pm Sat; 11am-7pm Sun. **Credit** AmEx, Disc, MC, V. **Map** p331 C7.
Covetable designer togs at high prices? Welcome to 21st-century Wicker Park, where Akira draws loyal crowds. This is the women's store; also on North Avenue, there's a men's shop (no.1922) and a shoe store (no.1849).

Alcala's Western Wear
1733 W Chicago Avenue, at N Ashland Avenue, West Town (1-312 226 0152/www.alcalas.com). Bus 66. **Open** 9.30am-8pm Mon, Thur, Fri; 9.30am-7pm Tue, Wed, Sat; 9.30am-5pm Sun. **Credit** AmEx, Disc, MC, V. **Map** p331 C9.
Wanna rodeo? Slip on the stetson to wallow in this shop's selections of jeans, hats and cowboy boots

(some 10,000 pairs). Menswear predominates, with a smattering of shirts and jackets for cowgirls.
► *When you've cowboyed up, head to happy hour at the Empty Bottle on Fridays and catch excellent local honky-tonk act the Hoyle Brothers; see p259.*

Apartment No.9
1804 N Damen Avenue, at W Churchill Street, Bucktown (1-773 395 2999/www.apartment number9.com). El: Blue to Damen. **Open** 11am-7pm Tue-Fri; 11am-6pm Sat; noon-5pm Sun. **Credit** AmEx, Disc, MC, V. **Map** p331 B7.
It's virtually impossible to look bad after shopping here, so stylish and timeless are the clothes. Staff specialise in helping men who need fashion guidance. The back room generally has great discounts on fashion by the likes of Rogan and Paul Smith.

Belmont Army
1318 N Milwaukee Avenue, at N Paulina Street, Wicker Park (1-773 384 8448). El: Blue to Division. **Open** 11am-8pm Mon-Sat; noon-5pm Sun. **Credit** AmEx, Disc, MC, V. **Map** p331 C8.
You can dress like a soldier if you like, but most shoppers at this bright, tidy store prefer to choose from the selections of cool trainers and youthful streetwear by the likes of Ben Sherman and Diesel. **Other locations** 855 W Belmont Avenue, at N Clark Street, Lakeview (1-773 549 1038).

Brooklyn Industries
1426 N Milwaukee Avenue, at W Evergreen Avenue, Bucktown (1-773 360 8182/www. brooklynindustries.com). El: Blue to Damen. **Open** 11am-7pm daily. **Credit** AmEx, Disc, MC, V. **Map** p331 C8.

Make the most of London life

INSIDE TRACK THREADLESS

It pays to be a repeat customer at **Threadless** (*see below*). The store runs a programme in which buyers get $1 off every non-sale shirt purchased when they bring in the bag from their previous purchase.

Just like its NYC outposts, the first Brooklyn Industries location to open outside of the Big Apple offers messenger bags, graphic T-shirts, hoodies and other reasonably priced items.

Krista K Boutique

3458 N Southport Avenue, at W Roscoe Street, Wrigleyville (1-773 248 1967/www.kristak.com). El: Brown to Southport. **Open** 11am-7pm Mon-Fri; 10am-6pm Sat; noon-5pm Sun. **Credit** AmEx, Disc, MC, V. **Map** p329 D2.

Neighbourhood gals rely heavily on Krista K for its all-occasion sensibilities. There's a little bit of everything for sale here, from jeans and dresses to suits, and even a maternity line.

★ Penelope's

1913 W Division Street, at N Damen Avenue, Wicker Park (1-773 395 2351/www.shop penelopes.com). El: Blue to Division. **Open** 11am-7pm Mon-Sat; noon-6pm Sun. **Credit** AmEx, MC, V. **Map** p331 B8.

Recovering indie rockers swarm to this adorable store, where guys and girls get their fill of slightly mod clothes, shoes and accessories.

★ Threadless

3011 N Broadway, between W Wellington & W Barry Avenues, Lakeview (1-773 525 8640). El: Red, Brown or Purple to Belmont. **Open** 11am-8pm Mon-Sat; noon-6pm Sun. **Credit** AmEx, Disc, MC, V. **Map** p329 F3.

The two-storey shop has a typical retail space full of newly designed T-shirts ($12-$25) and hoodies ($40) on the first floor, and an upstairs gallery space featuring artwork from Threadless.com designers.

Tula

3738 N Southport Avenue, between W Grace Street & W Waveland Avenue, Wrigleyville (1-773 549 2876/www.tulaboutique.com). El: Brown to Southport. **Open** 11am-7pm Mon-Fri; 10am-5pm Sun. **Credit** MC, V. **Map** p329 D1.

Ageless dressing with a European bent is the theme at this women's shop, which highlights casual clothing by mostly continental designers. Because a mother and daughter team run this shop, women of all ages should find something that works.

Vive la Femme

2048 N Damen Avenue, between W Dickens Avenue & W McLean Avenue, Bucktown (1-773 772 7429/www.vivelafemme.com). El: Blue to Damen. **Open** 11am-7pm Tue-Fri; 10am-5pm Sat, Sun. **Credit** AmEx, Disc, MC, V. **Map** p331 B6.

Plus-sized women don't deserve frumpy frocks, which is why this big-girl boutique is a must-visit if you're a size 12 (UK size 14) or larger. The styles here complement curves rather than hide them; size-two twiglets often envy the designs.

Threadless.

Used & vintage

Beatnix

3400 N Halsted Street, between W Roscoe Street & W Newport Avenue, Wrigleyville (1-773 281 6933). El: Brown, Purple or Red to Belmont. **Open** noon-9pm Mon-Thur, Sun; 11am-11pm Fri, Sat. **Credit** MC, V. **Map** p329 F2.

This colourful Boystown bazaar has outfits and accessories, both new and used, to keep club kids, drag queens and muscle boys all looking their best. If you head on past the 'pimp shoes' at the back you'll find a great collection of wigs.

★ Haystack

2934 N Broadway Street, between W Oakdale Avenue & W Wellington Avenue, Lakeview (www.haystackvintage.com). El: Red, Brown or Purple to Belmont. **Open** noon-8pm daily. **Credit** AmEx, Disc, MC, V. **Map** p329 F3.

The hipster owners of Haystack up in Lakeview describe their shop as Anthropologie meets a thrift store. In addition to a fine collection of old-school clothes, the shop also features new graphic T-shirts by Isotope (two for $30) and a growing collection of Schwinn bikes with banana seats.

Hollywood Mirror

812 W Belmont Avenue, at N Halsted Street, Lakeview (1-773 404 2044/www.hollywood mirror.com). El: Brown, Purple or Red to Belmont. **Open** 11am-9.30pm Mon-Thur; 11am-10pm Fri, Sat; 11am-7pm Sun. **Credit** AmEx, Disc, MC, V. **Map** p329 F2.

This retro shop has a huge selection of weathered jeans, bowling shirts and jackets, plus old-school furniture on the lower level and a wide array of nostalgic items upstairs.

★ Knee Deep Vintage

1425 W 18th Street, at S Bishop Street, Pilsen (1-312 850 2510/www.kneedeepvintage.com). El: Pink to 18th Street. **Open** noon-8pm Mon-Thur; 11am-9pm Fri, Sat; noon-6pm Sun. **Credit** AmEx, Disc, MC, V.

The co-owners of this fine shop, which is pretty representative of Pilsen's changing face, scour the country and local thrift shops for the best men's and womens's vintage finds and keep the mark-ups at very reasonable levels.

LuLu's at the Belle Kay

3862 N Lincoln Avenue, between W Byron Street & W Berenice Avenue, Lakeview (1-773 404 5858/www.lulusbellekay.com). El: Brown to Addison. **Open** 11am-6pm Tue-Fri; 11am-5pm Sat; noon-5pm Sun. **Credit** AmEx, MC, V. **Map** p330 C1.

An elegant fainting couch completes the salon setting for LuLu's neatly arranged vintage handbags, furs, couture clothing and jewellery.

Silver Moon

1755 W North Avenue, at N Wood Street, Wicker Park (1-773 235 5797/www.silvermoon vintage.com). El: Blue to Damen. **Open** noon-8pm Tue-Sat; noon-5pm Sun. **Credit** MC, V. **Map** p331 C7.

This shop features an exquisite collection of men's and women's clothes, some of them dating back to the 1890s. Coming more into the modern era, there's a heavy focus on Vivienne Westwood items, and everything is in immaculate condition.

FASHION ACCESSORIES & SERVICES

Cleaning & repairs

Brooks Shoe Service

55 E Washington Street, between N Michigan Avenue & S Wabash Avenue, the Loop (1-312 704 6805/www.brooksshoeservice.com). El: Brown, Green, Orange, Pink or Purple to Madison/Wabash; Blue or Red to Monroe. **Open** *June-Aug* 8am-5.30pm Mon-Fri. *Sept-May* 8am-5.30pm Mon- Fri; 10am-3pm Sat. **Credit** AmEx, Disc, MC, V. **Map** p325 J12.

The third generation of the Morelli family is still here at this Loop staple, repairing footwear for socialites, retailers and everyday Joes. They're also experts at restoring vintage shoes and bags. A delivery service is available.

Greener Cleaner

1522 N Damen Avenue, at N Milwaukee Avenue, Wicker Park (1-773 784 8429/www. greenercleaner.net). El: Blue to Damen. **Open** 7am-7pm Mon-Fri; 8am-6pm Sat. **Credit** MC, V. **Map** p331 B7.

As the name suggests, this dry cleaner is strictly eco-friendly. Your clothes will smell fresh rather than vaguely chemicalesque, and a delivery service is also available.

Hats

Hats Plus

4706 W Irving Park Road, between N Milwaukee Avenue & N Kilpatrick Avenue, Irving Park (1-773 286 5577/www.hats-plus.com). El: Blue to

Knee Deep Vintage.

Irving Park. **Open** 10am-6pm Mon-Wed, Fri, Sat; 10am-8pm Thur; 11am-5pm Sun. **Credit** AmEx, Disc, MC, V.

It's a hike from downtown, but men who take their headgear seriously will want to venture north for the city's largest choice in felt, fur, wool, straw and more. There's a small women's department.

Jewellery

For salt-of-the-earth shopping, hit Jeweler's Row, a strip of jewellery stores on S Wabash Avenue between Washington and Jackson in the Loop. In particular, try the **Jeweler's Center** (5 S Wabash Street, at E Washington Street, 1-312 424 2664, www.jewelerscenter. com), home to 150 jewellers. On a rather grander note, **Tiffany & Co** (no.730, at E Superior Street, 1-312 944 7500, www. tiffany.com) and **Cartier** (no.630, at E Ontario Street, 1-312 266 7440, www.cartier.com) both have shops on the Magnificent Mile.

★ Helen Ficalora

2014 N Halsted Street, between W Armitage Avenue & W Dickens Avenue, Lincoln Park (1-773 883 2014/www.helenficalora.com). El: Brown or Purple to Armitage. **Open** 11am-7pm Mon-Fri; 11am-5pm Sat; noon-5pm Sun. **Credit** AmEx, MC, V. **Map** p327 F6.

New York-based Ficalora was one of the pioneers of the alphabet-charm craze and has opened shops in SoHo, Beverly Hills and Palm Beach. The Lincoln Park outpost features letter charms (starting at $115 for 14-carat yellow gold), as well as chains and rings inspired by nature.

K Amato Designs

1229 W Diversey Avenue, at N Magnolia Avenue, Lakeview (1-312 882 1366/www.k-amato.com). El: Blue to Diversey. **Open** by appointment. **Credit** AmEx, Disc, MC, V. **Map** p328 E4.

This local jewellery designer's huge work space doubles as a by-appointment boutique. The line ($30-$100) includes strands of beads, delicate chokers and golden chains with adornments, as well as dangling earrings and matching bracelets.

Left Bank

1155 W Webster Avenue, between N Racine Avenue & N Clifton Avenue, Lincoln Park (1-773 929 7422/www.leftbankjewelry.com). El: Brown, Purple or Red to Fullerton. **Open** noon-7pm Mon, Wed, Thur; noon-6pm Fri; 11am-5pm Sat; noon-4pm Sun. **Credit** Disc, MC, V. **Map** p328 E5.

The owner specialises in jewellery made in France, as well as unique gift items with that Parisian *je ne sais quoi*. This romantic boutique also features dazzling, bejewelled bridal tiaras and custom veils.

Silver Room

1442 N Milwaukee Avenue, between W Evergreen Avenue & N Honore Street, Wicker Park (1-773 278 7130/www.thesilver room.com). El: Blue to Damen. **Open** 11am-8pm Mon-Sat; 11am-6pm Sun. **Credit** AmEx, Disc, MC, V. **Map** p331 C8.

The in-house weekend DJ says it all really: this is one style-conscious shop. Specialising in semi-precious jewellery, the Silver Room also sells hats and super-fly sunglasses.

Lingerie

There are five **Victoria's Secret** (www.victoriassecret.com) stores in Chicago, including two branches on Michigan Avenue (no.830 and no.845 respectively), at North and Clybourn Avenues and in the Century Shopping Center (*see p190*).

G Boutique

2131 N Damen Avenue, between W Charleston Street & W Shakespeare Avenue, Wicker Park (1-773 235 1234/www.boutiqueg.com). El: Blue to Damen. **Open** 11am-7pm Mon-Sat; noon-5pm Sun. **Credit** AmEx, MC, V. **Map** p331 B6.

One look at the bright pink façade of this underwear boutique and you know what's in store: frills, lace, and sauciness. Cosabella thongs share space with sumptuous French underthings; if you're feeling naughty, pick up a vibrating rubber duckie.

Isabella Fine Lingerie

840 W Armitage Avenue, between N Dayton Street & N Fremont Street, Lincoln Park (1-773 281 2352/www.shopisabella.com). El: Brown or Purple to Armitage. **Open** 10am-7pm Mon-Fri; 10am-6pm Sat; noon-5pm Sun. **Credit** AmEx, MC, V. **Map** p328 E5.

Rising from a cocoon of whisper-soft silk, this glamorous boutique prides itself on its excellent customer service and is known for helping shoppers to find that elusive, perfectly fitting bra. Kick back on the lounge room sofa among the pyjamas, sleepwear, swimwear and cosy robes.

Luggage

★ Flight 001

1133 N State Street, at W Division Street, Gold Coast (1-312 944 1001/www.flight001.com). El: Red to Clark/Division. **Open** 11am-7pm Mon-Sat; 11am-6pm Sun. **Credit** AmEx, DC, Disc, MC, V. **Map** p326 H9.

The interior of this travel-themed shop, part of a small but popular nationwide chain, resembles an airplane from the days when flying was glamorous, and stocks everything from luggage and carry-on goods to in-flight gadgets.

Shebang

1616 N Damen Avenue, at W North Avenue, Wicker Park (1-773 486 3800/www.shopshebang. com). El: Blue to Damen. **Open** 11am-7pm Mon-Sat; 11am-5pm Sun. **Credit** AmEx, MC, V. **Map** p331 B7.

Shebang's good-quality handbags and rare jewellery designs draw everyone from indie rockers to smart-dressed office workers after a chic accessory.

Shoes

Nordstrom (*see p189*) and **Bloomingdale's** (*see p188*) are famous for their selections of women's shoes.

Akira State Street

122 S State Street, between E Monroe Street & E Adams Street, the Loop (1-312 345 3034/www.akirachicago.com). El: Red to

Akira State Street.

CONSUME

Monroe. **Open** 11am-9pm Mon-Sat; 11am-7pm Sun. **Credit** AmEx, Disc, MC, V. **Map** p325 H12.

Ladies who work in the Loop often spend at least one lunch break a week here, scooping up deals on trendy and sexy, yet affordable shoes.

★ City Soles/Niche

2001 W North Avenue, at N Damen Avenue, Wicker Park (1-773 489 2001/www.citysoles. com). El: Blue to Damen. **Open** 10am-8pm Mon-Wed, Sat; 10am-9pm Thur, Fri; 11am-6pm Sun. **Credit** AmEx, Disc, MC, V. **Map** p331 B7.

Step into this emporium for beautifully crafted designer heels and cool loafers for guys. Many of the kicks are eco-friendly.

Other locations 3432 N Southport Avenue, at W Roscoe Street, Wrigleyville (1-773 665 4233).

Leaders 1354

672 N Wells Street, between N Huron & N Erie Streets, River North (1-312 787 7144/www. leaders1354.com). El: Brown or Purple to Chicago. **Open** noon-8pm Mon-Fri; 11am-8pm Sat; noon-5pm Sun. **Credit** MC, V. **Map** p326 H10.

Hip-hoppers and hipsters clamour over the selection of limited-edition Nikes, Adidas and other trainers. The store also features graphic T-shirts and the occasional DJ spinning beats.

Other locations 1400 N Milwaukee Avenue, at N Wolcott Avenue, Wicker Park (1-773 489 1900).

Lori's Designer Shoes

824 W Armitage Avenue, at N Dayton Street, Lincoln Park (1-773 281 5655/www.lorisdesigner shoes.com). El: Brown or Purple to Armitage. **Open** 11am-7pm Mon-Thur; 11am-6pm Fri; 10am-6pm Sat; noon-5pm Sun. **Credit** AmEx, Disc, MC, V. **Map** p328 F6.

A favourite with the shoe-crazed woman, Lori's has one of the city's largest ranges of American and European designer shoes and boots, all at between 10% and 30% less than department store prices. Great bags, too.

FOOD & DRINK

Bakeries

Bittersweet

1114 W Belmont Avenue, between N Seminary & N Clifton Avenues, Lakeview (1-773 929 1100/www.bittersweetpastry. com). El: Brown, Purple or Red to Belmont. **Open** 7am-7pm Tue-Fri; 8am-7pm Sat; 8am-6pm Sun. **Credit** MC, V. **Map** p329 E2.

Pastry chef Judy Contino's café/bakery is a charming spot in which to linger over a salad, quiche or other bistro fare. The scones, cakes, croissants, tarts and cookies practically fly out of the store.

Lovely

1130 N Milwaukee Avenue, between W Haddon Avenue & W Thomas Street, Wicker Park (1-773 572 4766/www.lovelybakeshop.com) El: Blue to Division. **Open** 7am-7pm Mon-Fri; 9am-6pm Sat; 9am-4pm Sun. **Credit** MC, V. **Map** p331 D9.

From cakey, star-shaped muffins to flaky pain au chocolat, the pastries are just as sweet and delicious as they should be. The welcoming shop also sports a small selection of baking-inspired gifts.

★ Molly's Cupcakes

2536 N Clark Street, between W Wrightwood Avenue & W Deming Place, Lincoln Park (1-773 883 7220/www.mollyscupcakes.com). El: Brown, Purple or Red to Fullerton. **Open** noon-10pm Mon; 8am-10pm Tue-Thur, Sun; 8am-midnight Fri, Sat. **Credit** AmEx, Disc, MC, V. **Map** p328 G4.

The owner named this sweet spot after his beloved grade-school teacher. Snag a spot on the large wooden swing near the counter and enjoy the always-changing lineup of cupcakes.

Swedish Bakery

5348 N Clark Street, at W Summerdale Avenue, Andersonville (1-773 561 8919/www.swedish bakery.com). El: Red to Berwyn. **Open** 6.30am-6.30pm Mon-Fri; 6.30am-5pm Sat. **Credit** AmEx, Disc, MC, V.

You'll have to fight through a throng to get to the tantalising array of cookies, breads and pastries at this 70-year-old classic, which is why there's always free coffee on tap while you're waiting.

▶ *There's more fine Swedish fare at nearby Svea; see p161.*

Drinks

Argo Tea Café

958 W Armitage Avenue, at N Sheffield Avenue, Lincoln Park (1-773 649 9644/www.argotea. com). El: Brown or Purple to Armitage. **Open** 6am-10pm Mon-Fri; 7am-10pm Sat, Sun. **Credit** MC, V. **Map** p328 E6.

High ceilings lend a European feel to this purveyor of black, green, oolong, white and herbal teas, served hot (Carolina honey) or iced (sparkling passion fruit). The shop also offers tasty coffee and baked goods, plus free wireless access.

Other locations 16 W Randolph Street, at N State Street, the Loop (1-312 324 3899); 819 N Rush Street, at W Chicago Avenue, Gold Coast (1-312 546 4718).

House of Glunz

1206 N Wells Street, at W Division Street, Gold Coast (1-312 642 3000/www.thehouseofglunz. com). El: Red to Clark/Division. **Open** 10am-8pm Mon-Fri; 10am-7pm Sat; 2-5pm Sun. **Credit** AmEx, MC, V. **Map** p327 H8.

CONSUME

The House of Glunz is the city's oldest wine shop. It should come as no surprise then that it harbours some of the world's oldest wines: several vintages date back as far as the early 1800s.

Intelligentsia

53 E Randolph Street, between N Michigan Avenue & S Wabash Avenue, the Loop (1-312 920 9332/www.intelligentsiacoffee.com). El: Blue to Washington; Brown, Green, Orange, Pink or Purple to Randolph/Wabash; Red to Lake. **Open** 6am-8pm Mon-Thur; 6am-9pm Fri; 7am-9pm Sat; 7am-7pm Sun. **Credit** AmEx, Disc, MC, V. **Map** p325 J12.

The hip baristas at Intelligentsia compete for (and often win) awards for artistry in cappuccino creation. A variety of house-blend beans is for sale by the pound, as are sundry coffee-making essentials. **Other locations** 53 W Jackson Boulevard, at S State Street, the Loop (1-312 253 0594); 3123 N Broadway, between W Barry Avenue & W Briar Place, Lakeview (1-773 348 8058).

Julius Meinl

3601 N Southport Avenue, at W Addison Street, Wrigleyville (1-773 868 1857/www.meinl.com). El: Brown to Southport. **Open** 6am-10pm Mon-Thur; 6am-midnight Fri; 7am-midnight Sat; 7am-10pm Sun. **Credit** AmEx, Disc, MC, V. **Map** p329 D1.

Austrian Julius Meinl started roasting coffee beans in 1862. Modelled after his famous Viennese coffeehouses, this inviting spot certainly looks (and feels) the part. Order apple strudel to accompany your coffee or hot chocolate, served on a silver tray. **Other locations** 4363 N Lincoln Avenue, at W Montrose Avenue, Lincoln Square (1-773 868 1876).

Kafka Wine Co

3325 N Halsted Street, at W Buckingham Place, Lakeview (1-773 975 9463/www.kafkawine.com). El: Brown, Purple or Red to Belmont. **Open** noon-10pm Mon-Sat; noon-7pm Sun. **Credit** AmEx, Disc, MC, V. **Map** p329 F2.

CONSUME

Farmer in the City

Pick up a picnic at one of the city's many farmers' markets.

The Midwest is fertile farming territory, something reflected in the huge variety and popularity of farmers' markets in the city. There's one in almost every neighbourhood, at least during the warmer months, offering fresh and seasonal produce. The launch of **Chicago's Downtown Farmstand**, open Tuesday to Saturday at 66 E Randolph Street in the Loop, offers visitors a daily choice, but the one-day-a-week neighbourhood markets are really where it's at. Here are some of the more central markets.

WICKER PARK & AROUND

There's a weekly farmers' market in **Wicker Park** itself (W Schiller Street & N Damen Avenue, June-Oct), held every Sunday from 7am to 2pm. Three hours later, another market gets under way over in **Logan Square** (W Logan Boulevard & N Milwaukee Avenue, June-Oct), ending around 3pm.

THE LOOP

A pair of farmers' markets appear in the Loop on Tuesdays: at **Federal Plaza** (W Adams & S Dearborn Streets, mid May-Oct) and **Prudential Building Plaza** (E Lake Street & N Beaubien Court, June-Oct). Thursdays are also busy, with farmers' markets at **Daley Plaza** (W Washington

& N Dearborn Streets, mid May-mid Oct) and **Sears Tower** (*see p66*; mid June-Oct). On Saturdays, there's a market in the parking lot at Dearborn and Polk Streets on Printers' Row (mid June-Oct). All markets run from 7am to 3pm except the one at Printers' Row, which ends an hour earlier.

THE NEAR NORTH SIDE

There's a farmers' market held every Tuesday from 9am until 4pm by the **Museum of Contemporary Art** in Streeterville (June-Oct).

OLD TOWN & LINCOLN PARK

The city's most prestigious farmers' market, the **Green City Market** (www.chicagogreencitymarket.org) takes place every Wednesday and Saturday (7am-1pm, June-Oct) in Lincoln Park itself, north of N LaSalle Street along the path between N Clark Street and N Stockton Drive. The market occurs less regularly in winter and spring, usually only on selected Saturdays (and, mercifully, indoors, at the Peggy Notebaert Museum). There are more goods on offer at the separate **Lincoln Park Farmers' Market**, held 7am-2pm on Saturdays in the parking lot of a local high school (Armitage Avenue & N Orchard Street, mid May-Oct).

The knowledgeable staff are only too happy to help novices choose a bottle of vino before heading to a Lakeview BYOB restaurant. Polaroid pictures of customers with their favourite bottles are posted throughout the shop.

General

Jewel Food Stores, a workhouse of a supermarket, has numerous locations, including a 24-hour Gold Coast store (1210 N Clark Street, at W Division Street, 1-312 944 6950). Local favourite **Dominick's**, another general supermarket, also has many branches around town, including a 24-hour store in the South Loop (1340 S Canal Street, at W Roosevelt Street, 1-312 850 3915, www.dominicks.com).

On a more exotic level, the city contains several branches of **Whole Foods Market**, the wildly popular (and often wildly expensive) organic supermarket chain, the most central in River North (50 W Huron Street, at N Dearborn Street, 1-312 932 9600). All are open 8am-10pm daily. Cheery health, and more affordable, food chain **Trader Joe's** also has three Chicago locations:, including one in River North (44 E Ontario Street, at N Wabash Avenue, 1-312 951 6369) that opens 9am-10pm daily.

Fox & Obel

401 E Illinois Street, at N Fairbanks Court, Streeterville (1-312 410 7301/www.fox-obel.com). El: Red to Grand. **Open** *6am-midnight daily.* **Credit** *AmEx, Disc, MC, V.* **Map** *p326 J11.*
Just what Chicago really needs: a gourmet food emporium (cheeses, just-baked goods, fresh fish, etc) with an in-store café. Get a healthy snack here instead of opting for something fried at one of the chains on the nearby Navy Pier.

Provenance Food & Wine

2528 N California Avenue, at W Logan Boulevard, Logan Square (1-773 384 0699/ www.provenancefoodandwine.com). El: Blue to California. **Open** *noon-8pm Mon; noon-9pm Tue-Sat; noon-7pm Sun.* **Credit** *AmEx, Disc, MC, V.*
Everything you need for a perfect picnic in the park can be found inside this friendly gourmet shop. Sample wine from boutique vintners, then pick up some wonderfully stinky cheese and Red Hen bread.

Specialist

See also p204 **Farmer in the City**.

Aji Ichiban

2117-A S China Place, Chinatown Square, Chinatown (1-312 328 9998). El: Red to Cermak-Chinatown. **Open** *10am-8pm Mon-Thur, Sun; 10am-9pm Fri, Sat.* **Credit** *MC, V.* **Map** *p324 G16.*

Garrett Popcorn Shop. *See p206.*

CONSUME

Feeling like a food adventure? Head here for obscure Japanese gummy candies, seaweed-hugged crackers and, inexplicably, a knitting shop in the back.

Garrett Popcorn Shop

4 E Madison Street, between N State Street & N Wabash Avenue, the Loop (1-888 476 7267/www.garrettpopcorn.com). El: Green, Orange, Pink or Purple to Madison/Wabash. **Open** 10am-8pm Mon-Sat; 11am-7pm Sun. **Credit** AmEx, MC, V. **Map** p326 J10.

At all hours, customers craving Garrett's caramel corn form a line outside its small storefronts, lured by the sugary aroma that wafts down the block. Try the Chicago mix – caramel and cheese. *Photo p205.* **Other locations** 2 W Jackson Boulevard, at N State Street, the Loop; 26 E Randolph Street, at N State Street, the Loop.

L'Appetito

30 E Huron Street, at N Wabash Avenue, River North (1-312 787 9881/www.lappetito.com). El: Red to Grand. **Open** 7.30am-6.30pm Mon-Fri; 9am-6.30pm Sat. **Credit** AmEx, MC, V. **Map** p326 H10.

A great Italian grocery store with imported meats, cheeses and pastas, plus the best submarine sandwiches in the city. **Other locations** John Hancock Center, 875 N Michigan Avenue, at E Chestnut Street, Magnificent Mile (1-312 337 0691).

Vosges Haut-Chocolat

Shops at North Bridge, 520 N Michigan Avenue, at E Grand Avenue, Magnificent Mile (1-312 644 9450/www.vosgeschocolate.com). El: Red to Grand. **Open** 10am-8pm Mon-Sat; 11am-6pm Sun. **Credit** AmEx, Disc, MC, V. **Map** p326 H10.

Two childhood friends run this gourmet chocolatier, which specialises in truffles but also turns out chocs accented with rare spices and flowers. For instance, the Aztec hot chocolate contains cinnamon and chipotle powder and is better than it sounds. **Other locations** 951 W Armitage Avenue, between N Sheffield Avenue & N Bissell Street, Lincoln Park (1-773 296 9866).

GIFTS & SOUVENIRS

Chicago's museums conveniently offer some of the best souvenirs. Fun, funky objets d'art are available at the **Chicago Architecture Foundation** (*see p304*), while the **Museum of Contemporary Art** (*see p81*) features plenty of unusual items, and the **Art Institute of Chicago** (*see p56*) sells gifts and art books. The store at **Symphony Center** (*see p255*) has a range of high-culture souvenirs. Many of the gift shops located in the city's hotels offer the usual goods (postcards, T-shirts) but both W locations add some luxe items to the mix.

★ Art Effect

934 W Armitage Avenue, at N Bissell Street (1-773 929 3600/www.shoparteffect.com). El: Brown or Purple to Armitage. **Open** 11am-7pm Mon-Thur; 11am-6pm Fri; 10am-6pm Sat; noon-5pm Sun. **Credit** AmEx, MC, V. **Map** p328 E6.

This fun, airy shop has loads of nifty gift items: tiny calculators, antique brooches, Jonathan Adler pottery and vintage-looking toy robots, plus some thoroughly cool, casual clothing (for women and children), and wonderful jewellery.

Oprah Store

37 N Carpenter Street, at W Washington Boulevard, West Loop (1-312 633 2100/www.theoprahstore.com). El: Green to Clinton. **Open** 10am-5.30pm Mon-Sat; noon-4pm Sun. **Credit** AmEx, Disc, MC, V. **Map** p330 E11.

Get a piece of the city's most famous resident at her store across the street from Harpo Studios. Items in the shop include many of Oprah's favourite things and even clothes from her closet.

▶ *For more on Oprah, see p101.*

Paper Boy

1351 W Belmont Avenue, at N Southport Avenue, Lakeview (1-773 388 8811/www.unclefunchicago.com). El: Brown to Southport. **Open** noon-7pm Mon-Fri; 11am-7pm Sat; 11am-5pm Sun. **Credit** AmEx, MC, V. **Map** p329 D3.

A large selection of cards and one-of-a-kind gift wrap is supplemented by a great range of stationery, wedding invites and other funky impulse items. It's owned by the same man behind nearby collectibles shop Uncle Fun (*see p194*).

Paper Doll

2048 W Division Street, at N Damen Avenue, Wicker Park (1-773 227 6950/www.paperdollchicago.com). El: Blue to Damen. **Open** 11am-7pm Tue-Fri; 11am-6pm Sat; 11am-5pm Sun. **Credit** Disc, MC, V. **Map** p331 B8.

House pug Maude welcomes you to this treasure trove of fantastic and funky items you don't really need but simply have to have. It'll be difficult to tear yourself away from the cool letterpress stationery, journals and quirky knick-knacks.

RR#1

814 N Ashland Avenue, at W Chicago Avenue, West Town (1-312 421 9079/www.rr1chicago.com). Bus 9, 66. **Open** 11am-7pm Mon-Sat; noon-5pm Sun. **Credit** AmEx, Disc, MC, V. **Map** p331 C9.

Set in a 1930s apothecary, this dimly lit but brilliantly stocked store has something for everyone. Along with a selection of hard-to-find natural bodycare lines, it also carries fun items and postcards with an international bent.

CONSUME

Shop Class

Columbia College brings students' work to the storefront.

Few phrases terrify parents more than, 'I want to go to art school.' But **Shop Columbia**, a new initiative from artsy Columbia College Chicago, might help allay their fears. The 750-square-foot boutique in the Loop (623 S Wabash Avenue, at E Balbo Avenue, 1-312 369 8616, www.colum.edu/shopcolumbia) provides real-world lessons in making a living through creative work: every item for sale was produced by a Columbia student.

The store sells clothing and accessories, prints, photographs, films, jewellery, temporary tattoos and more, all of it vetted by a rotating curatorial committee that includes five Columbia professors. Shop Columbia puts each item up for sale for at least three months, but Kari Sommers, Columbia's associate dean of student affairs, predicts that most will sell out earlier because they are 'one-of-a-kind and small editions'. Prices range from $2 for a tiny cake sculpture sold through a gum-ball machine to $500 for an original painting.

'The reason [Shop Columbia] exists is to support our students,' says Sommers. She adds that students receive 75 per cent of the proceeds from their goods; part of the other 25 per cent defrays the store's operating expenses, which were 'intentionally kept very low', with the rest going towards scholarships.

Considering how intertwined Shop Columbia seems to be with the school's curriculum – an undergraduate retail-management course devised the store's business plan, and some professors are already encouraging students to create products for it – what happens to students who don't want to make ironic stationery?

'We have no intention of turning students into worker drones for the store,' says Kevin Cassidy, the shop's manager. 'They're here to learn and to develop their art, and that comes first. In that process, they'll often produce something that ought to be out in the world. At that point, we'll step in and say, "You should think about this."'

Cassidy and Sommers portray the store as a teaching tool that will enable students to learn how to price and present their work in a supportive environment. 'Students have been making things all along,' concludes Sommers. 'All we had to do was give them a venue for showcasing it.'

CONSUME

CONSUME

HEALTH & BEAUTY
Complementary medicine

Cortiva Institute
18 N Wabash Avenue, between E Madison Street & E Washington Street, the Loop (1-312 753 7990/www.cortiva.com). El: Brown, Green, Orange, Pink or Purple to Madison/Wabash; Blue or Red to Monroe. **Open** *9am-9pm Mon-Fri; 9am-5pm Sat, Sun.* **Credit** *AmEx, Disc, MC, V.* **Map** *p325 J12.*
Massage-therapy students offer low-priced massages in this spa-like environment. A small retail area in the lobby sells healing massage oils, neck supports and other homeopathic remedies.

Ruby Room
1743-1745 W Division Street, at N Wood Street, Wicker Park (1-773 235 2323/www.rubyroom. com). El: Blue to Damen. **Open** *10am-7pm Mon-Fri; 9am-7pm Sat; 10am-6pm Sun.* **Credit** *AmEx, MC, V.* **Map** *p331 C8.*
This enormous yet cosy 'healing sanctuary' has guides to help visitors select crystals, traditional Chinese medicine herbs and flower essences. The vibe is slightly New Age, but the luxurious environment and fees are far from earthy.

Hairdressers & barbers

Art + Science
1971 N Halsted Street, at W Armitage Avenue, Lincoln Park (1-312 787 4247). El: Brown or Purple to Armitage. **Open** *10am-9pm Tue-Thur; 10am-8pm Fri; 9am-6pm Sat.* **Credit** *Disc, MC, V.* **Map** *p328 F6.*
Trendsetters are loathe to give up the secrets to their hip haircuts, but this place is almost always the source. The glass-fronted location is something of a see-and-be-seen place.
Other locations 1554 N Milwaukee Avenue, at N Damen Avenue, Wicker Park (1-773 227 4247).

State Street Barbers
1151 W Webster Avenue, at N Racine Street, Lincoln Park (1-773 477 7721/www.statestreet barbers.com). El: Brown or Purple to Armitage. **Open** *8am-9pm Mon-Thur; 10am-7pm Fri; 8am-5pm Sat; 9am-5pm Sun.* **Credit** *MC, V.* **Map** *p328 E5.*
An inviting, old-fashioned barbershop that provides haircuts and hot lather shaves, as well as shoe shines and repairs. Ask about the first-visit discount.
Other locations 1547 N Wells Street, at W North Avenue, Old Town (1-312 787 7722).

Opticians

In the Loop, **Macy's** (*see p188*) and **Sears** (*see p189*) have optical counters.

Eye Want
1543 N Milwaukee Avenue, at N Damen Avenue, Wicker Park (1-773 782 1744/www.eyewanteye wear.com). El: Blue to Damen. **Open** *noon-7pm Mon-Fri; noon-5pm Sat.* **Credit** *AmEx, Disc, MC, V.* **Map** *p331 B7.*
The high-end styles on offer at this laid-back Wicker Park eye store are made for fashionistas. There's also an optometrist on site.

Pharmacies

You're never far from one of two chain pharmacies. **Walgreens** (www.walgreens.com) has 24-hour branches on the Magnificent Mile (757 N Michigan Avenue, at E Chicago Avenue, 1-312 664 8686) and in River North (641 N Clark Street, at W Ontario Street, 1-312 587 1416), while **CVS** (www.cvs.com) has 24-hour stores on the Gold Coast (1201 N State Street, at W Division Street, 1-312 640 2842) and in Lincoln Park (1714 N Sheffield Avenue, at N Clybourn Avenue, 1-312 640 5160).

★ Merz Apothecary
4716 N Lincoln Avenue, at W Lawrence Avenue, Lincoln Square (1-773 989 0900/www.merz apothecary.com). El: Brown to Western. **Open** *9am-6pm Mon-Sat.* **Credit** *AmEx, Disc, MC, V.*
This classic apothecary attracts a diverse crowd to its Lincoln Square store, with a wide range of mind- and body-friendly products including organic toothpaste, aromatherapy kits and all-natural soaps.
▶ *There's a Merz counter in Macy's on State Street; see p188.*

Shops

Benefit
852 W Armitage Avenue, at N Halsted Street, Lincoln Park (1-773 880 9192/www.benefit cosmetics.com). El: Brown or Purple to Armitage. **Open** *11am-7pm Mon-Wed; 10am-8pm Thur; 10am-7pm Fri, Sat; noon-5pm Sun.* **Credit** *AmEx, MC, V.* **Map** *p328 F6.*
Drop in for a brow wax at this cheekily retro beauty spot. Its cosmetics counter majors in smart solutions for common problems such as redness, puffy eyes and fine lines.

CO Bigelow Apothecary
Water Tower Place, 835 N Michigan Avenue, at Chicago Avenue, Magnificent Mile (1-312 642 0551/www.bigelowchemist.com). El: Red to Chicago. **Open** *10am-9pm Mon-Sat; 11am-6pm Sun.* **Credit** *AmEx, Disc, MC, V.* **Map** *p326 J9.*
A more modern sister store to New York's first pharmacy, this is a veritable repository of hard-to-find personal care items from around the world. The house lines of tonics and lotions are based on decades-old formulas.

INSIDE TRACK
MAKE-UP TUITION

After you've paid $18 for the perfect arch at **Benefit** (*see p208*) brow bar, a beauty artist leads you through a free five-minute complimentary mini make-up lesson. You'll walk out 20 minutes later with your face set for the night's festivities.

MAC Pro

910 W Armitage Avenue, at N Fremont Street, Lincoln Park (1-773 327 4902/www.macpro. com). El: Brown or Purple to Armitage. **Open** 11am-7pm Mon-Fri; 10am-7pm Sat; noon-6pm Sun. **Credit** AmEx, Disc, MC, V. **Map** p328 F6.
In addition to core products such as foundation and lipstick, this location also carries the PRO collection. It's tailored for TV and theatrical use, meaning anyone can prepare for that high-def close-up. **Other locations** throughout the city.

Ulta

114 S State Street, between W Adams & W Monroe Streets, the Loop (1-312 279 5081/ www.ulta.com). El: Red to Monroe. **Open** 10am-8pm Mon-Sat; 11am-5pm Sun. **Credit** AmEx, Disc, MC, V. **Map** p325 H12.
A large selection of high-end and drug store cosmetics and fragrances fill this multi-storey cosmetic shop. The salon on the top level provides haircuts and facials. **Other locations** throughout the city.

Spas

For hotel spas, *see p129* ...**And, Relax**.

Asha Gold Coast

1135 N State Street, between E Elm & E Cedar Streets, Gold Coast (1-312 664 1600/www. ashasalonspa.com). El: Red to Clark/Division. **Open** 9am-9pm Mon-Fri; 8am-7pm Sat; 10am-6pm Sun. **Credit** AmEx, Disc, MC, V. **Map** p326 H9.
This spa boasts 5,000sq ft dedicated entirely to pampering. The exotic menu of massages ($45-$160), facials (from $60) and waxes ($15-$110) are carried out in six spa rooms decorated with bamboo. Most luxurious is the enclosed slate-tile steam shower room with heated floors, in which you can customise your rain shower with aromatherapy.

Avanti Skin Centers

409 W North Avenue, at N Sedgwick Street, Old Town (1-312 988 7546/www.avanticenters.com). El: Brown to Sedgwick. **Open** 9am-8pm Tue-Thur; 10am-6pm Fri; 9am-5pm Sat; 11am-4pm Sun. **Credit** AmEx, MC, V. **Map** p327 G7.

You won't find day-spa luxuries such as gourmet nibbles and gratis wine at Avanti. But what you will find makes up for the lack of frills: thorough facials, medical-grade chemical peels and surprisingly gentle microdermabrasion provide all the essentials needed for beautiful skin.

★ Exhale

945 N State Street, at E Oak Street, Gold Coast (1-312 753 6500). El: Red to Chicago. **Open** 8am-8pm daily. **Credit** AmEx, MC, V. **Map** p326 H9.
This Gold Coast spa is all about luxury. The spin is spa treatments and fitness education that focus on healing: acupuncture, Thai massage and drop-in core fusion classes are among the options.

Honey Child Salon & Spa

735 N LaSalle Street, at W Chicago Avenue, River North (1-312 573 1300/www.spasalon.com/ honeychild). El: Brown or Red to Chicago. **Open** 10am-6pm Tue, Sun; 10am-9pm Wed-Fri; 9am-6pm Sat. **Credit** AmEx, MC, V. **Map** p326 K10.
Catering primarily to an African-American clientele, the salon's menu includes treats for body, face, hands and feet. The Brown Sugar scrub ($110-$170) and Honey on the Rocks massage ($150) are good.

John Allan's

111 W Jackson Boulevard, at S Clark Street, the Loop (1-312 663 4600/www.johnallans.com). El: Blue to Jackson; Orange, Pink, Brown or Purple to Quincy/Wells. **Open** 10am-6pm Mon-Thur; 10am-7pm Fri. **Credit** AmEx, Disc, MC, V.
Situated on the top floor of a high rise adjoining the Chicago Board of Trade, this gentlemen's grooming club features a bar, pool table, flat-screen TVs and an outdoor terrace. Of course, the real reason for hanging out here is to take advantage of the services, which include facials ($78) and pedicures ($49).

Kaya

112 N May Street, between W Randolph Street & W Washington Boulevard, West Loop (1-312 243 5292/www.kayadayspa.com). El: Green or Pink to Ashland. **Open** 9am-7pm Tue, Wed, Fri; 9am-9pm Thur; 9am-5pm Sat; 11am-5pm Sun. **Credit** AmEx, Disc, MC, V. **Map** p330 E11.
Pampering options at Kaya range from green tea facials to an 'East Meets West' body wrap designed to make skin tighter and fresher. Hydrotherapy and massage offerings are also on the menu.

Massage Envy

345 E Ohio Street, between N McClurg & N Fairbanks Courts, Streeterville (1-312 222 0808/ www.massageenvy.com). El: Red to Grand. **Open** 8am-10pm Mon-Fri; 8am-6pm Sat; 10am-6pm Sun. **Credit** AmEx, Disc, MC, V. **Map** p326 J10.
The downtown location of this massage parlour chain specialises in rub downs for under $100 and often advertises introductory deals.

★ Sir Spa

5151 N Clark Street, between W Winona Street & W Foster Avenue, Andersonville (1-773 271 7000/www.sirspa.com). El: Red to Berwyn. **Open** 11am-9pm Mon-Thur; 10am-9pm Fri; 10am-7pm Sat; 10am-6pm Sun. **Credit** AmEx, MC, V.

At this lads' spa in Andersonville, men don't have to endure crimes against masculinity. The robes fit the male body, foot treatments are performed from the comfort of a barber's chair and facials address the specific problems of testosterone-buffeted skin.

Urban Oasis

12 W Maple Street, between N State Street & N Dearborn Street, Gold Coast (1-312 587 3500/www.urbanoasis.biz). El: Red to Clark/Division. **Open** noon-8pm Mon; 10am-8pm Tue-Thur; 9am-7pm Fri; 9am-5pm Sat; 11am-5pm Sun. **Credit** AmEx, Disc, MC, V. **Map** p326 H9.

Every massage (from $60) on the map is offered at Urban Oasis, including reflexology, deep tissue, sport, hot stone and pregnancy massages. The Oasis salon offers aromatherapy wraps and yoga classes.

Tattoos & piercings

Deluxe Tattoo

1459 W Irving Park Road, at N Greenview Avenue, Lakeview (1-773 549 1594/www.deluxe tattoo.com). El: Brown to Irving Park. **Open** noon-8pm daily. **Credit** AmEx, Disc, MC, V.

Tribal tats, trompe l'oeil, 3-D layering and pin-up girls are the specialities at this in-demand shop.

Jade Dragon Tattoo

5331 W Belmont Avenue, at N Lockwood Avenue, Northwest Side (1-773 736 6960/ www.jadedragontattoo.com). Bus 77. **Open** noon-2am daily. **Credit** AmEx, Disc, MC, V.

Fat Joe heads up this ink shop, which draws thousands of locals (and, reputedly, DMX and Kid Rock). The emphasis is on safety, and staff are welcoming.

HOUSE & HOME

Antiques

Andersonville, especially Clark Street between Foster and Bryn Mawr, has become the city's unofficial home decor district, and the number of new and vintage home and furniture shops seems to multiply every couple of months.

Chicagoland is also home to a number of regular antiques markets, the most central of which is the prosaically titled **Chicago Antique Market** (www.chicagoantique market.com). Held from 10am to 4pm on the last Saturday and Sunday of the month (May-Sept only) around the junction of N Randolph Street and W Ogden Avenue, the show draws hundreds of dealers.

Broadway Antiques Market

6130 N Broadway Street, at W Hood Avenue, Rogers Park (1-773 743 5444/www.bamchicago.com). El: Red to Granville. **Open** 11am-7pm Mon-Sat; noon-6pm Sun. **Credit** AmEx, Disc, MC, V.

This two-level antiques mall represents 75 dealers, showcasing everything from Victoriana to '70s collectibles. There's an emphasis on art deco, Arts and Crafts, and modern movements.

Salvage One

1840 W Hubbard Street, at N Wood Street, West Town (1-312 733 0098/www.salvageone.com). El: Green or Pink to Ashland. **Open** 11am-6pm Fri; 9am-5pm Sat; noon-5pm Sun. **Credit** AmEx, Disc, MC, V.

Love the thrill of the dig? Take a tour of this massive three-floor warehouse, which is filled to the rafters with beautiful and unusual furniture. Highlights include mantelpieces, claw-foot bathtubs and bathroom fixtures.

Urban Remains

410 N Paulina Street, at W Kinzie Street, West Town (1-312 523 4660/www.urbanremains chicago.com). El: Green or Pink to Ashland. **Open** 11am-6pm daily. **Credit** MC, V. **Map** p330 C11.

Housed in a former turn-of-the-century bottling company, this unconventional shop stocks architectural artefacts and antiques. You might find Victorian-era doorknobs, sconces from the Chicago Board of Trade, or the owner's series of old-timey photographs – a steal at just $25.

Garden stores

★ Sprout Home

745 N Damen Avenue, at W Chicago Avenue, West Town (1-312 226 5950/www.sprouthome.com). Bus 50, 66. **Open** 9am-8pm Mon-Fri; 9am-7pm Sat, Sun. **Credit** AmEx, Disc, MC, V. **Map** p331 B10.

You'll find clever modern design pieces for the home at Sprout, including some interesting mod-print plates and stick-on decals for walls. During the warmer months, an outside garden is filled with beautiful plants and trees.

General

ID

3337 N Halsted Street, between W Roscoe Street & W Buckingham Place, Wrigleyville (1-773 755 4343/www.idchicago.com). El: Brown, Purple or Red to Belmont. **Open** 11am-7pm Tue-Sat; noon-5pm Sun. **Credit** AmEx, Disc, MC, V. **Map** p329 F2.

This über-minimalist home accessories store features expertly selected gadgets, exquisite Swedish furniture, bath products, stylish eyewear and a small range of unusual wooden clutch bags.

The Vinyl Score

If MP3s don't rock your boat, fret ye not: Chicago has record stores galore.

Chicago has long been a cradle for crate-digging. Japanese collectors, Ibiza DJs and Northern Soul junkies from far and wide have long hunted through used vinyl stores searching for rare platters, and the digital era still hasn't managed to kill off all the city's mom-and-pop record stores. For new records, head to the three **Reckless Records** locations (*see p212*), **Permanent Records** (*see p211*) and **Gramaphone Records** (2843 N Clark Street, at W Diversey Parkway, Lakeview, 1-773 472 3683, www.gramaphonerecords.com), which caters to the techno set. Those in search of vintage vinyl also have a sound selection, stretching from **Record Dugout** (*see p212*) to a host of other operations.

The rarest funky stuff is at **Dusty Groove** (1120 N Ashland Avenue, at W Haddon Street, West Town, 1-773 342 5800, www.dustygroove.com), where a clean, unassuming layout belies a vast quantity of soul, jazz, reggae and Latin reissues. Some scour the globe looking for obscure Serge Gainsbourg and Caetano Veloso records. The smart ones just cut to the chase and shop here.

On a typical weekday, just a few souls wander in to **Mr Peabody's** (11832 S Western Avenue, at W 119th Street, Mount Hope, 1-773 881 9299, www.mrpeabodyrecords.com), down on the South Side. But this is perhaps the best place in the Midwest to get boogie and disco records – especially rare, original pressings and independent releases.

For rare classic rock, new wave, psych and mod LPs, try **Vintage Vinyl** (925 Davis

Street, at Maple Avenue, Evanston, 1-847 328 2899, www.vvmo.com). Sheltered under the Metra station, the shop keeps only a fraction of its stock in the tidy front room. If you can't find that Stones bootleg you need, just ask: it's probably in the back. Prices are steep (it's like shopping in 1977 with 2020 costs) but the records are always mint.

Jazz hounds, meanwhile, are directed to **Jazz Record Mart** (27 E Illinois Street, at N Wabash Avenue, River North, 1-312 222 1467, www.jazzrecordmart.com). It's cluttered and dusty, with the requisite air of chaos about the place. But the range of rare jazz vinyl is unmatched in the Midwest.

MUSIC & ENTERTAINMENT

CDs & records

K-Starke
1109 N Western Avenue, between W Haddon Avenue & W Thomas Street, Wicker Park (1-773 772 4880/www.myspace.com/kstarke). El: Blue to Division. **Open** noon-9pm Mon-Sat; noon-5pm Sun. **Credit** MC, V. **Map** p331 A9.
Specialising in rare vinyl and hard-to-find 45s, this off-the-beaten-path shop draws hunter-gatherer DJs with its selections of obscure house, jazz, soul, reggae, Italo disco and punk wax. If what you're looking for is underground, it may well be available here. Enthusiastic and knowledgeable staff.

Laurie's Planet of Sound
4639 N Lincoln Avenue, between W Eastwood Avenue & W Leland Avenue, Lincoln Square (1-773 271 3569/www.lauriesplanetofsound. tripod.com). El: Brown to Western. **Open** 10am-10pm Mon-Sat; 11am-7pm Sun. **Credit** AmEx, Disc, MC, V.
Apart from the usual records and CDs, Laurie's sells pop culture items such as Johnny Cash action figures, Alf stuffed animals and even a little Social Distortion skeleton guy.

Permanent Records
1914 W Chicago Avenue, between N Wolcott Avenue & N Winchester Avenue, Ukrainian Village (1-773 278 1744/www.permanent

recordschicago.com). Bus 66. **Open** 11am-8pm
Mon-Thur, Sun; 11am-9pm Fri, Sat. **Credit**
AmEx, Disc, MC, V. **Map** p331 C10.
Permanent is as much a record label as it is a shop,
and in fact the tiny room doesn't have a huge variety
of stock. But it's a cordial cool-kids hangout, with frequent, free in-store performances. Even Zaireeka, the
cat, seems to dig the sounds of the underground.

★ Reckless Records
*1532 N Milwaukee Avenue, at N Damen Avenue,
Wicker Park (1-773 235 3727/www.reckless.
com). El: Blue to Damen.* **Open** 10am-10pm Mon-
Sat; 10am-8pm Sun. **Credit** AmEx, Disc, MC, V.
Map p331 B9.
Perhaps the best used CD all-rounder in the city, the
Wicker Park branch of Reckless has decent selec-
tions of CDs in more or less all genres.
Other locations 26 E Madison Avenue, at S
Wabash Avenue, the Loop (1-312 795 0878); 3161
N Broadway Street, at W Belmont Avenue,
Lakeview (1-773 404 5080).

Record Dugout
*6053 W 63rd Street, between S McVicker Street
& S Meade Avenue, South Side (1-773 586
1206). El: Red to 63rd.* **Open** noon-7pm daily.
No credit cards.
Vinyl geeks sift through the quite breathtakingly
large piles of used records at this South Side hangout, hunting for hyper-rare rock, pop, soul and R&B
singles. A must-visit.

SPORTS & FITNESS

Niketown (669 N Michigan Avenue, between
E Huron Street & E Erie Street, 1-312 642 6363,
www.nike.com), located on the Magnificent
Mile, is something of a tourist trap but it
does offer just about everything from
Nike's collection.

Lululemon Athletica
*2104 N Halsted Street, between W Dickens
Avenue, Lincoln Park (1-773 883 8860/www.
lululemon.com). El: Brown or Purple to Armitage.*

Open 10am-6pm Mon-Thur; 10am-7pm Fri,
Sat; 11am-6pm Sun. **Credit** AmEx, MC, V.
Map p328 F6.
Super-stylish yoga gear, from mats to clothing,
draws a crowd that insists on looking alluring while
doing downward dog poses.

Sports Authority
*620 N LaSalle Street, at W Ontario Street, River
North (1-312 337 6151/www.sportsauthority.
com). El: Red to Grand.* **Open** 9am-9.30pm Mon-
Sat; 10am-8pm Sun. **Credit** AmEx, Disc, MC, V.
Map p326 H10.
This eight-storey flagship store has entire floors
given over to virtually every athletic pursuit. Watch
out for the busloads of tourists who create a frenzy
over the pro sports memorabilia.
Other locations 3134 N Clark Street, at W
Belmont Avenue, Lakeview (1-773 871 8501).

Viking Ski Shop
*3422 W Fullerton Avenue, between N Kimball
Avenue & N Bernard Street, Logan Square
(1-773 276 1222/www.vikingskishop.com). El:
Blue to Logan Square.* **Open** May-Sept call for
details. Oct-Apr 11am-9pm Mon, Tue, Thur, Fri;
11am-6pm Wed; 10am-5pm Sat; 11am-5pm Sun.
Credit AmEx, Disc, MC, V.
Arguably *the* destination for skiers in the Midwest,
Viking has more than 30 years of experience fitting
the entire family with ski equipment and general
cold-weather gear.

TICKETS

For theatre shows, discounted tickets
are available for same-day and advance
performances at **Hot Tix**, which is situated
inside the Chicago Tourism Center at 72 E
Randolph Street, a half-block west of
Millennium Park. Hot Tix is also at Water
Works Visitor Center, 163 E Pearson Street,
at N Michigan Avenue. Half-price tickets
are also sold online every day through
www.chicagoplays.com. Check with theatres
for rush tickets, that is discounted seats
sometimes sold at box offices one hour before
the start of performances. Most other tickets
can be purchased at www.ticketmaster.com.

TRAVELLERS' NEEDS

If you need to rent a mobile phone during
your stay, try **Cellhire** (www.cellhire.com),
which can deliver phones to your hotel in
advance of your stay. (For more on mobile
phones, *see p309.*)
   The Loop is dotted with stores selling cheap
luggage. For nicer varieties, *see p202,* or any
of the department stores listed on *pp188-190.*
For shipping firms, *see p305.*

INSIDE TRACK FREE TICKETS

The **Empty Bottle** (*see p182*) teams up
with **Reckless Records** (*see above*) to
offer free concert tickets each week.
Just buy a new copy of the latest album
from one of the bands playing the Bottle
that week, and you and a friend will
automatically be put on that band's
guest list. But you'd better move fast:
each of the three Reckless locations
only has two pairs of tickets to dole out.

CONSUME

Arts & Entertainment

Navy Pier. *See p224.*

Calendar

Winter keeps things quiet, but summer in Chicago is a non-stop party.

'They just love to shut a street down, fry up a bunch of food and play some music,' said talk-show host Conan O'Brien, reflecting on Chicagoans' enthusiasm for street festivals. That sums up the city's summer, when Windy City denizens take to the streets for a flurry of celebrations. Mammoth festivals fill the parks; further out, street fairs and block parties are a great way to escape the crush. Even when temperatures plunge, Chicagoans brush off the wind chill and head to an outdoor party.

For information on events, contact the **Mayor's Office of Special Events** (1-312 744 3315) or the **Chicago Office of Tourism** (1-312 744 2400); see www.explorechicago.org for both. *Time Out Chicago* magazine offers weekly listings in its 'Around Town' section, and publishes an annual guide to summer festivals that's available both as a pull-out guide and at www.timeoutchicago.com/festivals. The Friday editions of the *Chicago Tribune* and the *Chicago Sun-Times* do their bit with regular pull-out guides. All events in this section are free and family-friendly unless stated.

ARTS & ENTERTAINMENT

SPRING

Chicago Flower & Garden Show
Navy Pier, Streeterville (1-773 435 1250/ www.chicagoflower.com). El: Red to Grand. **Date** mid Mar. **Map** p325 H11-H13.
An annual harbinger of spring, this green fingered delight brings horticulture and flower-arranging competitions, gardening-supply and landscape vendors, and life-size theme gardens to Navy Pier. Chef demos, seminars and appearances by top national gardeners are also featured.

St Patrick's Day
Columbus Drive, from E Balbo Drive to E Monroe Street, the Loop (1-312 744 2400/ www.cityofchicago.org). El: Blue or Red to Jackson; Brown, Green, Orange, Pink or Purple to Adams/Wabash. **Date** Sat before 17 Mar. **Map** p325 H11-H13.
During election years, the candidates magically become Irish for the duration of St Patrick's Day, which is celebrated with serious abandon by locals and suburbanites regardless of whether or not they

have any connection to the Emerald Isle. Downtown, the Chicago River is dyed green at 10.45am on the nearest Saturday to St Patrick's Day (it's best viewed from the upper level of the Michigan Avenue Bridge), before a parade rumbles through the Loop.
▶ *There was a separate parade on the South Side until 2009, but organisers gave up the ghost after the notoriously enthusiastic revellers got too rowdy to control.*

★ Great Chicago Places & Spaces
Around the city (1-312 744 3370/www.cityof chicago.org). **Date** 1 day, late May.
This event devoted to Chicago's architecture allows entry to many places and spaces that aren't ordinarily accessible to the public – the mayor's rooftop garden, wetlands occupying former steel mill properties and so on. The dozens of excursions cover

---

About the author
Martina Sheehan *is a staff writer at* Time Out Chicago *magazine, and a freelance travel writer.*

> **INSIDE TRACK**
> **CULTURAL EVENTS**
>
> Many other cultural festivals are listed in their arts-specific chapter. For **movie festivals**, *see p236*; for **music festivals**, *see p256*; and for **gay and lesbian events**, *see p244*.

other special-interest topics, including labour history, hidden-gem restaurants and skyscrapers. The Chicago Architecture Foundation (www.architecture.org) oversees the tours by bus, train, trolley and foot; most are free but require registration at the CAF's ArchiCenter, from 7.30am each day.

▶ *For more on the city's architecture, see pp34-44; for more on the CAF's tours, see p304.*

SUMMER

Summer in Chicago is awash with small neighbourhood festivals, block parties and other similar events. For details of these celebrated neighbourhood festivals, held just about every weekend during summer, *see p219* **Profile**.

Andersonville Midsommarfest

N Clark Street, between W Foster Avenue & W Berwyn Street, North Side (1-773 665 4682/ www.starevents.com). El: Purple or Red to Berwyn. **Date** *wknd, June.*
The Andersonville neighbourhood was first known as a Swedish immigrant hub, then as a vibrant lesbian hangout, and more recently for its condo-dwelling urban professionals. Today, the area boasts a bit of all three, as evidenced at this festival. Some 50,000 locals descend to watch Maypole dancers, munch street food and generally make merry at this free summer solstice celebration.

▶ *For more on Andersonville, see p95.*

St Patrick's Day.

Printers' Row Book Fair

S Dearborn Street, between W Congress Parkway & W Polk Street, South Loop (1-312 527 8132/ www.printersrowbookfair.org). El: Blue to LaSalle; Red to Harrison. **Date** *wknd, June.* **Map** p324 H13.
Pick a few books for your travels at this outdoor event held in what was once the wellspring of the city's publishing prosperity. Printers' Row rekindles its heritage once a year, as more than 150 booksellers hawk new, used and rare items; authors are on hand to give readings and sign copies of their works. Show up early for the best selection; but for true bargains, stroll up at closing time, when vendors weigh up the benefit of packing less. Advance tickets are available for many author appearances, which take place in tents and surrounding buildings.

★ Taste of Chicago

Grant Park, the Loop (1-312 744 2400/www.taste ofchicago.us). El: Brown, Green, Orange, Pink or Purple to Adams/Wabash; Red to Monroe. **Date** *10 days, late June-early July.* **Map** pp324-325 J11-J14.
More than 70 restaurants representing every corner of the city serve more than 3.5 million food fans over ten days at this, the city's largest festival. Entry is free; instead, you pay for tickets that you then exchange for either sample-sized 'taste portions' or only slightly more generous entrée servings. Large crowds at weekends and evenings make it tricky to find a seat, or even a peaceful place to stand. Entertainment comes from big-name music acts, and there are also family-friendly activities.

▶ *You can buy discount food tickets in advance from Dominick's grocery stores around town.*

★ Independence Day Fireworks

Grant Park, the Loop (1-312 744 2400/ www.tasteofchicago.us). El: Brown, Green, Orange, Pink or Purple to Adams/Wabash; Red to Monroe. **Date** *3 July.* **Map** pp324-325 J11-J14.
On the day before Independence Day, huge crowds descend on Downtown to sway to live bands, before turning their eyes to the sky for a spectacular fireworks display at around 9.30pm. The display is best viewed from Grant Park (where the Taste of Chicago is in full swing) or along the lakefront.

▶ *There are further festivities (and more fireworks) on Independence Day itself at Navy Pier; see p81.*

ARTS & ENTERTAINMENT

Dearborn Garden Walk

*N Dearborn, N State, N Astor & N LaSalle Streets
& N Sandburg Terrace, between W Goethe Street
& W North Avenue, Gold Coast (1-312 632 1241/
www.dearborngardenwalk.com). El: Red to Clark/
Division.* **Date** Sun, mid July. **Map** p327 G8-H8.
It's rare that common folk are afforded a peek behind
the iron gates protecting Gold Coast mansion-
dwellers from the outside world. This horticultural
celebration – America's oldest garden walk, running
since the 1950s – works its way around 20 or so luxurious homes and private gardens. Garden items
and refreshments are sold en route. You'll also
encounter live music and garden vignettes in some
of the yards. Tickets, which usually cost around $30,
include a copy of a coffeetable book entitled *The
Gardens of Chicago's Gold Coast.*

Old St Pat's World's Largest Block Party

*Old St Patrick's Church, 700 W Adams Street,
at N Des Plaines Avenue, West Loop (1-312 648
1590/www.worldslargestblockparty.com). Bus: 8,
126, 156.* **Date** wknd, mid July. **Map** p327 G8-H8.
This fest has a reputation with singles, having
apparently brought together more than 70 sets of
spouses over the years. It probably helps that five
free drinks are included with admission. Still, the
friendly, open atmosphere provides visitors with a
great opportunity to mingle with locals. Expect performances by local music acts.
▶ *For more on the church, see p101.*

Venetian Night

*Lake Michigan, from the Adler Planetarium to
Monroe Harbor, the Loop (1-312 744 2400/www.
cityofchicago.org). El: Brown, Green, Orange, Pink
or Purple to Adams/Wabash; Red to Harrison.*
Date Sat, late July. **Map** pp324-325 K12-K14.
For this festival, inspired by Venice's boat parade,
about 35 vessel owners dress up their crafts with
lights and decorations for a procession along the
waterfront. Brilliant fireworks conclude the evening.

Bud Billiken Day Parade & Picnic

*From 39th Street, at S King Drive, to
Washington Park, at E 51st Street, Hyde Park
(1-312 744 2400/www.budbillikenparade.com).
El: Green to 51st or Indiana.* **Date** 2nd Sat, Aug.
Map p332 X16.
This huge kid-centred parade was first launched in
1929 by Robert S Abbott, founder of African-
American newspaper the *Chicago Defender*. Since
then, the South Side procession has grown to include
upwards of 160 floats and vehicles, marching bands,
community groups and a reliable assortment of big-
time politicos acting as grand marshal (Barack
Obama once held the title). Drawing about 1.5 million
spectators annually, it's thought to be the largest and
oldest parade of its kind in the nation. The procession
ends with a picnic in Washington Park.

Chicago Air & Water Show.

★ Chicago Air & Water Show

*North Avenue Beach, at North Avenue &
from W Oak Street to W Diversey Parkway
(1-312 744 3370/www.explorechicago.org).
Bus: 72, 151.* **Date** wknd, Aug. **Map** pp326-
328 G4-H9.
If you didn't know this free event was scheduled, the
sonic booms that bounce off the Gold Coast high-
rises as planes soar over your hear should wake you
up to its existence in a hurry. Don't duck for cover:
instead, join about two million other people in heading to the lakefront to take in the spectacular aero-
batic and aquatic stunts. The roaring Navy Blue
Angels, and the Army Golden Knights Parachute
Team are typically part of the line-up. Great views
of the sky show can be had just about anywhere near
the water; the boat show is best seen from the North
Avenue Beach.

Chicago Carifete

*Around Hyde Park, centred on E 59th Street
(1-773 944 1444/www.chicagocarifete.com).
Metra: 59th Street.* **Date** Sat, late Aug.
Map p332 Y18.
Chicago's Caribbean community shows off its car-
nival finery with a masquerade procession through
the streets of Hyde Park on the city's South Side.
Check out scantily clad marchers donning elaborate
carnival-style feathered headdresses and sequinned
bodices as costumed bands with steel drummers
keep the parade in stride.

AUTUMN

German-American Festival
4700 N Lincoln Avenue, at W Lawrence Avenue, Lincoln Square (1-630 653 3018/www.germanday. com). El: Brown to Western. **Date** wknd, Sept.
Held in Lincoln Square, this Oktoberfest hasn't changed much over the decades. Revellers pack the neighbourhood annually for a German-American celebration that includes generous mugs of beer, brass bands for dancing and juicy sausages. The festival coincides with the Von Steuben Day Parade down Lincoln Avenue on the Saturday.

Wells Street Crush, Music & Comedy Fest
N Wells Street, at W North Avenue, Old Town (1-773 868 3010/www.chicagoevents.com). El: Brown or Purple to Sedgwick. **Date** wknd, mid Sept. **Map** pp324-325 J11-J14.
The Wells Street Crush has expanded its offerings to include more food, music and laughs. The comedy element seems apropos; famed comedy clubs Second City and Zanies are nearby. You'll still find an art market, food from local restaurants, crafts, a music stage and plenty of wine-tasting pavilions.
▶ *For comedy venues in Old Town, see pp226-229.*

★ Renegade Craft Fair
W Division Street, from N Hermitage Avenue to N Damen Avenue, Wicker Park (1-312 744 2400/www.renegadecraft.com). El: Blue to Division. **Date** wknd, mid Sept. **Map** p325 J13.
Browse crafty handmade creations from more than 150 local and national indie designers. Showcasing everything from clothing and handbags to poster art and jewellery, Renegade Craft is a great chance to pick up one-of-a-kind gifts.

★ Around the Coyote Festival
Plumbers Union Hall, 1340 W Washington Boulevard, at Ada Street, West Loop (1-773 342 6777/www.aroundthecoyote.org). El: Green or Pink to Ashland. **Date** wknd, mid Oct. **Map** p330 D12.
This two-decade-old arts fest is named for Wicker Park's Coyote building, the venue that once acted as an anchor for the festival's multi-venue exhibitions and events. But a few years back, it was moved to a new West Loop location, ostensibly to give its artists more space. Though ATC began as an artists' open house, with painters and sculptors welcoming the public into their studios, it now also incorporates readings, screenings and other performances.
▶ *A smaller winter edition is held in February.*

★ Bank of America Chicago Marathon
Start/end: Grant Park, nr Buckingham Fountain, the Loop (1-312 904 9800/www.chicagomarathon. com). El: Blue or Red to Monroe; Brown, Green, Orange, Pink or Purple to Adams/Wabash. **Date** Sun, mid Oct. **Map** p325 J13.

The city all but shuts down as nearly 40,000 sweaty athletes race along a 26.2-mile course, one of the fastest in the world. Starting from Grant Park, runners head up north via Lincoln Park to Wrigleyville, then turning on their heels before coming back down through Old Town, out into the West Loop, south through Pilsen and across via Chinatown into Grant Park to the finish line at Buckingham Fountain.
▶ *Keen on running in Chicago but maybe not quite that far? See p280.*

Chicago Humanities Festival
Around Chicago (1-312 661 1028/www.ch festival.org). **Date** 3wks, Oct/Nov.
Get up close and personal with big (and small) names in literature, film and art. The programme of lectures, readings and panel discussions is vast; the fest's theme changes each year to reflect current issues of interest.

Hallowe'en
Around Chicago (www.explorechicago.org). **Date** 31 Oct.
As the pagan-rooted holiday approaches, don't be surprised to see adults roaming the streets in scary costumes, from barely-there, sexy devil outfits to much-loathed politicos. Of course, kids are the real focus: three weeks of Hallowe'en celebrations, fronted by the suitably scary Mayor Daley, deliver a downtown costume parade, a haunted house in Daley Plaza, and other festivities for the wee ones.

Day of the Dead
National Museum of Mexican Art, 1852 W 19th Street, at S Damen Avenue, Pilsen (1-312 738 1503/www.nationalmuseumof mexicanart.org). El: Blue or Pink to 18th. **Date** 1 day, early Nov.
Tiny skeletons placed in colourful scenarios within shadowbox-like altars honour gone-but-not-forgotten loved ones for this Mexican All Souls' Day tradition. The elaborate displays of macabre but oddly joyous folk art offerings to the dead are complemented by a procession that kicks off at the St Precopious School (1625 S Allport Street, at W 16th Street, Pilsen) and ends up at the museum.
▶ *For more on Pilsen's Mexican culture, see p104.*

INSIDE TRACK
RUNNING ON EMPTY

For the first time in its 30-year history, the **Chicago Marathon** (*see above*) ground to a halt mid-race in 2007. One runner died and hundreds of others fell ill as temperatures soared into the upper 80s (more than 30°C), about 25°F above the average October high. As a result, the race was suspended.

ARTS & ENTERTAINMENT

WINTER

In addition to the events below, the City of Chicago stages a variety of events in January and February for its **Winter Delights** series; see www.choosechicago.com for details.

McDonald's Thanksgiving Parade

State Street, from Congress Parkway to Randolph Street, the Loop (1-312 781 5681/www.chicago festivals.org). El: Blue or Red to Jackson, Monroe or Washington; Brown, Green, Orange, Pink or Purple to Adams/Wabash, Madison/Wabash or Randolph/Wabash. **Date** Thanksgiving Day (4th Thur in Nov). **Map** pp325 H11-H13.

While most shops and attractions close for the big holiday, there's still fun to be had downtown. This big parade along 'that great street' in the Loop stars everything from monster-size floats and gigantic helium-balloon characters to upbeat marching bands and countless performance groups. Events start at 8.30am and conclude by 11am.

Christmas Around the World

Museum of Science & Industry, 5700 S Lake Shore Drive, at E 57th Street, Hyde Park (1-773 684 1414/www.msichicago.org). Metra: 55th-56th-57th Street. **Date** mid Nov-early Jan. **Map** p332 Z17.

For the last 60-plus years, the Museum of Science & Industry has staged a simultaneous exhibition on, and celebration of, the ways in which the festive season is observed all over the globe. In addition to Christmas, there are events based around Diwali, Hanukkah, Kwanzaa and Chinese New Year, with theatre, dance and music shows to jolly along the proceedings.
▶ *For more on the museum, see p121.*

★ Zoolights

Lincoln Park Zoo, 2200 N Cannon Drive, at W Webster Avenue, Lincoln Park (1-312 742 2000/ www.lpzoo.com). El: Brown, Purple or Red to Fullerton. **Date** late Nov-early Jan. **Map** p328 H5.

The zoo stays open late through the holidays, and the atmosphere is dazzling. Evening visitors are guided along the winding pathways by a sprawling display of illuminated designs, many of them shaped like animals, and there's a synchronised musical light show. If the two million bulbs leave you dazed, the hot cider and chainsaw-wielding ice sculptors are sure to give you a jolt.
▶ *For more on the zoo itself, see p89.*

Christkindlmarket & Holiday Tree Lighting Ceremony

Daley Plaza, W Washington Boulevard & N Dearborn Street, the Loop (1-312 644 2662/ www.christkindlmarket.com). El: Blue to Washington; Brown, Green, Orange, Pink or Purple to Randolph/Wabash; Red to Lake. **Date** late Nov-late Dec. **Map** p325 H12.

The night after Thanksgiving, usually around 4pm, a giant 80-foot (25-metre) tree constructed from piles of smaller evergreens is illuminated at Daley Plaza. Four giant toy sentries tower over onlookers and an enormous toy train roams around the plaza's corner. At around the same time, the plaza is converted into a traditional German-style market, complete with German food and handicrafts, and twinkling lights. Small stands are packed full of gifts and culinary delicacies; wooden huts brim with candy, blown glass, Christmas decorations and other delights.

Winter WonderFest

Navy Pier, 600 E Grand Avenue, at Streeter Drive, Streeterville (1-312 595 7437/tickets 1-312 595 1212/www.ticketmaster.com). El: Red to Grand. **Tickets** $12-$18. **Date** early Dec-early Jan. **Map** p326 K10.

This seasonal wonderland of holiday-themed indoor amusements in the Pier's Festival Hall lets kids cut loose with inflatable games, a carousel, slides, a crafts area and an indoor ice-skating rink. Trees, lights and decorations set the festive mood.

★ Chinatown New Year Parade

Along S Wentworth Avenue, Chinatown (1-312 326 5320/www.chicagochinatown.org). El: Red to Cermak-Chinatown. **Date** 1st Sun after Chinese New Year (early Feb). **Map** p324 H16.

The streets of Chinatown come alive for this annual event. The Lunar New Year is ushered in with a colourful parade that includes marching bands, floats, lion teams, the 100-foot Mystical Dragon dance and a fanfare of firecrackers. Revellers would be wise to stick around Chinatown to stroll the shops and fill up at neighbourhood restaurants.
▶ *For more on Chinatown, see p72.*

Chicago Auto Show

McCormick Place, 2301 S Lake Shore Drive, South Side (1-312 791 7000/www.chicago autoshow.com). Bus 2, 3, X3, 4, 6, 10, 14, 21, 26, 28. **Tickets** $10. **Date** 10 days, early Feb.

Petrolheads can be among the first to check out what's new in motoring at this car showcase that's been running for more than a century. Close to 1,000 different vehicles are on display, along with accessories, collectibles and car-themed exhibits.

Snow Days Chicago

Grant Park, the Loop (1-312 742 4007/www. explorechicago.org). El: Brown, Green, Orange, Pink or Purple to Adams/Wabash; Red to Monroe. **Date** 5 days, mid Feb **Map** pp324-325 J11-J14.

Leave it to Chicagoans to embrace the bone-chilling cold wholeheartedly. This newer winter fest draws all ages outdoors to frolic in the snow, check out the snow-sculpting competition, cheer on canines in dog-sled demonstrations and gasp at gravity-defying snowboarding stunts. An activities igloo keeps kids warm and engaged with crafts and games.

Profile Neighbourhood Festivals

The 'hoods come alive in summer with block parties, bashes and blowouts.

When winter is at its fiercest and the snow feels like it'll never melt, Chicagoans go into huddled hibernation. But when warmer weather rolls around, nothing can keep them off the streets. Payback for the often vicious winters arrives around May or June, and locals hardened by the ice and snow are anxious to make the most of the sun-soaked summer months before the mercury starts to fall again.

The City of Chicago organises a number of huge summer events, most of which take over Grant Park and the lakefront. But a more charismatic window into summer in the city can be found in the city's neighbourhoods, which celebrate the sunny months with glorious enthusiasm at a variety of block parties. There are dozens of these low-key events around the city each year. Streets are blocked off for the weekend, vendors provide food and drinks, and musicians of varying talent offer entertainment.

Many block parties reflect the neighbourhoods in which they're set. **Wicker Park Fest** (late July) features an array of indie-rock bands spread over two days, while the Near West Side's

West Fest (mid July) is even artier. A number reflect the melting-pot make-up of the city: Greektown's **Taste of Greece** (late August); the Polish-oriented **Taste of Polonia** (www.copernicus fdn.org), held each year in Jefferson Park on the first weekend in September; and August's **Ukrainian Festival** in (where else?) Ukrainian Village. But others are more straightforward: a couple of bands, a couple of kegs and a couple of cops, all combined into an opportunity for the locals to hang out and celebrate the city at its most jubilantly beautiful.

GET THE LOWDOWN
A schedule of events can be obtained from the **Mayor's Office of Special Events** (*see p214*); it's also worth looking out for the free guide to festivals published by *Time Out Chicago* each summer.

Children

Chicago welcomes kids of all ages with a spread of attractions.

Whether you're travelling with junior culture vultures, pint-sized sports fans, little foodies or bored babies, Chicago is a tremendously family-friendly place. The city offers a rich blend of world-class museums and performance groups, parks and beaches, hot-dog stands and gourmet restaurants with high chairs. Along with the laid-back, friendly Midwest attitude, it's a combination that makes Chicago a perfect destination for parents and kids.

For details of family events in Chicago, check the Kids section of *Time Out Chicago* magazine. Look out, too, for *Time Out Chicago Kids* magazine, or see www.timeoutchicago.com/kids.

ARTS & ENTERTAINMENT

SIGHTSEEING
Museums & attractions

Kiddie culture is serious business in Chicago. Almost all the city's museums and cultural institutions acknowledge young visitors, and many do considerably more than that – a few museums are even aimed purely at youngsters. However, for kid-friendliness, five of the city's big attractions stand out from the pack.

In 2006, *Child* magazine named the **Art Institute of Chicago** (*see p56*) the best art museum in the US for children. Since then, things have only improved. Most of the superb kids' programming is centred around the Ryan Education Center, which expanded with the opening of the new Modern Wing in May 2009. The multi-purpose space, now with its own entrance, has a teacher resource area and a larger space where families can get hands-on with arts, crafts and other activities. Special events include storytelling sessions, treasure hunts and a variety of other shows; see the website for details.

The **Field Museum** (*see p68 & p70*) is home to Sue, the world's largest T-Rex; as such, it's perpetually packed with bands of little dino-lovers. If the kids tire of Sue's charms, lead them to the Crown Family Play Lab, a sizeable

permanent exhibit for kids aged two to six. Six individual play areas are each linked to other parts of the museum, including a woodland area, a dinosaur field station and an art studio. Little ones can make fossil rubbings, 'harvest' corn and enjoy the 'safe zones' for crawlers.

The **Spertus Museum** (*see p61*), the city's Jewish museum, occupies a spectacular new space in Michigan Avenue containing the Gray Children's Center, designed to present a universally appealing look at Judaism through displays that bring to life ancient folktales about water, the alphabet and other subjects. Kids can climb though tunnels to get the middle of a doughnut-shaped aquarium, make Hebrew letters in an art studio, and basically run, skip and jump their way through the space.

Like their grown-up counterparts, kids can get lost for days inside the **Museum of Science & Industry** (*see p121*), where they flock to the genetics exhibit to watch as chicks break from their shells and the model railroads of the Great Train Story. The submarine *U505*,

---

INSIDE TRACK TOUR THE TOWN

Tell junior to grab his headphones for the **Chicago for Kids** audio tour, a free and downloadable taste of downtown hotspots created by the Chicago Office of Tourism (*see p310*) and available at www.downloadchicagotours.com.

About the author
Judy Sutton Taylor *is the Kids editor for* Time Out Chicago *magazine and the editor of* Time Out Chicago Kids.

captured in battle during World War II, is another fave, but the famous coal mine tends to have the longest queues. Make time, too, for Colleen Moore's fairy castle.

The superb **Shedd Aquarium** (*see p68*), the largest indoor aquarium in the world, can keep kids happy for hours. The Wild Reef section displays a coral reef habitat, from the shoreline surf to creatures that lurk in deeper waters. Kids can view anaconda and piranhas in Amazon Rising: Seasons of the River; the newly redesigned Oceanarium affords improved views of dolphins, sea otters, harbour seals and whales (including a baby beluga born in July 2006). Time your visit to coincide with a poolside feeding session, though the daily hand-feeding of fish by divers in the main aquarium's Caribbean Reef tank is just as popular. The new Polar Play Zone in the Oceanarium gives kids a chance to explore extremes (cold to warm, smooth to scaly) in touch pools, dress-up areas and play submarine. Tots on Tuesdays offers storytelling, crafts and animal touch events designed for pre-schoolers.

Bronzeville Children's Museum

Evergreen Plaza, 9301 S Stony Island Avenue, at 93rd St, Bronzeville (1-773 721 9301/www.bronze villechildrensmuseum.com). Bus 14. **Open** 10am-4pm Tue-Sat. **Admission** $6. **No credit cards.**
The only African-American children's museum in the country recently moved to bigger digs in this historic section of town on the South Side. Interactive exhibits include a look at African-Americans' journey from Africa to Chicago, neighbourhood

---

INSIDE TRACK GOING UP...

Kids love a tall building, but the cost of getting the whole family to the top of a skyscraper can reach stratospheric proportions. Instead of paying for the entire gang to visit the **John Hancock Observatory** (*see p79*; $9 for kids ages 4-11 and $18 for adults), stump up for drinks or snacks at the **Signature Room** on the 95th, just one floor below.

---

landmarks and the story of the African-American man who invented the traffic light. Tours are conducted hourly from 10am until 2pm.

★ Chicago Children's Museum

700 E Grand Avenue, at Navy Pier, Streeterville (1-312 527 1000/www.chichildrensmuseum.org). El: Red to Grand. **Open** 10am-5pm Mon-Wed, Fri-Sun; 10am-8pm Thur. **Admission** $10; $9 over-65s; free under-1s; free to families 5-8pm Thur, & under-15s on 1st Mon of mth. **Credit** AmEx, Disc, MC, V. **Map** p326 K10.
Kids will have a blast at this Navy Pier museum dedicated to under-11s, but they might also learn something at the 15 permanent exhibits and the one or two touring shows usually on display in the massive, three-floor space. Aspiring archaeologists can dig for dinosaur bones in a replica excavation pit; cooped-up urban kids can get a dose of green space in the indoor Big Backyard, which combines technology and art to create a fantastical Chicago backyard that changes with the seasons.

ARTS & ENTERTAINMENT

Navy Pier.

INSIDE TRACK OUTSIDE ART

Give kids an education in the arts while they run themselves ragged by visiting one of Chicago's many outdoor sculptures. A couple of our faves: Picasso's very climbable **Untitled** piece in Daley Plaza, and Anish Kapoor's kidney bean-shaped **Cloud Gate** in Millennium Park (the mirrored surface is perfect for making silly faces). For both, see p62 **Walk**.

The museum also runs Kids on the Fly, a free interactive exhibition on the departures level of Terminal 2 at O'Hare.

Kohl Children's Museum

2100 Patriot Boulevard, Glenview (1-847 832 6600/www.kohlchildrensmuseum.org). Metra: North Glenview. **Open** *June-Aug* 9.30am-5pm Mon-Sat; noon-5pm Sun. *Sept-May* 9.30am-noon Mon; 9.30am-5pm Tue-Sat; noon-5pm Sun. **Admission** $7.50; $6.50 over-55s; free under-1s. **Credit** AmEx, Disc, MC, V.

Catering to kids aged eight and under, the state-of-the art, eco-friendly Kohl has plenty of indoor exhibition space, including a pint-sized grocery store and a water play area where budding seafarers can design their own boats and control movement with water and air jets (clothes dryers are available, free of charge). Habitat Park, the museum's two acres of outdoor exhibition space, provides year-round access to the outdoors in a fenced-off site with a landscaped garden, a sculpture trail and interactive tools to encourage kids to connect with the environment – in other words, get good and dirty for the ride back.

Wonder Works

6445 W North Avenue, at Elmwood Avenue, Oak Park (1-708 383 4815/www.wonder-works.org). Bus 72/El: Green to Oak Park. **Open** 10am-5pm Wed-Sat; noon-5pm Sun. **Admission** $5; free under-1s. **No credit cards.**

Oak Park's Wonder Works is a small museum that feels more like a big playroom, with an emphasis on exhibits that encourage learning through creative play. There's something for kids of all ages: at Lights, Camera, Action!, young 'uns can dress up and act on stage, while North Avenue Art Works is an art studio where creative types can work with paint, crayons and other crafty tools.

Parks & gardens

Over in **Millennium Park** (*see p54*), kids get a kick out of kicking off their shoes and frolicking in the water around the two 50-foot (15-metre) glass-brick towers that face one another at Crown Fountain. The faces of 1,000 Chicagoans flash continually across screens on the towers; periodically, one will purse their lips and water will spout out, making it seem like the person is spitting on the crowd below.

The highlight of a visit to **Lincoln Park** (*see p89*) for many kids is a wander around the **Lincoln Park Zoo**. The Children's Zoo offers an up-close-and-personal view of more than a dozen species of North American animals in a wooded landscape and throws in a crash course on conservation, while the Farm-in-the-Zoo is a working replica of a Midwestern farm, complete with red barns housing cows, sheep and horses. There's also a carousel, children's train ride and safari ride. Best of all, admission is free.

Not far from Lincoln Park sits **Oz Park**, famous for its silver statue of the Tin Man from *The Wizard of Oz* (the story's author, L Frank Baum, lived in Chicago) along with later additions of the Cowardly Lion, the Scarecrow, Dorothy and Toto. Facilities include basketball, volleyball and tennis courts, and everyone loves following the requisite yellow brick road.

If the rug rats still have some leftover energy you'd like them to expend, head to the 185-acre **Garfield Park** (*see p106*) about four miles west of the Loop, where you'll find a playground, baseball diamonds, soccer fields, basketball and tennis courts, a pool, a lagoon, a bike path and a couple of sandpits. The conservatory (*see p106*) is a delightful spot when it's gloomy outside. The children's garden is open 365 days a year and contains a tube slide through the trees and lots of climbable sculptures. The conservatory hosts all kinds of free, drop-in activities for little nature lovers; check the online calendar.

CONSUME

Restaurants

Children are welcome at all but the smartest spots in town. Here are a few family favourites.

★ Big Bowl

60 E Ohio Street, at N Wabash Avenue, River North (1-312 951 1888/www.bigbowl.com). El: Red to Grand. **Open** 11am-10pm Mon-Thur; 11am-11pm Fri; 11.30am-11pm Sat; 11.30am-10pm Sun. **Main courses** $8-$18. **Credit** AmEx, Disc, MC, V. **Map** p326 H10.

Looking to expand Junior's culinary repertoire beyond chicken tenders and fries? Try this Chinese-Thai restaurant, where the kids' menu lists steamed dumplings, satays, stir-frys, and is printed with games that go beyond the usual mazes and word-searches. The restaurant is especially festive around Chinese New Year, when young guests receive red envelopes with crisp dollar bills and 'feed' oranges to dragons that dance their way through the room.

Other locations 6 E Cedar Street, at N State Street, Gold Coast (1-312 640 8888).

Eleven City Diner

1112 S Wabash Avenue, at 11th Street, South Loop (1-312 212 1112/www.elevencitydiner.com). El: Green to Roosevelt. **Open** 8am-9pm Mon-Thur; 8am-11pm Fri; 9am-11pm Sat; 9am-9pm Sun. **Main courses** $9-$13. **Credit** AmEx, Disc, MC, V. **Map** p324 H14.

Old-fashioned egg creams, penny candy, soul-soothing chicken soup and hearty sandwiches are all on the menu at the South Loop's Eleven City Diner. The Jewish-style deli has cushy booths and an easy-going retro feel. Kids especially love that you can order breakfast all day and follow it up with a banana split. Placemats printed with kids' activities were created with the help of the owner's young son, so they pass muster with the quiz-and-maze set.

★ Foodlife

Water Tower Place, 835 N Michigan Avenue, at E Pearson Street, Magnificent Mile (1-312 335 3663/www.foodlifechicago.com). El: Red to Chicago. **Open** 8am-8pm Mon-Thur; 8am-8.30pm Fri, Sat; 8am-7.30pm Sun. **Main courses** $7-$10. **Credit** AmEx, Disc, MC, V. **Map** p326 J9.

Your suddenly-vegan teenager and her burger-loving little brother will both find meals to please at this fun and festive food court on the mezzanine level of Water Tower Place. The 13 kiosks offer everything from roadside barbecue and made-to-order Mexican fare to Asian noodles and wheatgrass smoothies.

▶ *For more on the mall, see p190.*

★ Margie's Candies

1960 N Western Avenue, at W Armitage Avenue, Bucktown (1-773 384 1035/www. margiescandies.nv.switchboard.com). El: Blue to Western. **Open** 9am-midnight daily. **Main courses** $4-$8. **Credit** AmEx, Disc, MC, V. **Map** p331 A6.

The slightly surly waitstaff are as old as the decor at this soda fountain, here since 1921, but that's all part of the charm. The other part is the ice-cream, served in an array of tempting sundae, milkshake and malted combinations. Little ones love the saucer of hot fudge served next to their dish of ice-cream, along with a couple of wafer cookies. Margie's also makes its own boxed chocolates and candies, so you can keep the kids' sugar highs going after you leave.

Orange

3231 N Clark Street, between W School Street & W Belmont Avenue, Lakeview (1-773 549 4400/www.orangerestaurantchicago.com). El: Brown, Purple or Red to Belmont. **Open** 9am-3.30pm Mon-Fri; 8am-3.30pm Sat, Sun. **Main courses** $8-$10. **Credit** AmEx, Disc, MC, V. **Map** p329 F2.

Pancake 'flights' include flavours such as cinnamon roll and jelly donut at this funky Wrigleyville spot. Adventurous little eaters love the restaurant's signature 'Frushi', a breakfast sushi made with fruit, not fish, and the rainbow-hued array of freshly squeezed fruit juices. There's a menu of less inspired (but still tasty) salads and sandwiches for lunch, too.

Shops

For children's shops, *see p193.*

Margie's Candies.

ARTS & ENTERTAINMENT

In addition to the venues below, the touristy but fun **Navy Pier** (*see p81*) offers plenty for the young 'uns, including an IMAX cinema, the Chicago Children's Museum, a Ferris wheel and a massive maze. Seasonal entertainment includes the **Winter WonderFest** (*see p218*).

Dave & Buster's

1030 N Clark Street, at W Oak Street, Gold Coast (1-312 943 5151/www.daveand busters.com). El: Red to Clark/Division. **Open** 11.30am-midnight Mon-Wed, Sun; 1.30am-1am Thur-Sat. **Admission** $5 after 10pm Fri, Sat. **Credit** AmEx, Disc, MC, V. **Map** p326 H9.
Although the focus is on arcade games, Dave & Buster's offers everything from shuffleboard to high-tech virtual reality kits. Frazzled adults can take the edge off with a cocktail. School groups, birthday parties and the like frequent the space during the day, but at night and on days of big sporting events, it turns into more of a grown-up party space.

Different Strummer

4544 N Lincoln Avenue, at W Wilson Avenue, Lincoln Square (1-773 728 6000/www.old townschool.org). El: Brown to Western. **Open** 9am-10pm Mon-Thur; 9am-5pm Fri-Sun. **Credit** AmEx, Disc, MC, V.
The Different Strummer store offers plenty for the budding muso: CDs, videos and toy instruments, as well as real ones made especially for younger players (little girls especially dig the Hello Kitty electric guitar). Check out the school's concert schedule for kids' performances by lauded local artists who often play to grown-up audiences.
▶ *It's part of the Old Town School of Folk Music; see p261.*

Down in the Basement

Blue Chicago (South), 536 N Clark Street, at W Grand Avenue, River North (1-312 661 0100/www.bluechicago.com). El: Red to Grand. **Admission** $5; under-12s free. **Open** 8pm-midnight Sat. **Credit** AmEx, MC, V. **Map** p326 H10.

INSIDE TRACK PUPPET BIKE

A mobile playhouse built on the back of a cargo tricycle, **Puppet Bike** tours around Chicago neighbourhoods performing short street shows. The puppeteers and their characters have developed something of a cult following around the city; visit www.puppetbike.com to see where they're playing while you're in town.

Little ones get glum, too, but the Gloria Shannon Blues Band feels their pain every Saturday at this all-ages, alcohol-free show in the Blue Chicago Store.
▶ *For the sister clubs, see p264.*

WhirlyBall

1880 W Fullerton Avenue, at N Wolcott Avenue, Wicker Park (1-773 486 7777/www.whirlyball. com). Bus 50, 74. **Open** 11am-midnight Mon-Thur; 11am-2am Fri; noon-3am Sat; noon-midnight Sun. Over-21s only after 5pm; under-21s in large parties allowed with restricted access. **Admission** *Walk-ins* $12/30mins. *Pre-bookings* $180/hr Mon-Thur; $200/hr Fri-Sun. **Credit** AmEx, Disc, MC, V. **Map** p331 C5.
Two teams spin around a 4,000sq ft (370sq m) court, attempting to scoop up a ball and whip it at a backboard. Think polo in bumper cars that go at an average of 3-5mph. Kids must be aged 12 or over, and be at least 54in (137cm) tall. After 5pm, it's strictly 21 and over for folks without reservations.

Theatre

There's no shortage of original musicals and plays for kids in Chicago, thanks to a bevy of professional children's theatre companies (and a few grown-up ones that also put on some stellar shows for younger audiences). **Chicago Shakespeare Theatre** offers the Bard to babes with its Family Series; productions have included *MacHomer*, with Homer Simpson as the tragic King Macbeth. Its Short Shakespeare! series puts teachers and students on stage to perform abbreviated versions of the classics.

★ Chicago Children's Theatre

1-773 227 0180/www.chicagochildrenstheatre.org. **Tickets** $7.50-$35. **Credit** AmEx, Disc, MC, V.
This multi-million-dollar venture launched in 2006 with the aim of bringing high-end children's productions to young theatregoers. The company doesn't yet have a home of its own, and instead stages shows at venues across the city. Productions have ranged from a musical version of the book *Go, Dog. Go!*, in a big top tent in Grant Park, to *The Selfish Giant*, with the help of huge papier-mâché puppets.

Emerald City Theatre

Apollo Theater, 2540 N Lincoln Avenue, at W Wrightwood Avenue, Lincoln Park (1-773 935 6100/www.emeraldcitytheatre.com). El: Brown, Purple or Red to Fullerton. **Tickets** $15; $12 children. **Credit** AmEx, Disc, MC, V. **Map** p328 E4.
Expect productions of everything from children's favourites such as *James and the Giant Peach* to modern, multi-culti takes on classics such as *Cinderella* and *The Nutcracker* from this top-notch kids' theatre company. The audience gets to ask questions and interact with the cast after each performance. *See also right* **A New Way to Play**.

A New Way to Play

Emerald City Theatre takes a fresh approach to creating kids' shows.

It's no secret that plenty of parents, and even some kids, get a sinking feeling at the thought of having to sit through a children's theatre production. Karen Cardarelli, executive director of **Emerald City Theatre** (*see p224*) knows this first-hand, as she's always struggling to find fresh works that meet the theatre's high standards for both entertainment and educational value. 'The quality of scripts available for young theatregoers,' she admits, 'is nowhere near the calibre of what's out there for adults.'

When several works by the Lincoln Park children's company were commissioned by eight other theatre groups in the US and Canada, Cardarelli realised Emerald City wasn't alone in looking for better scripts. However, she also felt that the

company was in a position to help change things. 'We want to address both the community and industry needs, and feel we can do that in a city with so much amazing writing talent.'

With that in mind, the company formed Emerald City PlayGround, a lab that stages readings in front of test kid audiences to serve as an incubator for its original works. *If You Take a Mouse to School*, the Playground's first production, underwent several script changes following these readings. 'The kids gave us ideas about what they would and wouldn't like to see the character of Mouse do,' Cardarelli says.

The PlayGround also uses advisers from government-funded education initiative Head Start and other learning programmes to provide feedback. The benefits work both ways, claims Cardarelli. 'It helps us to get advice from educators out in the field, and by inviting them to our staged readings, they learn theatre techniques they can use for storytelling in their classrooms.'

Among the things Cardarelli has learned is the need for 'character education' at preschool level; in other words, teaching kids to be good citizens and be kind to others. 'Theatre can help by providing good role models by way of characters. We've heard from parents that they love it when we have characters who brush their teeth and listen to their mothers.'

Lookingglass Theatre

Water Tower Water Works, 821 N Michigan Avenue, at E Pearson Street, Magnificent Mile (1-312 337 0665/www.lookingglasstheatre.org). El: Red to Chicago. **Tickets** $30-$60. **Credit** AmEx, Disc, MC, V. **Map** p326 J9.

Young and old watch in awe as this company performs daring, acrobatic interpretations of everything from Greek myths such as *Hephaestus* to funky airy tales (*Lookingglass Alice*) in a space carved from the pipes within the Water Tower Water Works building. During select Sunday matinée performances, parents can drop off kids ages five through 14 for classes while they take in the show.

DIRECTORY

Babysitting & childcare

Your hotel may be able to arrange childcare; ask front desk staff or the concierge.

North Shore Nannies

1-847 864 2424/www.northshorenannies.com.
This suburban service is thought to be one of the best for providing both temporary and permanent childcare throughout Chicagoland. North Shore Nannies rates range from $12 to $18 per hour (bear in mind there's a four-hour minimum) plus parking, or $120 for overnight service, plus $5 per night for each additional child. Add in a $25 agency fee, and an extra $15 for same-day service when available. It's advisable to book ahead, especially for weekends.

Sitter's Studio

1-312 890 8194/www.sitterstudio.com.
Parents of budding creative types will appreciate this specialised babysitting service that hires 'artist babysitters' who do everything from stage plays with kids to sing them arias to soothe them to sleep. Rates are $15 an hour with a four-hour minimum, plus a $10 cab fare after 9pm.

Comedy

The Second City's comedy scene is second to none.

Comedy has been synonymous with improv in Chicago ever since a handful of University of Chicago brainiacs started experimenting with the form in the 1950s. Under the direction of David Shepherd and Paul Sills, the Compass Players improvised their performances based on audience suggestions. When the group dissolved in 1959, a new ensemble called **Second City** filled the gap in the market.

The rest is (living) history. Comics such as Mike Nichols, Elaine May, Tina Fey, Amy Sedaris, Stephen Colbert and Steve Carell cut their teeth at Second City; others, including Amy Poehler, Mike Myers, Stephanie Weir and Andy Dick, did the same at rival improv house **iO Chicago**, co-founded by the legendary actor Del Close. Many Chicago comics aim to tickle the funny bone in the old-fashioned way: alone on stage, with a mic and a routine. The city's stand-up scene is certainly growing, but improv still rules the roost.

COMEDY VENUES

Improv is performed most visibly at the **Annoyance Theatre**, **Gorilla Tango Theater**, the **Playground Theater** and **ComedySportz**, while the spotlight gets shined on both local and touring stand-up comics at the **Lakeshore Theater**, **Zanies**, the **Lincoln Lodge**, **Jokes & Notes** and many local taprooms around town.

For weekly listings, pick up a copy of the weekly *Time Out Chicago* magazine, which covers almost every venue in town. Tickets can be bought directly from theatre box offices. Some improv troupes don't perform in a set location; check listings for details of their movements.

★ Annoyance Theatre & Bar

Annoyance Theatre, 4840 N Broadway, at W Gunnison Street, Uptown (1-773 561 4665/ www.annoyanceproductions.com). El: Red to Lawrence. **Shows** 8pm Mon, Tue; 8pm & 10.30pm Thur; 8pm, 10.30pm & midnight Fri, Sat. **Tickets** $5-$15. **Credit** MC, V.

The ever-irreverent Annoyance sits alone on a particular echelon of respectability in Chicago's comedy scene, mostly because performers love to curse and offend (the theatre rose to fame with a musical entitled *Co-ed Prison Sluts*). However, the shows are better than that description might indicate: behind the in-your-face bombast lies some of the city's best improv and sketch comedy writing. Mick Napier, one of the founders, is held to be something of a comedy guru. As such, the shows he directs are often the most reliable, although Susan Messing's *Messing With a Friend* is not to be missed.

Chicago Center for the Performing Arts

777 N Green Street, at W Chicago Avenue, West Town (1-312 733 6000/www.theaterland.com). El: Blue to Chicago. **Shows** 8pm & 9.30pm Tue-Sat. **Tickets** $10-$15. **Credit** AmEx, Disc, MC, V. **Map** p326 F11.

This theatrical multiplex actually holds four theatres: the Green Street Theater, the West Town Studio and two cabarets. It's not all comic in nature, but you can find sketch, improv and stand-up here almost every night. The Edge Comedy Club (in the West Town Studio) often presents a line-up of comics on a set theme: Down with Brown, for instance, a night of Indian and Pakistani comics, or ChiHAgo, jokes aimed at the Windy City. The big draw these days seems to be Bye Bye Liver, an interactive night of sketch comedy and drinking aimed at, well, getting the audience utterly wasted.

ComedySportz of Chicago

929 W Belmont Avenue, between N Clark Street & N Sheffield Avenue, Lakeview (1-773 549 8080/www.comedysportzchicago.com).

El: Brown, Purple or Red to Belmont. **Shows**
8pm Thur; 8pm & 10pm Fri; 6pm, 8pm & 10pm
Sat. **Tickets** $21. **Credit** AmEx, Disc, MC, V.
Map p329 E2.
ComedySportz is the Starbucks of its field, though
it's no surprise that Chicago hosts one of its
stronger franchises. The schtick is simple: two
teams battle each other at improv games, complete
with a scoreboard. The performers are generally
talented, but the place is aimed more at providing
PG-rated fun for the masses than pushing the
boundaries. That said, the filth is allowed to fly
every now and then, especially at late-night shows
such as 'The Hot Karl'.

Gorilla Tango Theater

*1919 N Milwaukee Avenue, at N Western
Avenue, Bucktown (1-773 598 4549/www.gorilla
tango.com). El: Blue to Western.* **Shows** 9.30pm
Wed; 8pm & 9.30pm Thur; 8pm & 10pm Fri; 2pm,
4pm, 6pm, 8pm 10pm & 11.30pm Fri; 1pm, 3pm,
5pm & 7pm Sun. **Tickets** $10-$17. **Credit**
AmEx, Disc, MC, V. **Map** p331 A6.
A little like the Lakeview's Playground Theater
(*see p228*), Gorilla Tango is the place to see high-
energy youngsters eager to make their mark (and
make it big). There's a lot of untrained talent running around, but occasionally a bunch of up-and-
comers break away from the pack with genuinely
solid improv and sketch material. Two to three
troupes perform a night.

★ iO Chicago

*3541 N Clark Street, at W Addison Street,
Wrigleyville (1-773 880 0199/www.ioimprov.
com). El: Red to Addison.* **Shows** times vary,
daily. **Tickets** free-$14. **Credit** Disc, MC, V.
Map p329 E1.
The most respected Chicago venue for hardcore
improv (alumni include Andy Richter, Tim
Meadows and founder Charna Halpern), iO Chicago
takes as its house speciality a long-form style
called the Harold. Created by Del Close, it features

\Lakeshore Theater.

improvising teams creating fluid acts that loosely
revolve around a single audience suggestion.
However, it's just one of numerous shows at this
two-space venue, busy every night with a young,
party-hearty crowd. The name? It was formerly
called the ImprovOlympic, but the International
Olympic Committee felt violated.

Jokes & Notes

*4641 S King Drive, at E 46th Place,
Bronzeville (1-773 373 3390/www.jokesand
notes.com). El: Green to 47th Street.* **Shows**
8.30pm Wed, Thur; 8.30pm & 10.30pm Fri, Sat;
8pm Sun. **Tickets** $10-$20 (2-drink min).
Credit MC, V.
In the 1940s, Bronzeville was the centre of
Chicago's black culture, a hotbed of jazz musicians,
writers and others of an artistic bent. Six decades
later, Jokes & Notes is helping to return the neighbourhood to the primacy of its glory days by
putting African-American comics front and centre.
National acts such as Bill Bellamy and Mo'Nique
swing through all the time, but owner Mary
Lindsey honours hometown talent by offering top
billing to local joke-makers.

Lakeshore Theater

*3175 N Broadway Street, at Belmont Avenue,
Lakeview (1-773 472 3492/www.lakeshore
theater.com). El: Brown, Purple or Red to
Belmont.* **Shows** times vary, weekends.
Tickets $15-$40. **Credit** AmEx, Disc, MC, V.

INSIDE TRACK AFTER HOURS

If you're unable to nab a ticket to the
latest Second City revue or simply lack
the funds for a full night of sketch, fear
not. Every show at both the Mainstage
and Etc at **Second City** (except Friday;
see p228) is followed by a fully improvised
set of material, with no admission
charge. One caveat: it's free but it's
not a free-for-all, so do call ahead and
ask what time you should show up to grab
a seat. Visiting celebs sometimes join
the cast; the likes of Jim Belushi and Tim
Meadows have shown up in the past.

Formerly a first-run movie theatre, the Lakeshore reinvented itself in 2002 as a 'comedic art house' and has remained true to its mission ever since. In addition to delivering top-notch alternative comics, including Maria Bamford, Eugene Mirman, Kumail Nanjiani and Louis CK, you can also catch sketch comedy (Upright Citizens Brigade), indie bands (Iron & Wine), modern composers (Nico Muhly) and local cabaret acts (Amy & Freddy). But first and foremost, the Lakeshore is all about comedy.

▶ *For the music side of the operation, see p261.*

Lincoln Lodge.

★ Lincoln Lodge
4008 N Lincoln Avenue, at W Irving Park Avenue, Lincoln Square (1-773 251 1539/ www.thelincolnlodge.com). El: Brown to Irving Park. **Shows** 9pm Thur, Fri. **Tickets** $10 (1-drink min). **Credit** Disc, MC, V. **Map** p330 B0.
Perhaps *the* place to see locally grown stand-up comedy, the Lincoln Lodge has cultivated a cult following. Shows routinely sell out (reservations can be made in advance, but are only guaranteed until 8.45pm), and comedians are encouraged to perform their edgiest material. Located in the back of the Lincoln Restaurant, the room itself feels like a second-tier supper club, complete with old-timey waitresses who call you 'honey'. Performers vary week to week, but you're guaranteed a few good sets at each show.

Playground Theater
3209 N Halsted Street, at W Belmont Avenue, Lakeview (1-773 871 3793/www.the-playground. com). El: Brown, Purple or Red to Belmont. **Shows** times vary, daily. **Tickets** free-$15. **Credit** Disc, MC, V. **Map** p329 F3.
This improv specialist features plenty of nascent troupes and even hosts something called the Incubator, where lonely improvisers pay a small fee to meet each other. Purely in terms of entertainment, it's a little hit and miss. That said, on a typical night, you can catch three or four different troupes each performing 30-minute long-form acts, one of which is bound to be funny. There are usually two shows a night, with three on Fridays and Saturdays (and one on Mondays).

INSIDE TRACK
GOING UNDERGROUND

One of the best places in town to uncover up-and-coming local comics is a music venue: the **Beat Kitchen** (*see p258*). The intimate Lakeview venue majors in music but gives over Tuesdays to **Chicago Underground Comedy** (www.chicago undergroundcomedy.com), a cheap-ass smörgåsbord of rising-star joke-throwers that always entertains.

★ Second City
1616 N Wells Street, at W North Avenue, Old Town (1-312 337 3992/www.secondcity.com). El: Brown or Purple to Sedgwick. **Shows** *Mainstage* 8pm Tue-Thur; 8pm & 11pm Fri, Sat; 7pm Sun. *Etc stage* 8pm Thur; 8pm & 11pm Fri, Sat; 7pm Sun. *Donny's Skybox* times vary. **Tickets** *Mainstage & Etc stage* $12-$25. *Donny's Skybox* $3-$12. **Credit** AmEx, Disc, MC, V. **Map** p327 G7.
The grandaddy of all comedy theatres and a temple of social-political satire, Second City is the brand name for funny business. Founded in 1959, it's a well-polished machine and a top tourist attraction. The city's top improvisers perform here, waiting to be snatched away by *Saturday Night Live* or *Mad TV*, but the humour is still cutting-edge: recent shows focused on the president (*Between Barack and a Hard Place*) and Illinois' disgraced governor (*Rod Blagojevich Superstar!*). A different and often gutsier revue plays on the Etc stage, with Donny's Skybox given over to student shows. Get there early on weekends or book ahead, as most shows sell out.
▶ *Mere steps away, the Old Town Ale House (see p179) has hosted countless Second City comics. Portraits of many alumni line the walls; you might find their successors at the bar post-show.*

Zanies
1548 N Wells Street, at W North Avenue, Old Town (1-312 337 4027/www.zanies.com). El:

Sketching Out Your Week

Our night by night guide to Chicago comedy.

With dozens of sketch comedy troupes appearing on stages all over town each week, it's near-impossible to figure out which shows are worth seeing, especially since so many are here today and gone tomorrow. But some shows have garnered enough belly laughs to become permanent fixtures on the scene. Here are our top picks.

On Monday, many theatres go dark, but the long-running (14 years and counting) **Armando Diaz Experience** at iO Chicago (*see p227*) sheds a little light on the city's scene. Each week, a single monologist recalls stories from his or her childhood based on an audience suggestion, while improvisers create scenes around these monologues to mesmerising effect.

On Tuesday, you can choose between **Chicagoland** at the Annoyance (*see p226*) or **Cook County Social Club** at iO (*see p227*). The former features a handful of the city's veteran improvisers; and the boys at CCSC aren't afraid to rock the boat with bold on-stage moves and untraditional scenic transitions.

When Wednesday rolls around, don't miss **TJ & Dave** at iO (*see p227*). Master improvisers TJ Jagodowski and David Pasquesi perfect the art of long-form improvisation in what many regard as the best show in town. Wednesday also offers a night of social-political satire on the **Second City Mainstage** (*see p228*), attended mostly by locals.

Devote your Thursday night to **Messing with a Friend** at the Annoyance (*see p226*). In this two-person show, Susan Messing invites a different improviser to perform a set with her each week. Messing's limitless bag of characters is reminiscent of a more disciplined Amy Sedaris; it's exciting – and rare – to see a show in which a female improviser dominates.

Hit the Apollo Theater (1-773 935 6100, 2540 N Lincoln Avenue, at Lill Avenue, Lincoln Park, www.apollo chicago.com) on Fridays for the fully improvised musical **Baby Wants Candy**. Improvisers perform a full-length musical (no joke) and the results are often jaw-droppingly impressive. Alternatively, hit the Chemically Imbalanced Theater (1420 W Irving Park, between N Janssen Avenue & N Southport Avenue, Wrigleyville, 1-773 865 7731, www.cicomedy.com) for **Pimprov**, improv with a gigolo twist.

The best improv on Saturday is **Whirled News Tonight** at iO (*see p227*), at which top-notch improvisers perform intelligent scenes based on news clippings ripped straight out of daily newspapers. If you're travelling with youngsters, the family-friendly comedy at the ComedySportz (*see p226*) includes early shows on Saturday night.

Save some comic appetite for the Sabbath. **Your Sunday's Best** at Schubas (*see p262*), ordinarily a music venue, is a fast-paced open-mic night frequented mostly by local stand-ups. Some are mediocre but others are amazing.

Brown or Purple to Sedgwick. **Shows** 8.30pm Mon-Thur, Sun; 8.30pm, 10.30pm Fri; 7pm, 9pm, 11.15pm Sat. **Tickets** $22-$50 (2-drink min). **Credit** MC, V. **Map** p327 G7.

Imagine a stand-up room, Zanies is what springs to mind – 'old school' suitably describes this local institution, where glossy black-and-white photos of visiting comics hang wall to wall and the crowd is skewed toward fortysomethings. Still, this oldie's still a goodie, booking established local comics and touring giants such as Richard Lewis, Will Durst and *Curb Your Enthusiasm*'s Susie Essman.

CLASSES

As the likes of Bill Murray and Chris Farley have graduated from the Chicago stage to the national TV screen, a few souls have sat in the

audience thinking 'I can do that'. Most can't, of course. But some venues offer courses to help wannabes improve at improv. Classes start at around $240 for an eight-week programme, though some of the theatres offer unpaid internships in exchange for free classes.

Second City (*see p228*) offers numerous classes in its Old Town space, from beginners' lessons to the Conservatory Level. Those more interested in long-form should try **IO Chicago** (*see p227*), which offers five tiers of classes alongside performance-level lessons. For *Whose Line is it Anyway?*-style laughs, head to **ComedySportz** of Chicago (*see p226*). **Annoyance Productions**, meanwhile, teaches its brand of offbeat and slightly offensive humour at its theatre (*see p226*).

Dance

Chicago's movers and shakers.

Chicago's dance scene is broad and diverse. Whether you're looking for experimental dance or traditional ballet, flamenco or *bharata natyam*, you'll find it here, particularly if you visit when the season is at its height between September and May.

Time Out Chicago and the *Chicago Reader* are best for listings and reviews; it's also worth checking the *Tribune* and the *Sun-Times*, and the searchable calendar at www.seechicagodance.com. For tickets, contact the theatres, Ticketmaster (*see p212*) or Ticketweb (www.ticketweb.com); for discounts, *see p232*. And for classes or studio space, go to www.chicagoartistsresource.org or www.takechicagodance.com.

About the author
Asimina Chremos is the Dance Editor of Time Out Chicago *and a member of the city's Lucky Plush troupe.*

MAJOR COMPANIES

★ Hubbard Street Dance Chicago
Information & tickets 1-312 850 9744/ www.hubbardstreetdance.com.
Founded in 1977 by jazz-dance choreographer Lou Conte, Hubbard Street has built up a deserved reputation as Chicago's premier dance company. Under the artistic direction of Jim Vincent from 2000 to 2009, the company entered the realm of contemporary dance with an international flavour, performing a repertoire that takes in works by the likes of Naharin, Forsythe and Duato. The group is often on tour, but performs annually at the Harris Theater for Music & Dance (*see right*).

★ Joffrey Ballet of Chicago
Information 1-312 739 0120/tickets 1-312 386 8905/www.joffrey.com.
One of the major American ballet companies, Joffrey emigrated to Chicago from New York in 1995. It's now resident at the Auditorium Theatre (*see right*), but also has a glamorous new offstage headquarters: the highrise Joffrey Tower on the north-east corner of State and Randolph. The troupe's eclectic repertoire is strong on American choreographers and reconstruction of Ballet Russe-era works.

Luna Negra Dance Theater
Information 1-312 337 6882/www.lunanegra.org.

Founded in 1999 by Cuban-born Eduardo Vilaro, this skilled, vibrant company creates and performs contemporary dance by Latino choreographers from the US and beyond. The repertoire includes choreography by José Limón and Stephanie Martinez.

Muntu Dance Theatre of Chicago
Information 1-773 241 6080/www.muntu.com.
This dynamic group is strongly connected to its South Side community, but also keeps ties with dancers and musicians in Africa. The company draws on traditional African and African-American dance and music to create new works, and is in the midst of a project to build its own arts centre.

River North Chicago
Information 1-312 944 2888/www.rivernorth chicago.com.
For 20 years, this hip and sexy touring troupe has created a trademark breezy style combining jazz and modern dance with a strong emphasis on accessibility. The current repertoire includes works by artistic director Frank Chaves as well as Robert Battle, Daniel Ezralow and Ginger Farley.

MAJOR VENUES

★ Athenaeum Theatre
2936 N Southport Avenue, at W Oakdale Avenue, Lakeview (1-773 935 6860/www.athenaeum theatre.com). El: Brown or Purple to Wellington.
Box office 3-7pm Tue-Fri. **Tickets** $15-$30.
Credit AmEx, Disc, MC, V. **Map** p329 D3.
Built in 1911 as a recreation centre for the German community, the 900-seat Athenaeum has old-

fashioned red velvet seats and a gilded ceiling with allegorical paintings. However, the rest of the building recalls one of its past lives as a girls' high school.
▶ *The main stage is used for the annual Dance Chicago in November; see p232.*

Auditorium Theatre
50 E Congress Parkway, at S Wabash Avenue, the Loop (1-312 922 2110/www.auditorium theatre.org). El: Blue or Red to Jackson; Brown, Orange, Pink or Purple to Library. **Box office** noon-6pm Mon-Fri. **Tickets** $25-$130. **Credit** AmEx, Disc, MC, V. **Map** p325 J13.
This gorgeous palace (*see p60*) is home to the Joffrey Ballet (*see left*), but also hosts an international dance series that includes world-class companies such as the Kirov Ballet. Depending on your cashflow and connections, you can find yourself sitting pretty in the orchestra or communing with the gods near the golden ceiling.

Dance Center of Columbia College
1306 S Michigan Avenue, at W 13th Street, South Loop (information 1-312 369 8300/tickets 1-312 369 6600/www.colum.edu/dance_center). El: Green, Orange or Red to Roosevelt. **Box office** 9am-5pm Mon-Fri. **Tickets** $15-$30. **Credit** AmEx, Disc, MC, V. **Map** p324 H15.
The only dance-dedicated theatre in Chicago is managed by the dance department of Columbia College, the city's most progressive centre for dance education. The programming reflects this, with appearances by touring and national artists mixed in with performances by local choreographers, faculty programmes and student workshops. The level of the touring work is high: in 2009, the modern 272-seat

centre hosted Delfos Danza Contemporenea from Mexico and the much-lauded New York-based Trisha Brown Dance Company, among others.
▶ *For Columbia College, see also p59 and p207.*

★ Harris Theater for Music & Dance
205 E Randolph Street, between N Stetson Avenue & N Columbus Drive, the Loop (1-312 334 7777/ www.harristheaterchicago.org). El: Brown, Green, Orange, Pink or Purple to Randolph/Wabash; Red to Lake. **Box office** noon-6pm daily. **Tickets** $20-$90. **Credit** AmEx, MC, V. **Map** p325 J12.
Completed in 2003 as part of the Millennium Park complex, this ultra-modern 1,500-seater can house large productions. The interior is pared-down and white, with Dan Flavin-esque neon lighting. Inside the vast theatre itself, sightlines are excellent. Most of Chicago's major dance companies perform here.

★ Links Hall
3435 N Sheffield Avenue, at N Clark Street, Wrigleyville (1-773 281 0824/www.linkshall.org). El: Red to Addison. **Box office** 9am-5pm Mon-Fri. **Tickets** $10-$15. **Credit** AmEx, MC, V. **Map** p329 E2.
Founded in 1979 by a group of choreographers, this intimate studio/theatre offers multidisciplinary programming that takes in a healthy portion of experimental dance by local and international artists.

Museum of Contemporary Art
220 E Chicago Avenue, at N Mies van der Rohe Way, Streeterville (1-312 280 2660/www.mca chicago.org). El: Red to Chicago. **Box office** 10am-8pm Tue; 10am-5pm Wed-Sun. **Tickets** free-$35. **Credit** AmEx, MC, V. **Map** p326 J10.

ARTS & ENTERTAINMENT

Compagnie Marie Chouinard, at the **Museum of Contemporary Art**.

The Seldoms.

The MCA's elegant theatre is set up perfectly for viewing dance: the 300-odd seats are arranged on a deep slope, starting at the same level as the stage and rising to look down on it. The programming is excellent: the MCA is one of the city's most important theatres for touring companies.

▶ *For more on the museum, see p81.*

Ruth Page Center for the Arts

1016 N Dearborn Avenue, at W Oak Street, Gold Coast (1-312 337 6543/www.ruthpage.org). El: Red to Clark/Division. **Box office** 9am-9pm daily. **Tickets** $10-$30. **Credit** MC, V. **Map** p326 H9.

Heiress, dancer and choreographer Ruth Page established this home for dance in the middle of the swanky Gold Coast. In addition to studios and a dance library, the building houses a 200-seat theatre, which is rented out to small- or medium- sized dance companies and independent choreographers.

FRINGE COMPANIES

Chicago has hundreds of smaller troupes that together make up a healthy fringe scene. Some aspire to the aesthetic of the more established companies, while others represent cultural diversity and/or artistic experimentation. All perform off the beaten path in smaller theatres; a few stage shows in unconventional locations.

Roving contemporary companies include the dancer-run collective **Same Planet Different World Dance Theatre** (www.spdwdance. org), which boasts a repertory of works by edgy young choreographers; **Thodos Dance Chicago** (www.thodosdancechicago.org), which showcases the talents of choreographer Melissa Thodos and develops its members' talents through its New Dances programme; and **Lucky Plush** (www.luckyplush.com), which features original, lush choreography with compelling imagery by artistic director Julia Rhoads and other interdisciplinary collaborators.

At the Chicago Cultural Center (*see p59*), look out for resident modern dance troupe **Hedwig Dances** (www.hedwigdances.com). Further north, the **Chicago Moving Company** (www.chicagomoving company.org) hosts an annual alternative dance festival every autumn at the Hamlin Park Field House (3035 N Hoyne Avenue, at W Berry Avenue).

Molly Shanahan (www.madshak.com) is one of the city's most compelling experimental choreograpgers; her solos, duets and works for small ensembles have gained recognition in Montreal and New York. **The Seldoms** (www.theseldoms.org), led by Carrie Hanson, offer intellectually stimulating dance-theatre with multidisciplinary components. And for something different, **Natya Dance Theatre** (www.natya.com) brings classical Indian *bharata natyam* into a contemporary context.

FESTIVALS

The big event on the calendar is **Dance Chicago** (www.dancechicago.com). Founded in 1995, the festival aims to highlight the quality and variety of local dance, and features local companies performing throughout November at the Athenaeum Theatre (*see p230*). Tickets are available from the Athenaeum box office.

During the summer, members of the public are invited to dig out their dancing shoes for **Chicago SummerDance** (www.cityofchicago. org/summerdance), a free festival held in a number of city parks (on a rotating basis) that invites the public to trip the light fantastic through a variety of dance styles. One-hour lessons in everything from ballroom dancing to Irish step-dance are followed by two hours of hoofing, often to live bands.

New on the scene is the **Chicago Dancing Festival** (www.chicagodancingfestival.com), a summer extravaganza of nationally recognised companies with several free events at Millenium Park in August.

INSIDE TRACK
CHEAP TICKETS

The website **seechicagodance.com** has a page titled Hot Deals, which offers codes you can use to get significant discounts off the price of tickets to performances when ordering online. You must become a member of the site to get these deals by offering an email address and mailing address... but if you'd like to forego offering your own information, simply sign in with the user name 'timeoutguest' and the password 'timeout'.

ARTS & ENTERTAINMENT

Film

Filmmakers and filmgoers both have reason to celebrate the Windy City.

Chicago has a long and storied movie history, both on and off the screen. It was the centre of production during the silent era; and, for decades, Chicago controlled the distribution side of the business. The cityscape has since lured filmmakers with its screen-friendly architecture and gritty landscape, playing in everything from *Call Northside 777* to *Ferris Bueller's Day Off*, *The Fugitive* to *The Dark Knight*.

The city once boasted some of the country's finest picture palaces downtown, and intimate neighbourhood mini-palaces all across the city. Regrettably, the downtown palaces have been shuttered or repurposed as theatre venues, while the Music Box is one of only a few surviving mini palaces still showing films. But the city still scores highly, offering a variety of idiosyncratic alternatives to the multiplex experience – you can watch movies in galleries, bars and museums, and even in an old bank.

CINEMAS

Weekly film listings are available in *Time Out Chicago* and at www.timeoutchicago/film, as well as in the *Chicago Tribune*, the *Chicago Sun-Times*, *RedEye* and the *Chicago Reader*. To buy tickets in advance, either visit the theatre in person, call the numbers listed below or visit the theatre's website. Parents should note that many Chicago movie theatres won't admit children under six years old after 6pm.

Mainstream & first-run

There are multiplexes galore dotted around the Chicagoland region; those listed below are among the best. The **Century 12** in Evanston is favoured by purists (the sound quality is excellent) and drivers (there's free parking across the street).

AMC Loews 600 N Michigan

N Michigan Avenue, entrance at N Rush Street & E Ohio Street, Magnificent Mile (1-312 255 9347/ www.amctheatres.com). El: Red to Chicago.

About the author
Hank Sartin *is the Film editor at* Time Out Chicago *magazine.*

Tickets $10.50; $8.50 before 6pm Mon-Thur, before 4pm Fri-Sun; $7.50-$9.50 discounts. **Credit** AmEx, Disc, MC, V. **Map** p326 J10.

★ AMC River East 21

322 E Illinois Street, at N Columbus Drive, Streeterville (1-312 596 0333/www.amctheatres. com). El: Red to Grand. **Tickets** $10.50; $8.50 before 6pm Mon-Thur, before 4pm Fri-Sun; $7.50-$9.50 discounts. **Credit** AmEx, Disc, MC, V. **Map** p326 J11.

★ Century 12 Evanston & CinéArts 6

1715 Maple Avenue, at Church Street, Evanston (1-847 491 9751/www.cinemark.com). El: Purple to Davis. **Tickets** $9.50-$10; $6.75 before 6pm Mon-Fri, before 2pm Sat, Sun; $5.50-$8.50 discounts. **Credit** MC, V.

Davis Theater

4614 N Lincoln Avenue, at W Montrose Avenue, Lincoln Square (1-773 784 0893/ www.davistheater.com). El: Brown to Montrose. **Tickets** $8; $5.50 before 6pm; $5.50 discounts. **Credit** AmEx, Disc, MC, V.

Kerasotes Webster Place 11

1471 W Webster Avenue, at N Clybourn Avenue, Lincoln Park (1-773 327 3100/www.kerasotes. com). El: Brown, Purple or Red to Fullerton.

Tickets $10.75; $8.75 before 6pm Mon-Thur, before 4pm Fri-Sun; $5 before noon Fri-Sun; $7.50-$9.75 discounts. **Credit** AmEx, Disc, MC, V. **Map** p328 D5.

Indie & revival

In addition to the theatres below, there are also regular screenings at venues as varied as the **Skokie Public Library** and the **Center on Halsted** (*see p249* **Center of Attention**).

Bank of America Cinema
4901 W Irving Park Road, at N Lamon Avenue, Irving Park (1-312 904 9442). Bus 54, 54A, 80. **Tickets** $5; $3 discounts. **No credit cards**.
Classic, vintage and forgotten films, including some silent movies, are given new life in the back of this old bank building on Saturdays at 8pm. The tickets are cheap, the retrospectives complete and scholarly, and the overall experience is terrific.

Block Cinema
Mary & Leigh Block Museum of Art, Northwestern University, 1967 S Campus Drive, Evanston (1-847 491 2448/www.blockmuseum. northwestern.edu). El: Purple to Davis. **Tickets** $6; $4 discounts. **No credit cards**.
This campus series screens an interesting mix of classic and contemporary films from around the world in a small but state-of-the-art facility. Programming is sometimes tied to art exhibits in the museum, and some screenings are introduced by Northwestern scholars. In summer, weather permitting, the series moves outdoors.
▶ *For the museum, see p98.*

Brew & View at the Vic
3145 N Sheffield Avenue, at W Belmont Avenue, Lakeview (1-773 929 6713/www.brewview.com). El: Brown, Purple or Red to Belmont. **Tickets** $5. **No credit cards**. **Map** p329 E3.
Some movies are better seen with a few drinks under your belt, and that's the mission of the Brew & View. Screenings of newish movies and older flicks cost five bucks, and pitchers of beer are cheap. If the mood takes you, follow the drunken crowd and start yelling retorts at the screen. The best seats are on the balcony.
▶ *The Vic also hosts concerts; see p257.*

Chicago Filmmakers
5243 N Clark Street, at W Berwyn Avenue, Andersonville (1-773 293 1447/www.chicago filmmakers.org). El: Purple or Red to Berwyn. **Tickets** $8; $7 discounts. **Credit** AmEx, Disc, MC, V.
This Andersonville set-up, one of two operations run by the not-for-profit Chicago Filmmakers enterprise, screens a selection of experimental films a few times a month (often with the filmmaker in attendance), with occasional screenings at other venues such as the Cinema Borealis in Wicker Park. The group also stages classes and workshops, and provides behind-the-scenes support for local moviemakers.

★ Doc Films, University of Chicago
Max Palevsky Cinema, Ida Noyes Hall, 1212 E 59th Street, at S Woodlawn Avenue, Hyde Park (1-773 702 8575/www.docfilms.uchicago.edu). Metra: 55th-56th-57th Street. **Tickets** $5. **No credit cards**. **Map** p323 Y18.
For serious film buffs, no trip to the city is complete without a pilgrimage to Hyde Park to catch a flick presented by Doc Films, where the eclectic programming is all over the cinematic map. 'Doc' is short for 'documentary', reflecting this film society's origins as the International House Documentary Film Group; founded in 1940 but with its origins eight years earlier, it's purportedly the longest-running student film society in the country. These days, the programme is wider: the range of titles, screened every night of the academic year at the 490-seat Max Palevsky Cinema, is a shrewdly selected mix of arthouse, cult and classic work during the week, balanced by more popular fare on weekends.
▶ *For more on UC, see p120.*

Facets Multimedia
1517 W Fullerton Avenue, at N Ashland Avenue, Lincoln Park (1-773 281 4114/www.facets.org). El: Brown, Purple or Red to Fullerton. **Tickets** $9. **Credit** AmEx, Disc, MC, V. **Map** p328 D5.
This no-nonsense, not-for-profit Lincoln Park venue has always been the place to go for low-budget American indies and foreign revivals, but it's recently shifted its focus to include more documentaries. The seats are a little hard on the back, but cinephiles don't mind putting up with it to see movies that would never

Profile Roger Ebert

The world's most famous film critic is still unstoppably prolific.

Never mind the tens of thousands of film reviews, the worldwide following and the Pulitzer Prize (the first awarded for film criticism). For many, Roger Ebert's name comes with an '&'. For years, it was Siskel & Ebert. Then it was Ebert & Roeper.

But for those who know Ebert well, there's another partnership, one that has been getting increasing public notice during his recent battle with cancer. For the last 16 years, it's been Roger & Chaz, as in Chaz Hammelsmith Ebert – his wife and, since Ebert lost the ability to speak after a tracheostomy in 2006, often his public voice. Sometimes he uses a voice-synthesising program to deliver short speeches. But freqeuntly, Chaz does the speaking for him as part of her increasingly visible role.

'We didn't sit down and say, "Let's be the public face of cancer or cancer survival or rehabilitation,"' says Chaz. 'It was to us more of a natural, organic outgrowth of how we are as people. Roger was always public and out there and enjoyed meeting people. He decided, why should this stop him?'

Being without a voice seems to have made Ebert all the more avid about writing. 'I started out by writing in the first person, and now I do it more strongly than ever. It's how I talk.' His direct, personal approach to criticism – in print and on television – has been the hallmark of his career. As if the remarkable volume of reviews wasn't enough, Ebert uses his blog (blogs.suntimes.com/ebert) to muse on everything from the Olympics' opening ceremony to his early days as a newspaperman.

Faced with serious health issues at age 66, some people might choose to take it easy. Not Ebert. 'Writing is my life's blood. I always said that I couldn't retire until I'd written a book about Scorsese. Now I have [*Scorsese by Ebert*, published in 2008] and I'm still not retiring.'

WHERE TO READ EBERT
Roger Ebert's reviews appear in the *Chicago Sun-Times* every Friday, and can be found online at http://rogerebert.suntimes.com.

ARTS & ENTERTAINMENT

Film

get screened at bigger venues. Many of the 40,000-plus titles housed in this esteemed video library are all but impossible to find elsewhere. The New French Cinema series (*see p237*) in December is a must.

Film Row Cinema

Columbia College, 1104 S Wabash Avenue, at W 11th Street, South Loop (no phone/www.colum. edu). El: Green, Orange or Red to Roosevelt. **Tickets** free. **No credit cards. Map** p324 H14. Columbia has been working hard to make its shiny new facility a destination with novelties such as the Cinema Slapdown, in which two 'experts' are brought in to argue pro and con for cult films such as *Bad Santa*. Screenings aren't on a set schedule, but it's worth checking Columbia's website – you never know when something amazing will appear, whether an advance screening of a new indie with the director in attendance or a revival of a rare experimental work.
▶ *For more on Columbia College, see p59* The Old College Try *and p207* Shop Class.

★ Gene Siskel Film Center

164 N State Street, at W Randolph Street, the Loop (showtimes 1-312 846 2800/office 1-312 846 2600/www.artic.edu/webspaces/siskelfilm center). El: Brown, Green, Orange, Pink or Purple to State; Red to Lake. **Tickets** $9; $7 discounts. **Credit** AmEx, MC, V. **Map** p325 H12.
The Siskel Center is named for the former *Tribune* critic who found national fame when TV producers paired him with *Sun-Times* critic Roger Ebert (*see p235* **Profile**). Though Siskel died in 1999, his spirit lives on in this refined, modern complex. The two state-of-the-art theatres, with some of the best projection equipment in the country outside New York and LA, feature experimental American work, new foreign movies, classic revivals, themed retrospectives and other festivals.

INSIDE TRACK
SIPPING AND SCREENING

Some movies are best seen with a good stiff drink in hand. Alas, most movie theatres in Chicago aren't allowed to serve alcohol, but a few do have drinkers' dispensation. **Brew & View at the Vic** (*see p234*) is the most obvious place to quaff while you watch, particularly for budget boozers. For something more highbrow, venture down to the classy **Gene Siskel Film Center** (*see p236*), which has a liquor licence: buy a beer at the concession stand and drink through some of the finest examples in world cinema. You can also catch movies at **Delilah's** (*see p179*), a bar that programmes a mix of weird '70s schlock and cool concert films.

Landmark's Century Centre Cinema

2828 N Clark Street, at W Diversey Parkway, Lakeview (1-773 509 4949/www.landmark theatres.com). El: Brown, Purple or Red to Belmont. **Tickets** $10; $8 before 5pm Mon-Fri, 1st show Sat, Sun; $8-$8.50 discounts. **Credit** AmEx, MC, V. **Map** p328 F4.
Though it's located in a yuppie mall, this seven-screen cinema concentrates on films at the artier end of the spectrum, and does a great job of screening them. Upon purchasing your ticket, ask the disillusioned but very funny and friendly punk-rock staff their opinion of the movie you're about to see.

★ Music Box

3733 N Southport Avenue, at W Waveland Avenue, Wrigleyville (1-773 871 6604/www. musicboxtheatre.com). El: Brown to Southport. **Tickets** $9.25; $8.25 1st show Mon-Thur. **Credit** MC, V. **Map** p329 D1.
The darling of Chicago movie houses, Music Box has two intimate theatres screening first-run arthouse and foreign films, supplemented by matinée and midnight screenings of everything from Marx Brothers classics to cheesy 1970s 3-D porn. But the vintage organ (sometimes employed to accompany silent films) and Moorish meets Tinseltown decor are even more memorable, with stars twinkling in the ceiling and projected clouds rolling by. The midnight shows offer old chestnuts of the midnight circuit (*Rocky Horror*, *The Warriors*) mixed with popular recent titles.

Navy Pier IMAX Theatre

600 E Grand Avenue, at Lake Michigan, Streeterville (1-312 595 5629/www.imax.com/ chicago). El: Red to Grand. **Tickets** *IMAX films* $11; $9-$10 discounts. *Other* $15; $13-$14 discounts. **Credit** AmEx, MC, V. **Map** p326 K10.
When it comes to cinema, bigger does not always equal better – the projection is great, but this theatre can feel a little soulless. Still, this IMAX set-up persists in its programme of large-format movies, some of which can be spectacular. Alongside the obligatory nature films and high-budget animations, the cinema also screens occasional 35mm blockbusters.
▶ *The Omnimax Cinema at the Museum of Science & Industry (see p121) offers similar fare.*

FILM FESTIVALS

As befits a city with such a long and illustrious cinematic history, Chicago abounds with film festivals of all stripes. The biggest and the best are detailed below, listed in chronological order. However, there are many others throughout the year, including a plethora of outdoor screenings in summer and a programme of experimental short films screened as part of September's **Around the Coyote** festival in Wicker Park (*see p216*). Check *Time Out Chicago* each week for details.

ARTS & ENTERTAINMENT

Gene Siskel Film Center.

European Union Film Festival
Gene Siskel Film Center; details p236 (1-312 846 2600/www.siskelfilmcenter.org). **Date** Mar.
This expertly vetted showcase of new European works runs for a good portion of March each year.

Chicago Asian American Showcase
Gene Siskel Film Center; details p236 (1-312 846 2600/www.faaim.org). **Date** Apr.
This two-week event offers an eclectic selection of features, docs and films by or about Asian-Americans.

Chicago Latino Film Festival
Various venues (1-312 431 1330/www.latino culturalcenter.org). **Date** Apr-May.
Established in 1984, the two-week CLFF is usually the strongest of the city's ethnic film festivals.

Onion City Experimental Film & Video Festival
Various venues (1-773 293 1447/www.chicago filmmakers.org). **Date** June.
Sponsored by Chicago Filmmakers (*see p234*), this weekend-long event is a bit more earnest and cerebral than its psychotronic cousin, the Chicago Underground Film Festival (*see below*).

★ Chicago Outdoor Film Festival
Grant Park; details p55 (1-312 744 3315/www. cityofchicago.org/specialevents). **Date** July-Aug.
This ever-popular series offers screenings every Tuesday each summer. If you don't want to be stuck behind a pole or thousands of people, arrive hours ahead of time, drop a blanket and get picnicking.

Black Harvest International Festival of Film & Video
Gene Siskel Film Center; details p236 (1-312 846 2600/www.siskelfilmcenter.org). **Date** Aug.
Filmmakers and artists attend screenings at Chicago's annual two-week showcase for films that explore or celebrate black culture around the world.

★ Chicago International Film Festival
Various venues (1-312 683 0121/www.chicago filmfestival.org). **Date** Oct.
Truly international in scope, the oldest competitive film festival in North America programmes over 100 features and documentaries, making it an appealing compromise between the dauntingly comprehensive Toronto International Film Festival and the hyper-exclusive New York Film Festival. Most screenings are at the AMC River East 21 (*see p233*) and the AMC Loews 600 N Michigan (*see p233*).

Chicago International Children's Film Festival
Facets Multimedia; details p234 (1-773 281 9075/www.cicff.org). **Date** Oct-Nov.
Presented annually by Facets but with regular screenings further afield, this ten-day event is the largest children's film festival in North America.

Chicago Underground Film Festival
Viaduct Theatre, 3111 N Western Avenue, at W Fletcher Street, Roscoe Village (www.cuff.org).
Date Oct-Nov.
Transgression, subversion and complete indifference to mainstream production values are the order of the day at this hard-partying, week-long film and video fest. Leave the kids at home.

Reeling: The Chicago Gay & Lesbian International Film Festival
Various venues (1-773 293 1447/www.reeling filmfestival.org). **Date** Nov.
Chicago Filmmakers' ten-day production is the second-oldest gay film festival in the US.

New French Cinema
Facets Multimedia; details p234 (1-773 281 9075/www.facets.org). **Date** Dec.
Facets presents this carefully curated ten-day round-up of new Gallic moviemaking, putting an emphasis on films that haven't played the festival circuit.

Galleries

Apartment studios and recent graduates make for an approachable scene.

Chicago is a rare city where galleries don't make you feel unwelcome – even in the event that you have no intention of dropping tens of thousands on an artwork your mother wouldn't understand. Many of the emerging artists whose work you'll see here recently graduated from prestigious masters' programmes at the **School of the Art Institute of Chicago (SAIC)**, **Columbia College** or the **University of Illinois at Chicago (UIC)**. Some bide their time until they're famous enough to move to New York or LA, but others have no intention of leaving, having noted the success of longtime locals such as Kerry James Marshall. The city's most upscale galleries show a mix of Chicago stalwarts and international stars, while apartment galleries in artists' homes will connect you with the alternative scene.

ARTS & ENTERTAINMENT

COMMERCIAL GALLERIES

The **West Loop** is your safest bet for a satisfying art walk, but slightly more staid **River North** (near the intersection of Superior and Franklin Streets) always has several worthwhile shows at any one time. Smaller, edgier spaces, some in artists' apartments (*see p240*), are scattered throughout the city.

Pick up a copy of *Time Out Chicago* for reviews and listings, and see www.timeout chicago.com/art for more on the local scene. *Chicago Gallery News* (www.chicagogallery news.com), a free glossy available at many galleries, offers helpful maps of the city's various art districts.

Gallery hours often change; call ahead to check. New shows usually open with public receptions on Friday or Saturday nights, which are a blast and often attended by the artists.

River North

In 1976, about a dozen pioneering galleries settled in River North, an area previously dominated by factories and warehouses. Dealing in everything from mid-century to contemporary American art, they thrived until 1989, when a fire that wrecked several galleries led some to flee the area for the West Loop. Plenty of galleries remain, most of them open 11am-5pm (if not later) from Tuesday to Saturday. The best are detailed below; we've omitted those that cater to wealthy older couples looking for art to match their new sofas.

Start at 311 W Superior Street, at Orleans Street. Run by the former director of the Milwaukee Art Museum, **Russell Bowman Art Advisory** (Suite 115, 1-312 751 9500,

About the author

As Time Out Chicago*'s Art & Design Editor*, **Lauren Weinberg** *reviews exhibitions, mocks ugly condos and searches for new ways to explain performance art. She also writes for* ARTNews.

> ### INSIDE TRACK
> ### MAJOR GALLERIES
>
> Major art museums and non-commercial galleries are listed on the following pages:
> **Art Institute of Chicago** *p56*
> **Arts Club of Chicago** *p81*
> **Loyola University Museum of Art** *p79*
> **Mary & Leigh Block Museum of Art** *p98*
> **Museum of Contemporary Art** *p81*
> **Museum of Contemporary Photography** *p61*
> **National Museum of Mexican Art** *p106*
> **National Vietnam Veterans' Art Museum** *p71*
> **Renaissance Society** *p121*
> **Smart Museum of Art** *p124*
> **Ukrainian Institute of Modern Art** *p110*

www.bowmanart.com) presents the cream of the mid-century to contemporary crop. It hosted Kiki Smith's first solo show in Chicago, with life-sized bronze sculpture and nature-oriented prints. Also here are **Stephen Daiter** (Suites 404 & 408, 1-312 787 3350, www.stephendaiter gallery.com), which specialises in documentary photography, and **Printworks** (Suite 105, 1-312 664 9407, www.printworkschicago.com), which carries prints and other works on paper by artists at all stages of their careers.

Across the street at 300 W Superior Street, **David Weinberg Gallery** (Suite 203, 1-312 529 5090, www.davidweinberggallery.com) runs solid exhibitions of contemporary photography and painting; **Catherine Edelman Gallery** (1-312 266 2350, www.edelmangallery.com) is a reliable source of intriguing photography; and **Judy Saslow** (1-312 943 0530, www.jsaslow gallery.com) specialises in self-taught or 'outsider' artists, especially popular in Chicago. For such a well-heeled address, **Zg Gallery** (1-312 654 9900, www.zggallery.com) comes off as unusually young and cheeky.

A few blocks north-east, **Roy Boyd Gallery** (739 N Wells Street, at W Chicago Avenue, 1-312 642 1606, www.royboydgallery.com) mainly highlights abstract painting by local legends such as William Conger. The exceptional roster of 20th-century and contemporary artists at the nearby **Carl Hammer Gallery** (740 N Wells Street, at W Chicago Avenue, 1-312 266 8512, www.hammergallery.com) ranges from forgotten outsiders to icons such as cartoonist Chris Ware, who lives in Oak Park.

INSIDE TRACK IN THE LOOP

Most of the notable art in the Loop is found at the **Art Institute of Chicago** (*see p56*) and in the streets (for a tour of the area's best public art, *see p62*). However, there is one commercial gallery worth a look: **Donald Young** (Suite 266, 224 S Michigan Avenue, 1-312 322 3600, www.donaldyoung.com), one of the best (and unfortunately, snootiest) places to see art in the city. Come here for museum-quality new work by critical darlings such as Josiah McElheny, Rodney Graham and Mark Wallinger.

The Magnificent Mile

The majority of the 'galleries' on Michigan Avenue just want to sell you Obama tat, but the **John Hancock Center** (875 N Michigan Avenue, at E Delaware Place; *see p79*) does contain two major exceptions. **Richard Gray** (Suite 2503, 1-312 642 8877, www.richardgraygallery.com) has been promoting outstanding contemporary art for decades; he was an early supporter of the likes of David Hockney and Jaume Plensa, the creator of Millennium Park's beloved *Crown Fountain*. **Valerie Carberry** (Suite 2510, 1-312 397 9990, www.valeriecarberry.com) showcases post-war American artists with a Chicago connection.

Carl Hammer Gallery.

The North Side

The North Side lacks a critical mass of galleries, but the spaces here are special – and normally only open on the weekend. **Audible at ESS** (5925 N Ravenswood Avenue, at Thorndale Avenue, 1-773 769-1069, www.exsost.org), located in the Experimental Sound Studio, is the only gallery in Chicago that specialises in sound art. The young, well-connected co-directors of **Golden** (No.1, 816 W Newport Avenue, at N Halsted Street, 1-773 209 8889, www.golden-gallery. org) might show artists from Finland one month, and others from School of the Art Institute of Chicago (SAIC) the next. And the exhibitions at **Art on Armitage** (4125 W Armitage Avenue, at Kedvale Avenue,

Home Is Where the Art Is

For Chicago's cutting edge, head not to a gallery but a local apartment...

Old Gold.

Chicago's ample real estate, relatively low cost of living and ready supply of emerging artists are the three essential ingredients for the city's apartment gallery scene. These spaces are labours of love for their young proprietors – it figures that anyone who is willing to give up their weekends and their bedrooms in the name of art will be thrilled to discuss their shows with all-comers. All the same, call or double-check the hours online before you visit in case they've changed.

Bill Gross started **65Grand** (1378 W Grand Avenue, at N Noble Street, www. 65grand.com; noon-5.30pm Fri, Sat) in his kitchen before relocating it to two rooms in his West Town apartment, where he now shows a mix of painting and sculpture. A mile north in Wicker Park is the **Lloyd**

Dobler Gallery (2nd floor, 1545 W Division Street, at Milwaukee Avenue, 1-312 961 8706, www.lloyddoblergallery.com; 6-9pm Thur, noon-5pm Sat), named after John Cusack's endearing character in *Say Anything* and founded by two recent SAIC graduates.

Steadily gentrifying Logan Square is home to **Mini Dutch** (1st floor, 3111 W Diversey Parkway, at Troy Street, 1-773 235 5687, www.minidutchgallery.org; 11am-3pm Sun) and the recently relocated **Old Gold** (3102 W Palmer Street, at N Whipple Street, www.oldgoldexhibitions andevents.com; hours vary). Both have been around for a few years, and both present an appealing mix of popular up-and-coming Chicago artists and surprisingly well-known outsiders.

Other apartment galleries are open to the public for raucous receptions or by appointment only. On the South Side, Bridgeport's **Second Bedroom Project Space** (Apt 4R, 3216 S Morgan Street, at 32nd Place, 1-630 849 7750, www. secondbedroomproject.blogspot.com) is run by curators with a strong sense of humour. They recently expanded the gallery to include **Medicine Cabinet** (www.the-medicine-cabinet.blogspot.com), a venue that specialises in dioramas – in their bathroom.

Serious art fans should consider making a pilgrimage to Oak Park, where galleries **Shane Campbell** (125 N Harvey Avenue, at W North Avenue, 1-630 697 0609, www.shanecampbellgallery.com) and **the Suburban** (244 W Lake Street, at N Wells Street, 1-708 763 8554, www.the suburban.org) host some of the brightest art stars in the US. **He Said-She Said** (831 S Grove Avenue, at S Canal Street, 1-708 310 2607, www.hesaid-shesaid.us) also stages phenomenal solo shows by artists from outside Chicago.

Moniquemeloche.

1-773 235 8583, www.artonarmitage.com) are always on view – the 'gallery' is a ground-floor window display.

The West Loop

It's more than a decade since the first galleries trickled into the West Loop. The area still feels gritty, but it's a magnet for exceptional contemporary art. Most galleries are open Wednesday to Saturday from noon to 5pm, if not later and/or more often; call to check.

Start at 835 W Washington Street, just west of Halsted Street. While the group shows at **Carrie Secrist** (1-312 491 0917, www.secristgallery.com) tend to include almost every medium, the **McCormick Gallery** (1-312 226 6800, www.thomasmccormick.com) focuses on Abstract Expressionist painting. The founder of **Kavi Gupta Gallery** (1-312 432 0708, www.kavigupta.com) organises the chic Volta art fair, and the paintings, videos and installations on display are some of the trendiest the US and Europe have to offer. **Andrew Rafacz Gallery** (1-312 404 9188, www.andrewrafacz.com) also shows a cool mix of young artists, many from Chicago.

Just north of Washington Street, there's plenty to see at 118 N Peoria Street. **Rhona Hoffman** (1-312 455 1990, www.rhoffman gallery.com) shows excellent work by both 20th-century masters such as Sol Lewitt and Fred Sandback and breakout stars like Mickalene Thomas. **Moniquemeloche** (1-312 455 0299, www.moniquemeloche.com)

displays hip conceptual installations and videos with substance. The **Walsh Gallery** (1-312 829 3312, www.walshgallery.com) seems to be the only place in Chicago that regularly promotes contemporary art from India and China. And the **Peter Miller Gallery** (1-312 951 1700, www.petermillergallery.com) presents contemporary art – mostly painting – from around the country. Down the block, **GR N'Namdi** (110 N Peoria Street, at Washington Boulevard, 1-312 563 9240, www.grnnamdi. com) highlights some of the nation's best-known black artists.

Across the street at 119 N Peoria, a crew of sophisticated gallery directors produce exhibitions that are both fun and intellectually rigorous. The not-for-profit **ThreeWalls** (Suite 2D, 1-312 432 3972, www.three-walls.org) alternates edgy group shows and solo

INSIDE TRACK
FIRST THURSDAYS

Bribing people is the Chicago way. On the first Thursday of every month (except January), the **Art Dealers Association of Chicago** (1-312 649 0065, www. chicagoartdealers.org) offers free snacks and booze at galleries in River North (W Superior Street, between Orleans & Wells Streets) and the West Loop (W Washington Boulevard, at Peoria Street). The venues remain open until 7pm.

residencies, while **Western Exhibitions** (Suite 2A, 1-312 480 8390, www.western exhibitions.com) and **Tony Wight Gallery** (Suite 2C, 1-312 492 7261, www.tonywight gallery.com) emphasise young and mid-career avant-garde artists who work in painting, printmaking and video.

Not sated yet? Walk north to **Thomas Robertello** (939 W Randolph Street, at Sangamon Street, 1-312 421-1587, www.thomas robertello.com) and **Packer Schopf** (942 W Lake Street, at Morgan Street, 1-312 226 8984, www.packergallery.com). Both specialise in contemporary American art, as do nearby **Kasia Kay** (1044 W Fulton Market, at Aberdeen Street, 1-312 492 8828, www.kasia kaygallery.com) and **Linda Warren Gallery** (1052 W Fulton Market, at Aberdeen Street, 1-312 432 9500, www.lindawarrengallery.com).

Pilsen

Pilsen is the traditional home of Chicago's Mexican artists, who made the politically oriented murals that tie the community together. Miguel Cortez has fostered tech-savvy and socially conscious art for several years and continues to do so at **Antena** (1765 S Laflin Street, at 18th Street, www.ante napilsen.com). Don't leave the neighbourhood without browsing the posters, books and other goods at **No Coast** (1500 W 17th Street, at Laflin Street, 1-312 850 2338, www.no-coast. org) and **Golden Age** (1744 W 18th Street, at Wood Street, 1-312 850 2574, www.shopgolden age.com). Nearly all of their funky products

are made by artists, many of them locals, and they're shockingly affordable.

Unfortunately, the so-called 'Chicago Arts District' at Pilsen's eastern edge, south of UIC, has fewer worthwhile venues than its name suggests. One of the best is **Vespine** (1st floor, 1907 S Halsted, at W 19th Street, www.vespine. org), which specialises in works on paper and artists' books.

West Town & Wicker Park

A number of not-for-profit galleries dot the neighbourhoods north of the West Loop scene. West Town's **ARC Gallery** (832 W Superior Street, suite 204, at N Green Street, 1-312 733 2787, www.arcgallery.org) and **Woman Made Gallery** (685 N Milwaukee Avenue, at Erie Street, 1-312 738 0400, www.womanmade.or) are both of a feminist bent.

Heading north, **Roots & Culture Contemporary Art Center** (1034 N Milwaukee Avenue, at W Cortez Street, 1-773 235 8874, www.rootsandculturecac.org) and **Alogon Gallery** (3rd floor, 1049 N Paulina Street, at W Cortez Street, www.alogon gallery.com) champion emerging artists. The subversive **Heaven Gallery** (1550 N Milwaukee Avenue, at N North Avenue, no phone, www.heavengallery.com) and **Around the Coyote** (1815-25 W Division Street, at N Honore Street, 1-773 342 6777, www.around thecoyote.org) are Wicker Park institutions, though the latter still takes flak for moving its 20-year-old annual art fairs (*see p216*) out of the hopelessly gentrified locale.

The area's commercial galleries share their neighbours' commitment to strong work; take **Corbett vs Dempsey** (3rd floor, 1120 N Ashland Avenue, at W Haddon Avenue, 1-312 278 1664, www.corbettvsdempsey.com), which unearths neglected 20th-century artists with a Chicago connection. Fine contemporary art is always on view at **Shane Campbell** (1431 W Chicago Avenue, at N Bishop Street, 1-312 226 2223, www.shanecampbellgallery.com), which has an annex in Oak Park (*see p113*).

The nearby neighbourhood of **East Garfield Park** marks the new frontier of Chicago's ever-changing art scene. **Devening Projects + Editions** (3039 W Carroll Avenue, at N Whipple Street, 1-312 420 4720, www. deveningprojects.com) makes the trek to its desolate industrial block worthwhile with thoughtful exhibitions, most frequently of prints and other works on paper. Down the street, the young artists who run **Julius Caesar** (3144 W Carroll Avenue, at N Albany Avenue, www.juliuscaesarchicago.com) show impressive paintings, sculptures and videos by their art-school classmates and instructors.

INSIDE TRACK
HAYMARKET MEMORIAL

In the West Loop, be sure to visit Chicago artist Mary Brogger's evocative **Haymarket Memorial** (N Desplaines Street, at Randolph Street). The bronze sculpture, which was commissioned by the city and completed in 2004, marks the precise spot where the 1886 Haymarket riot occurred – a protest by striking workers that turned violent when a bomb was thrown at police, killing officers and protesters. Brogger places faceless workers on a stylised wagon symbolising the one used by the anarchist protesters; some figures appear to be in the midst of fiery speeches. The cement pedestal is covered with a curious mix of plaques donated by trade unions – including one from Iraqi oil workers – alongside anarchist graffiti.

Gay & Lesbian

The third coast in the Second City comes first for queer life.

To the casual queer observer, miles upon miles of cornfields may not look like they lead to much. But when those barren interstates lead to a thriving, thumping metropolis that's home to more than 400,000 corn-fed homos, the pancake-flat prairie suddenly doesn't seem so bad after all. Chicago continues to be a 'mo mecca for people in the LGBT community seeking escape from the conservative confines of middle America, as well as coastal queers wanting the comforts of urban life in an attitude-free zone.

And why wouldn't they? Chicago's own **Boystown** contains more than 20 nightlife venues within a five-block radius; mega-watt festivals such as International Mr Leather and Northalsted Market Days continue to draw thousands from all over the world; and the city's benevolent dictator – that would be Mr Richard M Daley – proudly caters to his LGBT constituents by giving full support to same-sex marriage.

GAY NEIGHBOURHOODS

A subsection of Lakeview bordered by Addison Street to the north, Broadway to the east, Belmont Avenue to the south and Halsted Street to the west, **Boystown** is the city's out and proud, feather-boa-wearin' gaybourhood; indeed, the name is now officially recognised by the city. Broadway is best for shopping and dining, while Halsted Street's bar scene delivers a host of party palaces.

Andersonville, an old Swedish enclave to the north, is Chicago's other key gay area. The queer scene here has its origins in the 1990s, when lesbians dug it for its low-key vibe and cheap rents. The boys soon followed; today, it's a laid-back if slightly smug enclave of trendy restaurants, gay hangouts and furniture stores, all centred along Clark Street.

While Boystown and Andersonville scream 'queer', gay life thrives all over town. **Wicker Park**, **Ukrainian Village** and **Pilsen** are all meccas for alterna-queers who eschew gay-identified bars in favour of metrosexual hipster hangouts, while an older crowd can be found in

River North and **Lincoln Park**. Muggings sometimes occur and homophobia still exists outside the gay enclaves, but most problems are verbal and generated by out-of-towners.

Cruising is common in Chicago. Popular haunts include Lincoln Park (the park itself, not the yuppie neighbourhood); you can also score pretty much anywhere from Montrose Harbour up to the Hollywood Beach (also an excellent gay beach by day). If a car flashes its lights at you or a furtive glance is cast your way, you're

---

About the author
Jason A Heidemann *is the Gay & Lesbian editor at* Time Out Chicago, *and has co-authored and contributed to seven guidebooks.*

INSIDE TRACK SOUTH SIDE

Andersonville and Boystown tend to hog the spotlight, but there's also a queer scene on Chicago's massive South Side. Both **InnExile** (5758 W 65th Street, at S Menard Avenue, 1-773 582 3510, www.innexilechicago.com) and **Jeffrey Pub** (7041 S Jeffery Boulevard, at E 71st Street, 1-773 363 8555) are aimed at the African-American crowd. And just over in Blue Island, **Club Krave** (1326 Western Avenue, 1-708 597 8379) caters to South Siders and suburbanites with retro dance parties, barbecues and bingo nights.

in business. But the Chicago police are no fools: either head somewhere else with your new-found friend or make sure that you conduct yourselves with discretion.

LESBIAN LIFE

The easiest way for girls to come out of the closet is to walk into the **Closet** (*see p247*) on Broadway, or to take the Red line to Berwyn and head into **Andersonville**. **T's Bar & Grill** (*see p247*) shines brightest, boasting the biggest diversity of babes and a bodacious patio, while classy dykes should try lesbian wine bar **Joie de Vine** (*see p246*).

In general, though, you'll fare better at the city's weekly and monthly events. **FKA** at **Big Chicks** (*see p246*) brings in hot ladies and trans men on the first Thursday of the month for a sweaty night of drinking and dancing. **Chances**, a queer dance party at Subterranean (2011 W North Avenue, at N Damen Avenue, Wicker Park, 1-773 278 6600, www.subt.net), draws a pretty even male/female mix, as does its sibling party **Off-Chances** at Danny's Tavern (*see p184*). The regular girlie parties hosted by ChixMix and Girlbar (of LA fame) at **Circuit** (*see p251*) are worth a look, as is **Femistry Fridays**, a monthly party aimed at black women (see www.bblyss.com).

THE QUEER CALENDAR

Gays, straights and more or less everyone in between jam Boystown during the first weekend in June for **Pride** (www.chicagopride calendar.org). The whole month is dotted with Pride-related events, leading up to a weekend of partying and Sunday's huge Pride Parade.

Six weeks later, the largest street festival in the Midwest rolls into Boystown: **Northalsted Market Days** (www.northalsted.com), staged over the first weekend in August on Halsted

between Belmont and Addison. It's basically a two-day outdoor gay bar with bands, DJs and street vendors galore.

For **Reeling**, the annual gay film festival, *see p237*.

INFORMATION & MEDIA

Time Out Chicago lists plenty of gay events each week. In addition, the vestibule of any eaterie or meeterie in Andersonville and Boystown will have high-rise stacks of the multifarious gay freesheets.

The *Chicago Free Press* and the *Windy City Times*, twin sufferers of an acrimonious media divorce, delve into local and national issues while also including all-important nightlife information. *Nightspots*, with its compact map and addresses of manjoints, fits snugly into a back pocket. *Boi* contains listings, fluff pieces and occasional articles on abs or amphetamines. *Gay Chicago* has full listings. And quarterly *Pink* magazine is the glossiest of them all, supplementing generally well-written articles with a queer business directory.

Online, the city has become a hotbed of queer podcasting: check out the wildly popular **Feast of Fools** (www.feastoffools.net), musical podcast **Think Pink Radio** (www.thinkpink radio.com) and the **Daily Purge** (www.the dailypurge.net), among others.

Consume

RESTAURANTS & CAFES
Andersonville

★ Anteprima

5316 N Clark Street, between W Summerdale Avenue & W Berwyn Avenue (1-773 506 9990/www.anteprimachicago.net). El: Red to Berwyn. **Open** 5.30-10pm Mon-Thur; 5.30-11pm Fri, Sat; 5.30-9.30pm Sun. **Main courses** $20. **Credit** AmEx, Disc, MC, V.

This place is quickly becoming everyone's new favourite neighbourhood restaurant, thanks to rustic, home-style dishes that are perfectly executed and reasonably priced and servers that are refreshingly attentive. Local homos come there to impress their visiting friends and relatives.

Francesca's Bryn Mawr

1039 W Bryn Mawr Avenue, at N Sheridan Road (1-773 506 9261/www.miafrancesca.com). El: Red to Bryn Mawr. **Open** 11.30am-2pm, 5-9pm Mon; 11.30am-2pm, 5-9.30pm Tue-Thur; 11.30am-2pm, 5-10.30pm Fri; 5-11pm Sat; 5-9pm Sun. **Main courses** $22. **Credit** AmEx, Disc, MC, V.

**INSIDE TRACK
THE MAYOR OF BOYSTOWN**

It's true: Chicago's gaybourhood has its very own mayor. Except that he's self-appointed and no one really understands what he does. In 2001, Seattle native **Bill Pritchard** (then 32) moved to Chicago in 2001 and annointed himself as B-town's unofficial king. Hubristic? Perhaps, but he's a likeable enough guy. And as Senior Vice-President of Community Affairs for www.chicago pride.com, an LGBT website, he promotes his mission of 'making a difference'.

ARTS & ENTERTAINMENT

Hamburger Mary's.

There are a dozen or so versions of this hip Italian hangout in Chicagoland, but only this one is nick-named Mancesca's. You can't swing a fettuccini noo-dle without hitting same-sex couples chowing down good pasta, or (less frequently) large parties of gup-pies ordering tons of vino and checking out both the daily specials and the handsome waitstaff.

Hamburger Mary's
5400 N Clark Street, at W Balmoral Avenue (1-773 784 6969/www.hamburgermarys.net). El: Red to Bryn Mawr. **Open** 11am-11pm Mon-Fri; 10am-11pm Sat, Sun. **Main courses** $10. **Credit** AmEx, Disc, MC, V.
Chicago gets its very own version of the queer ham-burger chain. The burgers come in every combina-tion of ingredients (Buffy the Hamburger Slayer, anyone?) and are quite tasty. Supplement them with beer, before your bill arrives in a high heel.
▶ *Upstairs, Mary's Attic is a casual cocktail spot.*

Jin Ju
5203 N Clark Street, at W Foster Avenue (1-773 334 6377/www.jinjuchicago.com). El: Red to Berwyn. **Open** 5-9.30pm Tue, Wed; 5-10.30pm Thur; 5-11.30pm Fri, Sat. **Main courses** $15. **Credit** AmEx, Disc, MC, V.
Brick walls and a subdued sexiness draw a mixed crowd, who nibble on fiery spare ribs (you must) and sip Sojutinis, a potable crafted with a Korean grain liquor that's made from sweet potatoes (again, you must). Finish with the ginger ice-cream.

★ M Henry
5707 N Clark Street, at W Hollywood Street (1-773 561 1600/www.mhenry.net). El: Red to Bryn Mawr. **Open** 7am-2.30pm Tue-Fri; 8am-3pm Sat, Sun. **Main courses** $10. **Credit** AmEx, MC, V.
Come the weekend, you can't get through the door here. However, you'll still want to try to make an entrance, simply to taste the most scrumptious blue-berry and walnut pancakes this side of the Mississippi. The wait can be long, but it's a friendly queue full of attractive possibilities.

Tweet
5020 N Sheridan Road, at W Argyle Avenue (1-773 728 5576/www.tweet.biz). El: Red to Argyle. **Open** 9am-3pm Mon, Thur, Sat, Sun; 9am-3pm, 7-10pm Fri. **Main courses** $10. **No credit cards**.
Michelle Fire's Uptown brunch spot serves up slam-min' helpings of breakfast favourites, with a won-derful coffee-cake *amuse-bouche* to start. Most of the food is made with organically grown and locally pro-duced ingredients, and the clientele is über-queer. The restaurant recently started opening for dinner.

Boystown

Ann Sather
909 W Belmont Avenue, between N Clark Street & N Sheffield Avenue (1-773 348 2378/ www.annsather.com). El: Brown, Purple or Red to Belmont. **Open** 7am-3pm Mon-Fri; 7am-4pm Sat, Sun. **Main courses** $10. **Credit** AmEx, MC, V. **Map** p329 E2.
Known for its sticky buns, this hospitable, gay-run Swedish enclave has been around for half a century. The place is cheap, cosy and, despite its Nordic roots, emphatically all-American in its cuisine. Ann Sather's owner, Tom Tunney, was elected as the city's first openly gay alderman in 2003.
Other locations 3411 N Broadway, Boystown (1-773 305 0024); 3416 N Southport Avenue, Lakeview (1-773 404 4475); 5207 N Clark Street, Andersonville (1-773 271 6677).

Caribou Coffee
3300 N Broadway, at W Aldine Avenue (1-773 477 3695/www.cariboucoffee.com). El: Brown, Purple or Red to Belmont. **Open** 5.30am-11.30pm Mon-Thu; 5.30am-midnight Fri; 6.30am-midnight Sat; 7am-11pm Sun. **Credit** AmEx, Disc, MC, V. **Map** p329 F2.
Caribou has multiple locations, but this branch – aka Cruisabou – is in the heart of Boystown. Come here to chat with your mates, but look elsewhere if you're looking to… well, look elsewhere.

Halsted's
3441 N Halsted Street, at W Newport Avenue (1-773 348 9696/www.halstedschicago.com). El:

ARTS & ENTERTAINMENT

Red to Addison. **Open** 5pm-midnight Mon-Thur; 5pm-1am Fri; 11am-1am Sat; 11am-3pm, 11am-midnight Sun. **Main courses** $15. **Credit** AmEx, Disc, MC, V. **Map** p329 F2.

The servers are flighty and the hours are erratic. But on the plus side, multiple TVs mean you can watch the newest Beyoncé video, the football game and CNN while simultaneously eating respectable bar food. As an added bonus, the backyard patio is brilliant when the weather's warm.

Home Bistro Chicago

3404 N Halsted Street, between W Roscoe Street & W Newport Avenue (1-773 661 0299/www.homebistrochicago.com). El: Red to Addison. **Open** 5.30-10pm Tue-Thur; 5-10.30pm Fri, Sat; 5-9pm Sun. **Main courses** $20. **Credit** AmEx, Disc, MC, V. **Map** p329 F1.

There's almost nothing but tables for two in this cramped Boystown spot. Just make sure you get the seat facing the window, so your partner has his eyes on you and not the boys on Halsted. Dig into new American dishes such as cider-brined loin of pork or slow-cooked chicken *harira*. A $30 three-course *prix fixe* is offered on Wednesdays.

Intelligentsia

3123 N Broadway, between W Barry Street & W Briar Place (1-773 348 8058/www.intelligentsiacoffee.com). El: Brown, Purple or Red to Belmont. **Open** 6am-10pm Mon-Fri; 7am-10pm Sat, Sun. **Credit** AmEx, Disc, MC, V. **Map** p329 F3.

Putty-toned walls, soothing tunes, scattered-pattern seating, Adirondack chairs out front in summer… yep, it's Boystown's very own independent coffeehouse, popular with the anti-Starbucks crowd. **Other locations** throughout the city.

Kit Kat Lounge & Supper Club

3700 N Halsted Street, at W Waveland Avenue (1-773 525 1111/www.kitkatchicago.com). El: Red to Addison. **Open** 5.30pm-2am Tue-Sun. **Main courses** $20. **Credit** AmEx, Disc, MC, V. **Map** p329 F1.

Get ready for diva overload at Boystown's boisterous cocktail joint. The martini list is exhaustive (root beer float martini, anyone?), and on Sundays and Tuesdays they're all half-off. But it's the ebullient female impersonators that make this a favourite among gays, bachelorettes and even straight dudes. The sidewalk patio is among the best in B-town.

Melrose

3233 N Broadway, at W Melrose Street (1-773 327 2060). El: Brown, Purple or Red to Belmont. **Open** 24hrs daily. **Main courses** $10. **Credit** MC, V. **Map** p329 F2.

It's 4am, you're mid-hangover, and there's a frighteningly tall pile of greasy food staring you in the face. It really doesn't get much better than this.

Besides, the Melrose is your last chance to decide if that bar pick-up sitting across from you is really worth the trouble of taking home.

Nookies Tree

3334 N Halsted Street, at W Buckingham Place (1-773 248 9888/www.nookiesrestaurant.net). El: Brown, Purple or Red to Belmont. **Open** 7am-midnight Mon-Thur, Sun; 24hrs Fri, Sat. **Main courses** $10. **Credit** MC, V. **Map** p329 F2.

March in here for munchies, brunchies and grilled American cheese sandwiches. It's an inevitable, even obligatory destination, and right on the Boystown strip; pretty well everybody goes there, night and day, and so should you. There are two other branches, but this one's got the gaydar.

Other locations Nookies, 1746 N Wells Street, at W St Paul Avenue, Old Town (1-312 337 2454); Nookies Too, 2114 N Halsted Street, at W Dickens Avenue, Lincoln Park (1-773 327 1400).

★ Ping Pong

3322 N Broadway, at W Buckingham Place (1-773 281 7575/www.pingpongrestaurant.com). El: Brown, Purple or Red to Belmont. **Open** 5pm-midnight daily. **Main courses** $15. **Credit** AmEx, Disc, MC, V. **Map** p329 F2.

Several years ago, restaurateur Henry Chang doubled the size of his pint-sized Asian eatery. Since then, it's been the most happening restaurant on Broadway. Every gay in town heads here with a date or a group of mates to chow down on succulent Chinese classics and an ever-evolving cocktail menu (BYOB is also allowed, with $5 corkage).

► *If you're not in the mood to stand and model for A-list gays, check out Chang's impressive sushi joint Wakamono across the street.*

BARS

Andersonville

★ Big Chicks

5024 N Sheridan Road, at W Argyle Avenue (1-773 728 5511/www.bigchicks.com). El: Red to Argyle. **Open** 4pm-2am Mon-Fri; 10am-3am Sat; 10am-2am Sun. **No credit cards.**

This charming speakeasy-style saloon is more akin to an East Village hangout than it is to a Chicago joint. Owner Michelle Fire doles out shots at midnight and rolls out an all-you-can-eat Sunday buffet at no charge. The clientele is a mixed bag of scruffy neighbourhood locals, relaxed twentysomethings and lesbians on the loose. Everyone gets along, especially on the tiny, packed dancefloor.

Joie de Vine

1744 W Balmoral Avenue, at N Ravenswood Avenue (1-773 989 6846). Bus 22. **Open** 4pm-midnight Mon-Thur; 4pm-2am Fri; 4pm-3am Sat; 4pm-midnight Sun. **Credit** AmEx, Disc, MC, V.

Hotel Homo

Where to hit the hay in Boystown and beyond.

Provincetown this ain't. But if you're looking to stay gay on the third coast, you do have a few options. In the heart of Boystown, the **Villa Toscana** (3447 N Halsted Street, at W Cornelia Avenue, 1-773 404-2643, www.thevillatoscana.com, $99-$159) offers an unbeatable location smack in the middle of the 'hood; enjoy breakfast on the sundeck during the summer months while the city hums around you. Also in the area, neither the **Best Western Hawthorne Terrace** (3434 N Broadway, at W Hawthorne Place, 1-773 244 3434, www.hawthorneterrace.com), or **City Suites** (*see p144*) are exclusively gay, but proximity to Boystown guarantees a homo-heavy clientele.

Further north on the tree-lined streets of Edgewater, **Ardmore House** (1248 W

Ardmore Avenue, at N Magnolia Avenue, 1-773 728 5414, www.ardmorehousebb.com, $99-$179) is a gay-owned bed and breakfast. It's admittedly a ten-minute cab ride to Boystown but just a stone's throw from Andersonville and über-gay Hollywood Beach.

And to the west, the five-room **Ashland Arms** (6408 N Clark Street, at W Devon Avenue, 1-312 498 9979, www.ashlandarms.com, $99-$250) entices the fetish and kink community with themed guestrooms, including the leather, bunk and rubber rooms. The Ashland is located above Jackhammer bar (*see p248*) and Mephistor Leathers, and the owners go out of their way to make sure guests have all the fetish gear they desire.

Romantics will quickly fall in love with this lesbian wine bar, where flickering candles and soft house music are combined with international wines and some light bites. Most nights, it's just a regular bar, popular with oenophiles of all orientations. But on weekends, it looks like a casting call for *The L Word*.

Marty's
1511 W Balmoral Avenue, at N Clark Street (1-773 561 6425). El: Red to Berwyn. **Open** 5pm-2am daily. **No credit cards**.
Sure, it's teeny tiny, but the forty-plus crowd can't get enough of this classic cocktail joint. No thumping music, no whiny twentysomethings: just spot old-fashioned martinis, the kind your boozy great aunt drank back in the '40s. The bar staff are handsome, attentive and know everybody's name.

★ T's Bar & Grill
5025 N Clark Street, between W Winnemac Avenue & W Argyle Street (1-773 784 6000/ www.tsbarchicago.com). El: Red to Argyle. **Open** 5pm-2am Mon-Fri; 11am-3am Sat; 11am-2am Sun. **Credit** AmEx, Disc, MC, V.
T's isn't exclusively lesbian, but you wouldn't know it by the throngs of women that have christened this bar and grill the best lady hangout in town. Boys congregate in the front room, but this is Sappho territory.

Boystown

★ Closet
3325 N Broadway Street, at W Buckingham Place (1-773 477 8533). El: Brown, Purple or Red to Belmont. **Open** 5pm-4am Mon-Fri; noon-5am Sat; noon-4am Sun. **No credit cards**. **Map** p329 F2.

This Lilliputian bar, a safe stone's throw away from the hustle and muscle of Halsted Street, is the perfect place to have a beer with the ladies while watching the straight folk push their strollers down Broadway. Things really get rolling after 2am on weekends, when boys and girls mix as easily as a vanilla-chocolate swirl ice-cream.

Cocktail
3359 N Halsted Street, between W Roscoe Street & W Buckingham Place (1-773 477 1420/ www.cocktailbarchicago.com). El: Brown, Purple or Red to Belmont. **Open** 4pm-2am Mon-Fri; 2pm-3am Sat; 2pm-2am Sun. **Credit** AmEx, Disc, MC, V. **Map** p329 F2.
A much-needed facelift helped catapult this corner taproom into the 21st century. Go-go boys rule the stage here almost every night; they're awfully flirty, so bring singles. Otherwise, Cocktail is a low-key if perpetually bustling place in which to loosen the tie and throw down some Long Islands.

Minibar
3341 N Halsted Street, between W Roscoe Street & W Buckingham Place (1-773 871 6227/www.minibarchicago.com). El: Red to Addison. **Open** 5pm-2am Mon-Fri; 11am-3am Sat; 11am-2am Sun. **Credit** AmEx, Disc, MC, V. **Map** p329 F2.
Hold your martini glass and your nose up in the air at this tiny jet-set lounge for the pretentious and beautiful. Music is kept to a low roar, which enables conversation, and the bar staff are beautiful. Penny-pinchers should head elsewhere.
▶ *While you're here, check out the wine bar and tasting lounge next door.*

ARTS & ENTERTAINMENT

Roscoe's

3356 N Halsted Street, at W Roscoe Street
(1-773 281 3355/www.roscoes.com). El: Red to
Addison. **Open** 3pm-2am Mon-Thur; 2pm-2am
Fri; 1pm-3am Sat; 1pm-2am Sun. **Admission**
$5 after 10pm Sat. **Credit** Disc, MC, V.
Map p329 F2.

This horny Gen-Y romper room has everything a
queer kid could ask for, including drinks specials,
loads of cute boys and plenty of entertainment courtesy of Chicago's 'finest' drag queens. It's a lovely
tavern, with loads of exposed brick, a cosy outdoor
patio, and plenty of nooks and crannies for making
out in. Expect queues on weekends.

★ Scarlet Bar

3320 N Halsted Street, at W Buckingham Place
(1-773 348 1053/www.scarletbarchicago.com)
El: Brown, Purple or Red to Belmont. **Open**
6pm-2am Mon-Wed; 4pm-2am Thur, Fri, Sun;
4pm-3am Sat. **Credit** AmEx, Disc, MC, V.
Map p329 F2.

The community was devastated when this attitude-
free newcomer suffered a fire just one year after
opening in 2008. But the bar promises to come back
stronger than ever, which should hopefully mean the
return of the insanely popular Frat Boy Thursdays
and the edgier Art Haus Mondays.

★ Sidetrack

3349 N Halsted Street, at W Roscoe Street
(1-773 477 9189/www.sidetrackchicago.com).
El: Red to Addison. **Open** 3pm-2am Mon-Fri,
Sun; 3pm-3am Sat. **Credit** AmEx, Disc, MC, V.
Map p329 F2.

This juggernaut of a bar is famous not just in
Boystown but across the US. Stare at videos or stare
at men in any number of rooms, including the cavernous glass bar, the sparkling roof deck or a new
addition that the locals are affectionately calling 'new
bar'. Showtune nights (Sun, Mon) are legendary –
and participatory, so be warned. Girls are welcome,
but will find themselves in the minority. *Photo p250.*

Elsewhere

Crew Bar & Grill

4804 N Broadway Street, between W Lawrence
Avenue & W Gunnison Street, Uptown (1-773
784 2739/www.worldsgreatestbar.com). El: Red
to Lawrence. **Open** 11.30am-midnight Mon-Thur;
11.30am-2am Fri; 11am-2am Sat; 11am-midnight
Sun. **Credit** MC, V.

Sports bar Crew has broken away from the
Boystown pack with a novel Uptown location, a
crowd that's welcoming to men and women, and fun
monthly parties such as Frat Boy Fridays.
► *The owners also run the nearby Wild Pug*
(4810 N Broadway Street, at W Gunnison Street,
1-773 784 4811), a Brit-themed queer pub that's
chatty in front and clubby in back.

★ Jackhammer

6406 N Clark Street, between W Devon
Avenue & W Schreiber Avenue, Rogers Park
(1-773 743 5772/www.jackhammer-chicago.com).
Bus 22. **Open** 4pm-4am Mon-Fri; 2pm-5am Sat;
2pm-4am Sun. **Credit** AmEx, Disc, MC, V.

This sprawling bar and dance club in the far North
Side draws a mix of adventurous Boystowners,
leather folk and thirtysomethings on the prowl. The
main room is dominated by a dancefloor; once a
month, it hosts Flesh Hungry Dog Show, a queer
rock cabaret. The upstairs lounge is all about kicking back with a beer; the downstairs Hole bar
devotes itself to hardcore cruising and most nights
is dress code-enforced.

Manhandler Saloon

1948 N Halsted Street, between W Armitage
Avenue & W Wisconsin Street, Old Town
(1-773 871 3339). El: Brown or Purple to
Armitage. **Open** noon-4am daily. **No**
credit cards. **Map** p328 F6.

If someone had managed to cryogenically freeze the
1970s gay life and then defrost it in the 21st century,
it would look a lot like this place. Located amid aromatherapy shops and yuppie bistros, Manhandler
Saloon is a dimly lit watering hole that is the kind
of place where old men stare at you too long. Still,
it's nice to come here to imagine those heady days
of gay lib when moustaches and short shorts ruled,
and safer sex was still light years away.

SHOPS & SERVICES

Andersonville

For queer-friendly bookstore **Women &**
Children First, *see p193*.

Early to Bed

5232 N Sheridan Road, between E Foster
Avenue & E Berwyn Avenue (1-773 271 1219/
www.early2bed.com). El: Red to Berwyn. **Open**
noon-7pm Tue; noon-9pm Wed-Fri; noon-8pm
Sat; noon-6pm Sun. **Credit** AmEx, Disc, MC, V.

Chicago would be full of grumpy and undersexed
queer (and straight) ladies if not for this local institution. Stock up on all your favourite harnesses, dil-
dos and battery-operated goodies, and feel free to
ask the staff *anything* while you're at it.

His Stuff

5314 N Clark Street, between W Summderdale
Avenue & W Berwyn Avenue (1-773 989 9111/
www.hisstuffchicago.com). El: Red to Berwyn.
Open 11am-9pm Mon-Fri; 11am-7pm Sat;
noon-6pm Sun. **Credit** AmEx, Disc, MC, V.

In case anybody needed the final and definitive
proof that Andersonville has gentrified, this haber-
dasher offers an undeniably stylish choice of
menswear for the modern homo.

Center of Attention

Chicago's gay community welcomes a new Boystown hub.

In 2007, a brand new LGBT community centre was unveiled in Boystown. Such initiatives are usually worthwhile, important and, to be honest, not terribly exciting. The **Center on Halsted** (3656 N Halsted Street, at W Addison Street, 1-773 472 6469, www.centeronhalsted.org), however, is a little different from the usual well-intentioned community project.

For starters, it's quite a looker. The Center was built above an old art deco parking structure; elements of the old building remain artfully intact, but there's now a sleek modern façade built over it. The building sits at the intersection of Halsted and Addison, and reveals itself with conspicuous pride through three storeys of floor-to-ceiling windows. The Center is also a LEED-certified building, meeting high standards on environmental friendliness. Tours are offered once a month (check online for a schedule); alternatively, visit during summer to admire the building and its stellar views from the lovely rooftop garden.

As hard economic times force belt-tightening around town, several local theatre groups have taken shelter inside the Center's 161-seat black-box performance space, the Hoover-Leppen Theater. **GayCo**, the city's only all-queer sketch comedy troupe, appears regularly; so do **About Face Theatre** (www.aboutface theatre.com), which remains committed to enhancing dialogue on issues of sexual orientation and gender identity. The Hoover-Leppen also offers an all-inclusive worship service each Sunday.

It took a ton of cash to make the Center happen – $40 million, to be exact – and it couldn't be done alone. That's why the south wall of the Center is joined to a branch of all-conquering chain Whole Foods. An entryway between the two spaces encourages a flow of people from one building to the other; not only is the selection of food impressive, the cruising is relentless. Indeed, this may be the only Whole Foods in Chicago where the produce isn't the number one draw.

Sidetrack. *See p248.*

ARTS & ENTERTAINMENT

Boystown

For the **Unabridged Bookstore**, which stocks gay and lesbian literature, *see p192.*

Batteries Not Included

3420 N Halsted Street, between W Roscoe Street & W Newport Avenue (1-773 935 9900/ www.toysafterdark.com). El: Brown, Purple or Red to Belmont. **Open** 11am-midnight Mon-Thur, Sun; 11am-1am Fri; 10am-2am Sat. **Credit** AmEx, MC, V. **Map** p329 F2.

They don't call Batteries Not Included bachelorette party headquarters for nothing. This cheerful adult toy store and novelty shop rules with ladies, but its Boystown location ensures that boys make a mad dash here when they're out of condoms and lube.

Beatnix

3400 N Halsted Street, at W Roscoe Street (1-773 281 6933). El: Red to Addison. **Open** noon-8pm Mon-Thur, Sun; 11am-10pm Fri, Sat. **Credit** MC, V. **Map** p329 F2.

This vast vintage store in the middle of Boystown is a favourite clothes closet for club kids, drag queens, bull dykes and muscle boys. It offers a sexy selection of tuxes (the queers must cater, you know) and a cute vortex in the corner devoted to wigs.

Gay Mart

3457 N Halsted Street, at W Cornelia Avenue (1-773 929 4272). El: Red to Addison. **Open** 11am-7pm Mon-Thur, Sat; 11am-8pm Fri; noon-6pm Sun. **Credit** Disc, MC, V. **Map** p329 F2.

The gaudy and goofy rooms here are overflowing with gay-themed cards, novelties, jewellery and stuff adorned with rainbows and schlongs. Shop 'til you drop your inhibitions and then cross over to Hydrate (*see p251*) for a drink.

Universal Gear

3153 N Broadway, between W Belmont Avenue & W Briar Place (1-773 296 1090/www.universal gear.com). El: Brown, Purple or Red to Belmont. **Open** 11am-9pm Mon-Thur; 11am-10pm Fri, Sat; 11am-8pm Sun. **Credit** AmEx, Disc, MC, V. **Map** p329 F3.

Pretty boys do the folding in this menswear-only shop, which hawks threads from the likes of Diesel, Energie and Modern Amusement, as well as more underwear than you could sniff in a lifetime.

Arts & Entertainment

BATHHOUSES & BOOTHSTORES

Andersonville

Man's Country

5015 N Clark Street, at W Argyle Street (1-773 878 2069/www.manscountrychicago.com). El: Red to Argyle. **Open** 24hrs daily. **Admission** $10 lifetime member. **No credit cards.**

This Andersonville bathhouse, which bills itself as 'more fun than a barrel of hunkies', contains three floors of nakedness, with singles, doubles and fantasy rooms. It's a bit worn around the edges, but it's taken over the space of the old Chicago Eagle, and renovation and expansion is underway.

Boystown

Leather Sport
3505 N Halsted Street, at W Brompton Avenue (1-773 868 0914). El: Red to Addison. **Open** 11am-midnight daily. **Admission** free. **Map** p329 F1.
The friendly dudes working the counter at this leather fetish emporium are helpful and sex-positive, and the vast selection of leather fetish gear, sex toys and jock straps is impressive, to say the least.

Steamworks
3246 N Halsted Street, between W Belmont Avenue & W Melrose Street (1-773 929 6080/ www.steamworksonline.com). El: Brown, Purple or Red to Belmont. **Open** 24hrs daily. **Admission** $5 one-mnth membership; $14-$17 lockers; $20-$55 room rentals. **Credit** AmEx, MC, V. **Map** p329 F2.
Some 70 private rooms, a gym, a sauna, gang showers, a jacuzzi and hot hunks galore. The attitude quotient can be high, especially on weekends, but furry guys are in vogue during the monthly Bears, Bath & Beyond party.

Elsewhere

Bijou Theater
1349 N Wells Street, at W Evergreen Avenue, Old Town (1-312 943 5397/www.bijouworld. com). El: Brown or Purple to Sedgwick; Red to Clark/Division. **Open** 24hrs daily. **No credit cards. Map** p327 H8.
Owned and operated by porn producer Steven Toushin since 1970, this pioneering establishment screens dirty movies in a Victorian townhouse. It sounds slightly quaint, until the hardcore flicks and exotic dancers unreel and undress.

NIGHTCLUBS
The venues below are specifically gay-oriented, but many other clubs are also big with queers; chief among them is **Berlin** (*see p272*), a huge part of the local scene. Queues are long at weekends, Sundays are a local favourite, and on Tuesdays everybody stays in and rents a DVD.

Boystown

Charlie's
3726 N Broadway, at W Waveland Avenue (1-773 871 8887/www.charlieschicago.com). El: Red to Addison. **Open** 3pm-4am Mon-Fri, Sun; 3pm-5am Sat. **Admission** free-$20. **Credit** AmEx, MC, V. **Map** p329 F1.

If you don't know how to dance country style, head down to Charlie's – lessons are held several nights a week. But it's not homos doin' the hoedown that pack this queer country club: it's the circuit queens and the style-conscious who join the queues around 2am, when the crowds ditch their cowboys hats in exchange for some high-energy fun.

Circuit
3641 N Halsted Street, at W Addison Street (1-773 325 2233/www.circuitclub.com). El: Red to Addison. **Open** 9pm-4am Thur, Fri; 10pm-5am Sat; 7pm-4am Sun. **Admission** $5-$15. **Credit** AmEx, Disc, MC, V. **Map** p329 F1.
This venerable club has had its fair share of woes, including a dispute with local condo dwellers that gave it a bruising some years back, but it still knows how to churn out a late-night dance party. Latin men dish and dance together on Thursdays and Sundays, while hip hop homos and lady-lovin' ladies each get a monthly party of their own.

Hydrate
3458 N Halsted Street, between W Cornelia Avenue & W Newport Avenue (1-773 975 9244/www.hydratechicago.com). El: Brown, Purple or Red to Belmont. **Open** 8pm-4am Mon-Fri, Sun; 8pm-5am Sat. **Admission** $3-$10 Fri, Sat. **Credit** MC, V. **Map** p329 F2.
Hydrate manages to lure some of the city's best DJs for its wildly busy after-hours scene, but there's plenty going on here every night, including the Hydrag review on Wednesdays, a Latin night on Tuesdays and a lube-wrestling contest the first Friday of every month.

Spin
800 W Belmont Avenue, at N Halsted Street (1-773 327 7711/www.spin-nightclub.com). El: Brown, Purple or Red to Belmont. **Open** 4pm-2am Mon-Fri; 2pm-3am Sat; 2pm-2am Sun. **Admission** free-$5. **Credit** MC, V. **Map** p309 F2.

INSIDE TRACK
SCREEN QUEENS

Indie queer cinema thrives in the Windy City. **Threat Level** is an evening of queer shorts, held bimonthly at the Elegant Mr Gallery (www.elegantmrgallery.com) in Wicker Park; hosted monthly at Chicago Filmmakers (*see p234*), **Dyke Delicious** offers lesbian moviemaking. Head to **Landmark's Century Centre Cinema** (*see p236*) to catch more mainstream indie fare. And don't miss **Reeling** (*see p237*), the city's annual festival of gay and lesbian cinema.

INSIDE TRACK PARTY PEOPLE

In Chicago, finding the coolest queer parties is all about knowing who the best promoters are. While you're in town, keep your ears pricked for names such as **Scott Cramer** (www.myspace.com/scottcramer), **Jenae Williams**, **Bobby Pins** (www.myspace.com/b_pins) and **Social Flare Productions** (www.myspace.com/socialflareprod), which produces interesting event nights for Chicago's women.

This video bar and dance club was looking a little worn until it bought the building next door and transformed itself into a mega-watt dance club and lounge. The new space is pumping out high-energy dance music on weekends, while the dollar drink night on Wednesdays is nearly an institution.

THEATRE & PIANO BARS

For **Jackhammer**, which hosts queer-oriented indie-rock night Flesh Hungry Dog Show on the third Friday of each month, *see p248.*

Baton Lounge

436 N Clark Street, between W Illinois Street & W Hubbard Street, River North (1-312 644 5269/www.thebatonshowlounge.com). El: Brown
or Purple to Merchandise Mart; Red to Grand. **Shows** 8.30pm, 10.30pm, 12.30am Wed-Sun. **Admission** $10-$15 (2-drink min). **Credit** Disc, MC, V. **Map** p326 H10.

Chicago's prime drag venue allows only pre-ops to perform; these quasi-queens are so strut-alicious that straight men, as well as gay men's moms, have been known to swoon. Clap your mitts for Mimi Marks, the Marilyn Monroe-esque belle of the circuit ball, and don't miss October's Miss Continental Pageant.

Homolatte

Big Chicks, 5024 N Sheridan Road, between Argyle Street & W Carmen Avenue, Uptown (1-773 728 5511/www.homolatte.com). El: Red to Argyle. **Open** 1st & 3rd Tue/mth. **Admission** free. **No credit cards**.

With performances by, for and about word-hungry queers, this weekly showcase of gay, lesbian and transgendered musicians and writers is hosted by Scott Free, the angry, talented one-time falsetto soprano for the Lavender Light Gospel Choir.

3160

3160 N Clark Street, between W Fletcher Street & W Belmont Avenue, Lakeview (1-773 327 5969/www.chicago3160.com). El: Brown, Purple or Red to Belmont. **Shows** times vary; call for details. **Admission** free. **Map** p329 F3.

Homos wept when both of the city's queer piano bars (Gentry on State and Gentry in Boytown) finally closed for good, but this out-of-the-way cabaret is making nice with musical homos by presenting a nonstop barrage of crooners and ivory ticklers.

Spin. *See p251.*

Music

From grand opera to scuzzy rock – and, yes, the blues…

Covering grand old concert halls and grimy blues clubs, Chicago's musical past is famous and oft-documented. With good reason, too; it's a story worth telling. The present, though, is just as interesting. The classical music and indie-rock scenes continue to satisfy, much as they've done for decades, while the blues is a tourist industry in its own right. Yet much of the most interesting stuff is happening on the fringes: from intriguing electronica to freeform jazz, avant-garde classical ensembles to shape-shifting rock sounds, Chicago's music scene doesn't want for innovation.

ARTS & ENTERTAINMENT

Classical & Opera

Chicago's classical music scene starts with the **Chicago Symphony Orchestra** and the **Lyric Opera of Chicago**, which both cling to stellar national reputations and draw enormous crowds. However, there's more to the scene than these two big players. The wealth of smaller ensembles includes **Music of the Baroque** (www.baroque.org) and **Eighth Blackbird** (www.eighthblackbird.com), which join the cutting-edge **Chicago Opera Theater** (www.chicagooperatheater.org) at the Harris Theater; the **Chicago Sinfonietta** (www.chicagosinfonietta.org), which offers creatively programmed shows at Dominican University and Orchestra Hall; and the all-female **Orion Ensemble** (www.orionensemble.org) and the **Chicago Chamber Musicians** (www.chicagochambermusic.org), which stage imaginative chamber music shows. Contemporary music has a strong following thanks to the likes of **Dal Niente** (www.dalniente.com), **Fulcrum Point** (www.fulcrumpoint.org), the **International Contemporary Ensemble** (www.iceorg.org) and the CSO's youthful MusicNOW series, which allows ticketholders to mingle with composers and musicians. Also boasting plenty of fans is **WFMT** (98.7 FM), the city's beloved classical station.

About the author
Bryant Manning *(Classical & Opera) writes about classical music for* Time Out Chicago *and the* Chicago Sun-Times. **Brent DiCrescenzo** *(Rock & Roots, Blues & Jazz) is the Music Editor of* Time Out Chicago *magazine.*

INFORMATION & TICKETS

Tickets for the CSO, Lyric Opera and Ravinia are sold at their respective box offices and by **Ticketmaster** *(see p212)*; try to book ahead, as many concerts are part of subscription series and sell out ahead of time. Tickets may not be sold in advance for smaller chamber concerts. The selection of free and cheap events is rich throughout the year, especially at the Chicago Cultural Center. For information on concerts, check the weekly *Time Out Chicago* magazine.

VENUES

★ Civic Opera House
20 N Wacker Drive, at E Madison Street, the Loop (1-312 419 0033/www.lyricopera.org). El: Brown, Green, Orange or Purple to Washington. **Box office** *noon-6pm Mon-Fri.***Tickets** *$40-$170.* **Credit** *AmEx, Disc, MC, V.* **Map** *p325 G12.*
As soon as you clap eyes on the elegant architecture and opulent lobby at this hall, built by Samuel Insull in 1929 *(see pp21-22)*, you'll realise that subtlety isn't the order of the day at the Civic Opera House. The prestigious Lyric Opera of Chicago has made its home

---

INSIDE TRACK HALLELUJAH!

Every December, the Civic Opera *(see right)* hosts the **Do-It Yourself Messiah**, a Chicago tradition in which have-a-go locals join a local orchestra of amateurs in a rousing rendition of Handel's classic. Tickets are free, but you'll need to book your place in advance.

here since 1954, and now presents eight productions each season. It's regularly ranked as one of the top opera companies in the country, boasting a talented stable of singers alongside an excellent orchestra under the musical direction of Sir Andrew Davis (formerly of the BBC Symphony Orchestra), and is also seen as one of the most traditional in terms of both repertoire and style of production. However, the last few years have seen the company stage a handful of more unexpected operas – John Adams' brand new *Doctor Atomic*, Gershwin's *Porgy and Bess* – with astounding success. And the numbers speak for themselves: on average, the company draws in excess of 90% capacity, no mean feat in a room that holds 3,500.

Ganz Hall at Roosevelt University

430 S Michigan Avenue, at E Van Buren Street, the Loop (1-312 341 3780/www.roosevelt.edu). El: Blue or Red to Jackson; Brown, Orange, Pink or Purple to Library. **Tickets** *usually free.* **No credit cards. Map** p325 J13.
Formerly a hotel banqueting hall and a masonic lodge, this impressive space now stages recitals by student and faculty members at Roosevelt's Chicago College of Performing Arts, alongside regular concerts by visiting soloists and ensembles. The acoustics lend every instrument a rich resonance.

★ Harris Theater

Millennium Park, 205 E Randolph Drive, at N Columbus Drive, the Loop (1-312 334 7777/ www.harristheaterchicago.com). El: Brown,

Green, Orange, Pink, Purple to Randolph/ Wabash. **Box office** *noon-6pm Mon-Fri.* **Tickets** *$25-$120.* **Credit** *AmEx, MC, V.* **Map** p325 J12.
The sleek Harris Theater prides itself on being the area's least pretentious theatre for brand-name acts. The home of numerous forward-thinking new music groups (Fulcrum Point New Music Project, Eighth Blackbird), the Chicago Opera Theater and the Chicago Symphony's MusicNOW series, the Harris is the city's best mainstream-alternative hall, if that's not a contradiction in terms. The theatre's mostly underground design means concertgoers have to walk up and down several flights of stairs to enter and leave, though the dificult-to-locate elevators do provide an alternative.
► *The Harris also hosts dance and ballet troupes such as Hubbard Street Dance Chicago and Garth Fagan Dance; see pp230-232.*

Ravinia Festival. *See p256.*

Lyon & Healy Hall

168 N Ogden Avenue, at W Randolph Street,
West Loop (1-800 595 4849/www.lyonhealy.com/
hall). El: Green or Pink to Ashland. **Box office**
from 6.45pm on performance nights. **Tickets**
$30. **Credit** Disc, MC, V. **Map** p330 D11.
A 200-capacity hall housed in (and run by) the Lyon
& Healy harp factory, this relatively recent addition
to the local music scene is highlighted by its unusual
design: the stage is backed by a huge window that
affords concertgoers breathtaking views of downtown. The music's pretty good, too: L&H's own
recitals series includes some impressive names, and
many local musicians also rent the space and stage
their own independent concerts.

Mandel Hall

1131 E 57th Street, at S University Avenue,
Hyde Park (1-773 702 8069/http://music.
uchicago.edu). Metra 55th-56th-57th Street. **Box**
office times vary; call for details. **Tickets** $5-
$35. **No credit cards. Map** p332 X17.
Part of the University of Chicago, the distinguished,
century-old Mandel Hall plays host to internation-
ally recognised string quartets, opera singers (in
recital) and early music groups. Many of today's
classical stars, among them violinist Hilary Hahn,
made their Chicago debuts here.
▶ *UC also stages occasional concerts in the lovely*
Rockefeller Memorial Chapel; see p122.

Merit School of Music, Gottlieb Concert Hall

38 S Peoria Street, between W Monroe & W
Madison Streets, West Loop (1-312 786
9428/www.meritmusic.org). El: Blue to UIC-
Halsted. **Box office** times vary; call for details.
Tickets free-$20. **Credit** varies. **Map** p330 F12.
This cosy 372-seat hall, which opened in 2005 at a
local music college, has been embraced by the city's
chamber ensembles: the Rembrandt Chamber
Players, Chicago a cappella and the Chicago
Chamber Musicians have all played here in recent
times. The near-downtown location is a boon both
to musicians and concertgoers.

Pick-Staiger Concert Hall

50 Arts Circle Drive, Evanston (1-847 467
4000/www.pickstaiger.com). El: Purple to Davis.
Box office 10am-6pm Mon-Fri; noon-3pm Sat.
Tickets $7-$24. **Credit** AmEx, MC, V.

INSIDE TRACK RADIO DAYS

Chicago showcases its overflowing young
pre-collegiate classical talent every Saturday
at 11am on **WFMT**'s 'Introductions'. These
always-entertaining performances (98.7 FM)
are broadcast live and open to the public.

This somewhat sterile mid-1970s structure on the
campus of Northwestern University all the way up
in Evanston provides good sightlines, a sun-lit
lobby and warm acoustics for its local and international acts. The annual Winter Chamber Music
Festival, Segovia Classical Guitar Series and opera
productions are star attractions; local ensembles
such as the Chicago Chamber Musicians, the
Chicago Philharmonic and the Evanston Symphony
Orchestra regularly rent the space. The theatre also
doubles as a performance and rehearsal space for
the university's acclaimed School of Music; senior
and doctoral recitals are free and open to the public.
▶ *For more on Northwestern University,*
see p98.

Preston Bradley Hall at the Chicago Cultural Center

78 E Washington Boulevard, at N Michigan
Avenue, the Loop (1-312 744 6630/www.cityof
chicago.org). El: Blue to Washington; Brown,
Green, Orange, Pink or Purple to Randolph/
Wabash; Red to Lake. **Open** 8am-7pm Mon-Thur;
8am-6pm Fri; 9am-6pm Sat; 10am-6pm Sun.
Tickets free. **No credit cards. Map** p325 J12.
The original site of Chicago's public library hosts
regular concerts under the world's largest (and, for
that matter, most expensive) Tiffany dome, which
was renovated beautifully in the summer of 2008.
Any number of classical music events are staged
here, with musicians from the nearby Chicago
Symphony often among the artists. You're guaranteed to find free classical performances at 12.15pm
every Monday (as part of the hall's LunchBreak
series) and Wednesday (in the Dame Myra Hess
Memorial Concert Series), and at 3pm on Sundays.
▶ *For details of other activities at the Chicago*
Cultural Center, see p59.

Sherwood Conservatory of Music, Columbia College

1312 S Michigan Avenue, at E 13th Street,
South Loop (1-312 369 3100/www.colum.edu/
sherwood_conservatory). El: Green, Orange or
Red to Roosevelt. **Tickets** free. **Map** p324 J15.
The Sherwood Conservatory is home to the weekly
PianoForte Salon Series, broadcast live every Friday
afternoon on WFMT. Tickets are still free since the
series relocated from the Fine Arts Building in the
fall of 2008. The hall, with its no-frills decor, also
hosts a variety of educational music programmes
that feature musicians of all ages and experience.

★ Symphony Center

220 S Michigan Avenue, at E Adams Street,
the Loop (1-312 294 3000/www.cso.org).
El: Blue or Red to Jackson; Brown, Green,
Orange, Pink or Purple to Adams. **Box office**
10am-6pm Mon-Sat; 11am-4pm Sun. **Tickets**
$10-$200. **Credit** AmEx, Disc, MC, V.
Map p325 J12.

As the architectural centrepiece in Chicago's classical music landscape, Symphony Center is appropriately multifunctional. Its primary role, of course, is as the home of the Chicago Symphony Orchestra, which performs in Orchestra Hall every weekend from autumn to early summer. Principal Conductor Bernard Haitink has elevated the orchestra to new heights both home and abroad; Riccardo Muti takes over at the top in 2010, with the fiercely precise Pierre Boulez continuing to serve as Conductor Emeritus.

The CSO's main programme is supplemented by occasional visits from touring soloists, small ensembles and orchestras; Saturday morning family concerts; sporadic pop and jazz shows; and occasional concerts from the Civic Orchestra of Chicago (the CSO's training orchestra for young musicians) and the Chicago Youth Symphony Orchestra (www.cyso.org). Also on site is the Buntrock Hall, an auxiliary space for chamber music; the elegant Grainger Ballroom, which stages lectures and small ensemble performances; plus a learning centre, a music-themed restaurant (Rhapsody) and a shop selling gifts and CDs, including many from the CSO's own Resound label.

▶ *The Art Institute of Chicago (see p56), just a 30-second walk across the street, gives Symphony Center its ideal cultural companion.*

FESTIVALS

In addition to the major events below, look out for the **Winter Chamber Music Festival** at Northwestern University's Pick-Staiger Hall (Dec & Jan; www.pickstaiger.org); and March's **Four Score Festival** at the Music Institute of Chicago (www.musicinstituteof chicago.org), a four-day multimedia celebration with concerts, lectures, exhibits and workshops.

Grant Park Music Festival
Jay Pritzker Pavilion, Millennium Park, the Loop (www.grantparkmusicfestival.com). El: Blue to Washington; Brown, Green, Orange, Pink or Purple to Randolph/Wabash; Red to Lake. **Date** June-Aug.
Having celebrated its 75th anniversary in 2009, the Grant Park Music Festival continues to invite some of the industry's most notable soloists to perform with its resident Grant Park Orchestra at Frank Gehry's handsome Jay Pritzker Pavilion in Millennium Park. The pavilion has room for 11,000 listeners, 4,000 on permanent seating and the rest camped out on the lawn, and the acoustic set-up is astonishing: the trellis that loops over the lawn carries a crystal-clear sound system.

★ Ravinia Festival
Ravinia Park, Green Bay Road, Highland Park (www.ravinia.org). Metra: Ravinia Park. **Date** June-Aug.

INSIDE TRACK
COVER TO COVER

Take an album-cover tour of the city. Riverside condo complex Marina City (*see p42*) graced the cover of *Yankee Hotel Foxtrot*, the revered 2002 album from local brainy roots rockers **Wilco**, having earlier cropped up on the sleeve of the **Revolting Cocks'** *Big Sexy Land*. The Art Institute (*see p56*) houses a couple of Gerhard Richter's candle paintings, made famous by **Sonic Youth** on *Daydream Nation*, while the Museum of Contemporary Art (*see p81*) holds water stills from photographer Hiroshi Sugimoto (**U2**'s *No Line on the Horizon*) and an ink work from Raymond Pettibon, designer of **Black Flag**'s logo and **Sonic Youth**'s *Goo* album.

The oldest outdoor music festival in North America, keeps the classical music scene hopping in the otherwise dog days of summer. The biggest and most famous of the three stages is the Ravinia Pavilion, which presents concerts by the Chicago Symphony alongside occasional big-name galas, concert performances of popular operas and pop gigs. The 3,200 covered seats at the pavilion are supplemented by a huge expanse of picnic-friendly lawn; tickets run from pocket change up to three-figure sums. Also on site, the 850-seat Martin Theatre hosts concerts by chamber groups, and the smaller Bennett-Gordon Hall features a variety of college-age performers. Ravinia's Steans Institute trains young musicians, and the concerts feature top-shelf talent. *Photo p254.*

Rock & Roots

These days, 2120 S Michigan Avenue, the former home of Chess Records, houses nothing more than a memorial and gift shop (*see p73*). The same brand of harmonica-fuelled electric shuffle that kick-started rock 'n' roll contines to thrive in countless clubs around town – but the latter-day rock scene is even more vital.

The 1980s saw the emergence from the city of such disparate styles as industrial metal (courtesy of Ministry and the Wax Trax label), and house (which takes its name from the now-defunct Warehouse club), while the 1990s spawned post-rock and an insurgent country scene that continues to thrive under the banner of Bloodshot Records. At the other end of the spectrum, Kanye West and Common gave local hip hop international currency, while a new wave of MCs, like Kid Sister and the Cool Kids, are donning '80s threads and splashing Day-Glo paint on a scene that continues to evolve.

INFORMATION & TICKETS

For reviews and listings of the latest concerts and events, check the weekly *Time Out Chicago* magazine and see www.timeoutchicago.com.

In giant venues such as the Allstate Arena and the United Center, shows keep regular hours, starting around 7.30pm and wrapping up by 10.30pm. The smaller clubs, up to the size of Metro or even House of Blues, run later: gigs start about 9pm and finish between midnight and 1am, with everything an hour later on Fridays and Saturdays. Shows not designated 'all-ages' are only open to those over the age of 21. Always carry a photo ID.

Tickets for many club shows are available at the door. Tickets for bigger bands are sold in advance, either through the venue or via an agency such as **Ticketmaster** (1-312 902 1500, www.ticketmaster.com), while smaller clubs such as the Bottom Lounge, Empty Bottle and Abbey Pub peddle admission through **Ticketweb** (www.ticketweb.com).

VENUES

Major arenas & stadiums

In addition to the venues listed below, several major sporting venues host occasional rock and pop gigs. **Soldier Field** (*see p277*), home of the Chicago Bears, welcomes the likes of the Rolling Stones or Fall Out Boy when it's not too cold, while the University of Illinois at Chicago's UIC Pavilion (525 S Racine Avenue, at W Congress Parkway, West Loop, 1-312 413 5740, www.uicpavilion.com) occasionally stages big-name indie acts when not holding home games for its fightin' Flames. On the South Side, the Chicago Fire's **Toyota Park** (*see p277*) also presents large-scale gigs, while the Sears Centre (www.searscentre.com) draws arena-fillers of old, middle-aged hair bands and country superstars to the north-west suburbs. Multi-band summer extravaganzas such as Warped Tour and jam bands often roll into the First Midwest Bank Amphitheatre (19100 S

Ridgeland Avenue, at Flossmoor Road, 1-708 614 1616, www.livenation.com) in Tinley Park.

Other outdoor venues include **Charter One Pavilion at Northerly Island** (1300 S Lynn White Drive, 1-312 540 2000, www.livenation. com), which hosts a handful of concerts, and the **Skyline Stage at Navy Pier** (www. navypier.com). The **Jay Pritzker Pavilion** in Millennium Park (*see p256*) and the **Petrillo Music Shell** in Grant Park stage free shows in summer, and the **Ravinia Festival** (*see p256*) supplements its classical line-ups with pop and jazz shows for the wine-sipping set.

Allstate Arena

6920 Mannheim Road, Rosemont (1-847 635 6601/www.allstatearena.com). El: Blue to Rosemont, then Pace bus 223 or 250. **Box office** 11am-7pm Mon-Fri; noon-5pm Sat. **Tickets** $20-$100. **Credit** AmEx, Disc, MC, V. The venue known to many longtime locals as the Rosemont Horizon attracts mainstream star power, from Queen to Justin Timberlake, as well as Latin, country and world music acts.

United Center

1901 W Madison Street, between S Damon Avenue & S Wood Street, West Loop (1-312 455 4500/www.unitedcenter.com). El: Green or Pink to Ashland-Lake. **Tickets** vary; call for details. **Credit** AmEx, Disc, MC, V. **Map** p330 C12. When the city's NBA and NHL franchises hit the road, this comfortable cavern lures the likes of Madonna, U2, Jay-Z and any other act that needs 100 feet of overhead for massive mechanised props and video screens. On the bright side, the upper tier is so steep that even the cheap seats offer decent views.

Rock & roots venues

Several major theatres stage regular shows, among them the **Chicago Theatre** (175 N State Street, at W Lake Street, the Loop, 1-312 902 1500, www.thechicagotheatre.com), the **Auditorium Theatre** (50 E Congress Parkway, at S Wabash Avenue, the Loop 1-312 922 2110, http://auditoriumtheatre.org) and the more casual **Vic Theatre** (*see p234*).

Darkroom and **Sonotheque** (for both, *see p274*) host shows by hot local acts when they're not majoring in DJ culture, while **Cal's Liquors** (*see p174*) stages free shows on Fridays and Saturdays by noisy local acts. There are also art-rock and laptop shows at the **Museum of Contemporary Art** (*see p81*) and great free gigs at the **Chicago Cultural Center** (*see p255*).

Abbey Pub

3420 W Grace Avenue, at N Elston Avenue, Avondale (1-773 478 4408/www.abbeypub.com).

INSIDE TRACK
RAINBO COALITION

The cheap suds at Wicker Park's **Rainbo Club** (*see p183*) have drawn starving artists for decades. Liz Phair shot the cover of her seminal album *Exile in Guyville* inside the bar's infamous photobooth. Sidle up to the bar, next to one of the Chicago's indie rock heroes... or get served by one.

ARTS & ENTERTAINMENT

El: Blue to Addision. **Tickets** free-$25. **Credit** AmEx, Disc, MC, V.

There are two sides, literally, to this spot on the city's Northwest Side. On one is a small Irish pub that hosts energetic folk and traditional performances most nights. On the other is one of the city's premier venues for independent hip hop, where you can catch anyone from local act the Cool Kids to conscious hip hop artists such as Little Brother. Indie rock and electro pop acts such as Cut Copy and Jamie Lidell also stop by.

Aragon Ballroom

1106 W Lawrence Avenue, at N Winthrop Avenue, Uptown (1-773 561 9500/www.aragon. com). El: Red to Lawrence. **Tickets** $30-$50. **Credit** AmEx, MC, V.

This beautiful, ornate and capacious space opened as a ballroom in 1926. These days, though, it serves as one of the biggest music venues within the city limits. The 4,500-capacity room hosts acts such as My Bloody Valentine, Morrissey and Beck, as well as Spanish-language gigs.

★ Beat Kitchen

2100 W Belmont Avenue, at N Hoyne Avenue, Lakeview (1-773 281 4444/www.beatkitchen. com). Bus 50, 77. **Tickets** $5-$20. **Credit** AmEx, MC, V.

This tidy, welcoming little corner bar in the north of the city has hosted innumerable debut shows, many of them of the punk, garage and power-pop varieties. However, it also stages sporadic gigs from more well-known acts such as a residency from bubble-grunge heroes Local H.

▶ *Beat Kitchen also hosts Chicago Underground Comedy on Tuesday nights; see p228.*

Bottom Lounge

1375 W Lake Street, at N Loomis Street, West Loop (1-312 666 6775/www.bottomlounge.com). El: Green or Pink to Ashland. **Tickets** $12-$15. **Credit** AmEx, Disc, MC, V. **Map** p330 D11.

Forced to relocate from its old train-side home due to mass transit expansion, the Bottom Lounge has risen again as a swank two-storey club, with a killer sound system and some of the most consistently

The E-Town Shuffle

Musical youths, vinyl vaults and jazzers make Evanston worth the trip.

Threaded by the Purple Line, on the northern tip of the CTA, and a quick 20-minute ride up Metra's Union Pacific North line, Evanston is Chicago's nearest lakeside suburb. Though home to Northwestern University, the city hardly fits the notion of a college town. Prohibition laws kept the town dry until the late 1970s, which explains the proliferation of liquor stores just over the Chicago border in neighbouring Rogers Park. Fret not, however, as the taps now flow with copious suds and the condensed, quaint downtown area offers a surprisingly well-rounded musical microscene.

Just off the CTA Dempster stop, **2nd Hand Tunes** (800 Dempster Street, at Sherman Avenue, Evanston, 1-847 491 1690, www.2ndhandtunes.com) has been a purveyor of used platters for decades, which explains the wide selection of Rush albums and used Superchunk CDs. There's often a whiff of garage sale about the titles on hand, but it's a great place to rediscover that album you regretfully lent to an ex. And, despite the name, the store stocks new releases on wax.

A block down the street, a gutted old car dealership holds **SPACE** (1245 Chicago Avenue, at Dempster Street, Evanston, 1-847 492 8860, www.evanstonspace. com). Sleek, modern and attached to a joint selling delicious wood-fired pizzas, the club books everything from venerable delta bluesman David 'Honeyboy' Edwards to Spinal Tap bassist Harry Shearer, as well as some hip indie gigs with the help of student station WNUR.

A quick jog north gets you to the heart of the city, just off the CTA and Metra Davis stations. Before settling into a bar stool, pop into **Vintage Vinyl** (*see p211* **The Vinyl Score**) to peruse the killer assortment of immaculately kept LPs and 45s. A fraction of its classic rock, new wave, psych and mod LPs is kept in the tidy front room. If you can't find that Stones bootleg you need, just ask; it's probably out back.

Bill's Blues Bar (1029 Davis Street, at Oak Avenue, Evanston, 1-847 424 9800, www.billsbluesbar.com) books much of the same rotating slate of howlin' wolves as Chicago's tourist-choked juke joints. Regulars and students pack the intimate room, which also brings in folk and roots acts. **Pete Miller's** (1557 Sherman Avenue, at Grove Street, 1-847 328 0399, www. petemillers.com) serves up steaks – and equally sizzlin' jazz Tuesday through Saturday evenings. Acts range from the jumping ragtime of the Joel Paterson Trio to Green Mill regulars Deep Blue Organ Trio. There's no cover charge.

Bottom Lounge.

solid rock 'n' roll bills in town. Everyone from local chicano kraut-popper Allá to blog-buzzing hypes such as Glasvegas have played here, helping the venue give Metro (*see p261*) competition for the city's top rock spot. A tiki bar slings rum upstairs, with an immense patio overlooking the skyline.

▶ *The alcoholic side of the operation is run by Mike Miller of rock 'n' roll bar Delilah's; see p179.*

Congress Theater

2135 N Milwaukee Avenue, between W Maplewood Avenue & W Rockwell Street, Humboldt Park (1-773 276 1235/www.congress chicago.com). El: Blue to Western. **Tickets** $20-$50. **Credit** AmEx, Disc, MC, V.

This sizeable, slightly oddball venue hosts a diverse range of shows, with everyone from mainstream alt-rockers such as My Chemical Romance and Modest Mouse to nationally known Latino groups and even hip hop and techno acts. The calibre of the bookings has improved of late, having been taken over by Lollapalooza promoters C3 Events.

Double Door

1572 N Milwaukee Avenue, at N Damen Avenue, Wicker Park (1-773 489 3160/www.doubledoor. com). El: Blue to Damen. **Tickets** $5-$20. **Credit** AmEx, Disc, MC, V. **Map** p331 B7.

Located in the heart of the nightlife action in Wicker Park, the Double Door is essentially the little brother to the Metro (*see p261*). Many older local bands play here, leaning towards the tattooed set, alongside turns from touring groups (especially Brit invaders like Bloc Party). With a pool room downstairs and a small cocktail balcony, the venue offers respite from noisome opening acts.

Elbo Room

2871 N Lincoln Avenue, between W George Street & W Diversey Parkway, Lakeview (1-773 549 5549/www.elboroomchicago.com).

El: Brown or Purple to Diversey. **Tickets** $7-$10. **Credit** AmEx, Disc, MC, V. **Map** p329 D3.

The music may be played in the basement, but don't mistake the Elbo Room for a dive. With a rotating roster of usually undiscovered rock bands, and comfortable, eye-level sightlines, there might not be a better place to find out that the homegrown alt-rock scene offers some low-key appeal.

★ Empty Bottle

1035 N Western Avenue, at W Cortez Street, Wicker Park (1-773 276 3600/www.emptybottle. com). Bus 49, 70. **Tickets** $7-$20. **Credit** AmEx, Disc, MC, V. **Map** p331 A8.

Don't be fooled by its unassuming storefront: this is Chicago's premier indie rock club, hosting cutting-edge bands from home and abroad. If you need to get away from the noise for a while, the club has a comfortable front room, complete with a pool table and a friendly cat named Radley curled up on the couch. 'Cheap Sundays' and free Mondays remove the financial risk from gambling on an unknown bill. In September, look out for the Adventures in Modern Music festival, sponsored by *The Wire. Photo p260.*

▶ *To score free tickets for Empty Bottle shows, see p212 Inside Track.*

Epiphany

201 S Ashland Avenue, at W Adams Street, West Loop (1-773 276 3600/www.emptybottle. com). Green or Pink to Ashland-Lake.

Tickets $13-$30. **Credit** AmEx, Disc, MC, V. **Map** p330 D12.

No need to genuflect, but the Empty Bottle's latest branch functions as an Episcopal church by day. Bands set up on the altar before a backdrop of ornate wooden panelling and faux-Renaissance depictions of the passion. Rev Meigan Cameron bans hip hop and metal from her holy stage, but the unique spot has made a fittingly solemn setting for acts such as Low, Jenny Lewis and Tindersticks.

Empty Bottle. *See p259.*

FitzGerald's

6615 W Roosevelt Road, at East Avenue,
Berwyn (1-708 788 2118/www.fitzgeralds
nightclub.com). El: Blue to Oak Park. **Tickets**
$8-$20. **Credit** AmEx, Disc, MC, V.
Perhaps Chicago's premier roots music showcase,
this homey haunt out in Berwyn – it's about 20 minutes from the Loop on the Blue line – features an
array of zydeco, country, rockabilly and blues acts,
alongside occasional big-band jazz of the deeply
nostalgic variety. All-acoustic country bands perform in a side bar. Food comes courtesy of barbecue
specialists Wishbone; they can deliver your dishes
to the venue from their stand next door.

Heartland Café

7000 N Glenwood Avenue, at W Lunt Avenue,
Rogers Park (1-773 465 8005/www.heartland
cafe.com). El: Red to Morse. **Tickets** free-$5.
Credit Disc, MC, V.
This Rogers Park restaurant offers acoustic entertainment of a country/folk bent. Local regulars the
Long Gone Lonesome Boys are typical of the kind
of thing you can expect, though the venue also features a weekly open-mic poetry and music night on
Wednesdays, as well as a Saturday radio show
broadcast on WLUW 88.7 FM.
► *Adjacent to the venue (and sharing the same*
fantastic kitchen), the Red Line Tap (1-773 338
9862) books small-time but usually endearing
rock, folk, country and punk bands.

INSIDE TRACK
EMPTY, NEVER FULL

The **Empty Bottle** (*see p259*) never truly
sells out before showtime. If a listing says
'sold out' online, get to the gig before the
doors open and, nine times out of ten,
they'll let you in.

★ Hideout

1354 W Wabansia Avenue, between Elston
Avenue & Throop Street, Wicker Park (1-773
227 4433/www.hideoutchicago.com). Bus 72.
Tickets $5-$12. **Credit** AmEx, Disc, MC, V.
Appropriately named (it's tucked away in an industrial corridor), the Hideout serves as both an unpretentious, friendly local bar and a don't-miss roots
venue. Some of the city's best alt-country acts got
their start in the backroom, which also plays host to
rock groups, readings and other non-music events.
Its block party (*see p263*) is always a blast.

House of Blues

329 N Dearborn Street, at W Kinzie Street,
River North (1-312 923 2000/www.hob.com).
El: Red to Grand. **Tickets** $10-$60. **Credit**
AmEx, Disc, MC, V. **Map** p326 H11.
Presenting some of the best national and international touring acts through one of the city's finest
sound systems, the Chicago edition of this chain is
especially beautiful (check out the lush bathrooms).
Purists scorn the place, but any venue that runs the
gamut from Eli 'Paperboy' Reed to Katy Perry to the
Game in a single week must have something going
for it. The majority of bands on the smaller Back
Porch stage are blues acts, playing in a well-lit setting meant to look like a juke joint but actually
resembling a modern art museum. Every Sunday,
the venue hosts a Gospel Brunch.

Kinetic Playground

1113 W Lawrence Avenue, at N Winthrop
Avenue, Uptown (1-773 769 5483/www.the
kineticplayground.com). El: Red to Lawrence.
Tickets $5-$25. **Credit** AmEx, Disc, MC, V.
The Summer of Love vibe lives on at the Kinetic
Playground, an Uptown Hacky Sack haven in the
same block as the Aragon Ballroom and the Riveria.
Jam bands and bluegrass acts dominate the sched-
ule, but the 500-person room has a knack for spot-
lighting conscious backpack hip hop and trance.

Lakeshore Theater

3175 N Broadway Street, at W Belmont Avenue, Lakeview (1-773 472 3492/www.lakeshore theater.com). El: Brown, Purple or Red to Belmont. **Tickets** $15-$40. **Credit** Disc, MC, V. **Map** p329 F2.

Better known as a theatre venue, this North Side spot has recently started featuring all-ages music shows booked by the Empty Bottle crew (*see p259*). It's an intimate venue with comfy bucket seats and excellent sightlines, ideal for acoustic sets from acts such as Bon Iver and Iron & Wine.

▶ *There's also comedy here; see p227.*

Logan Square Auditorium

2539 N Kedzie Boulevard, at W Albany Avenue, Logan Square (1-773 252 6179/www.logan squareauditorium.com). El: Blue to Logan Square. **Tickets** $8-$20. **No credit cards.**

This all-ages, 750-capacity Logan Square spot resembles nothing so much as a high-school gym – it's no wonder local radio station WLUW hosts its annual indie rock prom here. The acoustics leave much to be desired, but some of the gigs (many booked by the team at the Empty Bottle; *see p259*) really are can't-miss, starring everyone from the Fall to the Eagles of Death Metal.

Martyrs'

3855 N Lincoln Avenue, at W Berenice Avenue, Lakeview (1-773 404 9494/www.martyrslive. com). El: Brown to Irving Park. **Tickets** $6-$30. **Credit** Disc, MC, V.

This plain, mid-sized space has hosted big names such as Wilco and Bernie Worrell in the past, but in recent years has exposed Chicago to a welter of jazz-fusion, world music and jam acts. On first Thursdays, it stages the Big C Jamboree, Chicago's only all-rockabilly showcase and open mic night.

Metro

3730 N Clark Street, between W Waveland & W Racine Avenues, Lakeview (1-773 549 0203/www.metrochicago.com). El: Red to Addison. **Tickets** $5-$25. **Credit** AmEx, MC, V. **Map** p329 E1.

This two-level room, one of the city's older and more famous clubs, hosts a variety of mid-sized national touring acts of all genres, from metal and main-stream indie to emo and electronica; mascara-wearing band members are likely to draw screaming teens. It's also known for hosting larger showcases of local bands, especially budding one-hit-wonders from the suburbs (think Plain White T's).

▶ *Downstairs, you'll find excellent DJs at the Smart Bar; see p272.*

Morseland

1218 W Morse Avenue, between N Lakewood Avenue & N Sheridan Road, Rogers Park (1-773 764 8900/www.morseland.com). El: Red to Morse. **Tickets** free-$10. **Credit** AmEx, Disc, MC, V.

After a makeover, this Rogers Park club has become the single best destination on the Far North Side for hip hop, dub and jazz. Whether you're watching a live jazz band or a bona fide turntablist, the cushy environment aids enjoyment. Mondays are free.

★ Old Town School of Folk Music

4544 N Lincoln Avenue, between W Sunnyside & W Wilson Avenues, Ravenswood (1-773 728 6000/www.oldtownschool.org). El: Brown to Western. **Tickets** $12-$30. **Credit** AmEx, Disc, MC, V.

Hideout.

There are some shows at the Old Town School's Old Town location (909 W Armitage Avenue). However, the bigger concerts staged by this loveable local institution, featuring folk, blues, country and world music acts, are held up in the roomier Ravenswood space. Take in everything from Senegalese hip hop to Tropicalia for little to no cost on World Music Wednesdays, and don't miss the annual Old Town Folk & Roots Festival in July.

▶ *It's still a school too, so you can satisfy your undying urge to learn the autoharp or the oud.*

Park West

322 W Armitage Avenue, at N Clark Street, Lincoln Park (1-773 929 1322/www.parkwest chicago.com). El: Brown or Purple to Armitage. **Tickets** $15-$25. **Credit** AmEx, MC, V. **Map** p328 G6.

This smarter-than-average venue in Lincoln Park books anyone from Cat Power to Sharon Jones & the Dap Kings. Note that it's a 15-minute walk from Armitage station; if you can't be bothered taking it, the 11 or 22 buses will drop you closer.

Reggie's

2109 S State Street, at E 21st Street, Chinatown (1-312 949 0121/www.reggieslive.com). El: Red to Cermak-Chinatown. **Tickets** $5-$10. **Credit** AmEx, Disc, MC, V. **Map** p324 H16.

This punk sanctuary draws the youngest crowds into its two distinct rooms, Reggie's Music Joint and Reggie's Rock Club. The latter is heir to the much-loved, now-deceased Fireside Bowl (the same dude books the gigs here now), and regular offers all-ages shows. Dig for used Screeching Weasel CDs at the adjacent Record Breakers before taking in the likes of Jay Reatard and the Queers.

Riviera Theatre

4746 N Racine Avenue, at N Broadway Street, Uptown (1-773 275 6800/www.rivieratheatre. com). El: Red to Lawrence. **Tickets** $20-$45. **No credit cards.**

The Riv is generally considered to be the sister rock club to the Aragon (*see p258*), a few blocks away. With a capacity of around 2,500, the jazz-age theatre isn't quite as big as its neighbour, but the acoustics are much better. Those afraid of heights should probably give the steep balcony seating a miss.

★ Schubas Tavern

3159 N Southport Avenue, at W Belmont Avenue, Lakeview (1-773 525 2508/www.schubas.com). El: Brown, Purple or Red to Belmont. **Tickets** $8-$15. **Credit** AmEx, Disc, MC, V. **Map** p309 D3.

This small club books some of the best indie touring acts around but also leans toward the acoustic singer-songwriter end of the spectrum, and offers month-long residencies from local groups with a national profile. You can hang out in the front bar area without paying cover for the shows; if you're

under 21, go straight to the back room, which stages plenty of all-ages and over-18 shows. The Harmony Grill serves up a mean brunch at weekends.

▶ *Look out for Lincoln Hall, a new venue from the Schubas folk housed in the old 3 Penny Cinema in Lincoln Park (2424 N Lincoln Avenue).*

Subterranean

2011 W North Avenue, at N Damen Avenue, Wicker Park (1-773 278 6600/www.subt.net). El: Blue to Damen. **Tickets** $5-$15. **Credit** AmEx, Disc, MC, V. **Map** p331 B7.

This upstairs club (pity the drummers lugging gear up the stairs) rarely disappoints sound-wise. There's a lofty balcony high above the stage for those who don't want to rub shoulders with the crowd, which packs in to see typically heavy rock and hip hop.

Uncommon Ground

3800 N Clark Street, at W Grace Street, Lakeview (1-773 929 3680/www.uncommonground.com). El: Red to Addison. **Tickets** $20 min purchase. **Credit** AmEx, Disc, MC, V. **Map** p329 E1.

One of Chicago's most beloved coffeehouses hosts the city's best weekly open-mic night alongside shows from folk artists. Nodding to a much-ballyhooed set by the then-unknown Jeff Buckley in 1994, the cosy shop holds a tribute to the late singer-songwriter in November that draws big crowds.

▶ *A newer second location on the Far North Side focuses on reggae, jazz and bluegrass.*

Wild Hare

3530 N Clark Street, between W Cornelia Avenue & W Eddy Street, Lakeview (1-773 327 0868/ www.wildharemusic.com). El: Red to Addison. **Tickets** $5-$12. **No credit cards. Map** p329 E2.

One of the few places left to see authentic Caribbean music in the city, the Wild Hare boasts live reggae and dub seven nights a week. Come on a Monday and you might also catch some local hip hop.

Festivals

In addition to the festivals below, you can catch seemingly every working band in the biz at the proliferation of neighbourhood festivals and block parties around the city each summer (*see p219* **Profile**). The line-ups at the **Do Division Street Fest** (www.do-divisionstreet fest.com) and **Wicker Park Fest** (www. myspace.com/wickerparkfest), in particular, have begun to give Pitchfork a run for its money. There's also music staged as part of the **Taste of Chicago** (*see p215*).

Chicago Country Music Festival

www.chicagocountrymusicfestival.us. **Date** Oct.

This two-day October event moved from Grant Park to the Soldier Field Parkland (a pleasant way of saying 'parking lot') in 2008. It isn't as high-profile as

Blues & Jazz

Without Chicago, the blues wouldn't be the same. And without the blues, Chicago would be a different town. From the 1910s to the '50s, African Americans from the south flocked to the city in what became known as the Great Migration. A handful plugged in their guitars and invented the Chicago blues, an electrified, energetic take on traditional Delta sounds. The reverberations of Muddy Waters, Howlin' Wolf and Bo Diddley bounced around the world, influencing the likes of the Rolling Stones. Many clubs in Chicago these days cater to tourists, but you can still find musicians playing with the passion of their predecessors.

The jazz scene here is vibrant, too, with international touring acts supplementing a vibrant local scene. The **Association for the Advancement of Creative Musicians** (http://aacmchicago.org), which stages shows at the Velvet Lounge, is a powerhouse of African American jazz.

The weekly *Time Out Chicago* magazine carries comprehensive listings and previews. Few club shows start before 9pm; many kick off nearer 10pm. At many jazz venues, the band will play two sets, wrapping up at 1am or later. A few clubs sell tickets or accept reservations in advance, especially for bigger-name acts (Buddy Guy at Buddy Guy's Legends, for example). If in doubt, call ahead or check online.

the city's other genre celebrations, but 2008 saw big names Taylor Swift and Gretchen Wilson head-lining the free event.

Chicago World Music Festival
www.cityofchicago.org/worldmusic. **Date** Sept. This week-long wing-ding allows Chicagoans to travel the globe without leaving town via a sprawl-ing bill of more than 40 artists from across the world. Events are held everywhere from Millennium Park to the Empty Bottle; check online for details.

Lollapalooza
www.lollapalooza.com. **Date** Aug. Starting life as an alt-rock travelling show in the '90s, Lollapalooza has made Chicago its permanent home at least until 2018. Big names – Depeche Mode and the Killers in 2009 – play a variety of stages over three days. A pass costs around $200.

Hideout Block Party
www.hideoutblockparty.com. **Date** wknd in Sept. The tiny dive's reputation shines at its annual Block Party (tickets around $25/day), when diverse head-lining acts such as Neko Case and Vieux Farka Touré choose to bypass larger events in favour of playing a strip of pavement in an industrial quarter of town. The old hippie reading poetry between acts is Hideout part-owner Tim Tuten, who now also works for the Obama administration in DC.

Pitchfork Music Festival
www.pitchforkmusicfestival.com. **Date** July. The locally based but globally known online tastemaker stages a three-day festival each year in Union Park. Expect to see the blog-hyped likes of Animal Collective and Bon Iver alongside a few nos-talgia acts and a horde of the tragically hip. Friday evenings are given to iconic acts (in 2009, the Jesus Lizard and Tortoise) running their crowd-pleasers. Tickets run around $30 for individual days, $50 for a Saturday/Sunday pass, or $65 for the whole thing.

BLUES & R&B

Blues fans should also check the line-ups at the **Chicago Cultural Center** (*see p254*), the **Old Town School of Folk Music** (*see p261*) and the **Red Line Tap** (*see p260* **Heartwood Café**), all of which regularly feature blues acts on their rosters. In addition, the 4,200-capacity, 45-year-old **Arie Crown Theatre** (2301 S Lake Shore Drive, 1-312 791 6190, www.ariecrown.com) often hosts shows by middle-of-the-road blues and R&B acts.

Venues

B.L.U.E.S.
2519 N Halsted Street, between W Altgeld Street & W Lill Avenue (1-773 528 1012/www.chicago bluesbar.com). El: Brown, Purple or Red to Fullerton. **Tickets** $5-$8. **Credit** AmEx, Disc, MC, V. **Map** p328 F5.
The 'other' popular Lincoln Park blues club is more traditional and down-home than Kingston Mines. Popular acts include local stalwarts such as Peaches Staton and Vance 'Guitar' Kelly.
▶ *On 'Blues Alley' Sundays, admission to B.L.U.E.S. also gets you into Kingston Mines; see p264.*

ARTS & ENTERTAINMENT

New Checkerboard Lounge.

Blue Chicago

Blue Chicago North *736 N Clark Street, at W Superior Street, River North (1-312 642 6261). El: Brown, Purple or Red to Chicago.*
Blue Chicago South *536 N Clark Street, at W Ohio Street (1-312 661 0010). El: Brown or Purple to Merchandise Mart; Red to Grand.*
Both www.bluechicago.com. **Tickets** $5-$8.
Credit AmEx, MC, V. **Map** p326 H10.
These two related nightclubs are so similar in style that they're virtually interchangeable. Both focus primarily on local female blues vocalists like Shirley Johnson and Big Time Sarah, and draw a crowd thick with tourists.

▶ *There are kids' shows here on Saturdays nights; see p224.*

★ Buddy Guy's Legends

754 S Wabash Avenue, at E 8th Street, South Loop (1-312 427 1190/www.buddyguys.com). El: Red to Harrison. **Tickets** $10-$15. **Credit** AmEx, Disc, MC, V. **Map** p325 H13.
If you want to see Guy perform at his own club, stop by in January when he takes over the schedules. If you show up the other 11 months of the year, you may see him sitting at the bar, overseeing the whole operation. If you like Louisiana cuisine, the kitchen has just what you need. The club has been due to relocate ever since the land was granted to Columbia College in 1999. A decade later, the move is still in the air, as Guy hunts for a suitable haunt.

Kingston Mines

2548 N Halsted Street, at W Wrightwood Avenue, Lincoln Park (1-773 477 4646/www. kingstonmines.com). El: Brown, Purple or Red to Fullerton. **Tickets** $12-$15. **Credit** AmEx, Disc, MC, V. **Map** p328 F4.
This polite Lincoln Park club has an unusual set-up – two different bands in two different rooms on two different stages, with MC Frank Pellegrino keeping things moving at all times. Expect to find local bands that lean in a rock direction while playing the standards, though the club occasionally hooks out-of-town acts as well.

★ Lee's Unleaded Blues

7401 S South Chicago Avenue, at E 74th Street, South Side (1-773 493 3477). Bus 30, 71, 75.
Tickets free. **No credit cards**.
Since the demise of the original Checkerboard, Lee's has inherited the title of the South Side's leading blues bar, and with good reason. The unassuming brick house, across from an auto wrecker in the shadow of the I-90 overpass, books a variety of local acts for seasoned regulars ready to hop – and there's never a cover. Perhaps the last truly authentic juke joint in the city.

New Checkerboard Lounge

5201 S Harper Court, at 52nd Street, Hyde Park (1-773 684 1472). Metra 55th-56th-57th Street.
Tickets $10. **No credit cards**. **Map** p332 Y16.

Forced out of its old Bronzeville digs, this legendary old blues club has found a new and rather swankier home in a Hyde Park strip mall. The booking policy remains the same as ever, with popular blues performers such as Vance Kelly appearing regularly.

Rosa's Lounge
3420 W Armitage Avenue, at N Kimball Avenue, Logan Square (1-773 342 0452/www.rosas lounge.com). Bus: 73. **Tickets** $7-$15. **Credit** AmEx, Disc, MC, V.
Located in a working-class West Side neighbourhood, this family-run spot is owned by fine local drummer Tony Mangiullo and his mother, after whom the place is named. The schedule mixes local musicians (including a weekly jam hosted by Tony) and underground out-of-town acts with growing reputations. A full crowd makes Rosa's seem cosy rather than congested.

Festivals

Chicago Blues Festival
www.chicagofestivals.net. **Date** June.
Held over three days in early June, the Chicago Blues Festival is the biggest of all the city's free music festivals, attracting more than half a million visitors each year. The biggest names play at the Petrillo Music Shell in Grant Park. Even if corporate sponsorship has led to goofy side stage names such as the Zone Perfect All-Natural Nutrition Bars Route 66 Roadhouse, it's hard to deny the authenticity and draw of headliners like BB King and Koko Taylor.

Chicago Gospel Festival
www.chicagofestivals.net. **Date** June.
The big-name performers at this two-day free event perform at the Pritzker Pavilion. However, there's also a side stage, often spotlighting young praisers.

JAZZ & EXPERIMENTAL MUSIC

The **Chicago Cultural Center** (*see p254*) regularly presents free jazz shows both at lunchtime and occasionally in the evening. On Wednesdays, the **Hideout** (*see p260*) stages an ambitious programme led by local treasure Ken Vandermark as part of the Immediate Sound Series, spotlighting local cats and cutting-edge improvisers. Thursdays finds similar programming at Logan Square performance space **Elastic Arts Foundation** (2830 N Milwaukee Avenue, at W Diversey, www.elasticrevolution.com); Sundays see experimental musicians play over at the **Hungry Brain** (*see p180*).

Venues

Andy's
11 E Hubbard Street, at N State Street, River North (1-312 642 6805/www.andysjazzclub.com). El: Red to Grand. **Tickets** $5-$15. **Credit** AmEx, MC, V. **Map** p326 H11.
This mainstream jazz haven runs regular, low-key residencies with some of Chicago's most respected scene elders, Von Freeman and Mike Smith among

Jazz Showcase. *See p266.*

them. It's a comfortable, intimate space; on top of the music, the restaurant boasts a respectable menu that tempts jazzheads to make an evening of it.

Davenport's

1383 N Milwaukee Avenue, at W Wolcott Avenue, Wicker Park (1-773 278 1830/http://davenports pianobar.com). El: Blue to Division. **Tickets** $15-$30. **Credit** AmEx, Disc, MC, V. **Map** p331 C8.
On the edge of Wicker Park's vibrant nightlife quarter, Davenport's specialises in old-fashioned cabaret reinterpreted by younger, hipper performers. The venue itself is colourful and modern, a far cry from what you might expect given the line-ups. There's often more than one show on any given night.
▶ *For other piano bars, see p252.*

Green Dolphin Street

2200 N Ashland Avenue, at W Webster Avenue, Lincoln Park (1-773 395 0066/www.jazzitup. com). Bus 9, 73. **Tickets** free-$20. **Credit** AmEx, MC, V. **Map** p328 D5.
This capacious spot by the river is as much restaurant as jazz club, but the food's decent enough that no one's grumbling. The jazz tends toward the light side, though there are also regular Latin sessions.
▶ *On Mondays, the venue hosts quasi-legendary house night Boom Boom Room; see p272.*

★ Green Mill

4802 N Broadway, at W Lawrence Avenue, Uptown (1-773 878 5552/www.greenmilljazz. com). El: Red to Lawrence. **Tickets** free-$15. **Credit** MC, V.
Al Capone used to hang here in the 1920s, but these days it's all about the music: mainstream jazz in a variety of stripes, from the idiosyncratic vocal jazz of Patricia Barber (every Monday) to the ferociously swinging Deep Blue Organ Trio (Tuesdays). Come early, as it's often understandably busy.

Hotti Biscotti

3545 W Fullerton Avenue, at N Drake Avenue, Logan Square (1-773 292 6877). El: Blue to Belmont. **Tickets** free. **No credit cards**.
This Logan Square dive may not be as well-funded as its competition, but its idiosyncratic Tuesday weekly with free-jazz synth wizard Jim Baker and NRG Ensemble alumni is worthy of diversion.

★ Jazz Showcase

806 S Plymouth Court, at W Polk Street, South Loop (1-312 360 0234/www.jazzshowcase.com). El: Red to Harrison. **Tickets** $10-$20. **Map** p324 H14.
Long heralded as Chicago's leading jazz venue, the venerable club has been forced to move more than once since its inception in 1947. However, since relocating to swank new digs in 2008, the Showcase has re-established its reputation for bringing in top-shelf talent of the ilk of David Sánchez. *Photo p265.*

Katerina's

1920 W Irving Park Road, between N Wolcott & N Damen Avenues, Lakeview (1-773 348 7592/www.katerinas.com). El: Brown to Irving Park. **Tickets** free-$10. **Credit** AmEx, MC, V.
Den mother Katerina supports local jazz and world music like few others in the city of Chicago. Inside her cosy venue, you can catch gypsy violinist Alfonso Ponticelli, jazz chanteuse Typhanie Monique, sporadic world music gigs and, occasionally, local jam bands.

Lampo

2nd floor, 216 W Chicago Avenue, between Franklin & Wells Streets, River North (1-312 282 7676/www.lampo.org). El: Brown or Purple to Chicago. **Tickets** vary. **No credit cards**. **Map** p326 G10.
Concerts are infrequent at this not-for-profit performance space, but it remains one of the best places in which to see experimental music. Artists from all over the world show up and make everything from provocative tape experiments to sax skronking.

Pops for Champagne

601 N State Street, at E Ohio Street, River North (1-312 266 7677/www.popsforchampagne.com). El: Red to Grand. **Tickets** free-$15. **Credit** AmEx, Disc, MC, V. **Map** p326 H10.
Having relocated from its Lakeview premises at the tail end of 2006, Pops hopes to continue its tradition of showing high-quality mainstream jazz in a very upmarket setting. Even if you're not a champagne type, it's still worth a look, thanks to residencies from a number of the city's finest straight-ahead pianists and vocalists.

Velvet Lounge

67 E Cermak Road, between E Michigan & E Wabash Avenues, Chinatown (1-312 791 9050/www.velvetlounge.net). El: Red to Cermak-Chinatown. **Tickets** free-$20. **No credit cards**.
The address is different but the booking policy remains the same at this pioneering venue and informal showcase for members of Chicago's trailblazing Association for the Advancement of Creative Musicians. Run by veteran saxophonist Fred Anderson, the club concentrates on free jazz, with high-calibre guests such as Henry Grimes and former Chicagoan Matana Roberts joining the locals.

Festivals

Chicago Jazz Festival

www.chicagojazzfestival.org. **Date** Sept.
Held over the Labor Day weekend, this three-day festival welcomes many big names to Grant Park. In 2008, the opening show at the Jay Pritzker Pavilion (with Sonny Rollins) was followed by free shows from the likes of Isotope 217, Eddie Palmieri and Ornette Coleman. Admission is free.

Nightlife

The home of house still raises the roof.

As the birthplace of house music, Chicago will always have a place near to the hearts of clubbers. Four-to-the-floor electronic beats were first interwoven with disco by Frankie Knuckles at the legendary, long-departed Warehouse club in the late 1970s. Older clubbers sometimes obsess about a lack of respect on the local scene for Chicago's original DJs. But in reality, the city does an incredible job at accommodating all-comers, from innovative young artists to down-and-dirty house purists, through to glamour-loving party people and the casual cool kids.

The Local Scene

River North remains the hottest and most densely concentrated nightlife district. The area still favours velvet ropes, high covers, pricey bottle service and strict dress codes; long lines preclude club-hopping. But despite the stilettos and bouncers, the tone is more naughty than haughty. Stars of European techno and minimal house can be found at **Spy Bar** (*see p269*); Crimson Lounge in the **Hotel Sax** (*see p136*) and **Angels & Kings** (*see p175*) have upped the celeb and youth factors respectively.

In the West Loop, the **Fulton Market** area is simmering but not yet boiling over, while pockets of the **Lake Street** nightlife corridor have been troubled by violence. Police are keeping an eye on the area.

The real action is further north in **Ukrainian Village** and **Wicker Park**, both dotted with mid-sized spots that vie for locals' attention. Slightly lighter on cover charges but higher on edgy attitude, **Debonair** (*see p274*), **Empire Liquors** (*see p184*) and the hip hop-oriented **Ohm** (*see p274*) are new landmarks. Further north in **Logan Square**, low-key and looser DJ bars such as the **Burlington** (*see p186*) and **Whistler** (*see p187*) are following in the footsteps of **Danny's** (*see p184*) and **Rodan** (*see p170*), perennial bohemian hangouts with soul and mutant disco nights.

INFORMATION & TICKETS

The weekly *Time Out Chicago* magazine carries the most comprehensive listings, previews and features. It's also worth checking stores such as

Reckless (*see p212*), **Gramaphone** (*see p211*), **Borderline** (3333 N Broadway Street, at W Buckingham Place, Lakeview, 1-773 975 9533, www.borderlinemusic.com) and **Kstarke** (*see p211*) for flyers. You'll also find many events listed at www.deephousepage.com and www.5chicago.com.

Tickets for **Smart Bar**, **Crobar**, **Spy Bar** and some other venues are sold in advance via their own websites or are available at www.wantickets.com. For some clubs, you can call or email ahead (or sign up with a promoter) to get on a list offering cheaper admission, often dependent on early arrival. The city's public transport system runs all night but doesn't cover every corner of town; always carry a cab number. For more on getting around town, *see pp302-304*.

Clubs

THE NEAR NORTH SIDE

River North

Crescendo

222 W Ontario Street, at N Franklin Street (1-312 787 6060/www.clubcrescendo.com). El: Brown to Chicago. **Open** 10pm-4am Wed, Fri; 10pm-5am Sat. **Admission** free-$20. **Credit** AmEx, Disc, MC, V. **Map** p326 G10.

This compact club has joined the Sound-Bar (*see p269*) and Y Bar (*see p270*) family, serving a younger, fashion-conscious crowd amid vaguely Moroccan decor. It's geared toward bottle service; tables are elevated but are extra-visible, which

Manor/Stay.

explains the high density of cocktail dresses and slim suits. Music comes from big-name electro and house DJs, from Green Velvet to Louie Vega.

Enclave

220 W Chicago Avenue, between N Wells & N Franklin Streets (1-312 654 0234/www.enclave chicago.com). El: Brown or Purple to Chicago. **Open** 10pm-2am Thur; 9pm-2am Fri; 9pm-3am Sat. **Admission** free-$20. **Credit** AmEx, Disc, MC, V. **Map** p326 G10.

The handsome, open and woody loft look of this spacious club balances the sexed-up, usually hip hop-fuelled parties that happen from Thursday through the weekend. Big-name radio DJs, celeb appearances, platform dancers and MCs keep it lively. When it closes, traffic heads to RiNo (*see below*), Crescendo (*see p267*) or Stone Lotus Lounge (*see p268*).

★ Manor/Stay

642 N Clark Street, at W Erie Street (1-312 475 1390/www.manorchicago.com). El: Red to Grand. **Open** 10pm-2am Tue, Thur; 10pm-3am Sat. **Admission** free-$20. **Credit** AmEx, Disc, MC, V. **Map** p326 H10.

With decor suggesting an old-world millionaire's opulent library, lovely ladies serving bubbly with sparklers, and frisky hip hop and club cuts on the Funktion One sound system, Manor creaks and booms with the trappings of the good life. Its cash-slinging crowd might be the city's best-dressed; they don't mind reminding you of this by dancing on the banquettes. Bottle service isn't a must, but you'll need to take a table to feel at home.

▶ *Stay has a speakeasy entrance by a side door, a late-night licence and a more relaxed atmosphere.*

Ontourage

157 W Ontario Street, between N Wells Street & N LaSalle Drive (1-312 573 1470/www. ontouragechicago.com). El: Brown or Purple to Merchandise Mart. **Open** 9pm-2am Thur, Fri; 9pm-3am Sat. **Admission** $10-$20. **Credit** AmEx, MC, V. **Map** p326 H10.

Ontourage caters to a big-night-out crowd from the 'burbs with money to burn. The bi-level club, bathed in pink and blue light, has two dancefloors, both often packed to the limit for glossy hip hop and club remixes. Occasional special events spice things up.

Religion

720 N Wells Street, at W Superior Street (1-312 787 2375/www.religionchicago.com). El: Brown to Chicago. **Open** 11pm-4am Fri; 11pm-5am Sat. **Admission** $10-$20. **Credit** AmEx, Disc, MC, V. **Map** p326 G10.

The upper floor of this recently remodelled building – partygoers trudge up three flights of stairs – has the trappings of a place of dance music worship: DJs spin house, club classics and hip hop from a giant pulpit; the sound system and dancefloor are tuned for serious dancers; and bottle-service addicts are consigned to a crow's nest. It works as a more populist spot in a sea of elite joints.

RiNo

343 W Erie Street, at N Orleans Avenue (1-312 587 3433/www.rinolounge.com). El: Brown or Purple to Merchandise Mart. **Open** 10pm-4am Wed-Fri; 10pm-5am Sat. **Admission** $10-$20. **Credit** AmEx, MC, V. **Map** p326 G10.

If location is everything, then the cosy Ri(ver)No(rth) makes sure you know where it's at. Inside, it feels like a wealthy socialite's loft party for pretty people. The casually trendy girls seem to love dancing on the furniture, which makes sense when you consider that they're usually already drunk when they arrive.

Sound-Bar

226 W Ontario Street, at N Franklin Street (1-312 787 4480/www.sound-bar.com). El: Brown or Purple to Chicago. **Open** 10pm-4am Fri; 10pm-5am Sat. **Admission** $10-$20. **Credit** AmEx, Disc, MC, V. **Map** p326 G10.
After opening in 2003, the sleek, modern Sound-Bar quickly became a prime Chicago venue in which to hear big-name DJs spinning techno and house. It's since turned to more Miami-style beats, but some of its biggest nights have been bhangra blowouts, while hip hop always predominates downstairs. Each of the three rooms, including the VIP-only round bar, features a DJ.

★ Spy Bar

646 N Franklin Street, at W Erie Street (1-312 337 2191/www.spybarchicago.com). El: Brown or Purple to Chicago. **Open** midnight-4am Wed; 10pm-4am Thur, Fri, Sun; 10pm-5am Sat. **Admission** $5-$20. **Credit** AmEx, MC, Disc, V. **Map** p326 G10.
At least once a week, the underground Spy Bar (refurbished in 2008 to feature bottle service and better sound) brings in headline-grabbing DJ talent with the latest in techno, progressive and house. On the whole, it's moderate on attitude and high on intimacy, but don't let the photogenic crowd intimidate you – this is one of the city's best clubs.

Stone Lotus Lounge

873 N Orleans Street, between W Chestnut & W Locust Streets (1-312 440 9680/www.stonelotus lounge.com). El: Red to Chicago. **Open** 9pm-2am Tue-Fri; 9pm-3am Sat. **Admission** $10-$20. **Credit** AmEx, Disc, MC, V. **Map** p326 G9.
An overly ambitious concept, this 'liquor spa' features DJs and gourmet food in an Asian-themed space. But aside from the opportunity to nibble and canoodle in the carpeted basement lounge, it's basically business as usual for the posing and dancing clubbers that jam its narrow confines.

Sub 51

Lower Level, 51 W Hubbard Street, at N Dearborn Street (1-312 828 0051/www.sub51. com). El: Brown or Purple to Merchandise Mart; Red to Grand. **Open** 10pm-2am Thur, Fri; 10pm-3am Sat. **Admission** 1-bottle min. **Credit** AmEx, Disc, MC, V. **Map** p326 H11.
The clubby portion of Hub 51 (*see p154*), the first dining venture from the Melman brothers, is about as exclusive as it gets (table reservations are essential). They've hired some of the most shameless, young, in-the-know party DJs to play upstairs and down, so the sonics are in good hands.

Underground

56 W Illinois Street, at N Dearborn Street (1-312 644 7600/www.theundergroundchicago.com). El: Red to Grand. **Open** 9pm-4am Thur, Fri; 9pm-5am Sat. **Admission** $20. **Credit** AmEx, Disc, MC, V. **Map** p326 H10.
With a military bunker theme and waitresses in form-fitting khaki, Billy Dec's below-street-level venture might seem a tad absurd. Its door policy, which often overloads the place with females, certainly can be. But it boasts the most congenial bar service and drink pours in the neighbourhood, which, combined with star drop-ins from the pop, MTV and hip hop world, make it a major player in River North.

Vision/Excalibur

640 N Dearborn Street, at W Ohio Street (1-312 266 1944/www.excaliburchicago.com). El: Red to Grand. **Open** 7pm-4am Mon-Fri, Sun; 7pm-5am Sat. **Admission** *Mon-Wed, Sun* free. *Thur-Sat* $10-$20. **Credit** AmEx, Disc, MC, V. **Map** p326 H10.
Housed in a historic castle-like building, this multi-faceted mega-club is big enough to be many things

---

INSIDE TRACK STEP ON

Chicago stepping grew out of the dance crazes of the pre-war years, with the walking dance evolving into more formal couple steps during the R&B era. The craze continued in discos and dancefloors on Chicago's South Side, and came to greater prominence via R Kelly's hit 'Step in the Name of Love' and movies such as 1997's *Love Jones*. Websites such as www.steppersusa.com now list parties from coast to coast. But Chicago lays claim to this elegant subculture, which is, unusually, a grown-ups' phenomenon.

The most welcoming and regular steppers' nights are at the **50 Yard Line** (69 E 75th Street, at S Michigan Avenue, South Side, 1-773 846 0005), where Big Jeff spins for after-work experts. It's also worth checking out the **New Celebrity Lounge** (2020 E 83rd Street, at Jeffrey Boulevard, South Side, 1-773 375 1348) on Mondays from 5pm. And mainstream venues have been getting in on the action, too, with the **House of Blues** (*see p260*) experimenting with a steppers' night. It's not easy to waltz right in and fake it, so lessons are something of a must. For gung-ho students, **Dusty Groove America** (*see p211*) sells a wide range of stepper's instructional and documentary DVDs, so you can at least gen up before you step out.

ARTS & ENTERTAINMENT

at once; it even hosts ghost tours. Late-night yuppies, suburbanites and tourists rub shoulders with trance, house and techno heads. Its sound system can rattle your cartilage, with sets from globe-trotting big names in progressive and electro in Vision's main room on Fridays and Saturdays.

★ Y Bar
224 W Ontario Street, at N Franklin Street (1-312 787 2355/www.ychicago.com). El: Red to Grand. **Open** 9pm-2am Wed-Fri; 9pm-3am Sat. **Admission** $20. **Credit** AmEx, Disc, MC, V. **Map** p326 G10.
The upmarket sibling to the nearby Sound-Bar plays up the bottle service angle with luxury seating and model-like bartenders. But with the aid of a big sound system that pumps out house and hip hop, the designer-clad clientele raises the temperature.

The Magnificent Mile & Streeterville

★ J Bar
610 N Rush Street, between E Ontario & E Ohio Streets (1-312 660 7200/www.jameshotels.com). El: Red to Grand. **Open** 8pm-2am Wed-Fri; 8pm-3am Sat; 10pm-2am Sun. **Admission** free. **Credit** AmEx, Disc, MC, V. **Map** p326 J10.
Hotel bars and clubs aren't as integral to Chicago's nightlife as they are in other cities, but J Bar (aligned with the James Hotel, but with its own entrance) is the exception. It has a prominently placed DJ booth for purveyors of hip hop, club and house but only room for dancing between tables. Many downtown movers and shakers start out here on weekends.

The Gold Coast

Level
1045 N Rush Street, at W Cedar Street (1-312 397 1045/www.levelchicago.com). El: Red to Clark/Division. **Open** 10pm-4am Tue-Thur, Sun; 9pm-4am Fri; 9pm-5am Sat. **Admission** $5-$20. **Credit** AmEx, Disc, MC, V. **Map** p326 H9.
Simply for its second-level window on the Rush Street circus of seduction, Level is worth the price of admission. This being the Gold Coast, bottle service is big. Seasoned DJs deliver trance, house and hip hop to martini-fuelled partygoers.

OLD TOWN & LINCOLN PARK
Old Town

Boutique
809 W Evergreen Avenue, at N Halsted Street (1-312 751 2900/www.theboutiquelifestyle.com). El: Red to North/Clybourn. **Open** 10pm-4am Fri; 10pm-5am Sat. **Admission** $5-$20. **Credit** AmEx, MC, V. **Map** p327 F8.
Chicago hip hop's reputation for tailored chic with street cred is realised in this three-tiered lounge. Hip

hop manager John Monopoly is a partner in the venture, and you can't move without bumping into an aspiring actress/model/whatever. The likes of Diddy and Kanye West (plus entourages) can be seen on occasion, but the veneer of elitism is mostly a ruse: the members-only policy has never taken hold.

★ Crobar
1543 N Kingsbury Street, at W Weed Street (1-312 266 1900/www.crobar.com). El: Red to North/Clybourn. **Open** 10pm-4am Thur, Fri; 10pm-5am Sat. **Admission** $20. **Credit** AmEx, Disc, MC, V.
The young and rich returned in droves to the original member of a now-international franchise following a mid-aughts renovation, and have pretty much stayed in residence. Crobar books big names in Gallic house and New York legends such as Erick Morillo, as well as Aussie male dancers and celeb nights to keep 'em coming in. Hang in the mezzanine and watch the fashion show unfold.

Republic
1520 N Fremont Street, at W Weed Street (1-312 787 1130/www.republicchicago.com). El: Red to North/Clybourn. **Open** 9pm-4am Fri; 9pm-5am Sat. **Admission** $10-$20. **Credit** AmEx, Disc, MC, V.
Going against the trend for intimate clubs, this late entrant Weed Street district spot is something of a giant. There are two rooms side by side (one usually pumps house, the other hip hop and rap), each with an enormous dancefloor. The mass-market offerings and steep drink prices don't agree with everyone, and the place seems a love it or hate it proposition.

Zentra
923 W Weed Street, between N Sheffield Avenue & N Fremont Street (1-312 787 0400/www.zentranightclub.com). El: Red to North/Clybourn. **Open** 10pm-4am Thur, Fri, Sun; 10pm-5am Sat. **Admission** $7-$20. **Credit** AmEx, Disc, MC, V.
Zentra's eastern decor has faded over the years; you won't be finding any hookahs around here these days. Instead, Jack night on Fridays has become the raging home of big names in Chicago house – from Roy Davis Jr to Derrick Carter, with some Detroit techno and classic hip hop thrown in on occasion. In the basement and lounges, less experienced spinners and hip hop residents hone their sets.

Lincoln Park

Krem
1750 N Clark Street, between W Menomonee Street & W Eugenie Street (1-312 932 1750/www.kremchicago.com). Bus: 22. **Open** 8pm-2am Thur, Fri, Sun; 8pm-3am Sat. **Admission** free. **Credit** AmEx, Disc, MC, V. **Map** p327 H7.

The Soul of the City

How to find Chicago's soul flame flickering in the shadows.

Chicago's association with the music genres that it spawned – house, electric blues, gospel – is so strong that its contribution to soul history tends to be neglected. Yet soul stars such as Sam Cooke, the Impressions and the Chi-Lites called the city home, as did the influential **Brunswick** label (in the 1449 S Michigan Avenue building that was formerly home to blues and R&B imprint Vee Jay). And with retro-style soul back in the charts, Chicago again has a lot for soul lovers to love, even if the scene isn't exactly groomed for music tourism – this is, after all, a city that can't seem to get a proper blues museum up and running.

Even before soul came back into fashion across the country as a whole, Chicago was already ahead of the curve. Held at Danny's Tavern (*see p184*), **Soul Night** (formerly Sheer Magic; *pictured*) is the longest-running monthly soul party in Chicago. On the last Wednesday of every month, Dante Carfanga and Courtland Green spin all-original vinyl 45s of vintage soul and funk, plus a sprinkling of whatever else works on the dancefloor. Also worth a look: the **East of Edens Soul Express** DJ team (www.myspace.com/eastofedenssoul express), which drops the needle monthly at the Hideout (*see p260*) and also plays other sessions in town, and the **Windy City Soul Club** (www.myspace.com/windycity

soulclub), which lost its residency at the Viaduct Theatre in 2009 but regularly plays at other venues around town.

Hearing live soul music is an all too rare event in Chicago, though it has been sneaking into North Side venues through the garage rock and retro funk circles. Down at **Lee's Unleaded Blues** (*see p264*), there are often fine soul singers on the bill: Super Percy & His Soul Clique, in particular, is worth the trip. It's also worth keeping an eye on the line-ups at the **Chicago Blues Festival** (*see p265*), which often has soul acts in its vast mix.

There's more of Chicago's soul history on the radio. Tune in to **V-103** (WVAZ, 102.7 FM) on Saturday (8am-noon) and Sunday (noon-7pm) and you'll find Herb Kent (aka 'the Cool Gent'), who's been on the air since 1949. Kent's known for spinning 'love dusties', and he was mixing Motown and Stax with a call for civil rights before everyone else.

Failing all that, there is one more way to sample Chicago soul – through the stomach. While the city is often modest about its soul food offerings, **Edna's** (3175 W Madison Street, at S Kedzie Avenue, West Side, 1-773 638 7079) excels, and not just for the home-cooked flavours of the food – owner Edna Stewart has helped over 100 felons get off the street and into the kitchen.

The South Beach-inspired Krem attracts an unusually tanned young clientele for mainstream house, pricey bites and cocktails. The white beds and red VIP room make it clear that this isn't a sports bar, but it's not exactly a downtown boogie palace either. The preponderance of eligible, extra-friendly singles makes up for the hit-or-miss service.

MaxBar
2247 N Lincoln Avenue, between W Belden & W Webster Avenues (1-773 549 5884/www. maxbarchicago.com). El: Brown, Purple or Red to Fullerton. **Open** 9pm-4am Wed-Fri; 9pm-5am Sat. **Admission** free-$5. **Credit** AmEx, Disc, MC, V. **Map** p328 F5.

The owners made over this space in 2006 to give Lincoln Parkers a more upmarket option just steps away from all the pubs and sports bars. It's a bit on the schizophrenic side, playing the fancy saloon up front but turning fully modern and clubby in the rear. There's an overlooking VIP area, a compact and crowded dancefloor, and platforms for vogueing. It draws a post-collegiate, young professional crowd still getting its sea legs for nightlife.
▶ *It's run by the owners of Crobar; see p270.*

Neo
2350 N Clark Street, bwtween W Fullerton Avenue & W Belden Avenue (1-773 528 2622/ www.neo-chicago.com). El: Brown, Purple or Red to Fullerton. **Open** 10pm-4am Mon-Fri, Sun; 10pm-5am Sat. **Admission** free-$5. **No credit cards**. **Map** p328 G5.

Somehow, the unrepentantly goth Neo has survived since 1979 in the yuppified air of Lincoln Park. Down an alley off Clark Street, you'll find a dark cave with bargain-basement drinks, sparse decor and unpre-

tentious staff. DJs spin plenty of classic industrial along with punk, electronica and new wave. Creative attire is encouraged but in no way required.

LAKEVIEW & AROUND

For gay nightclubs in **Boystown**, *see p247.*

Berlin
954 W Belmont Avenue, at N Sheffield Avenue (1-773 348 4975/www.berlinchicago.com). El: Brown, Purple or Red to Belmont. **Open** 8pm-4am Mon; 5pm-4am Tue-Fri; 5pm-5am Sat; 8pm-4am Sun. **Admission** free-$5. **No credit cards**. **Map** p329 E2.

Anything goes at this libidinous late-night perennial from the *Liquid Sky* and Tenax era. The music ranges from industrial and '80s to new club sounds; Ralphi Rosario spins disco on the last Wednesday of the month. It's very gay-friendly, but all freaks-of-the-week are welcome.

★ Smart Bar
3730 N Clark Street, between W Waveland & W Racine Avenues (1-773 549 0203/www. smartbarchicago.com). El: Red to Addison. **Open** 10pm-4am Wed-Fri, Sun; 10pm-5am Sat. **Admission** $5-$15. **Credit** AmEx, MC, V. **Map** p329 E1.

A makeover in 2006 slicked up this award-winning Wrigleyville joint, adding a world-class Funktion One sound system. Cutting-edge DJs from Europe, Detroit and Chicago form the bulk of the house, techno, nu disco, dubstep and electro bookings, but local mash-up, industrial and indie jocks rule on bargain weeknights.
▶ *It's twinned with the Metro; see p261.*

THE NEAR WEST SIDE
The West Loop

★ Butterfly Social Club
722 W Grand Avenue, at N Halsted Street (1-312 666 1695). El: Blue to Grand. **Open** 10pm-2am Wed-Fri; 10pm-3am Sat. **Admission** free. **Credit** AmEx, MC, V. **Map** p326 F10.

Intended as the earth-friendly sister to next-door Funky Buddha (*see below*), Butterfly offers healthy organic drinks along with the usual libations. It tends to have lower covers for reggae and hip hop DJs than its popular neighbour. It lost some points for green-inspired audacity when it got rid of its mud walls and went with a slicker look.

★ Funky Buddha Lounge
728 W Grand Avenue, at N Halsted Street (1-312 666 1695/www.funkybuddha.com). El: Blue to Grand. **Open** 9pm-2am Thur, Fri, Sun; 9pm3am Sat. **Admission** $5-$20. **Credit** AmEx, MC, V. **Map** p326 F10.

INSIDE TRACK
TRACKING DOWN THE HOUSE

After years spent in the shadows, more popular abroad than at home, Chicago house has made a comeback in the city that spawned it. Wednesday's Movement at **Evil Olive** (*see p274*), the house party at **Betty's Blue Star Lounge** (1600 W Grand Avenue, at N Ashland Avenue, Ukrainian Village, 1-312 243 1699, www. bettysbluestarlounge.com) and the Fridaynighter at **Zentra** (*see p270*) are all heavy with local talent, while **Smart Bar** (*see above*) usually reserves one weekend night for a top Chicago DJ. But they're all kids compared to the hyper-diverse, gay-friendly **Boom Boom Room,** still going strong every Monday at Green Dolphin Street (*see p266*) after more than 16 years. Note: it doesn't even get warm until midnight.

Debonair Social Club. *See p274.*

These two cosy but well-ventilated rooms bulge with hip hop, bhangra, frequent live PAs and cameos from R&B and rap stars, all of which combine to keep the lines long. Earlier in the week, local mash-up jocks and visitors from Berlin and New York drop in for guest turns.

★ Lumen

839 W Fulton Market Street, between N Green Street & N Peoria Street (1-312 733 2222/www.lumen-chicago.com). El: Green or Pink to Clinton. **Open** 10pm-2am Tue; 9pm-2am Fri; 9pm-3am Sat. **Admission** $20. **Credit** AmEx, Disc, MC, V. **Map** p330 F11.

Originally opened as an arty, airy cocktail lounge, this Fulton Market area hotspot eventually darkened its decor and moved its DJ booth to the main floor to please the bottle-ordering party people that its promoters were bringing in. It's still an elegant open space that draws a crowd for celebrity nights, plus periodic live sets from indie-dance acts.

Mannequin

306 N Halsted Street, at W Fulton Street (1-312 850 0065/www.mannequinchicago.com). El: Green or Pink to Clinton. **Open** 10pm-4am Thur, Fri; 10pm-5am Sat. **Admission** $10-$20. **Credit** AmEx, Disc, MC, V. **Map** p330 F11.

This bi-level club has nice sightlines, a varied DJ mix (progressive to techno and beyond) and reasonable drink prices, but between the hassles at the door and the trendy suburban-dwelling crowd, it's a bit more work having fun than it should be. The mannequin theme tends to invite more mockery than marvel.

Rednofive

440 N Halsted Street, at W Hubbard Street (1-312 733 6699/www.rednofive.com). El: Blue to Grand. **Open** 10pm-4am Tue-Fri; 10pm-5am Sat. **Admission** $10-$20. **Credit** AmEx, Disc, MC, V. **Map** p326/p330 F11.

Outside, this bi-level club strings up the velvet rope to block the rabble; behind the bouncers, it goes for old-world elegance, chiefly by offering more celeb-friendly booths upstairs. Hip hop, house and Medusa's throwback nights get spiked by live percussion and usually provoke go-for-broke dancing.

Victor Hotel

311 N Sangamon Street, between W Wayman Street & W Fulton Market (1-312 733 6900/ www.victorhotelchicago.com). Bus: 8. **Open** 9pm-2am Fri; 9pm-3am Sat. **Admission** $20. **Credit** AmEx, Disc, MC, V. **Map** p330 F11.

Sushi, house DJs and modern furnishings made this Meatpacking District spot hot for a while with fashionistas and boogie addicts. It's not the centre of attention any more, but there are still some interesting electro and techno nights.

WICKER PARK & AROUND
Ukrainian Village

Every boho's favourite DJ bar, **Danny's Tavern** (*see p184*) has been kicking it since the grunge era with little sign of losing its cool. More recently, it's become a hotbed for international scenester DJ Lono Brazil.

Cat's Meow

2700 W Chicago Avenue, between N Washtenaw Avenue & N Fairfield Avenue (1-773 489 6998). Bus: 66. **Open** 5pm-2am Thur, Fri; 5pm-3am Sat; 8pm-2am Sun. **Admission** free. **Credit** AmEx, Disc, MC, V.

Run by Music 101, one of Chicago's mainstay house music promoters, this bar with food turns clubby downstairs, where house, Brazilian beats, techno and electro nights are booked most nights of the week. Best of all, there's never a cover.

★ Darkroom

2210 W Chicago Avenue, between N Leavitt Street & N Oakley Boulevard (1-773 276 1411/ www.darkroombar.com). Bus: 50, 66. **Open** 9pm-2am Mon-Fri, Sun; 9pm-3am Sat. **Admission** free-$10. **Credit** AmEx, Disc, MC, V. **Map** p331 D9.

This unpretentious Ukrainian Village nightspot has upgraded its sound and stage features, enabling it to make the transition from rock bar to DJ den. Reggae, hip hop and house predominate, but rock, indie and electro nights are still frequent. Somehow, it's never become too hip, which might be because it needs a headcount of 100 before it starts to fizz.

★ Sonotheque

1444 W Chicago Avenue, at N Ashland Street (1-312 226 7600/www.sonotheque.net). Bus: 66. **Open** 7pm-2am Mon-Fri, Sun; 7pm-3am Sat. **Admission** free-$15. **Credit** AmEx, Disc, MC, V. **Map** p331 D9.

There's no sign outside this lounge club for serious music lovers, but you'll find exceptional programming and top-flight sound within. Black-clad hipsters queue outside the matte-silver building for popular monthly get-downs such as Dark Wave

INSIDE TRACK
JOIN THE INDUSTRY

Looking for an eclectic mix of people, cheap admission and cheaper drinks? Well, who isn't. Chicago insiders and savvy party people go where the pros go: **industry nights**. The concept – a weekly low- or no-cover party on a night when business would otherwise be slow – isn't original to Chicago, but it's on a firm footing. 'Industry' can refer to nightlife and dining staffers who don't have weekends off, but it also includes folks from the music, fashion and salon trades. DJs tend to be local and the atmosphere's usually extra-lively. To find out about industry nights, check *Time Out Chicago*, visit club websites or, best of all, ask a club bartender.

Disco; the likes of Diplo and Four Tet unleash beats for a tight-knit crowd of creative types. The beer and wine list slays those of its competition.

Wicker Park & Bucktown

★ Debonair Social Club

1575 N Milwaukee Avenue, at W North Avenue (1-773 227 7990/www.debonairsocialclub.com). El: Blue to Damen. **Open** 10pm-2am Mon-Fri, Sun; 10pm-3am Sat. **Admission** free. **Credit** AmEx, MC, V. **Map** p331 B7.

Debonair combines star-quality bookings (Tommie Sunshine and Steve Aoki among them) with dark and modern design. Video art screens on an upstairs wall; downstairs comes with an illicit red-light-district vibe, as DJs play electro, rock and club hits to frisky hipsters making out on the dancefloor. It's usually jammed with young folks sporting magazine-ready looks. *Photo p273.*

Evil Olive

1551 W Division Street, at N Ashland Avenue (1-773 235 9100/www.evil-olive.com). El: Blue to Division. **Open** 9pm-4am Mon, Wed-Fri; 9pm-5am Sat. **Admission** free-$20. **Credit** AmEx, Disc, MC, V. **Map** p331 D8.

No one likes the name, but this easy-to-reach late-night spot has become one of the city's most street-savvy clubs. Monday night's indie hipster party Rehab packs them in; a midweek house night does well; and open-ended bounce music sets keep it raging late on the weekends.

★ Lava

1270 N Milwaukee Avenue, at N Paulina Street (1-773 342 5282/www.lavachicago.com). El: Blue to Division. **Open** 7pm-2am Mon-Fri, Sun; 7pm-3am Sat. **Admission** $5-$10. **Credit** AmEx, Disc, MC, V. **Map** p331 C8.

This boutique club is tiny even by Tokyo standards. But for a time, the breakbeat and dub-loving owners were booking some of the most adventurous house, techno and electro DJs coming through town. Alas, the economic realities have forced it to ease up, but the low covers and the local talent still make it a Chicago essential.

Ohm

1958 W North Avenue, at N Damen Avenue (1-773 278 4646/http://ohmnightlife.com). El: Blue to Damen. **Open** 10pm-4am Fri; 10pm-5am Sat. **Admission** $10. **Credit** AmEx, Disc, MC, V. **Map** p331 B7.

This spacious dancer's club hit Wicker Park a few years back, playing up its handsome classic looks and formidable sound system. The Chicago-centric DJ programming leans toward current hip hop with more niche music in the upstairs room. Ohm's biggest attraction might be space: with a vast dancefloor, there's room to freak out properly.

Sports & Fitness

For sportspeople and spectators, Chicago comes out on top.

Even though the local pro teams leave their fans perpetually hungry, you'd be hard-pressed to find a more sports-mad city in the US than Chicago. But don't be fooled into thinking the sporting life is solely enjoyed from the sidelines. Thanks to a great lake and an emerald necklace of parks, the citizens of Chicago are almost always on the move. Biking, swimming, jogging and in-line skating are just a few ways to see the city, its lakefront and its people. While spring and summer are the best times to enjoy the great outdoors, Chicagoans stay active through the year, as the city's winter ice skaters (and lake jumpers) can attest.

For information on upcoming games and opportunities for participation, see the Around Town section in the weekly *Time Out Chicago* magazine.

SPECTATOR SPORTS

Baseball

Chicago is home to two major league baseball teams, and the locals make the most of the rivalry. The two teams play in different leagues, but the six inter-league games they play against one another every year are raucous occasions. And when the teams stay on their own sides of town, the division remains strong – in many ways, no single characteristic says more about a longtime Chicagoan than whether they root for the Cubs or the White Sox.

Despite winning the National League Central division several times in recent years, the **Chicago Cubs** are destined to disappoint fans every year until they win the World Series, breaking a losing streak that dates to 1908. Still, they have one great asset: Wrigley Field (*see p94* **Field of Nightmares**). Built in 1914, the old ballpark is a bit rough around the edges but is still a terrific stadium, especially for afternoon games. Many games sell out, so book far ahead. And if you don't score tickets, vibrant, boozy Wrigleyville on game day is still worth a visit.

The rivalry between the North Side Cubs and the **Chicago White Sox**, who play in the American League Central Division to a devoted South Side fanbase, only intensified after the White Sox won the 2005 World Series. US Cellular Field, the Sox's ballpark, isn't as characterful as Wrigley, but it's a pretty good place to see a game. What's more, tickets are cheaper than at Wrigley, and far fewer games sell out. Smart fans head here on Mondays, when most seats are half-price.

The baseball season runs from the start of April to the end of September. The best teams in each league enter October's play-offs.

Chicago Cubs

Wrigley Field, 1060 W Addison Street, at N Clark Street, Wrigleyville (1-773 404 2827/ www.cubs.com). El: Red to Addison. **Tickets** $9-$350. **Credit** AmEx, Disc, MC, V. **Map** p329 E1.

Chicago White Sox
US Cellular Field, 333 W 35th Street,
between S Stewart Avenue & S Wentworth
Avenue, Bridgeport, Chicago IL 60616
(1-312 674 1000/1-866 769 4263/http://
chicago.whitesox.mlb.com). El: Red to
Sox-35th. **Tickets** $9.50-$67. **Credit**
AmEx, Disc, MC, V.

Basketball

The **Chicago Bulls** dominated the NBA in the 1990s, but when Michael Jordan, arguably the greatest player ever to step on to a court, quit in 1997, the team fell apart. Now another star has arrived on the scene, and home-grown Derrick Rose has led the team back to the play-offs from

Woman's World

Chicago's female athletes bring home the medals.

If women skating around a track and bashing each other is your thing – and, judging by their popularity, it's quite a lot of people's thing – then the **Windy City Rollers** (www.windycityrollers.com), the local roller derby team are for you. There's action just about all year, with the hot and heavy part of the season taking place from January to June at the University of Illinois-Chicago Pavilion. The team was only founded in 2005, but they've already been ranked as high as second in the country.

Another squad on the rise is the **Chicago Force** (www.chicagoforcefootball.com), the city's women's tackle football team. In 2008, the women made quite an impression on their fans (as well as their opponents) as they posted a perfect season, only to come up short in the championship. The season runs from April until June at the Holmgren Athletic Complex on the campus of North Park University.

In 2009, women's pro soccer got another chance in the US with the creation of the Women's Professional Soccer League. Locally, the **Chicago Red Stars** (www.womensprosoccer.com/chicago) is one of the teams hoping to translate the excitement built up around the Olympics on to pitches nationwide. The team shares the Toyota Park field with the Chicago Fire (*see right*), and battle it out from April to August.

If you really want to get the blood pumping, **Fleet Feet Sports**, a local outfitter for all your active needs, hosts women's fun runs on Tuesday nights (1620 N Wells Street, at W North Avenue, Old Town, 1-312 587 3338) and Wednesday nights (4555 N Lincoln Avenue, at W Wilson Avenue, Lincoln Square, 1-773 271 3338). Expect three- to five-mile runs with talks on everything from wine to breast cancer afterwards in the store. For more information, see www.fleetfeetsports.com.

the Eastern Conference Central Division. With many of the building blocks in place, tickets at the United Center are getting harder to come by as fans see another championship looming.

The NBA regular season runs from November to mid April, with the best teams competing in the play-offs until June.

Chicago Bulls

United Center, 1901 W Madison Street, at N Damen Avenue, West Town (1-312 462 2849/www.nba.com/bulls). El: Blue to Medical Center. **Season** Nov-Apr. **Tickets** $12-$145. **Credit** AmEx, Disc, MC, V. **Map** p330 C12.

Football

After pulling the strings on a trade that brought Jay Cutler to Soldier Field, the **Chicago Bears** aim to stop leaning on its defence in a bid to bring home some wins. For some fans, the glory days in the mid 1980s under Mike Ditka were the be-all and end-all. But if the team can find some success through the air, Cutler & Co just might make some memories of their own.

The team plays at Soldier Field, a Chicago institution built in the early '20s as a monument to America's war dead but brutalised by renovations a few years ago. The NFL season runs from September to December, with the play-offs leading up to the Super Bowl on the first Sunday in February.

Chicago Bears

Soldier Field, 425 E McFetridge Place, at S Lake Shore Drive, Museum Campus (1-847 615 2327/ www.chicagobears.com). El: Green, Orange or Red to Roosevelt. **Tickets** $68-$350. **Credit** AmEx, DC, Disc, MC, V. **Map** p324 J15.

Hockey

Ever since 'Dollar' Bill Wirtz, the former owner of the **Chicago Blackhawks**, died in 2007, his son Rocky has been battling to make Chicago a hockey town once more. Just like the Bulls, with whom they share the United Center, the Hawks are banking on a core of young studs for titles; success came with a trip to the play-offs during the 2008-09 season. Keep an eye out for the team's annual Blackhawks Fest, where fans can get up close and personal with their hockey heroes. The season runs October to April, with the play-offs following until June.

Chicago Blackhawks

United Center, 1901 W Madison Street, at N Damen Avenue, West Town (1-312 943 4295/ www.chicagoblackhawks.com). El: Blue to Medical Center. **Tickets** $15-$300. **Credit** AmEx, Disc, MC, V. **Map** p330 C12.

INSIDE TRACK
RUN WITH THE LOCALS

Most travellers throw their exercise regime out the window when on holiday. But you don't have to if you join the **Chicago Hash House Harriers** (www.chicagohash.com), the self-proclaimed 'running club with a drinking problem', for its weekly runs that always finish at a local watering hole.

Soccer

Despite the large numbers of people playing the sport, soccer will never be more than a marginal interest in the United States. However, the **Chicago Fire** has found itself a tidy little market in Chicago, drawing crowds of more than 10,000 to the 15 games the team plays each year at shiny new Toyota Park. The regular season runs from April to November, followed by the play-offs.

Chicago Fire

Toyota Park, 7000 S Harlem Avenue, at W 71st Street, Bridgeview (1-888 657 3473/ http://chicago.fire.mlsnet.com). El: Orange to Midway, then shuttle bus. **Tickets** $20-$45. **Credit** AmEx, Disc, MC, V.

ACTIVE SPORTS & FITNESS

Sure, Chicago has spring, summer, autumn and winter like everywhere else. But there are really only two seasons here so far as sports lovers are concerned: when it's warm enough to leave the house and when it isn't.

While Chicago's weather is notorious, recent years have seen a succession of relatively mild winters, and the sight of people jogging by the water in February is not as unusual or odd as it once was. But summer is when the city really goes berserk. The **Lakefront Trail** (*see p278*) gets packed with skaters, cyclists and runners during warmer weather, all competing for the best views over the city. A ride or a jog along this stretch is one of the finest sightseeing bargains in town.

Before you get out and about, pick up the invaluable monthly **Windy City Sports** magazine (www.windycitysports.com), which offers information on just about every amateur sport in the Chicago area. The magazine is available free in sporting goods stores, bookshops and health clubs.

Many sporting facilities are found in locations administered by the **Chicago Park District** (1-312 742 7529, www.chicagopark district.com); see its website for full details.

Basketball

The **Chicago Park District** (*see p277*) maintains more than 1,000 basketball courts in the city. Many are in fine nick, while others are in disrepair. Regardless of condition, though, almost all are packed on sunny summer afternoons.

Bowling

For whatever reason, Chicagoans love to bowl. The city is dotted with alleys of every stripe, from the ragged **Timber Lanes** via the wilfully old-school **Southport Lanes** (where the pins are manually reset) to the slick, shiny **Lucky Strike Lanes**.

Lucky Strike Lanes

322 E Illinois Street, at N Columbus Drive, Streeterville (1-312 245 8331/www.bowllucky strike.com). El: Red to Grand. **Open** noon-midnight Mon-Thur; noon-2am Fri; 11am-midnight Sat, Sun. **Rates** *Per game* $4.95-$6.95. *Per lane* $45-$65/hr. *Shoes* $3.95. **Credit** AmEx, Disc, MC, V. **Map** p326 J10.

Southport Lanes

3325 N Southport Avenue, at W Henderson Street, Lakeview (1-773 472 6600/www.spare timechicago.com). El: Brown to Southport. **Open** noon-2am Mon-Fri; noon-3am Sat; noon-1am Sun. **Rates** *Per lane* $10-$20/hr. *Shoes* $3. **Credit** AmEx, DC, Disc, MC, V. **Map** p329 D2.

Timber Lanes

1851 W Irving Park Road, between N Ravenswood & N Wolcott Avenues, North Side (1-773 549 9770). El: Brown to Irving Park. **Open** 11am-2am Mon-Fri; 11am-3am Sat; 10am-2am Sun. **Rates** *Per game* $2.50-$3. *Per lane* $20/hr. *Shoes* $2. **Credit** MC, V. **Map** p330 C0.

Cycling

If you're used to riding in big cities, cycling around Chicago should be straightforward and, if it's not too cold, enjoyable. Few US cities are as bike-friendly as Chicago: the roads are wide, straight and flat, and drivers generally pay attention to cyclists and to the increasingly impressive network of bike lanes. What's more, cycling is just about the best way to get views of the lake and the city's famous skyline. As usual in a big city, though, be sure to use a sturdy lock if you want to retain your steed.

Dedicated bike lanes and trails are springing up around the city all the time. In 2006, Mayor Daley announced ambitious plans to increase the network to a total of 500 miles as part of his Bike 2015 strategy (www.bike2015plan.org). However, the best route in town is one of the oldest: the 18-mile **Lakefront Trail**, which runs between Kathy Osterman Beach near Andersonville and 71st Street on the South Side. Whether you choose to do all or part of the trail, it's an easy and often beautiful ride, especially if you steer clear of busy summer weekends (watch out for in-line skaters). Finding the path is as easy as riding a bike: head for the lake (east of wherever you are, unless you're swimming in it), and look for the yellow lines.

For more on riding in Chicago, contact the **Active Transportation Alliance** (1-312 427 3325, www.activetrans.org), which publishes the excellent Chicagoland Bike Map of local bike trails ($6.95 non-members). There's more useful information at http://chicagobikes.org.

Critical Mass.

Chicago's **Critical Mass** rides (www.chicago criticalmass.org) ensure a large group setting where cyclists take over the streets, if only for a few hours. Taking place on the last Friday of the month, the outings have fun themes (the January Polka Ride is popular) to ensure an enjoyable time and a safe ride.

Bike rentals are available from **On the Route**, a Lakeview specialist store; **Bike Chicago**, a touristy operation with branches in Millennium Park (part of the McDonald's Cycle Center, which also offers repais and secure bike parking; www.chicagobikestation.com, Navy Pier, and the Ohio Street, Oak Street, North Avenue and Foster Avenue Beaches; and **Bobby's Bike Hike** (*see p304*). However, the best deals are offered at the **Working Bikes Cooperative**, a charitable organisation that sells serviceable bikes at knockdown prices (*see right* **Inside Track**).

The town is also awash with bike stores. Among the best are **Irv's Bikes** in Pilsen (1725 S Racine Avenue, at W 18th Street, 1-312 226 6330), **Rapid Transit** in Wicker Park (1900 W North Avenue, at N Wolcott Avenue, 1-773 227 2288, www.rapidtransitcycles.com) and **Johnny Sprockets** (with two branches, the most central of which is at 3001 N Broadway, at W Wellington Avenue, 1-773 244 1079, www.johnnysprockets.com).

Bike Chicago

McDonald's Cycle Center, Millennium Park, the Loop (1-888 245 3929/www.bikechicago.com). El: Blue to Washington; Brown, Green, Orange, Pink or Purple to Randolph; Red to Lake. **Open** *Summer* 6.30am-8pm Mon-Fri; 8am-8pm Sat, Sun. *Spring, autumn* 6.30am-7pm Mon-Fri; 9am-7pm Sat, Sun. *Winter* 6.30am-6.30pm Mon-Fri. **Rates** $8-$12/hr; $30-$49/day. **Credit** AmEx, Disc, MC, V. **Map** p326 K10. **Other locations** throughout the city; see website for details.

On the Route

3144 N Lincoln Avenue, at N Ashland Avenue, Lakeview (1-773 477 5066/www.ontheroute. com). El: Brown to Southport. **Open** 11am-8pm Mon-Thur; 11am-7pm Fri; 10am-6pm Sat; 11am-5pm Sun. **Rates** $35-$50/day; $125-$195/week. **Credit** AmEx, Disc, MC, V. **Map** p329 D3.

Fishing

The easiest fish to catch in Lake Michigan are alewives, which float to the shore in summer. Dead. A whiff of defunct alewife, and you'll know to leave 'em be. Thankfully, most of the alewives have now been eaten by the Pacific salmon that in turn spawned a huge charter fishing industry. The lake also boasts many

INSIDE TRACK RIDE FOR LIFE

The **Working Bikes Cooperative** salvages Chicago's discarded and unwanted bikes, which are then revived by volunteer mechanics. Roughly 5,000 such bikes are shipped from Chicago to developing countries each year, but the WBC also sells around other bikes to Chicagoans for $50-$100 from its store (2434 S Western Avenue, at W 24th Place, 1-312 421 5048, http://workingbikes.org). If you fancy cycling around town, you could do worse than buy a WBC bike, ride it during your stay, then donate it when you leave – the price may be lower than a standard rental, and it's all in a good cause.

other live fish: perch are the most sought-after catch among pier anglers, while the smelt fishing season is a sight to behold.

You'll need a licence to fish legally in Illinois; they're available to over-16s at bait stores (check the *Yellow Pages*), sporting goods stores, currency exchanges or the City Clerk's office. The **Illinois Department of Natural Resources** (1-312 814 2070/www.dnr.state.il. us) offers guides on where to fish. For starters, try Chicago's parks (details from the **Chicago Park District**; *see p277*); the **Forest Preserve District of Cook County** (1-800 870 3666, www.fpdcc.com); and, of course, Lake Michigan. You can cast off the shore at **Belmont Harbor** (3200 North, 1-312 742 7673), **Diversey Harbor** (2800 North, 1-312 742 7762), **Monroe Harbor** (100 South, 1-312 742 7643) or **Burnham Harbor** (1600 South, 1-312 742 7009); for all, see www.chicagoharbors.info.

Fitness clubs

Many hotels have a fitness facility on site or offer an 'in' at a nearby club. However, if yours doesn't, there are plenty of options. Among the more popular clubs are **Bally Total Fitness** (25 E Washington Street, at N State Street, the Loop, 1-312 372 7755, www.ballyfitness.com), a chain with numerous local branches, or one of the three **Lakeshore Athletic Clubs** (there's one at 1320 W Fullerton Avenue, Lincoln Park, 1-773 477 9888, www.lsac.com). Daily membership is available at all, costing around $15-$20 a day.

Golf

The **Chicago Park District** (*see p277*) runs a half-dozen courses around the city, details of which can be found at www.cpdgolf.com.

ARTS & ENTERTAINMENT

Cog Hill Golf & Country Club

*12294 Archer Avenue, at W 123rd Street,
Lemont (1-866 264 4455/www.coghillgolf.com).
Metra Lemont.* **Open** *Summer* 6am-9pm daily.
Winter 6am-5pm daily. **Rates** $37-$150. **Credit**
Disc, MC, V.

A series of no fewer than four 18-hole courses out in
Lemont. The most expensive and most impressive
is Dubsdread, the on-again, off-again home to the
BMW Championship in September, but the other
three offer a decent challenge. Call for details of afternoon and twilight rates.

Jackson Park

*6401 S Richards Drive, at E Maruette Drive,
South Side (1-312 245 0909/www.cpdgolf.com).
Metra: 63rd Street.* **Open** sunrise-sunset daily.
Rates *Non-residents* $23-$26. **Credit** MC, V.
Map p331 Z18.

The Chicago Park District's (and the city's) only 18-
holer runs down by the lakefront on the South Side,
and should challenge even low handicappers. Club
rental is available.

Sydney R Marovitz Course

*3600 N Recreation Drive, in Lincoln Park (1-312
245 0909/www.cpdgolf.com). El: Red to Addison.*
Open sunrise-sunset daily. **Rates** *Non-residents*
$20.50-$23.50. **Credit** MC, V. **Map** p329 G1.

This nine-hole Lincoln Park course enjoys a fantastic setting alongside the lake. The course is good,
too, but you'll need to book ahead (allow up to 14
days in advance).

In-line skating

Chicago drivers tend not to notice skaters
until one slams against the hood of their car.
However, there's safety in numbers at the
Road Rave, a summer skate similar to the
Friday Night Skate events held in other cities
around the world. The skate leaves from Daley
Plaza, (corner of Dearborn and Washington
Streets in the Loop) at 7.30pm on the first
Friday of the month from May to October,
and is suitable for skaters of all grades.
Experienced street skaters can also join a
longer Road Rave event on the third Friday
of the month (May to September).

Off the road, the **Lakefront Trail** (*see
p278*) is a pleasant way to while away an
afternoon in the company of cyclists and
runners. Skates can be hired from **Bike
Chicago** (*see p279*).

Pool

In many Chicago bars, the unspoken pool-table
rule is that the winner keeps the table. However,
you can rent a table by the hour at Chris's
Billiards, one of the town's better pool halls.

Chris's Billiards

*4637 N Milwaukee Avenue, at W Lawrence
Avenue, Jefferson Park (1-773 286 4714). El:
Blue to Jefferson Park.* **Open** 9.30am-2am daily.
Rates $5-$8/hr. **Credit** AmEx, Disc, MC, V.

Sequences for *The Color of Money* were filmed at
this BYOB North Side joint, which has been drawing pool hounds and sharks for years.

Running

The **Chicago Area Runners Association**
(1-312 666 9836, www.cararuns.org) has details
on races and running routes, though you might
be fine just jogging along the **Lakefront Trail**
(*see p278*) or with the **Chicago Hash House
Harriers** (*see p277* **Inside Track**).

Good road surfaces, amenable weather
and a pancake-flat landscape combine to make
the **Chicago Marathon** one of the fastest
marathons in the world. The race draws plenty
of international runners. For more, *see p217*.

Skating & sledding

Wintertime visitors can sled courtesy of the
Chicago Park District (*see p277*), which
operates a number of toboggan runs with
wooden chutes. City-run rinks, such as
those in **Millennium Park** and at **Daley
Bicentennial Plaza**, are generally open from
late November to mid March. From December
until early January, there's also a fairly
expensive ice rink on **Navy Pier**.

McCormick Tribune Ice Skating Rink at Millennium Park

*McCormick Tribune Plaza, Millennium Park,
55 N Michigan Avenue, at E Randolph Street,
the Loop (1-312 742 5222/http://millenniumpark.
net). El: Blue to Washington; Brown, Green,
Orange, Pink or Purple to Randolph; Red to Lake.*
Open *late Nov-mid Mar* 10am-10pm daily.
Admission free. *Skate rental* $10. **Map** p325 J12.

This 16,000sq ft outdoor skating rink, open for about
four months during winter is free, but there's a catch:
skate rental costs $10.

INSIDE TRACK LAKE PLACID

Although it helps, you don't have to be
Donald Trump to enjoy Lake Michigan up
close and personal. Several organisations
offer sailing lessons, among them the
Chicago Sailing Club (Belmont Harbor,
1-773 871 7245, www.chicagosailing
club.com). And the lake's relative calm
makes it a good place for novices to
take to the water.

Daley Bicentennial Plaza.

Soccer

Given Chicago's large Latin American
population, it's no surprise that the beautiful
game is popular in the city. Some of the liveliest
action happens just off the lake at Montrose
Avenue. For details of local games, contact
the **Illinois Soccer Association** (1-312 226
7920, www.illinoissoccer.org) or the **National
Soccer League of Chicago** (1-708 589 5599,
www.nslchicago.org).

If you're just interested in watching your
team from back home, visit one of the city's
soccer-friendly bars; *see p185* **Inside Track**.

Swimming

In summer, thick-skinned aquanauts swim from
Navy Pier north towards the Oak Street Beach.
Buoys protect swimmers from boats, at least
theoretically. The season runs from Memorial
Day to Labor Day, but some beaches are
sporadically closed due to high water toxicity.

The **Chicago Park District** (*see p277*)
operates numerous indoor swimming pools
that are both free and, on the whole, well
maintained. Among the best is **Welles Park**,
a full-size pool in a great Lincoln Square
building (2333 W Sunnyside Avenue, at
N Western Avenue, 1-312 742 7511).

Tennis

With more than 600 courts around Chicago, it's
easier to find a net than a partner. Fees vary
wildly. If you prefer to play indoors, there are
courts at a few health clubs in the city, such as
the Lincoln Park branch of the **Lakeshore
Athletic Club** (*see p279*). The most central
public court is along the lakefront; for others,
call the **Chicago Park District** (*see p277*).

Daley Bicentennial Plaza
*337 E Randolph Street, at N Columbus
Drive, the Loop (1-312 742 7648). El: Blue to
Washington; Brown, Green, Orange, Pink or
Purple to Randolph; Red to Lake.* **Open** 7am-
10pm Mon-Fri; 9am-5pm Sat, Sun. **Rates** $5-
$7/hr. **Credit** Disc, MC, V. **Map** p325 J12.
Rally beneath the skyscrapers on the city's most
stunningly located tennis court, threatened with
redevelopment but still currently intact.

Volleyball

Along the lake, there are pick-up games
galore. Try **Foster Beach** (at Foster Avenue),
Montrose Beach (at Montrose Avenue), and
the **North Avenue Beach** (at North Avenue),
the Centre Court of Chicago beach volleyball.
See also p84 **Summer Lovin'**.

Theatre

A theatrical hub for years, Chicago continues to impress.

Since the days of Maurice Brown's Little Theatre movement at the turn of the 20th century, Chicago has been a hotbed of independent theatrical innovation. A longstanding tradition in performance arts, a vibrant ethnic mix and strong educational programmes have made it a great place for hopeful visionaries to try and make their mark.

The city's theatrical alumni include blazing mavericks (David Mamet, John Malkovich), comfort-TV stars (Laurie Metcalf, David Schwimmer) and acting titans (Brian Dennehy, Joan Allen), most of whom cut their teeth in the storefront scene. The majority of these scrappy enterprises – along with those, like Steppenwolf, that have grown into institutions – demonstrate Chicago's commitment to actor-centred takes on contemporary and canonical plays. But the scene today has space for all kinds of visions, from experimental spectacles to Broadway glitz.

Theatre

INFORMATION & TICKETS

The weekly *Time Out Chicago* magazine carries comprehensive theatre listings, plus reviews of major shows. Other resources include the free *Chicago Reader* weekly, the *Chicago Tribune*'s 'Friday' section (which has most theatre ads), and the generally accurate monthly listings magazine published by the League of Chicago Theatres (LCT; www.chicagoplays.com), freely available in many hotels.

Many Chicago theatres, especially the small ones, stage performances only from Thursday to Sunday. On Fridays and Saturdays, late-night shows typically begin around 11pm. It's generally best to buy tickets direct from theatre box offices in order to avoid surcharges; however, most shows also sell seats via **Ticketmaster** (*see p212*), with smaller companies preferring **Ticketweb** (www.ticketweb.com). Prices are all over the map, from $10-$20 at fringe venues to $60 or more at big theatres.

Many theatres sell half-price tickets for that day's performance through the LCT's three **Hot Tix** booths: in the Loop (78 E Randolph Street, at N Michigan Avenue), at the **Water Works** (163 E Pearson Street, at N Michigan Avenue) and in **Skokie** (at the North Shore Center for

the Performing Arts, 9501 N Skokie Boulevard). All are open from 10am to 6pm Tuesday to Saturday, and 11am to 4pm on Sunday. Each morning, a list of shows for which cheap seats are available is posted at www.hottix.org. Some theatres list shows several days in advance, which allows you to buy, say, half-price tickets for Saturday's show on a Thursday.

MAJOR COMPANIES

There are so many theatres in Chicago that what follows is a necessarily selective list. Check *Time Out Chicago* for reviews of the latest shows when you're in town.

Note that the box office hours listed in this section apply when there is no performance at the specified theatre. On days when there is a scheduled show, hours are generally extended until showtime and occasionally beyond.

★ American Theater Company

1909 W Byron Street, at N Lincoln Avenue, Irving Park (1-773 409 4125/www.atcweb.org). El: Blue to Irving Park. **Box office** 10am-6pm Tue-Fri. **Tickets** $10-$40. **Credit** AmEx, MC, V. **Map** p330 C0.

ATC has a long track record of straightforward productions of classic and occasionally new American plays. PJ Papparelli has shaken up the company,

Midnight Express

After two raucous decades of after-hours theatre, the Neo-Futurists still reign.

From an evolutionary standpoint, natural selection should surely have killed off the **Neo-Futurists** (*see p285*) long ago. The ragtag fleet of performers isn't exactly famous for being organised. Or mainstream. Or well funded.

Yet remarkably, the group's show *Too Much Light Makes the Baby Go Blind* celebrated its 20th anniversary in 2008. Featuring a game if somewhat scrappy ensemble of writer-performers attempting to perform 30 miniature plays in 60 minutes, it's part block party and part accessible performance art. Strangely populist yet also resolutely underground, the show has produced multiple generations of hard-working writer-performers and won untold legions of fans, many of them non-traditional theatregoers.

Too Much Light started as an experiment at the old Stage Left Theatre in Lakeview, made a brief stop at Live Bait Theater and eventually moved north to pre-gentrified Andersonville in 1992. There, in a makeshift space above a funeral parlour, the Neo-Futurists and *Too Much Light...* carved themselves a perfectly unusual niche.

The show was originally a hit with suburban punks who came into the city craving alternative culture, lining up around the block in the dead of winter to score a seat. But its frenzied party energy and up-to-the-minute commentary on politics and pop culture helped secure the show a permanent place in Chicago theatre.

With only a quicksilver moment in the national spotlight – the Broadway musical *Urinetown*, which had a darkly comic Neo-Futurist point of view, won a 2002 best-book Tony for Neo-Futurist alumnus Greg Kotis and earned a Tony nomination for ensemble actor Spencer Kayden – the company has somehow kept

itself under the radar. But without the charismatic accessibility these hard-driving artists have shared with generations of first-time theatre patrons, Chicago wouldn't have half the scene it has today.

Bookings aren't accepted; show up by 10.45pm if you want to get in. (If the show sells out, they'll order a pizza for the entire audience.) Tickets cost $7 plus whatever number shows up when you roll a dice; roll a five, for example, and you'll pay 12 bucks. The company also produces full-length shows, more notable for their goofy charm and political sensibility than for their polish. But it's *Too Much Light...* that continues to draw the crowds.

with a colourblind repertory production of Sam Shepard's *True West* and Suzan-Lori Parks's *Topdog/Underdog*. The 2009 departure of several ensemble members has left the company's future open, but it should continue to innovate. *Photo p284.*

Chicago Shakespeare Theater
800 E Grand Avenue, at Navy Pier, Streeterville (1-312 595 5600/www.chicagoshakes.com). El: Red to Grand. **Box office** noon-5pm

Tue-Sat; noon-4pm Sun. **Tickets** $23-$70. **Credit** AmEx, Disc, MC, V. **Map** p326 K10. Bardolators of all stripes will want to check out the lavish digs that CST has secured amid the Ferris wheels and peel-and-eat shrimp of Navy Pier. Winners of a regional theatre Tony in 2008, artistic director Barbara Gaines' solid crew of journeymen actors deliver rousing performances in productions that tend toward the crowd-pleasing, with interpretive decisions generally more Renaissance air than lower Manhattan. Visiting international productions spice up the proceedings, and the CST Family Series offers the Bard abridged.

Congo Square Theatre Company

Chicago Center for the Performing Arts, 777 N Green Street, at W Chicago Avenue, West Town (information 1-773 296 1108/tickets 1-312 733 6000/www.congosquaretheatre.org). Bus: 66. **Box office** 11am-5pm Mon-Wed; 11am-8pm Thur-Sat; 11am-4pm Sun. **Tickets** $20-$30. **Credit** AmEx, Disc, MC, V.

Derrick Sanders, Congo Square's founding artistic director, was a protégé of the late American playwright August Wilson, and Congo Square follows Wilson in its commitment to a regional theatre centred on the African-American experience. The company has produced several of Wilson's plays, as well as work by such up-and-coming writers as Lydia Diamond. Its commitment to emerging writers sometimes leads to uneven scripts, but the company boasts consistently sharp performances, direction and design.

Court Theatre

5535 S Ellis Avenue, at E 55th Street, Hyde Park (1-773 753 4472/www.courttheatre.org). Metra: 55th-56th-57th Street. **Box office** noon-5pm daily. **Tickets** $36-$54; 10-25% off discounts. **Credit** AmEx, Disc, MC, V. **Map** p332 X17.

Fitting with its Hyde Park location, the Court delivers brainy and meticulous productions of modern and contemporary plays by the likes of Stoppard, Ionesco and Beckett. Directorial work by Joanne Akalaitis has introduced a spiky, deconstructive tone to the Court's seasons, while co-productions at the Museum of Contemporary Art's performance space (*see p81*) have been noteworthy for combining visual flair with acute dramaturgy.

Gift Theatre Company

4802 N Milwaukee Avenue, at W Lawrence Avenue, Jefferson Park (1-773 283 7071/ www.thegifttheatre.org). El: Blue to Jefferson Park. **Box office** call to reserve tickets or order online. **Tickets** $20-$30. **Credit** AmEx, Disc, MC, V.

American Theater Company present *Speech and Debate. See p282.*

The Gift is almost an archetypal Chicago storefront theatre. Packed into an impossibly intimate performance space, audience members practically share the stage with the company's young and dynamic performers. It's the acting and directing talent that sets the Gift apart: actors such as Paul D'Addario, Brendan Donaldson, and Mary Fons throw themselves into roles with abandon, and director Michael Patrick Thornton has acquired a stellar reputation.

Goodman Theatre

170 N Dearborn Street, at W Randolph Street, the Loop (1-312 443 3800/www.goodman theatre.org). El: Blue, Brown, Green, Orange, Pink or Purple to Clark/Lake; Red to Lake. **Box office** 10am-5pm Mon-Fri; noon-5pm Sat, Sun. **Tickets** *Albert Theatre* $20-$68. *Owen Theatre* $20-$68. **Credit** AmEx, Disc, MC, V. **Map** p325 H12.

The Goodman has long stood as one of the country's première theatrical destinations outside New York, and an anchor of Chicago's serious dramatic scene. Artistic director Robert Falls favours lush, starstudded productions of the classic American repertory (Brian Dennehy's a repeat performer), but forays such as 2009's Eugene O'Neill festival, which featured provocative productions by NY's Wooster Group and Chicago's own Hypocrites, keep the theatre's offerings puckishly unpredictable.

INSIDE TRACK
WHAT'S IN A NAME?

It sounds dainty, but **A Red Orchid Theatre** (*see right*) takes its name from *Naked Lunch* by anything-but-dainty Beat writer William Burroughs. When one of the book's characters shoots up heroin into the arm of another, Burroughs describes the blood sucked into the vial as 'a red orchid'.

Lookingglass Theatre Company

Water Tower Water Works, 821 N Michigan Avenue, at E Pearson Street, Magnificent Mile (1-312 337 0665/www.lookingglasstheatre.org). El: Red to Chicago. **Box office** 10am-showtime Tue-Fri; noon-showtime Sat, Sun. **Tickets** $20-$58. **Credit** Disc, MC, V. **Map** p326 J9.

You may not associate David Schwimmer – or *Boston Public*'s Joey Slotnik, for that matter – with circus-flavoured productions of *The Arabian Nights*, Dickens and Dostoevsky, but they're both ensemble members of this company, which blends an interest in literary adaptation with spectacular physical theatre. The troupe also includes Mary Zimmerman, maybe the most influential Chicago theatrical export since David Mamet; her gorgeously precise approach to visual design has earned her plaudits, including a Tony and a MacArthur 'genius grant'.

★ Neo-Futurists

Neo-Futurarium, 5153 N Ashland Avenue, between W Winona Street & W Foster Avenue, Andersonville (1-773 275 5255/www.neofuturists. org). El: Red to Berwyn. **Tickets** $8-$13. **No credit cards.**

See p283 **Midnight Express.**

Next Theatre

927 Noyes Street, at Ridge Avenue, Evanston (1-847 475 1875 ext 2/www.nexttheatre.org). El: Purple to Noyes. **Box office** noon-6pm Tue-Sat; from 2hrs prior to showtime Mon, Sun. **Tickets** $20-$40; $10-$36 discounts. **Credit** AmEx, Disc, MC, V.

Over the last decade, Evanston's Next Theatre has built a reputation as a première destination for new, intellectually challenging and theatrically exploratory plays. As a result, it's given regional premières of work by many of the country's most adventurous playwrights, including John Patrick Shanley and Christopher Shinn. The company's musical version of *Adding Machine*, adapted from Elmer Rice's 1923 play, garnered multiple awards after it moved to New York.

★ Profiles Theatre

4147 N Broadway Street, at W Gordon Terrace, Lakeview (1-773 549 1815/www.profilestheatre. org). El: Red to Sheridan. **Box office** 1pm-showtime daily. **Tickets** $25-$30. **Credit** AmEx, Disc, MC, V.

Profiles works very much in the Chicago tough-guy tradition pioneered by Mamet. Edgy work by the likes of Neil LaBute, Adam Rapp and Rebecca Gilman tends to exploit the tension inherent in the theatre's close-quarters space.

★ A Red Orchid Theatre

1531 N Wells Street, at W North Avenue, Old Town (1-312 943 8722/www.aredorchid theatre.org). El: Brown or Purple to Sedgwick. **Box office** noon-5pm Mon-Fri. **Tickets** $14-$20. **Credit** AmEx, Disc, MC, V. **Map** p327 G7.

A Red Orchid mixes the contemporary and the classical: bang-up productions of Ionesco work sit alongside the work of Brett Neveu, one of Chicago's hottest writing talents and an ensemble member. With any luck, 2008's hilarious and surprisingly touching *A Very Merry Unauthorized Children's Scientology Pageant* will become a regular holiday attraction.

Redmoon Theater

1438 W Kinzie Street, at N Ashland Avenue, West Loop (1-312 850 8440/www.redmoon.org). El: Green or Pink to Ashland. **Box office** 9am-5pm Mon-Fri. **Tickets** free-$35. **Credit** AmEx, MC, V. **Map** p330 D11.

They build puppets; they organise massive pageants (for years, their Hallowe'en parade was an annual highlight in Logan Square); they're as likely to put on a performance in a park as in a traditional theatre space. There's nothing quite like Redmoon in Chicago, and its commitment to large-scale spectacle has made it a significant influence on a younger generation of theatre artists.

Side Project

1439 W Jarvis Avenue, at N Greenview Avenue, Rogers Park (1-773 973 2150/www.theside project.net). El: Red to Jarvis. **Box office** call to reserve tickets or order online. **Tickets** $15. **No credit cards.**

Occupying a super-intimate space, the Side Project has had a solid decade of potent and edgy productions. The group specialises in premièring new plays by writers including Stephen Cone, Sean Graney and Adam Rapp, but has also had success with festivals of shorter works. With consistently solid direction and acting, it's a reliable venue for seeking out contemporary theatre's bleeding edge.

★ Steppenwolf Theatre Company

1650 N Halsted Street, at W North Avenue, Lincoln Park (1-312 335 1650/www.steppen wolf.org). El: Red to North/Clybourn. **Box office** 11am-5pm Mon-Sat; 1-5pm Sun. **Tickets** *Main theatre* $50-$65. *Garage* $20-$30. **Credit** AmEx, Disc, MC, V. **Map** p327 F7.

There was a period when it was starting to look as though the legacy of Malkovich and Sinise, of John Mahoney and Joan Allen and Laurie Metcalf, was mostly resting on its laurels. But the company can thank Tracy Letts for ushering in a newly revitalised Steppenwolf in time for the Age of Obama. *August: Osage County* took Chicago by storm when it premièred here in 2007, garnering a Pulitzer and a Tony after moving to Broadway. The company continues to offer a repertoire balancing the classic and the contemporary, centred on focused performances.

Alan Bennett's *The History Boys*, at the **TimeLine Theatre Company**.

Strawdog Theatre Company

3829 N Broadway Street, at W Grace Street, Lakeview (1-773 528 9696/www.strawdog.org). El: Red to Sheridan. **Box office** from 1hr before show. **Tickets** $15-$20. **Credit** Disc, MC, V. **Map** p329 F1.

The sizeable ensemble at this storefront stalwart gets put to use mainly for staging stripped-down versions of the classics – its 2009 staging of *The Cherry Orchard*, in Curt Columbus's translation, won plaudits – but it's also mounted original productions. The cabaret space next door allows for abundant post-show hijinks.

TimeLine Theatre Company

615 W Wellington Avenue, at N Broadway Street, Lakeview (1-773 281 8463/www.time linetheatre.com). El: Brown or Purple to Wellington. **Box office** noon-5pm Tue-Fri; noon-9pm (on performance days) Sat; noon-3pm (on performance days) Sun. **Tickets** $25-$35; $15 discounts. **Credit** MC, V. **Map** p329 F3.

Up in tony Lincoln Park, TimeLine mounts productions dedicated to exploring historical themes. Their educational mission is reflected in the extensive programme notes and dramaturgical displays accompanying the plays. TimeLine has one of the more seasoned ensembles working the Chicago storefront scene; performers such as David Parkes and artistic director PJ Powers have powerfully interpreted plays including *Hannah and Martin* and *Fiorello!*.

Trap Door Theatre

1655 W Cortland Street, at N Paulina Street, Humboldt Park (1-773 384 0494/ www.trapdoortheatre.com). Bus: 9X.

Box office call or book online. **Tickets** $20. **Credit** AmEx, Disc, MC, V.

Given the mazelike walkway one navigates to get to this cosy space, Trap Door's name seems appropriate. Inside, artistic director Beata Pilch and associates devote themselves to classic and contemporary plays centred on the Eastern European avant garde. Expect to see some diatribes against the soullessness of modern consumer life, maybe accompanied by scantily clad ingénues.

Victory Gardens Theater

2433 N Lincoln Avenue, at W Fullerton Avenue, Lincoln Park (1-773 871 3000/www.victory gardens.org). El: Brown, Purple or Red to Fullerton. **Box office** noon-8pm Tue-Sat; noon-4pm Sun. **Tickets** $26-$45. **Credit** AmEx, Disc, MC, V. **Map** p328 F5.

Lincoln Park's Biograph Theater remains best known as the spot where notorious bank robber John Dillinger drew his last breath. However, its occupant for the last few years, theatre company Victory Gardens, has some claims to fame of its own, supporting emerging and established playwrights through residencies and stand-alone productions – and nurturing talent through its training centre. The work here isn't always groundbreaking, but Victory Gardens's consistent professionalism makes it Chicago's analogue to the mainstream outlets of Off-Broadway.

ITINERANT COMPANIES

House Theatre of Chicago

Information 1-773 769 3832/tickets 1-773 251 2195/www.thehousetheatre.com.

It's a staple of theatre coverage to bemoan the lack of interest in theatre among under-40s, but the people at House have no such worries: their formula of visual spectacle, rock soundtracks and pop-culture obsession has made them a destination for hipsters and hipster-haters alike. The group's home base is the Chopin Theatre (*see p288*) in Wicker Park.

Hypocrites

1-773 989 7352/www.the-hypocrites.com.
Artistic director Sean Graney has developed a theatrical language one part Artaud, one part David Lynch, and several parts his own disturbing and strangely moving vision. The Hypocrites have staged several original pieces, but they're best known for their skewed takes on works from the classic and contemporary canon, from Arthur Miller to Sarah Kane. The company's version of *Our Town*, directed by David Cromer, enjoyed a high-profile New York transfer in 2009. *Photo p288.*

Porchlight Music Theatre

1-773 327 5252/www.porchlighttheatre.com.
Porchlight's not the place to find mind-blowing spectacle. However, it does reliably offer emotionally nuanced and heartfelt versions of some underperformed gems by the likes of Stephen Sondheim and William Finn, and its commitment to supporting new musical works helps keep this vital American form from going completely Hollywood. Its unofficial digs are in the Theatre Building (*see p288*) in Lakeview.

Teatro Vista

1-312 666 4659/www.teatrovista.org.
Teatro Vista ('Theatre with a View') regularly premières new plays and translations by Latino dramatists, from inside America's borders and out. Often engaging in a poetic magical realism, its productions have included adaptations of García Lorca, and the recent *Our Lady of the Underpass*, chronicling the 2005 sighting of the Virgin in a Fullerton underpass water stain, and playing at the Victory Gardens Theater Greenhouse (*see p288*). In addition to the fine work it produces solo, the company often gangs up with other local groups for hybrid co-productions.

INSIDE TRACK OPEN BAR

For small Chicago theaters, liquor licences are famously difficult to secure, which is why so many storefront operations can sell you nothing stronger than a Dr Pepper. One exception is Wicker Park's **Chopin Theatre** (*see p288*), which plays host to many of Chicago's best young companies and has at long last snagged the proper paperwork to allow them to serve alcohol.

OTHER VENUES

Athenaeum Theatre

2936 N Southport Avenue, at W Oakdale Avenue, Lakeview (information 1-773 935 6860/Ticketmaster 1-312 902 1500/www. athenaeumtheatre.com). El: Brown or Purple to Wellington. **Box office** *Theatre* 3-7pm Tue-Fri. *Ticketmaster* 24hrs daily. **Tickets** $10-$35. **Credit** *Ticketmaster* AmEx, Disc, MC, V. **Map** p329 D3.
This antiquated, cathedral-like building was once an annex to a mammoth neighbouring church. Now it has several studio theatres and a large proscenium main stage; between them they play industry to shows of all shapes and sizes, including dance and performance art. Prices vary, but most of the performances cost less than $20.

Briar Street Theatre

3133 N Halsted Street, at W Belmont Avenue, Lakeview (1-773 348 4000/www.blueman.com). El: Brown, Purple or Red to Belmont. **Box office** 10am-6pm Mon-Wed; 10am-8pm Thur; 10am-7pm Fri; 10am-10pm Sat; noon-4pm Sun. **Tickets** $49-$59. **Credit** AmEx, Disc, MC, V. **Map** p329 F3.
This bigger-than-it-looks theatre might appear rather prosaic from the outside. Most nights, though, it's packed to the hilt with crowds who thrill to the colourful techno antics of Blue Man Group, which has occupied the space for years (and shows no signs of vacating soon).

Broadway in Chicago

Bank of America Theatre *18 W Monroe Street, between S State & S Dearborn Streets, he Loop. El: Blue or Red to Monroe; Brown, Green, Orange, Pink or Purple to Madison/Wabash.* **Map** p325 H12.
Cadillac Palace Theatre *151 W Randolph Street, at N LaSalle Street, the Loop. El: Blue, Brown, Green, Orange, Pink or Purple to Clark/Lake; Red to Lake.* **Map** p325 H12.
Drury Lane Theatre *Water Tower Place 175 E Chestnut Street, at N Michigan Avenue, Magnificent Mile. El: Red to Chicago.* **Map** p326 J9.
Ford Center for the Performing Arts Oriental Theatre *24 W Randolph Street, between N State & N Dearborn Streets. El: Blue, Brown, Green, Orange, Pink or Purple to Clark/Lake; Red to Lake.* **Map** p325 H12.
All venues *Information 1-312 977 1700/Ticketmaster 1-312 902 1400/www.broadway inchicago.com.* **Box office** *Ticketmaster* 24hrs daily. **Tickets** $15-$85. **Credit** AmEx, Disc, MC, V.
Three of the Loop's glorious old theatres have received a new lease of life courtesy of Broadway in Chicago, which uses them as a roadhouse for big-ticket touring shows. Gorgeous and resplendent, the

ARTS & ENTERTAINMENT

The Threepenny Opera, as performed by **Hypocrites**. *See p287.*

1926 **Cadillac Palace** retains the opulence of Golden-era vaudeville palaces, and now stages large-scale productions such as *The Lion King*. The spectacularly renovated **Bank of America Theatre** (formerly the Majestic Theatre) is the cosiest of the trio, and mixes touring shows with pre-Broadway try-outs of productions such as *Jersey Boys*. The ornate **Oriental Theatre**, former long-time home of *Wicked*, plays host to a rotating crop of crowd-pleasers. Broadway in Chicago also administers the **Drury Lane Theatre**, at Water Tower Place, which features a variety of light musical fare.

★ Chopin Theatre

1543 W Division Street, at N Ashland Avenue, Wicker Park (1-773 278 1500/www.chopin theatre. com). El: Blue to Division. **Box office** 10am-8pm daily. **Tickets** $5-$40. **Credit** varies by show. **Map** p331 C8.
The home base for some of the city's most dynamic storefront troupes, Wicker Park's Chopin is a resolutely funky venue that consistently draws young audiences. In addition to a rotating door for visiting European companies, many of them Polish, the Chopin regularly hosts innovative companies such as Tuta, a Chicago-based ensemble with strong European ties, and the House Theatre (*see p286*).

Royal George Theatre

1641 N Halsted Street, at W North Avenue, Old Town (1-312 988 9000/www.theroyalgeorge theatre.com). El: Red to North/Clybourn. **Box**

office 10am-6pm Mon-Tue; 10am-7.30pm Wed; 10am-8pm Thur-Sat; noon-5pm Sun. **Tickets** $25-$50. **Credit** AmEx, MC, V. **Map** p327 F7.
This dependable and tourist-friendly outlet is located across the street from Steppenwolf (*see p285*). The mainstage favours light comedy and musicals. Those looking to relive Catholic school days should make a beeline for the Great Room's sweetly satirical *Late Nite Catechism*.

Theatre Building Chicago

1225 W Belmont Avenue, at N Southport Avenue, Lakeview (1-773 327 5252/http://theatre building chicago.org). El: Brown, Purple or Red to Belmont. **Box office** noon-6pm Wed; noon-showtime Thur-Sun. **Tickets** $10-$32. **Credit** AmEx, Disc, MC, V. **Map** p329 D3.
Since the 1970s, this three-stage rental house has been the incubator for countless storefront companies. Some feature the city's top-shelf Equity actors, while others are produced on tight budgets; in other words, the reviewers are your friends. And as the bartenders never tire of reminding you, you can bring your drinks into the theatre. The resident company regularly produces workshops and new musicals.

Theatre on the Lake

2400 N Lake Shore Drive, at W Fullerton Avenue, Lincoln Park (1-312 742 7529/www. chicagopark district.com). Bus 151. **Box office** mid June-mid Aug. **Tickets** $15-$20. **Credit** MC, V. **Map** p328 H5.
Offering a selection of the season's best storefront plays, the Theatre on the Lake is a decades-old summer tradition for Chicago families. The partially open-air space on Lake Michigan changes the feel of many of the plays from their original venues; the drafty acoustics and the sea-salt air can feel like a day at the docks. But, miraculously, more troupes overcome it than not, and the variety of the plays makes this a terrific sampler of the local scene.

Victory Gardens Theater Greenhouse

2257 N Lincoln Avenue, at W Webster Avenue, Lincoln Park (1-773 871 3000/www.victorygardens. org). El: Brown, Purple or Red to Fullerton. **Box office** noon-8pm Tue-Sat; 10am-4pm Sun. **Tickets** $20-$35. **Credit** AmEx, Disc, MC, V. **Map** p328 F5.
Once home to the Tony-winning Victory Gardens company (*see p286*), this facility now simply serves as a rental house, with four theatres of varying sizes. Among the many dependable companies that call it home are the Eclipse Theatre, which devotes each of its seasons to a single American playwright; Shattered Globe, a long-standing producer of mostly middle-class dramas; Remy Bumppo, a dapper and intelligent company producing high-minded literary classics; MPAACT, which produces new and non-traditional African-American works; and the Latino-themed Teatro Vista (*see p287*).

Escapes & Excursions

Milwaukee Art Museum. *See p296.*

Escapes & Excursions

Head out of the Windy City for a breath of fresh air.

Simple geography makes Chicago an ideal base for touring the Midwest. Drive south-east from the Loop and within half an hour you're in Indiana; in an hour, you're in Michigan. Wisconsin is only an hour's drive north, with **Milwaukee** a mere 90 minutes away.

Shared by Illinois, Indiana, Michigan and Wisconsin, **Lake Michigan** is a great source of recreation. Day trips to the **Indiana Dunes** and Michigan's **Harbor Country** offer plenty of ways to enjoy the great inland sea, whether by fishing, boating or just watching the waves while you daydream.

Although **Amtrak** (*see p302*) runs services to several places listed in this chapter, you'll need a car to reach most of them. Bring a handful of both single-dollar bills and change: tolls range from 30 cents to $3, and some unmanned tollbooths don't offer change.

Illinois

SMALL-TOWN CHARM

Galena

Welcome to presidential country: Grant, Lincoln and Reagan all took root here. Driving the back roads east of Galena over the rolling terrain of one of the few hilly regions in prairie-flat Illinois, you may encounter a bright red stagecoach pulled by a pair of brown Belgian draught horses. An authentic reproduction of a 19th-century Concord stagecoach, it's one of many living history experiences that await in Galena, the quintessential time-warp town.

Established in the 1820s, Galena grew into a lead-mining boomtown at a time when Chicago was a tiny military outpost on the swampy lake shore. Today, the quaint little town is calmer, but does offer a tourist-friendly motherlode of arts and crafts, antiques shops, winery tours, stylish bistros and about 40 B&Bs. More than 85 per cent of its buildings appear on the National Register of Historic Places.

Housed in an 1858 Italianate mansion, the **Galena/Jo Daviess County Historical Society & Museum** (211 S Bench Street, 1-815 777 9129, www.galenahistorymuseum.org, free-$4.50) takes visitors back to the time when Galena was the richest port north of St Louis, attracting more than 350 steamboats a year. It offers an audio-visual presentation and a peek into the original shaft of one of the lead mines to which Galena owes its existence.

You can soak up more history at the **Ulysses S Grant Home State Historic Site** (500 Bouthillier Street, 1-815 777 3310, www.granthome.com, closed Mon & Tue, $3), a reminder of the day (18 August 1865) when, with a jubilant procession, speeches and fireworks, proud citizens welcomed home their returning Civil War hero. Before going to war, Grant had worked at a Galena store owned by his father and run by his younger brothers. Upon his return, Grant was presented with a handsome, two-storey furnished brick mansion on Bouthillier Street, purchased for $2,500 by a group of wealthy Republicans a few months prior to his homecoming. Following his death, his children bequeathed the mansion to the city of Galena in 1904, which later turned it over to the state of Illinois. The house has since been restored to the way it appeared in drawings published in an 1868 edition of Frank Leslie's *Illustrated Newspaper*, with the addition of assorted Grantabilia.

Take time to wander away from touristy Main Street to discover the 'Artists' Row' section of Spring Street, dotted with a wide variety of one-of-a-kind shops, galleries and B&Bs. A few minutes from Main Street, you'll also find a chunk of Ireland. Opened in 2003, the **Irish Cottage & Frank O'Dowd's Irish Pub** (9853 US Route 20 W, 1-815 776 0707,

www.theirishcottageboutiquehotel.com) nestle on a 20-acre site, containing a 75-room inn, and an Irish-themed pub and restaurant created by two first cousins from Ireland.

Galena is tucked away in Illinois's north-west corner, where Iowa, Wisconsin and Illinois converge near the Mississippi. A ten-minute drive north-east takes you to spectacular views from Charles Mound, the highest point in what otherwise is a monotonously flat state.

Getting there

Galena is 165 miles north-west of Chicago. By car, take I-90 (Northwest Tollway) to Rockford, then take US 20.

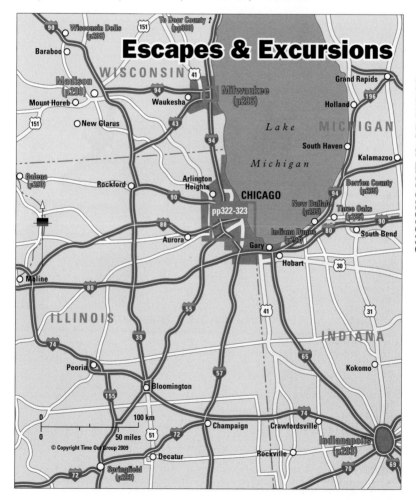

Springfield.

LAND OF LINCOLN
Springfield

Let's be honest: the reason to visit Springfield is Abraham Lincoln – he lived, worked and raised a family there from 1837 until 1861, when he was inaugurated as the 16th President of the United States. The town is chock-full of Lincoln memorabilia and sites, from the humble (his home) to the grand (his tomb). And Springfield has recently acquired a little more presidential polish, as the former stomping ground of then-state senator, now-commander-in-chief Barack Obama.

You can get a personal glimpse of Lincoln's life at his home: located in a leafy neighbourhood, the house is operated by the National Park Service as the **Lincoln's Home National Historic Site** (S 8th Street, 1-217 492 4241, www.nps.gov/liho, free), with guided tours by park rangers.

For a more Disneyfied take on America's greatest president, hit the fantastic **Abraham Lincoln Presidential Library & Museum** (212 N Sixth Street, 1-800 610 2094, free-$10) for its memorabilia, high-end exhibits and immersive presentations. In particular, check out 'Lincoln's Eyes', where smoke machines and 3-D projection are used in the presentation, and the seats actually shake (to mimic a cannon's boom) during a Civil War retelling.

The **Old State Capitol** (1 Old State Capitol Plaza, 1-217 785 7961, closed Mon & Sun, $2-$4), built in 1837, is a fine example of Greek revival architecture. Lincoln made his 'house divided' speech on slavery here in 1858; a scant seven years later, the body of the slain president lay in state in the same building. More recently, Obama announced his candidacy for the US presidency on the steps of the Old State Capitol.

Across from the Old State Capitol are the **Lincoln-Herndon Law Offices** (Adams Street, between 5th & 6th Streets, 1-217 785 7960, closed Mon, $1-$2), where Lincoln practised law. Cases were tried in the federal court below; Lincoln would sometimes lie on the office floor and observe courtroom proceedings through a peephole in the floorboards.

Springfield's most moving site is surely **Lincoln's Tomb** (1500 Monument Avenue, 1-217 782 2717, closed Sun & Mon, free). Most Tuesday evenings at 7pm between June and August (call ahead to confirm), a retreat ceremony is held in front of the tomb, with a drill, musket firing and the haunting sound of *Taps* played by a bugler. Captured in an inscription are the words spoken by Secretary of War Edwin M Stanton at Lincoln's death: 'Now he belongs to the ages.'

INSIDE TRACK
LUCKY HORSESHOE

If you ask after local delicacies in Springfield, locals will insist you partake of a 'horseshoe' sandwich, an open-faced sandwich on toasted sourdough bread with a hamburger patty or ham, topped with french fries and cheese sauce. It's every bit as messy as it sounds. The best version can be found at **D'arcys Pint** (661 W Stanford Avenue, 1-217 492 8800, closed Sun).

Although Lincoln is Springfield's most famous citizen (and Obama it's most famous visiting legislator), another of Springfield's native sons had an international reputation. Vachel Lindsay (1879-1931) was one of America's best-known poets during the early decades of the 20th century, and the **Vachel Lindsay Home** (603 S 5th Street, 1-217 524 0901, open Sat only, $2-$4) has been restored as a State Historic Site.

Getting there
Springfield is 200 miles south-west of Chicago. Take I-55 from Chicago to Springfield, exit 98-B (Clearlake).

Indiana
WINDY CITY TO INDY CITY
Indianapolis

Indianapolis buzzes with a cosmopolitan vibe mixed with a classically Midwestern warmth, prividing sights and sounds that can only be found here. Diagonal Massachusetts Avenue, or Mass Ave (www.discovermassave.com), is the artsy section; shops such as **At Home in the City** (434 Massachusetts Avenue, 1-317 955 9925) feature city-smart designs at small-town prices. Catch music at the **Chatterbox Jazz Club** (435 Massachusetts Avenue, 1-317 636 0584) or rub elbows with artists and sports fans at the **Lockerbie Pub** (631 E Michigan Street, 1-317 631 9545).

Mass Ave borders **Lockerbie Square** (www.lockerbiesquare.org), a quaint collection of cobbled streets and historic homes. The **Fountain Square** neighbourhood (www.discoverfountainsquare.com), on the south-east side of town, is anchored by the architecturally impressive **Fountain Square Theatre Building** (1105 Prospect Street, 1-317 686 6010), which contains a vintage 1950s soda fountain and diner, a rooftop restaurant and two duckpin bowling alleys (a regional version of bowling).

Plenty of more heady delights are available, too. The intriguing **Eiteljorg Museum of American Indians and Western Art** (500 W Washington Street, 1-317 636 9378, $5-$8) boasts a couple of minor O'Keeffes and an impressive collection of photography from indigenous peoples. While you're there, don't miss the scenic White River Canal Walk, which winds through ten and a half blocks between 11th and Washington Streets, linking the Eiteljorg Museum, the **NCAA Hall of Champions** and the **Indiana State Museum**. Jog along the paved walkways, or rent a paddleboat and cruise down the river.

The city boasts one of the best kids museums in the country: the **Children's Museum of Indianapolis** (3000 N Meridian Street, 1-317 334 3322, www.childrensmuseum.org, $9.50-$14.50). Wee naturalists can peer into a realfreshwater pond and backyard daredevils can scale a 20-foot climbing wall. Just before 1pm, watch the 26-foot water clock overflow in a dramatic siphon.

The works of Georges Seurat and a number of other neo-Impressionists are among the 50,000-plus pieces in the permanent collection at the striking **Indianapolis Museum of Art** (4000 Michigan Road, 1-317 923 1331, www.imamuseum.org, free), founded all the way back in 1883. The museum sits on an impressive 152-acre site; be sure to save some time to meander through the park and gardens.

A gastro mecca Indy isn't, so skip the newfangled and head straight for the classics. Steamy hot bagels and pastrami sandwiches stacked higher than Indy's tallest building rule at **Shapiro's** (808 S Meridian Street, 1-317 631 4041), an old-school Jewish deli and cafeteria on the south side of town. Foamy beer and schnitzels are mainstay items at the near-legendary **Rathskeller** (401 E Michigan Street, 1-317 636 0396), a German restaurant and brewpub, with an outstanding beer garden that's open in the warmer months.

Getting there

Indianapolis is 185 miles south-east of Chicago. Take the I-90 East tollway toward Indiana, then merge onto I-65 South which goes directly to Indianapolis.

THE GREAT OUTDOORS
Indiana Dunes & vicinity

Just as Easterners cherish a trip to 'the shore', thousands of Chicagoans grow up looking forward to visiting 'the dunes'. Located along

Indiana's north-western corner, this beach playground offers swimming, bodysurfing and the exhilaration of a romp down steep, sandy slopes after a leg-wearying climb to the summit. On a clear day, the Chicago skyline is visible from the shore, shimmering on the horizon.

The sloping white expanses of the dunes encompass the **Indiana Dunes State Park** (1600 North 25 E, Chesterton, 1-219 926 1952, www.state.in.us/dnr), Chicago's closest beach getaway and just an hour's drive from the city. Relax along the park's three miles of Lake Michigan-hugging shoreline, or explore more than 15,000 acres of dunes, bogs, marshes and prairie grounds in the surrounding **Indiana Dunes National Lakeshore** (Highway 12 & County Line Road, Chesterton, 1-219 926 7561, www.nps.gov/indu, free). The federal nature reserve spans 15 miles of shoreline and offers canoeing, hiking and other outdoor activities.

If you're up for a little more exertion than lying around on the beach, take a hike along the Mt Baldy Trail (Highway 12, Michigan City). It's less than a mile long, but hiking a sand dune isn't easy and you'll definitely feel it the next day. But the pay-off is well worth it, particularly at sunset: a spectacular view of the Chicago skyline from an entirely new vantage point. Less adventurous types can take a flatter path around the 126-foot (38-metre) 'mountain' of sand, but be sure to snag a map at the **Dorothy Buell Memorial Visitor's Center** (Indiana Highway 49 & Munson Road, Chesterton, 1-219 395 8914). The centre boasts several interactive exhibits about the surrounding terrain, as well as a pleasant bookstore.

Getting there

By car, take the Chicago Skyway and I-80/90 and I-94 to Highway 49.

By train, the Chicago South Shore & South Bend Railroad follows the curve of the Lake Michigan shoreline into Indiana and makes several stops in Lake and Porter Counties. Trains leave from Randolph Street station in the Loop.

INSIDE TRACK
GAMBLING ON INDIANA

A trip to the dunes isn't complete without a stop at one of the area's clutch of riverboat casinos, the king of which is **Hammond's Horseshoe Casino** (777 Casino Center Drive, Hammond, 1-866 711 7463, www.horseshoe.com). It's the closest casino to the city: you can't miss its massive sign from the Chicago Skyway.

Michigan

HARBOR COUNTRY

Just an hour and a half's drive from the city, Michigan's Harbor Country is a pretty amalgam of shabby-chic shops, bucolic B&Bs, tree-shaded paths and white-sand beaches. Here are three ways in which you can experience it.

New Buffalo & vicinity

Red Arrow Highway, which runs through the heart of Harbor Country, connects dozens of tiny beach towns that come to life during Michigan's balmy summer. The largest and most central destination is New Buffalo (population 2,200), roughly an hour from the Loop. It's a sweet place, well worth a wander.

Stroll down Whittaker Street towards the centre of town. Lined with a few chic clothing shops, Whittaker is home to the **Stray Dog Bar & Grill** (245 N Whittaker Street, New Buffalo, 1-269 469 2727, www.thestraydog.com), packed in summer with locals vying for a spot on its rooftop deck. Continue down the block to the New Buffalo Beach, which offers casual surfing and an outpost of the popular Oink's ice-cream chain. After working up an appetite in the outdoors, head to **Redamak's** (616 E Buffalo Street, New Buffalo, 1-269 469 4522), where the tasty, no-frills burgers and fries have been satisfying locals since 1975.

About 20 miles up the road at **Warren Dunes State Park** (12032 Red Arrow Highway, Sawyer, 1-269 426 4013), giant piles of sand, some nearly 250 feet (75 metres) high, make a perfect perch from which to take in the lake. The surrounding woods provide more than six miles of trails, making it a great place for spotting wood ducks, opossum, foxes and all sorts of woodland creatures.

Getting there
New Buffalo is approximately 60 miles east of Chicago. Take I-90 east to the La Porte exit IN-39 (La Porte Road).

Berrien County wineries

The tri-county south-west region of Michigan has been designated an American Viticultural Area by the name of 'Lake Michigan Shore'. Tucked into the rolling hills and fertile valleys of Berrien County, little more than an hour's drive from the Loop, nearly a dozen wineries take advantage of the micro-climate, producing a range of wines that are sold locally and nationally. Visitors are generally welcome.

Among the best of the bunch is **Tabor Hill Winery** (185 Mount Tabor Road, Buchanan,

1-800 283 3363, www.taborhill.com, tours Apr-Nov, tastings year-round, free), which attracts couples in search of fine dining and romantic sunsets. Windows look out over the vineyards; on the horizon sit the dark, brooding humps of the dune ridges along Lake Michigan.

Rick Moersch was a winemaker at Tabor Hill for 14 years before he opened the **Round Barn Winery, Distillery & Brewery** (10983 Hills Road, Baroda, 1-800 716 9463, www.heartofthe vineyard.com, $5 for a tasting), in 1992. Wine, beer and vodka tastings are conducted in the eponymous round Amish barn. Discovered in northern Indiana, it was dismantled, transported 90 miles to this site and rebuilt by Amish craftsmen. A crescent-shaped copper bar features matching wall sconces decorated with alchemical symbols from the Middle Ages.

Family-owned and family-oriented **Lemon Creek Fruit Farm & Winery** (533 East Lemon Creek Road, Berrien Springs, 1-269 471 1321, www.lemoncreekwinery.com, $5 for a tasting) is a vast working farm with a fruit stand, pick-your-own orchards, tractor rides for children and abundant wildlife, including deer, foxes, hawks and owls, plus waterfowl that settle on a five-acre pond. The vineyards produce white wines ranging from dry chardonnay to sweet vidal blanc, reds that include an award-winning cabernet sauvignon, grape and raspberry sparkling wines, and three non-alcoholic sparkling juices. Just down the road is the **Domaine Berrien Cellars & Winery** (398 E Lemon Creek Road, Berrien Springs, 1-269 473 9463, hours vary, www.domaineberrien.com), a popular picnic venue. The winery was opened in 2001 by Wally Maurer, who himself pours during the week.

The best of the bunch is **St Julian Winery** (716 S Kalamazoo Street, Paw Paw, 1-269 657 5568, www.stjulian.com, free), established in 1921 and Michigan's oldest winery by far. Located in Paw Paw, St Julian also has a tasting room at downtown Union Pier (9145 Union Pier Road, Union Pier, 1-269 469 3150), with a selection of fairly priced favourites.

Getting there
At the heart of the Lake Michigan Shore viticultural region is St Joseph, approximately 95 miles north-east of Chicago. Take I-94 east to the Stevensville exit. The winery exits are posted along I-94. Amtrak runs a service from Chicago to St Joseph.

Three Oaks

Modest in comparison to its neighbouring beach towns, Three Oaks (population 1,900) is a cultured gem amid the cluster of tourist destinations along the lake. A second home for many Chicagoans, the town provides big-city comforts – fine dining, arts and entertainment – on a small-town scale.

Every summer, hundreds of visitors descend on the place for the annual Sound of Silents Film Festival at the restored, turn-of-the-century **Vickers Theatre** (6 N Elm Street, Three Oaks, 1-269 756 3522, www.vickers theatre.com). The Vickers sponsors live music in the town's Dewey Cannon Park during the summer, and screens indie and art-house films all year round. Down the street is the **Acorn Theater** (107 Generations Drive, Three Oaks, 1-269 756 3879, www.acorntheater.com), a beautifully updated performance space located in the town's historic featherbone factory.

Three Oaks is also known for its visual arts and antiques. **Ipso Facto** (1 W Ash Street, Three Oaks, 1-269 756 3404, closed Tue-Thur) concentrates on accessories, artefacts, and vintage-modern and antique finds.

A handful of popular dining establishments are worth the quick drive from the lakeshore. **Froehlich's** (26 N Elm Street, Three Oaks, 1-269 756 6002, www.shopfroehlichs.com), pronounced 'fray-licks', oozes small-town charm. Nibble on delicious breads, sandwiches, cheeses, home-canned jams and other delights at this gourmet deli and bakery. Housed in a 100-year-old storefront, the heart-stoppingly cute **Viola** (102 N Elm Street, Three Oaks, 1-269 756 9420, closed Tue) opened in April 2005, and now serves breakfast, lunch and afternoon tea.

Getting there

Three Oaks is approximately 80 miles east of Chicago. Take I-94 east to the US-12 E exit 4A to Three Oaks/Niles.

Wisconsin

THE SECOND CITY'S SECOND CITY
Milwaukee

Milwaukee is as traditional as the oompah bands that it trots out periodically to celebrate its German heritage, and as contemporary as the experimental theatre that flourishes in the revitalised downtown historic districts. It has big-city assets: museums, galleries, orchestra, opera and ballet companies, lively nightlife, plenty of parkland and major league sports. Yet it's also quiet enough to please families, and compact enough to reward the day tripper up in town from its rival city to the south: the 90-minute commute from Chicago is well worth the effort, whether for an afternoon of art or a Friday night fish-fry.

While Milwaukee's German roots have ensured its reputation as a mecca for beer (Pabst, Schlitz, Blatz and, most famously, Miller were all started in Milwaukee by German families), it's recently become known for its architecture. Chief among the town's marvels is the **Milwaukee Art Museum** (700 N Art Museum Drive, 1-414 224 3200, www.mam.org, closed Mon, free-$8). The original building has a showy extension designed by world-renowned architect Santiago Calatrava. The extension was inspired by the museum's lakeside location: check out the cabled pedestrian bridge with a mast suggested by the form of a sailing boat, the curving single-storey galleria reminiscent of a wave and, most strikingly, the moving steel louvres, which pay homage to the wings of a bird. It's a credit to the museum's 20,000 works,

Milwaukee Art Museum.

including a significant number by Milwaukee native Georgia O'Keeffe, that the art itself isn't overshadowed.

In addition to its growing architectural reputation, Milwaukee's beer legacy remains. Although Miller is Milwaukee's only surviving megabrewery, it's complemented by several microbreweries that have started up over the past decade. At the same time, swathes of the admittedly small downtown area have been redeveloped to pleasing effect, most notably the Historic Third Ward, and new businesses are springing up around the city.

Much of the town's prosperity is mirrored in a recent downtown renaissance, especially on the RiverWalk along the Milwaukee River, which the city hopes will bring in more visitors. A prime example of the city's revitalisation and flourishing performing arts scene is the 4,100-seat **Milwaukee Theatre** (Wisconsin Center District, 400 W Wisconsin Avenue, 1-414 908 6000), a $32 million makeover of the historic Milwaukee Auditorium, which opened in

November 2003. The theatre features an elegant domed rotunda lobby and reception area, and hosts a range of Broadway shows as part of its programme of entertainments.

Culturally, Milwaukee's on the up. Aside from festivals, the biggest of which is late June's **Summerfest** (1-800 273 3378, www.summerfest.com), the **Milwaukee Symphony Orchestra** (www.mso.org) draws the crowds, and a number of theatre groups push drama further up the town's agenda. Incidentally, make sure you don't get the **Marcus Center for the Performing Arts** (929 N Water Street, 1-414 273 7121, www.marcuscenter.org), downtown's main entertainment venue, confused with **Art's Performing Center** (144 E Juneau Avenue, 1-414 271 8288), a creatively named strip joint nearby.

Families love the **Milwaukee Public Museum** (800 W Wells Street, 1-414 278 2702, www.mpm.edu, free-$11), a three-floor natural history museum that holds some six million exhibits, but there are other attractions nearby;

not for nothing is the area known informally as Museum Center. **Discovery World** (500 N Harbor Drive, 1-414 765 9966, www. discoveryworld.org, closed Mon, free-$16.95) is full of interactive exhibits; the **Humphrey IMAX Dome Theater** (800 W Wells Street, 1-414 319 4629, www.mpm.edu, boasts a six-storey high screen and a 12,000-watt sound system.

The town's real must-see is the **Milwaukee County Zoo** (10001 W Bluemound Road, 1-414 771 3040, www.milwaukeezoo.org, prices vary). With 3,000 animals across 200 acres, it's one of the nation's largest and best zoos. Elsewhere, **Betty Brinn Children's Museum** (929 E Wisconsin Avenue, 1-414 390 5437, www. bbcmkids.org, closed Mon from Sept to May, free-$6) is an interactive place designed for under-10s, while one of Milwaukee's newer and most fascinating museums, the **Eisner American Museum of Advertising & Design** (208 N Water Street, 1-414 847 3290, www.eisnermuseum.org, closed Mon & Tue, free-$5) provides colourful, interactive exhibits on how advertising effects our culture. And the most recent buzz has been about the **Harley-Davidson Museum** (400 Canal Street, 1-877 436 8738, www.h-dmuseum.com, free-$16), which opened in 2008. The huge, sleek, industrial-style exhibition space features more motorcycles than you can shake a stick at, and is part of a sprawling new complex set in 20 park-like acres along the river.

For a chance to soak up Brew City's history, along with some suds, head to the **Miller Brewing Co** (4251 W State Street, 1-800 944 5483, www.millerbrewing.com, free), which is open for free (albeit self-aggrandising) tours. Learn how the brewery churns out six gazillion bottles of Miller Lite a minute and how Miller has five of the top ten selling beers in the US. Gratis beers are a fitting end to the brisk tour. Beer connoisseurs (as opposed to beer guzzlers) might prefer a trip to the **Lakefront Brewery**

**INSIDE TRACK
CUSTARD CRAZE**

Roadfood, Jane and Michael Stern's invaluable guide to diners, mom-and-pop joints and other low-key, high-reward local eateries across the US, contains a huge array of recommendations for Milwaukee. If you only have time for one, make it an order of frozen custard from **Leon's Frozen Custard Drive-In** (3131 S 27th Street, 1-414 383 1784), which reputedly acted as the inspiration for Arnold's Drive-In on *Happy Days*.

(1872 N Commerce Street, 1-414 372 8800, www.lakefrontbrewery.com, tours $6). The tour includes a souvenir pint glass, four pours of (good) beer and a coupon for another free beer at various local bars.

Shoppers and diners will be charmed by the Historic Third Ward, where boho boutiques, gastropubs and posh eateries line the refurbed blocks. In the heart of the district is the **Milwaukee Public Market** (400 N Water Street, 1-414 336 1111, www.milwaukee publicmarket.org), built in autumn 2005 in an effort to preserve the neighbourhood's history as a public marketplace. In it you'll find dozens of vendors selling gourmet and organic produce, seafood from around the world, baked goods, flowers and, of course, pounds and pounds of cheese.

Getting there

By car, Milwaukee is approximately 90 miles north of Chicago on I-94. Milwaukee is a 90-minute train ride from Chicago's Union Station; services are frequent.

WATER WORLD
The Wisconsin Dells

Dispensing Hoopla with a capital 'H', the Wisconsin Dells remains one of the Midwest's great child-pleasers. Adventure parks and video arcades, helicopter rides and go-kart races, minigolf and hot dogs… The Dells is the place to head when the kids whine about wanting something to do.

The Dells is forever reinventing itself, adding new attractions every season. None, though, has had as much impact as the indoor waterparks that have popped up all over town; indeed, the place now touts itself as the 'Waterpark Capital of the World'. Among the biggest and best are the elegant **Kalahari Resort & Convention Center** (1305 Kalahari Drive, 1-877 253 5466, www.kalahariresort.com); the golfer-friendly **Wilderness Hotel & Golf Resort** (511 E Adams Street, 1-800 867 9453, www.wildernessterritory.com); and the enormous **Mt Olympus Water & Theme Park** (1701 Wisconsin Dells Parkway, 1-608 254 2490, www.mtolympusthemepark.com), which expanded in 2006 by adding six new outdoor theme-park rides in addition to its 37 waterslides, two floating rivers, water basketball and shallow play-water areas. These wet and wild destinations have helped to transform the Dells from a strictly seasonal resort into a year-round tourist hub.

Despite its brash, noisy front, the Dells somehow remains the scenic destination it was back when 19th-century photographer Henry

Madison.

Hamilton Bennett first set out to capture the landscape. The towering sandstone cliffs and cool, fern-filled gullies remain unspoiled, and a tour of the upper and lower rivers by boat or aboard an amphibious 'duck', a World War II landing craft, are enjoyable outings (try **Wisconsin Ducks**, 1-608 254 8751, www.wisconsinducktours.com, closed Dec-Mar, $11.85-$21.70). To see the Dells as Bennett saw them, visit the **HH Bennett Studio & History Center** (215 Broadway, 1-608 253 3523, www.hhbennett.wisconsinhistory.org, closed Mon-Fri from Nov to Apr, $6-$7).

A number of shows keep children on their toes. The **Famous Tommy Bartlett Thrill Show** (560 Wisconsin Dells Parkway, 1-608 254 2525, www.tommybartlett.com, closed Labor Day-Memorial Day, $9-$23) has been entertaining visitors for a while; magician **Rick Wilcox** (1666 Wisconsin Dells Parkway, 1-608 254 5511, www.rickwilcox.com, times & prices vary) is also a popular figure here.

Getting there

Wisconsin Dells is 188 miles north-west of Chicago. Take I-90 from Chicago to Dells exits 92, 89, 87, 85 (the best exit for downtown is 87).

LITTLE TOWN ON THE PRAIRIE
Madison

Every Saturday, 20,000 locals and tourists flock to the square around Wisconsin's neo-classical Capitol building. Although the building dates from 1917 and boasts a quite singular granite dome, it's neither history nor architecture that attracts the crowds. This is the **Dane County Farmers' Market** (www.dcfm.org), awash with the aroma of freshly brewed coffee, the sweet scent of basil and the distinctive tang of hand-made cheeses. When you're ready for a break, rest on the lawn or on the Capitol steps, where there's often a concert going on.

This weekly ritual illustrates why Madison is so highly regarded by those who live here and those who visit. Built on an isthmus bordered by Lake Monona and Lake Mendota, it's a beautiful town. Five lakes, 13 public beaches, 50 miles of bike paths and more than 200 parks draw the crowds in summer for cycling, hiking, fishing and canoeing. But Madison has a full calendar of events and activities year-round. Winter sees the locals ice-skating, ice-fishing, skiing and sledding.

Culturally, Madison punches above its weight, with a resident orchestra, a theatre and a full performing arts schedule at the University of Wisconsin at Madison. It keeps improving, too: the **Overture Center for the Arts** (201 State Street, 1-608 258 4177, www.overture center.com), added in 2004, focuses on local artists in a multitude of disciplines, including an International Festival in February (www. cityofmadison.com/overture/if.htm).

Downtown's 'Museum Mile' includes the **Madison Children's Museum** (100 State Street, 1-608 256 6445, www.madisonchildrens museum.org, free-$4); the **Madison Museum of Contemporary Art** (227 State Street, 1-608 257 0158, www.mmoca.org, closed Mon, free); the **University of Wisconsin-Madison's Chazen Museum of Art** (800 University Avenue, 1-608 263 2246, www.chazen.wisc.edu, closed Mon, free); the **Wisconsin Historical Museum** (30 N Carroll Street, 1-608 264 6565, www.wisconsinhistory.org/museum, closed Mon, $3-$4); and the **Wisconsin Veterans' Museum** (30 W Mifflin Street, 1-608 267 1799, http://museum.dva.state.wi.us, closed Sun Oct–Mar only, free).

The **Monona Terrace Community & Convention Center** (1 John Nolen Drive, 1-608 261 4000, www.mononaterrace.com, free), located on the shores of Lake Monona, was conceived by Frank Lloyd Wright more than 60 years ago, but wasn't completed until 1997 after decades of architectural and civic controversy. This world-class, five-level facility hosts conventions, meetings and special events; tours are offered daily (1pm, $3).

Elsewhere, clusters of boutiques, speciality shops and restaurants on King, Monroe and Williamson streets capture the city's eclectic character. The antiquarian bookstores around State Street draw collectors from Chicago and beyond in search of rare first editions.

Getting there

Madison is 145 miles north-west of Chicago. Take I-90 to Beltline Highway (US 12/18); follow signs to downtown (look for the Capitol dome symbol).

INSIDE TRACK MICKIE'S

At weekends, it sometimes feels as if the whole of Madison is queueing for breakfast at **Mickie's Dairy Bar** (1511 Monroe Street, 1-608 256 9476). Don't worry: the line moves fast, and so does the kitchen, dishing up huge, messy breakfasts to a crowd of appreciative locals (many students) in an old-school ambience. Prices could hardly be lower.

BACK TO NATURE
Door County

Those who say the Midwest is landlocked have clearly never ventured to Door County, the long, elegant peninsula home to a serenely isolated cluster of communities anchored along Lake Michigan's westernmost dip into Wisconsin. Engulfing about a dozen towns and numerous tiny villages on either side of the peninsula, and many surrounding islands, this 300-mile curved stretch of shoreline is popular in summer for sailing, fishing, hiking, canoeing and other water-based activities, but also serves as a peaceful winter getaway.

Door County's mainland peninsula has two sides – literally. The west side faces mild **Green Bay**, where winding roads connect tourist towns such as **Egg Harbor**, **Fish Creek** and **Ephraim**. The county's first inhabitants developed the sweeping **Sturgeon Bay** on the Lake Michigan (east) side of the land, the peninsula's county seat and only real city. With a population of 865, it's a typically friendly Midwestern town, but its spectacular surroundings stand in stark contrast to the cow-towns and corn country that surrounds Chicago.

Travel north a few miles along the peninsula for a real escape. Just south of the town of **Jacksonport**, you'll find **Cave Point and Whitefish Dunes State Park** (3275 Clarks Lake Road, Sturgeon Bay, 1-920 823 2400), which is know for its picturesque wave-worn limestone caves.

For those in search of island life with all the amenities, **Washington Island** (www. washingtonislandchamber.com), Door County's largest, offers an easy respite from the main peninsula's hustle and bustle. After arriving in Detroit Harbor, mellow and relaxed recreation awaits: Washington Island plays host to arts and gallery scenes, as well as a handful of museums, shopping districts and a first-rate golf course, the **Deer Run Golf Course & Resort** (1885 Michigan Road, 1-920 847 2017, seasonal hours). Take it all in from **Mountain Park**. Or if you're visiting during summer, stick around for a performance by the **Peninsula Players** (W4351 Peninsula Players Road, Fish Creek, 1-920 868 3287, www.peninsulaplayers.com), where top-notch actors imported from around the Midwest perform in an open-air theatre tucked into the woods.

Getting there

By car, Door County is around 250 miles north of Chicago. Take I-94 to Milwaukee, then I-43 to Green Bay.

Directory

Getting Around

DIRECTORY

ARRIVING & LEAVING

By air

Chicago is served by two airports.

O'Hare International *1-773 686 2200/www.flychicago.com.* O'Hare (ORD) is one of the busiest airports in the world. All domestic flights and international departures by domestic airlines use Terminals 1, 2 and 3. Non-US international airlines use T5, with two exceptions: Lufthansa and Iberia, which arrive at T5 but depart from T1 and T3 respectively. The terminals are linked by an airport train system.

The CTA provides a 24-hour El service on its Blue line between O'Hare and downtown. The journey takes 45-50mins, plus 15-20mins to travel between the station and the airport. Follow signs marked 'Trains to the city'. Like all CTA fares (*see below*), the fare is $2.25

The next cheapest option for getting into town is by **shuttle bus**. Continental Airport Express (1-888 284 3826, www.airport express.com), which has a booth in the baggage reclaim area, charges $25 for the journey downtown (a round-trip ticket costs $46).

There's a **taxi** rank outside the baggage reclaim area of each terminal. The fare to downtown should come to about $35-$40 plus tip. Note that traffic on I-90 can extend the half-hour travel time, and the fare, at busy times. Money can be saved by using the Shared Ride scheme: up to four passengers can share a cab from O'Hare to downtown (as far north as Fullerton Avenue and as far south as McCormick Place) for $15 per person. During quiet spells, it can take time to assemble a shared ride.

Midway International *1-773 686 2200/www.flychicago.com.* Smaller than O'Hare, Midway (MDW) is used mostly by lower-cost airlines. However, it's also closer to the Loop, and easier to negotiate than sprawling O'Hare.

Travelling to and from town on the **El** is easy on the Orange line, which runs to the Loop. The journey time is around 35mins, and the fare is the standard $2.25.

As with O'Hare, Continental Airport Express (1-888 284 3826, www.airportexpress.com) operates a **shuttle bus** into the city. The firm has a booth in the baggage reclaim; it costs $20 for a single or $36 for a round-trip ticket.

The **taxi** ride to downtown from Midway should cost around $25-$30 plus tip and will take 20-25mins. The Shared Ride scheme allows for a flat fee of $10 per person.

By bus

Greyhound services (1-800 231 2222, www.greyhound.com) use the city's main bus station (630 W Harrison Street, at S Desplaines Street, West Loop, 1-312 408 5821).

By rail

Amtrak trains (1-800 872 7245, www.amtrak.com) pull into **Union Station** (225 S Canal Street, at W Jackson Street, the Loop).

PUBLIC TRANSPORT

Chicagoland transport is overseen by the **Regional Transportation Authority** (**RTA**). The service is split between the **Chicago Transit Authority** (**CTA**), which runs buses and the elevated/subway train system (aka the 'El') in the

city; the **Metra** rail network, which links the city to its suburbs; and **Pace**, a suburban bus system.

CTA *567 W Lake Street, IL 60661 (1-888 968 7282/1-312 664 7200/ www.transitchicago.com).* **Open** *By phone* 7am-8pm Mon-Fri.
Metra *547 W Jackson Boulevard, IL 60661 (1-312 322 6777/www. metrarail.com).* **Open** *By phone* 8am-5pm Mon-Fri.
Pace *550 W Algonquin Road, Arlington Heights, IL 60005 (1-847 364 7223/www.pacebus.com).* **Open** *By phone* 8am-5pm Mon-Fri.
RTA *Suite 1550, 175 W Jackson Boulevard, IL 60604 (1-312 913 3200/www.rtachicago.com).* **Open** *By phone* 4.45am-1am daily.

CTA fares & tickets

The CTA operates a simple fare structure across its network of buses and trains, but prices vary depending on how you pay.

Short-term visitors might be best off with a **Visitor Pass**, which allows unlimited travel across the El and bus network for a flat fee. A one-day pass costs $5.75, with a three-day ticket priced at $14 and a seven-day pass retailing at $23. Tickets are valid for 24, 72 or 168 hours from the first time the card is used, and are available from O'Hare (Blue line), Midway (Orange) and Chicago (Red) El stations, Union Station, the Chicago Cultural Center (*see p310*), the Water Works Visitor Center (*see p310*) and a number of other locations (including many drugstores but excluding all other stations). For a full list of locations, see www.transitchicago.com.

Visitors planning to travel less often should consider a **Transit Card**, which bills travellers on a per-journey basis. The customer decides how much value to add to their card, available from vending machines at all El stations; when the money runs out or runs low, cards can be recharged at any machine. The flat fare of $2.25 is deducted when passengers pass the card through the reader on entering each bus or station. If you make another journey within two hours, you'll be charged a 'transfer' rate of 25¢; a further transfer is free.

The **Chicago Card** and **Chicago Card Plus** are electronic passes valid on El trains and on CTA and Pace buses. (UK residents may recognise the technology as similar to that of London's Oyster card.) When money runs low, it's topped up through a debit system tied to the user's credit or debit card. Fares on the El cost $2.25, with bus fares at $2. For each $20 added to the card, the customer receives a $2 bonus. For short-term visitors, the disadvantages are that the card costs $5 and is less widely available than other tickets (you can apply online, by mail, by phone or in person from selected locations; see www.chicago-card.com).

If you don't have a ticket, you can pay **cash** on buses, but the $2.25 fare doesn't allow for any transfers.

CTA trains

The CTA's elevated/subway train system, or the 'El', consists of eight colour-coded lines. It's generally fast and reliable, if a little creaky. For a map of the network, *see p335*.

Most lines run every 5-15mins, between 4.30-5am and 12.30-1.30am daily. The main exceptions are the Red and Blue lines, which run 24 hours (every 15-20mins in the dead of night), and the Purple line, which runs south of Howard only in rush hours (roughly 6-10am and 3-7pm). Care should be taken late at night. Destinations are shown on the front and side of trains, and on platforms.

Several El stations share a name. For instance, there are three different stations called 'Chicago' (on the Red, Purple/Brown and Blue lines). For clarity, our listings include each station's parent line.

There are plenty of El stations in the Loop: in the area bounded by Wells Street, W Wacker Drive, Michigan Avenue and Van Buren Street, 48 blocks square, there are no fewer than 16 stops. We've listed the nearest one or two stations to each venue, but if you're travelling between two points within the Loop, it may be quicker to walk.

CTA buses

CTA bus stops are marked by white signs listing the names and numbers of the routes they serve. Most routes run every 10-15mins from dawn until at least 10.30pm daily. Night buses ('Night Owls') run every half-hour on some routes.

Most routes stick to one north-south or east-west street, unless they're forced off it by one-way systems. Some of the more popular and useful routes are listed below.

6: Jackson Park Express The Jackson Park Express is useful for visitors wanting to travel between the Loop/Museum Campus and Hyde Park. Southbound, it runs down State Street between the river and Balbo Drive, then turns east on Balbo and heads south to Museum Campus at 11th and Columbus. From here, the bus runs non-stop down Lake Shore Drive as far as 47th; here, it resumes a stopping service along Lake Park Avenue and Hyde Park Boulevard to 57th Street by the Museum of Science & Industry, then continues south. The bus follows the same route north until Balbo, where it heads north up Michigan Avenue rather than State.

20: Madison Westbound, the 20 runs on Madison from Michigan Avenue to Austin Boulevard in Oak Park. Eastbound, it turns on to Washington at Halsted Street, then terminates at Washington and Michigan. In rush hours, its route is extended to the Illinois Center.

22: Clark Southbound, the 22 runs on Clark between the far North Side and Polk Street in the Loop. The northbound route runs up Dearborn from Polk Street to Washington Square, where it joins Clark Street.

29: State The 29 runs up State Street from the far South Side to Illinois Street, where it turns east and heads to Navy Pier. The return journey follows the same route, but leaves Navy Pier along Grand Avenue until it connects with State.

36: Broadway Southbound, the 36 runs from the far North Side down Broadway to Diversey, then heads south to Clark before joining State Street at Division and continuing south to Polk Street. Northbound, it runs up Dearborn from Polk to Illinois Street where it joins State. At Division, it joins Clark; at Diversey, it joins Broadway and heads north.

56: Milwaukee Northbound, the 56 runs west on Madison from Michigan to Jefferson, then north on Jefferson, west on Fulton and north-east on Milwaukee through Wicker

Park. Southbound, it runs on Milwaukee to Desplaines, then east to the Loop on Washington.

66: Chicago The eastbound 66 runs on Chicago Avenue between the far West Side and Fairbanks Court in Streeterville, then heads south on Fairbanks to Illinois Street and then east to Navy Pier. The westbound route is near-identical, but leaves Navy Pier along Grand Avenue instead of Illinois.

72: North The 72 runs along North Avenue between Lincoln Park and the far West Side.

Metra rail

The Metra is an 11-line rail system that serves 243 stations in Illinois and parts of Indiana. The termini, all in the Loop or West Loop, are **LaSalle Station** (414 S LaSalle Street, at E Congress Parkway); **Millennium Station** (E Randolph Street, at N Michigan Avenue); the **Ogilvie Transportation Center** (500 W Madison Street, at S Canal Street); and **Union Station** (*see p302*). Fares run from single-route fares to a $5 ticket that allows unlimited weekend travel.

Pace buses

Pace buses serve the suburbs. A regular fare costs $1.75, with premium fares (on four routes that serve the Loop) at $4. Reduced-price fares are available for 7-11s; under-7s ride free. CTA Chicago Cards are valid on all Pace routes; Transit Cards are accepted on most services. Pace also offers a number of reduced-rate passes; among them is the Pace/CYA Seven-Day Pass ($28).

TAXIS

Taxis are prevalent in most locales covered in this guide, and can be hailed on the street. Further out, and on the South Side, you'd be better off booking a taxi; staff in bars and restaurants can help.

Meters start at $2.25, rising by 20¢ for every one-ninth of a mile or 36 seconds of waiting time. The first extra passenger (aged 12-65) is charged $1, with additional passengers adding a further 50¢ to the fare. Journeys to or from either airport incur an additional $1 charge. There is no fee for baggage. Tipping is optional, but expected.

Taxis are usually safe and reliable. If you have a complaint, call the **Department of Consumer Services** on 1-312 744 4006 or on 311. Four taxi firms are listed below.

DIRECTORY

American United *1-773 248 7600.*
Checker Cab *1-312 243 2537.*
Flash Cab *1-773 561 4444/*
www.flashcab.com.
Yellow Cab *1-312 829 4222/*
www.yellowcabchicago.com.

DRIVING

Traffic in Chicago can be wearying,
especially in the Loop and River
North. The city's grid system
makes it easy to negotiate. But if
you're staying in the centre of town
and not planning to travel far,
there's no point hiring a car.

The **American Automobile
Association** (**AAA**) offers maps,
guides and other perks to members
of affiliated organisations, such as
the British AA. See www.aaa.com
or call 1-866 968 7222.

Parking

Parking in Chicago is expensive.
Street parking is limited and meter-
controlled; parking in a car park
costs upwards of $15 per day, at
least twice that at hotels. If you're
towed, call the police on 311 or 1-
312 744 4000. You'll end up paying
the cost of retrieving your car from
the car pound plus a separate fine.

Car hire

Some firms will rent cars to over-
21s, but you'll usually need to be
25 or older. Tax is 16 per cent.

Renters will be offered required
insurance and a collision-damage
waiver. If you're not covered by
your home policy, take both. UK
travellers should note that while
deals struck with the UK offices of
the major firms include insurance,
it's often cheaper for long rentals to
rent the car from the US operation
and rely for insurance on the good-
value, year-long policy available
from www.insurance4carhire.com.

All major firms have outlets at
O'Hare; most are also at Midway.

Alamo *US: 1-800 462 5266/www.
alamo.com. UK: 0870 400 4562/
www.alamo.co.uk.*
Avis *US: 1-800 331 1212/www.
avis.com. UK: 0870 606 0100/
www.avis.co.uk.*
Budget *US: 1-800 527 0700/
www.budget.com. UK: 0844 581
2231/www.budget.co.uk.*
Dollar *US: 1-800 800 3665/
www.dollar.com. UK: 0808 234
7524/www.dollar.co.uk.*
Enterprise *US: 1-800 261 7331/
www.enterprise.com. UK: 0870 350
3000/www.enterprise.co.uk.*

Hertz *US: 1-800 654 3131/www.
hertz.com. UK: 0870 844 8844/
www.hertz.co.uk.*
National *US: 1-800 227 7368.
UK: 0870 400 4581. Both: www.
nationalcar.com.*
Thrifty *US: 1-800 847 4389/
www.thrifty.com. UK: 0808 234
7642/www.thrifty.co.uk.*

CYCLING

Chicago is very bike-friendly, with
plenty of wide roads and bike lanes.
For more on cycling in the city and
details of bike hire firms, *see p278.*

The **CTA** and **Metra** allow bikes
on trains outside of weekday rush
hours (7-9am and 4-6pm on CTA;
trains arriving in Chicago before
9.30am and departing 3-7pm on
Metra). Bikes can be transported
on the front of all CTA buses.

WATER TRANSPORT

During summer, **Chicago Water
Taxi** (1-312 337 1446, www.chicago
watertaxi.com) runs a taxi service
on the river, linking Michigan
Avenue, LaSalle Street, Madison
Avenue and Chinatown. Single
rides are $2-$4; an all-day pass
costs $4 ($6 covering Chinatown).

From May to August, **Shoreline
Sightseeing** (1-312 222 9328,
www.shorelinesightseeing.com)
operates water taxi services that
link Navy Pier with the Shedd
Aquarium and Sears Tower.
For boat tours, *see below.*

GUIDED TOURS

Bobby's Bike Hike *1-312 915
0995/www.bobbysbikehike.com.*
Tours *Late May-early Sept* 9am,
1.30pm, 7pm daily. *Apr-late May,
early Sept-Nov* 10am, 1.30pm Mon-
Fri, Sun; 10am, 1.30pm, 7pm Sat.
Tickets *$32-$49.50; $5-$39.50
discounts.* **Credit** AmEx, MC, V.
A selection of non-strenuous bike
tours, exploring central districts
and the lakefront. Tours leave from
Bobby's office at 465 N McClurg
Court; rates include bike hire.
Bobby's also offers bike rentals
($14-$37/half-day, $18-$50/day).
**Chicago Architecture
Foundation** *Information 1-312
922 3432/tickets 1-312 902 1500/
www.architecture.org.* **Tours**
times vary. **Tickets** prices vary.
Credit AmEx, DC, Disc, MC, V.
The most popular of the CAF's
huge range of excellent tours is the
Architecture River Cruise (May-mid
Nov; $28-$32), the best of the city's
water cruises; other itineraries

take in everything from modern
skyscrapers to quiet locales, and
are conducted on foot, by coach and
by bike. Book ahead for the River
Cruise, by phone or online.
Chicago Greeter *1-312 744 8000/
www.chicagogreeter.com.* **Tours**
by appt. *InstaGreeter* 10am-3pm
Fri-Sun. **Tickets** free.
See the city through the eyes of
volunteer locals, who guide guests
through their neighbourhoods with
personal anecdotes. Some tours
focus on downtown, but it's a great
way to experience off-the-beaten-
track but fascinating parts of town.
You need to register at least 7-10
business days in advance; if not,
try the walk-up InstaGreeter tours
of the Loop. Tours leave from the
Chicago Cultural Center (*see p310*).
Chicago Hauntings *1-888 446
7891/www.chicagohauntings.com.*
Tours 7pm Tue-Thur, Sun; 7pm,
10pm Fri, Sat. **Tickets** $28; $20
discounts. **Credit** AmEx, MC, V.
Kicking off at the Rock 'n' Roll
McDonald's (Clark & Ohio Streets),
noted historian, author and
parapsychology enthusiast Ursula
Bielski and her staff of guides visit
haunted spots in Chicago.
Chicago Neighbourhood Tours
*1-312 742 1190/www.chicago
neighborhoodtours.com.* **Tours**
June-Aug 10am Thur-Sat. *Sept-
May* 10am Sat. **Tickets** $25-$50;
$20-$45 discounts. **Credit** AmEx,
MC, V.
Leaving from the Chicago Cultural
Center (*see p310*), these city-run
tours focus on different locales, or
on subjects as diverse as Greek
immigrants and the Chicago Fire;
Summertime Samplers take visitors
around three 'hoods in one go.
Chicago Trolley Company *1-773
648 5000/www.coachusa.com/
chicagotrolley.* **Tours** *mid Mar-Oct*
9am-6.30pm (last pick-up 5pm)
daily. *Nov-mid Mar* 9am-5pm (last
pick-up 4pm) daily. **Tickets** *1-day*
$29; $17-$24 discounts. *2-day* $45;
$17-$24 discounts. **Credit** AmEx,
DC, Disc, MC, V.
This hop-on/hop-off service trawls
landmarks in the Loop and the Near
North Side. There's a route map
online, where rates are 10% lower.
Lake cruises Numerous operators
offer cruises on the lake from
Navy Pier, including **Shoreline
Sightseeing** (*see above* **Water
taxis**), **Mystic Blue** (1-877 299
7783, www.mysticbluecruises.
com) and **Seadog** (1-888 636 7737,
www.seadogcruises.com/chicago).
An alternative is provided by the
150-foot schooner **Windy** (1-312
595 5555, www.tallshipwindy.com).

Resources A-Z

ADDRESSES

Addresses follow the standard US format. The room and/or suite number appears after the street address, followed on the next line by the city name and the zip code.

AGE RESTRICTIONS

Buying/drinking alcohol 21.
Driving 16.
Sex (hetero- & homosexual) 17.
Smoking 18.

ATTITUDE & ETIQUETTE

Chicago is a buzzing metropolis, but it's also in the Midwest, and comes with all the relaxed good manners that characterise its location. Some high-end restaurants will insist on jacket or jacket and tie (call to check), while some clubs operate a dress code (no gym shoes, baggy jeans or sports gear). But mostly, casual clothes are fine.

BUSINESS

Chicago's central location, not to mention its natural and man-made travel links, has long made it attractive to industry and business. It's still an economic powerhouse: the city is visited by millions of business travellers each year, many of whom are here for a convention.

Conventions

The majority of Chicago's conventions occur at the vast **McCormick Place**: 2.2 million square feet (205,000 square metres) of exhibition space, 170,000 square feet (16,000 square metres) of banqueting, ballroom and meeting room space, spread over 27 acres. It's so large that you'll need to factor journey time into your appointments. The facilities are modern, but there's nothing to do within several blocks of the centre.

Two other venues also stage conventions and exhibitions: **Festival Hall** at Navy Pier, and the **Donald E Stephens Convention Center** in Rosemont.

Donald E Stephens Convention Center 5555 N River Road (near O'Hare Airport), Rosemont (1-847 692 2220/www.rosemont.com).

Festival Hall Navy Pier, 600 E Grand Avenue, at Lake Michigan, Near North (1-312 595 5300/ www.navypier.com). El: Red to Grand. **Map** p326 K10.
McCormick Place Convention Complex 2301 S Lake Shore Drive, at E 23rd Street, South Side (1-312 791 7000/www. mccormickplace.com). Metra: 23rd Street.

Couriers & shippers

DHL 1-800 225 5345/www.dhl. com. **Credit** AmEx, Disc, MC, V.
FedEx 1-800 463 3339/www. fedex.com/us. **Credit** AmEx, Disc, MC, V.
UPS 1-800 742 5877 (US)/1-800 782 7892 (international)/www.ups. com. **Credit** AmEx, Disc, MC, V.

Office services

All of the companies listed below have branches around the city; check online for others.

AlphaGraphics 208 S LaSalle Street, at W Adams Street, the Loop (1-312 368 4507/ www.alphagraphics.com). El: Brown, Orange, Pink or Purple to Quincy. **Open** 8am-6pm Mon-Fri. **Credit** AmEx, Disc, MC, V. **Map** p325 H12.
FedEx Kinko's 700 S Wabash Avenue, at E Balbo Drive, South Loop (1-312 341 0975/http://fedex. kinkos.com) El: Red to Harrison. **Open** 7am-10pm Mon-Fri; 10am-5pm Sat, Sun. **Credit** AmEx, DC, Disc, MC, V. **Map** p325 H13.
Office Depot 6 S State Street, at W Madison Street (1-312 781 0570/www.officedepot.com). El: Blue or Red to Monroe; Brown, Green, Orange, Pink or Purple to Madison/Wabash. **Open** 8am-8pm Mon-Fri; 10am-8pm Sat; 10am-5pm Sun. **Credit** AmEx, Disc, MC, V. **Map** p325 H12.

Useful organisations

For **libraries**, see p307.

CONSULATES

Foreign embassies are located in Washington, DC, but many countries also have a consulate in Chicago.

British Consulate General Suite 1300, Wrigley Building, 400 N Michigan Avenue, at E Hubbard Street, Magnificent Mile (1-312 970 3800/www.britainusa. com/chicago). El: Red to Grand. **Open** 8.30am-5pm Mon-Fri. **Map** p326 J11.
Canadian Consulate General Suite 2400, Two Prudential Plaza, 180 N Stetson Avenue, the Loop (1-312 616 1860/www.chicago.gc.ca). El: Brown, Green, Orange, Pink or Purple to State/Lake; Red to Lake. **Open** 8.30am-12.30pm, 1-4.30pm Mon-Fri. **Map** p325 J11.
Irish Consulate Suite 911, Wrigley Building, 400 N Michigan Avenue, at E Hubbard Street, Magnificent Mile (1-312 337 1868/ www.irishconsulate.org). El: Red to Grand. **Open** 10am-noon Mon-Fri. **Map** p326 J11.

CONSUMER

For complaints about shops, cabs, restaurants and the like, contact the **City of Chicago Department of Consumer Services** on 1-312 744 4006 or 311, or see www.cityof chicago.org/consumerservices.

CUSTOMS

International travellers go through Customs directly after Immigration. Give the official the filled-in white form you were given on the plane.

Foreign visitors can import the following goods duty free: 200 cigarettes or 50 cigars (not Cuban; over-18s) or 2kg of tobacco; one litre of wine or spirits (over-21s); and up to $100 in gifts ($800 for returning Americans). You must declare and maybe forfeit plants or foodstuffs. Check **US Customs** for details (www.cbp.gov/xp/cgov/travel).

UK Customs & Excise allows returning travellers to bring in up to £145 worth of goods.

DISABLED

Chicago is reasonably accessible to disabled visitors: a lot of the buses are fitted with lifts, there are lifts on elevated CTA platforms and the sidewalks have ramps. However, it's always wise to call ahead to check accessibility.

The **Mayor's Office for People with Disabilities** (1-312

DIRECTORY

744 7050, TTY 1-312 744 4964,
www.cityofchicago.org) is a good
source of information about all
aspects of disabled access. Try the
RTA (1-312 836 7000, TTY 1-312
836 4949, www.rtachicago.com) or
the **CTA** (1-888 968 7282, TTY 1-
888 282 8891, www.transitchicago.
com) for information on public
travel, or **Special Services** on
1-800 606 1282 well in advance to
arrange accessible transportation.

DRUGS

A visit to any local bar brings home
how strict the local authorities are
about drugs: if they're going to be
that wary about serving beers to
under-21s, then drugs must be
policed with caution. Foreigners
caught in possession of anything
illegal may be treated harshly.

ELECTRICITY

US electricity voltage is 110-120V
60-cycle AC. Except for dual-
voltage, flat-pin shavers, foreign
appliances will need an adaptor.

EMERGENCIES

For helplines, *see below*. For police,
see p308. For hospitals, *see below*.

Ambulance, fire, police *911*.
Illinois Poison Control
1-800 222 1222.

GAY & LESBIAN

For more gay and lesbian resources,
including the **Center on Halsted**,
see pp243-252.

**Chicago Area Gay & Lesbian
Chamber of Commerce** *3656
N Halsted Street, at W Addison
Street, Lakeview (1-773 303
0167/www.glchamber.org)*.
Gerber-Hart Library *1127 W
Granville Avenue, at N Broadway,
North Side (1-773 381 8030/
www.gerberhart.org). El: Red
to Granville*. **Open** 6-9pm
Wed, Thur; noon-4pm Fri-Sun.
Admission free. *Membership* $40.
A gay and lesbian archive.

HEALTH

Accident & emergency

Foreign visitors should ensure they
have full travel insurance: health
treatment can be pricey. Call
the emergency number on your
insurance before seeking treatment;
staff should be able to direct you

to a hospital that deals with your
insurance company.
For information, call **Advocate
Health** (1-800 323 8622, www.
advocatehealth.com), which can
connect you to a hospital. There are
24-hour emergency rooms at the
locations below.

Northwestern Memorial Hospital
*251 E Huron Street, at N
Fairbanks Court, Streeterville
(1-312 926 2000/www.nmh.org).
El: Red to Chicago*. **Map** p326 J10.
Rush University Medical Center
*1653 W Congress Parkway, at
S Ashland Avenue, West Loop
(1-312 942 5000/www.rush.edu).
El: Blue to Medical Center*.
Map p330 D13.
Stroger Cook County Hospital
*1900 W Polk Street, at S Wood
Street, West Loop (1-312 864
6000/www.ccbh.org). El: Blue to
Medical Center*. **Map** p330 C14.
University of Chicago Hospital
*5841 S Maryland Avenue, at E
58th Street, Hyde Park (1-773
702 1000/www.uchospitals.edu).
Metra: 59th Street*. **Map** p332 X17.

Contraception & abortion

Planned Parenthood *6th floor,
18 S Michigan Avenue, at E
Madison Street, the Loop (1-312
592 6700/www.plannedparenthood.
org). El: Blue or Red to Monroe;
Brown, Green, Orange, Pink or
Purple to Madison/Wabash*.
Open 11.45am-4.45pm Thur.
Map p325 H13.
A non-profit organisation that can
supply contraception, treat STDs
and perform abortions.
Other locations around the city.

Dentists

For referrals, call 1-800 577 7322.

Hospitals

See above **Accident &
emergency**.

Opticians

For opticians, *see p208*.

Pharmacies

For pharmacies, *see p208*.

STDs, HIV & AIDS

Howard Brown Health Center
*4025 N Sheridan Road, at W Irving
Park Road, Lakeview (1-773 388
1600/www.howardbrown.org).*

El: Red to Sheridan. **Open**
9am-9pm Mon-Thur; 9am-5pm
Fri; 9am-3pm Sat.
Comprehensive health services
for the gay community, including
primary care, HIV testing, support
groups and research, as well as
supplies of free condoms.

HELPLINES

Alcoholics Anonymous *1-312
346 1475/www.chicagoaa.org.*
Illinois HIV/STD Hotline *1-312
814 2608/www.idph.state.il.us.*
LGBT Info Line *1-773 929 4357/
www.centeronhalsted.org.*
Narcotics Anonymous *1-708 848
4884/www.chicagona.org.*
Rape Crisis *1-888 293 2080/www.
rapevictimadvocates.org*

ID

If you're planning on drinking
in Chicago, then carry photo ID
that contains your date of birth
(a driving licence, say): you'll be
carded if staff think there's even a
tiny chance that you're under 21.

INSURANCE

Non-nationals should arrange
baggage, trip-cancellation and
medical insurance before they
leave. US citizens should consider
doing the same. Read the small
print: consequences of security
scares, including cancelled flights,
may not be covered.

INTERNET

Travellers with laptops should
find it easy to get a Wi-Fi hook-up.
Aside from **Screenz** (*see below*),
there are few internet cafés here,
but all branches of the Chicago
Public Library have terminals. The
**Harold Washington Library
Center** (*see p307*) has 78 terminals
on which anyone can sign up for a
free one-hour session, and 18
terminals for 15-minute sessions.

Screenz *2717 N Clark Street, at
W Diversey Parkway, Lincoln Park
(1-773 572 0090/www.screenz.
com). El: Brown or Purple to
Diversey*. **Open** 8am-midnight Mon-
Fri; 9am-midnight Sat, Sun. **Credit**
AmEx, Disc, MC, V. **Map** p328 F4.

LEFT LUGGAGE

Neither O'Hare nor Midway offer
any luggage storage facilities.
However, you can leave bags in
lockers at Union Station (*see p302*).

DIRECTORY

LEGAL HELP

Your first call in any serious legal embroilment should be to your insurance company or your consulate (*see p305*). The **Chicago Bar Association** offers a lawyer referrals service; call 1-312 554 2001.

LIBRARIES

In addition to the **Harold Washington Library Center**, the Chicago Public Library has branches on the **Near North Side** (310 W Division Street, at N Wells Street, 1-312 744 0991), in **Lincoln Park** (1150 W Fullerton Avenue, at N Racine Avenue, 1-312 744 1926) and in **Lakeview** (644 W Belmont Avenue, at Broadway, 1-312 744 1139). All are open 9am-9pm Monday to Thursday, 9am-5pm on Friday and Saturday. For other locations, see www.chipublib.org.

Harold Washington Library Center *400 S State Street, at W Congress Parkway, the Loop (1-312 747 4300/www.chipublib.org). El: Blue or Red to Jackson; Brown, Orange, Pink or Purple to Library.* **Open** 9am-9pm Mon-Thur; 9am-5pm Fri, Sat; 1-5pm Sun. **Map** p325 H13.
The main branch of the Chicago Public Library, the second largest library in the world, houses two million volumes, plus a theatre, meeting rooms and a large number of free-access computer terminals.

LOST PROPERTY

Airports

If you lose an item at either Chicago airport near the ticket counters or close to the gates, contact your airline. If you lose anything in other areas, call the numbers below.

Airport public areas *O'Hare* 1-773 686 2385. *Midway* 1-773 838 3003.
Airport transit system *O'Hare* 1-773 601 1817.
Food courts *O'Hare* 1-773 686 6148.
Parking facilities *Both airports* 1-773 686 7532.
Security checkpoints *O'Hare* 1-773 894 8760. *Midway* 1-773 498 1308.

Public transport

If you lose something on public transport, contact the relevant company (*see p302*).

Taxis

If you lose something in a cab, call the taxi company (there are several different firms in the city). You'll need the number of the cab.

MEDIA

Home to the country's third-largest media market, with a newspaper heritage to rival that of New York, Chicago is one of the US media's big hitters.

Daily newspapers

Chicago Tribune
www.chicagotribune.com.
Founded in 1847, the *Tribune* is the most powerful paper in Illinois. Its strengths include sports and Friday's entertainment supplement. However, thanks to cost-cutting and questionable editorial decisions, it's not the paper it once was. Under new owner Sam Zell, the paper's parent company filed for Chapter-11 bankruptcy protection in 2008, and its future appears uncertain.
The *Tribune* also publishes **RedEye**, a flimsy morning tabloid comprised of articles from that morning's paper and extra entertainment pieces. It's available for free at or near most El stations.

Chicago Sun-Times
www.suntimes.com.
The *Sun-Times* is the *Trib*'s tabloid competitor. Though it offers gritty reporting and good coverage of Chicago sports, arts coverage is weak (with the notable exception of movie critic Roger Ebert), and in-depth news is largely absent.

Daily Herald & SouthtownStar
www.dailyherald.com & www.southtownstar.com.
The *Daily Herald* and the *Southtown Star* cover the Chicagoland suburbs. The *Herald* publishes zoned suburban editions, while the *Star* concerns itself with the southernmost area of the city.

Magazines

Time Out Chicago
www.timeoutchicago.com.
Obviously we're biased, but we think our sister magazine is the essential publication for locals and visitors wanting to know what's going on in town. Retailing for $1.99, available every Wednesday at newsstands and bookshops around the city, *Time Out Chicago* covers every corner of the city's arts and entertainment scene,

with substantial coverage of shopping, eating and drinking.
Chicago Reader
www.chicagoreader.com.
Much diminished in recent years, the *Reader* is the city's dominant free weekly, distributed in bars, cultural venues and distribution boxes around town. The paper no longer carries the gravitas with which it made its name, and its listings are a little spotty. But it does still carry some good writing, and includes Dan Savage's notorious 'Savage Love' sex advice column.
The Onion *www.theonion.com.*
In addition to the satire for which it's best known, *The Onion* offers coverage of music and movies, and (like the *Reader*) the 'Savage Love' column. It's available free every week in bars and some stores.

Other publications

Other streetcorner boxes are filled with a variety of freesheets. A few are specific to the locale in which they're found; others, such as the **Windy City Times** (www.wctimes.com) and the **Chicago Free Press** (www.chicagofreepress.com), are targeted at the gay community. **Newcity** (http://newcity.com) is a scrappy culture rag. Paid-for monthlies include the surprisingly cultured **Chicago** magazine (www.chicagomag.com), and **Where** (www.wheretraveler.com), tilted at the tourist market.

Radio

The more interesting sounds on Chicago's dial emanate from college stations: Northwestern's **WNUR** (89.3 FM, www.wnur.org); Columbia College's **WCRX** (88.1 FM, www.wcrx.net); **WDCB** (90.9 FM, www.wdcb.org) from the College of DuPage; Loyola's **WLUW** (88.7 FM, www.wluw.org); the University of Chicago's **WHPK** (88.5 FM, http://whpk.org); and St Xavier University's **WXAV** (88.3 FM, www.wxav.com). The pick of the pack is **WBEZ** (91.5 FM, www.wbez.org), the city's public radio station.
The major FM rock stations, among them **WXRT** (93.1 FM, www.93xrt.com), **WKQX** (101.1 FM, www.q101.com) and **WTMX** (101.9 FM, www.wtmx.com), are generally pretty bland. Pop kids may like **WKSC** (103.5 FM, www.kisschicago.com) and **WBBM** (96.3 FM, www.b96hits.com), while those after classic rock should head for **WLUP** (97.9 FM, www.wlup.com).

News, sport and mindless chat dominate the AM dial. Sportswise, **WBBM** (780 AM, www.wbbm780.com) is the home of the Bears; **WGN** (720 AM, www.wgn radio.com) broadcasts Cubs games; and **WSCR** (670 AM, www.670 thescore.com) broadcasts the White Sox and the Blackhawks.

Television

In addition to the local affiliates of the major networks – **CBS2** (aka WBBM, http://cbs2chicago.com), **NBC5** (aka WMAQ, www.nbc5.com), **ABC7** (aka WLS, http://abc local.go.com/wls) and **Fox** (channel 32, aka WFLD, www.myfoxchicago.com) – the biggest station is **WGN-9** (www.wgntv.com).

MONEY

The US dollar ($) is divided into 100 cents (¢). Coins run from the copper penny (1¢) to the silver nickel (5¢), dime (10¢), quarter (25¢), less-common half-dollar (50¢) and very rare dollar. Green notes or 'bills' come in denominations of $1, $5, $10, $20, $50 and $100.

Bring at least one major credit card: they are accepted at nearly all hotels, restaurants and shops. The most widely accepted cards are American Express (AmEx), Diners Club (DC), Discover (Disc), MasterCard (MC) and Visa (V); in our listings, we've indicated where a venue accepts cards.

Banks & ATMs

Most banks are open 9am-5pm during the week. You'll need photo ID to cash travellers' cheques. Not all banks offer currency exchange.

There are ATMs throughout the city: in banks, stores and even bars. ATMs accept Visa, MasterCard and AmEx, as well as other cards, but may charge a usage fee. If you've forgotten your PIN, most banks will dispense cash to cardholders.

Bureaux de change

Try and travel with some US dollars. You can change money at the airport, but the rates may not be great. If you want to cash travellers' cheques at a shop, note that some require a minimum purchase.

Stores that bill themselves as 'currency exchanges' will not help you exchange your currency: they're basically cheque-cashing services and don't accept foreign funds. Instead, try an AmEx office.

American Express 605 N Michigan Avenue, at E Ohio Street, Magnificent Mile (1-312 943 7840). El: Red to Chicago. **Open** 8.30am-6pm Mon-Fri; 9am-5pm Sat. **Map** p326 J10.
Other locations 55 W Monroe Street, at N Dearborn Street, the Loop (1-312 541 5440).

Lost or stolen credit cards

Call the appropriate number below.

American Express Cards 1-800 992 3404. Travellers' cheques 1-800 221 7282.
Diners Club 1-800 234 6377.
Discover 1-800 347 2683.
MasterCard 1-800 622 7747.
Visa Cards 1-800 847 2911. Travellers' cheques 1-800 227 6811.

Tax

In Chicago, standard sales tax is a huge 10.25 per cent. The tax isn't included in the marked price of goods and will be added at the till. For hotel rooms and services, the tax rate is a nasty 15.4 per cent.

OPENING HOURS

For banks, see left; for post offices, see below; for public transport, see p303. General office hours in the city are 9am to 5pm during the week. Most bars are open until 2am, or 3am on Saturday; however, a few bars remain open until 4am.

POLICE

For emergencies, call **911**. You don't have to report non-emergency crimes in person: phone them in on **311** (or, from out of town, 1-312 746 6000). The details will be taken and paperwork can be sent to you. The city's most central police station is at 1718 S State Street (1-312 745 4290); for others, see www.cityof chicago.org/police.

POSTAL SERVICES

Post offices in Chicago are usually open 9am to 5.30pm Monday to Friday; most are closed on Sundays. The main office is open 24 hours. Phone 1-800 275 8777 or check www.usps.com for locations.

Stamps can be bought at any post office and at some hotels, vending machines and drugstores. Stamps for postcards within the US cost 27¢; for Europe, the charge is 94¢. A regular stamp is 44¢. For couriers and shippers, see p305.

Main Chicago Post Office 433 W Harrison Street, at S Canal Street, West Loop. El: Blue to Clinton. **Open** 24hrs daily. **Map** p325 G13.
The Loop 211 S Clark Street, at W Adams Street. El: Blue or Red to Jackson; Brown, Orange, Pink or Purple to Quincy. **Open** 7am-6pm Mon-Fri. **Map** p325 H12.
River North 540 N Dearborn Street, at W Grand Avenue. El: Red to Grand. **Open** 7.30am-6.30pm Mon-Fri; 7.30am-3pm Sat; 9am-2pm Sun. **Map** p327 H10.
Lincoln Park 2405 N Sheffield Avenue, at N Fullerton Avenue. El: Brown, Purple or Red to Fullerton. **Open** 8am-7pm Mon-Fri; 8am-3pm Sat. **Map** p328 E5.
Lakeview 1343 W Irving Park Road, at N Southport Avenue. El: Red to Sheridan. **Open** 7.30am-7pm Mon-Fri; 8am-3pm Sat.
Wicker Park 1635 W Division Street, at N Ashland Avenue. El: Blue to Division. **Open** 8.30am-7pm Mon-Fri; 8am-3pm Sat. **Map** p331 C8.

RELIGION

Baptist

Unity Fellowship Missionary Baptist Church 211 N Cicero Avenue, at W Maypole Avenue, West Side (1-773 287 0267). El: Green to Cicero. **Services** 7.30am, 11am Sun.

Buddhist

Buddhist Temple of Chicago 1151 W Leland Avenue, at N Racine Avenue, Uptown (1-773 334 4661/www.budtempchi.org). El: Red to Lawrence. **Services** 11am Sun. **Map** p326 G9.

Catholic

Holy Name Cathedral 735 N State Street, at E Superior Street, River North (1-312 787 8040/www.holynamecathedral.org). El: Red to Chicago. **Services** 6am, 7am, 8am, 12.10pm, 5.15pm Mon-Fri; 8am, 12.10pm, 5.15pm, 7.30pm Sat; 7am, 8.15am, 9.30am, 11am, 12.30pm, 5.15pm Sun. **Map** p326 H10.
Old St Mary's Church 1500 S Michigan Avenue, at S State Street, the Loop (1-312 922 3444). El: Green, Orange or Red to Roosevelt. **Services** 8.30am, noon Mon-Fri; noon, 5pm Sat; 8.30am, 11.30am, 6pm Sun. **Map** p325 H13.

Eastern Orthodox

St George Orthodox Cathedral
*917 N Wood Street, at W Iowa
Street, West Town (1-312 666
5179/www.saintgeorgecathedral.net).
El: Blue to Division.* **Services**
9.30am Sun. **Map** p331 C9.

Episcopal

St James Cathedral *65 E Huron
Street, at N Wabash Avenue,
Magnificent Mile (1-312 787 7360/
www.saintjamescathedral.org).
El: Red to Chicago.* **Services**
5.30pm Wed; 12.10pm Thur, Fri;
8am, 10.30am Sun. **Map** p326 H10.

Jewish

Chicago Loop Synagogue
*16 S Clark Street, at W Madison
Street, the Loop (1-312 346 7370/
www.chicagoloopsynagogue.org).
El: Blue or Red to Monroe.*
Services 8.05am, 1.05pm,
4.40-5pm (depends on sunset) Mon-
Fri; 9am, 3.45-4.30pm, 4.45-5.30pm
(depends on sunset) Sat; 9.30am,
4.15-4.45pm (depends on sunset)
Sun. **Map** p325 H12.
**Chicago Sinai Congregation
(Reform)** *15 W Delaware Place,
at N State Street, Gold Coast (1-312
867 7000/www.chicagosinai.org). El:
Red to Chicago.* **Services** 6.15pm
Fri; 11am Sun. **Map** p326 H9.

Lutheran

**First St Paul's Evangelical
Lutheran Church** *1301 N LaSalle
Street, at W Goethe Street, Gold
Coast (1-312 642 7172/www.
fspauls.org). El: Red to Clark/
Division.* **Services** 7am Wed;
8.30am, 11am Sun. **Map** p327 H8.

Methodist

**First United Methodist Church
at the Chicago Temple** *77 W
Washington Boulevard, at N Clark
Street, the Loop (1-312 236 4548/
www.chicagotemple.org). El: Blue,
Brown, Green, Orange, Pink or
Purple to Clark/Lake.* **Services**
7.30am, 12.10pm Wed; 5pm Sat;
8.30am, 11am Sun. **Map** p325 H12.

Muslim

Downtown Islamic Center *231 S
State Street, at E Jackson Boulevard,
the Loop (1-312 939 9095/www.
dic-chicago.org). El: Brown, Green,
Orange, Pink or Purple to Adams/
Wabash; Red to Jackson.* **Open** 9am-
5pm Mon-Fri. **Map** p325 H12.

Presbyterian

Fourth Presbyterian Church *126
E Chestnut Street, at N Michigan
Avenue, Magnificent Mile (1-312
787 4570/www.fourthchurch.org).
El: Red to Chicago.* **Services** 8am,
9.30am, 11am, 6.30pm Sun. **Map**
p326 J9.

SAFETY & SECURITY

Follow the same precautions as you
would in any urban area. Don't
draw attention to yourself by
unfolding a huge map and looking
lost, and do beware of hustlers.
Don't leave your purse or wallet
in a place where it could easily be
pickpocketed; leave valuables in
a hotel safe if possible, and don't
carry too much cash. And try to
avoid deserted areas late at night.
Potentially dangerous parts of town
include parts of the West Side and,
especially, parts of the South Side.

SMOKING

Smoking is outlawed in Chicago's
restaurants and bars.

STUDY

The most prestigious of Chicago's
many educational establishments
is the **University of Chicago**
in Hyde Park (1-773 702 1234,
www.uchicago.edu). Other
prominent institutions include
the **University of Illinois at
Chicago** (UIC) in the West Loop
(1-312 996 7000, www.uic.edu);
Loyola University (1-773 274
3000, www.luc.edu) and
Northwestern University
(1-847 491 3741, 1-312 503 8649,
www.northwestern.edu), both split
over big campuses on the Far North
Side and smaller downtown set-ups;
and **DePaul University** (1-312
362 8000, www.depaul.edu). And
then there are numerous specialist
establishments, such as the **School
of the Art Institute** and
Columbia College Chicago.

US universities are more flexible
about part-time study than their
European equivalents. Stipulations
for non-English-speaking students
might include passing the TOEFL;
most students also have to give
proof of financial support.

TELEPHONES

Dialling & codes

There are five area codes in the
Chicagoland area. **312** covers

downtown Chicago (roughly as far
north, west and south as 1600 on
the street grid); **773** covers the rest
of the city; **847** serves the northern
suburbs; **708** covers the southern
and western suburbs; and the areas
to the far west are served by **630**.
Numbers beginning **1-8—** (eg
1-800, 1-888) are toll-free within the
US. Numbers prefaced with **1-900**
are charged at premium rates.

If you're dialling outside your
area code, dial 1 + area code +
seven-digit number. On payphones,
an operator or recording will tell
you how much money to add.

For collect or when using a phone
card, dial 0 + area code + phone
number and listen for the operator
or recorded instructions.
For international calls, dial the
US international access code (011)
or the '+' symbol (from a mobile
phone), then the country code
(*see below*), then the number.

Australia 61.
Germany 49.
Japan 81.
New Zealand 64.
UK 44 (omit first '0' of area code).

Mobile phones

Chicago operates on the 1900
GSM frequency. Travellers from
Europe with tri-band phones
should be able to connect to one
or more of the networks, assuming
their home provider has an
arrangement with a local network;
check before leaving.

Check the price of calls before
you depart. Rates may be hefty
and, unlike in the UK, you'll
probably be charged for receiving
as well as making calls. It might
be cheaper to rent or buy a phone
while you're in town; for phone
rentals, *see p212*.

Operator services

Operator 0.
**Emergencies (ambulance,
fire, police)** 911.
**Local and long-distance
directory enquiries** 411.

Public phones

Payphones are hard to find. But if
you do come across one, it'll accept
nickels, dimes and quarters. Check
for a dialling tone before adding
change. Local calls usually cost
35¢. The rate rises steeply as the
distance between callers increases
(an operator or recorded message
will tell you how much to add).

DIRECTORY

TIME

Chicago operates under US Central Standard Time (CST), six hours behind Greenwich Mean Time (GMT) and one hour behind Eastern Standard Time (EST). The border between Eastern and Central Standard Times is just to the east: Michigan and much of Indiana are on EST. From the second Sunday in March until the first Sunday in November, Daylight Saving Time puts the clocks forward an hour.

TIPPING

Waiters, bellhops and the like are paid a menial wage, and depend on tips to get by. In general, tip cab drivers, wait staff, hairdressers and food delivery people 15-20 per cent of the total tab. Tip bellhops and baggage handlers $1-$2 a bag. And in bars, bank on tipping a buck a drink.

TOILETS

Public toilets are few and far between. Head to a mall, a hotel, a department store, a shop with a café attached (such as Borders) or a fast food outlet. Bars and restaurants can be a little on the sniffy side unless you buy something first.

TOURIST INFORMATION

The **Chicago Office of Tourism** dispenses information about the city for visitors online at www.choosechicago.com, by phone on 1-877 244 2246 (within the US) and 1-312 201 8847 (outside the US), and through three visitor centres.

The **Chicago Cultural Center**, the most useful of the three, is full of information on the town's attractions along with details of the centre's own excellent programme of events. It's also the starting point for all city-run guided tours (see p304). The visitor centre at the **Chicago Water Works** includes a tourist information booth; as does **Hot Tix**, which also sells tickets for theatres in the Chicago area (see p212). The newest of the visitor centres is in **Millennium Park**, and offers a fairly standard array of tourist information and other goodies.

Chicago Cultural Center *77 E Randolph Street, at N Michigan Avenue, the Loop (1-312 744 6630/ 1-877 244 2246/www.choose chicago.com). El: Blue to*

Washington; Brown, Green, Orange, Pink or Purple to Randolph/Wabash; Red to Lake. **Open** 8am-7pm Mon-Thur; 8am-6pm Fri; 9am-6pm Sat; 10am-6pm Sun. **Map** p325 J12.
Chicago Water Works *163 E Pearson Street, at N Michigan Avenue, Magnificent Mile (1-312 744 6630/1-877 244 2246/www. choosechicago.com).* **Open** 7.30am-7pm daily. **Map** p326 J9.
Millennium Park *201 E Randolph Street, in the Northwest Exelon Pavilion, the Loop (1-312 742 1168/1-877 244 2246/www. choosechicago.com). El: Blue or Red to Washington; Brown, Green, Orange, Pink or Purple to Randolph/Wabash.* **Open** *Apr-Sept* 9am-7pm daily. *Oct-Mar* 10am-4pm daily. **Map** p325 J12.

VISAS & IMMIGRATION

Under the **Visa Waiver Scheme**, citizens of 27 countries, including the UK, Ireland, Australia and New Zealand, don't need a visa for stays of less than 90 days (for business or pleasure). Mexicans and Canadians don't usually need visas but must have legal proof of citizenship. All other travellers must have visas.

Visa applications can be obtained from the nearest US embassy or consulate, or online. Apply at least three weeks before you plan to travel. UK citizens should call the Visa Information Line: 0904 2450 100 (£1.20/min) or see www.usembassy.org.uk. Immigration regulations apply to all visitors, regardless of visa status. During the flight, you'll be issued with an immigration form, which you must complete and present to an official on the ground. You'll have your fingerprints and

photograph taken as you pass through immigration.

WHEN TO GO

Climate

For average temperatures, *see below*. Summer can be very humid, winter brings 40 inches of snow and, year-round, there's the wind. In other words, prepare for anything.

Public holidays

New Year's Day (1 Jan); **Martin Luther King Jr Day** (3rd Mon in Jan); **President's Day** (3rd Mon in Feb); **Memorial Day** (last Mon in May); **Independence Day** (4 July); **Labor Day** (1st Mon in Sept); **Columbus Day** (2nd Mon in Oct); **Veterans' Day** (11 Nov); **Thanksgiving Day** (4th Thur in Nov); **Christmas Day** (25 Dec).

WOMEN

When walking at night, take plenty of care: avoid unlit, deserted streets, and be alert for people trailing you. When travelling on trains at night, always try to pick a busy carriage.

WORKING IN THE US

Foreigners must find a US company to sponsor their application for an **H-1 visa**, which permits work in the country for up to five years. For the H-1 visa to be approved, the employer must convince the Immigration Department that there is no American citizen qualified to do the job as well.

UK students can contact the **British Universities North America Club** (BUNAC) for help in arranging a temporary visa and, perhaps, a job (www.bunac.org/uk).

THE LOCAL CLIMATE

Average temperatures and monthly rainfall in Chicago.

	High (˚C/˚F)	Low (˚C/˚F)	Rainfall (mm/in)
Jan	0 / 32	-8 / 18	56 / 2.2
Feb	3 / 38	-4 / 24	46 / 1.8
Mar	8 / 47	0 / 32	76 / 3.0
Apr	15 / 59	6 / 42	93 / 3.6
May	21 / 70	11 / 51	94 / 3.7
June	27 / 80	16 / 61	109 / 4.3
July	29 / 84	19 / 66	94 / 3.7
Aug	28 / 83	18 / 65	98 / 3.9
Sept	24 / 76	14 / 57	81 / 3.2
Oct	18 / 64	8 / 46	69 / 2.7
Nov	9 / 49	2 / 35	84 / 3.3
Dec	3 / 37	-4 / 24	67 / 2.6

Further Reference

BOOKS

Fiction

Nelson Algren
The Neon Wilderness (1947)
This collection of short stories set the scene for novels such as *The Man with the Golden Arm* (1949).
Saul Bellow *The Adventures of Augie March* (1953)
A coming-of-age tale of sorts, and one of several Chicago novels by Bellow; check out, too, the magisterial *Humboldt's Gift* (1975).
Sandra Cisneros
Loose Woman (1994)
Poems by the author of the fine *A House on Mango Street*.
Theodore Dreiser
Sister Carrie (1900)
Perhaps the first great Chicago novel, a tale of the corruption of a young woman in the big bad city.
James T Farrell
Studs Lonigan (1935)
Farrell's three Lonigan stories tell of the coming of age of an Irish American in the early 20th century.
Sara Paretsky
Indemnity Only (1982)
The first outing for Paretsky's 'tec VI Warshawski, now a veteran of a dozen hard-boiled whodunnits.
Upton Sinclair *The Jungle* (1906)
Sinclair's masterpiece, which caused a sensation on publication, is set in the Chicago stockyards.
Scott Turow
The Laws of Our Fathers (1996)
One of many page-turners from the Chicago lawyer turned author.
Richard Wright *Native Son* (1940)
A prescient tale of murder and racial issues in Chicago.

Non-fiction

Eliot Asinof *Eight Men Out* (1963)
The story of how the Chicago White Sox threw the 1919 World Series; later adapted for cinema.
**Richard Cahan &
Michael Williams**
Richard Nickel's Chicago (2006)
This paean to Nickel, who fought an often solitary battle to save the city's architecture, is packed with beautiful photography.
Adam Cohen & Elizabeth Taylor *American Pharaoh* (2000)
It's lazily written, but this biography of Mayor Daley keeps the reader interested.

Nadine Cohodas
Spinning Blues into Gold (2000)
The story of Chess Records has been waiting to be told for years; Cohodas does a fine job telling it.
Robert Cromie
The Great Chicago Fire (1958)
How the city lost its innocence. And most of its buildings, too.
Peter Golenbock
Wrigleyville (1996)
Golenbock's history of the Chicago Cubs is a highly entertaining read.
**James R Grossman,
Ann Durkin Keating &
Janice L Reiff (eds)**
The Encyclopaedia of Chicago (2004)
Incomplete, almost wilfully so in places, but still a treasure trove of history, conjecture and anecdote.
LeAlan Jones & Lloyd Newman *Our America* (1997)
Subtitled 'Life and Death on Chicago's South Side', *Our America* tells of life in Chicago's ghettos through the eyes of two teenagers.
Erik Larson
The Devil in the White City (2004)
An imaginative jaunt around the 1893 World's Columbian Exposition in the company of architect Daniel Burnham and murderer HH Holmes.
Richard Lindberg
To Serve and Collect (1991)
A splendidly titled survey of police corruption in Chicago, between 1855 and 1960.
David Garrard Lowe
Lost Chicago (rev.2000)
A wonderful book detailing some marvellous Chicago buildings that didn't survive the wrecking ball.
Elizabeth McNulty
Chicago Then and Now (2000)
Containing some beautiful old photographs, this book places the emphasis firmly on the 'then'.
Donald L Miller
City of the Century (1996)
'The epic of Chicago', reads the appropriate subtitle for the definitive history of the city.
Mike Royko
One More Time (1999)
A collection of articles by the grand old man of Chicago journalism. Also worth a look: his biography of Richard J Daley, *Boss* (1971).
Richard Schneirov et al (eds)
The Pullman Strike and the Crisis of the 1890s (1999)
One of the city's defining moments gets the essay treatment in this surprisingly engrossing book.

Alice Sinkevitch (ed)
AIA Guide to Chicago (2004)
'AIA' stands for the American Institute of Architects, which, with the Chicago Architecture Foundation, is behind this excellent survey of the city's buildings.
Carl Smith *The Plan of Chicago: Daniel Burnham and the Remaking of the American City* (2006)
How Daniel Burnham went about rebuilding Chicago.
Studs Terkel
Division Street: America (1967)
One of many worthwhile books from the late local legend; others include *Working* (1974).
Bill Veeck with Ed Linn
Veeck As in Wreck (1962)
The autobiography of the one-legged baseball executive who planted the ivy at Wrigley Field.
Lynne Warren et al (eds)
Art in Chicago 1945-1995 (1996)
A survey of more than 100 artists who worked in Chicago.

Poetry & drama

Gwendolyn Brooks
Selected Poems (1963)
Poetry from the first African American to win the Pulitzer prize.
Ben Hecht & Charles MacArthur *The Front Page* (1928)
A classic stage work co-authored by Ben Hecht, a notable local hack.
David Mamet
Mamet Plays 1 (1994)
Stage works, including *Sexual Perversity in Chicago* (1977) and *American Buffalo* (1976).
Carl Sandburg
Selected Poems (1996)
This collection includes the classic *Chicago Poems* (1916).

FILMS

About Last Night...
dir. Edward Zwick (1986)
The singles scene on Division Street forms the basis for this lame 1980s flick based on David Mamet's play *Sexual Perversity in Chicago*.
Backdraft *dir. Ron Howard* (1991)
Fire in Chicago, albeit 120 years after the biggest fire of them all.
The Blues Brothers
dir. John Landis (1980)
Feeble sketch extended to breaking point, or riotous romp? Either way, Chicago should get a credit alongside Belushi and Aykroyd.

DIRECTORY

The Break-Up
dir. Peyton Reed (2006)
Jennifer Aniston and Vince Vaughn try to resolve their differences in this romantic comedy.
Chicago *dir. Rob Marshall* (2002)
A massively popular adaptation of the roaring '20s musical.
The Color of Money
dir. John Hughes (1986)
Paul Newman and Tom Cruise shoot some stick on the North Side.
The Dark Knight
dir. Christopher Nolan (2008)
Batman comes to Chicago.
Eight Men Out
dir. John Sayles (1988)
Sayles' retelling of the Black Sox tale, adapted from Eliot Asinof's book, succeeds despite its treacle-thick sympathies for 'Shoeless' Joe.
Ferris Bueller's Day Off
dir. John Hughes (1986)
Matthew Broderick skips school to hit countless local landmarks. 'Bueller? Bueller…? *Bueller!*'
The Fugitive
dir. Andrew Davis (1993)
Harrison Ford on the run.
Go Fish *dir. Rose Troche* (1994)
A winning Chicago-set romantic comedy with a twist: it's set on the lesbian scene.
Hardball *dir. Brian Robbins* (2001)
Keanu Reeves stars as a bum who takes over a Little League team from the projects of Cabrini-Green.
Henry: Portrait of a Serial Killer *dir. John McNaughton* (1986)
If you see anyone on Lower Wacker Drive claiming their car has broken down, keep driving.
High Fidelity
dir. Stephen Frears (2000)
Successful translation of Nick Hornby's London novel to Chicago.
Hoop Dreams
dir. Steve James (1994)
Enthralling documentary following two young MJ wannabes.
The Lake House
dir. Alejandro Agresti (2006)
Strained supernatural romance with an architectural undertone and some nice on-location shots.
My Best Friend's Wedding
dir. PJ Hogan (1997)
Julia Roberts and Cameron Diaz find love (kinda) in the Windy City.
Risky Business
dir. Paul Brickman (1983)
A ludicrous plot – Tom Cruise is a teenager on the make, Rebecca de Mornay his hooker acquaintance – is saved by sharp scripting.
Road to Perdition
dir. Sam Mendes (2002)
Tom Hanks plays a mob enforcer, and Chicago plays itself, in this dark period drama set in the '30s.

Running Scared
dir. Peter Hyams (1986)
Billy Crystal stars with Gregory Hines in this comic cop flick.
The Untouchables
dir. Brian de Palma (1987)
Competent, Costner-starring retelling of the Capone-Ness battles.

MUSIC

Patricia Barber
Mythologies (2006)
A song cycle based on the 2,000-year-old works of Roman poet Ovid. *The Cole Porter Mix* (2008) may prove an easier way in to the works of this intriguing singer-pianist.
Big Black
Songs About Fucking (1987)
Grim and grubby, fierce and fearsome. Leader Steve Albini has gone on to engineer a staggering number of indie notables.
Cheap Trick *Cheap Trick* (1977)
The debut set from the local kings of power-pop, formed in Rockford but relocated to Chicago.
Chicago Transit Authority
Chicago Transit Authority (1969)
After a name change, they carved out a career as cheesy soft rockers. But Chicago's debut is a peach.
Common *Be* (2006)
Lonnie Lynn, Jr's breakthrough album, co-produced by fellow local Kanye West.
Bobby Conn *Homeland* (2004)
Playful – or, perhaps, just plain silly – alt-pop.
Felix da Housecat
Kittenz and Thee Glitz (2001)
As a teenager, Felix Stallings, Jr was a protégé of DJ Pierre.
Robbie Fulks
Country Love Songs (1996)
Fulks defies categorisation, but this record – on local label Bloodshot – is an alt.country landmark.
Howlin' Wolf
The Genuine Article (1951)
The best of Chester Arthur Burnett.
Ahmad Jamal *At the Pershing: But Not for Me* (1958)
A jazz classic, recorded at the now-defunct Pershing Hotel on the city's South Side.
R Kelly *R* (1998)
Sprawling double-disc set from the now-disgraced singer.
The Jesus Lizard *Goat* (1991)
The best record by the recently reformed quartet, released on local label Touch & Go.
Curtis Mayfield *Curtis* (1970)
Mayfield's stunning debut contains 'Move on Up'.
Liz Phair *Exile in Guyville* (1993)
A startling rethink of the Stones' *Exile On Main Street.*

Tortoise *TNT* (1998)
The most accessible album from the post-rock doyennes.
Muddy Waters
The Anthology 1947-1972 (2001)
Two discs cover the essential cuts of the pioneering bluesman.
Kanye West
Late Registration (2005)
Dazzling 21st-century hip hop.
Waco Brothers
Freedom and Weep (2005)
The most recent album from the rabble-rousing troupe.
Wilco *Yankee Hotel Foxtrot* (2002)
The disc that saw Jeff Tweedy shed the alt.country tag. The cover shot stars the Marina City towers.
Various Artists
The Sound of Chicago House (2006)
Marshall Jefferson, Sterling Void and others appear on this 2-CD set, a summary of the scene that revolutionised dance in the '80s.
Various Artists
The Chess Story 1947-1975 (1999)
15 CDs, 335 tracks, and everything you ever wanted to know about Chess Records but were afraid to ask. Plenty of smaller compilations do a decent job for less money.

WEBSITES

www.chicagoist.com
Pithy, searching and occasionally laugh-out-loud news and comment on what's happening in town.
www.chicagoparkdistrict.com
Details on where to find the city's 500-plus parks, along with information on their amenities.
www.chicagotribune.com
The local news.
www.choosechicago.com
Masses and masses of information for visitors to the city, including maps and details of guided tours.
www.encyclopedia.chicago history.org
The content of this vast book (*see p311*), compiled by the Newberry Library and the Chicago Historical Society, is available online.
www.cityofchicago.org
The city's homepage needs an overhaul. However, if you've got the patience to wade through it, you'll eventually find what you need.
www.timeoutchicago.com
Listings, previews, reviews, features and plenty more. Your one-stop guide to what's on in the city.
www.transitchicago.com
Everything you ever wanted to know about the Chicago Transit Authority, including downloadable system maps and timetables.

Index A-Z

Page references in **bold** indicate chapters and main references; page numbers in *italics* indicate photographs.

INDEX

INDEX

INDEX

INDEX

INDEX

Advertisers' Index

Please refer to the relevant pages for contact details.

Maps

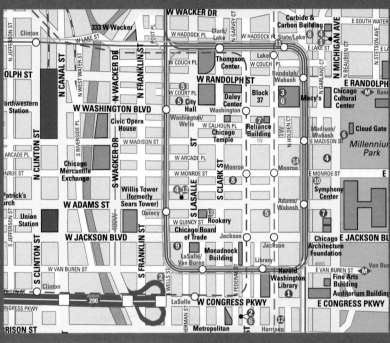

Legend:

Place of interest and/or entertainment ....
Railway stations ....
Parks ....
Hospitals/universities ....
Neighbourhood .... **LOOP**
Metra station .... Ⓜ
CTA station .... Clark
(colour denotes line)

© Copyright Time Out Group 2009

Chicago Overview

See p335

See p330

See pp328-329

See pp326-327

See p331

See p330

See pp324-325

See p332

Lake Michigan

Lincoln Park

Belmont Harbor

Grant Park

Humboldt Park

Garfield Park

Douglas Park

Washington Park

HYDE PARK

Jackson Park

CANADA

Winnipeg
Québec
Montreal
Minneapolis
Ottawa
Toronto
Boston
Detroit
Buffalo
New York
Chicago
Pittsburg
Philadelphia
Kansas City
St Louis
Washington
U S A
Oklahoma City
Memphis
Atlanta
Charleston
Dallas
Houston
New Orleans
Miami
CUBA

PETERSON AVE 6000N
N LINCOLN AVE
N BROADWAY
N RIDGE AVE ST
N ASHLAND AVE
W FOSTER AVE 5200N
N SHERIDAN RD
N CLARENDON AVE
W LAWRENCE AVE 4800N
N LINCOLN AVE
N PULASKI RD
N KEDZIE AVE
W MONTROSE AVE 4400N
W IRVING PARK RD 4000N
See p330
N BROADWAY ST
W ADDISON ST 3600N
N KIMBALL AVE
N NELSON AVE
N WESTERN AVE
N DAMEN AVE
W BELMONT AVE 3200N
N CLARK ST
N MILWAUKEE AVE
90
W DIVERSEY AVE
94
W DIVERSEY PKWY 2800N
N LINCOLN AVE
W FULLERTON AVE 2400N
N CALIFORNIA AVE
N KEDZIE BLVD
N SACRAMENTO AVE
W ARMITAGE AVE 2000N
N DAMEN AVE
N HALSTED ST
W NORTH AVE 1600N
N STATE ST
N CLARK ST
N PULASKI RD
W DIVISION ST 1200N
W CHICAGO AVE 800N
W LAKE ST
N HOMAN AVE
N CALIFORNIA AVE
S SACRAMENTO BLVD
W WASHINGTON BLVD
W MADISON ST 1N
N MICHIGAN AVE
290
S OGDEN AVE W
S RACINE AVE
S MORGAN ST
W ROOSEVELT RD 1200S
W 16TH ST 1600W
S BLUE ISLAND AVE
W 18TH ST
W 16TH PL
S STATE ST
W OGDEN AVE
W CERMAK RD 2200S
S WESTERN AVE
S DAMEN AVE
S CALIFORNIA AVE
55
W 26TH ST
W 31ST ST
S ARCHER AVE
W 31ST ST
E 31ST ST
S KING DR
W 35TH ST
E 35TH ST
90
W PERSHING RD
94
S MICHIGAN AVE
E 43RD ST
S COTTAGE GROVE AVE
S LAKE PARK AVE
S PULASKI RD
W 43RD ST
S ASHLAND AVE
S HALSTED ST
W 47TH ST
E 47TH ST
S STATE ST
See p332
W 51ST ST
E 51ST ST
E HYDE PARK BLVD
S WOODLAWN AVE
E 55TH ST
S KEDZIE AVE
S CALIFORNIA AVE
S DAMEN AVE
W GARFIELD BLVD
W 55TH ST
E 59TH ST
W 59TH ST
E 63RD ST
W 63RD ST

North Branch Chicago River

Time Out Chicago **323**

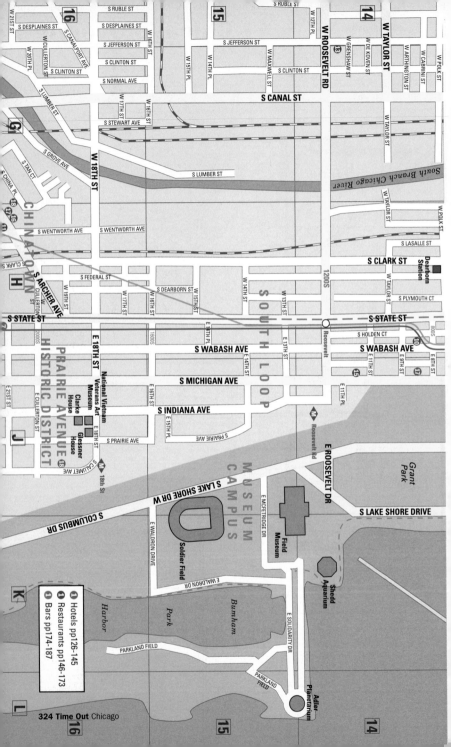

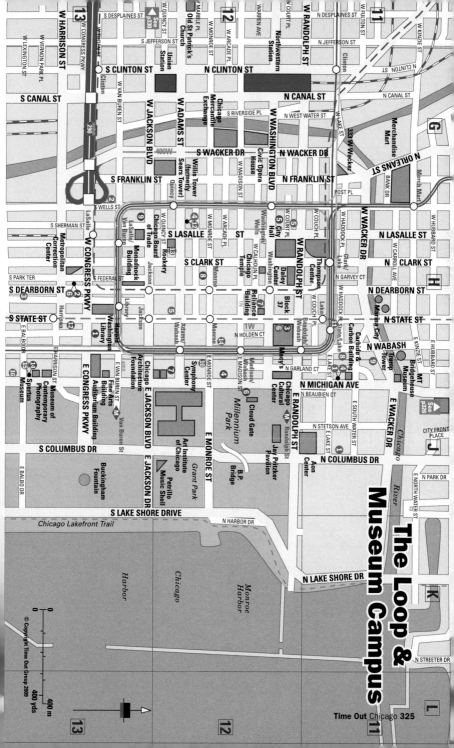

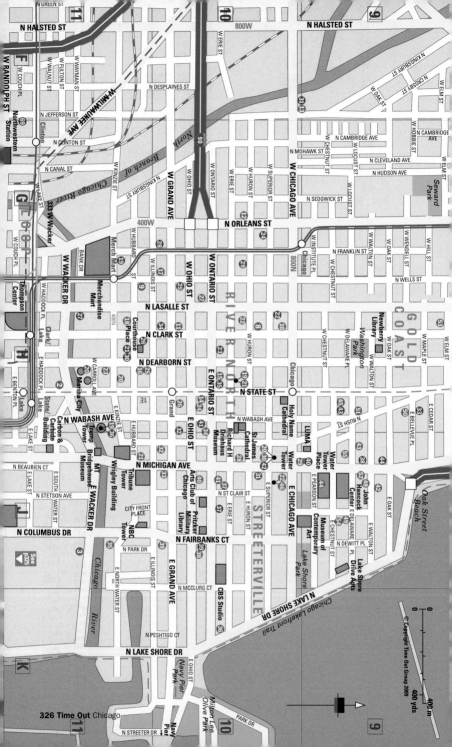

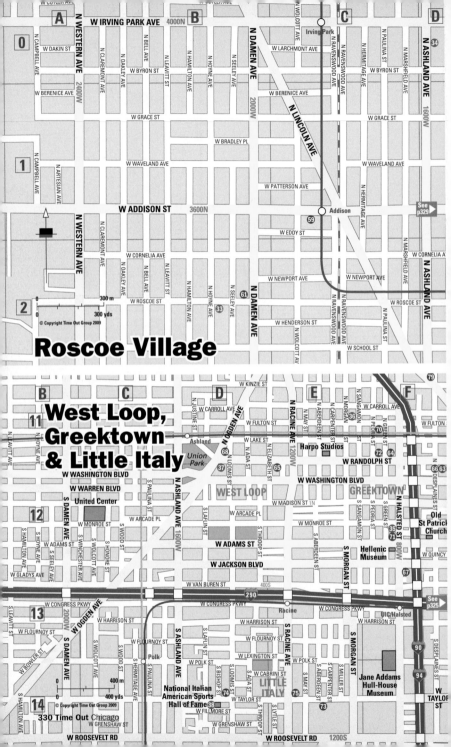

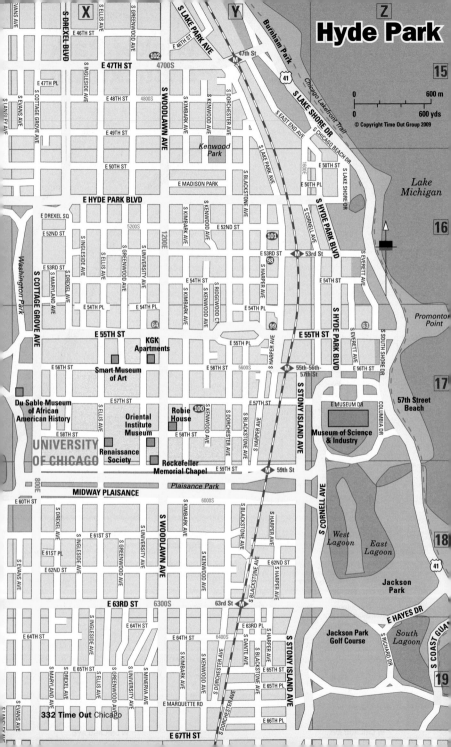

Hyde Park

© Copyright Time Out Group 2009

Street Index

For ease of use, all streets in this index are listed alphabetically without their various N, S, E or W prefixes.

Chicago Neighbourhoods

W FOSTER AVE 5200N

LINCOLN SQUARE
& RAVENSWOOD

W LAWRENCE AVE 2800N

ANDERSONVILLE,
EDGEWATER
& UPTOWN

N SHERIDAN RD

IRVING PARK &
ALBANY PARK

To O'Hare Airport

N PULASKI RD

N KEDZIE AVE

North Branch Chicago River

N LINCOLN AVE

N CLARENDON AVE

N BROADWAY ST

See pp328-329

W MONTROSE AVE 4400N

W IRVING PARK RD 4000N

See p330

W ADDISON ST 3600N

ROSCOE
VILLAGE

N KIMBALL AVE

N ELSTON AVE

N DAMEN AVE

N WESTERN AVE 2400N

LAKEVIEW &
WRIGLEYVILLE

W BELMONT AVE 3200N

Belmont
Harbor

Lake

AVONDALE

90

94

N CLARK ST

N LINCOLN AVE

Michigan

W DIVERSEY AVE

W DIVERSEY PKWY 2800N

Lincoln
Park

LOGAN SQUARE

N CALIFORNIA AVE 2800N

N LINCOLN AVE

W FULLERTON AVE 2400N

N KEDZIE BLVD

LINCOLN
PARK

See pp326-327

See p331

W ARMITAGE AVE 2000N

N CLYBOURN AVE

N HALSTED ST

OLD
TOWN

N STATE ST

BUCKTOWN

W NORTH AVE 1600N

N MILWAUKEE AVE

N CLARK ST

HUMBOLDT
PARK

N PULASKI RD 4000N

Humboldt
Park

WICKER
PARK

W DIVISION ST 1200N

N ASHLAND AVE 1600W

GOOSE
ISLAND

RIVER
NORTH

GOLD
COAST

W CHICAGO AVE 800N

UKRAINIAN VILLAGE
& WEST TOWN

W CHICAGO AVE

MAGNIFICENT MILE
& STREETERVILLE

GARFIELD PARK

W LAKE ST

See p330

WEST LOOP

GREEK-
TOWN

MICHIGAN AVE

THE
LOOP

LAKE SHORE DR

To Oak Park

Garfield
Park

N HOMAN AVE

SACRAMENTO BLVD

N CALIFORNIA AVE

W MADISON ST

AVE

S RACINE AVE

S MORGAN ST

Grant
Park

290

W OGDEN AVE

LITTLE ITALY

W ROOSEVELT RD 1200S

THE SOUTH
LOOP &
CHINATOWN

See pp324-325

Douglas
Park

W 16TH ST 1600S

S WESTERN AVE

S DAMEN AVE

1800S

S BLUE ISLAND AVE

W 18TH ST

W 15TH PL

S MICHIGAN AVE

W OGDEN AVE

PILSEN

W CERMAK RD 2200S

LAWNDALE

W 26TH ST 2600S

S CALIFORNIA AVE

HEART OF
CHICAGO

S HALSTED ST

S STATE ST

S KING DR

S PULASKI RD 4000S

W 31ST ST 3100S

55

S ARCHER AVE

W 31ST ST

90

94

E 31ST ST

BRONZEVILLE

MCKINLEY PARK

W 35TH ST

BRIDGEPORT

S MICHIGAN AVE

S STATE ST

To Hyde Park ↓

© Copyright Time Out Group 2009

0 _____ 2 km
0 _____ 1 mile

CTA Rail Map

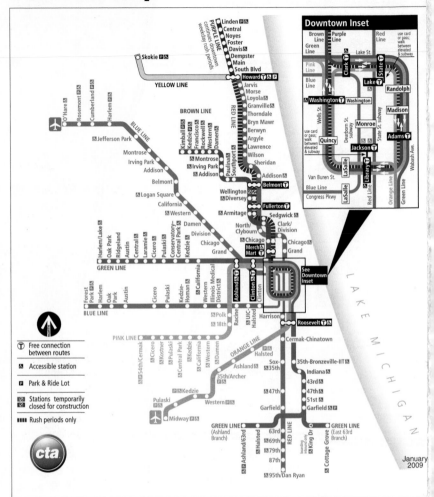

Map © 2009 Chicago Transit Authority